CONTENTS

FOUNDING EDITOR
Todd Hignite

ASSISTANT EDITOR
Sara Rowe Hignite

PUBLISHER
Alvin Buenaventura

DESIGN & PRODUCTION
Jonathan Bennett

COMIC ART ISBN 978-0-9766848-6-2 **ISSUE NUMBER NINE, FALL 2007**. ENTIRE CONTENTS © 2007 BY COMIC ART. COMIC ART IS PUBLISHED ANNUALLY BY BUENAVENTURA PRESS. ALL TEXT AND ARTWORK © THE RESPECTIVE CREATORS AND PUBLISHERS. NONE OF THE MATERIAL IN THIS PUBLICATION MAY BE REPRODUCED IN ANY FORM WITHOUT THE WRITTEN PERMISSION OF COMIC ART OR THE COPYRIGHT HOLDERS. ALL IMAGES UTILIZED HEREIN ARE REPRODUCED FOR HISTORICAL AND SCHOLARLY PURPOSES ONLY. EVERY EFFORT HAS BEEN MADE TO PROVIDE FACTUALLY ACCURATE INFORMATION. PRINTED AND BOUND IN CHINA.

CONTACT THE EDITOR AT: todd@comicartmagazine.com

PLEASE DIRECT ALL ORDERS AND ADVERTISING INQUIRIES TO THE PUBLISHER AT THE ADDRESS BELOW.

BUENAVENTURA PRESS, P.O. BOX 23661, OAKLAND, CA, 94623.
comicart@buenaventurapress.com • www.buenaventurapress.com

www.comicartmagazine.com

IVAN BRUNETTI

{ www.MURPHYDESIGN.com }

MARK MURPHY : MURPHY DESIGN ART BOOKS

RAY CAESAR : BOB DOB : SCOTT MUSGROVE *Collector Editions* MARTHA RICH : JOE SORREN : JEFF SOTO

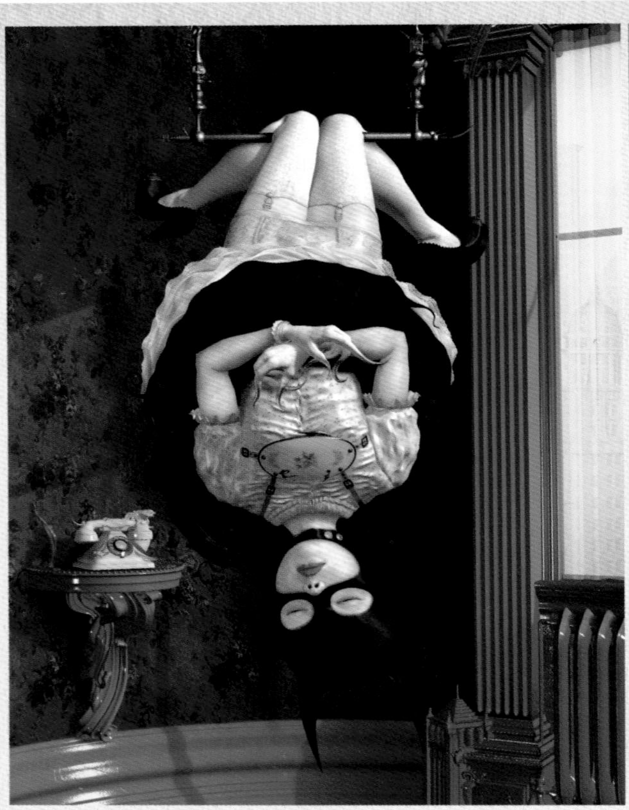

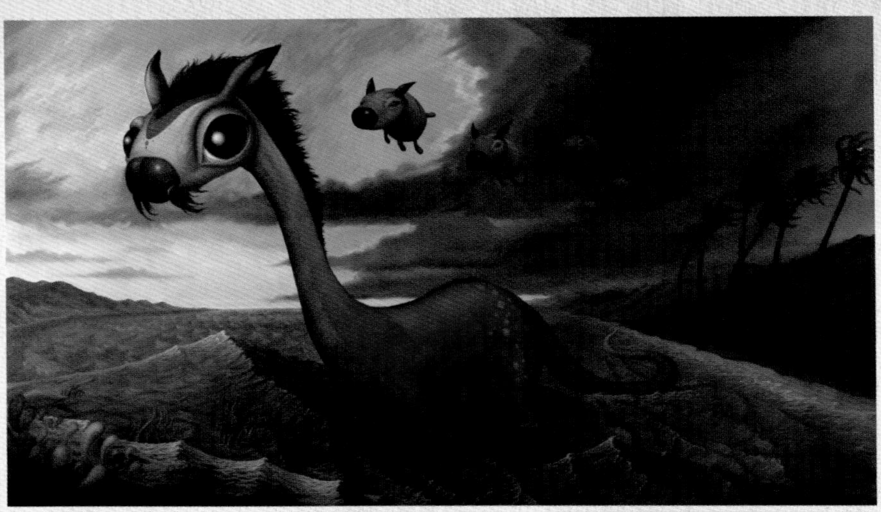

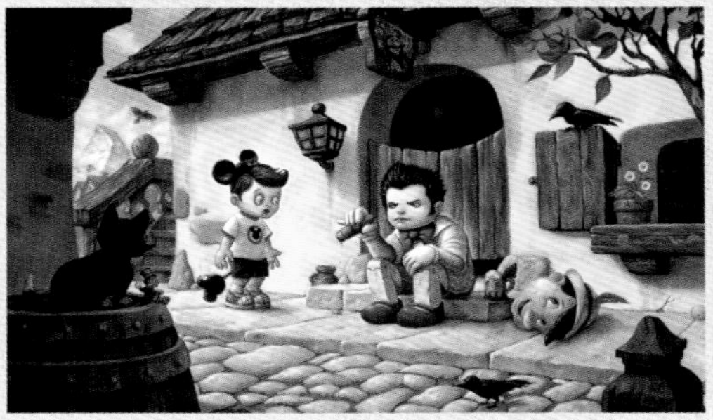

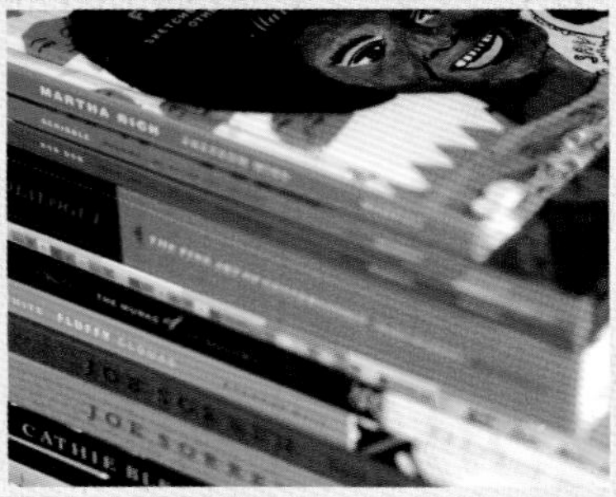
MARTHA RICH
JOE SORREN

: JEFF SOTO'S LUCKY THIRTEEN 2008 CALENDAR PACKAGE : FEATURES 32 PAGE — ARTIST SIGNED — MINI ZINE : STICKER PAGE : 13 MONTH CALENDAR :

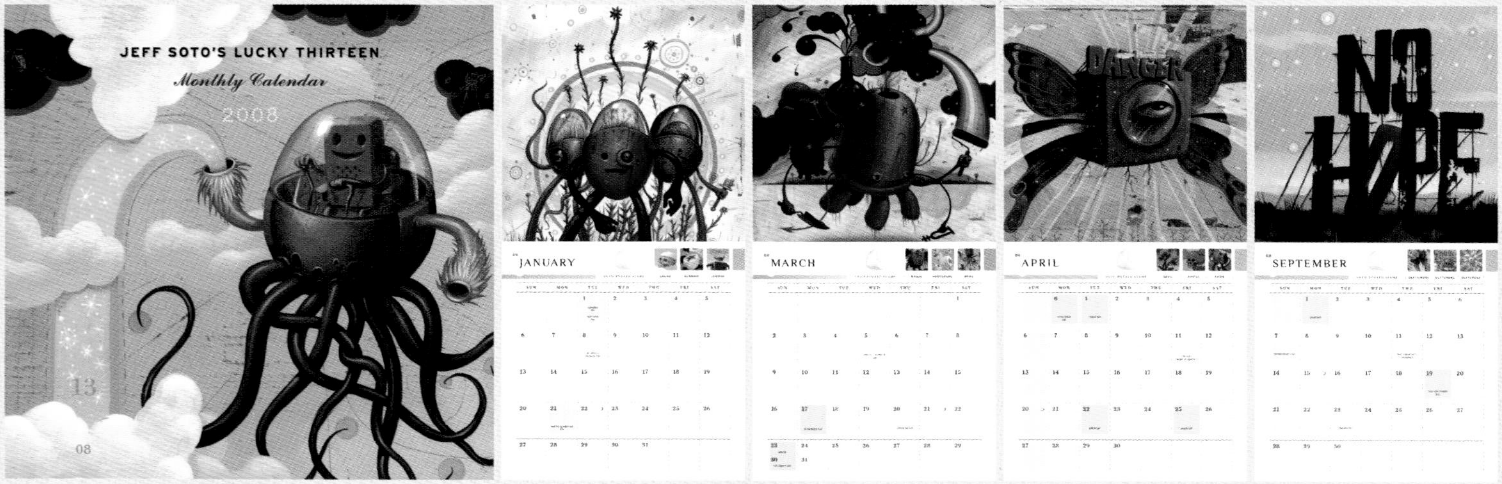
JEFF SOTO'S LUCKY THIRTEEN
Monthly Calendar
2008
JANUARY
MARCH
APRIL
SEPTEMBER
DANGER
NO HOPE

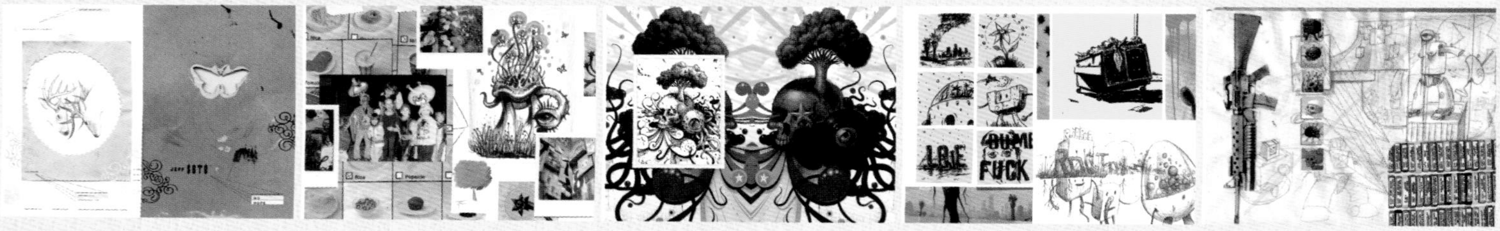

: DESIGN SERVICES AND WHOLESALE PRICING AVAILABLE : 619 743 0405 :

FAMILY

Yokoland · Mingering Mike · Ian Svenonius · Brian Chippendale · Miranda July · Gary Panter · Richard Brautigan · Osamu Tesuka · Russ Meyer · Paul Auster · Will Sweeney · Trinie Dalton · William Eggleston · Dan Zettwoch · Mika Miko · Kramers Ergot · The USA is a Monster · Trunk Records · David Shrigley · Daniel Pinchbeck · CF · Bobby Beausoleil · Haruki Murakami · Edogawa Rampo · Charles Willeford · Matthew Thurber · Dave Eggers · Anders Brekhus Nilsen · Ariel Pink · Sister Corita Kent · Napa · Tadanori Yokoo · Kim Deitch · Nieves · Georges Franju · Jordan Crane · Soyfriends · Tove Jansson · Fabio Viscogliosi · Islands Fold · Soiled Mattress and the Springs · Chris Johanson · Teardrops · Elvis Studio · Chris Ware · Masaki Kobayashi · Paper Rad · Mat Brinkman · Deathbomb Arc · Mario Bava · Not Not Fun · Kenneth Anger · Kevin Huizenga · Shobo Shobo · Little Wings · Sammy Harkham · No Age · Bald Eagles · Andrew Jeffrey Wright · Goblin · Kentura Miura · Harpo Marx · David Berman · Julie Doucet · Black Dice · Jason T. miles · Werner Herzog · More

436 N Fairfax Ave Los Angeles CA 90036
393 789 9991 FAMILYLOSANGELES.COM

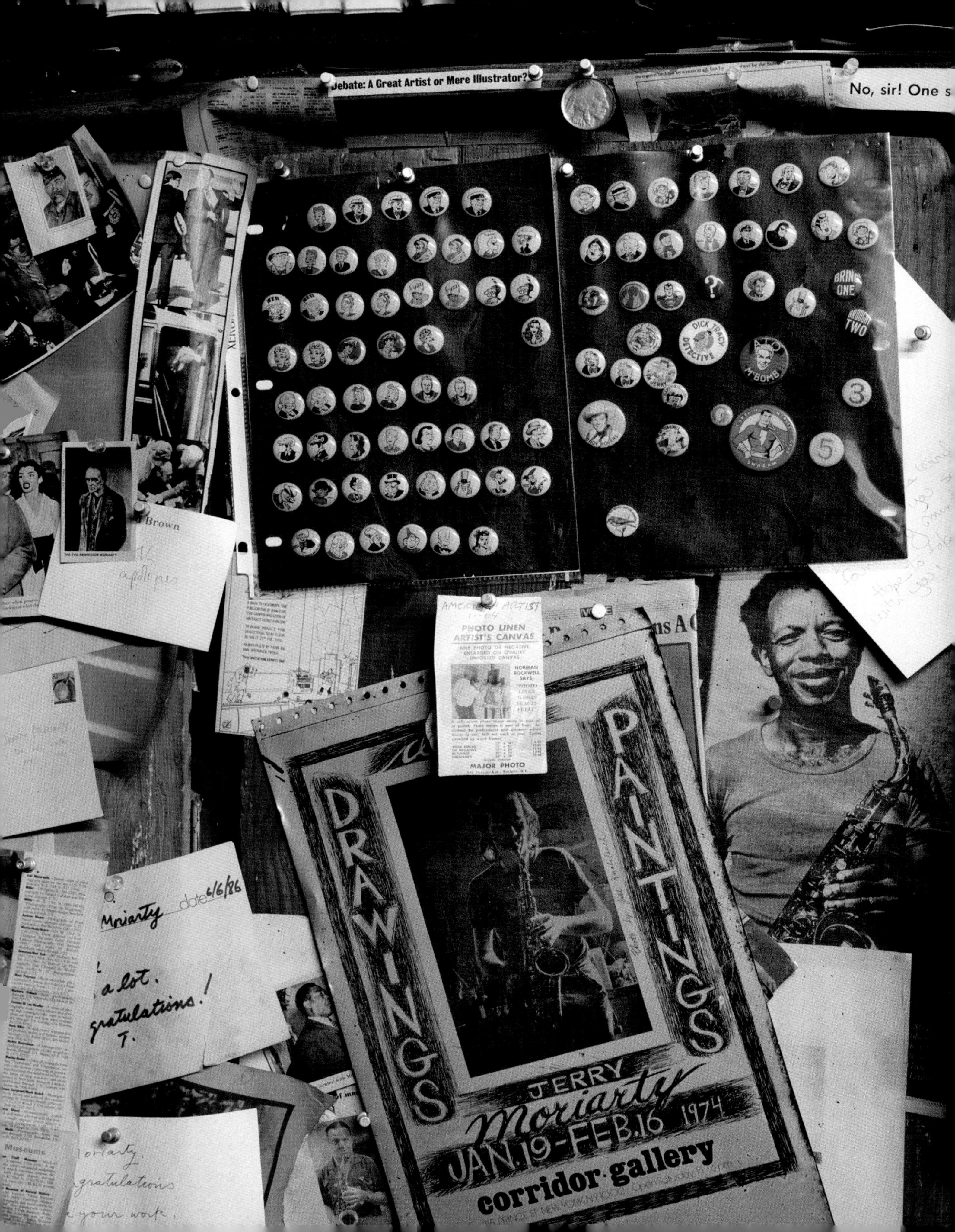

Debate: A Great Artist or Mere Illustrator?
No, sir! One s
DICK TRACY DETECTIVE
BRING ONE
BROUGHT TWO
3
5
Brown
PHOTO LINEN ARTIST'S CANVAS
NORMAN ROCKWELL SAYS,
MAJOR PHOTO
DRAWINGS
PAINTINGS
JERRY Moriarty
JAN. 19 - FEB. 16 1974
corridor·gallery
date 6/6/86
Museums

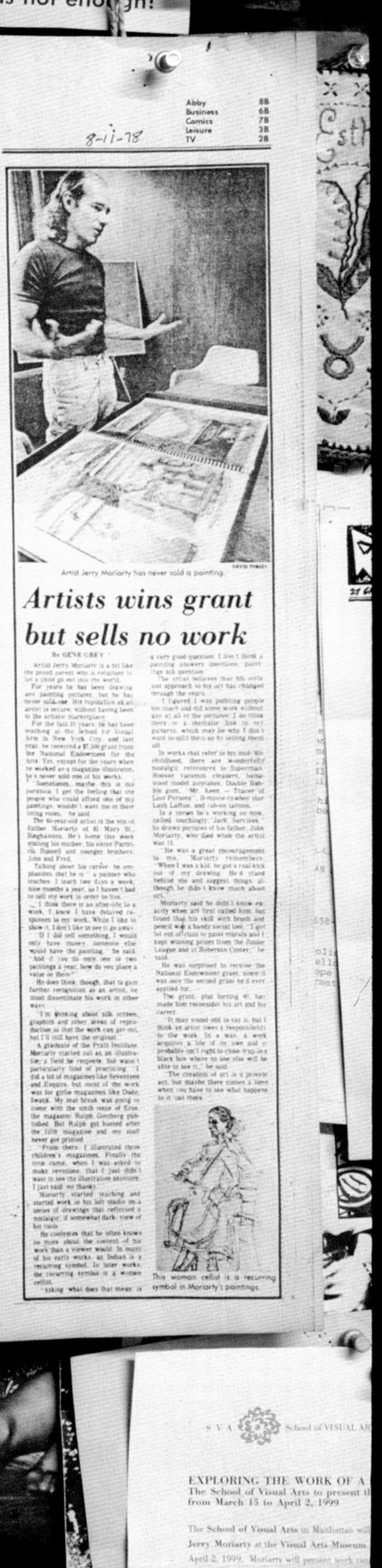
Artist Jerry Moriarty has never sold a painting.
Artists wins grant but sells no work
By GENE GREY
This woman cellist is a recurring symbol in Moriarty's paintings.
EXPLORING THE WORK OF A

Moriarty's studio, New York, New York, 2007. Photo by Jonathan Bennett.

JERRY MORIARTY

In 2002, I was shopping for the oversize issues of *RAW* at Lambiek, Europe oldest comix shop, when I bumped into cartoonist Chris Ware. From th shelf I was browsing, Chris pulled down a copy of Jerry Moriarty's *Jac Survives: A RAW One-Shot* and said, "Jeez, I actually traded an origin comic page of mine to someone years ago just to get a copy of this! Do yo have it?" I didn't. It looked interesting, was reasonably priced for a rar book, and coming so highly recommended, I bought it. The forty-pag comic featured twenty-two slice-of-life vignettes with everyman John V Jack, and it immediately became one of my favorites. These comics wer perfect and genuine in every way, from the playful and beautiful designed title lettering unique to each strip, to the slightly surreal y deadpan take on the humor inherent in small moments. After returning t California, I sought out more work by him but found only a few pages *RAW*. So I pegged Moriarty as one of those rare cartoonists who makes h mark on the history of comics with just a handful of top-quality strips, n unlike Lyonel Feininger or Richard McGuire.

Two years after discovering *Jack Survives*, I learned that Art Spiegelma was curating a show in New York of Moriarty's paintings. I enjoyed the fa that, though Moriarty had apparently retired from the drawing boar these paintings still showed a strong comics influence. Shortly after th show, Sammy Harkham and I were discussing whom he should include the next volume of *Kramers Ergot*. I was collaborating with Gary Panter o a series of prints at the time, and Jerry's name came up; I suggeste Moriarty's work to Sammy and he instantly agreed that he would b perfect. Panter told me Jerry was teaching at SVA with him, and he put u in contact. This led to Moriarty's stunning series of recent paintings an drawings appearing in *Kramers Ergot #6*.

During a 2006 trip to New York, I visited Jerry in the studio where he ha lived and worked for forty years. It was amazing to see his recent painting and to hear his countless fascinating stories about working for girlie ma azines in the '60s, collecting *Nancy* and talking with Ernie Bushmiller, an playing sax at CBGB's in 1979 with *Mutts* cartoonist Patrick McDonnel punk band The Steel Tips. I spent hours in the studio and returned th next day to look and listen some more. In the following illustrated essa Jerry tells many of these kinds of stories about his life and art, each o which offers a glimpse into his aesthetics and rich career. Enjoy.

—Alvin Buenaventura

Top left: Radio Corner with Superman,
casein on masonite, 16 x 12", 1974.

Top right: Ripping through Superman,
acrylic on Bristol board, 24 x 18", 1993.

Middle left: Roy, acrylic on Bristol board,
24 x 18", 1992.

Bottom left: Ripping through Roy,
pencil on paper, 24 x 18", 1992.

Right: Fella and the Garbage Men,
oil on canvas, 60 x 46", 2003.

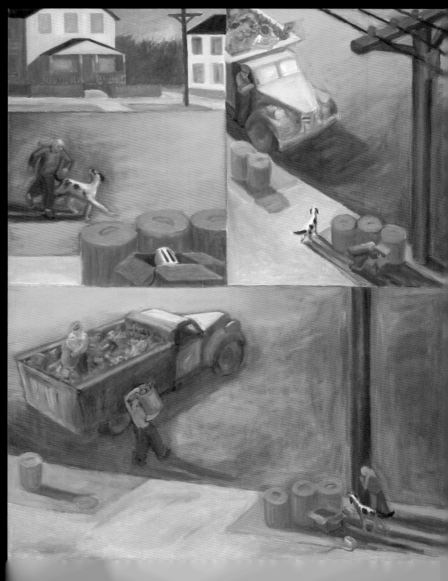

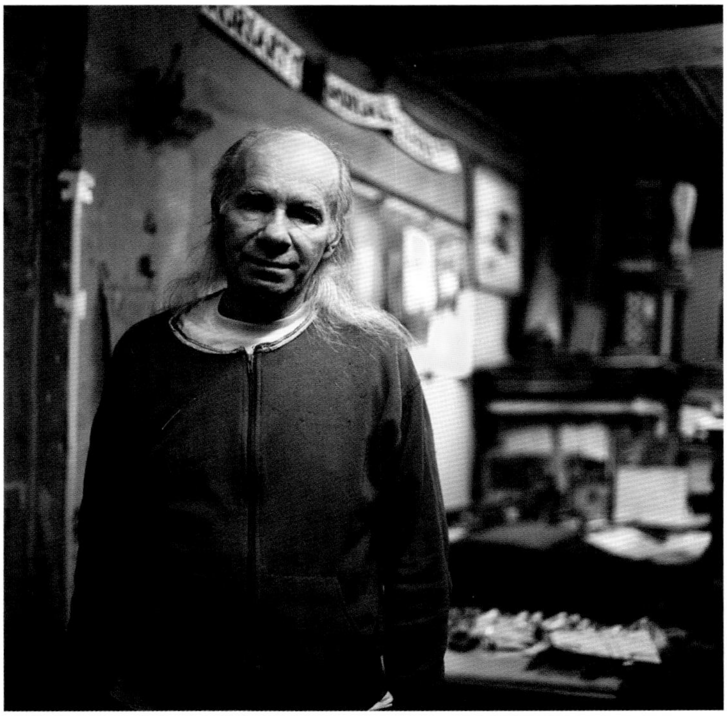

Moriarty in his studio, New York, New York, 2007. Photo by Jonathan Bennett.

Life Captions...

BY *Jerry Moriarty*

Superman on the radio sponsored by Kellogg's PEP cereal—staring at the yellow fabric speaker on the big floor radio as Superman transported a five-year-old.

Comic character pins in the bottom of PEP boxes; cereal got soggy fast.

A jigsaw puzzle that had a strong effect on me: you put the pieces together in a shallow box with a lid, closed the lid, turned the box over, opened another lid. There on the other side of the puzzle was a different image showing me that pictures can have a hidden image unlike the visible one. I was four years old.

Taken to my first movie at age five by an adult cousin, Betty. It was a Roy Rogers film and another hero was born in my picture brain along with a hero place—the West. Besides Trigger there were hero animals like Lassie, Flicka, and others.

Real-life heroes were the garbage men who worked in garbage on open dump trucks. Driving house to house, a garbage man would jump off the running board, pick up a full, steel garbage can and throw it up to the other garbage man. While I secretly watched with my hero dog, Fella, the garbage man on the truck would empty it and throw the steel can back to the guy on the ground.

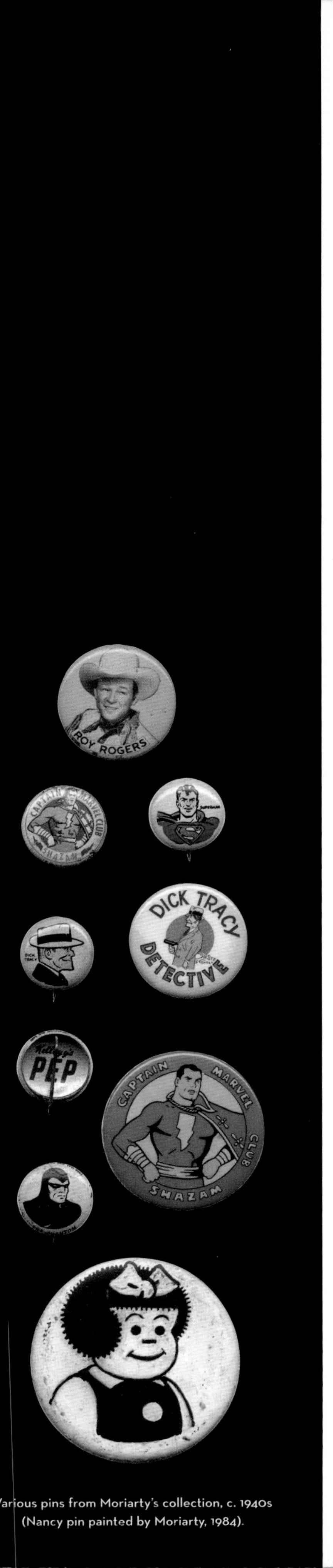
ROY ROGERS
DICK TRACY DETECTIVE
PEP
CAPTAIN MARVEL CLUB
SHAZAM

Various pins from Moriarty's collection, c. 1940s (Nancy pin painted by Moriarty, 1984).

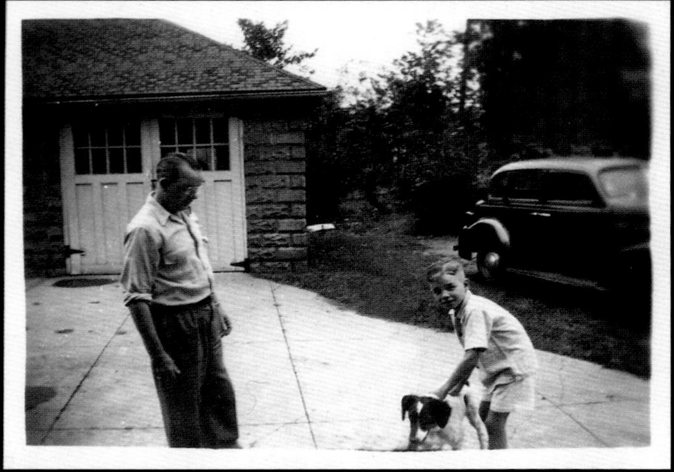

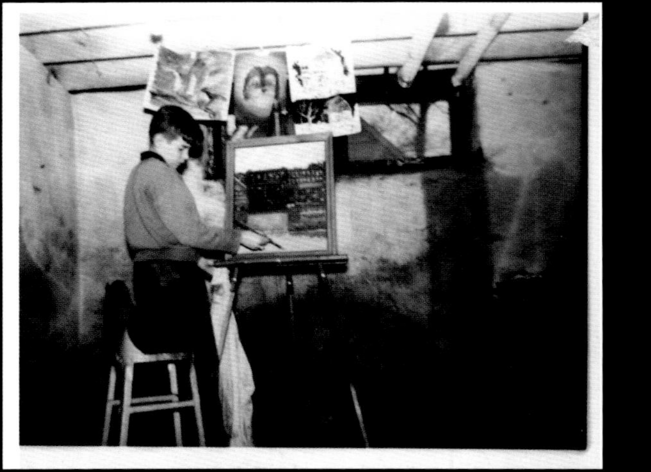

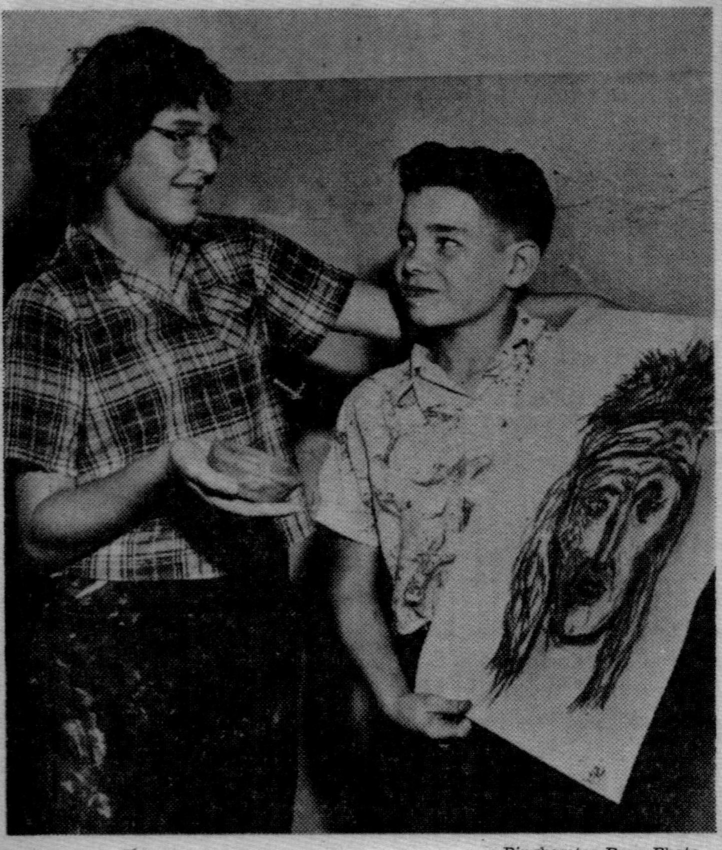

—Binghamton Press Photo.

ARMED WITH ART—These youngsters are two of 17 winners of scholarships in Binghamton Junior League Art Center classes. Lois Maston, 12, of 38 LaGrange Street was a winner in ceramics class. Jerry Moriarty, 11, of 8 Gary Street was successful in winning place in senior water color class.

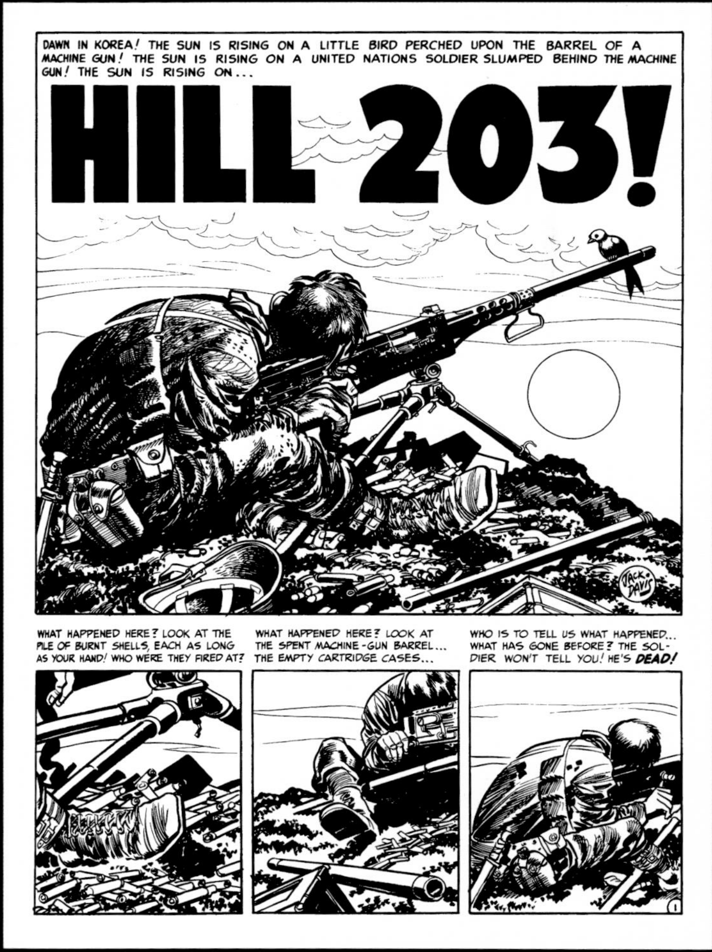
DAWN IN KOREA! THE SUN IS RISING ON A LITTLE BIRD PERCHED UPON THE BARREL OF A MACHINE GUN! THE SUN IS RISING ON A UNITED NATIONS SOLDIER SLUMPED BEHIND THE MACHINE GUN! THE SUN IS RISING ON...
HILL 203!
JACK DAVIS
WHAT HAPPENED HERE? LOOK AT THE PILE OF BURNT SHELLS, EACH AS LONG AS YOUR HAND! WHO WERE THEY FIRED AT?
WHAT HAPPENED HERE? LOOK AT THE SPENT MACHINE-GUN BARREL... THE EMPTY CARTRIDGE CASES...
WHO IS TO TELL US WHAT HAPPENED... WHAT HAS GONE BEFORE? THE SOLDIER WON'T TELL YOU! HE'S DEAD!
1

Top left: Moriarty at age seven with his father and their dog Fella, Binghamton, New York, 1945.

Top right: Moriarty at age eleven painting in cellar studio, Binghamton, New York, 1949.

Left: Binghamton, New York, newspaper clipping, 1949.

Above: Jack Davis, splash page from "Hill 203!," *Two-Fisted Tales* #24 (EC Comics, 1951).

-NAMELY, LOVE!! BUT, WOLF-GAL, AH IS A MARRIED ROACH!!

Top: Moriarty at age fourteen with his father in a photo booth, 1953.

Middle: Moriarty at age eleven with his father on their porch, Binghamton, New York, 1949.

Bottom: Al Capp, panel featuring Wolf Gal from L'il Abner, daily strip, 1960.

Captain Marvel began to edge out Superman for me because he was a human kid who said "Shazam," became Captain Marvel, and beat up bad adults.

I was jealous of kids who could draw well in school. Usually it was a cartoon character like Bugs Bunny or Donald Duck, so I began tracing gag cartoons from *True* magazine. Soon I was copying it by eye and more importantly getting noticed for it—an art kid was born. It was like I grew a cape.

Binghamton, N.Y., in the 1940s was an industrial town with little time for art. Art came from the outside in the form of comics, magazines, and illustrated books. No art in our house.

My father loved music and baseball and his four kids. He got a kick out of the drawings I did so he would bring home from work pencils, erasers, and paper for me. He was a white collar, working-class guy who knew nothing about art but even so encouraged me to make pictures. One Christmas I got an oil paint set and a bunch of white enamel painted shirt cardboards because the guy at the store told my dad that it was as good as canvas to paint on with oils. I was eleven years old.

By the time I was twelve in 1950, comic art had become less challenging to me and magazine illustrators like Norman Rockwell got my attention because I was painting in oils and he painted in oils, too.

Then EC comics appeared, *Two-Fisted Tales* and *Frontline Combat* especially. They showed that comics could be realistic and not boring and beautifully drawn. Jack Davis was my favorite. I did not relate to funny comics or talking animals or superheroes anymore.

There was a moment in puberty when Sheena, Queen of the Jungle and Al Capp's Wolf Girl became strangely interesting.

Reality war and puberty fantasy were well represented in comics by 1950. Remember Joe Orlando and Wally Wood putting statues of naked women in the background among the bric-a-brac with no connection to the story?

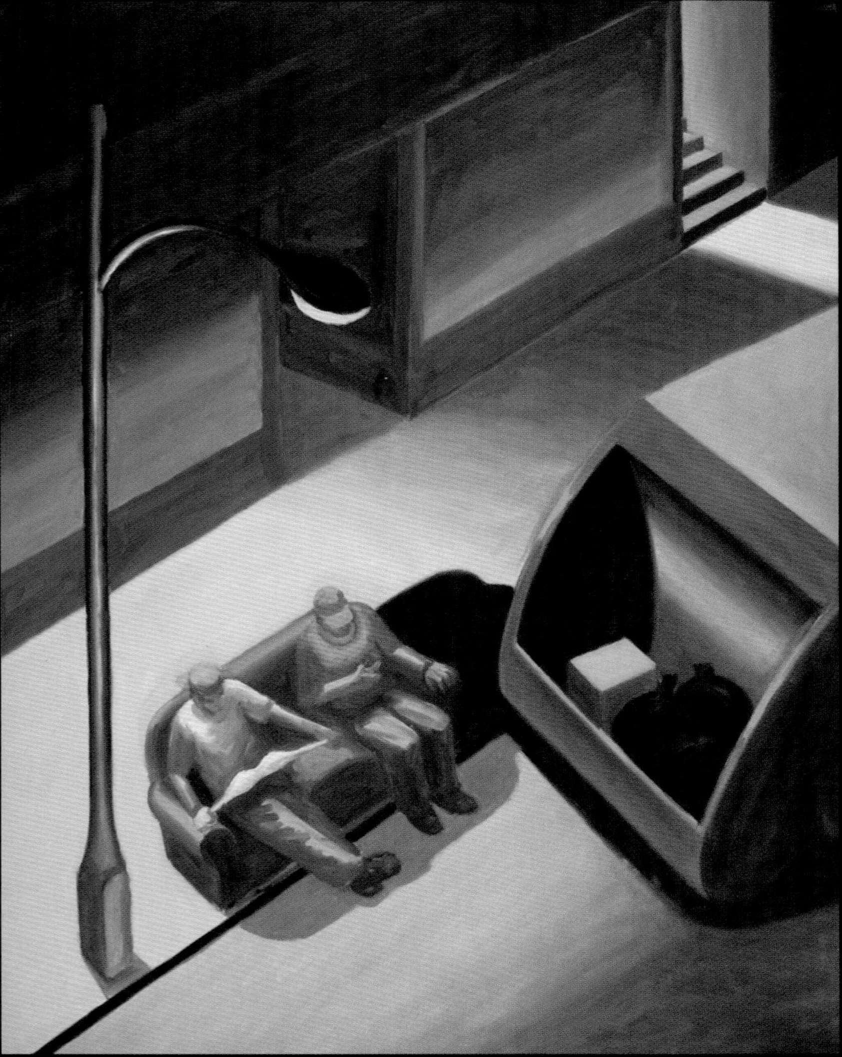

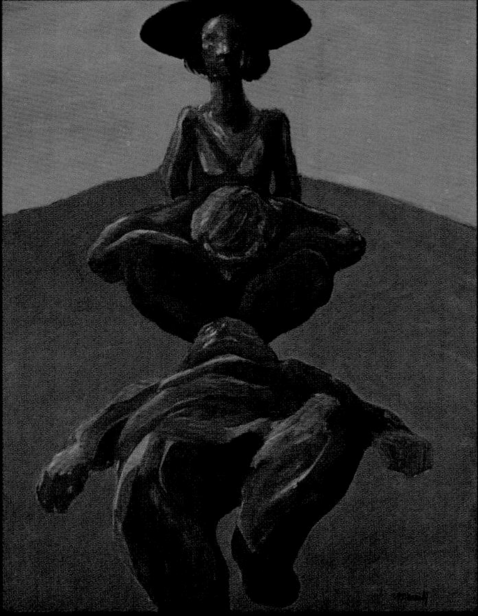

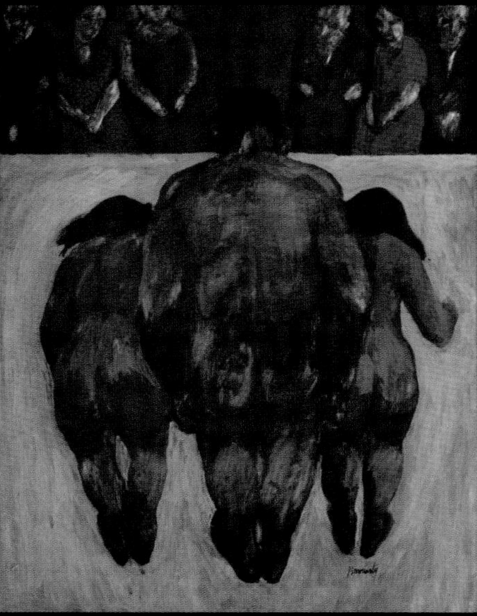

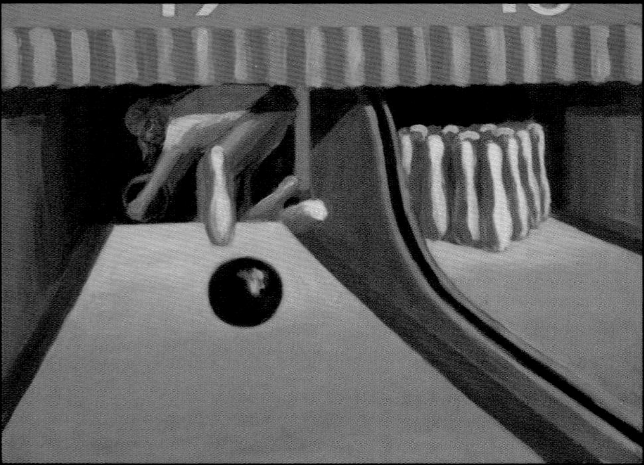

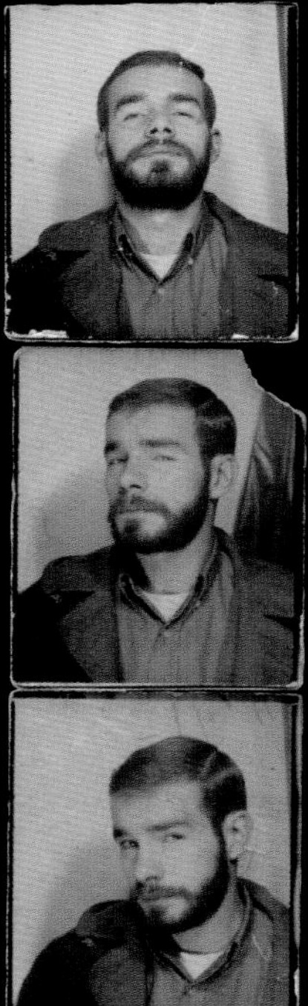

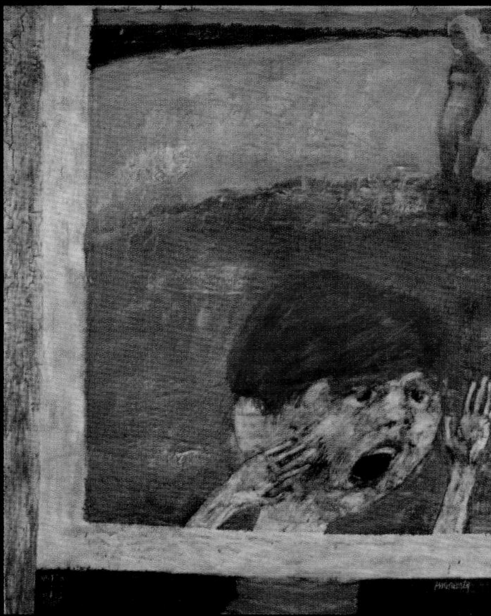

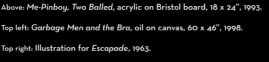

Above: *Me-Pinboy, Two Balled*, acrylic on Bristol board, 18 x 24", 1993.

Top left: *Garbage Men and the Bra*, oil on canvas, 60 x 46", 1998.

Top right: Illustration for *Escapade*, 1963.

Middle right: Tear sheet of unpublished illustration intended for *Eros* #5, 1963.

Bottom right: Moriarty's first published illustration, *Seventeen* magazine, 1960.

Right: Beatnik Moriarty at age nineteen in a photo booth, New York, New York, 1957.

ESCAPADE
PLEASURE FOR EVERY MAN
A LONDON "TOWEL" PARTY
COLLEGE CARTOONERY
IRISH HORSES

*America's 12 Most Famous Artists
*We're looking for people who like to draw
A Plan to Help Others
Find Out If You Have Talent
Famous Artists Schools
Studio 7251, Westport, Conn.
This is a postage-paid reply card
No stamp is needed
Just detach along the dotted line, fill out, and mail
Albert Dorne
Norman Rockwell
Al Parker
Jon Whitcomb
Austin Briggs
Ben Stahl
Fred Ludekens
Robert Fawcett
Harold Von Schmidt
George Giusti
Peter Helck
Stevan Dohanos

Famous Artists Course
Institute of Commercial Art, Inc.
JERRY MORIARTY

Top: *Escapade*, October 1961.

Middle: Famous Artists Course back-cover advertisement, c. 1950s.

Bottom: Moriarty's personal copy of the Famous Artists Course textbook.

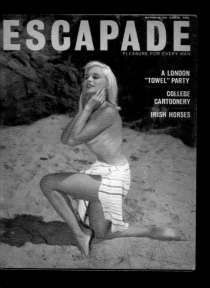

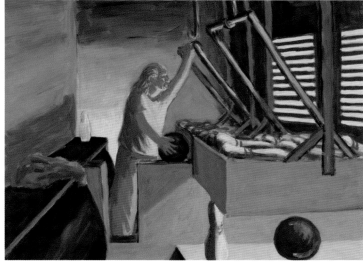

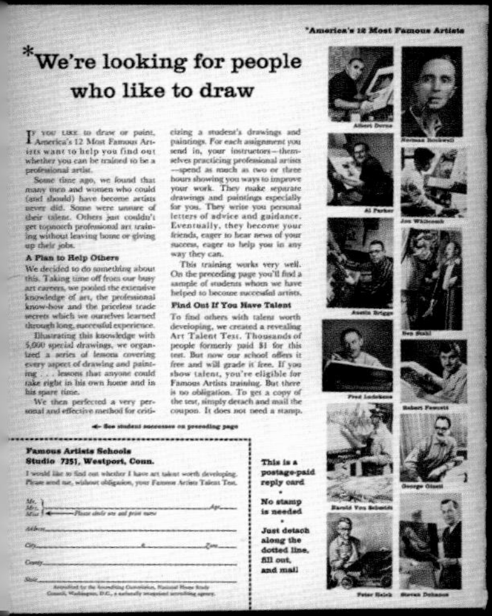

Me-Pinboy, acrylic on Bristol board, 18 x 24", 1993.

At age fifteen I took the Famous Artists Course that was advertised in the backs of comics. The twelve famous artists were magazine illustrators who were mostly in *The Saturday Evening Post*. It was a correspondence course that kept me focused on art when there was no other challenge in Binghamton at that time. I paid the $350 for it by working as a pin-boy in a local bowling alley.

Went to art school (Pratt) during the beatnik, cool jazz, Abstract Expressionist late 1950s. Embraced it all becoming an abstract beatnik art student.

Glad that I had illustration classes that kept me in touch with my story-telling self even though I saw illustration then as strictly commercial.

Graduated in 1960 and got my first freelance illustration jobs at different "girlie" magazines; in my free time I was painting abstractly. By 1962, I finally faced the fact that I was not an abstract painter after all. Still loved jazz, so I wasn't totally uncool.

My very first illustration job was for *Seventeen* magazine and my last was for *Eros* magazine (issue #5, which was never published). You might say I went from the little girls to the big girls.

When *Eros* got busted on a trumped-up charge of pornography, nothing was sacred anymore. I had counted on the premium exposure in that showcase magazine with Herb Lubalin as its art director and it crashed.

Couldn't pay my bills, got a job in a studio. Three months later someone recommended me to Scholastic Books to do a children's book. I quit my job, did the book, and started teaching in an art school.

In 1970 I had a student who sold comics at conventions. I asked him if he knew about *Two-Fisted Tales* and he said yes. He brought me a copy to borrow for a while. I couldn't believe how great it still was even after twenty years.

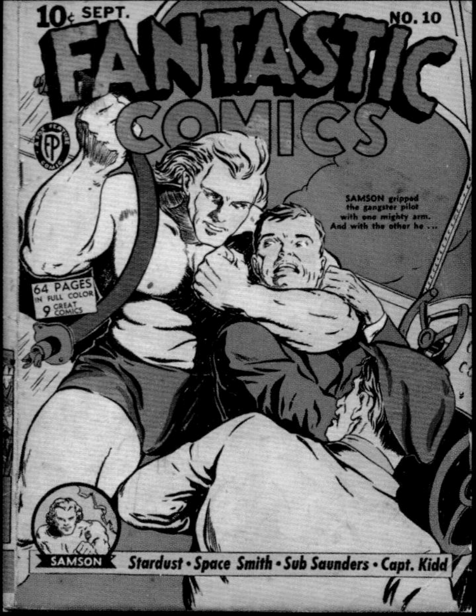
10¢ SEPT.
NO. 10
FANTASTIC COMICS
SAMSON gripped the gangster pilot with one mighty arm. And with the other he . . .
64 PAGES IN FULL COLOR
9 GREAT COMICS
SAMSON
Stardust • Space Smith • Sub Saunders • Capt. Kidd

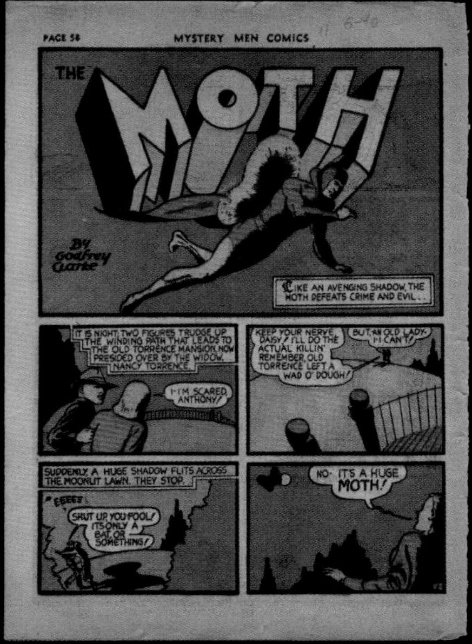
PAGE 58
MYSTERY MEN COMICS
THE MOTH
By Godfrey Clarke
LIKE AN AVENGING SHADOW, THE MOTH DEFEATS CRIME AND EVIL . .
IT IS NIGHT. TWO FIGURES TRUDGE UP THE WINDING PATH THAT LEADS TO THE OLD TORRENCE MANSION, NOW PRESIDED OVER BY THE WIDOW, NANCY TORRENCE.
I-I'M SCARED, ANTHONY!
KEEP YOUR NERVE, DAISY! I'LL DO THE ACTUAL KILLIN' REMEMBER, OLD TORRENCE LEFT A WAD O' DOUGH!
BUT, AN OLD LADY- I-I CAN'T!
SUDDENLY, A HUGE SHADOW FLITS ACROSS THE MOONLIT LAWN. THEY STOP.
"EEEEE"
SHUT UP, YOU FOOL! ITS ONLY A BAT, OR SOMETHING!
NO- IT'S A HUGE MOTH!

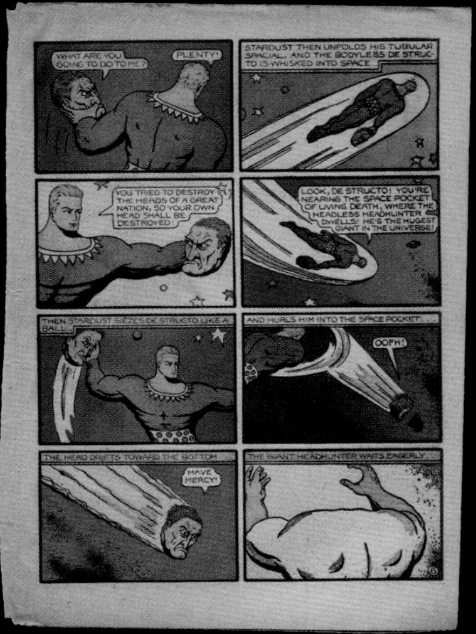
WHAT ARE YOU GOING TO DO TO ME?
PLENTY!
STARDUST THEN UNFOLDS HIS TUBULAR SPACIAL, AND THE BODYLESS DE STRUCTO IS WHISKED INTO SPACE.
YOU TRIED TO DESTROY THE HEADS OF A GREAT NATION, SO YOUR OWN HEAD SHALL BE DESTROYED!
LOOK, DE STRUCTO! YOU'RE NEARING THE SPACE POCKET OF LIVING DEATH, WHERE THE HEADLESS HEADHUNTER DWELLS! HE'S THE HUGEST GIANT IN THE UNIVERSE!
THEN STARDUST SIEZES DE STRUCTO LIKE A BALL . . .
AND HURLS HIM INTO THE SPACE POCKET . . .
OOFH!
THE HEAD DRIFTS TOWARD THE BOTTOM
HAVE MERCY!
THE GIANT HEADHUNTER WAITS EAGERLY . . .

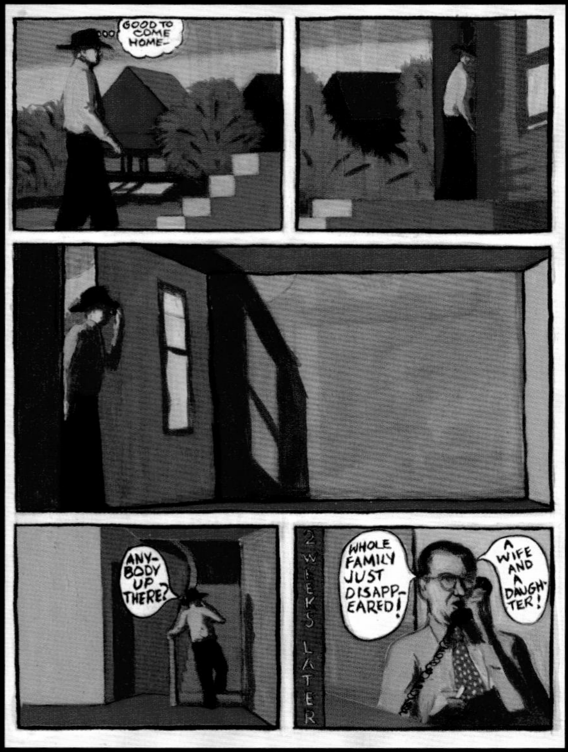
GOOD TO COME HOME-
ANY-BODY UP THERE?
2 WEEKS LATER
WHOLE FAMILY JUST DISAPP-EARED!
A WIFE AND A DAUGH-TER!

Top left: *Fantastic Comics* #10 (Fox, 1940).

Top middle: Jim Mooney, splash page from "The Moth," *Mystery Men Comics* (Fox, 1939).

Top right: Fletcher Hanks, interior page from "Stardust," *Fantastic Comics* (Fox, 1939).

Above: "Middleman," unpublished prototype for *Jack Survives*, acrylic on paper, 24 x 18", 1979.

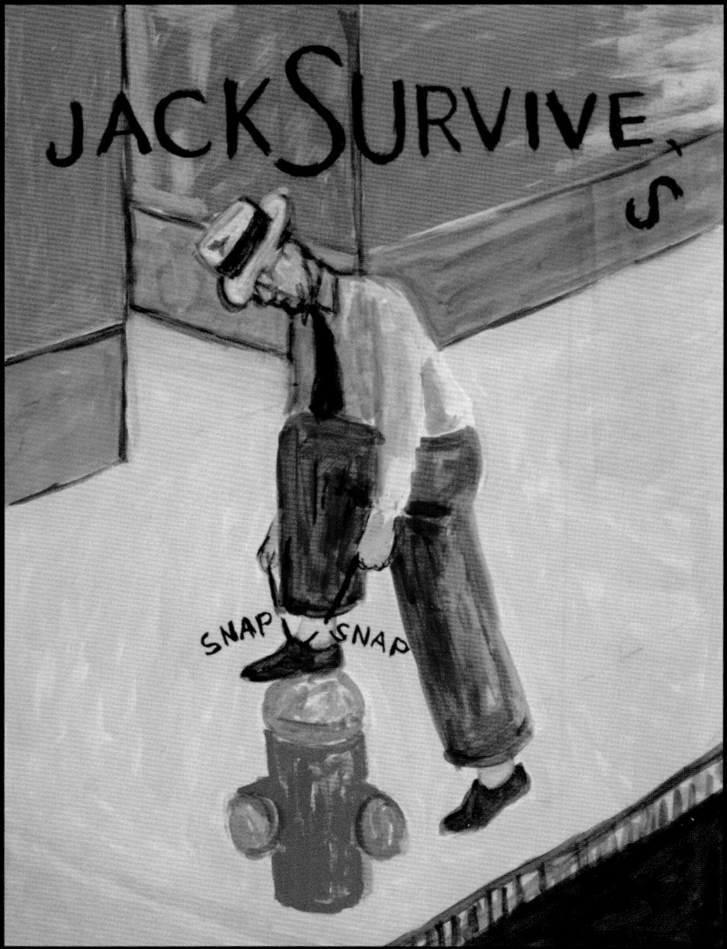
JACK SURVIVES
SNAP
SNAP

Unfinished cover art for the forthcoming *The Complete Jack Survives*, acrylic on paper, 24 x 18", 2007.

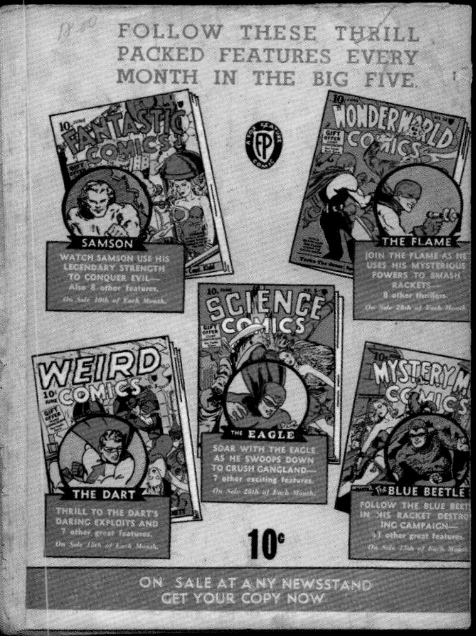
FOLLOW THESE THRILL PACKED FEATURES EVERY MONTH IN THE BIG FIVE.
FANTASTIC COMICS
WONDERWORLD COMICS
SAMSON
THE FLAME
SCIENCE COMICS
WEIRD COMICS
MYSTERY MEN COMICS
THE EAGLE
THE DART
BLUE BEETLE
10¢
ON SALE AT ANY NEWSSTAND
GET YOUR COPY NOW

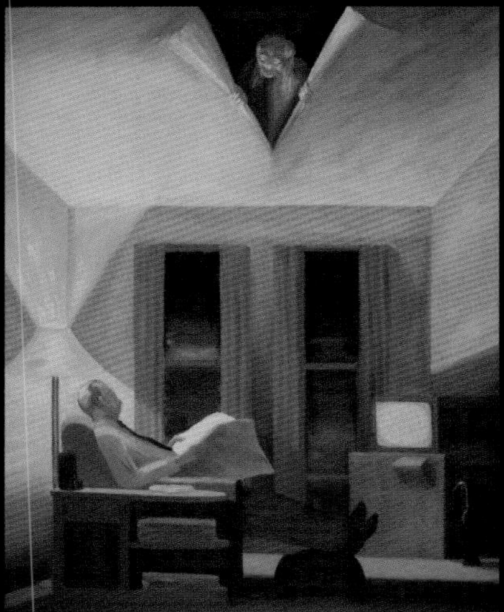

Top: Fox Publishing back-cover advertisement, 1939.

Above: *Visit*, oil on canvas, 60 x 45", 1993.

I started going to comic cons, which turned on my collecting gene. I am a black hole collector. Whatever I collect goes in but it never comes back out.

My comics taste shifted away from realistic comics to Golden Age second bananas like those published by Fiction House, Fox, and Centaur from 1939–45. They had weird superheroes like The Moth, Stardust, Blue Beetle, and The Flame.

I wasn't collecting out of nostalgia, these were comics I never saw as a kid. Then there were the Silver Age comics dominated by Marvel and Steve Ditko, who was the William Blake of comics—his Spider-Man and Dr. Strange were lyrical, other-worldly.

I discovered Warren Comics with the great Frazetta covers on *Creepy*, *Eerie*, and *Blazing Combat*, where a lot of former EC artists got work. Even Ditko did a number of stories in gray wash for Warren. As magazines, they beat the Comics Code.

There was the "underground" with its anger, sex, creativity, and goofiness along with its personal stuff. I loved Justin Green's *Binky Brown Meets the Holy Virgin Mary*.

My rediscovery of comics came at the point when the comics broke free from their masters and became an art form produced by artists—a unique form of self expression.

Meanwhile I got an NEA grant in painting, bought a cheap car, and rented a house in the country where a daily newspaper was delivered.

In that paper it was sad to see how the comic strips had been reduced in size—the only one that still looked good was *Nancy*.

I didn't like *Nancy* as a kid, so I feared for my mind now that I looked forward to it every day. The jokes were still lame but the art was better than I remembered because it was designed to tell stories at a minimum.

The paintings that got me an NEA were small and my most conservative up to that point, so I didn't feel a need to continue in that vein. Until I could come up with new painting ideas I decided to try and do a comic page. My visual life was more involved in comics than in painting by 1978. I'd go to comic cons more than art galleries or museums. I'd collect comics more than art books, so I didn't approach comics like a Pop artist and I wasn't slumming.

I had just turned forty, the age my father was when I first remembered him. I decided my comic character would look like my father, dressed in the clothes he'd have on when he came home from work. He wasn't called Jack until a year later.

Jack Survives took advantage of my new understanding of *Nancy*—that comics didn't have to be belly-laugh funny to engage you. I'd think of scenarios for Jack that were sort of funny. They were "hume" not humor or humest.

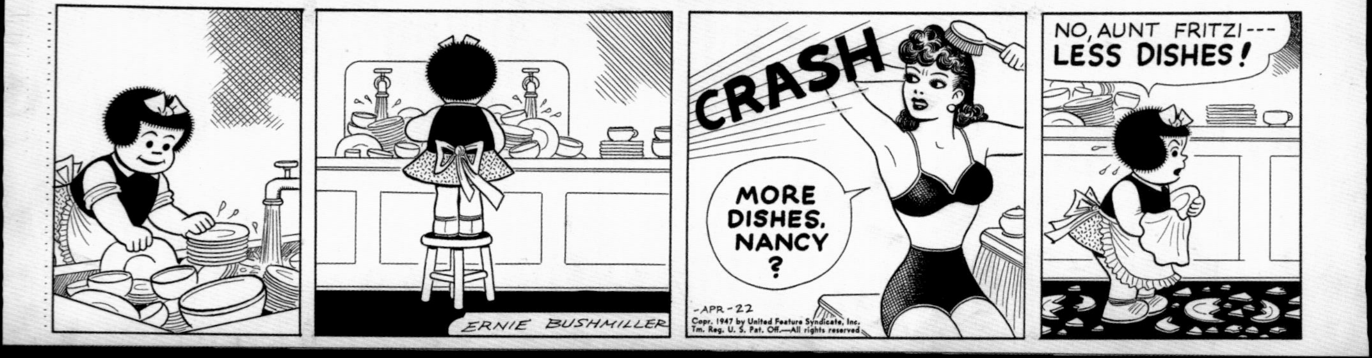
CRASH
MORE DISHES, NANCY?
NO, AUNT FRITZI--- LESS DISHES!
ERNIE BUSHMILLER
APR-22
Copr. 1947 by United Feature Syndicate, Inc. Tm. Reg. U. S. Pat. Off.—All rights reserved

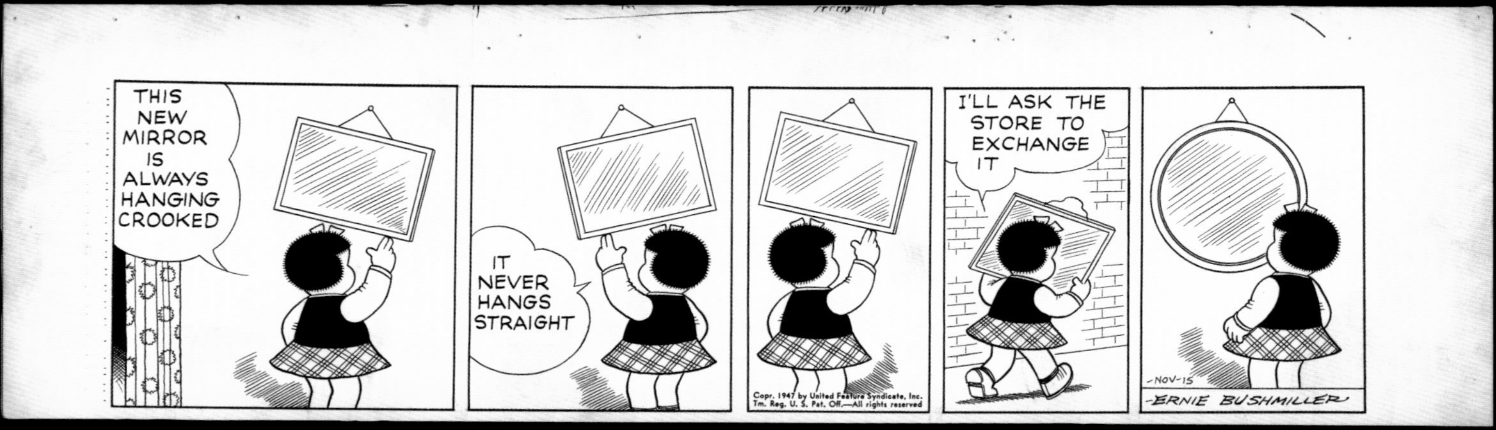
THIS NEW MIRROR IS ALWAYS HANGING CROOKED
IT NEVER HANGS STRAIGHT
I'LL ASK THE STORE TO EXCHANGE IT
Copr. 1947 by United Feature Syndicate, Inc. Tm. Reg. U. S. Pat. Off.—All rights reserved
NOV-15
ERNIE BUSHMILLER

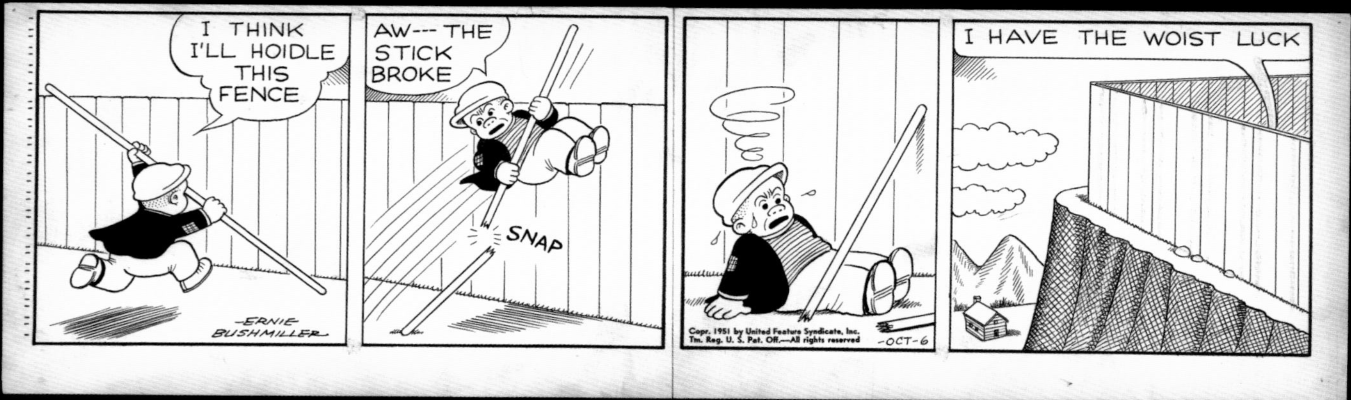
I THINK I'LL HOIDLE THIS FENCE
ERNIE BUSHMILLER
AW--- THE STICK BROKE
SNAP
Copr. 1951 by United Feature Syndicate, Inc. Tm. Reg. U. S. Pat. Off.—All rights reserved
OCT-6
I HAVE THE WOIST LUCK

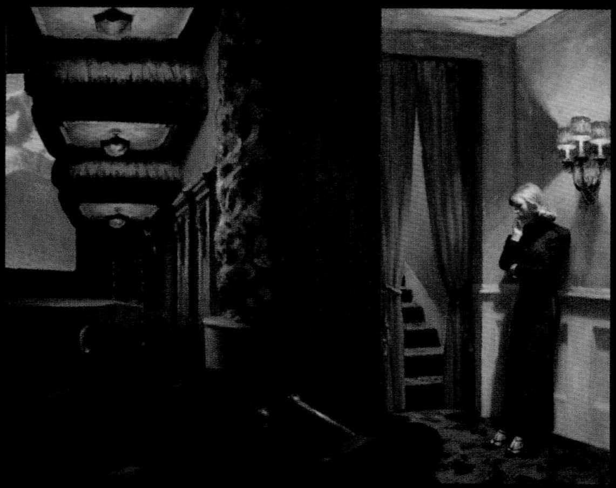

Edward Hopper, *New York Movie*, 1939.

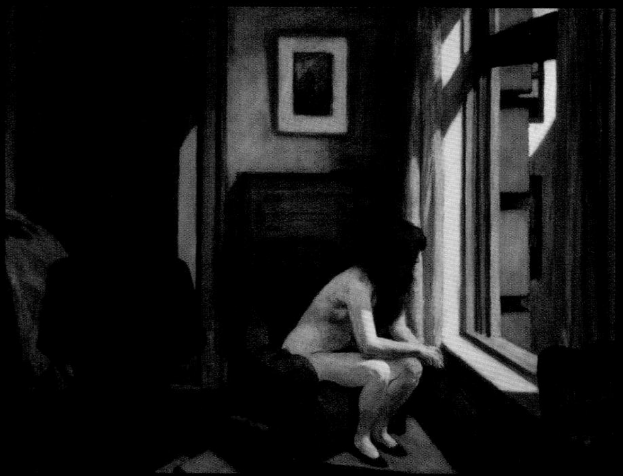

Edward Hopper, *Eleven A.M.*, 1926.

Opposite: Ernie Bushmiller, original art for three *Nancy* daily strips from Moriarty's collection, c. 1940s–50s.

Below: Moriarty's tryout for the *Nancy* Sunday strip, ink and acrylic on paper, 24 x 18", 1984.

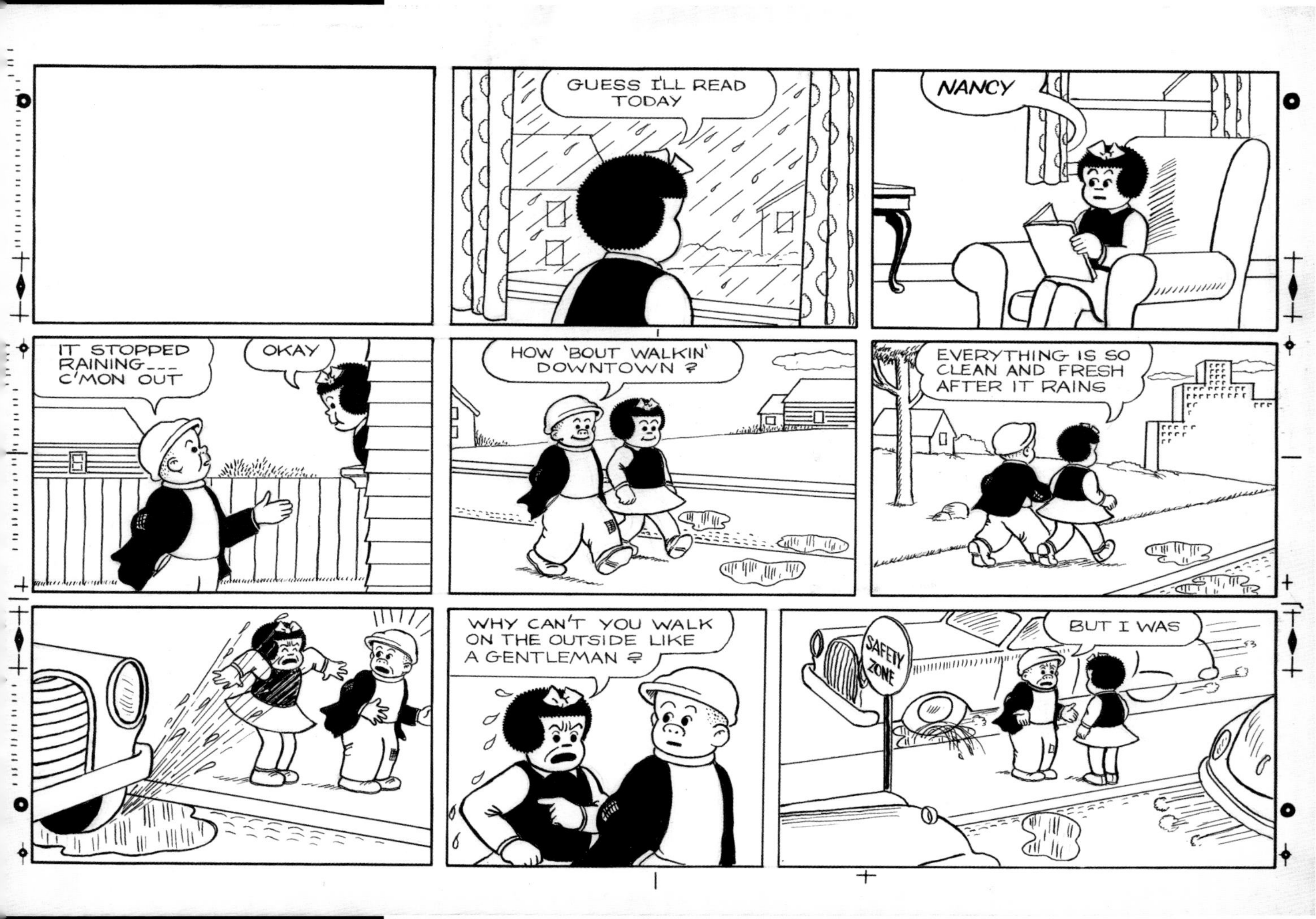
GUESS I'LL READ TODAY
NANCY
IT STOPPED RAINING--- C'MON OUT
OKAY
HOW 'BOUT WALKIN' DOWNTOWN ?
EVERYTHING IS SO CLEAN AND FRESH AFTER IT RAINS
WHY CAN'T YOU WALK ON THE OUTSIDE LIKE A GENTLEMAN ?
SAFETY ZONE
BUT I WAS

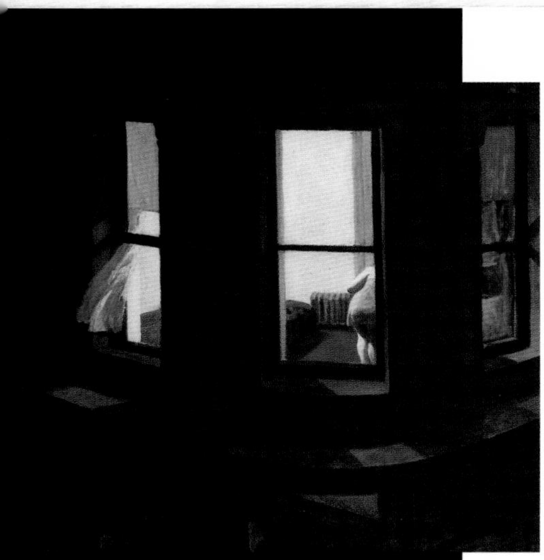
Edward Hopper, *Night Windows*, 1928.

Most people were not interested in *Nancy* then so I was able to collect a lot of originals of Bushmiller's best 1940s stuff. Collecting is my deepest form of studying something; especially with a limited income, I really have to weigh its true value.

I was even asked at one point to take over the Sunday page of *Nancy*. Ernie was still alive and doing the dailies. I took advantage of my position to call him up and talk to the great man. But it took me too long to do a page in his style because our styles were opposites. Got one Sunday page done but it never got printed.

My influences come in twos—one is conservative and shows realist art skills like Edward Hopper or Norman Rockwell, while the other is about ideas and less realist, like Philip Guston and Ernie Bushmiller. Both would be in my head at the same time.

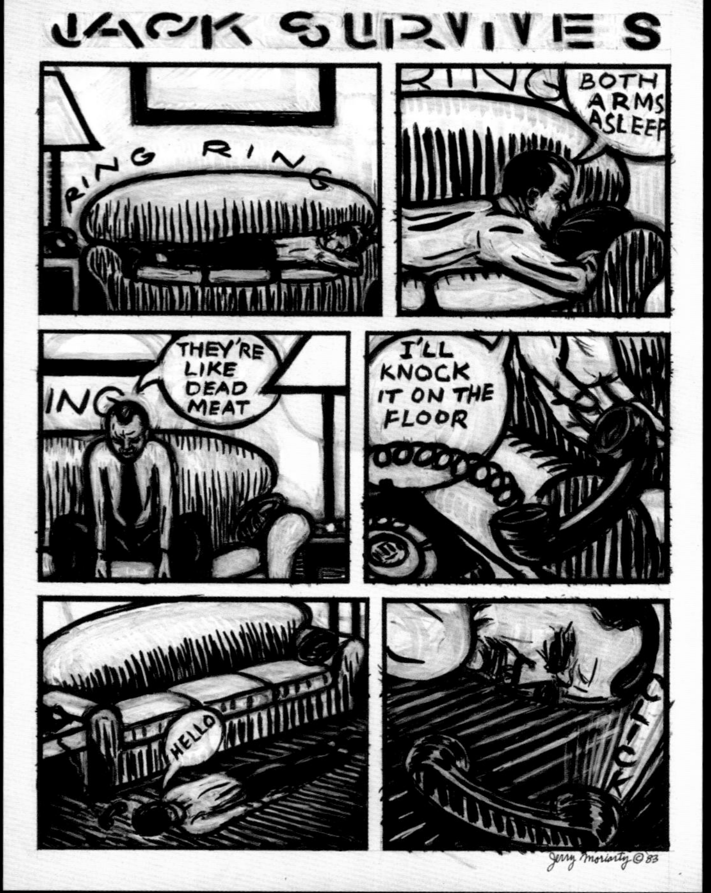
JACK SURVIVES
RING RING
RING
BOTH ARMS ASLEEP
ING
THEY'RE LIKE DEAD MEAT
I'LL KNOCK IT ON THE FLOOR
HELLO
Jerry Moriarty ©83

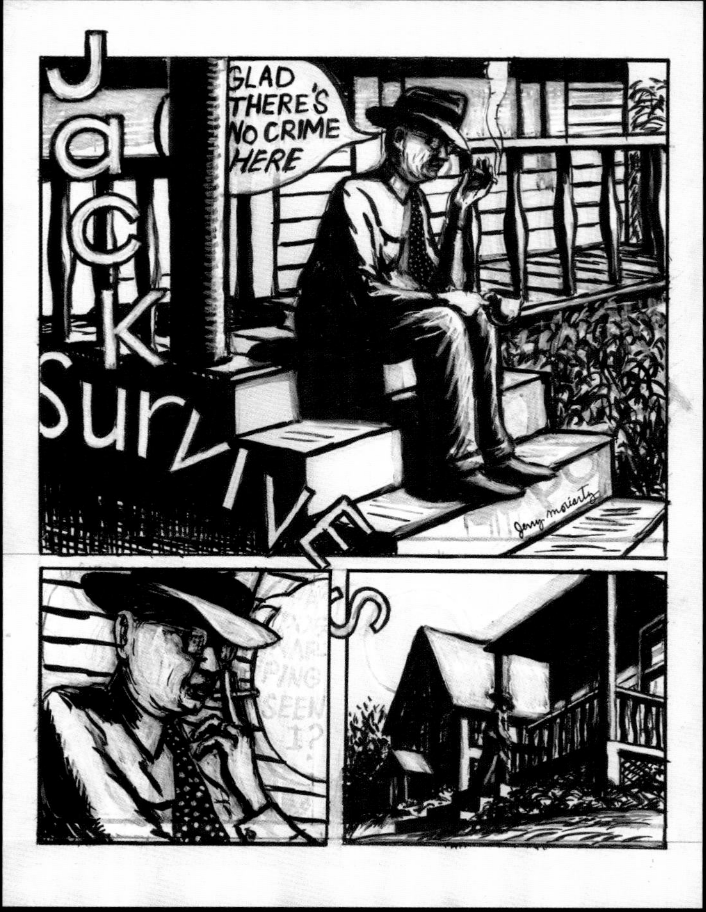
Jack Survives
GLAD THERE'S NO CRIME HERE
Jerry Moriarty

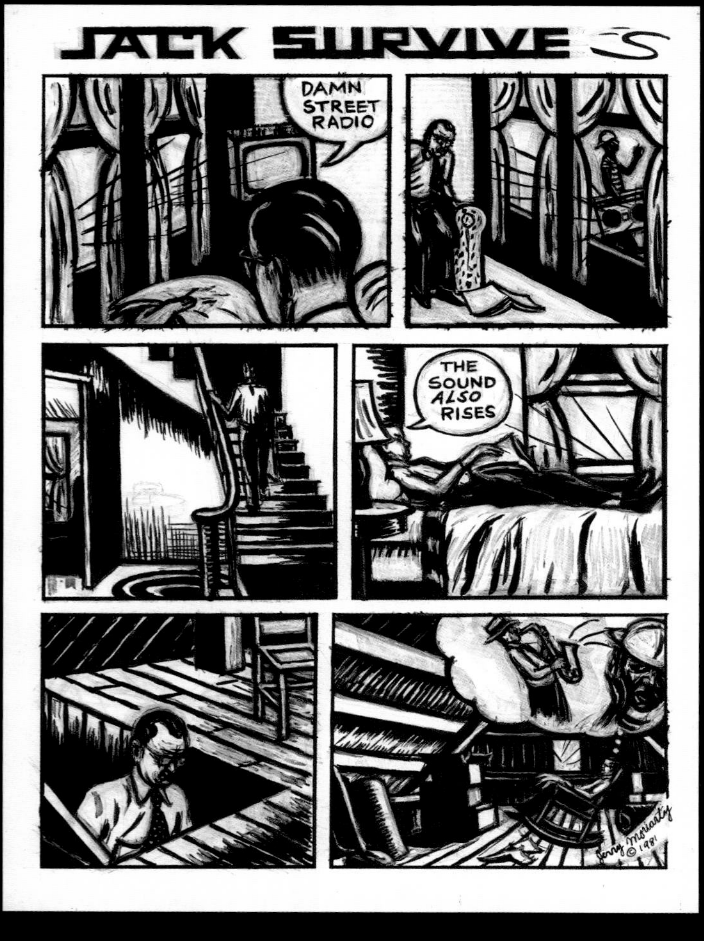
JACK SURVIVES
DAMN STREET RADIO
THE SOUND ALSO RISES
Jerry Moriarty ©1981

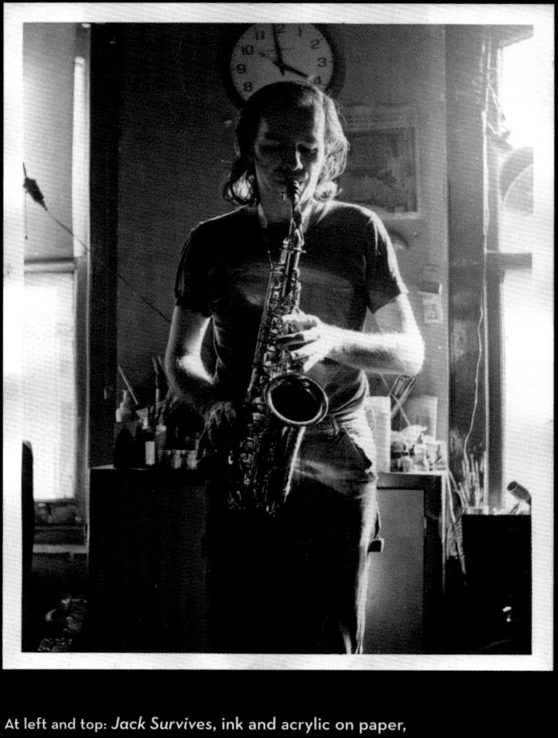

At left and top: *Jack Survives*, ink and acrylic on paper, three pages, each 24 x 18", 1983.

Above: Moriarty playing sax, 1974. Photo by Jill Knobelauch.

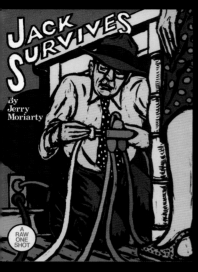

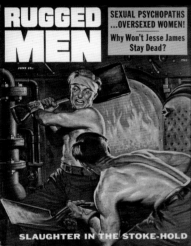

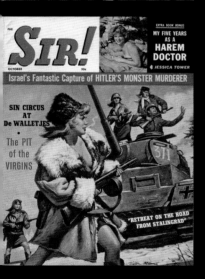

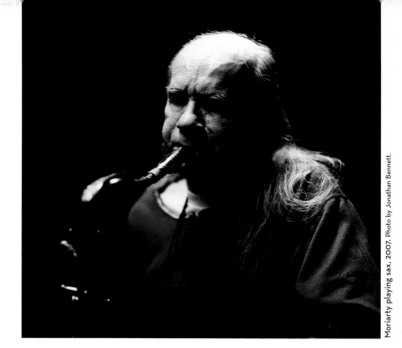

Moriarty playing sax, 2007. Photo by Jonathan Bennett.

Jack Survives was literally a painted cartoon and each page took a month. It was done with black ink and white acrylic on 18 x 24" Arches paper.

I showed Art Spiegelman and Françoise Mouly the seven pages of Jack I had done by 1980. They were very encouraging and invited me to be in the first *RAW*. I became a regular contributor. Later they published a book of *Jack Survives* (*RAW One-Shot* #3).

As a "loner" artist, *RAW* was the closest thing I have experienced to an artist's community. Twenty years later this is true of *Kramers Ergot* even though it is not centered in NYC but in LA.

When the *RAW One-Shot* was published that was the end of Jack for me. After five years and thirty-five pages Jack did not Survive. He had become predictable.

Saxophone music is a passion of mine. I have played my saxophones, an alto and a tenor, for thirty-five years. I have no skill but deep love. I make CDs of my practice and I make CDs of "out" solo sax improvisers to listen to when I make pictures. As I've gotten older my taste in sax music has got more radical, which is a foil against my conservative thinking in art. I want my jazz taste to inspire my art taste. I use the sax to express anger. I use art to express joy. I have never been successful when my art was done to express anger.

In 1984 at a flea market there was a pile of "men's adventure" magazines that got my attention. They were from the '50s and had lurid illustrations in them such as women in bras fighting Nazis, etc. They were painted realistically from photos set up by the artist. The images were meant to appeal to the average working-class American male. I was a "girlie" magazine illustrator and our pictures were directed at the aspiring urban bachelor so those images were more far out. We thought of the men's adventure guys as hacks. Twenty-five years later I was prepared to scoff at them, but was blown away by how Surreal, Noir, and well done they were. They had held up better than the pretentious arty stuff we "girlie" illustrators did.

JACK SURVIVES
By Jerry Moriarty
A RAW ONE SHOT

RUGGED MEN
SEXUAL PSYCHOPATHS ...OVERSEXED WOMEN!
Why Won't Jesse James Stay Dead?
SLAUGHTER IN THE STOKE-HOLD

SIR!
EXTRA BOOK BONUS
MY FIVE YEARS AS A HAREM DOCTOR
JESSICA TOWER
Israel's Fantastic Capture of HITLER'S MONSTER MURDERER
SIN CIRCUS AT De WALLETJES
The PIT of the VIRGINS
"RETREAT ON THE ROAD FROM STALINGRAD"

Top: *Jack Survives*: A *RAW One-Shot* #3 (RAW Books & Graphics, 1984).

Middle: *Rugged Men*, June 1956.

Bottom: *Sir*, October 1960.

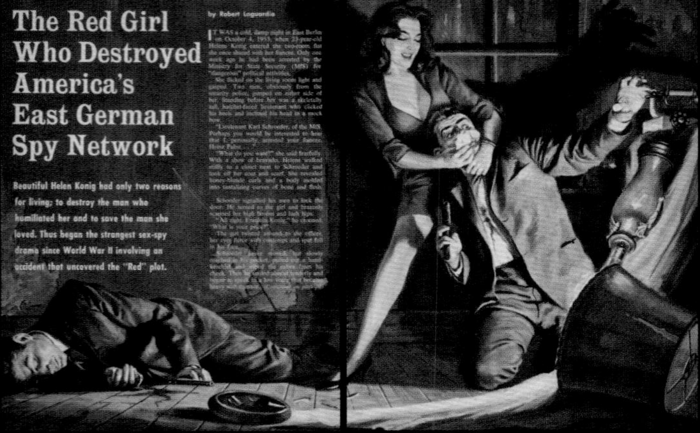
The Red Girl Who Destroyed America's East German Spy Network
by Robert Laguardia
Beautiful Helen Konig had only two reasons for living; to destroy the man who humiliated her and to save the man she loved. Thus began the strangest sex-spy drama since World War II involving an accident that uncovered the "Red" plot.

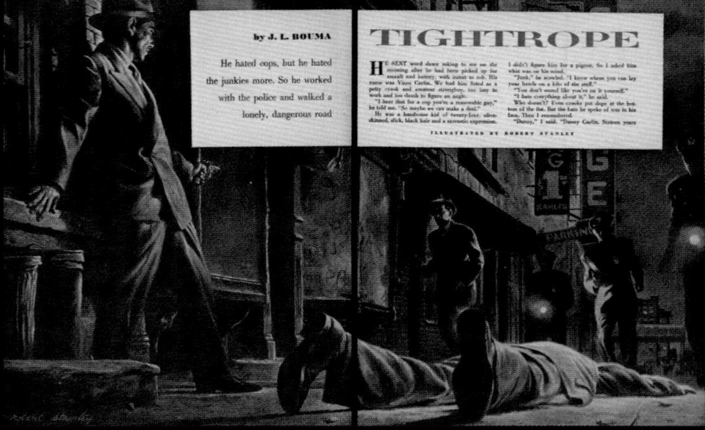
by J. L. BOUMA
He hated cops, but he hated the junkies more. So he worked with the police and walked a lonely, dangerous road
TIGHTROPE
ILLUSTRATED BY ROBERT STANLEY

Top and opposite: Interiors from various men's adventure magazines, c. 1950s–60s.

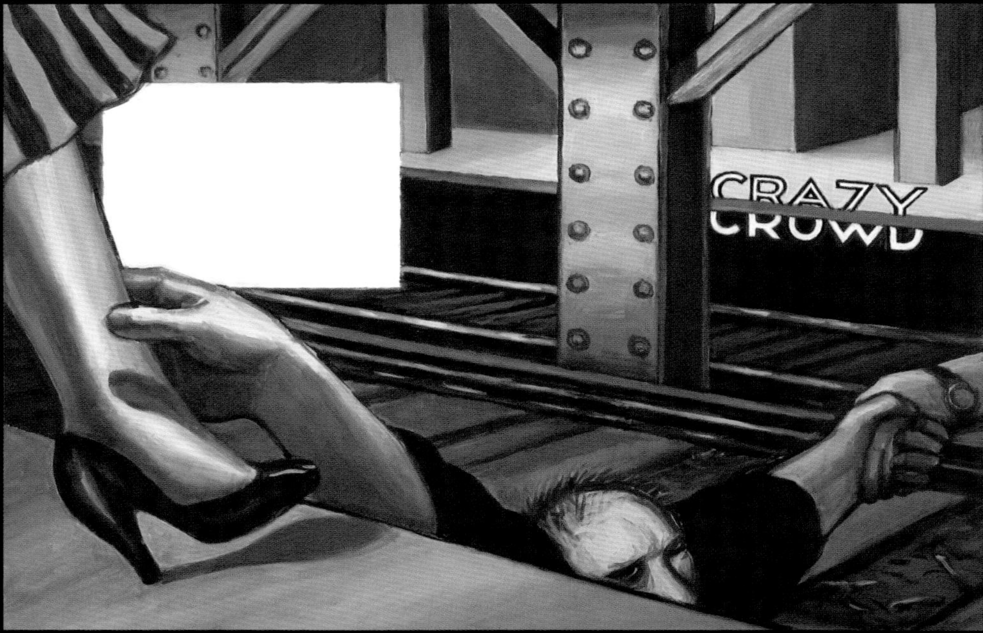
CRAZY
CROWD

Crazy Crowd, acrylic on masonite, 30 x 20", 1987.

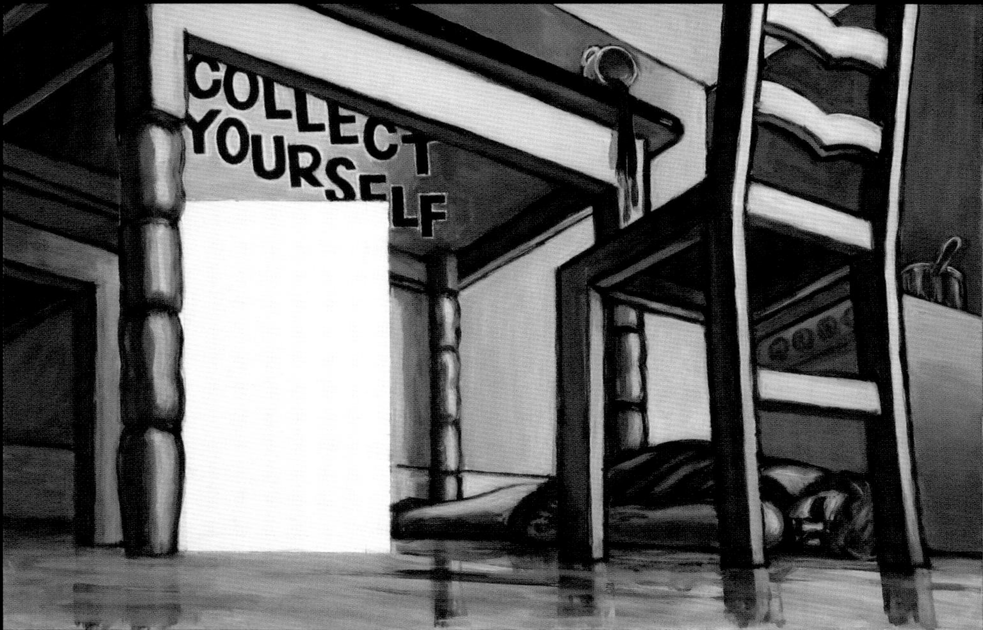
COLLECT
YOURSELF

Collect Yourself, acrylic on masonite, 30 x 20", 1987.

The Commies killed and raped their way through the countryside!

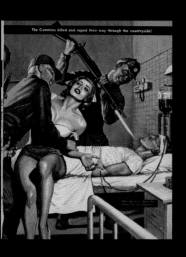

What appealed to me was the dramatic storytelling of the double-page-spread illustrations all done in a realistic manner. They were the heirs of the pulp covers of the 1930s but more Film Noir than Fu Manchu.

Once again I began collecting, this time men's adventure magazines. I cut them up for the best art. When I am collecting something I use the same part of my brain that I use to make art so rarely can I make art the same day. Once satiated, I turn from collector to creator.

By 1985 comics were dead to me, I stopped collecting or reading them because I was focusing on the single image form of storytelling that the men's adventure magazines had unleashed.

I wrote my own men's adventure stories and illustrated them for about four years. One was published in *RAW* and six more were published in other places.

One thing that helps me feel if I am on the right track as I change my art is when it shows opposites to the previous art. *Visual Crimes* (what I called my men's adventure stuff) were horizontal, single images, narrative not dialogue, words in a square box not round balloons, everything is painted in moody grays, everybody dies and there are no recurring characters. *Jack Survives* was none of the above.

In 1988 I turned fifty and had an urge to paint in oil on large canvases. The last time I painted large in oil was twenty years before. I was an entirely different artist then.

The paintings I did for the next ten years are forgettable, but I learned a lot. At the same time I was doing subway posters for SVA and when I did my last one I asked Silas Rhodes (SVA's founder) if I could have a show in the SVA museum. In 1999, my show went up with those forgettable (I liked them then) paintings and *Jack Survives* and *Visual Crimes* original art.

Once the art was shown it lost its relevance to me. Though I never sell my work it is like an old relationship has ended and rarely is revisited.

Back to collecting, this time it was art books and painters. I love reproduced things better than real things, preferring paintings seen in books than on walls, music on CDs, movies on DVDs. Things that cannot be experienced in reproduction have a "theater" need that demands a first hand audience. I like "intimate" art. An art installation cannot be reproduced by a photo in a flat form and still have its theater power.

I love art in its flattest form—reproduction. At the same time I love making the art object and having it as a physical thing. Once I photograph it and print it, the art reveals its magic. I have been moved and influenced by art that was only seen printed. Conversely, I have been disappointed by art that I've seen in person after first liking it reproduced.

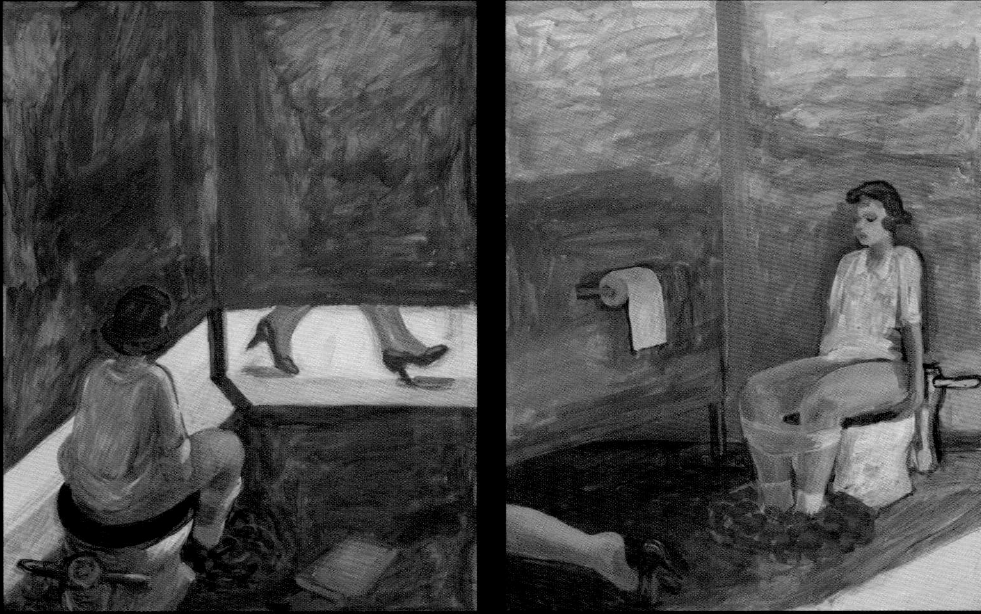

Top and opposite: *Sally in the Public Toilet*, acrylic on Bristol board, four panels, each 24 x 18", 2003.

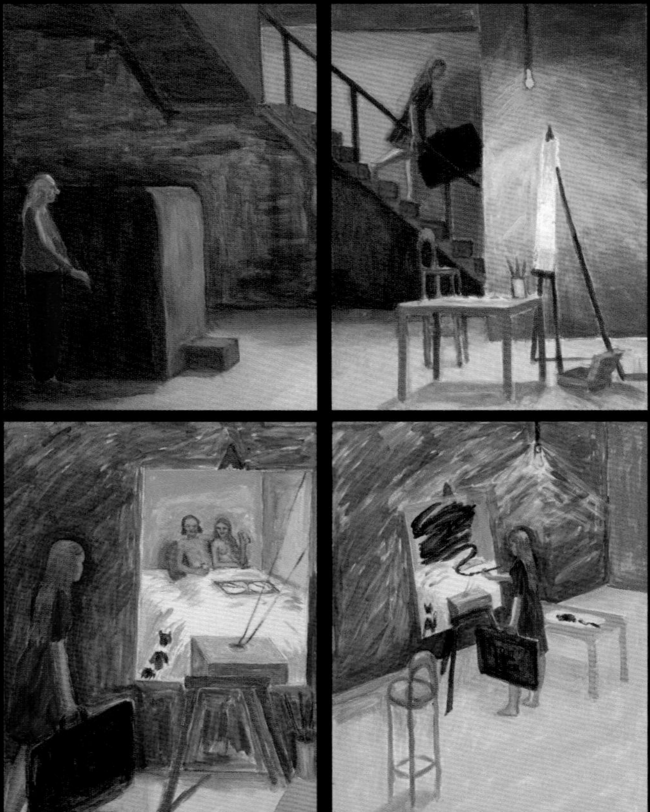

Annoyed X-girlfriend, acrylic on Bristol board, four panels, each 24 x 18", 2006.

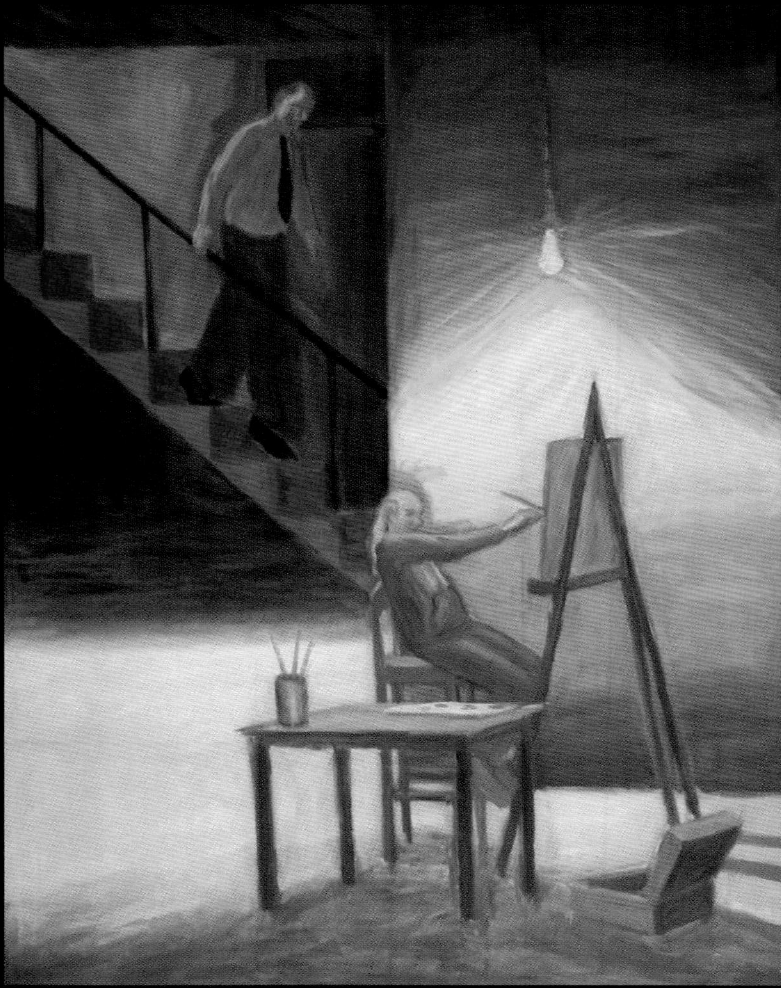

Dad Coming Down Cellar Stairs, oil on canvas, 60 x 46", 2005.

Sally in the Public Toilet, ink and acylic on paper, two pages, each 24 x 18", 2003.

By the year 2000 it was time to change. I was sixty-two, the fiftieth anniversary of my puberty in 1950. How could I do pictures celebrating this anniversary? Instead of doing a "fake" boy playing me, I decided to be a twelve-year-old girl in 1950.

Sally's Surprise is born. She forced me to use the "less-male" part of my brain, which is opposite of the "male" content pictures I had been doing since *Visual Crimes* started fifteen years earlier.

Along with *Sally's Surprise* I have been doing a series of paintings about loves of my life: my dog, my father, an ex-girlfriend. Memories of my dog and my father are from when I was a child in the 1940s. I call the series *Me-Now-Then*. I am in the memories as me, right now at sixty-eight, shrunk to a bald seven-year-old's size.

continues on page 27

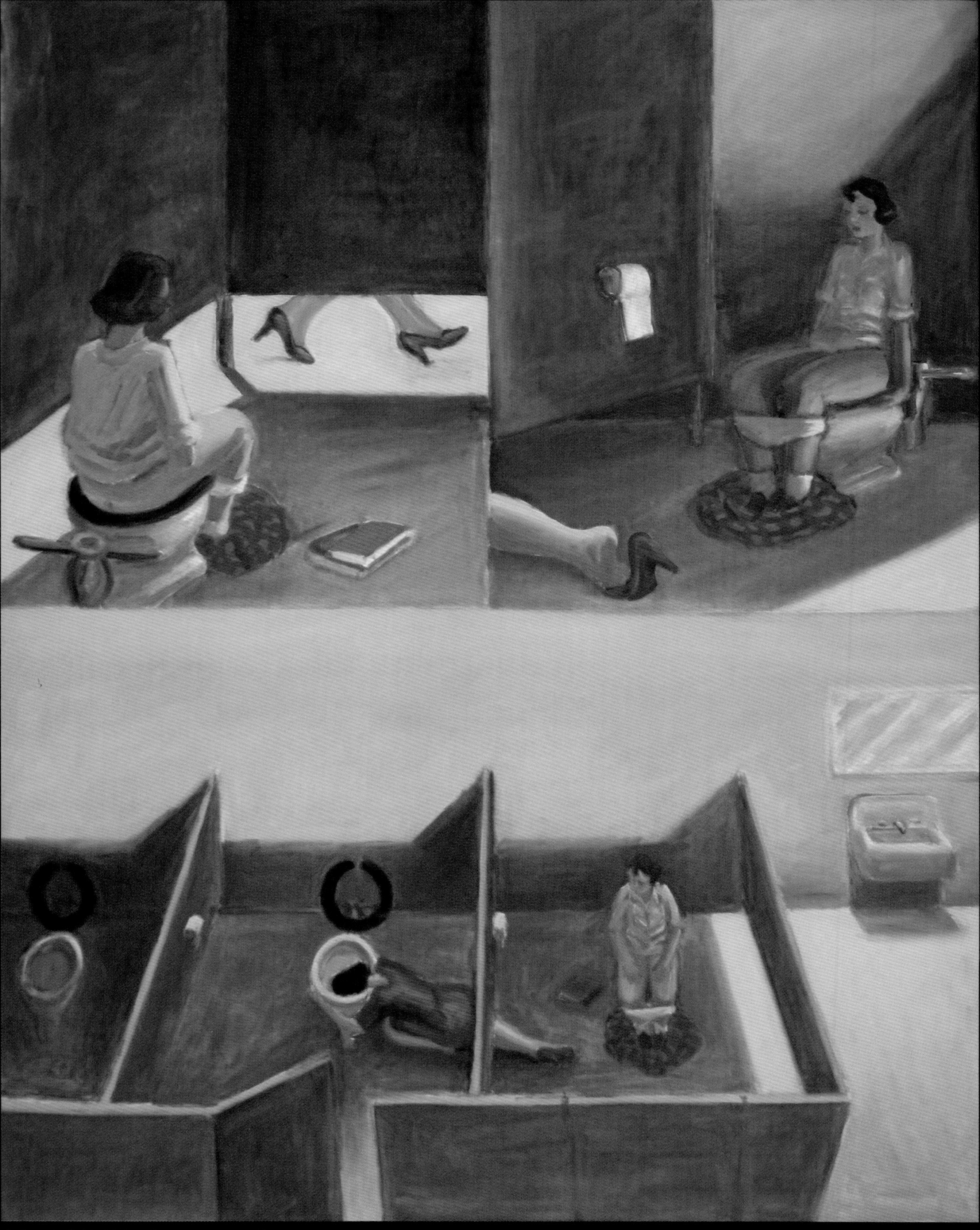

Sally in the Public Toilet, oil on canvas, 60 x 46", 2004.

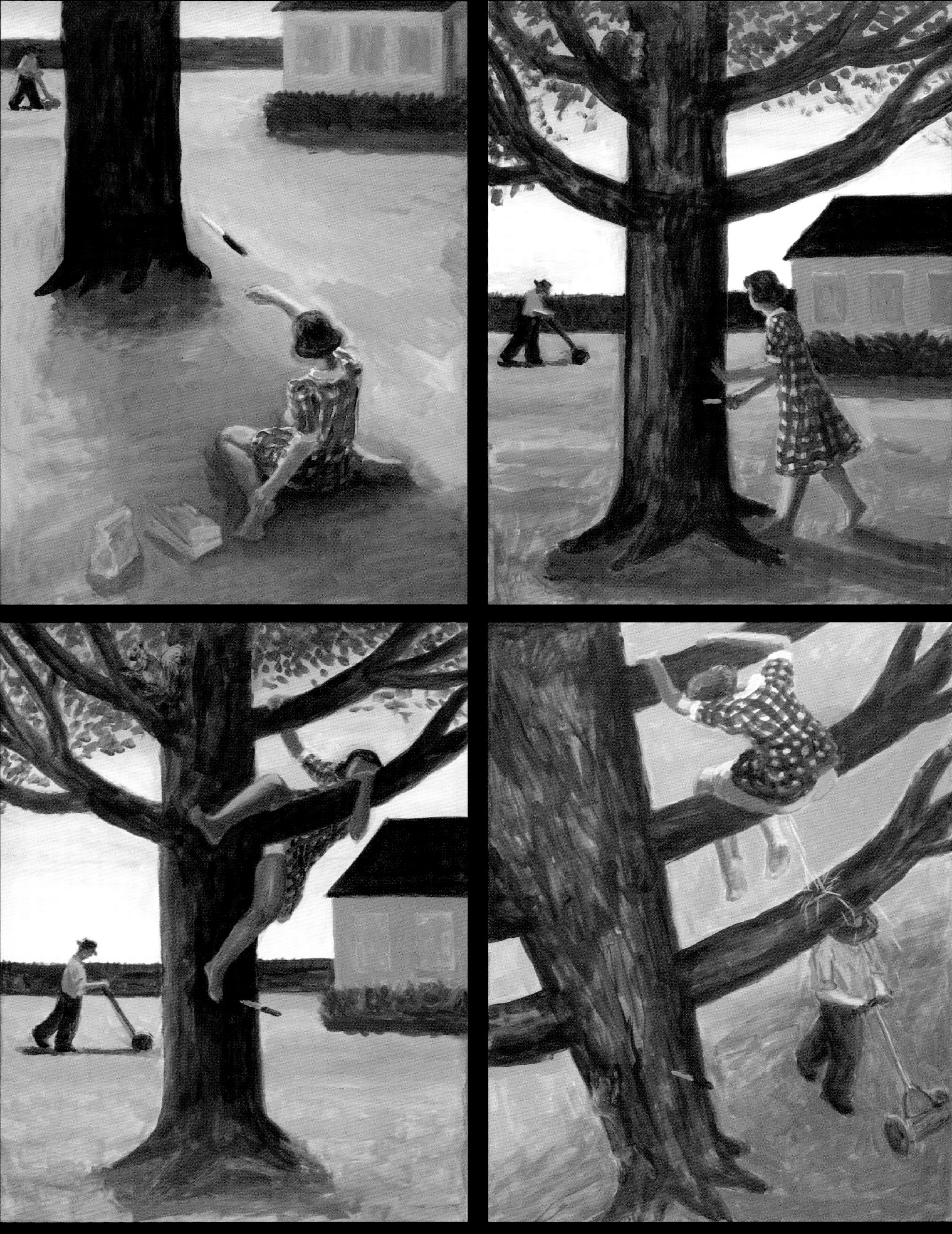

Tree Peé, acrylic on Bristol board, four panels, each 24 x 18", 2002.

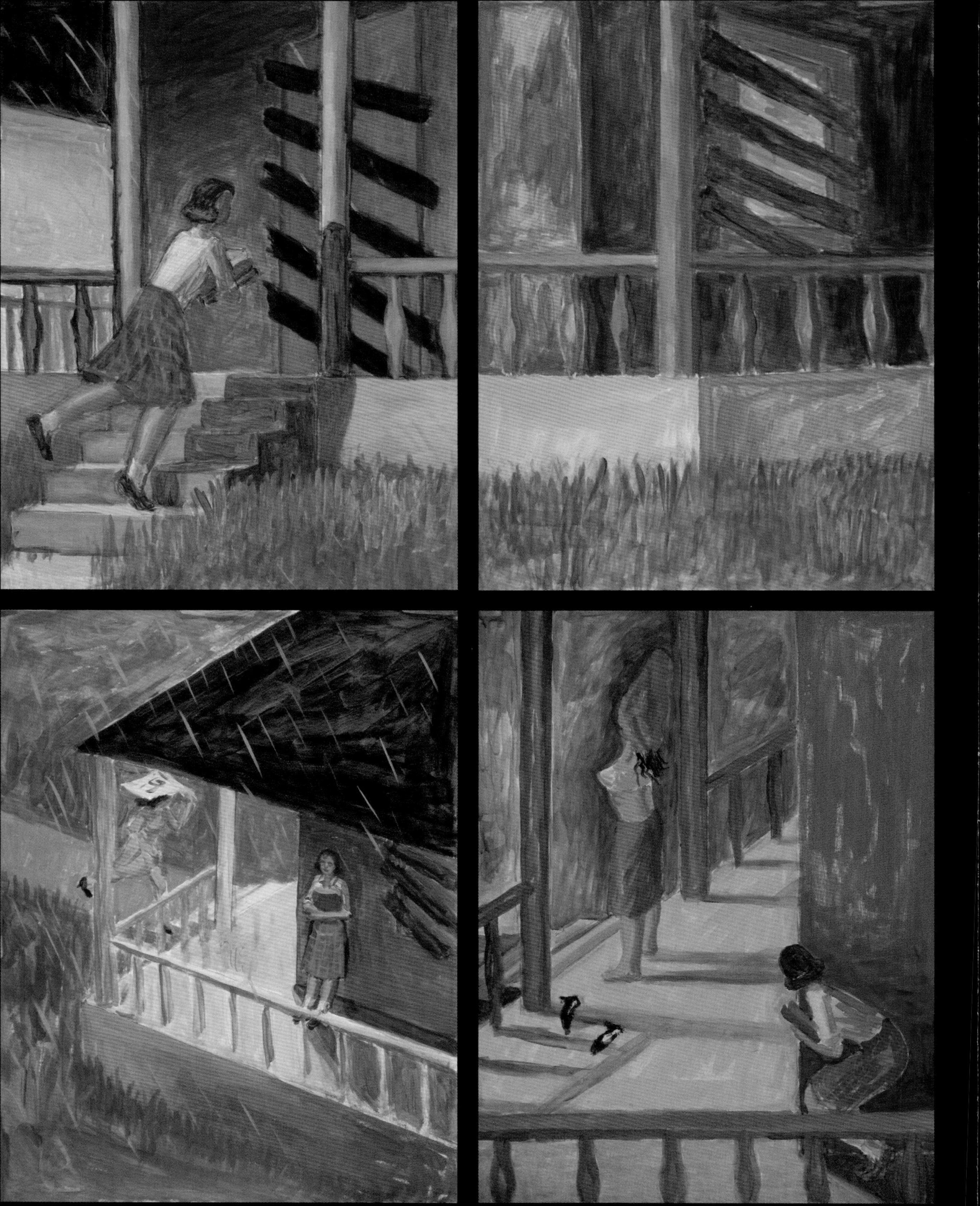

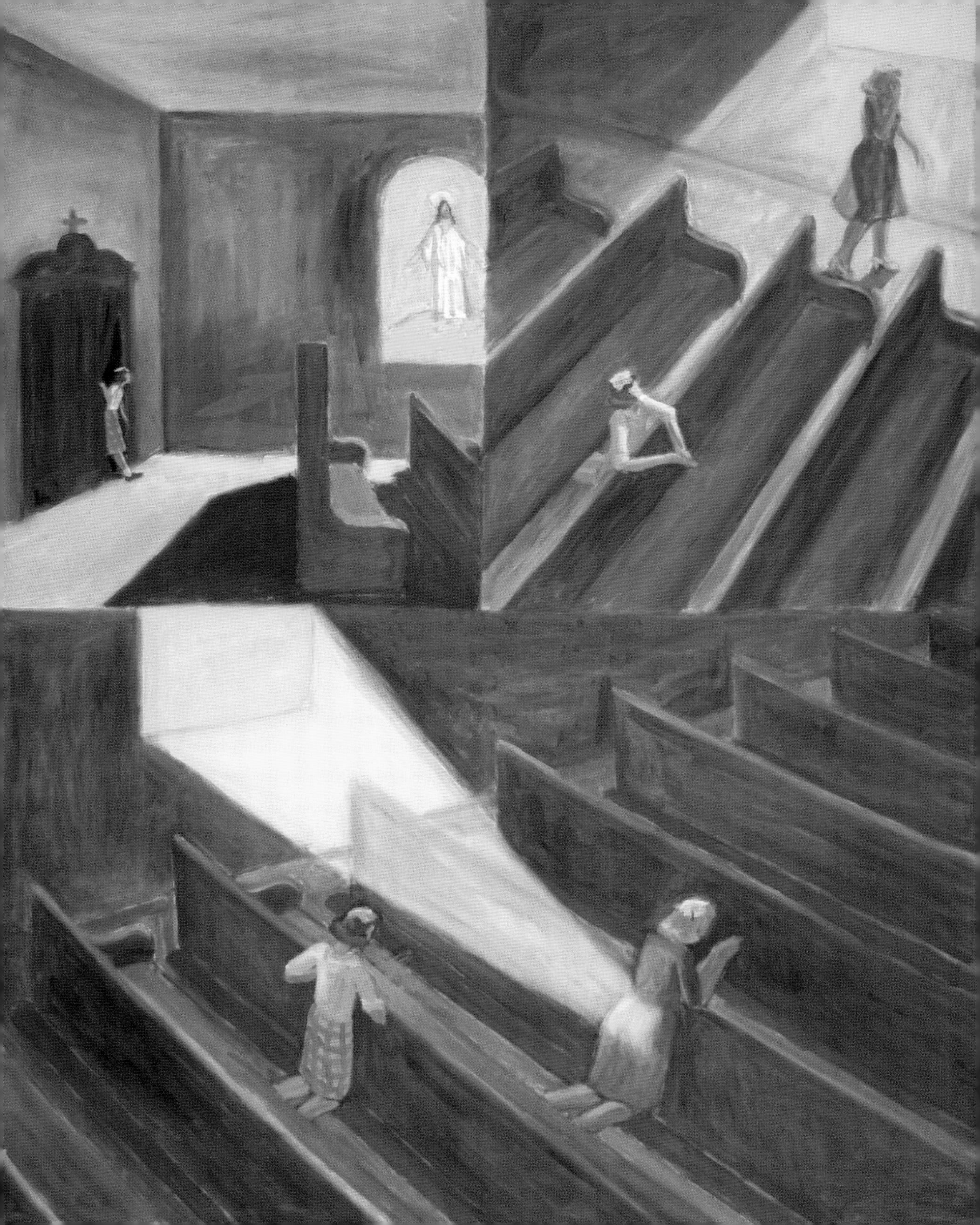

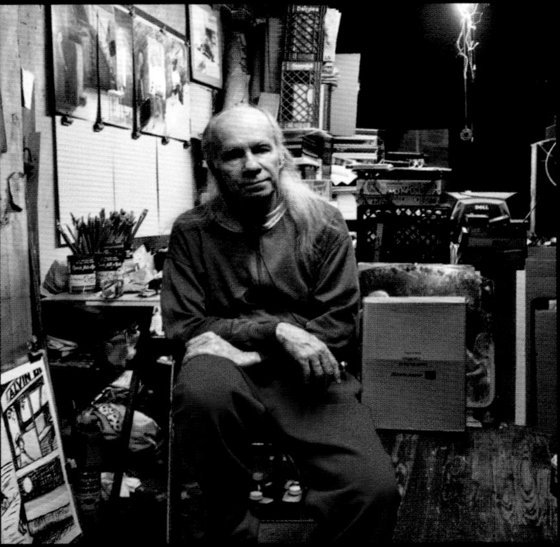

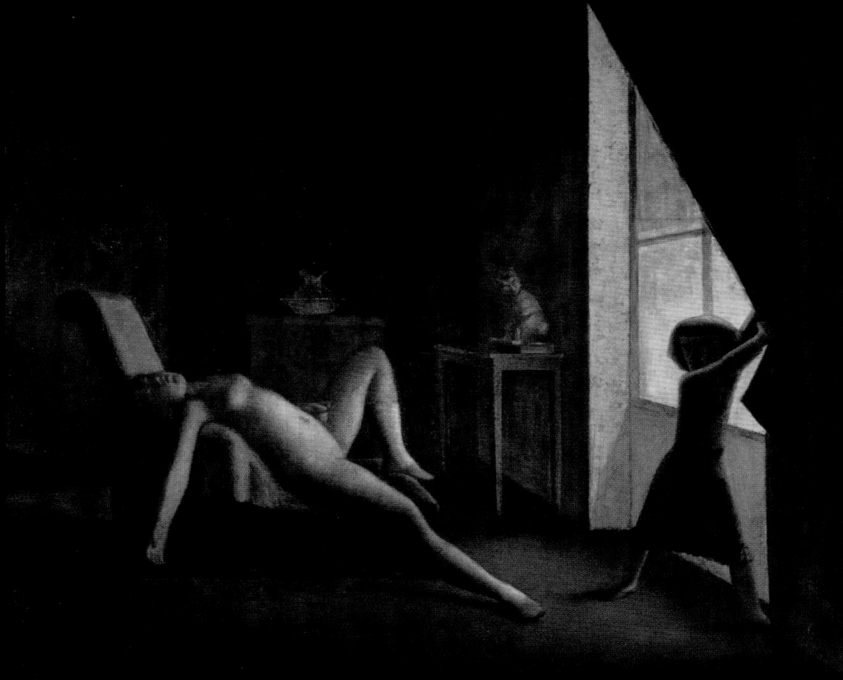

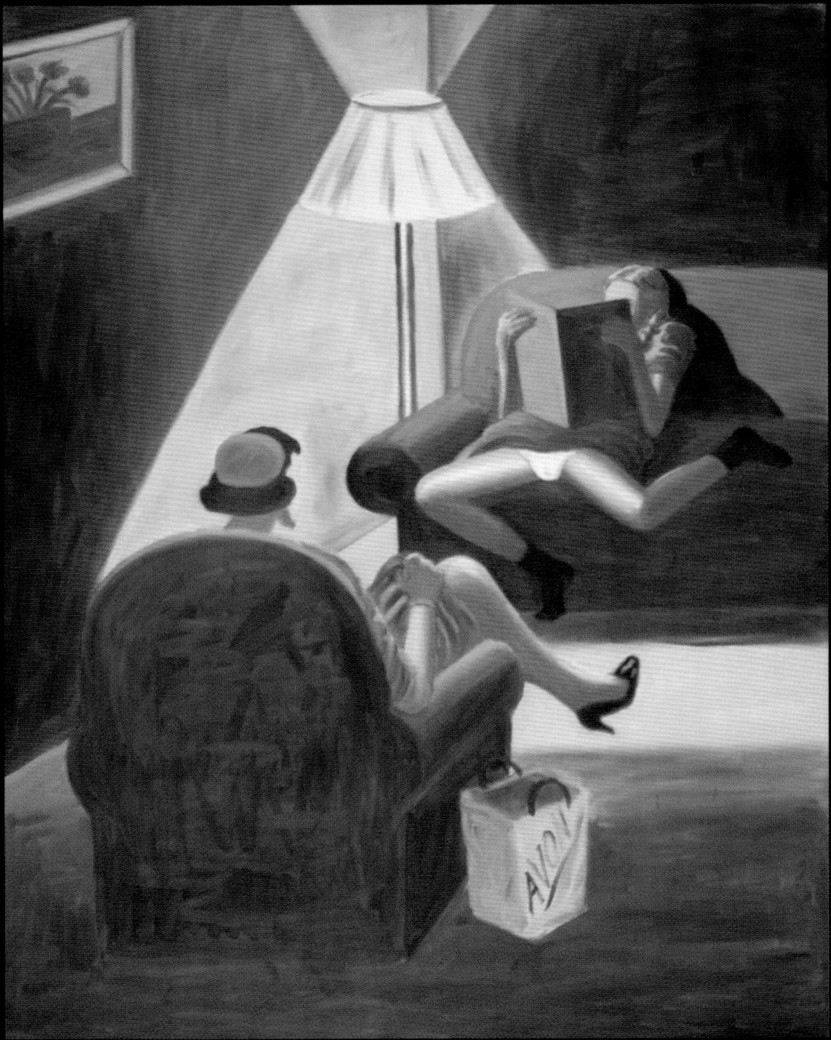

Avon Lady, oil on canvas, 60 x 46", 2000.

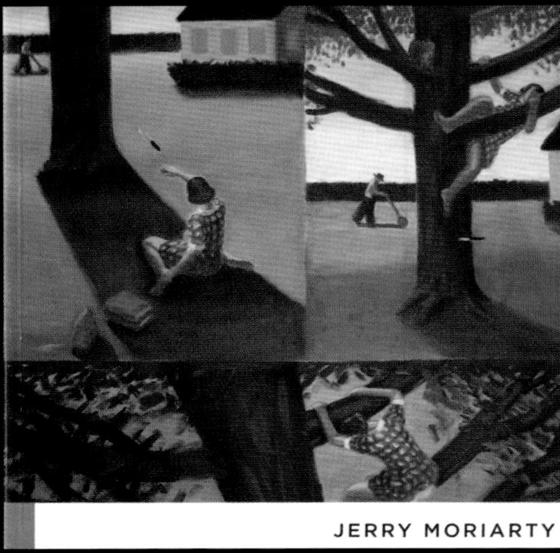
JERRY MORIARTY

Top left: Moriarty in his studio, 2007. Photo by Jonathan Bennett.

Top right: Balthus, *The Room*, 1954.

Above: *Jerry Moriarty*, exhibition catalogue (Cue Foundation, 2004).

Moriarty at Cue Foundation exhibition, 2004.

My influences in art at that time were Edvard Munch and Balthus—they both used emotional states of mind (usually sexual) as content.

Sally's Surprise is puberty without warning, as was common in 1950, those pre-*Playboy*, pre-Barbie, and pre-Britney days. I like imagining it from a girl's point of view, which seems even more innocent. I love the condition of surprise as the opposite of cool or worldly or professional.

Jack is innocent, too. Other than that, Sally and Jack have differences that keep me interested. I have stumbled a few times when I gave Sally male reactions instead of going to my "less-male" brain.

Sally has allowed me to work with a comic form of three panels on a canvas, bringing me back to the same feelings I had while doing *Jack Survives*. At 4 x 5 feet, it is a big comic page, but it doesn't feel like a painting either.

I have always been jealous of the power of movies and music being able to show time passing and movement. Comics does that and you don't have to collaborate with someone for it to happen. Very appealing to a "loner" artist like me.

In 2004 Art Spiegelman was asked to curate a gallery show of an artist's work he liked who was under-exposed and had no gallery. Art chose me and *Sally's Surprise* got her first public viewing at the Cue Art Foundation in Chelsea. A small *New York Times* review and an *Art News* review were very kind to Sally and me.

All my art is memory anyway. I do not use any photo reference and to drive it even further inside my head, I don't wear my glasses when making art. Later I put them on to see what I did.

I am a "recovering" collector, knowing that if a new passion arises it will consume me until it becomes art—for that reason I will not read the rest of this magazine. ᏩᎧ

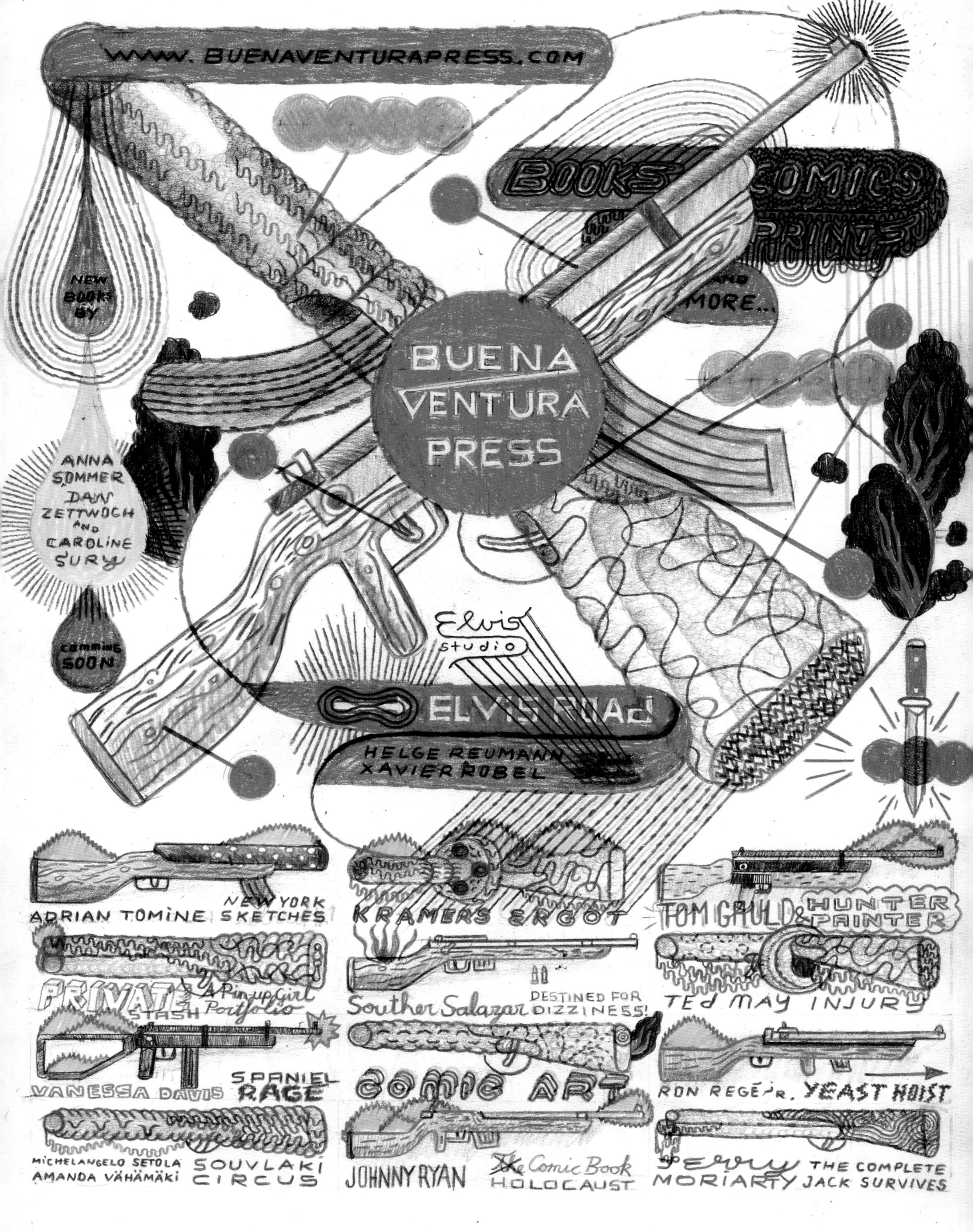
WWW. BUENAVENTURAPRESS.COM
BOOKS
COMICS
PRINTS
AND MORE...
NEW BOOKS BY
ANNA SOMMER
DAN ZETTWOCH AND
CAROLINE SURY
COMMING SOON
BUENA VENTURA PRESS
Elvis studio
ELVIS ROAD
HELGE REUMANN
XAVIER ROBEL
ADRIAN TOMINE
NEW YORK SKETCHES
KRAMERS ERGOT
TOM GAULD & HUNTER PAINTER
PRIVATE STASH
& A Pin-up Girl Portfolio
Souther Salazar
DESTINED FOR DIZZINESS!
TED MAY
INJURY
VANESSA DAVIS
SPANIEL RAGE
COMIC ART
RON REGÉ JR.
YEAST HOIST
MICHELANGELO SETOLA
AMANDA VÄHÄMÄKI
SOUVLAKI CIRCUS
JOHNNY RYAN
The Comic Book HOLOCAUST
JERRY MORIARTY
THE COMPLETE JACK SURVIVES

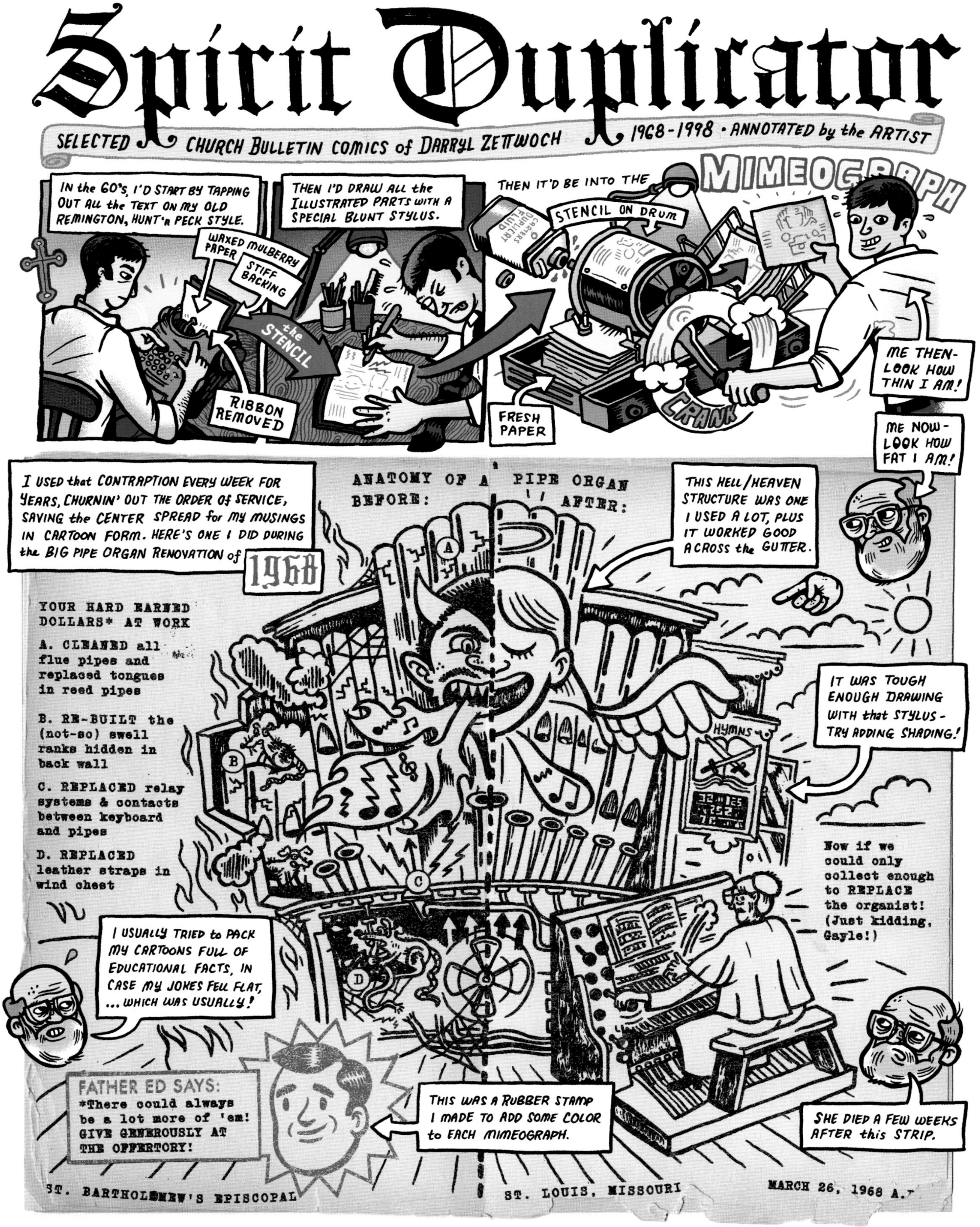
Spirit Duplicator
SELECTED CHURCH BULLETIN COMICS of DARRYL ZETTWOCH 1968-1998 • ANNOTATED by the ARTIST
IN the 60's, I'D START BY TAPPING OUT ALL the TEXT ON MY OLD REMINGTON, HUNT 'n PECK STYLE.
WAXED MULBERRY PAPER
STIFF BACKING
the STENCIL
RIBBON REMOVED
THEN I'D DRAW ALL the ILLUSTRATED PARTS WITH A SPECIAL BLUNT STYLUS.
THEN IT'D BE INTO THE MIMEOGRAPH
CARTERS DUPLICATING FLUID
STENCIL ON DRUM
FRESH PAPER
CRANK
ME THEN- LOOK HOW THIN I AM!
ME NOW- LOOK HOW FAT I AM!
I USED that CONTRAPTION EVERY WEEK FOR YEARS, CHURNIN' OUT THE ORDER of SERVICE, SAVING the CENTER SPREAD for MY MUSINGS IN CARTOON FORM. HERE'S ONE I DID DURING the BIG PIPE ORGAN RENOVATION of 1968
ANATOMY OF A PIPE ORGAN
BEFORE: AFTER:
THIS HELL/HEAVEN STRUCTURE WAS ONE I USED A LOT, PLUS IT WORKED GOOD ACROSS the GUTTER.
YOUR HARD EARNED DOLLARS* AT WORK
A. CLEANED all flue pipes and replaced tongues in reed pipes
B. RE-BUILT the (not-so) swell ranks hidden in back wall
C. REPLACED relay systems & contacts between keyboard and pipes
D. REPLACED leather straps in wind chest
HYMNS
IT WAS TOUGH ENOUGH DRAWING WITH that STYLUS - TRY ADDING SHADING!
Now if we could only collect enough to REPLACE the organist! (Just kidding, Gayle!)
I USUALLY TRIED to PACK MY CARTOONS FULL OF EDUCATIONAL FACTS, IN CASE MY JOKES FELL FLAT, ...WHICH WAS USUALLY!
FATHER ED SAYS:
*There could always be a lot more of 'em! GIVE GENEROUSLY AT THE OFFERTORY!
THIS WAS A RUBBER STAMP I MADE TO ADD SOME COLOR to EACH MIMEOGRAPH.
SHE DIED A FEW WEEKS AFTER this STRIP.
ST. BARTHOLOMEW'S EPISCOPAL
ST. LOUIS, MISSOURI
MARCH 26, 1968 A.D.

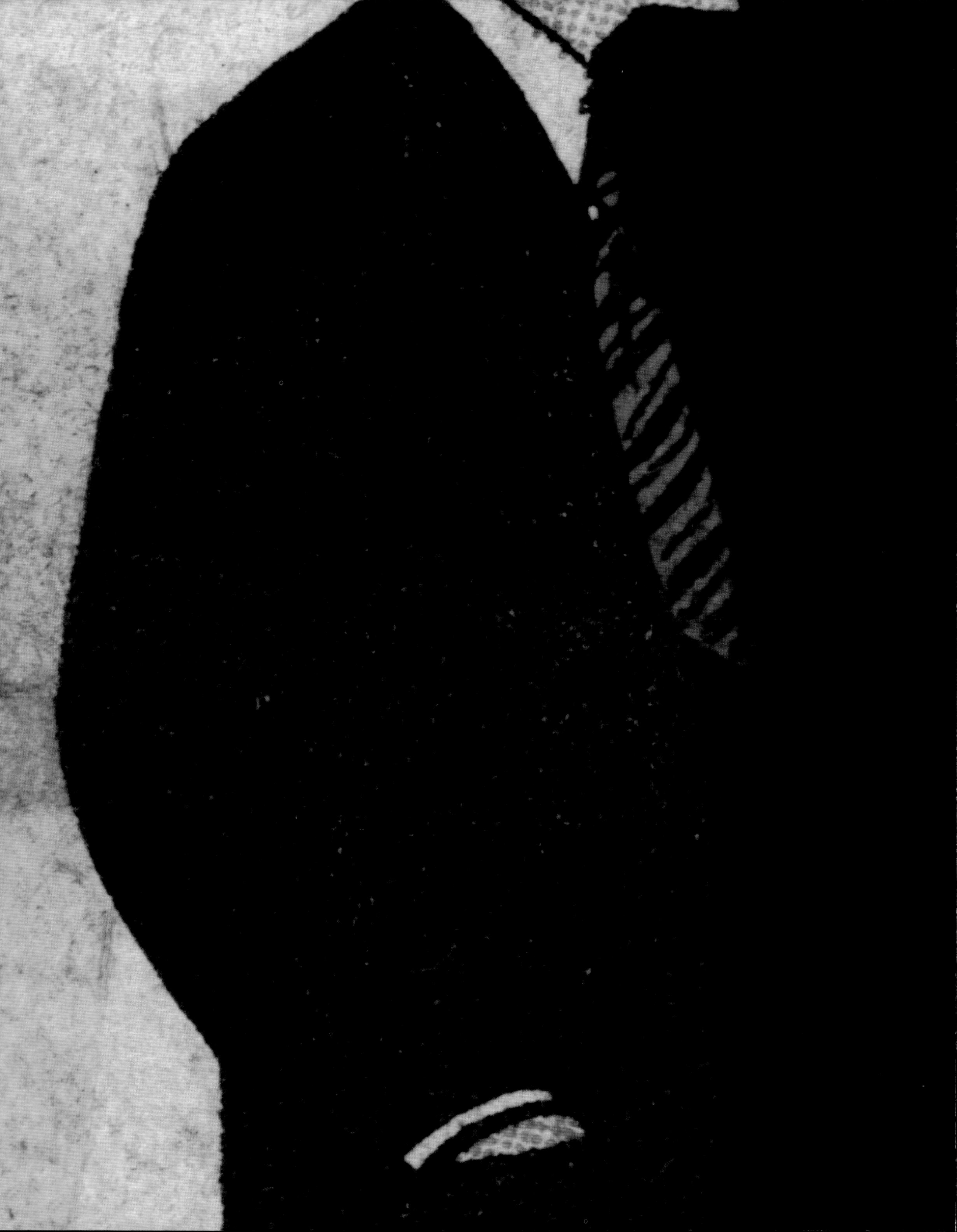

Heart of Gould: The Progress *of* Plainclothes Tracy

M—ME? YOU GHASTLY NIGHTMARE! WHAT ARE YOU?
Reg. U. S. Pat. Off.: Copyright, 1949, by The Chicago Tribune
GET AWAY—(BLUB-GURGLE-GLUB)—I'M DROWNING—
AH, HA, HA, HA—THIS TIME IT DID WORK! THE VERDICT WILL BE DROWNING.
8-28-49

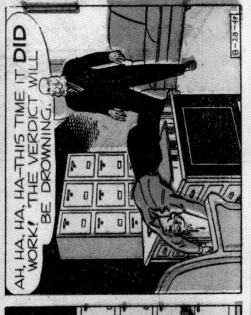

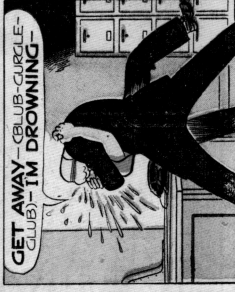

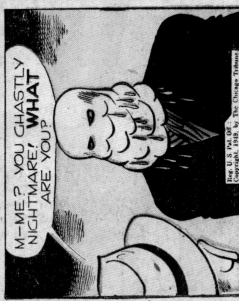

Dick Tracy, Sunday strip detail, August 28, 1949.

by Tom De Haven

"My production of *Dick Tracy* was mostly a case of *constant* application and *continuous* effort," Chester Gould wrote shortly after his retirement. Application. *Constant* application and continuous effort. The phrasing sounds antiquated, heartfelt but antiquated, something rote-learned in school rooms during the first and second decades of the twentieth century; and in the home too, of course, certainly in the home. Constant application and continuous effort. It's the phrasing, as well as the creed, of the morally Protestant man of his time, publicly educated in his time, a twentieth-century citizen with nineteenth-century values who never doubted the basic doctrine of American success or forgot its time-tested formula. Continuous effort. And constant application. The production of *Dick Tracy* was mostly a case of that. The *production* of *Dick Tracy* was. Not the *creation*, the production. Chester Gould, it should come as no surprise, earned a degree in marketing from Northwestern University. Commerce and Marketing. Night school. "Chet succeeded in everything he did," his wife said of her man. "Nothing daunted him."

Dauntless Chester Gould was born on November 20, 1900, in Pawnee, Oklahoma Territory. Born there and grew up there during the last years of the Old West, the West of the cattle-drive cowboys, when the Butch Cassidys were giving way to the Pretty Boy Floyds; during the oil boom years, the First World War. His grandparents were bona fide pioneers. His father was the owner, editor, publisher, and printer of the regional weekly newspaper. When Chester was ten or eleven, *Mutt and Jeff* started to run in his dad's paper. Practically from the moment he laid eyes on Bud Fisher's strip about a racing tout and an escapee from the lunatic asylum, he decided that this, *this*, was what he wanted to do. As a teenager he sent off twenty bucks to the Cleveland-based W.L. Evans School of Cartooning and doggedly completed its home-study course. He was not a natural draftsman, but he practiced and mastered the fundamentals, although in a wooden unimaginative way.

In 1921, he moved to Chicago, intending to make it big as a syndicated cartoonist. He had enormous self-confidence. He tried charming his way to success—pasting, for example, one of his own political drawings over the published drawing in an editor's copy of that morning's paper. If his charm sometimes fell short, and it could, he still had moxie. He'd get out there and fight, every day. Give it his best shot, every day. How could he fail? He came from pioneer stock.

Over the next ten years, the lawless Capone years, Gould wrote and drew a number of comic strips that were locally published—*Radio Cats*, *Fillum Fables*, *Why It's a Windy City*, *The Girl Friends*—but nothing clicked, nothing lasted. To support himself and his wife Edna (a nice girl from nearby Wilmette), Gould freelanced for different art services, and did salaried work in the art departments of every-paper-but-one published in the city of Chicago; like Harold Gray, he had a brief stint as Sidney Smith's background man on *The Gumps*. All the while he kept bombarding his primary target, "Captain" Joseph Patterson of the *Chicago-Tribune* syndicate, with different comic strip proposals, new samples (Gould claimed sixty separate submissions: funny animals, funny kids, funny office boys, funny beautiful girls, funny…) only to be told, over and over again, *no*.

"Chicago in 1931 was being shot up by gangsters," he recalled much later, "and I decided to invent a comic strip character who would always get the best of the assorted hoodlums and mobsters." Gould often said that he developed "Plainclothes Tracy" in late winter, early spring of '31. Warner Brothers' first talkie gangster movie, *Little Caesar*, was released on the last day of that January, then played widely throughout the early months of the year—and not only did it feature a gang leader called Big Boy, as did Gould's unsolicited submission, but Thomas E. Jackson, the rail-thin actor who played the detective hero Sergeant Flaherty, had the identical physique and Roman-nosed profile, the same mien, as the primordial Tracy. You just *know* Gould saw that picture. And probably more than once.

He worked up five dailies (in the first, Big Boy ignites a blow torch to burn the soles of a human rat's feet) and dropped them at the *Chicago Tribune*. It took a while for Patterson's response, but when it came, on August 31—Gould would always recall that it came while he was working a commercial job, laboring over a pen-and-ink drawing of a Persian rug—it was in the form of a telegram that started:

"YOUR PLAINCLOTHES TRACY HAS POSSIBILITIES…"

Patterson liked the idea, the *concept* of Gould's strip, but dismissed the title, too big of a mouthful. "Detectives are called dicks," he told the nervous cartoonist, who'd gone out and bought a new suit for this momentous, life-changing meeting—"so call it *Dick Tracy*."

The strip premiered in the *Detroit Mirror* on Sunday, the fourth of October. The daily debuted on Monday the twelfth. Patterson suggested the origin story: an undistinguished but upstanding young man—could be a retail clerk, could be a night-school student, we're never told—arrives at his fiancée's house for dinner. Her parents own a small grocery store. They all discuss the terrible neighborhood crime wave…and before the first week of *Dick Tracy* is through—on Friday—Emil Truehart, the father of Tracy's girlfriend, Tess, is shot and killed during a robbery. When Tess is dragged off, and by implication raped, Tracy vows to avenge her father *and* snatch her back, *and* bring the entire lot of murdering kidnappers to justice. Once he completes all of these self-imposed tasks, acting unofficially, mind you, he is invited to join the police force. From the very start, Tracy is the man in charge, answering only to the Chief, first Brandon, then Patton. To hell with the seniority system and Civil Service exams.

continues on page 39

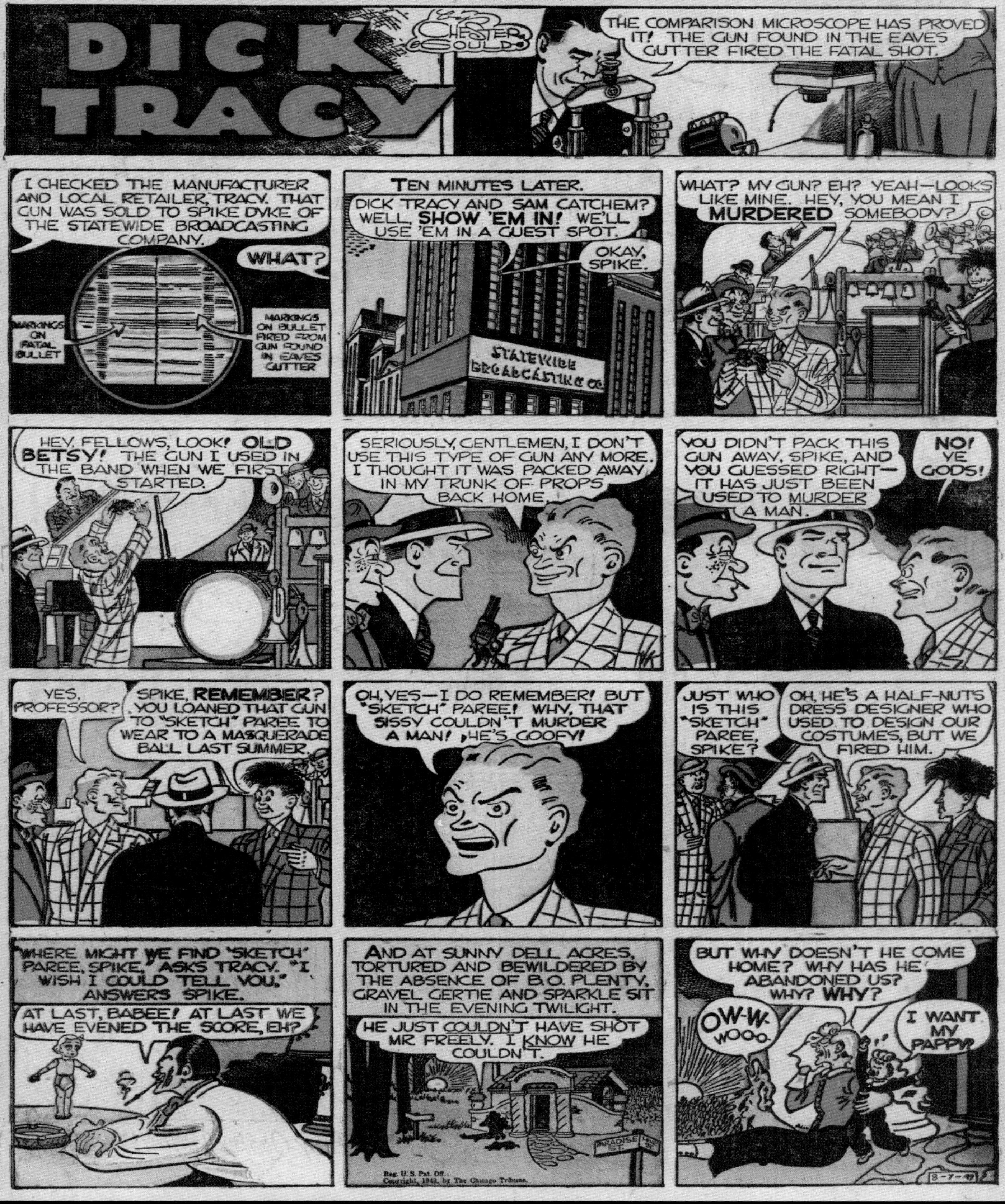
DICK TRACY
CHESTER GOULD
THE COMPARISON MICROSCOPE HAS PROVED IT! THE GUN FOUND IN THE EAVES GUTTER FIRED THE FATAL SHOT.
I CHECKED THE MANUFACTURER AND LOCAL RETAILER, TRACY. THAT GUN WAS SOLD TO SPIKE DYKE OF THE STATEWIDE BROADCASTING COMPANY.
WHAT?
MARKINGS ON FATAL BULLET
MARKINGS ON BULLET FIRED FROM GUN FOUND IN EAVES GUTTER
TEN MINUTES LATER.
DICK TRACY AND SAM CATCHEM? WELL, SHOW 'EM IN! WE'LL USE 'EM IN A GUEST SPOT.
OKAY, SPIKE.
STATEWIDE BROADCASTING CO.
WHAT? MY GUN? EH? YEAH—LOOKS LIKE MINE. HEY, YOU MEAN I MURDERED SOMEBODY?
HEY, FELLOWS, LOOK! OLD BETSY! THE GUN I USED IN THE BAND WHEN WE FIRST STARTED.
SERIOUSLY, GENTLEMEN, I DON'T USE THIS TYPE OF GUN ANY MORE. I THOUGHT IT WAS PACKED AWAY IN MY TRUNK OF PROPS BACK HOME.
YOU DIDN'T PACK THIS GUN AWAY, SPIKE, AND YOU GUESSED RIGHT—IT HAS JUST BEEN USED TO MURDER A MAN.
NO! YE GODS!
YES, PROFESSOR?
SPIKE, REMEMBER? YOU LOANED THAT GUN TO "SKETCH" PAREE TO WEAR TO A MASQUERADE BALL LAST SUMMER.
OH, YES—I DO REMEMBER! BUT "SKETCH" PAREE! WHY, THAT SISSY COULDN'T MURDER A MAN! HE'S GOOFY!
JUST WHO IS THIS "SKETCH" PAREE, SPIKE?
OH, HE'S A HALF-NUTS DRESS DESIGNER WHO USED TO DESIGN OUR COSTUMES, BUT WE FIRED HIM.
"WHERE MIGHT WE FIND 'SKETCH' PAREE, SPIKE," ASKS TRACY. "I WISH I COULD TELL YOU," ANSWERS SPIKE.
AT LAST, BABEE! AT LAST WE HAVE EVENED THE SCORE, EH?
AND AT SUNNY DELL ACRES, TORTURED AND BEWILDERED BY THE ABSENCE OF B.O. PLENTY, GRAVEL GERTIE AND SPARKLE SIT IN THE EVENING TWILIGHT.
HE JUST COULDN'T HAVE SHOT MR FREELY. I KNOW HE COULDN'T.
PARADISE ST.
BUT WHY DOESN'T HE COME HOME? WHY HAS HE ABANDONED US? WHY? WHY?
OW-W-WOOO
I WANT MY PAPPY!
Reg. U. S. Pat. Off.
Copyright, 1949, by The Chicago Tribune.
8-7-49

Dick Tracy, Sunday strip, August 7, 1949.

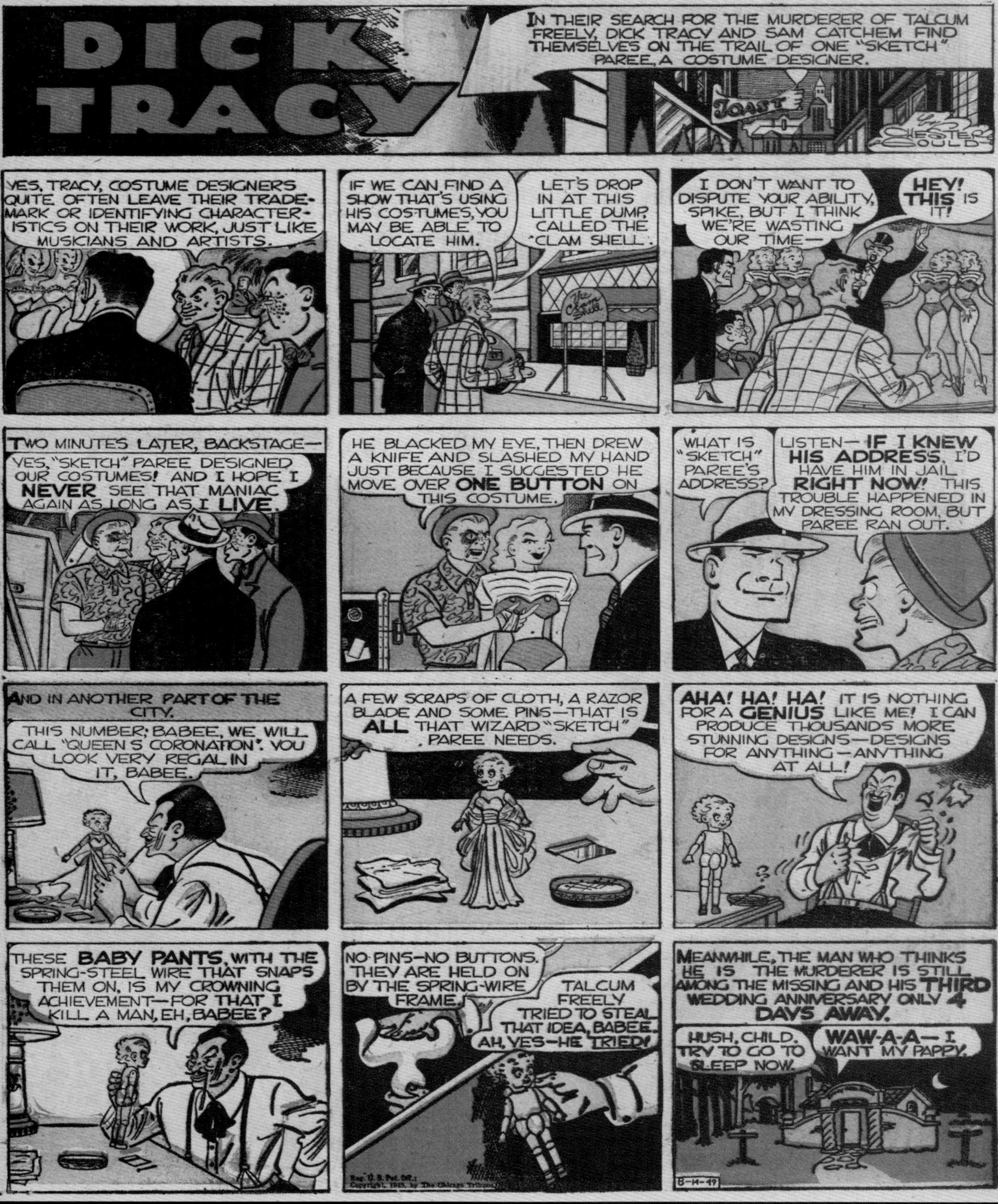
DICK TRACY
IN THEIR SEARCH FOR THE MURDERER OF TALCUM FREELY, DICK TRACY AND SAM CATCHEM FIND THEMSELVES ON THE TRAIL OF ONE "SKETCH" PAREE, A COSTUME DESIGNER.
TOAST
CHESTER GOULD
YES, TRACY, COSTUME DESIGNERS QUITE OFTEN LEAVE THEIR TRADE-MARK OR IDENTIFYING CHARACTER-ISTICS ON THEIR WORK, JUST LIKE MUSICIANS AND ARTISTS.
IF WE CAN FIND A SHOW THAT'S USING HIS COSTUMES, YOU MAY BE ABLE TO LOCATE HIM.
LET'S DROP IN AT THIS LITTLE DUMP, CALLED THE 'CLAM SHELL'.
The Clam Shell
I DON'T WANT TO DISPUTE YOUR ABILITY, SPIKE, BUT I THINK WE'RE WASTING OUR TIME—
HEY! THIS IS IT!
TWO MINUTES LATER, BACKSTAGE—
YES, "SKETCH" PAREE DESIGNED OUR COSTUMES! AND I HOPE I NEVER SEE THAT MANIAC AGAIN AS LONG AS I LIVE.
HE BLACKED MY EYE, THEN DREW A KNIFE AND SLASHED MY HAND JUST BECAUSE I SUGGESTED HE MOVE OVER ONE BUTTON ON THIS COSTUME.
WHAT IS "SKETCH" PAREE'S ADDRESS?
LISTEN— IF I KNEW HIS ADDRESS, I'D HAVE HIM IN JAIL RIGHT NOW! THIS TROUBLE HAPPENED IN MY DRESSING ROOM, BUT PAREE RAN OUT.
AND IN ANOTHER PART OF THE CITY.
THIS NUMBER, BABEE, WE WILL CALL "QUEEN'S CORONATION". YOU LOOK VERY REGAL IN IT, BABEE.
A FEW SCRAPS OF CLOTH, A RAZOR BLADE AND SOME PINS—THAT IS ALL THAT WIZARD "SKETCH" PAREE NEEDS.
AHA! HA! HA! IT IS NOTHING FOR A GENIUS LIKE ME! I CAN PRODUCE THOUSANDS MORE STUNNING DESIGNS—DESIGNS FOR ANYTHING—ANYTHING AT ALL!
THESE BABY PANTS, WITH THE SPRING-STEEL WIRE THAT SNAPS THEM ON, IS MY CROWNING ACHIEVEMENT—FOR THAT I KILL A MAN, EH, BABEE?
NO PINS—NO BUTTONS. THEY ARE HELD ON BY THE SPRING-WIRE FRAME.
TALCUM FREELY TRIED TO STEAL THAT IDEA, BABEE. AH, YES—HE TRIED!
MEANWHILE, THE MAN WHO THINKS HE IS THE MURDERER IS STILL AMONG THE MISSING AND HIS THIRD WEDDING ANNIVERSARY ONLY 4 DAYS AWAY.
HUSH, CHILD. TRY TO GO TO SLEEP NOW.
WAW-A-A— I WANT MY PAPPY.
8-14-49

Dick Tracy, Sunday strip, August 14, 1949.

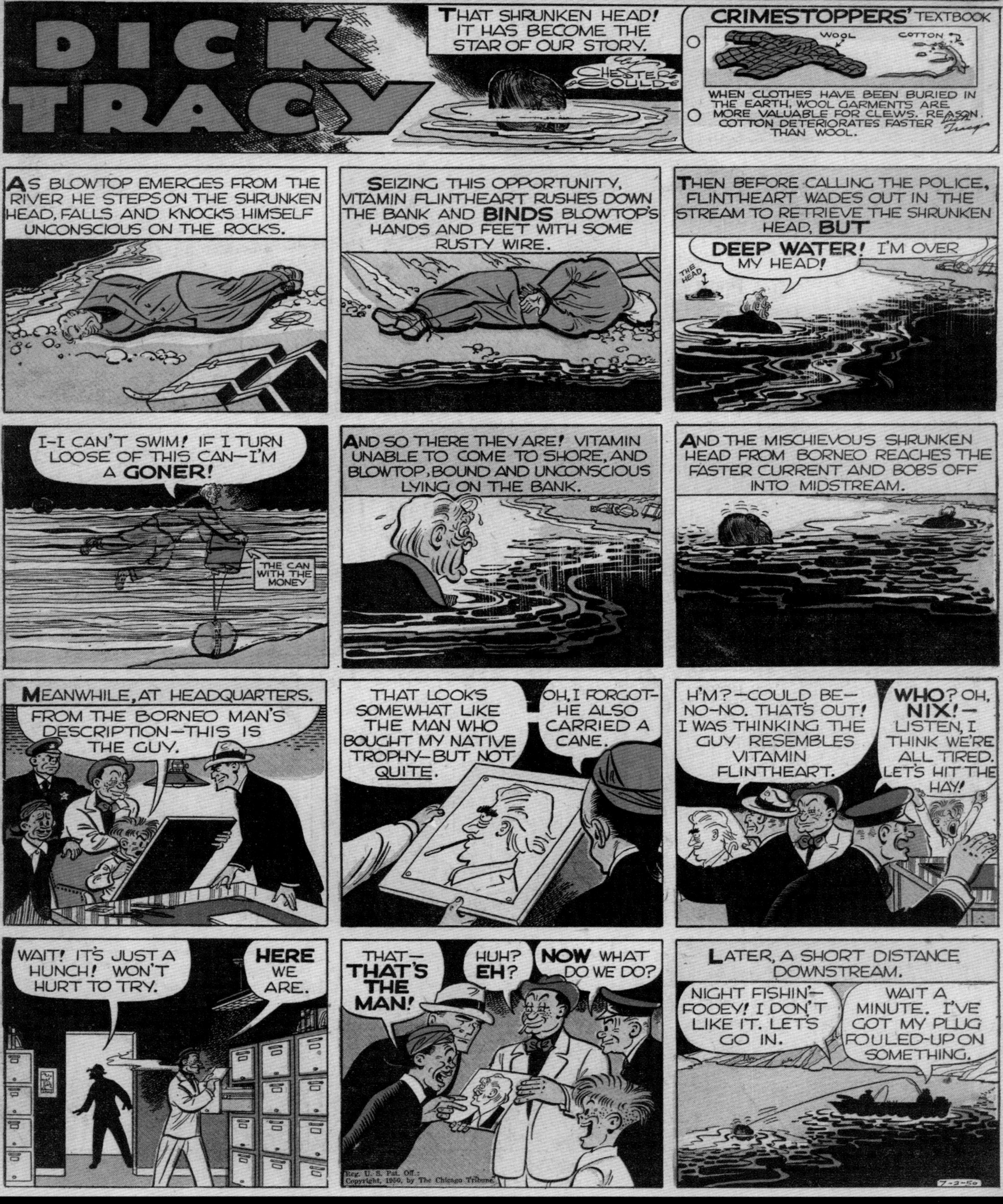
DICK TRACY
THAT SHRUNKEN HEAD! IT HAS BECOME THE STAR OF OUR STORY.
CHESTER GOULD
CRIMESTOPPERS' TEXTBOOK
WOOL
COTTON
WHEN CLOTHES HAVE BEEN BURIED IN THE EARTH, WOOL GARMENTS ARE MORE VALUABLE FOR CLEWS. REASON. COTTON DETERIORATES FASTER THAN WOOL.
AS BLOWTOP EMERGES FROM THE RIVER HE STEPS ON THE SHRUNKEN HEAD, FALLS AND KNOCKS HIMSELF UNCONSCIOUS ON THE ROCKS.
SEIZING THIS OPPORTUNITY, VITAMIN FLINTHEART RUSHES DOWN THE BANK AND BINDS BLOWTOP'S HANDS AND FEET WITH SOME RUSTY WIRE.
THEN BEFORE CALLING THE POLICE, FLINTHEART WADES OUT IN THE STREAM TO RETRIEVE THE SHRUNKEN HEAD, BUT
DEEP WATER! I'M OVER MY HEAD!
THE HEAD
I-I CAN'T SWIM! IF I TURN LOOSE OF THIS CAN—I'M A GONER!
THE CAN WITH THE MONEY
AND SO THERE THEY ARE! VITAMIN UNABLE TO COME TO SHORE, AND BLOWTOP, BOUND AND UNCONSCIOUS LYING ON THE BANK.
AND THE MISCHIEVOUS SHRUNKEN HEAD FROM BORNEO REACHES THE FASTER CURRENT AND BOBS OFF INTO MIDSTREAM.
MEANWHILE, AT HEADQUARTERS.
FROM THE BORNEO MAN'S DESCRIPTION—THIS IS THE GUY.
THAT LOOKS SOMEWHAT LIKE THE MAN WHO BOUGHT MY NATIVE TROPHY—BUT NOT QUITE.
OH, I FORGOT-HE ALSO CARRIED A CANE.
H'M?—COULD BE—NO-NO. THAT'S OUT! I WAS THINKING THE GUY RESEMBLES VITAMIN FLINTHEART.
WHO? OH, NIX!—LISTEN, I THINK WE'RE ALL TIRED. LET'S HIT THE HAY!
WAIT! IT'S JUST A HUNCH! WON'T HURT TO TRY.
HERE WE ARE.
THAT—THAT'S THE MAN!
HUH? EH?
NOW WHAT DO WE DO?
Reg. U. S. Pat. Off.: Copyright, 1950, by The Chicago Tribune
LATER, A SHORT DISTANCE DOWNSTREAM.
NIGHT FISHIN'—FOOEY! I DON'T LIKE IT. LET'S GO IN.
WAIT A MINUTE. I'VE GOT MY PLUG FOULED-UP ON SOMETHING.
7-2-50

Dick Tracy, Sunday strip, July 2, 1950.

World's Greatest Comics

10¢ SUNDAY NEWS 10¢
NEW YORK'S PICTURE NEWSPAPER®

Comic Section | New York 17, N.Y., Sunday, July 6, 1952★

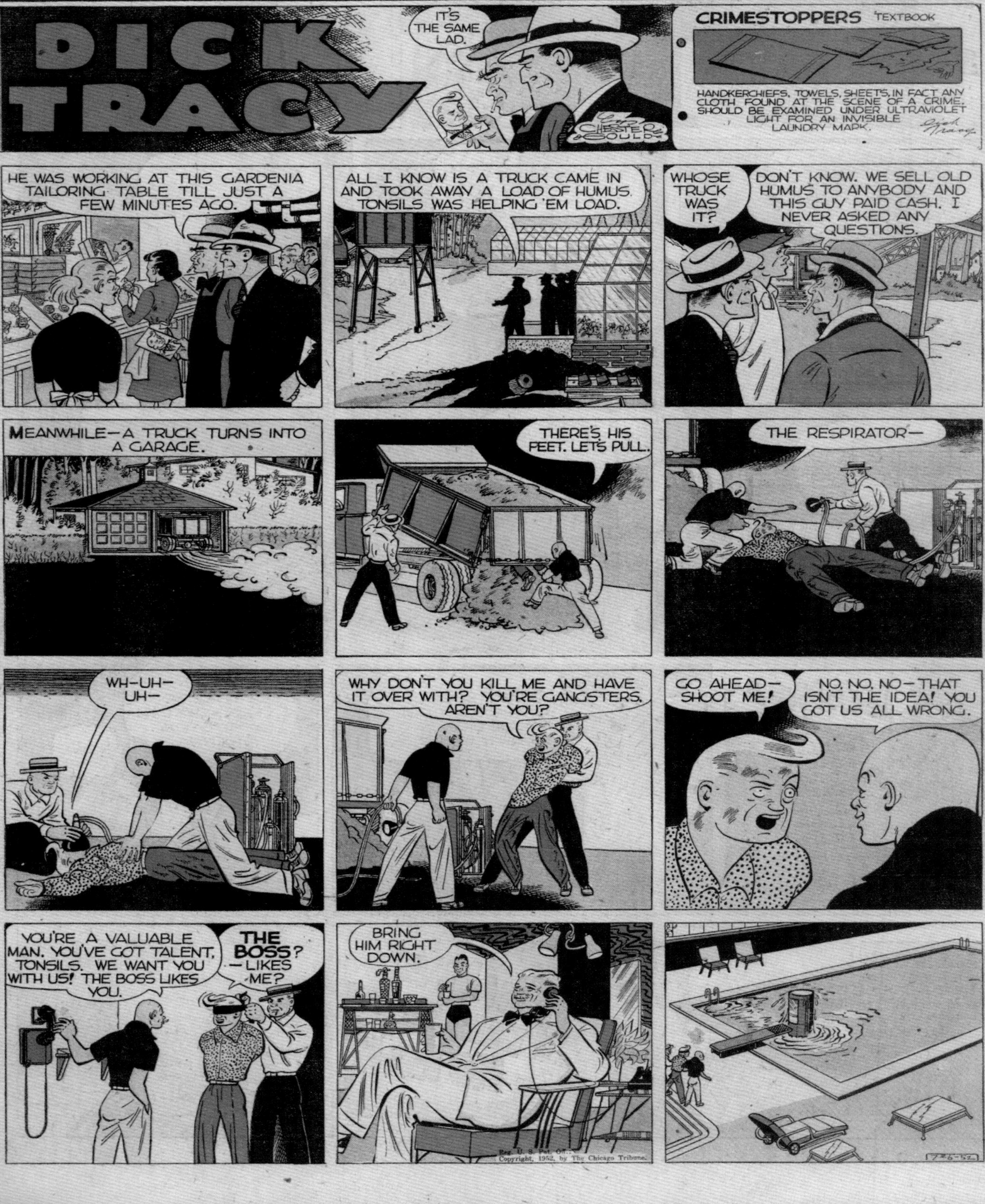
DICK TRACY
IT'S THE SAME LAD.
CHESTER GOULD
CRIMESTOPPERS TEXTBOOK
HANDKERCHIEFS, TOWELS, SHEETS, IN FACT ANY CLOTH FOUND AT THE SCENE OF A CRIME, SHOULD BE EXAMINED UNDER ULTRAVIOLET LIGHT FOR AN INVISIBLE LAUNDRY MARK.
Dick Tracy
HE WAS WORKING AT THIS GARDENIA TAILORING TABLE TILL JUST A FEW MINUTES AGO.
ALL I KNOW IS A TRUCK CAME IN AND TOOK AWAY A LOAD OF HUMUS. TONSILS WAS HELPING 'EM LOAD.
WHOSE TRUCK WAS IT?
DON'T KNOW. WE SELL OLD HUMUS TO ANYBODY AND THIS GUY PAID CASH. I NEVER ASKED ANY QUESTIONS.
MEANWHILE—A TRUCK TURNS INTO A GARAGE.
THERE'S HIS FEET. LET'S PULL.
THE RESPIRATOR—
WH-UH-UH-
WHY DON'T YOU KILL ME AND HAVE IT OVER WITH? YOU'RE GANGSTERS, AREN'T YOU?
GO AHEAD—SHOOT ME!
NO, NO, NO—THAT ISN'T THE IDEA! YOU GOT US ALL WRONG.
YOU'RE A VALUABLE MAN. YOU'VE GOT TALENT, TONSILS. WE WANT YOU WITH US! THE BOSS LIKES YOU.
THE BOSS?—LIKES ME?
BRING HIM RIGHT DOWN.
Reg. U. S. Pat. Off.
Copyright, 1952, by The Chicago Tribune.
7-6-52

World's Greatest Comics

10¢ SUNDAY NEWS 10¢

NEW YORK'S PICTURE NEWSPAPER®

Comic Section | New York 17, N.Y., Sunday, July 13, 1952★

Goodrich

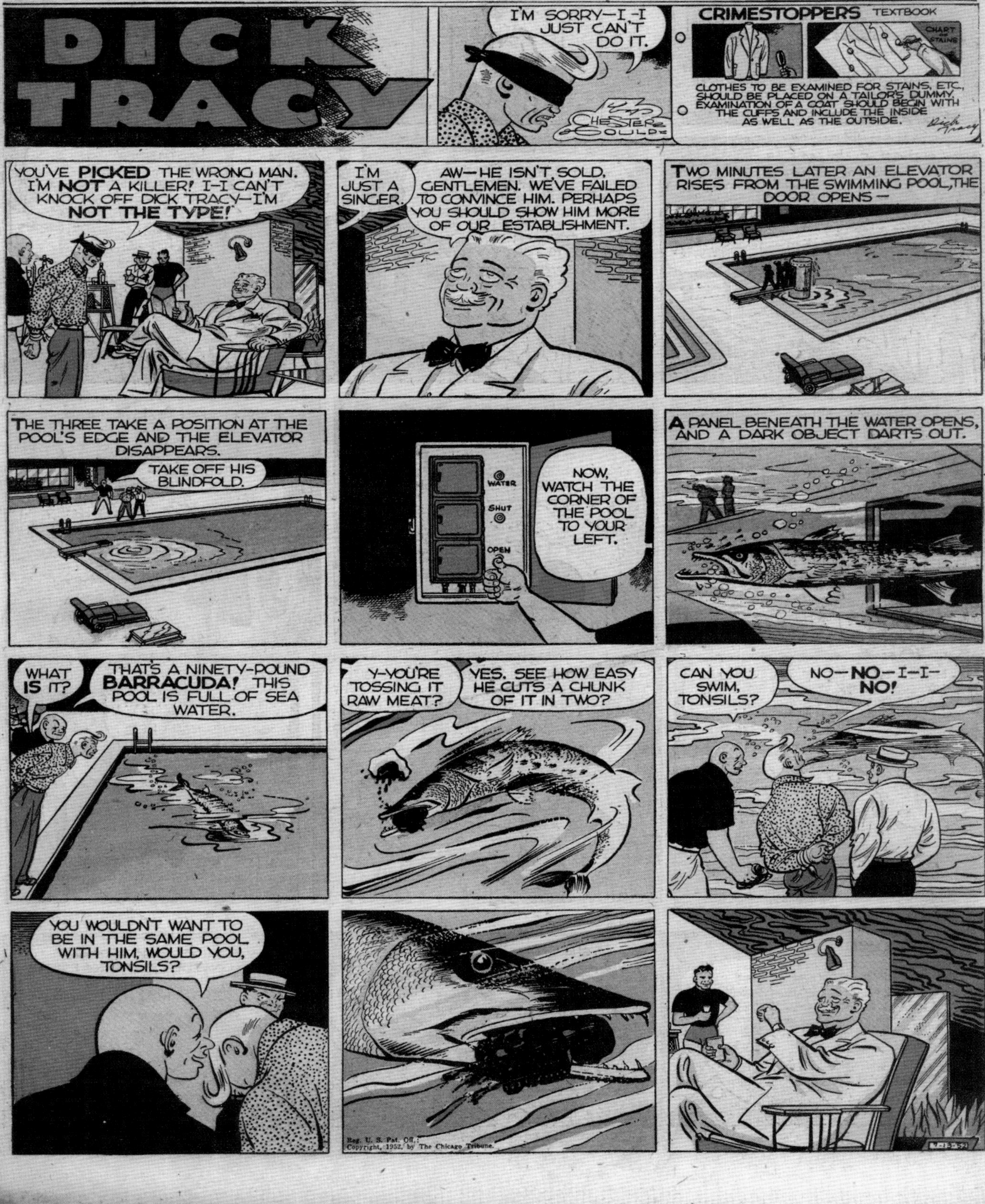

DICK TRACY
I'M SORRY—I-I JUST CAN'T DO IT.
CHESTER GOULD
CRIMESTOPPERS TEXTBOOK
CLOTHES TO BE EXAMINED FOR STAINS, ETC., SHOULD BE PLACED ON A TAILOR'S DUMMY. EXAMINATION OF A COAT SHOULD BEGIN WITH THE CUFFS AND INCLUDE THE INSIDE AS WELL AS THE OUTSIDE.
Dick Tracy
YOU'VE PICKED THE WRONG MAN. I'M NOT A KILLER! I-I CAN'T KNOCK OFF DICK TRACY—I'M NOT THE TYPE!
I'M JUST A SINGER.
AW—HE ISN'T SOLD, GENTLEMEN. WE'VE FAILED TO CONVINCE HIM. PERHAPS YOU SHOULD SHOW HIM MORE OF OUR ESTABLISHMENT.
TWO MINUTES LATER AN ELEVATOR RISES FROM THE SWIMMING POOL, THE DOOR OPENS —
THE THREE TAKE A POSITION AT THE POOL'S EDGE AND THE ELEVATOR DISAPPEARS.
TAKE OFF HIS BLINDFOLD.
WATER
SHUT
OPEN
NOW, WATCH THE CORNER OF THE POOL TO YOUR LEFT.
A PANEL BENEATH THE WATER OPENS, AND A DARK OBJECT DARTS OUT.
WHAT IS IT?
THAT'S A NINETY-POUND BARRACUDA! THIS POOL IS FULL OF SEA WATER.
Y-YOU'RE TOSSING IT RAW MEAT?
YES. SEE HOW EASY HE CUTS A CHUNK OF IT IN TWO?
CAN YOU SWIM, TONSILS?
NO—NO—I-I-NO!
YOU WOULDN'T WANT TO BE IN THE SAME POOL WITH HIM, WOULD YOU, TONSILS?
Reg. U. S. Pat. Off.; Copyright, 1952, by The Chicago Tribune.

World's Greatest Comics

10¢ SUNDAY NEWS 10¢

NEW YORK'S PICTURE NEWSPAPER®

Comic Section

New York 17, N.Y., Sunday, July 20, 1952★

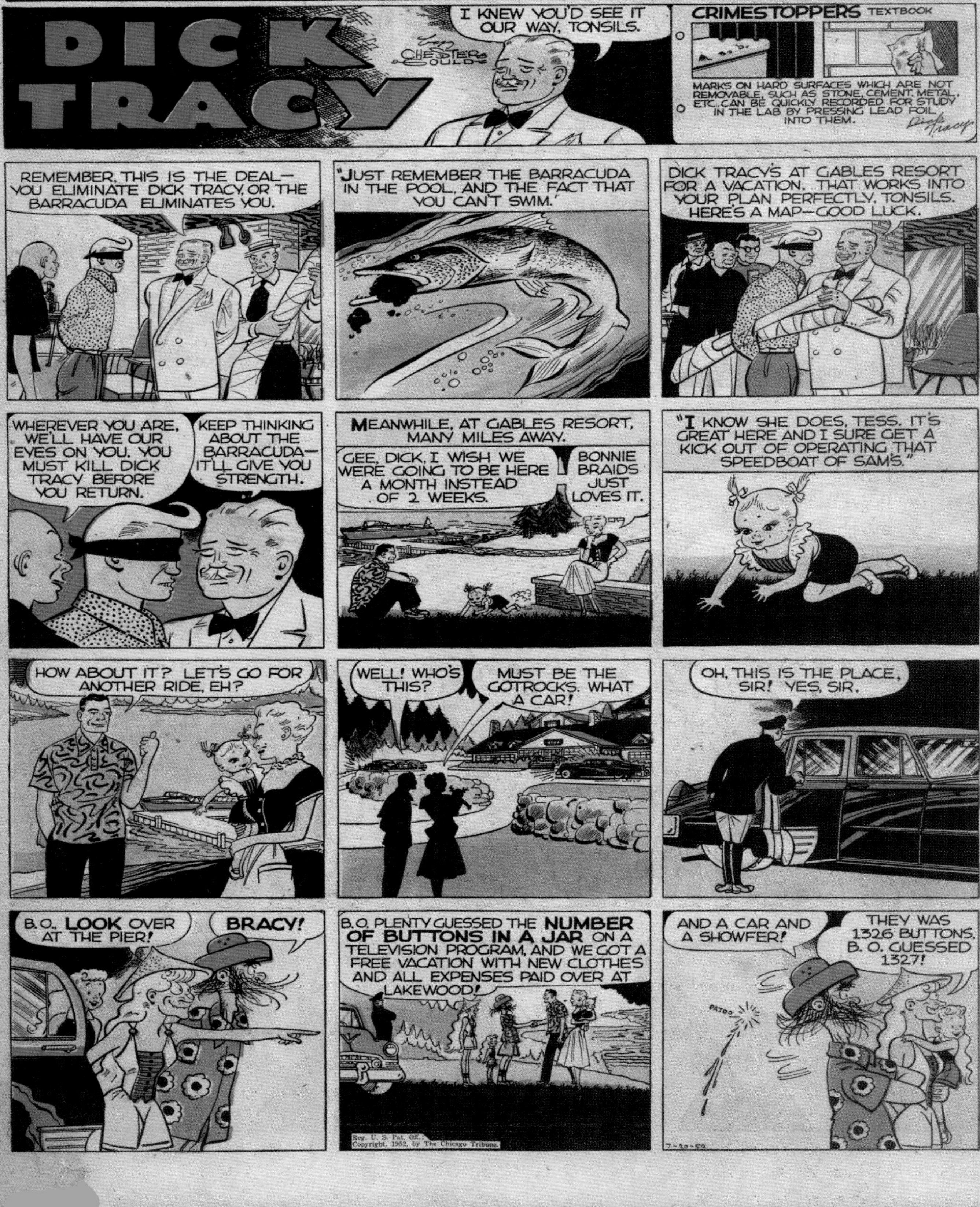
DICK TRACY
by CHESTER GOULD
I KNEW YOU'D SEE IT OUR WAY, TONSILS.
CRIMESTOPPERS TEXTBOOK
MARKS ON HARD SURFACES WHICH ARE NOT REMOVABLE, SUCH AS STONE, CEMENT, METAL, ETC., CAN BE QUICKLY RECORDED FOR STUDY IN THE LAB BY PRESSING LEAD FOIL INTO THEM.
Dick Tracy
REMEMBER, THIS IS THE DEAL— YOU ELIMINATE DICK TRACY, OR THE BARRACUDA ELIMINATES YOU.
"JUST REMEMBER THE BARRACUDA IN THE POOL, AND THE FACT THAT YOU CAN'T SWIM."
DICK TRACY'S AT GABLES RESORT FOR A VACATION. THAT WORKS INTO YOUR PLAN PERFECTLY, TONSILS. HERE'S A MAP—GOOD LUCK.
WHEREVER YOU ARE, WE'LL HAVE OUR EYES ON YOU. YOU MUST KILL DICK TRACY BEFORE YOU RETURN.
KEEP THINKING ABOUT THE BARRACUDA— IT'LL GIVE YOU STRENGTH.
MEANWHILE, AT GABLES RESORT, MANY MILES AWAY.
GEE, DICK, I WISH WE WERE GOING TO BE HERE A MONTH INSTEAD OF 2 WEEKS.
BONNIE BRAIDS JUST LOVES IT.
"I KNOW SHE DOES, TESS. IT'S GREAT HERE AND I SURE GET A KICK OUT OF OPERATING THAT SPEEDBOAT OF SAM'S."
HOW ABOUT IT? LET'S GO FOR ANOTHER RIDE, EH?
WELL! WHO'S THIS?
MUST BE THE GOTROCKS. WHAT A CAR!
OH, THIS IS THE PLACE, SIR! YES, SIR.
B.O., LOOK OVER AT THE PIER!
BRACY!
B.O. PLENTY GUESSED THE NUMBER OF BUTTONS IN A JAR ON A TELEVISION PROGRAM, AND WE GOT A FREE VACATION WITH NEW CLOTHES AND ALL EXPENSES PAID OVER AT LAKEWOOD!
AND A CAR AND A SHOWFER!
THEY WAS 1326 BUTTONS. B. O. GUESSED 1327!
PATOO
Reg. U. S. Pat. Off.: Copyright, 1952, by The Chicago Tribune.
7-20-52

Opposite: *Dick Tracy*, Sunday strip, July 20, 1952.
Previous spread: Left: *Dick Tracy*, Sunday strip, July 6, 1952.
Right: *Dick Tracy*, Sunday strip, July 13, 1952.

Every day for forty-six years, two months, and eleven days, Chester Gould's *Dick Trac* was a never-ending serial of crime and punishment, law and order, black and white Tracy himself had qualities (competence, doggedness, coolness under pressure), but n character to speak of, no personality quirks, nothing to particularize him, humanize him he had no catch phrases, no hobbies, no reader-endearing preferences for things lik exorbitant sandwiches or corned beef, he wasn't a Romeo or a jazz buff. In the strip everyone, even Tess most of the time, called him Tracy. He socialized only at Christmas and some years the situation was too grim or precarious for Tracy to socialize even then We almost never saw him at home when he was a bachelor and after he married Tess w saw him at home just briefly before the house was blown up. At first and throughout th 1930s he was the consummate pro, straight out of Hammett's Continental Op; later on h became a symbol. He was Pursuit, he was Vengeance. Either way he wasn't your bes friend. You couldn't warm to Dick Tracy.

It wasn't its star that quickly made the comic strip famous, but the casual violence. A time passed it became even more famous for its semi-annual sadistic slow-death trap (giant magnifying glass, hot paraffin bath, sinking room) and then, of course, for it rogue's gallery of grotesques—Coffyhead, Measles, Midget and Mama, Smallmouth Bass Empty Williams, Flyface, Itchy, Oodles, on and on.

In the beginning the strip was crudely drawn: the backgrounds seemed shabby, th figures were stiff, *hunched*, and everything was described monotonously by a thin an nervous line. But by the late '30s, after Gould had written and drawn the strip day afte day for several years, working out pictorial strategies, finding and changing rhythms sharpening focus, *Dick Tracy* had become glossily professional, confidently expressive bluntly informational. It grabbed your attention, insisted upon it.

Great big masses of solid black anchored and organized every panel. Gradually ther was less crosshatching, then far less, and then none. The brush line was fat and declarative. Gould developed a style notable for its selectivity, its subtractions; there was n clutter. It was spare, his filling of space, but not stark. There was a single source o intense light, always. Cartoonish figures existed, and behaved violently, in a world o geometrically precise objects; hyper-realistic things. (Tracy's plots often turned on th misuse or novel use of ordinary, instantly recognizable *things*.) By 1940, both the strip' graphics and narrative were indistinguishable, inextricable. During the Second Worl War the strip looked brutal and it was brutal, but it was also beautifully staged. Th pacing was a chaotic down-the-staircase tumble. Breathers occurred now and then, fo the birth of a baby or the celebration of an anniversary, but they never lasted long.

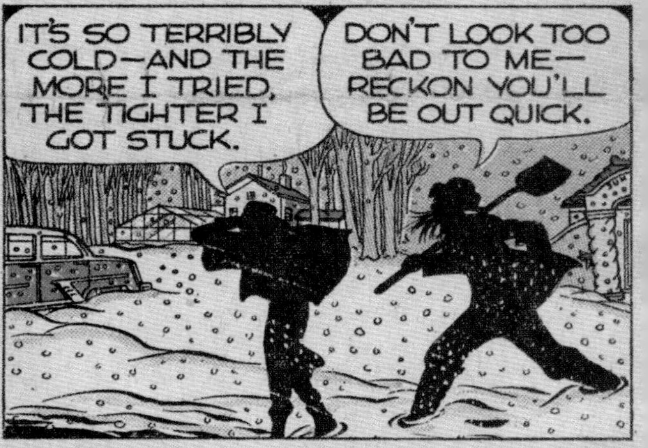
IT'S SO TERRIBLY COLD—AND THE MORE I TRIED, THE TIGHTER I GOT STUCK.
DON'T LOOK TOO BAD TO ME— RECKON YOU'LL BE OUT QUICK.

Dick Tracy, Sunday strip detail, March 15, 1953.

ORTY-SIX YEARS, two months, and eleven days. That was the cumu ative length of Chester Gould's lifework. One new strip every singl ay for forty-six years, two months, and eleven days. I've read mo f them. I guess at one time or another I've read every strip from th eginning through 1965 or '66. After that I read *Dick Tracy* intermit ently; it could break your heart, those final years. Tracy with h tupid mustache. All that sloganeering against judges, Miranda, th ifth Amendment. Very sad, most of the last years, the seventie ery goddamn sad. So no, I haven't read Gould's *entire run*, but '31 t 66 is a lot of comic strips. And a number of favorite sequences I'v ead many times over. This qualifies as an obsession, I think.

I first fell under Gould's spell in the middle 1950s. I was a youn id, eight years old, when I started following the strip in th *ew York Daily News*, which I had to get, usually a day late, from th ld lady in a wheelchair who lived diagonally across the street. M amily took, as they used to say, the *New York Journal-American*, earst rag but good for *Mandrake*, *The Phantom*, *Buz Sawyer*, Bu agendorf's *Popeye*, *The Heart of Juliet Jones*, *Drift Marlo*, and *M bernathy*.

Supplementing the new stuff that I read every day in a day-ol aper (Tracy versus the Kitten Sisters, the Clipso Brothers, Pants nd his gang of buried-treasure hunters) was the old stuff that ound in Harvey comic books, which, heavily edited and with colo sually out of register, reprinted Gould's strips from the 1930s, '40s nd very early '50s.

Gradually I developed a sense of, then got a handle on, the strip' ontinuity, such as it was (Gravel Gertie and B.O. Plenty wer illains first, *then* they were good guys), and came to recognize it raphic development. If the pictures had a lot of hay and the balloo ointers were dangling strings; if Tracy's nose came to a point; i unior was a little hobo and the villains looked like normal peopl even if they did smash other people in the face with blunt objects) hen I knew those stories dated from the strip's first years.

But if the drawings seemed rounder, more cartoonish, and if th rowl cars were long with dramatically curving hoods; if Dick Tracy' nose was hooked but his hair on the sides and in back was indicate y tiers of short parallel lines; and if—most importantly—if all of th ad guys looked like circus freaks or creatures from a horror movie hen for sure the stories dated from sometime during the 1940s

If, however, Tracy's hair was wavy on top and solid black all over (except when he sported a crew cut), and if his head seemed small (in relation to his body); if the villains looked *fairly* normal but principally preyed upon, or committed vicious crimes with their closest relatives; if Pat Patton was police chief and Sam Catchem was the sidekick; if the two-way wrist radio was in use; and if various small children (one of them invariably being Sparkle Plenty) were regularly tortured/bludgeoned/poisoned/shot or were lost in the wilderness or in some Weather Channel–type catastrophe (floods, fogs, blizzards), then I knew that *those* stories probably dated from the late 1940s through the early 1950s. They most closely resembled the new stuff that I was reading at the time in the daily paper. Those particular stories I eventually came to call (precocious schoolboy that I was) the "modern stuff."

I still call them the modern stuff.

Or when I'm trying to sound smarter, I'll say that those bleak and fugue-like strips from the 1950s belong to the "Modern Period."

I can even tell you, since I determined them, the exact years comprising *Dick Tracy*'s, or Chester Gould's, Modern Period: 1950 through 1959, from the wedding of Dick Tracy (Christmas 1949) to the Matty Munkie storyline, where Lizz the policewoman is accused on live television of participating in police brutality and its cover-up—in other words, from the famous matrimony, which made Dick Tracy the head of an instant family that could then be threatened, to the first indisputable sign of paranoia and political aggression, which in only a few years' time would poison the great strip.

Everything that came after 1959—the space coupe, the Moon Maid, the law and order tirades, the mustache, the sideburns, the embarrassing senior moments, the senility—I call that period the "Post-Modern."

And since I've already mentioned two periods, I might as well go ahead—whew! scholarship is backbreaking work!—and mention the others, just to be done with it. There are only two: the Primitive, lasting from 1931 till 1941, from the earliest lurching melodramas based on big-city gangsterism (at least as portrayed by the tabloids and Hollywood) to the appearances of Littleface and the Mole, first of the major grotesques, at which point the strip ceases to be cops-and-robbers and becomes instead a repeating morality tale,

individual sequences only kicking into high gear at the point when the monster/criminal flees arrest with Tracy in hot pursuit. The Classic Period.

All of the trials and tortures—preposterous, slapstick, mutilating, painful, lethal—that great villains like Pruneface, Flattop, Gargles, the Brow, etc. undergo before at last they're brought to ground (usually dead) are real jaw-droppers, marvels of ingenuity and sadism, lacking utterly in compassion, what Bruegel might have dreamed up if he'd drawn comic strips. (You look at it today and think, they actually printed this in the *newspaper*?)

For all of its nasty brilliance, though, the Classic Period is formulaic. Despite their delightful bits of macabre business, Gould's stories were pretty much all the same—crime/pursuit/pursuit/pursuit/the kill. Crime/pursuit/pursuit/pursuit/the kill. Endings were occasionally, and then always heavy-handedly, ironical (a Nazi spy impaled on an American flag pole). But much more often they simply were cruel and pitiless, bone crunching and/or filled with prolonged agony (suffocation, drowning, slow freezing). This is work done by the artist applying himself constantly, giving continuous effort, in his early middle age. He knows he's good, and good ideas come to him like the falling rain. So he showboats.

For my money, the best, most sustained work dates from the Modern Period, and I don't really feel like arguing with those Classic era bullies. It just is. The work Gould turned out beginning in the late '40s and continuing through the late '50s (*his* late forties, *his* late fifties, those feeling-your-own-mortality years) is darker than anything he'd ever done previously, by far, and not only because he used more black, which he certainly did. (He chose often to narrate now in silhouette, in long sequences of silhouette.) No, it wasn't the ink, it was the spirit: the *spirit* of the strip had darkened. Tracy looked older, his squint was tighter, and his pained grimace in profile—two curving slashes, one above the other, a graphic clamshell—was almost scary. While characters good and bad still were perfectly named (Little Wingy, 3-D Magee, Dot View, Acres O'Riley, Nothing Yonson), and remained striking in appearance (Gould did some of his best mug work in the '50s), they no longer were necessarily grotesques. Most of the Modern Era antagonists were not. A good number also happened to be women. Sleet, Pony, Mousey, Newsuit Nan, Cinn Ozone, Miss Egghead, Aunt Soso,

continues on page 47

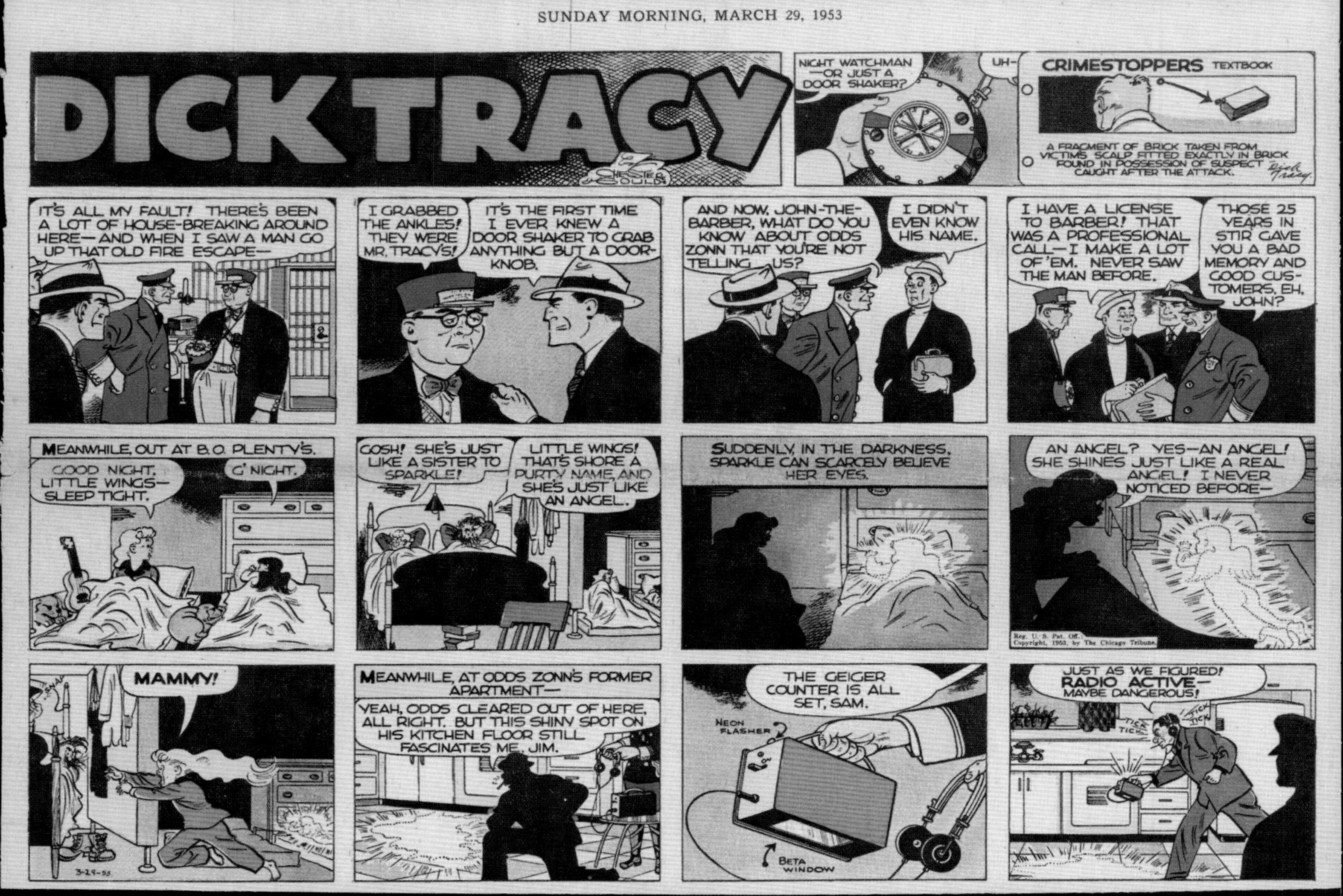
SUNDAY MORNING, MARCH 29, 1953
DICK TRACY
Chester Gould
NIGHT WATCHMAN —OR JUST A DOOR SHAKER?
UH—
CRIMESTOPPERS TEXTBOOK
A FRAGMENT OF BRICK TAKEN FROM VICTIM'S SCALP FITTED EXACTLY IN BRICK FOUND IN POSSESSION OF SUSPECT CAUGHT AFTER THE ATTACK.
Dick Tracy
IT'S ALL MY FAULT! THERE'S BEEN A LOT OF HOUSE-BREAKING AROUND HERE—AND WHEN I SAW A MAN GO UP THAT OLD FIRE ESCAPE—
I GRABBED THE ANKLES! THEY WERE MR. TRACY'S!
IT'S THE FIRST TIME I EVER KNEW A DOOR SHAKER TO GRAB ANYTHING BUT A DOOR-KNOB.
AND NOW, JOHN-THE-BARBER, WHAT DO YOU KNOW ABOUT ODDS ZONN THAT YOU'RE NOT TELLING US?
I DIDN'T EVEN KNOW HIS NAME.
I HAVE A LICENSE TO BARBER! THAT WAS A PROFESSIONAL CALL—I MAKE A LOT OF 'EM. NEVER SAW THE MAN BEFORE.
THOSE 25 YEARS IN STIR GAVE YOU A BAD MEMORY AND GOOD CUS-TOMERS, EH, JOHN?
MEANWHILE, OUT AT B.O. PLENTY'S.
GOOD NIGHT, LITTLE WINGS—SLEEP TIGHT.
G' NIGHT.
GOSH! SHE'S JUST LIKE A SISTER TO SPARKLE!
LITTLE WINGS! THAT'S SHORE A PURTY NAME, AND SHE'S JUST LIKE AN ANGEL.
SUDDENLY, IN THE DARKNESS, SPARKLE CAN SCARCELY BELIEVE HER EYES.
AN ANGEL? YES—AN ANGEL! SHE SHINES JUST LIKE A REAL ANGEL! I NEVER NOTICED BEFORE—
Reg. U. S. Pat. Off.: Copyright, 1953, by The Chicago Tribune.
SNAP
MAMMY!
3-29-53
MEANWHILE, AT ODDS ZONN'S FORMER APARTMENT—
YEAH, ODDS CLEARED OUT OF HERE, ALL RIGHT. BUT THIS SHINY SPOT ON HIS KITCHEN FLOOR STILL FASCINATES ME, JIM.
THE GEIGER COUNTER IS ALL SET, SAM.
NEON FLASHER
BETA WINDOW
JUST AS WE FIGURED! RADIO ACTIVE—MAYBE DANGEROUS!
TICK TICK
TICK TICK

Dick Tracy, Sunday strip, March 29, 1953.

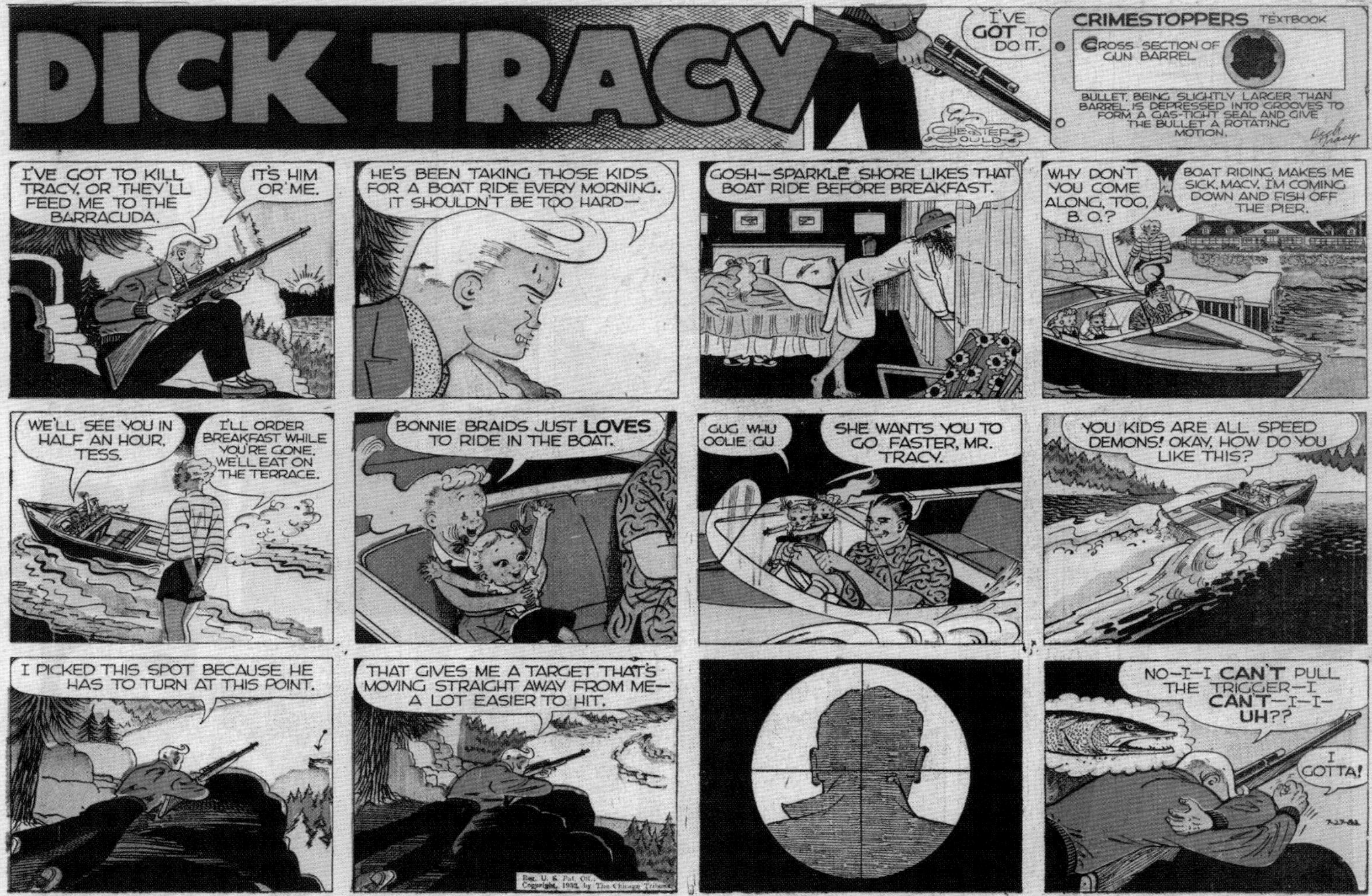
DICK TRACY
I'VE GOT TO DO IT.
CHESTER GOULD
CRIMESTOPPERS TEXTBOOK
CROSS SECTION OF GUN BARREL
BULLET, BEING SLIGHTLY LARGER THAN BARREL, IS DEPRESSED INTO GROOVES TO FORM A GAS-TIGHT SEAL AND GIVE THE BULLET A ROTATING MOTION.
I'VE GOT TO KILL TRACY, OR THEY'LL FEED ME TO THE BARRACUDA.
IT'S HIM OR ME.
HE'S BEEN TAKING THOSE KIDS FOR A BOAT RIDE EVERY MORNING. IT SHOULDN'T BE TOO HARD—
GOSH—SPARKLE SHORE LIKES THAT BOAT RIDE BEFORE BREAKFAST.
WHY DON'T YOU COME ALONG, TOO, B. O.?
BOAT RIDING MAKES ME SICK, MACY. I'M COMING DOWN AND FISH OFF THE PIER.
WE'LL SEE YOU IN HALF AN HOUR, TESS.
I'LL ORDER BREAKFAST WHILE YOU'RE GONE. WE'LL EAT ON THE TERRACE.
BONNIE BRAIDS JUST **LOVES** TO RIDE IN THE BOAT.
GUG WHU OOLIE GU
SHE WANTS YOU TO GO FASTER, MR. TRACY.
YOU KIDS ARE ALL SPEED DEMONS! OKAY, HOW DO YOU LIKE THIS?
I PICKED THIS SPOT BECAUSE HE HAS TO TURN AT THIS POINT.
THAT GIVES ME A TARGET THAT'S MOVING STRAIGHT AWAY FROM ME— A LOT EASIER TO HIT.
Reg. U. S. Pat. Off.
NO—I—I **CAN'T** PULL THE TRIGGER—I **CAN'T**—I—I— **UH**??
I GOTTA!
7-27-52

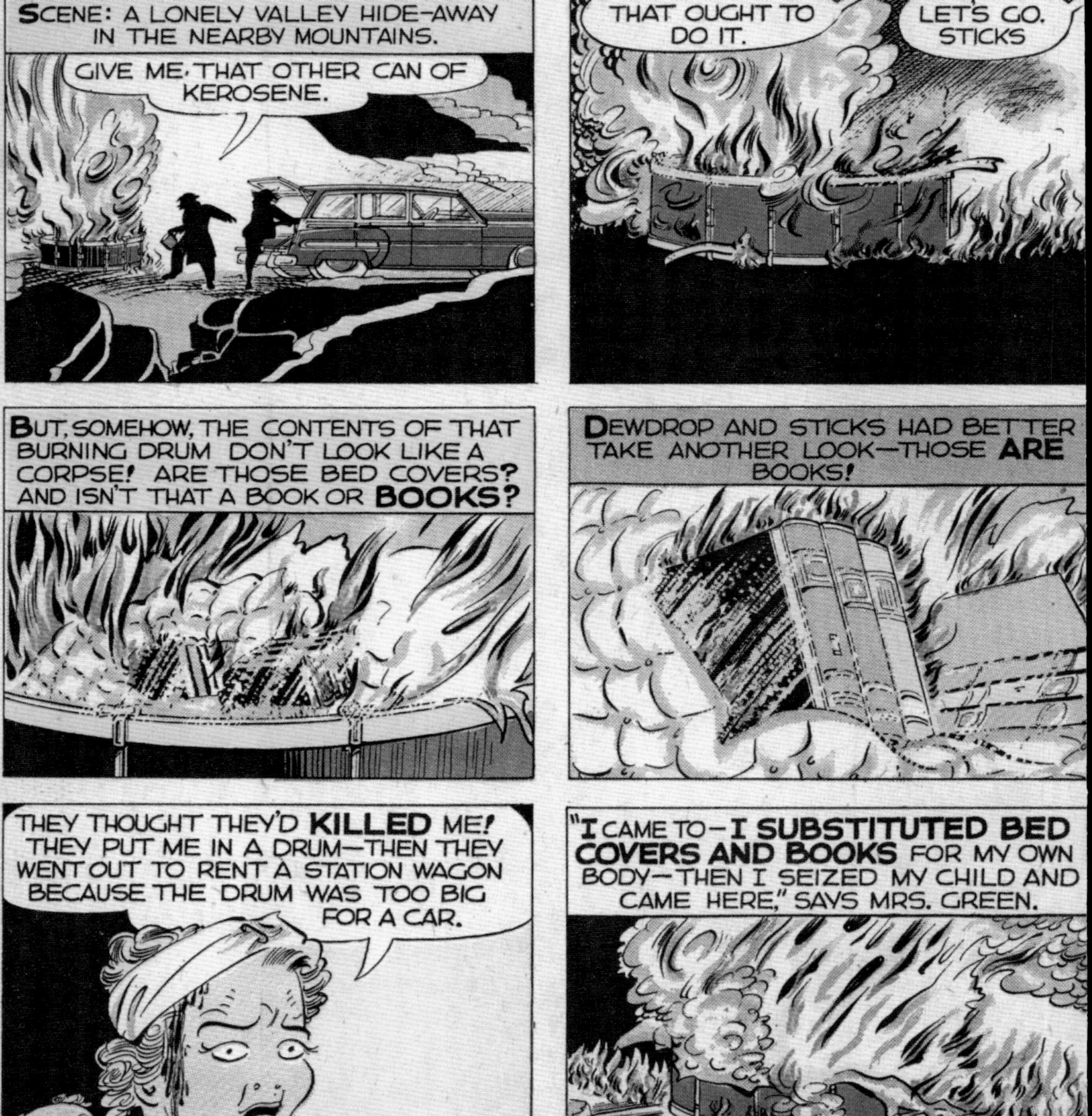
SCENE: A LONELY VALLEY HIDE-AWAY IN THE NEARBY MOUNTAINS.
GIVE ME, THAT OTHER CAN OF KEROSENE.
THAT OUGHT TO DO IT.
LET'S GO. STICKS
BUT, SOMEHOW, THE CONTENTS OF THAT BURNING DRUM DON'T LOOK LIKE A CORPSE! ARE THOSE BED COVERS? AND ISN'T THAT A BOOK OR BOOKS?
DEWDROP AND STICKS HAD BETTER TAKE ANOTHER LOOK—THOSE ARE BOOKS!
THEY THOUGHT THEY'D KILLED ME! THEY PUT ME IN A DRUM—THEN THEY WENT OUT TO RENT A STATION WAGON BECAUSE THE DRUM WAS TOO BIG FOR A CAR.
"I CAME TO—I SUBSTITUTED BED COVERS AND BOOKS FOR MY OWN BODY—THEN I SEIZED MY CHILD AND CAME HERE," SAYS MRS. GREEN.

hia Inquirer

L 11, 1954

GREATEST COMICS

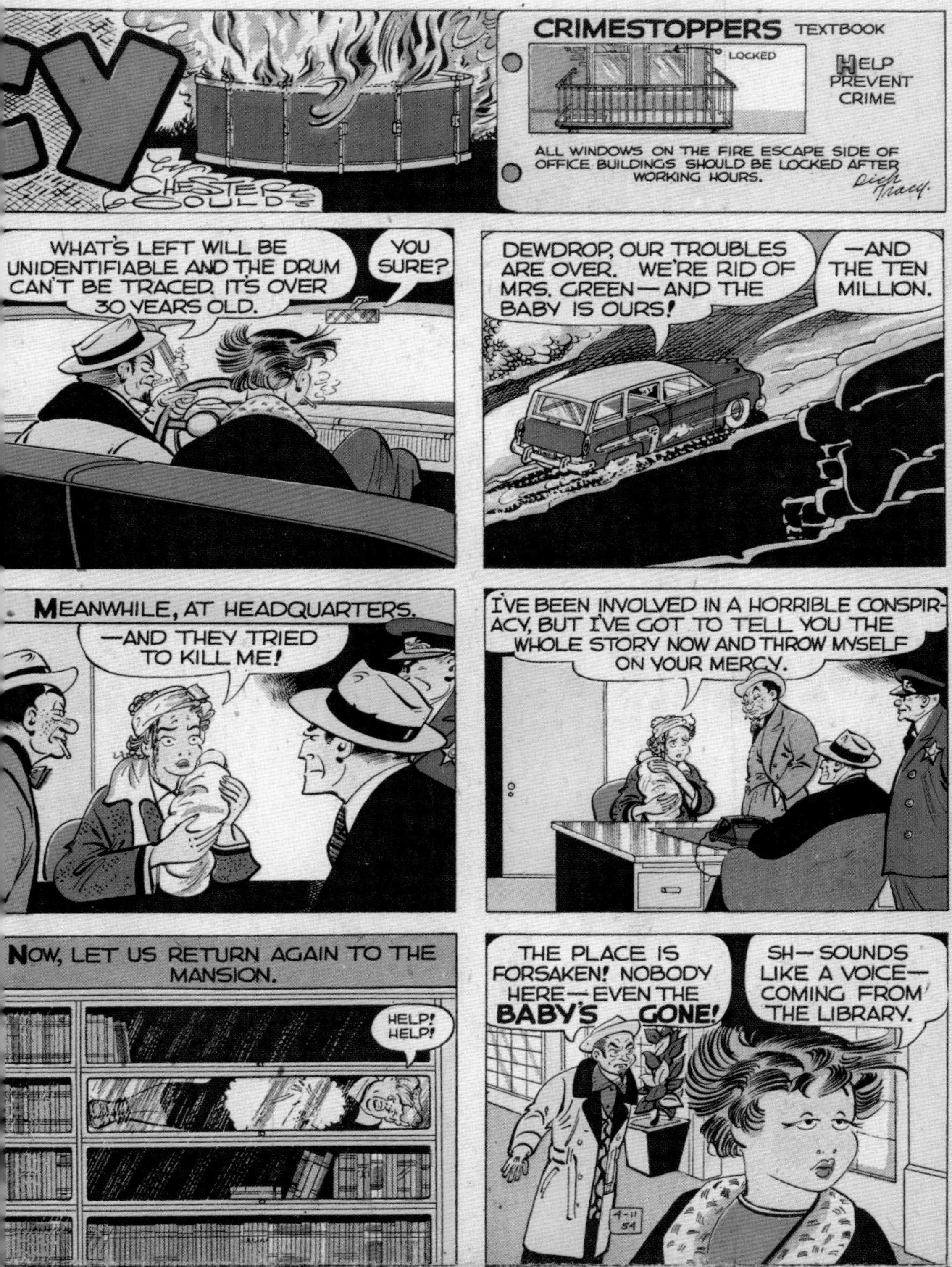
CY
CHESTER GOULD
CRIMESTOPPERS TEXTBOOK
LOCKED
HELP PREVENT CRIME
ALL WINDOWS ON THE FIRE ESCAPE SIDE OF OFFICE BUILDINGS SHOULD BE LOCKED AFTER WORKING HOURS.
Dick Tracy.
WHAT'S LEFT WILL BE UNIDENTIFIABLE AND THE DRUM CAN'T BE TRACED. IT'S OVER 30 YEARS OLD.
YOU SURE?
DEWDROP, OUR TROUBLES ARE OVER. WE'RE RID OF MRS. GREEN—AND THE BABY IS OURS!
—AND THE TEN MILLION.
MEANWHILE, AT HEADQUARTERS.
—AND THEY TRIED TO KILL ME!
I'VE BEEN INVOLVED IN A HORRIBLE CONSPIRACY, BUT I'VE GOT TO TELL YOU THE WHOLE STORY NOW AND THROW MYSELF ON YOUR MERCY.
NOW, LET US RETURN AGAIN TO THE MANSION.
HELP! HELP!
THE PLACE IS FORSAKEN! NOBODY HERE—EVEN THE BABY'S GONE!
SH—SOUNDS LIKE A VOICE—COMING FROM THE LIBRARY.
4-11 54

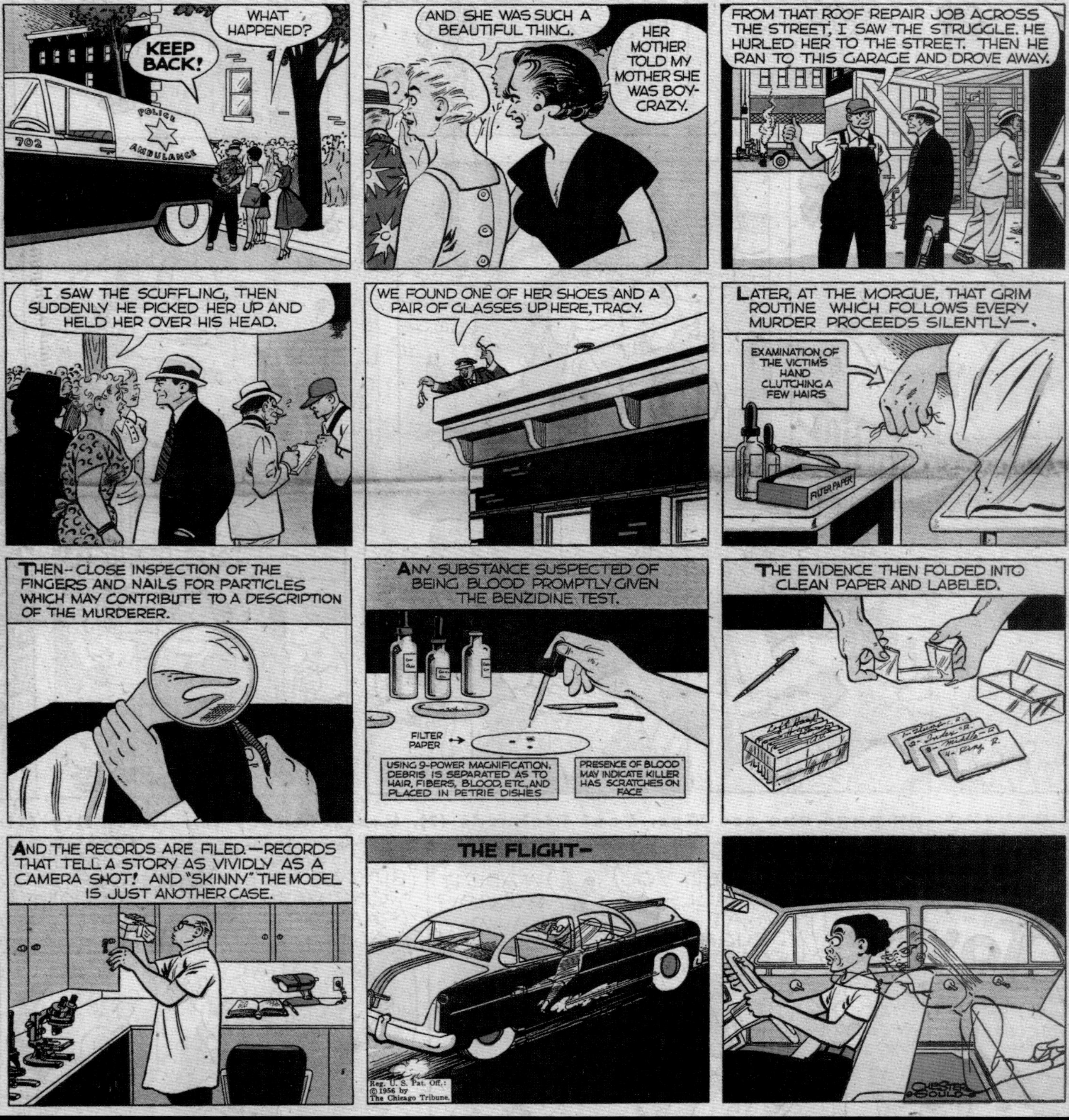
WHAT HAPPENED?
KEEP BACK!
702
POLICE
AMBULANCE
AND SHE WAS SUCH A BEAUTIFUL THING.
HER MOTHER TOLD MY MOTHER SHE WAS BOY-CRAZY.
FROM THAT ROOF REPAIR JOB ACROSS THE STREET, I SAW THE STRUGGLE. HE HURLED HER TO THE STREET. THEN HE RAN TO THIS GARAGE AND DROVE AWAY.
I SAW THE SCUFFLING, THEN SUDDENLY HE PICKED HER UP AND HELD HER OVER HIS HEAD.
WE FOUND ONE OF HER SHOES AND A PAIR OF GLASSES UP HERE, TRACY.
LATER, AT THE MORGUE, THAT GRIM ROUTINE WHICH FOLLOWS EVERY MURDER PROCEEDS SILENTLY—.
EXAMINATION OF THE VICTIM'S HAND CLUTCHING A FEW HAIRS
FILTER PAPER
THEN--CLOSE INSPECTION OF THE FINGERS AND NAILS FOR PARTICLES WHICH MAY CONTRIBUTE TO A DESCRIPTION OF THE MURDERER.
ANY SUBSTANCE SUSPECTED OF BEING BLOOD PROMPTLY GIVEN THE BENZIDINE TEST.
FILTER PAPER
USING 9-POWER MAGNIFICATION, DEBRIS IS SEPARATED AS TO HAIR, FIBERS, BLOOD, ETC., AND PLACED IN PETRIE DISHES
PRESENCE OF BLOOD MAY INDICATE KILLER HAS SCRATCHES ON FACE
THE EVIDENCE THEN FOLDED INTO CLEAN PAPER AND LABELED.
AND THE RECORDS ARE FILED.—RECORDS THAT TELL A STORY AS VIVIDLY AS A CAMERA SHOT! AND "SKINNY" THE MODEL IS JUST ANOTHER CASE.
THE FLIGHT—
Reg. U. S. Pat. Off.: © 1956 by The Chicago Tribune.
CHESTER GOULD

Dick Tracy, Sunday strip, August 5, 1956.

1950 through 1959, Gould's stories were longer than before, or very short, and far less formulaic. They were also, as I've said, more apt to revolve around families. Thematically, the '50s in *Dick Tracy* was about families, which Gould depicted alternately as being completely nuts, a source of anguish, a big nuisance, or just flat-out malignant. Big Frost arranges to have his irritating daughter Flossie taken for a ride and bumped off; Dew Drop smothers her rich old man with a pillow in his sick bed. Mother and son...father and sons...husband and wife...brother and sister...brother and brother...sisters...all commit crimes together. Poor wives rent out their babies, rich wives shoot their husbands. Or have their husbands shot. One even knocks hers on the head, then props him up on a soda crate in their basement home freezer.

There is no safety, either, in families, or in family life. Junior Tracy loses his first girlfriend in '52, policewoman Lizz loses a sister in '56. Both are murdered. Children keep born only to be thrust into immediate jeopardy, separated from their parents, menaced by killers and mountain lions, paralyzed by fire-ant venom.

And over the course of the 1950s most of the teenagers who showed up in *Dick Tracy* were criminals. Whether the products of bad parenting or just bad seeds, Gould had no pity on them. None. Zero. In fact he seemed to heap unusual scorn on shiftless coddled punks like Joe Period (the strip's James Dean figure) taking his first inevitable steps toward the soap box.

Oddly, though, this grimmest time in the strip's long run was also its funniest. While Gould could, and often did, overdo it with the antics of B.O. Plenty/Gravel Gertie, a lot of that stuff was pretty good buffoonery, it really was, and done with perfect timing. But there is no better low comedy/black comedy routine in all of Gould's work than when Vitamin Flintheart and his Indonesian shrunken head attached themselves to Flattop's easily irritated brother Blowtop. Summer, 1951. Because of its inspired clowning as much as for the astounding achievement of milking the same one joke (shrunken head, ventriloquism) for nearly a month, it rivals some of *Thimble Theatre's* greatest bits. You think I'm exaggerating? I'm not exaggerating. Look it up.

But why I most cherish those nine years of strips and hold them in higher esteem than the canonical "classic" years, finally—finally and most gratefully—are the images.

There are dozens of pictures and short multi-panel sequences that have startled me every time I've seen them again over the past fifty years. Every time. A long-haired lunatic "drowning" a six-inch dress-up doll by pressing it—*smashing* it—against a sopping wet sponge-mask attached to his face. A swaddled infant fitted inside a tiny insulated and weather-stripped closet cut directly into a tree—a tree standing in the middle of a forest in winter at night. A blond greaser with a haircut halfway between a Marine and a mullet peeling a derringer from a banana peel. A little girl who glows in the dark. A midget cobbler hunkered inside a supposedly automatic coin-operated shoe-heeling machine. A death threat printed vertically along a Popsicle stick: "THIS IS YOUR LAST DAY." Crazy combinations, inspired situations. An elevator rising from the bottom of a swimming pool, its doors opening onto the diving board. A lion prowling a *Playboy*-style swinger's pad; a black-jacketed juvenile delinquent with a D.A. standing to his knees in dill pickles and brine, one arm in a sling: he's trapped in a giant barrel, his mouth is open and he's screaming. A proto-beatnik girl (straight blond hair, Capri pants, cat's eye glasses) gliding through the air, following her murder, as a see-through ghost. A white-haired old lady in a shawl feeding beef brisket and flank steak to a flesh-eating plant (which, if you look closely, holds a full skeleton of a man tangled inside its vines). For me, the stuff is indelible. The laughing blond maniac leaping from a gym locker while bringing down a golf club hard upon the head of man in a tuxedo. Hip boots and a man's legs emerging from the carcass of a buck strung by rope from a barn's rafters. A black Plymouth floating down a river on a cake of ice in a blizzard. Stuff like that has been turning up in my dreams for fifty years. I'm not saying that what Gould made was art (all right, I'm saying it's art, but I'm not *insisting*), just that it can, and for me does, have the *impact* of art. That stuff is in there, way deep inside of me, and two hundred years from now if I have any descendants they'll be dreaming sometimes of twentieth-century Plymouths floating down a raging river on an ice floe. They'll wake up and wonder what the hell *that* was all about.

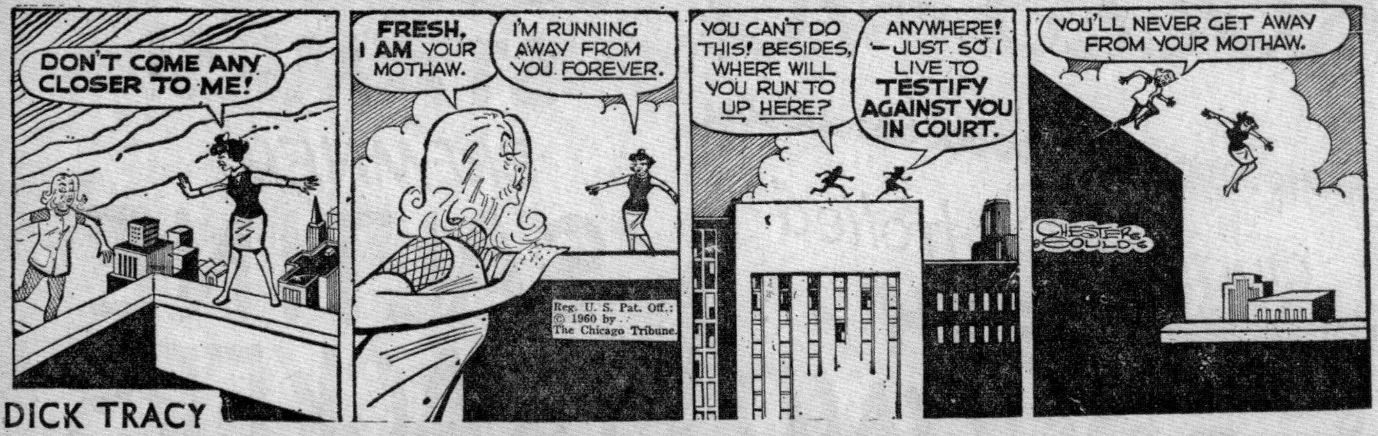
DON'T COME ANY CLOSER TO ME!
FRESH, I AM YOUR MOTHAW.
I'M RUNNING AWAY FROM YOU FOREVER.
Reg. U. S. Pat. Off.: © 1960 by The Chicago Tribune.
YOU CAN'T DO THIS! BESIDES, WHERE WILL YOU RUN TO UP HERE?
ANYWHERE! —JUST SO I LIVE TO TESTIFY AGAINST YOU IN COURT.
YOU'LL NEVER GET AWAY FROM YOUR MOTHAW.
CHESTER GOULD
DICK TRACY

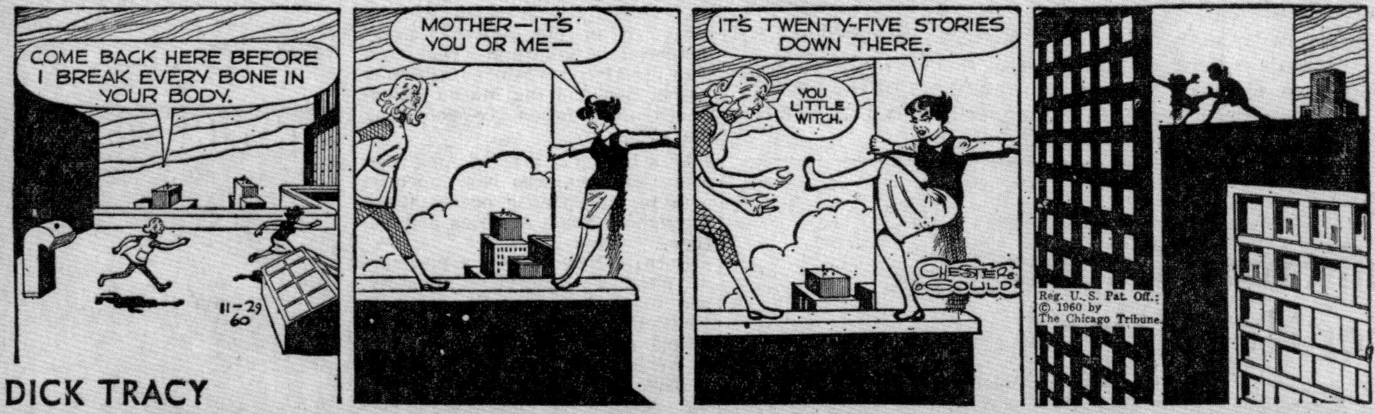
COME BACK HERE BEFORE I BREAK EVERY BONE IN YOUR BODY.
11-29 60
MOTHER—IT'S YOU OR ME—
IT'S TWENTY-FIVE STORIES DOWN THERE.
YOU LITTLE WITCH.
CHESTER GOULD
Reg. U. S. Pat. Off.: © 1960 by The Chicago Tribune.
DICK TRACY

Dick Tracy, three consecutive daily strips, November 28–30, 1960.

IN THE same autobiographical sketch that Chester Gould put together in 1977 soon after starting retirement, he said, "Of course, any work you like is not really hard work—it's a happy operation." Oh, I bet you it was—even during Gould's last years as operations manager, when story strips like his were dwindling, headed for extinction, their dimensions cut drastically (or as he once memorably put it, "locked in tiny cells like drunks"); I bet you it was a very happy operation. I *imagine* it was, even when his famous narrative power became blunted and groggy; when the strip turned into a lame-brained polemic for tough policing, and the poor guy himself, Gould himself, after thirty-five or forty years of lucrative celebrity and high repute was being name-called everything from a dinosaur to a callous crackpot. (The very idea of letting Dick Tracy fight crime with a vaporizing laser cannon!)

Through his last woozy days on *Dick Tracy* and despite everything—declining chops, declining health, declining popularity—it always seemed to me that Chester Gould was having serious fun. He may have been one of the few people in the world by then who was—by the end of Gould's tenure the stories made almost no sense—but you always felt that *he* was enjoying himself. Why wouldn't he? He'd distilled the strip's graphic look until it was nearly as emblematic as *Beetle Bailey*, he could still design a killer Sunday page even drawing at less than half the size he used to, and while it wasn't as reliable as before, his knack for image-making remained impressive. Currency, a few million bucks worth, orbiting the earth in a solid heap. A farmer's field where all of the cows are two-dimensional cutouts. Sparkly diamonds sailing away in helium balloons. Yeah, he could still knock 'em out from time to time.

The only photographs I've seen that don't show Chester Gould smiling, *beaming*, are the ones that show him drawing—and then he looks wholly absorbed. He often referred to himself as a mere newsboy ("The sole purpose of a comic strip is to sell newspapers; that makes me a newsboy"), but it was disingenuous modesty. Gould knew perfectly well what he was: a complete comic-strip man. Which meant, during his lifetime, a newspaper comic-strip man. A syndicated newspaper comic-strip man. For some mysterious reason, the sum total of Gould's scrappy driven personality plus his native talents, plus a lot of practice, plus luck, made him finally into a world-class cartoonist, a genius of his medium. Till he stopped, till he finally and for good stopped applying himself, till he quit making the daily effort, the effort daily, the man was in charge of his comic strip. *Dick Tracy*, Chester Gould, Prop. Of *course* he was happy.

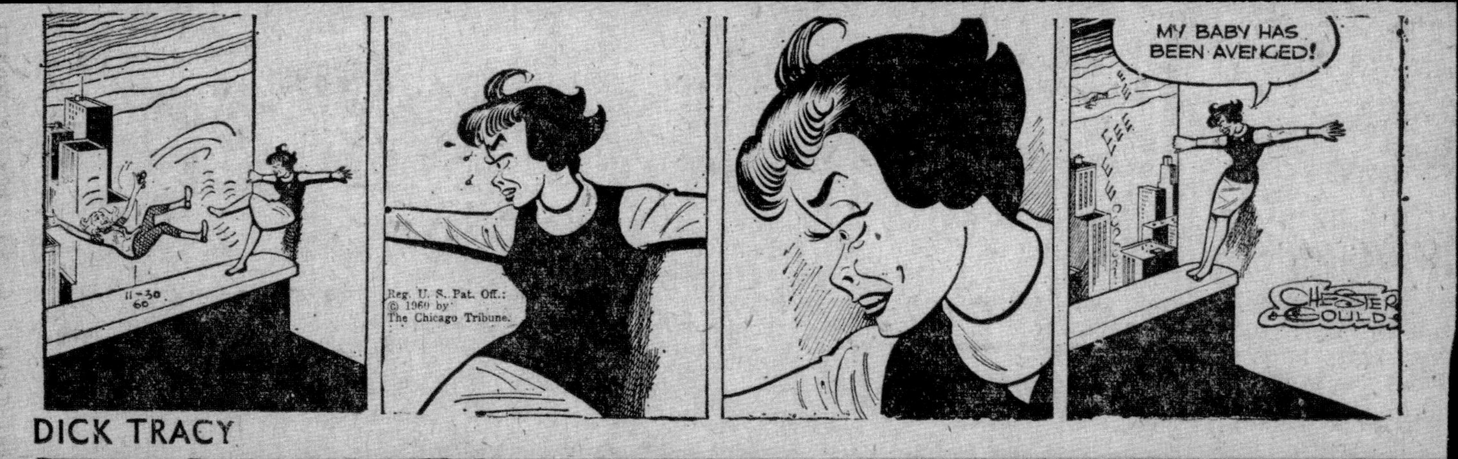

11-30 60
Reg. U. S. Pat. Off.: © 1960 by The Chicago Tribune.
MY BABY HAS BEEN AVENGED!
CHESTER GOULD
DICK TRACY

Opportunist in a Strange Land

"Sometimes

We're Lovable in Our Error "

THE CAREER OF ABNER DEAN

Left: "Opportunist in a Strange Land," *It's a Long Way to Heaven*, 1945.

After years of reading Abner Dean, I still can't answer a fundamental question: Are the drawings in the books he released from 1945 to 1954 cartoons? In one sense, of course, this question is irrelevant. They are thought-provoking and beautifully drawn images with text, and that's all that matters. Yet the question gets at issues central to Dean's philosophy of cartooning and to our understanding of his art. He had worked as an illustrator and cartoonist for fourteen years prior to releasing *It's a Long Way to Heaven* in 1945 and was unhappy with commercial work and the limitations of cartooning formulas. So, in the early '40s Dean took the familiar vocabulary of the gag cartoon and began to produce "drawings" (the term he preferred) that he thought were something new and "striking." These innovations expressed his belief in the power of the cartoon, not simply to get a laugh, but to get readers thinking about themselves in a new way. The typical gag cartoon only asks for a quick chuckle at how we—or, more often, other people—act. But for Dean, the combination of single-panel image and text could stimulate a wide range of responses: delight, frustration, provocation, sadness, or illumination. To bring about such reactions, Dean created cartoons (a term he also used) that placed a greater demand on readers than typical cartoons and generated more questions than answers. Take Dean's "Opportunist in a Strange Land." What's the opportunity presented to the protagonist? (To be a voyeur who can't be caught looking?) Why don't the others just remove the sacks from their heads? (Are they content in their blindness?) Why is he wearing a hat? (After all, no one can see it). But most importantly: What's in the bag he's carrying? If the opportunist represents Dean, then perhaps the bag contains not his drawing materials, but a sharp pair of scissors: he might cut eye-holes in the sacks of the others so they can view the world as he does.

Dean released five popular collections that displayed the unusual approach to cartooning evident in "Opportunist in a Strange Land." While mid-twentieth-century readers hadn't seen cartoons like this before, they certainly had seen Dean's commercial work in *Life*, *Time*, *Newsweek*, *Esquire*, *Collier's*, *Look*, *Ladies' Home Journal*, or dozens of other magazines. And Dean had a successful and varied career beyond cartooning; he collaborated on a ballet, lectured on psychoanalysis, published poetry, was involved in animation for TV and Broadway, and appeared on TV as a game show panelist and cultural critic. His drawings showed a similar kind of eclecticism; he constantly employed different mediums and styles, from silhouettes and woodcuts to aggressive brush work and a graceful, economical pen line. What follows is a biography of Dean's protean career told through images that trace his art from high school until shortly before his death, with an emphasis on the strange and compelling personal work of the '40s and '50s. This history tells the story of an innovative cartoonist celebrated during his lifetime as a "punch drunk prophet."

by KEN PARILLE

PORTRAIT

THE CLASS OF 19 3 1

Above left: "Portrait" (1926), *The Five Arts*, 1930.

Dean was born Abner Joseph Epstein on March 18, 1910, in New York City. His uncle, Jacob Epstein, was a pioneering modernist sculptor, and when Dean was young the two would talk about painting, drawing, and sculpture. While in high school, Dean was heavily involved in cartooning: he was cartoon editor of the school's monthly publication and art editor of both the newspaper and the annual. At sixteen he entered the National Academy of Design, starting in October of 1926 and attending for one year. Like most Academy students, Dean began in antique class—drawing casts of Greek and Roman sculptures—and was later "promoted" to life class, drawing live models. In a student show in April of 1927, Dean received an "honorable mention" for a drawing of a head, perhaps the one pictured here, which was done in December of the previous year.

Above middle and right: Two drawings, *Dartmouth Freshman Green Book*, 1927.

Dean entered Dartmouth College in Hanover, New Hampshire, in 1927, and was the first sophomore elected art editor of the campus's well-known humor periodical, the *Jack-O-Lantern*. Dean had mixed feelings about some of his work published there, later asking that his name be "routed" off the plates of several illustrations. Despite his misgivings, others recognized his considerable talents: in 1929 he won the "National College Comic Artist" competition sponsored by the magazine *College Humor*. Dean's creative interests always extended far beyond cartooning, and in 1930 he and another classmate pooled together $100 and founded "The Printer's Devil Press." The Press published Dean's first two books in 1931—*Simplicissimus* and *Twelve Silhouettes* (both in editions of ten)—and also released several other books, one of which featured linoleum cuts by Dean.

Left: Woodcut, *The Fall of the House of Usher*, 1931.

In 1931, Dean graduated from college and began to pursue a career in commercial art. His earliest work in this period included illustrations for two limited-edition books from small presses: *Thais* by Norman

SONGS TO BE SUNG WITH YOUR TONGUE IN YOUR CHEEK
ABNER DEAN
Many a girl
Who was never taught to,
Likes many a thing
That she hadn't ought to.

LINES TO BE MUTTERED TO YOURSELF
ABNER DEAN
Men don't get sexual
With girls intellectual.

Life
DECEMBER
15 CENTS
IN CANADA 20¢
CHRISTMAS NUMBER
ABNER DEAN

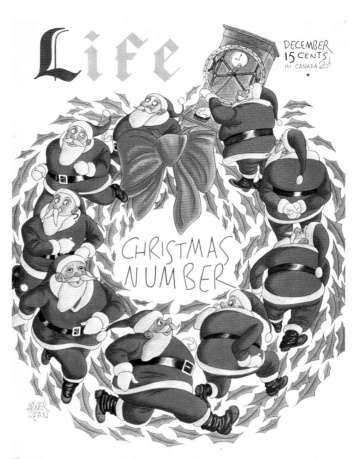

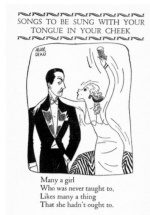

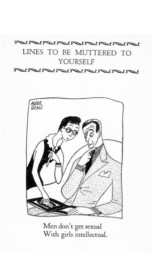

Levy—fine-line drawings done in an art deco style that Dean would occasionally use from 1927 to 1935—and the Cheshire House edition of Edgar Allan Poe's *The Fall of the House of Usher*—seven woodcuts that bear almost no trace of Dean's other styles. *Time* magazine recommended the Poe volume in a feature on holiday gifts, mentioning Dean's "frightening frontispiece." Earlier that year, Dean had painted a mural on the wall of the New York speakeasy *The Pilot's Club* with fellow Dartmouth graduate and *Jack-O-Lantern* contributor Dr. Seuss (Theodor Geisel, class of 1925) and friend Hugh Troy, in which Seuss imitated Dean's style and Dean imitated Troy. (No images of the mural are known to exist.) In 1932, Dean changed his last name from Epstein to one based on his mother's first name, "Deana," telling a correspondent that "the change was something I had intended many years ago." Dean's first national cover appeared in September of that year on *Life*. (The famous magazine with this title would begin four years later, and Dean would create many illustrations for it during the '40s.) Dean's cover, however, wasn't a drawing. He had made a series of paper masks of U.S. politicians and asked *Life*'s editor if the magazine could use them. A "caricature mask" of Franklin D. Roosevelt was made into a puppet and then photographed.

George Jean Nathan—Beginning This Issue
Life
OCTOBER
15 CENTS
IN CANADA 20¢
ABNER DEAN
"I always feel so conspicuous when I come in late!"
Don Herold—Paul Gallico—Ogden Nash—Kyle Crichton

Above: Two illustrated poems, *Slightly Sour Grapes*, 1934.

Right top and bottom: Two covers, *Life*, December 1934 and October 1934.

"All that happens to me here in New York is so much on the side of a mad, nervous hustle," Dean wrote in 1934. "It's so easy to be downed by petty discouragements in the profession of pictures." "My work," he continued, "is on the upgrade very definitely and I'm very hopeful for it at the moment...The drawings continue to develop and are approaching, at least, a starting point for a career. I feel that whatever I have done up till now, I have yet to get under way." During this year, Dean's work was on tour with the "Salon of American Humorists," a show sponsored by the College Art Association.

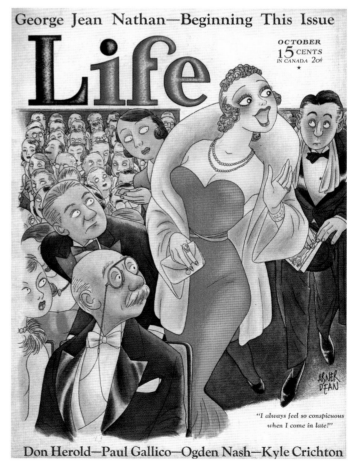

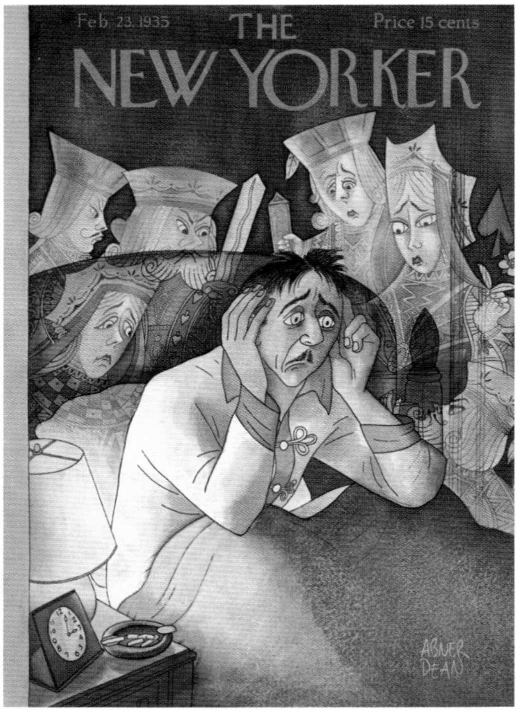
Feb. 23, 1935
THE
NEW YORKER
Price 15 cents
ABNER DEAN

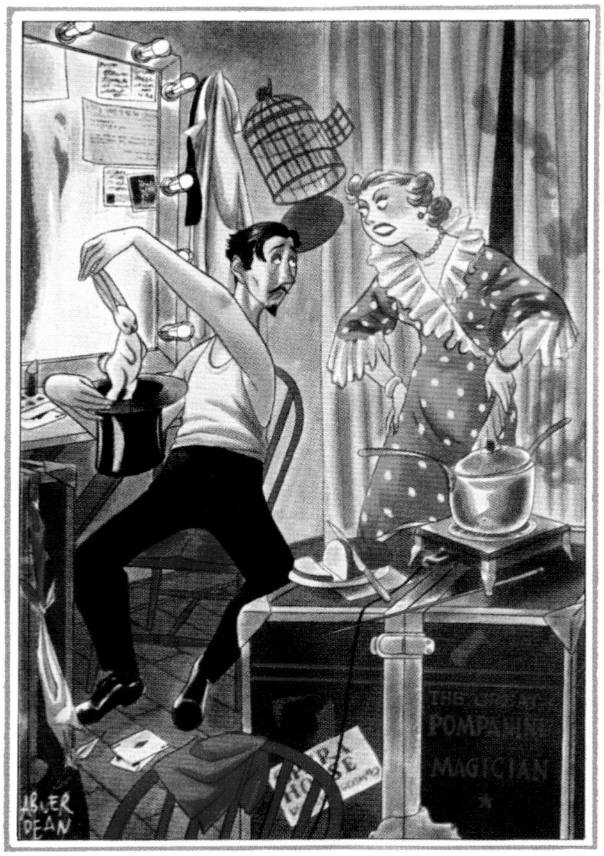
POMPANINI
MAGICIAN
ABNER DEAN

"I wish you'd get a real job—I'm sick of rabbit stew"

CORONET

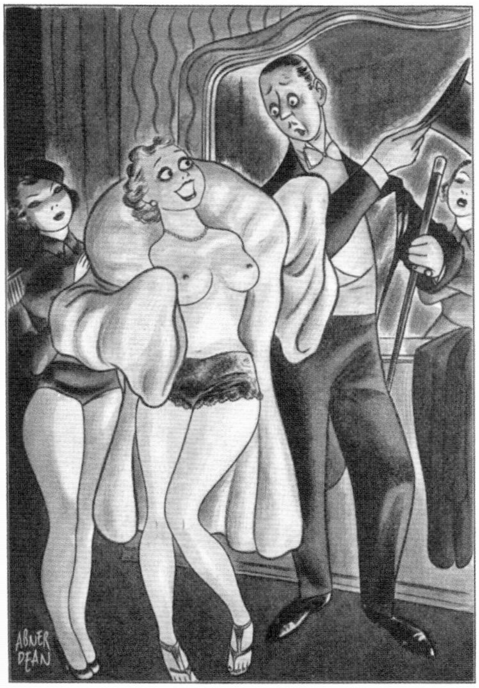
ABNER DEAN

"Remember, dear? I told you I forgot *something!*"

Above left: Cover, *The New Yorker*, February 23, 1935.

Perhaps Dean's highest profile cover work began in 1933, when the twenty-three-year-old artist created the first of five covers for *The New Yorker*. This cover from 1935 would be Dean's last for the magazine.

Left and below: "Remember, dear? I told you I forgot *something!*" and illustration, *The Bedroom Companion . . . A Steaming Bracer for the Forgotten Male*, 1935.

Above right: "I wish you'd get a real job–I'm sick of rabbit stew," *Coronet*, December 1936.

Dean produced more full-color gag cartoons in the 1930s than during any other time in his career. In 1934 he began an association with *Esquire* that lasted until the mid-'50s; the over forty color cartoons Dean created for the men's magazine were done in a style similar to this one from the second issue of the monthly *Coronet*. The '30s also saw the start of another long involvement: Dean began drawing cartoons for *Collier's* that would also appear in the magazine for over two decades.

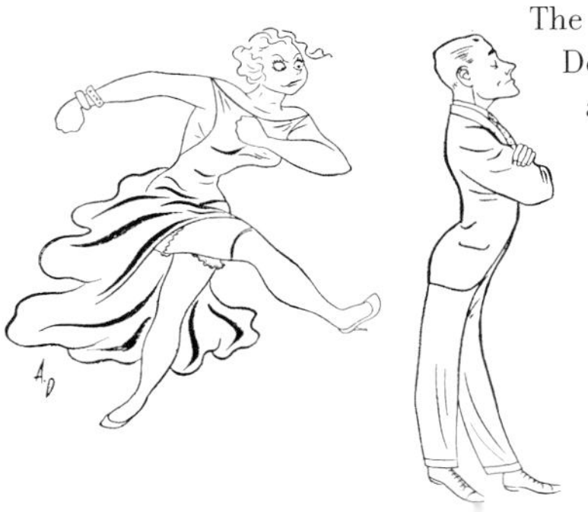

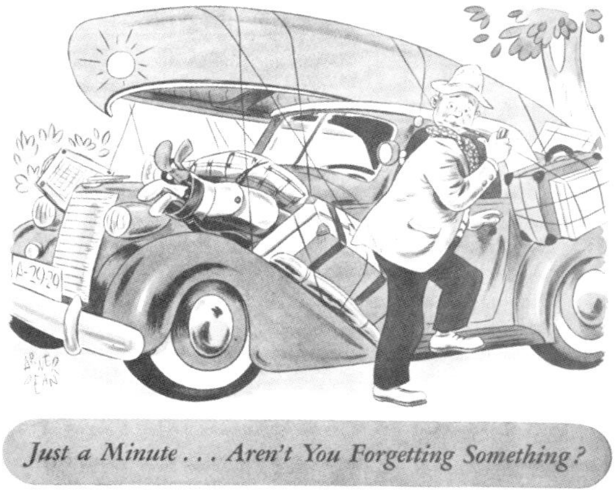
Just a Minute . . . Aren't You Forgetting Something?

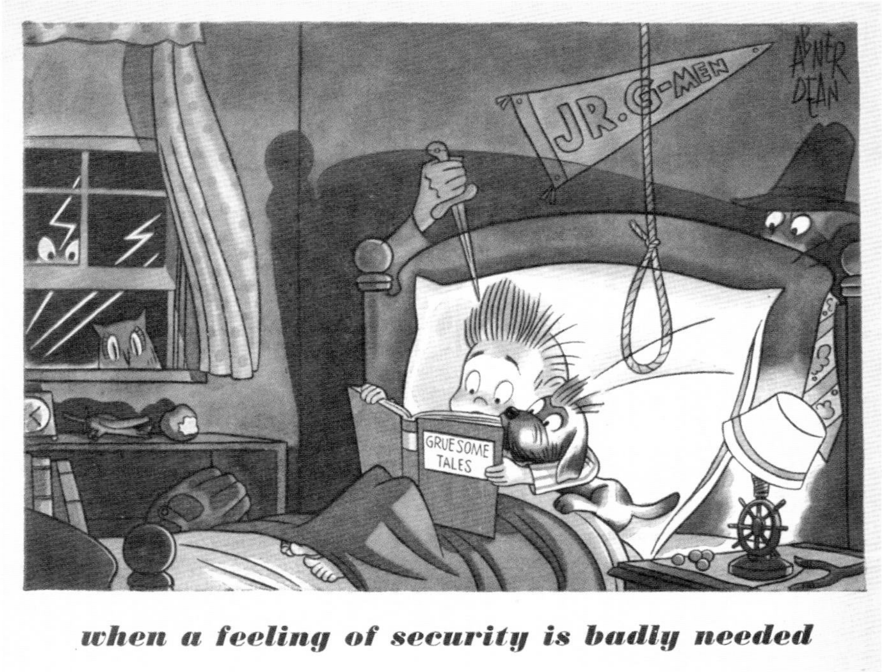
JR. G-MEN
GRUESOME TALES
when a feeling of security is badly needed

This page: Three *Aetna Insurance Company* advertisements, 1940, 1944, 1948.

Dean's most widely visible work, his drawings for Aetna Insurance, began to appear in prominent magazines such as *Time* and *Newsweek* in the summer of 1940. By the time the campaign ended in 1955, Dean had done over 110 ads. In *The Complete Guide to Cartooning* (1950), Gene Byrnes showed four versions of the third cartoon above, noting that Dean's stylization and careful choices about composition made him "one of the best draughtsmen in cartooning." This cartoon was reprinted in the mid-'50s in a fire safety pamphlet titled "Fire Foibles" that included nine of Dean's drawings for Aetna.

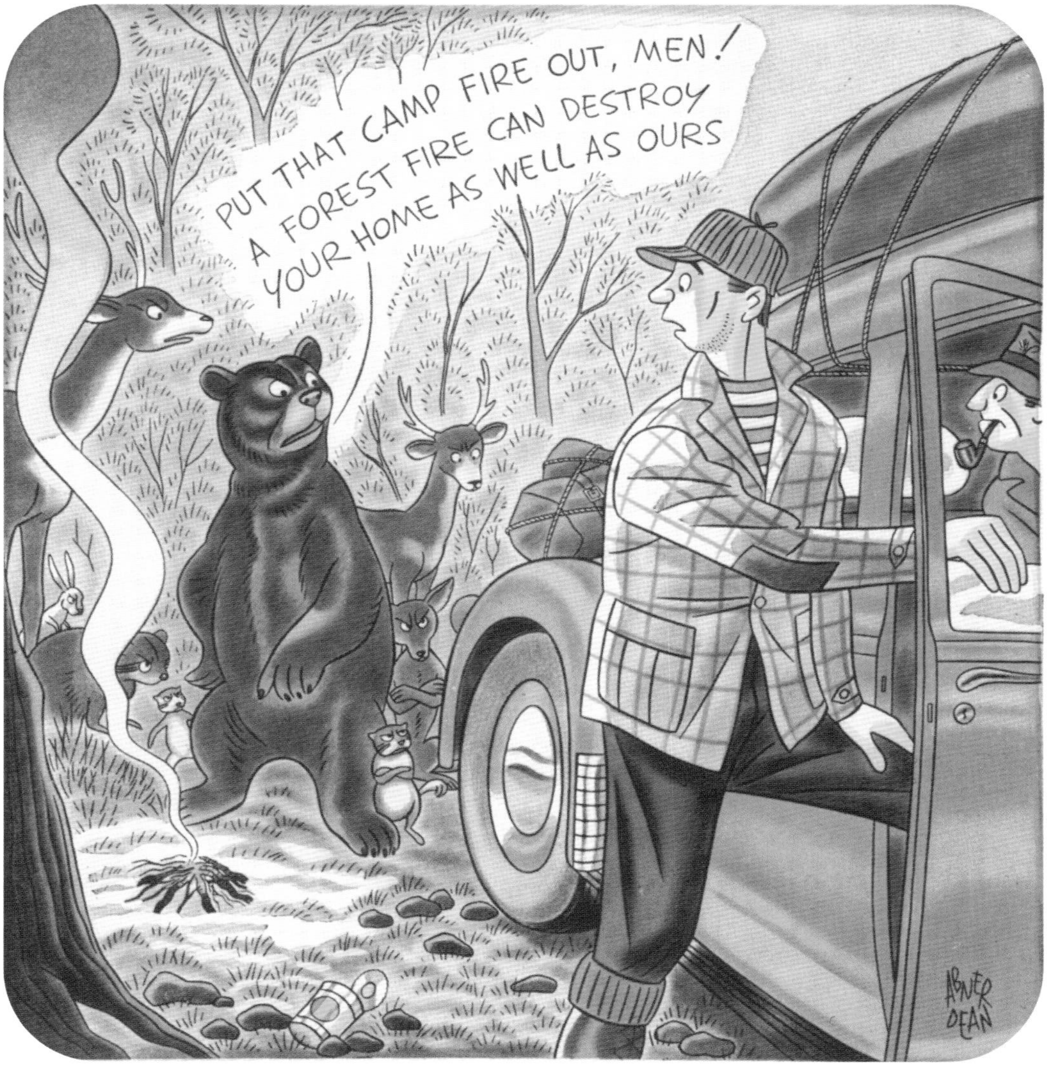
PUT THAT CAMP FIRE OUT, MEN!
A FOREST FIRE CAN DESTROY
YOUR HOME AS WELL AS OURS
ABNER DEAN

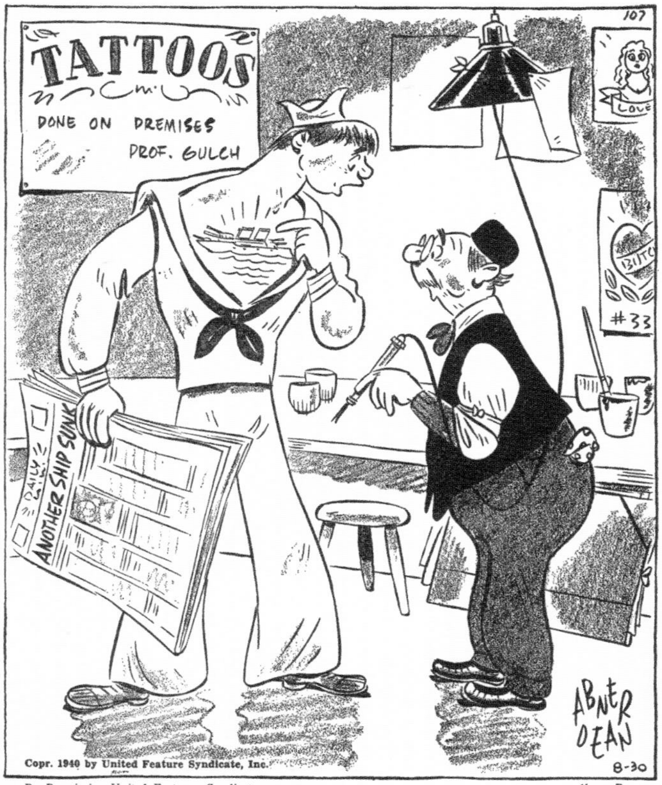
107
TATTOOS
DONE ON PREMISES
PROF. GULCH
LOVE
#33
ANOTHER SHIP SUNK
ABNER DEAN
8-30
Copr. 1940 by United Feature Syndicate, Inc.

By Permission United Features Syndicate *Abner Dean*

"I want you to add a convoy!"

Top left: Daily gag panel, *Funny Side Up*, August 30, 1940.

Another widely seen project also began in 1940. Dean was hired by United Features to do a cartoon similar to *Grin and Bear It* by George Lichty, who had recently left the syndicate. Dean's gag panel, which he named *Funny Side Up*, followed the template of Lichty's: a single-panel humor strip with no recurring characters, drawn in ink and shaded with crayon (a shading technique that Dean seldom used). In 1941, Dean wrote of the "ordeal" of creating over three hundred *Funny Side Up* cartoons: "For the greater part of the last year I was doing a daily and Sunday feature...It appeared in over a hundred papers, was a wonderful experience in discipline, but proved to be not sufficiently rewarding mentally to justify spending the next five years as its slave. After about ten months of a night and day routine I decided to abandon it and return to the work that syndication had forced me to leave." "I'm still unsettled in my work," Dean continued. "I've experimented a great deal and gone off on many tangents which justify themselves, but I haven't yet found the balance between the well known economic structure of things and the work I want to do. I find time occasionally to paint and experiment in clay, but the demands of commercial art are so great and lead so far away from the purer forms that I don't believe a compromise between the two is ever possible. Those who pretend it is are perhaps over-stating their validity in one or the other."

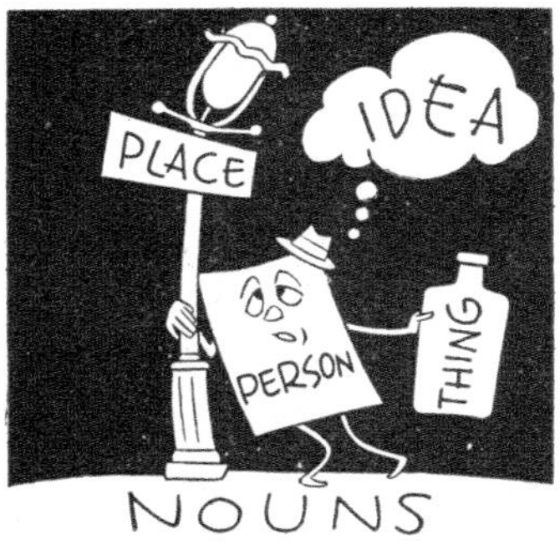
IDEA
PLACE
PERSON
THING
NOUNS

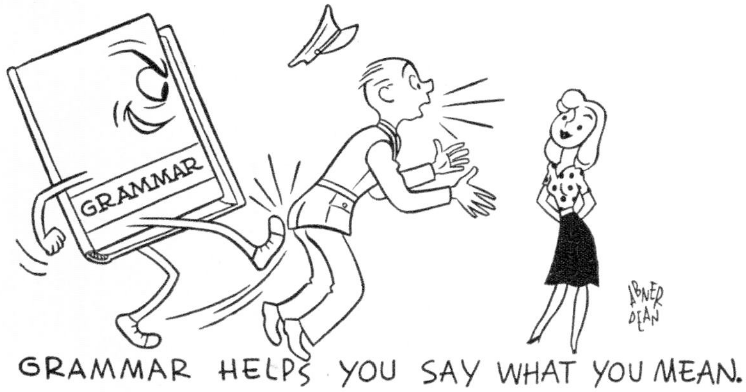
GRAMMAR
ABNER DEAN
GRAMMAR HELPS YOU SAY WHAT YOU MEAN.

Opposite: Six color gags, *Sparkler Comics* #26, October 1943.

Dean revived the *Funny Side Up* name for filler material in at least two United Features–owned comic books during 1943: *Sparkler Comics* and *Tip Top Comics*.

Middle and bottom left: Two illustrations, *English Grammar, a Self-Teaching Course Based on Functional Grammar*, 1943.

During World War II, Dean produced numerous drawings for military instructional materials, such as a fourteen-panel color poster warning soldiers about venereal disease, a short series about soldiers watching movies, and numerous drawings for a textbook on grammar. Although often referred to as an illustrator, Dean typically did not do traditional "spot" illustrations; his drawings usually took the form of cartoons that interpreted the text in unusual and often ironic ways. In 1944 and 1945 he created a series of conventional illustrations for a weekly newspaper feature by humorist Damon Runyon titled "Mr. Joe Turp Writes." This feature included some of the larger Dean illustrations ever printed.

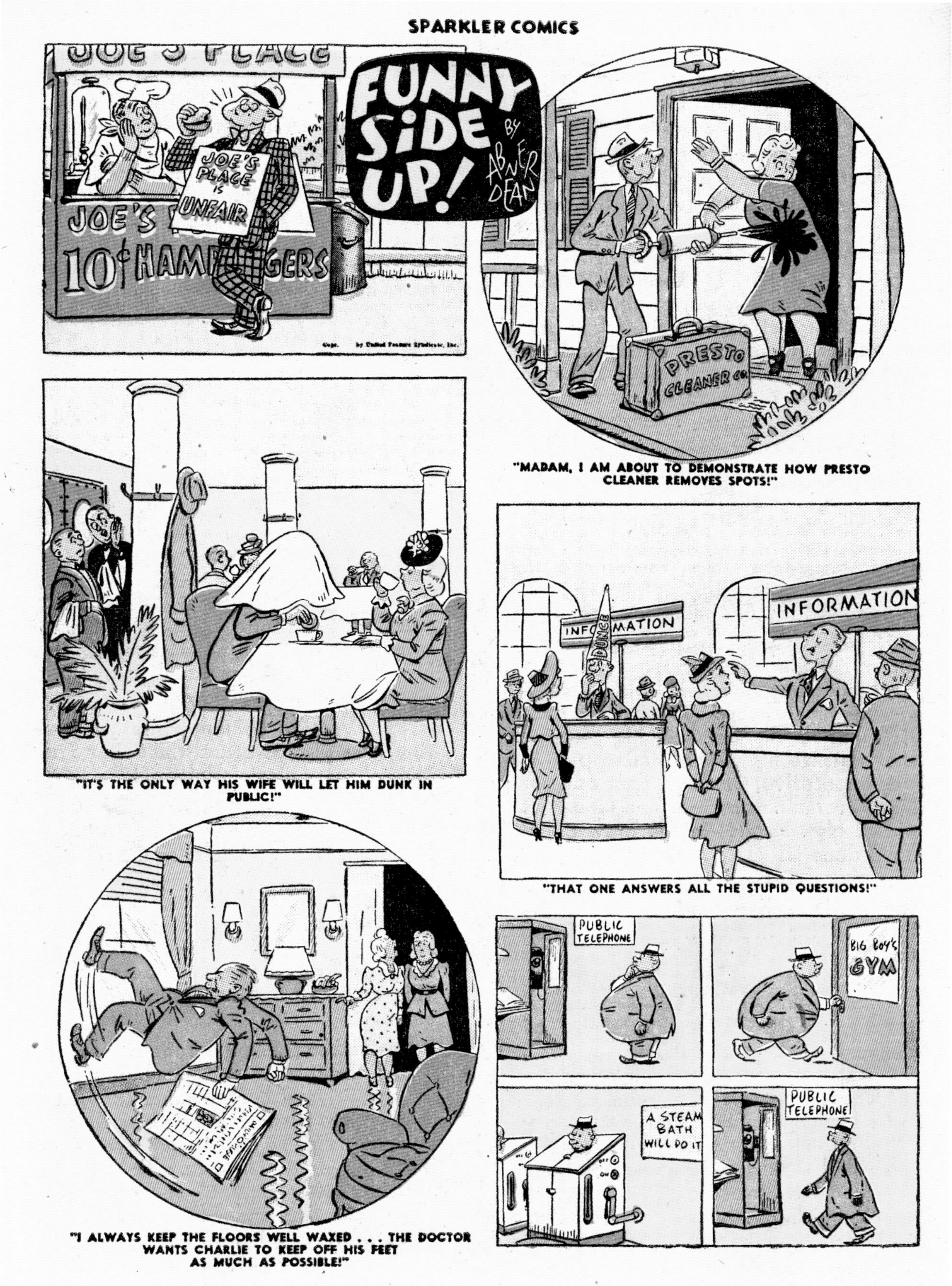
SPARKLER COMICS
FUNNY SIDE UP!
BY ABNER DEAN
JOE'S PLACE
JOE'S PLACE IS UNFAIR
JOE'S
10¢ HAMBURGERS
Copr. by United Feature Syndicate, Inc.
PRESTO CLEANER CO.
"MADAM, I AM ABOUT TO DEMONSTRATE HOW PRESTO CLEANER REMOVES SPOTS!"
"IT'S THE ONLY WAY HIS WIFE WILL LET HIM DUNK IN PUBLIC!"
INFORMATION
DUNCE
INFORMATION
"THAT ONE ANSWERS ALL THE STUPID QUESTIONS!"
"I ALWAYS KEEP THE FLOORS WELL WAXED . . . THE DOCTOR WANTS CHARLIE TO KEEP OFF HIS FEET AS MUCH AS POSSIBLE!"
PUBLIC TELEPHONE
BIG BOY'S GYM
A STEAM BATH WILL DO IT
PUBLIC TELEPHONE

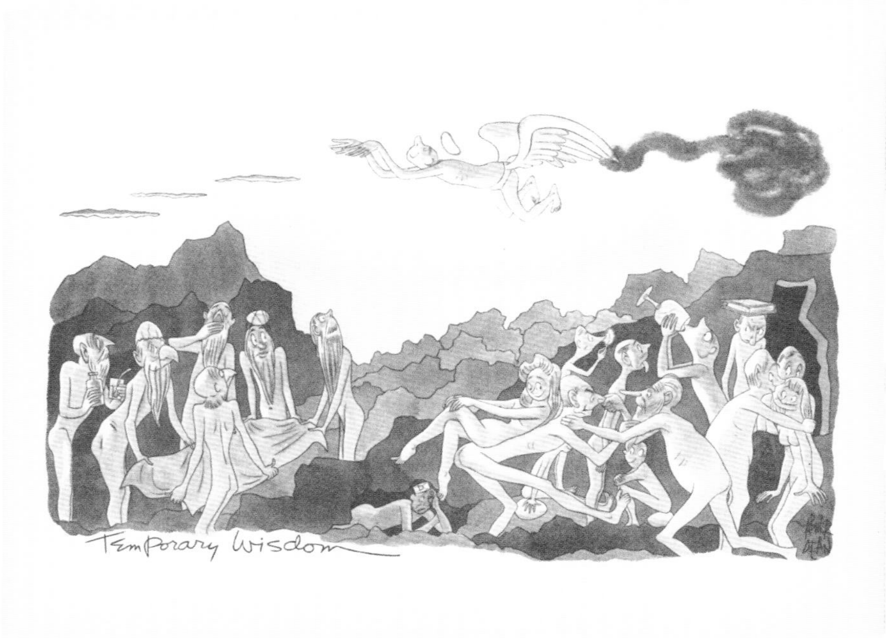
Temporary Wisdom

Above: **"Temporary Wisdom,"**
***It's a Long Way to Heaven*, 1945.**

1945 saw the publication of *It's a Long Way to Heaven*, the first of four books (with *What Am I Doing Here?*, *And on the Eighth Day*, *Cave Drawings for the Future*) upon which Dean's reputation rests. These books represent an unusual achievement in American cartooning before 1960: unlike most collections they feature cartoons that hadn't been previously published, and they showcase a new and philosophical approach to the gag cartoon. "Advance reports from the salesmen are staggering—and the first edition...will be about 25,000," Dean wrote. "The substance of the book was long accumulating." In 1941 he corresponded with a friend about commercial work he had sent to an exhibition at Dartmouth: "I hope Hanover likes the cartoons. Unfortunately they don't represent my best work. I'm at work on a long series of drawings now that are not intended for publication." It seems likely that this series, which Dean initially planned as a gallery show, became *It's a Long Way to Heaven*. Seven of the collection's cartoons first appeared in a 1942 article on Dean in *Life*, and these drawings (along with others in the volume) differ from conventional gag cartoons in two important ways: the text exists within the frame of the image; and the text is more like a title and less like the dialogue or narration typical of a gag panel's caption. In later books Dean would always place the text outside of the drawing, and he would often use type for the words (as did most gag cartoons) rather than the hand-lettering of *It's a Long Way to Heaven*. Seminal literary critic Northrop Frye said of the cartoons in this collection that "the best have a disturbingly haunting quality that one rarely finds in the more realistic captioned cartoons of the *New Yorker* school, and in fact are 'funny' only to the extent of making one giggle hysterically." Byrnes described Dean's technique: he "builds up his drawings in a series of overlays, wash over wash, usually on Whatman board. He uses all sorts of media but these drawings were done with lamp black and india ink after the first sketch in pencil. A brush rather than a pen is used for the line work in the finished drawing." In the first edition of *It's a Long Way to Heaven*, some of the cartoons were printed in a single color—either brown, gray, or green. Later editions, and all of Dean's other personal work, appeared in black and white.

Below: **"The Efficiency Expert,"**
***It's a Long Way to Heaven*, 1945.**

Dean was highly skeptical of any kind of specialized knowledge and repeatedly targeted "experts," be they Freudians, philosophers, scientists, or even cartoonists. His drawings show figures chained to books or using impressive-looking volumes as weapons in a competition for authority and in a quest for self-affirmation. He argued that we could begin to achieve a sense of "balance" (a main concern in his cartoons and notebooks) when we rejected the authority of others, questioned ourselves, developed a "plan," and realized our inherent connection with other people. "Knowledge" and "facts," Dean insisted, should be replaced with "doubt" and "wonder." In keeping with his bias against metaphysical and moral belief systems (which he called "voo-doo ideas"), he never offered any detailed program for change, for to do so would put him in the role of the expert. In "You missed life" (from *What Am I Doing Here?*), a man walks through an alley in which is housed a "pragmatist, "cultist," "authority," "expert," and many others who have labeled themselves; he attempts to rouse them to an awareness that has been suppressed by their belief in what Dean called "the false security" of specialization. Next to the main character is a sign that says "stand in," perhaps indicating that this provocateur is standing in for Dean.

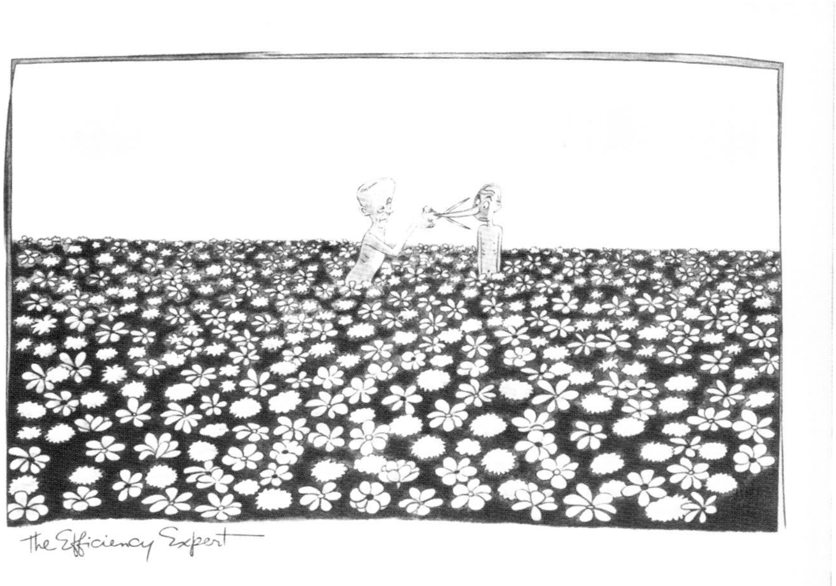
The Efficiency Expert

59

Below left: "The Understanding Wife,"
It's a Long Way to Heaven, 1945.

One of the most persistent themes of Dean's cartoons and poetry is male/female relationships. His commercial work until the mid-'40s often involved scenarios common in the world of men's humor, such as the dumb female and smart male, the inscrutable woman and inquisitive man, and the domineering wife and subjugated husband. (See *The Bedroom Companion* and *Slightly Sour Grapes* earlier.) Scenes like these appear throughout his 1945–1956 collections, and we may be tempted therefore to see such drawings as expressions of hostility towards women—but the work is more complex than that. This cartoon, for example, might appear to echo the third premise above: a husband is in thrall to his wife who, as the title ironically suggests, does not understand him. In his notebooks, Dean often asked questions about a character's self-awareness. And we could ask such questions here, ones that might affect our interpretation: If his wife doesn't understand him, is it because he doesn't understand either himself or her? If she's happy and he's not, is it her fault? Is he looking to her, and not himself, for liberation from the stocks? Perhaps, in the end, she does understand the predicament he has created for himself better than he does: "You are your own shackle," Dean said elsewhere. And in

cartoons like "The Bright Young Men" (*It's a Long Way to Heaven*), "Party Note" (*Come As You Are*), and many others, Dean was highly critical of what he saw as the often egotistical and destructive behaviors of males, and in *Cave Drawings for the Future* he visualized the ways that men use women as metaphors for their own confusion and conflicts.

Below right: "I made this," *What Am I Doing Here?*, 1947.

Dean left five notebooks in which he commented on dozens of cartoons from *What Am I Doing Here?* In this commentary he adopted different personas: in some he talked as if he were a character in the drawing; in others he sympathized with or scolded characters or the reader in his own voice; in many he offered either straightforward or obscure observations on the cartoon; and in others he moved between these approaches. "Our hero is part fool-part wise man," Dean said of "I made this," "but for one moment he partakes of greatness—ridiculous as his creation may be it is better than the plodding absence of consciousness. Within its hectic form is a plan—is self recognition—in its fumblings is the hope—." It might be easy to see this cartoon as ironic, mocking the foolishness of the immature artist. But Dean frequently displayed his sympathy for those who have a "plan" and attempt to create works of art or ways of thinking that will, if only in

some small way, make conditions better for themselves and others.

Because the cartoons in *What Am I Doing Here?* feature a recurring main character ("our hero"), the collection is more novelistic than Dean's other books and could be read as a kind of psychological narrative in which we follow the hero through an ever-shifting series of psychological states and social dilemmas. Interestingly, the cartoons in this collection and others may have been inspired by a template Dean used in the Aetna ads, especially those of the early '40s. They feature someone in a state of crisis or error and an understated title/caption that addresses both the character and the reader, such as "Things don't always turn out as you expect." Part of the interpretive openness of many cartoons in Dean's books comes from the fact that the pronouns in the titles do not have just one referent: An "I," for example, could refer to a main character, secondary character, and/or Dean himself; and "you" could refer to a character and/or the reader. And titles often include "it" or "this," either of which could reference any number of aspects of the drawing, or, in the case of "this," even the cartoon itself. Many of the titles (which are often unpunctuated sentences) appear to be words spoken by a character, but because Dean rarely used quotation marks, the text's status as dialogue is also an open question.

The Understanding Wife

I made this

It's good to own a piece of land

Sometimes we give up too soon

Above left: **"It's good to own a piece of land,"** *What Am I Doing Here?*, 1947.

"Don't search for hidden meanings in this drawing," Dean cautioned. "They're all apparent here—nothing hidden." Like many of Dean's titles, this one is to be taken literally: it's good to own land and everyone should. Yet Dean criticized the smugness of people who fail to extend sympathy to those in need: "What about those other people—do they own any land?" Dean worried that readers might bring their own philosophical bias to this cartoon, warning that "There is no implication here that the state should own the land." While many of Dean's cartoons are cryptic, others (like this one) communicate a simple premise in a clear way, and Dean's comments are a helpful reminder about over-reading and misinterpretation. If readers assume (as many have) that Dean is not sympathetic towards the plight of many of the characters he creates, then they might be bringing their own cynicism, and not Dean's, to the drawing.

Above right: **"Sometimes we give up too soon,"** *What Am I Doing Here?*, 1947.

"Competition on roller skates is my downfall," Dean lamented. "It demands of me responses that are foreign—it's not my fault— or yours. So I compete or withdraw...Don't talk of peace—of beauty—of culture of anything for that matter until we're rid of competition." Perhaps this cartoon expresses not only Dean's antagonism to competition in general, but his particular distaste for the commercial art world in which he was entangled, always competing for the scraps of advertising budgets. And Dean's views on competition may be related to his interest in psychoanalysis. Many have argued that Dean is heavily indebted to Freud, but I would argue his cartoons are more Adlerian than Freudian. Alfred Adler, one of the three main figures of modern psychoanalysis (Dean called Adler, Freud, and Jung "The Id Kids"), believed each of us suffers from an "inferiority complex" that leads us to compete with others to establish our sense of self-worth or superiority. Like "Sometimes we give up too soon," dozens of Dean's cartoons feature a character in a struggle with other people for self-definition. Following Adler, Dean argued that such "self-actualization" would occur when we rejected competition and embraced cooperation. Both Dean and Adler were less inclined than Freud to look to a person's past or to sexually based complexes as the source of neurosis. Adler believed that we based our lives on what he called "fictional finalism," an idealized self-image that we rarely understood but nevertheless spent a lifetime trying to achieve—Dean's drawings repeatedly show a single character wandering through a vast and barren landscape on a quest for such self-realization. Taken as a whole, Dean's cartoons offer a complex and thoughtful examination of the psychology of personal identity and social interaction, one that draws on numerous philosophical traditions. Using slides of his cartoons, Dean often lectured about psychology and psychoanalysis at colleges and medical schools, and Dean's publishers noted that his cartoons were used in psychiatric practice.

Opposite top: **"Can I help, maybe?,"** *What Am I Doing Here?*, 1947.

In picturing the jester as so small, tentative, and seemingly powerless when confronted with a mass of suffering people, Dean may reveal an ambivalence towards his career as a satirist. Although he has the lofty goal of arousing those who sleepwalk through life, most expect from a cartoonist only a fleeting, lowbrow laugh, the kind Dean had often delivered in his earlier commercial work: "I'm a rare one when it comes to lightening the moment—anyone got a lampshade I can wear as a hat—this'll kill ya!" Dean also wrote in his notes about this cartoon that although "humor never cured anything," "rightness... [will] have a twist of real humor in it," perhaps the kind of twist so often found in his drawings. The jester emerges unseen from the manhole, as if from the depths of the collective unconscious of the weeping characters. Though he can't cure the others (Dean believed you can only cure yourself), he can help them be happier and gain a deeper understanding of their own condition. Echoing his admiration for the artist of "I made this," Dean said of the jester and his efforts, "it's better to try than just to ignore."

Opposite bottom: **"We're all in it together,"** *What Am I Doing Here?*, 1947.

Dean: "It's to the good that one eye is open somewhere in this somnambulistic scene. Beware of mad dogs—sleep walking minds. This isn't dream world stuff. You can snap this with an ordinary Brownie any day. Pose Please! He's beginning to be conscious...it may be contagious...Meanwhile our hope is that we're all in it together—just that. No one is separate. There's an old wives' tale that it's dangerous to waken sleep walkers. Dangerous? More dangerous than what?"

Can I help, maybe?

We're all in it together

drawing by Abner Dean for "Amorous Adventure"

Don't anyone weep . . . the tragedy is all ours

Left: **"Don't anyone weep . . . the tragedy is all ours,"** *And on the Eighth Day,* 1949.

In each of the seven books released from 1945 to 1956, Dean used a different visual style. The art in *And on the Eighth Day* has a loose, deliberately unfinished look that contrasts with the polish of his earlier books and commercial work. A reviewer attacked Dean's cartoons as "vitriol martinis" and *Time* magazine criticized this collection as "a grim search through the weird subconscious levels of John Doe, a search that altogether misses heart & soul but finds a spirit crushed and shriveled." The claim of pessimism is more accurate for this book than previous ones, I would argue, not because the content is darker (though it is to some degree), but because the style is harsher: Dean's line is far more angular and aggressive. In particular, the characters' faces are often reduced to a series of marks, erasing the individuality they possessed in previous books. Reviewers and readers who have described Dean's oeuvre as "grim," though, have overlooked the way that the grace and charm of many drawings in other collections bring a lightness and humor that mitigate the darkness of the content. I wouldn't claim that Dean wasn't pessimistic, but I would say that his emotional, intellectual, and visual range showed more complexity than any term, or even set of terms, could capture.

Above: **Drawing,** *Dance,* 1951.

In 1949 Dean began collaborating with influential dancer and choreographer Pauline Koner on a ballet titled *Amorous Adventure.* Koner was searching for ideas for a new work, and a friend suggested Dean's cartoons. Months later she "came upon a book called *It's a Long Way to Heaven*": "His figures were full of movement ideas, and his strange world haunted me," Koner said. *Amorous Adventure* "dealt with a husband and a wife [with] transparent bags over their heads [that] kept them blissfully unaware of who they really were." (For a related image, see "Opportunist in a Strange Land" earlier.) The set consisted of three various-sized wishbones (objects that appear throughout Dean's cartoons), and the cast featured five dancers, some of whom wore portraits designed by Dean, painted on squares of silk, and then attached to costumes. Dean described the ballet in a program note as "the story of a girl with amatory hiccups, an unbalanced equation and several men who have peripheral influence on her personal mathematics. The dance resolves no world problems, and its conclusion 'X' still represents the unknown." The ballet premiered in August of 1951 at the American Dance Festival, and three years later Koner and Dean discussed another project: "Abner's idea had to do with an angel who, in her life on earth, had been jilted by her lover. She now decides to return and get even." The resulting solo piece, *Interlude for Angelica,* became a part of Koner's repertoire.

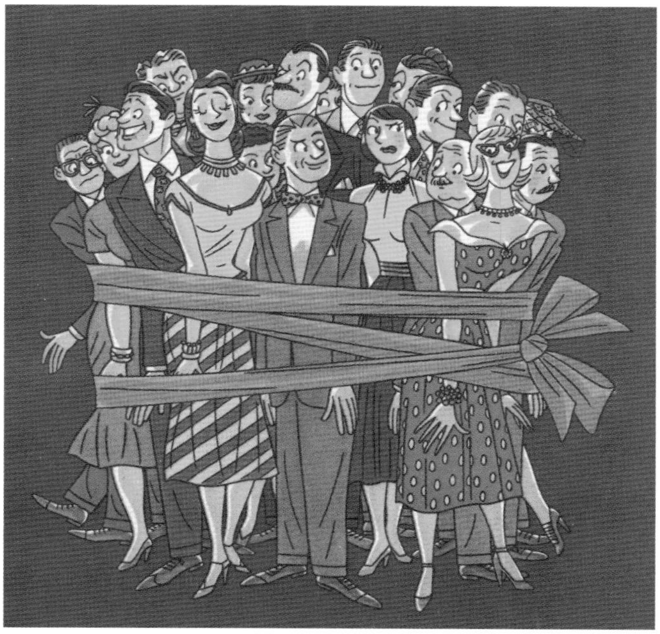

Above: Cover detail, *Come As You Are*, 1952.

Come As You Are again marked a dramatic style change for a Dean collection. These cartoons about the ways that people behave at parties looked less like the drawings in *And on the Eighth Day* or *What Am I Doing Here?* and more like his commercial cartooning from the '40s. Dean was acquainted with the upper-class social environment the cartoons satirize, associating with well-known figures like Koner, *Guys and Dolls* composer Frank Loesser, and Bartley Crum, an advisor to President Harry Truman and prominent opponent of the post-War Hollywood blacklist. In the year *Come As You Are* was released, Dean was on *Draw to Win*, a short-lived TV show with cartoonists Bill Holman and Syd Hoff. A TV reviewer characterized an episode: the cartoonists "plus a couple of guests—at least one of whom can't draw—play what amounts to charades on a drawing board. One of the cartoonists will compress an expression like 'eating high on the hog' into some sort of drawing and the other guests will make wild guesses about it. The drawings are pretty ingenious."

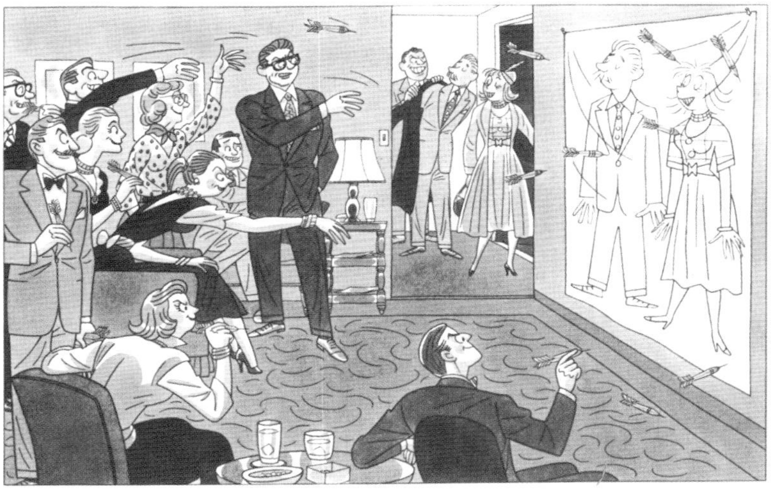

IT'S DANGEROUS TO LEAVE FIRST

Top right: "It's Dangerous to Leave First," *Come As You Are*, 1952.

Bottom right: "The glorification of the mediocre," *Cave Drawings for the Future*, 1954.

Dean appeared on CBS's morning show with Walter Cronkite in 1954 to promote *Cave Drawings for the Future*, the only Dean volume (except the anthology *Naked People*) to employ within it different styles. It's actually a collection of two groups of cartoons: those signed "Abner Dean," which are drawn in a loose, scratchy style that recalls the cartoons in *And on the Eighth Day*; and the polished drawings signed "A·D." Whereas many of Dean's drawings present interpretive dilemmas, "The glorification of the mediocre" represents an elegant and comic realization of a straightforward idea; though there's much to admire and discuss about the cartoon, there's not much to "get."

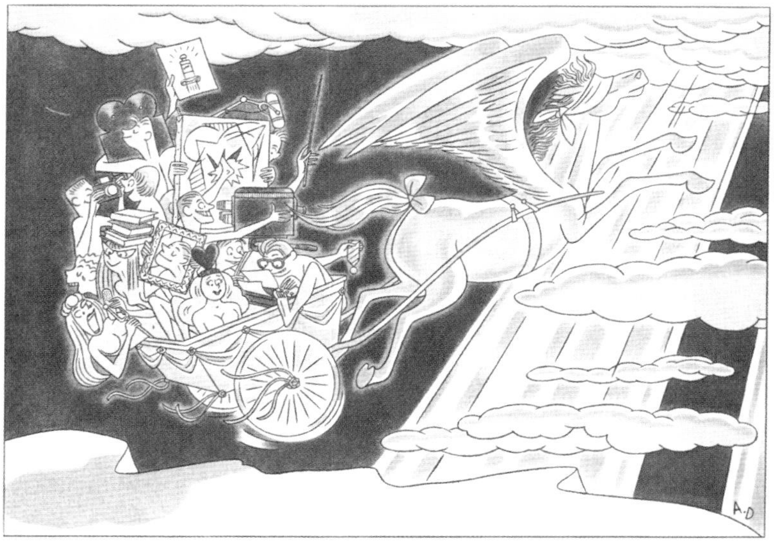
A·D

The glorification of the mediocre

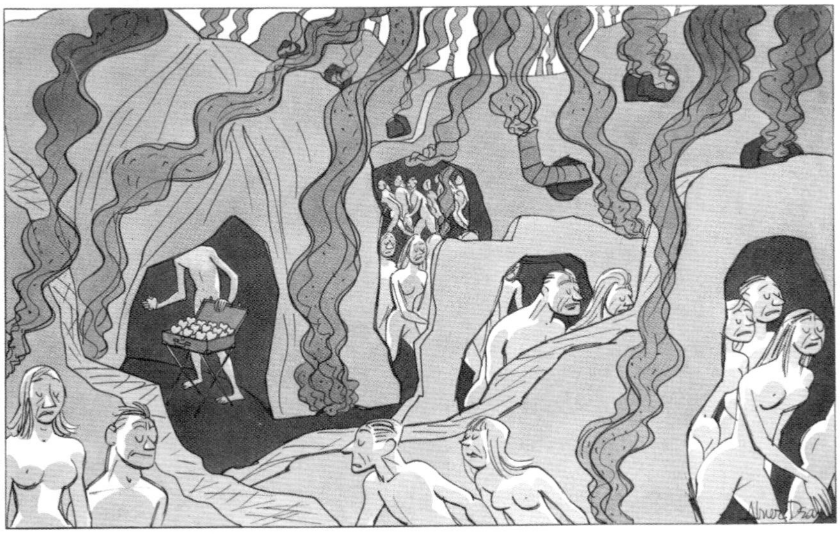

Pitchman on a side-street

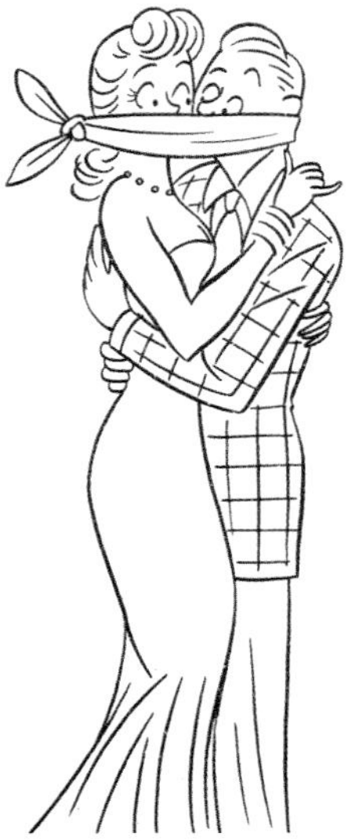
VALENTINE
If
Throughout the nation
They ever ration
Words —
I hope
They leave us
'I Love You' —
The rest is for the birds.

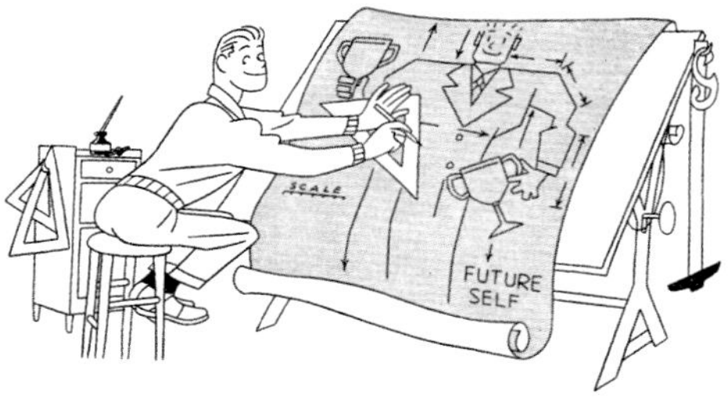
SCALE
FUTURE SELF

The future self needs planning, and we can achieve it only a step at a time.

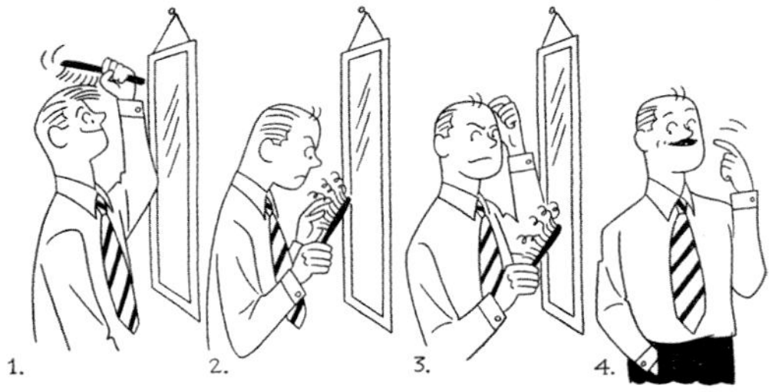
1.
2.
3.
4.

Some painful messages cannot be ignored; so we accept them finally — and change accordingly.

Top: **"Pitchman on a side-street,"**
***Cave Drawings for the Future*, 1954.**

In his introduction to *It's a Long Way to Heaven*, Philip Wylie described Dean's first volume as an examination of the hidden life of "Everyman," a term many have used when talking about Dean's characters. But if the "pitchman," for example, is an "everyman," who is everybody else? Dean continually sets his protagonist apart from a mass of people who are acting alike, signaling that he is not an "everyman." Sometimes Dean criticizes the protagonist for wrongfully separating himself, yet elsewhere, as in this cartoon, he endorses the character's actions. In the opening to *Cave Drawings for the Future*, Dean said that its cartoons illustrate "our latent ingredient—love," perhaps thinking of what this protagonist has for sale. Like many Dean "heroes," he's at an early stage of awareness about what he has to offer the others. But he needs to learn, Dean would likely argue, that if you want to make the sale, you should set up shop on a main street, where you can pitch your wares to the "everyman." (And there's another problem with the term "everyman": given the male/female conflict that drives some of Dean's cartoons, to invoke the term—which typically refers to both genders—is to ignore that Dean often characterized men and women differently.)

Above left and middle: **Two illustrations,**
***Introduction to Speech*, 1955.**

Above right: **"Valentine,"**
***Wake Me When It's Over*, 1955.**

Dean's last two books of new work, *Wake Me When It's Over* and *Not Far from the Jungle*, signaled yet another striking departure: he left the cartoon behind to focus on illustrated poems. Dean made changes in the books' design as well. Whereas earlier collections used mechanical type for captions, publication information, or table of contents, these employ drawing and lettering by Dean, suggesting that, though seldom discussed, these books deserve our attention as a more fully realized form of expression for Dean. *Wake Me When It's Over* is a collection of satirical poems about love and romance illustrated in a graceful and economical clear-line style, one he had used in the past (see *English Grammar* earlier) and would use often from the mid-'50s until the end of his career. As is frequently the case with Dean's work, the text and picture here tell different stories—the drawing may undermine the sentimentality of the poem.

overlooked offering
demonstration of sincerity

THE BOOK OF THE
IT
BY GEORG GRODDECK
INTRODUCTION BY
LAWRENCE DURRELL
A VINTAGE BOOK
V-195 $1.25

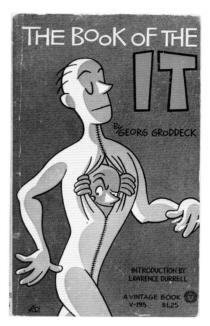

Hopeful Raconteur
Amateur Intriguer
Committee of One

Top left: Illustration for the poem "L'après-midi d'un cartoonist," *Not Far from the Jungle*, 1956.

Top middle: Two gags from "The Hand-off Play," *Esquire*, October 1956.

Above: Three gags from "Psycho-Pates," *Look*, March 5, 1957.

"Psycho-Pates" featured eight cartoons that illustrated "types found in every organization." Dean called these kinds of drawings "psycho-caricatures," and they usually appeared in a series of four or eight on a page. His first group was printed in the Dartmouth *Jack-O-Lantern* and others were published in *College Humor*, *Rockefeller Center Weekly*, and elsewhere.

Top right: *The Book of the It*, 1961. Middle right: "I wish it were more comfortable," *And on the Eighth Day*, 1949. Bottom Right: "How much of me is me?," *What Am I Doing Here?*, 1947.

Dean on "How much of me is me?": "If stained glass is an exalted medium of man's expression, then cover the world with stained glass pictorially reminding man of his real and urgent search—himself. If you understand you—you understand me." Though cartoons were certainly not seen as an exalted medium, Dean wanted his drawings to remind viewers of this same search, which he talked about in his notebooks in almost religious terms.

How much of me is me?

Image

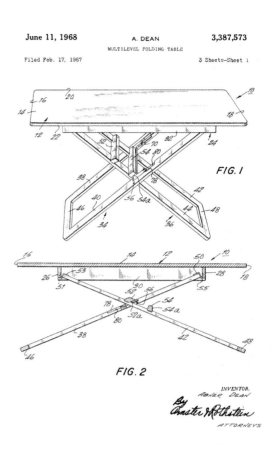

June 11, 1968   A. DEAN   3,387,573

MULTILEVEL FOLDING TABLE

Filed Feb. 17, 1967   3 Sheets-Sheet 1

FIG. 1

FIG. 2

INVENTOR.
ABNER DEAN
By
ATTORNEYS

Above left: **"Image,"** *The Relations Explosion*, 1963.

1963 saw the publication of Dean's last book, *Abner Dean's Naked People; A Selection of Drawings from Four of His Books*, which did not include any material from *Come As You Are* or the two volumes of poetry. This anthology's larger size solved a problem with earlier collections, which often printed a cartoon across two pages, causing key details to be lost near the inner margins of facing pages. (The images from *And on the Eighth Day* and *What Am I Doing Here?* that appear earlier in this biography have been taken from *Naked People* to avoid this problem and to benefit from its superior printing.) In 1963, Dean appeared with newscaster and journalist Hugh Downs on *The Shape of Things* to discuss architecture, a subject of great interest to Dean as a designer: "Working rapidly at his drawing board while conversing with Downs," a TV critic observed, "Dean illustrates some of his own ideas on the subject, starting with the concept that 'the space we occupy has an important effect on our well-being, our personalities and tempers,' and concluding with his own guess on what the small house of tomorrow will look like." Dean also helped to create animated scene transitions based on his drawings for a 1963 Broadway revival of the George Bernard Shaw play *Too True to Be Good*. In the 1950s and '60s he would produce illustrations for other Broadway comedies, such as *Dinny and the Witches*, *Don't Live over a Pretzel Factory*, and *The Heavenly Twins*.

Above right: **United States Patent, 1968.**

As Dean did less commercial work, he spent more time with design, painting, and sculpture. His papers at Dartmouth include drawings and plans from the mid-'60s and early '70s for a number of tables (including a "chess table" and a "materials table") and other pieces of furniture, as well as photos of a mock-up of a small house. In 1967 he filed a patent for a multilevel folding table that he intended to manufacture and sell. Many images that appear throughout his books are echoed in his clay sculptures: a woman carrying a wishbone, a man with a large egg on his head, and a woman looking through an empty frame that she holds in front of her face.

Opposite top left: **Illustration for the poem "Ten,"** *The Facts of Wife (For Teenage Girls from 13 to 53)*, 1968.

In the introduction to this book of poems by Robert Warren, comedian and actor Milton Berle discussed Dean's popularity and drawings: "most of us who won't see thirty again have long been familiar with the uncanny ability of Abner Dean to penetrate our superficial condition and, with great humor, lay bare our human frailties and shortcomings." Berle then addressed the female reader directly, recommending to her an unusual interpretive strategy: "let the pictures suggest whatever meaning you can accept, and give yourself time to come to them."

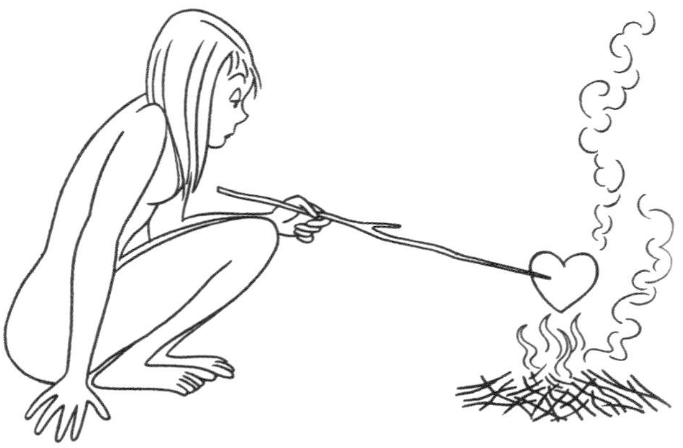

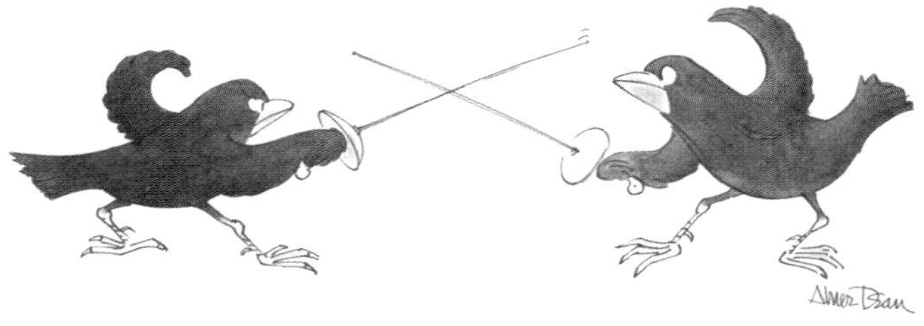

Bottom and above right: **Two drawings, *Animals, Animals, Animals*, 1979.**

The drawings in *Animals, Animals, Animals* are the only material from Dean's sketchbooks that, as far as I know, have ever appeared in print. In the mid-1960s, Dean had started a new aspect of his career that lasted until the late '70s: illustrations for medical journals. In fact, the last commercial work I have located is a drawing for the *American Journal of Nursing* from 1979. In 1981 he drew perhaps his last illustration, the logo for his 50th reunion at Dartmouth College, a place he always spoke of with great fondness. Abner Dean died at seventy-two on June 30, 1982, in New York City. The final piece in his last volume of new material is an illustrated poem, "Very Late Afternoon Thought." Dean drew an empty chair in front of a drawing table, upon which is pinned a cartoon of a question mark torn into four pieces:

> *What is there*
> *Will not be me—*
> *I will have left there*
> *Quietly*
> *On exit cue*
> *With cartoon done—*
> *And you can sit and watch the fun.*

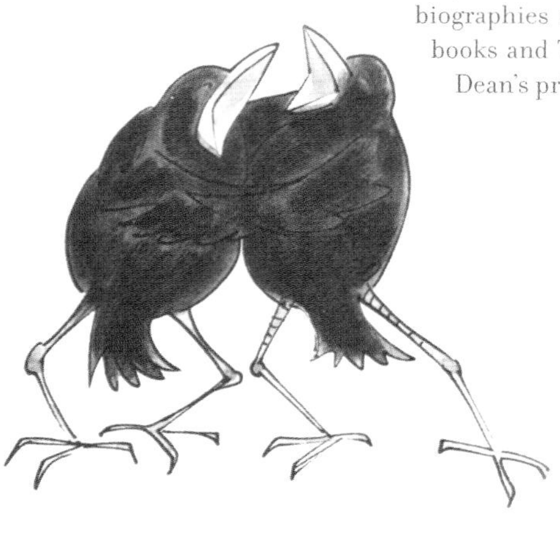

Author's note:

The excerpts from Dean's letters and notebooks are reprinted by kind permission of Dean's heirs and The Rauner Special Collections Library at Dartmouth College, where Dean's papers are housed. The examples of Dean's work are from my collection. I would like to thank Sarah Hartwell and the staff at The Rauner Library, the staff at the Dartmouth *Jack-O-Lantern*, Daniel Fulco at The New Britain Museum of American Art, Walter Reed at Illustration House, Marshall Price at the National Academy of Design, as well as Jude Epstein, Marc Clamage, and Kevin Huizenga. This essay has been assembled from numerous sources, including Dean's letters and notebooks, references to his work in books on cartooning and encyclopedias of cartoonists, materials in library and newspaper archives, biographies about those who knew Dean, contemporary reviews of his books and TV appearances, my correspondence with his relatives, and Dean's printed work.

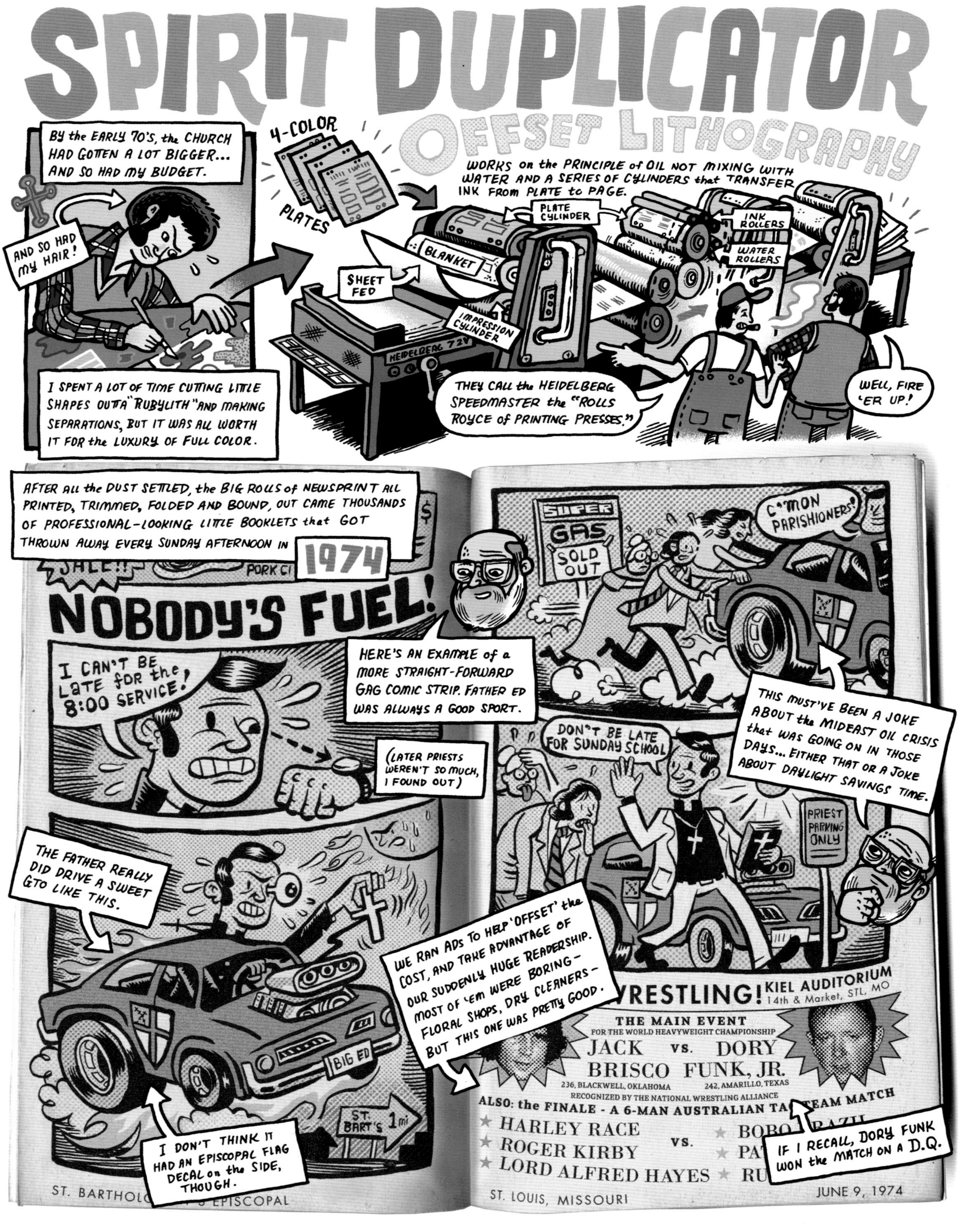

SPIRIT DUPLICATOR
OFFSET LITHOGRAPHY
BY the EARLY 70'S, the CHURCH HAD GOTTEN A LOT BIGGER... AND SO HAD MY BUDGET.
AND SO HAD MY HAIR!
I SPENT A LOT OF TIME CUTTING LITTLE SHAPES OUTTA "RUBYLITH" AND MAKING SEPARATIONS, BUT IT WAS ALL WORTH IT FOR the LUXURY OF FULL COLOR.
4-COLOR
PLATES
WORKS on the PRINCIPLE of OIL NOT MIXING WITH WATER AND A SERIES OF CYLINDERS that TRANSFER INK FROM PLATE to PAGE.
PLATE CYLINDER
INK ROLLERS
WATER ROLLERS
BLANKET
SHEET FED
IMPRESSION CYLINDER
HEIDELBERG 72V
THEY CALL the HEIDELBERG SPEEDMASTER the "ROLLS ROYCE of PRINTING PRESSES."
WELL, FIRE 'ER UP!
AFTER ALL the DUST SETTLED, the BIG ROLLS of NEWSPRINT ALL PRINTED, TRIMMED, FOLDED AND BOUND, OUT CAME THOUSANDS OF PROFESSIONAL-LOOKING LITTLE BOOKLETS that GOT THROWN AWAY EVERY SUNDAY AFTERNOON IN 1974
NOBODY'S FUEL!
I CAN'T BE LATE for the 8:00 SERVICE!
HERE'S AN EXAMPLE of a MORE STRAIGHT-FORWARD GAG COMIC STRIP. FATHER ED WAS ALWAYS A GOOD SPORT.
(LATER PRIESTS WEREN'T SO MUCH, I FOUND OUT)
THE FATHER REALLY DID DRIVE A SWEET GTO LIKE THIS.
BIG ED
ST. BART'S 1 mi
I DON'T THINK IT HAD AN EPISCOPAL FLAG DECAL on the SIDE, THOUGH.
SUPER GAS
SOLD OUT
C'MON PARISHIONERS!
THIS MUST'VE BEEN A JOKE ABOUT the MIDEAST OIL CRISIS that WAS GOING ON IN THOSE DAYS... EITHER THAT OR A JOKE ABOUT DAYLIGHT SAVINGS TIME.
DON'T BE LATE FOR SUNDAY SCHOOL
PRIEST PARKING ONLY
WE RAN ADS TO HELP 'OFFSET' the COST, AND TAKE ADVANTAGE OF OUR SUDDENLY HUGE READERSHIP. MOST OF 'EM WERE BORING - FLORAL SHOPS, DRY CLEANERS - BUT THIS ONE WAS PRETTY GOOD.
WRESTLING! KIEL AUDITORIUM 14th & Market, STL, MO
THE MAIN EVENT
FOR THE WORLD HEAVYWEIGHT CHAMPIONSHIP
JACK BRISCO vs. DORY FUNK, JR.
236, BLACKWELL, OKLAHOMA
242, AMARILLO, TEXAS
RECOGNIZED BY THE NATIONAL WRESTLING ALLIANCE
ALSO: the FINALE - A 6-MAN AUSTRALIAN TAG TEAM MATCH
HARLEY RACE
ROGER KIRBY
LORD ALFRED HAYES
VS.
IF I RECALL, DORY FUNK WON the MATCH ON A D.Q.
ST. LOUIS, MISSOURI
JUNE 9, 1974

Autographed portrait photo, undated. COURTESY OF TODD HIGNITE.

WHITE AND WILLIAMS

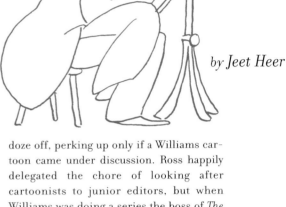

by Jeet Heer

*All artwork by Gluyas Williams
copyright the artist's estate.*

THEY WERE the last survivors of the old *New Yorker*. Throwbacks from the era of Calvin Coolidge, when they helped the freshly launched metropolitan weekly that was then finding its stylistic bearings, E.B. White and Gluyas Williams lived on until the Reagan presidency. White was the preeminent writer for the early *New Yorker*, Williams was arguably the magazine's most important cartoonist during its first three decades. Sharing a common sensibility and residing near each other in Maine, where the Whites had a farm and the Williamses a summer home, the writer and the cartoonist befriended each other in the 1930s and continued to correspond into their desolate old age, when they had both outlived their wives.

When E.B. White's wife Katherine, herself an editorial stalwart at *The New Yorker*, died in 1978, Williams penned a heartfelt note, particularly painful to read as one sees how the once fluid handwriting of the artist had grown craggy with arthritic shakiness. "The news of Katherine's going has left me very sad on my 89th birthday," Williams wrote. "She was my last and only tie with *The New Yorker*, and from the beginning did so much for me with advice and help in every way."

The importance of E.B. White, known as Andy to his friends, is beyond dispute. More than an acknowledged classic, he's a writer still beloved by countless readers, especially those who grew up reading his touching children's books *Stuart Little*, *Charlotte's Web*,

and *The Trumpet of the Swan*. In the history of *The New Yorker*, White's great achievement was to forge a crisp and direct style, which was clear without being simplistic, precise without being pedantic or fussy. This style became the governing tone of the magazine, often imitated by other writers although never with White's ease.

Harold Ross, founding editor of *The New Yorker*, held up White as the pinnacle that other writers should aim for. "It is not too much to say that Andy White was the most valuable person on the magazine," James Thurber argued in 1938. "His delicate tinkering with the works of *The New Yorker* caused it to move with a new ease and grace...His contributions to Talk of the Town, particularly his Notes and Comment on the first page, struck the shining note that Ross had dreamed of striking."

Williams was the cartooning counterpart to White. Just as White wrote clean prose, Williams drew a clean line. White purged his prose of clichés and journalistic heavy-handedness and Williams drew pictures startling in their linear directness. Even when drawing scenes with scores of characters, say a sidewalk teaming with shoppers or a crowded wedding pavilion, Williams was able to keep each figure distinct and individual while maintaining a perfect sense of design.

If White was Ross's favorite writer, then Williams was (along with Helen Hokinson and Peter Arno) the editor's most cherished artist. During art meetings Ross would often

doze off, perking up only if a Williams cartoon came under discussion. Ross happily delegated the chore of looking after cartoonists to junior editors, but when Williams was doing a series the boss of *The New Yorker* took a hands-on approach. This was especially true of the sixteen-page series chronicling a lavish upper-middle-class wedding that *The New Yorker* published in 1948.

Ross had the inspired idea of running the entire series all at once as a portfolio, on the model of the earlier issue given over entirely to John Hersey's Hiroshima. Ross wanted to keep this plan a secret from most of his staff and communicated with Williams surreptitiously, writing from home rather than the office and having the proofs shuttle back and forth away from the eyes of his secretaries. "Operation Shhh" was the name given to this cartoon caper. "From here on I will be completely underground and you won't hear from me unless there is a crisis of some kind, in which case I will probably endeavor to telephone you," Ross wrote on a blank sheet of paper (not daring to risk using *New Yorker* letterhead for this hush-hush affair). "If you get a call from Ulysses S. Grant talking in a low, husky voice, you will know who it is." All this skullduggery was justified, Ross felt, because Williams was one of the stars of the magazine and running a feature length portfolio of his cartoons in one issue was a surprise worth springing on the staff and readers alike.

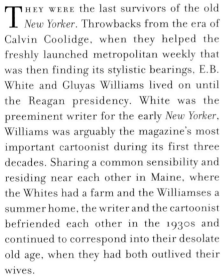

True to Life Sketches - - - - By Gluyas Williams
The Family Album—Mosquito Bites
READS AND SCRATCHES MOSQUITO BITE ON ANKLE
STOPS TO LOOK AT BITE
ANNOUNCES TO FAMILY HE'S GOT A MOSQUITO BITE RIGHT ON THE ANKLE
FAMILY PAYS NO ATTENTION TO HIS BITE. REPEATS IT'S RIGHT ON THE ANKLE, IT'S DRIVING HIM CRAZY
MILDRED REMARKS SHE'S GOT ONE ON HER EAR, THAT'S THE WORST PLACE YOU CAN HAVE A MOSQUITO BITE
ASKS FAMILY BUT PLEASE TO LOOK AT THIS ONE, IT'S THE WORST ONE HE'S EVER SEEN
FAMILY IS UNIMPRESSED, WILFRED REMARKING HE'S GOT ONE ON HIS SHOULDER BLADE WHERE HE CAN'T REACH IT
WIFE PUTS IN THAT IF HE'D STOP SCRATCHING HIS ANKLE IT WOULDN'T ITCH SO
SIGHS, AND GOES ON READING AND SCRATCHING
(Copyright, 1928, by The Bell Syndicate, Inc.)
8-9
GLUYAS WILLIAMS

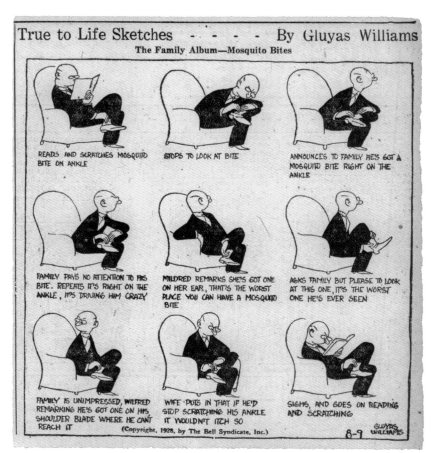

RIGHT: *True to Life Sketches, The Family Album—Mosquito Bites*, daily panel, August 9, 1928.

OPPOSITE: From "Mr. and Mrs. Melvin Davison Watts Request the Honour Of...." series of 16 drawings, *The New Yorker*, June 5, 1948.

It was Williams who convinced Ross that cartoons could be subtle. Avoiding the oppressive jokiness common to early-20th-century cartoons, Williams aimed for a sly, inward chuckle. Stylistically, this set Williams apart from the vaudevillian norm of magazine cartooning, the endless reliance on double-entendres, puns, and punch lines. Williams's low-key approach to cartooning won Ross over and influenced the overall tone of the magazine, making its cartoons distinct from the more blatant mirth-making found in competitors like *Life* and *Judge*.

Despite the high status he held in the era of Harold Ross, Williams enjoys nowhere near the posthumous prestige of White. While not quite forgotten, Williams has slowly faded over time. Early *New Yorker* cartoon anthologies always gave ample space to Williams. This is no longer the case. Roger Angell, the son of Katherine White and stepson of E.B. White, notes that the recently released volume titled *The Complete Cartoons of the New Yorker* has only two Williams drawings (to be sure, one of these drawings is used as the frontispiece). That's less than one percent of the 212 cartoons Williams drew for the magazine from 1926 to 1951. (All the Williams cartoons can be found on the compact disc that accompanies the book, but it's noteworthy that this magisterial collection relegates the paper-and-ink Williams to the margins.)

These days, when people think of the classic era of *The New Yorker*, the cartoonists that spring to mind are Charles Addams and Peter Arno. Part of the appeal of these artists is that it's easy to "get" them at a glace, although they of course repay close attention. Addams left a legacy of gothic comedy, an equal mixture of hearty good humor and creepiness; Arno created an equally distinct brand of naughty wit, a world populated by randy codgers chasing leggy chorus-girls.

The comedy of Gluyas Williams was more down to earth, lacking flights of morbid fantasy found in Addams or the wet-dream lushness of Arno. Williams was an observer, his wit grew out of a fidelity to life. In praising Williams's 1940 book *Fellow Citizens* in a private letter, E.B. White pointed to the cartoonist's ability to encapsulate everyday, shared experiences in a few deft strokes. "Probably a million American men have known the child in the seat ahead, but you were the guy that got it down on paper," White wrote.

What is remarkable about Williams's cartoons is the density of details found in them. While there is often a surface joke that is easy enough to understand, a full appreciation of his work requires spending time with each image. When he drew an elegant dinner party table or a teenage boy's messy bedroom, every little detail was expressive and significant. To really understand these cartoons we have to take the time needed to linger over them and enter into the world portrayed. Perhaps because readers are now conditioned to skim "gag" cartoons as quickly as possible, the audience for Williams has dwindled.

Despite changes in taste and reading habits, Williams is eminently worth reviving. Quieter and more subdued than his peers, he's also more gentle and humane. The befuddled little men that populate his cartoons, constantly beset by a malicious universe intent on placing them in socially awkward situations, belong in the same tradition as Eliot's Prufrock and Thurber's Walter Mitty. Williams at his best created cartoons that were alive with feeling. If we take the trouble to put as much effort into our reading of his cartoons as he did to the drawing of them, we'll discover why contemporaries like E.B. White and Harold Ross cherished Gluyas Williams.

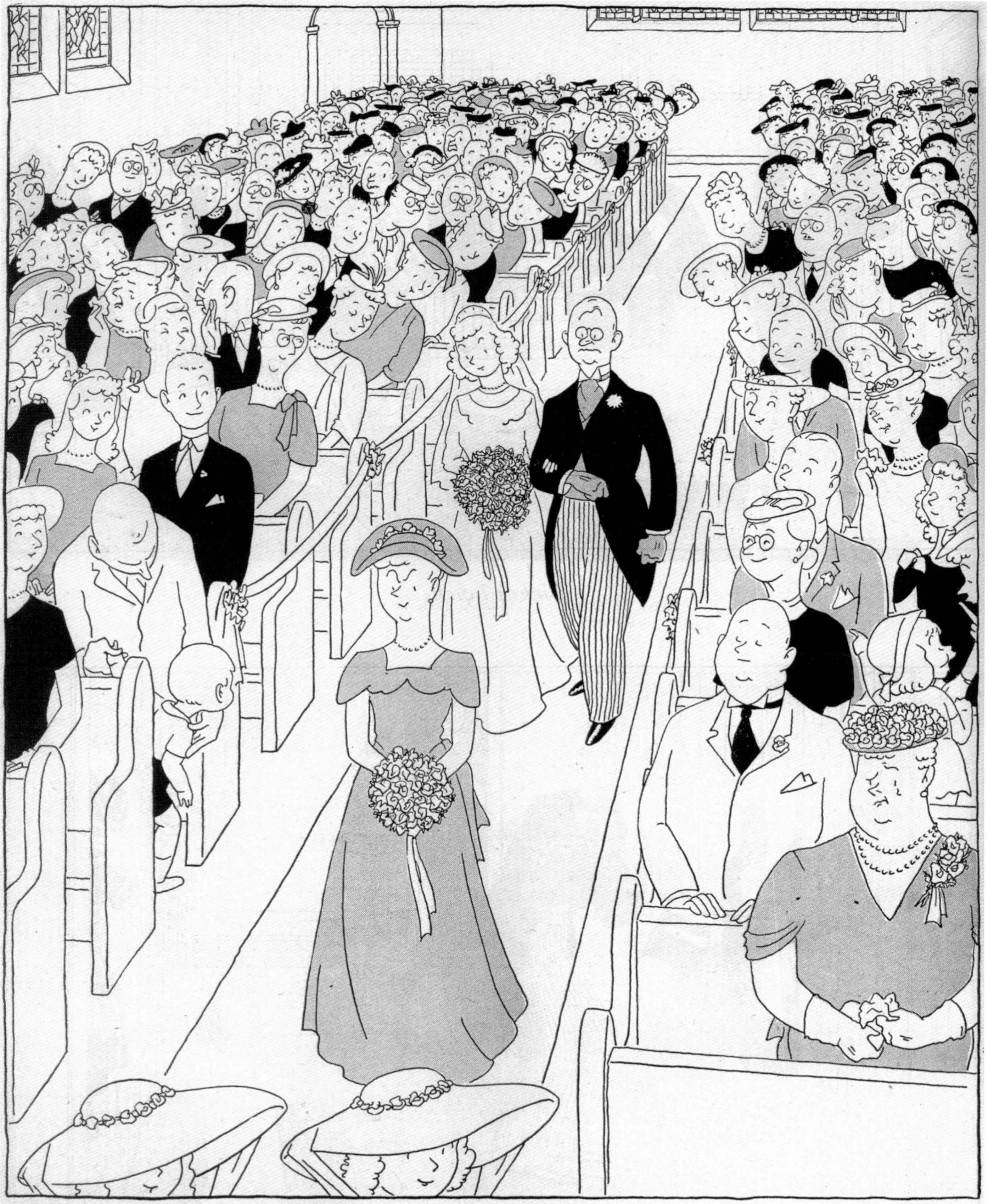

The wedding march.

THE YOUNGEST child in a large family, Gluyas Williams was born in San Francisco on July 23, 1888. His father, Robert Neil Williams, was a mining engineer who split his time between South America and the family's San Francisco residence (with occasional sojourns in Oregon and mining camps in the Sierras). The mother, Virginia Gluyas Williams, gave birth to eight kids in all, six of whom survived into adulthood, ranging from Mary Williams, born in 1869, to Gluyas, who was nearly two decades younger than his oldest sister. Perhaps because he was the baby of the family, Gluyas was particularly close to his mother (appropriately, his peculiar first name was his mother's Cornish maiden name). The family was well-to-do, and became more so due to a stroke of good luck. In 1892, Virginia won $40,000 in the Louisiana sweepstakes. She used the money to give her children a European education. Until he was a teenager, Gluyas lived mostly in Switzerland, Spain, and Germany.

As a family, the Williamses divided their energies between business and art. They were also unusually cosmopolitan. Mary Williams was a pioneering newspaper cartoonist and cultural journalist who won fame under the pen name Kate Carew. She spent her crucial working decades splitting time between England and America. Robert Williams, the eldest boy, was a businessman who lived in Java, representing Western companies doing commerce in Asia. Reed Williams, the middle brother, was a painter. The two younger girls, Weenonah and Ann, both married European men and spent the majority of their lives in Scandinavian countries.

Of all his siblings, Kate Carew had the greatest impact on young Gluyas. When he was still a teenager, she was making her first big splash. Although her star has faded over time, Kate Carew was a name to contend with at the turn of the century. Billboards and large newspaper ads hailed her as the first woman caricaturist. She had a knack for securing interviews with the top newsmakers of the day, ranging from Winston Churchill to the Wright Brothers to Pablo Picasso to Albert Einstein. She was the first woman to interview Mark Twain, who usually chased away journalists of whatever gender with a growl.

GLUYAS WILLIAMS
FELLOW
CITIZENS
COURTESY OF WARREN BERNARD.

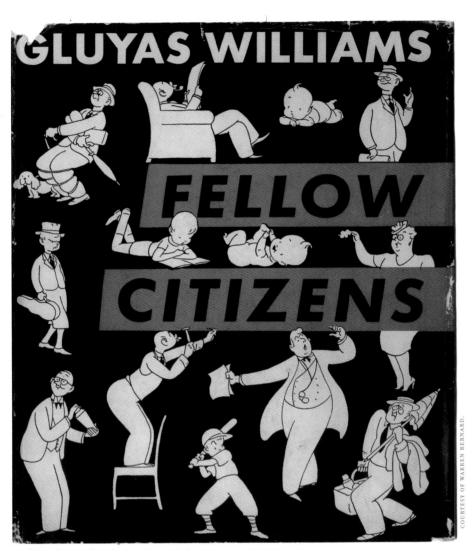

Fellow Citizens (Doubleday, Doran & Company, 1940). Williams's second collection.

Williams would recall that "a good deal of my inclination to draw came from watching my sister Kate Carew at work." Yet if Carew was an artistic inspiration, she was very different in temperament from her little brother. Thrice-married, living for a while as a single mother, shuttling back and forth from New York to London (with side trips in Hollywood), and at ease in theatrical and movie-making circles, Carew was a bohemian artist to the core. She was as unconventional as any woman of her time. Williams by contrast was always more of a homebody, kept warm by hearth and family.

Williams started classes at Harvard in 1908. Although his first year of studies was disrupted by the death of his father, he quickly graduated with the class of 1911. His initial goal at school was to be a lawyer, but he never seems to have pursued this ambition with any seriousness. The fact was, he already had an itching to be an artist and at Harvard, where he drew for the *Lampoon*, he quickly found an outlet for his talent.

Harvard left its mark on Williams. It was there that he met Robert Benchley, a future collaborator with a shared comedic sensibility. In fact, many of the writers whose books Williams would illustrate were fellow Harvard men, including Edward Streeter, Laurence McKinney, and David McCord. It is perhaps not an accident that Williams would go on to marry Margaret Kempton, sister of a Harvard graduate turned Harvard English instructor, Kenneth Kempton. Gluyas and Margaret would remain firm New Englanders, living in the Boston suburb of West Newton and summering in Maine. This allowed Williams to stay close to Harvard and go to their football games (which often disappointed him). In 1936, at the 25th reunion of the Harvard Class of 1911, Williams was named the most successful graduate of his year.

Williams's time at Harvard overlapped with another famous alumnus, T.S. Eliot. The two men were not close while students, having only a nodding acquaintance. But after graduation, they both ended up in Paris. As often happens with expatriates who run into familiar faces in a new environment, Williams and Eliot bonded in France and spent time reminiscing about home.

As a literate and literary cartoonist, Williams is most often associated with Benchley, but he had certain affinities with Eliot, particularly in the poet's early phase of poems like "The Love Song of J. Alfred Prufrock." It's easy to imagine one of Williams's patented middle-aged men, his balding head increasingly resembling an egg and ill at ease at a social function, muttering Prufrock's monologue:

And indeed there will be time
To wonder, "Do I dare?" and, "Do I dare?"
Time to turn back and descend the stairs,
With the bald spot in the middle of my hair—

Paris was perhaps as important to Williams as Harvard. He was now firm in his intention to become an artist, and borrowed money so he could learn the fundamentals of his craft. After six months, he returned to the United States but his brief French sojourn was the basis of his art career.

Back home, he freelanced as a cartoonist, selling a few cartoons to magazines like *Life* and *Collier's*. (This was the earlier incarnation of *Life*, a humor magazine with many cartoons rather than a home for photojournalism). He also briefly had a comic strip in the *Boston Journal*. He regarded this early effort as "terrible" and didn't like to talk about it in later life. Williams put a hold on his freelance career after he married Margaret in 1915. The couple had two kids: Margaret (known as Peggy) in 1917 and David in 1918. During these years, Williams was also looking after his mother. With family responsibilities weighing on his nervous shoulders, he took an editorial job at a magazine called *The Youth's Companion* in 1915. For the next few years, he confined his cartooning to his after hours, but steadily worked at improving his craft.

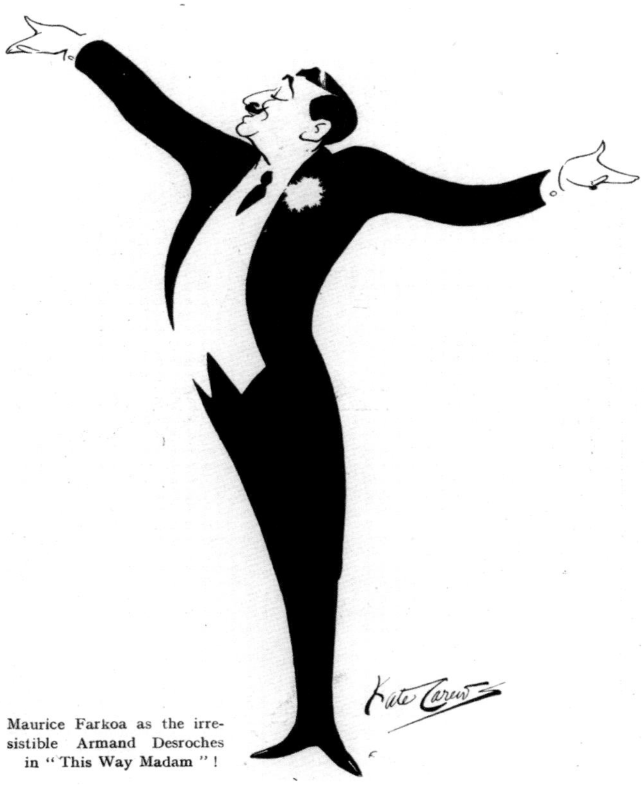
Kate Carew
Maurice Farkoa as the irresistible Armand Desroches in "This Way Madam"!

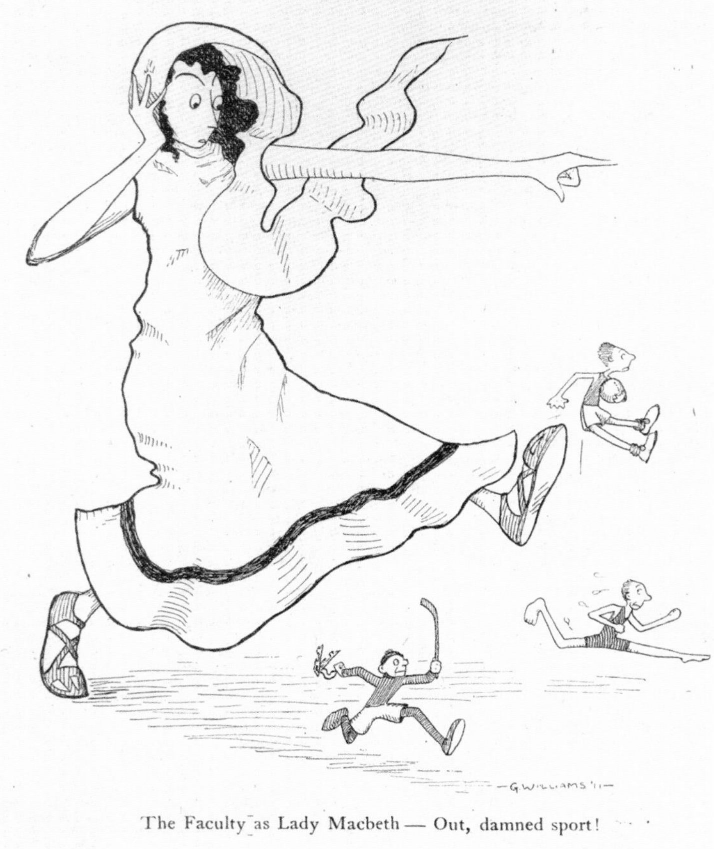
G. WILLIAMS '11
The Faculty as Lady Macbeth — Out, damned sport!

TOP: Kate Carew, caricature of Maurice Farkoa from *The Patrician*, c. 1913.

BOTTOM: From *The Harvard Lampoon*, vol. LV, #7, May 8, 1908.

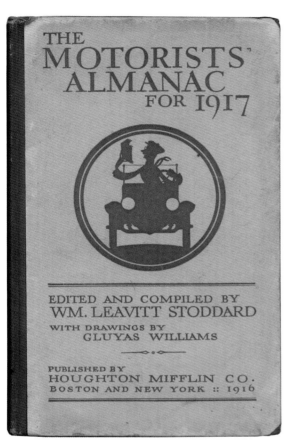

THE
MOTORISTS'
ALMANAC
FOR 1917
EDITED AND COMPILED BY
WM. LEAVITT STODDARD
WITH DRAWINGS BY
GLUYAS WILLIAMS
PUBLISHED BY
HOUGHTON MIFFLIN CO.
BOSTON AND NEW YORK :: 1916

The Motorists' Almanac for 1917 (Houghton Mifflin Company, 1916).
COURTESY OF CHRIS WARE.

In August of 1918, Charles Dana Gibson, the legendary illustrator who had just bought *Life* magazine, sent off a note to Williams. Gibson had liked a series of drawings Williams had done for *Collier's* and wanted to meet the young cartoonist. As Williams would recall, "the subsequent interview enabled me to give up my editorial job and begin freelance."

These early cartoons for *Life* occasionally had a mildly political tinge, but not in any deeply partisan sense. A recurring character was Senator Sounder, a distinguished windbag who bores everyone around him with campaign oratory. While not as polished as Williams's best work in the 1930s and 1940s, these early cartoons did display in rudimentary form his characteristic style. The sweep of his line can be traced back to Kate Carew and, more distantly, Aubrey Beardsley. The sureness with which Williams could portray the movement of a body in sequential drawings owes something to Caran d'Ache. But aside from these models, Williams had his own peculiar way of drawing people. Many of his figures look like squeezed balloons, with puffed-up chests and inflated rear ends.

Always a Nervous Nelly, filled with trepidations about the numerous ways life can go awry, Williams didn't take the decision to freelance easily. But it quickly proved to be the right move. He became a fixture not only at *Life* but also *Vanity Fair*. By 1920, both magazines carried advertisements listing Williams as a prominent contributor, with his name highlighted along with Norman Rockwell, G.K. Chesterton, and Walter Lippmann. By 1922, he was doing a daily strip for the *Boston Globe*, a series of panels with rotating titles (such as *Suburban Heights*, *The World at Its Worst*, and *Hello! Hello!*). Like similar series by Clare Briggs, this panel focused on the foibles and peeves of daily life. Two years later this series was picked up by the Bell Syndicate, giving Williams a national newspaper audience. The daily strip would run for a quarter of a century until Williams retired it.

Not long after *The New Yorker* started up in 1925, Ross approached Williams to contribute. The cartoonist was reluctant at first, since he regarded *Life* as his natural magazine home. But Williams was won over by the fact that *The New Yorker* was a genuinely cooperative enterprise. While the magazine's editors would often suggest changes or ideas, they also listened to their cartoonists and often deferred to his wishes. He was particularly impressed by the fact that Ross accepted the idea that humor based on understatement was preferable to slapstick. "I thought to myself that this was an editor I'd like to work for," Williams remembered in a late-life interview.

A sign of the respect *The New Yorker* accorded cartoonists could be seen in how they dealt with copycat advertisers. In 1932, an advertiser sent in a series of ads done by an artist imitating Williams's style. Ross refused to run the ads, prompting Williams to send in a note of gratitude. "Killing that advertisement was the sort of thing that makes it so pleasant to work for *The New Yorker*," Williams wrote to Katharine White. "I don't believe any other periodical in the country would have done it, and I am mighty grateful to you."

This happy relationship was troubled by a ruffle in 1934 when *Fortune* magazine ran an article about *The New Yorker* that claimed, falsely, that Williams received all his ideas from the magazine's editors. Williams wrote an angry note to Katharine White saying that he would no longer accept any editorial suggestions.

Ross wrote a long letter to placate Williams, condemning "that damned, as I call it, *Fortune* piece." In his letter Ross offered an impassioned defense of his magazine's editorial practice. "I don't know whether *Fortune* said so or not, but the one thing that has made *The New Yorker* successful is that it is a collaborative effort, switching ideas back and forth to find the man best adapted to doing them, and I hope to high heaven that you aren't going to be discouraged into not being willing to work collaboratively," the editor pleaded. "I'm a steadfast believer in collaboration and *The New Yorker* is a monument, or something to it." Ross's arguments proved convincing and Williams resumed his close working relationship with *The New Yorker*.

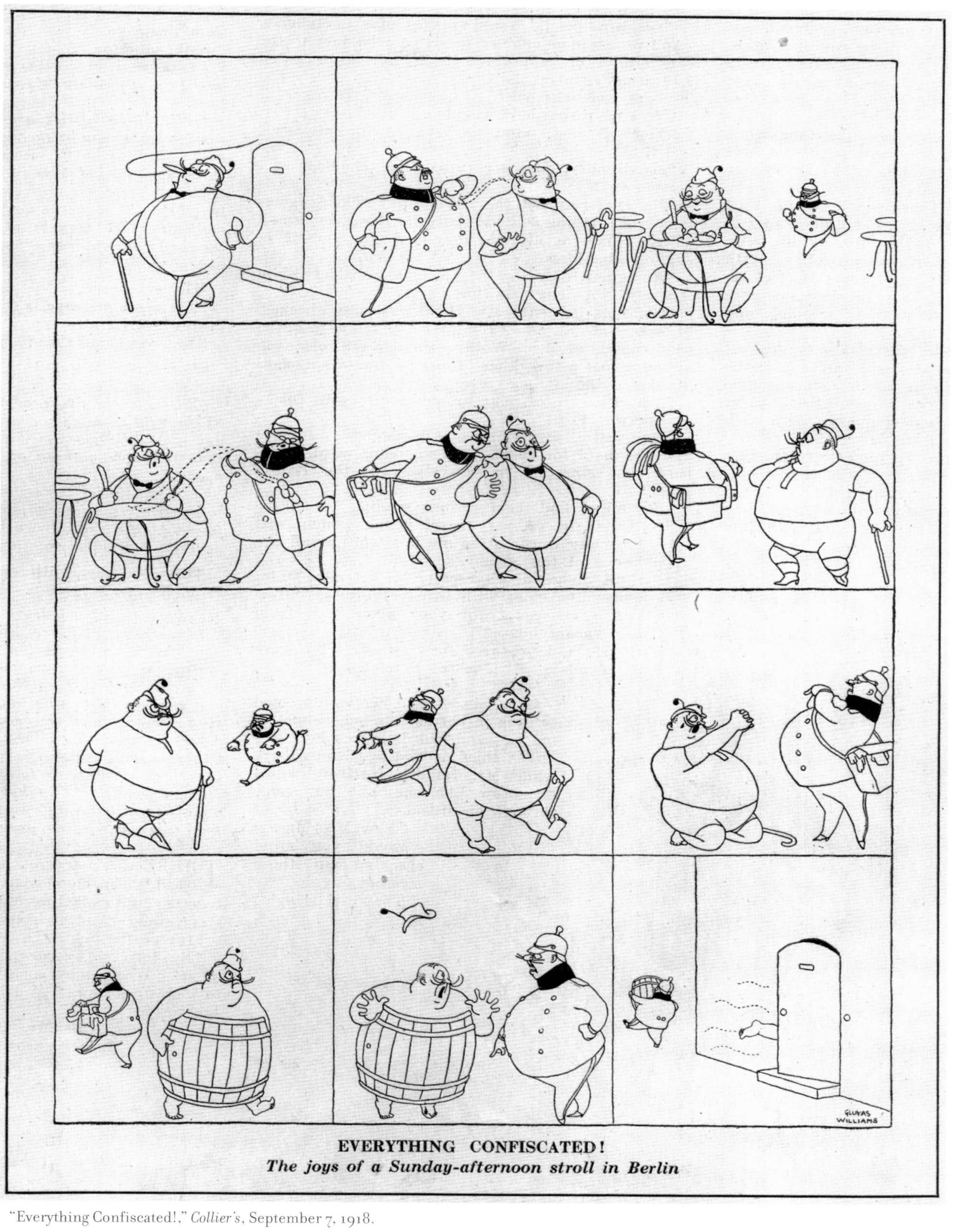
GLUYAS
WILLIAMS

EVERYTHING CONFISCATED!
The joys of a Sunday-afternoon stroll in Berlin

"Everything Confiscated!," *Collier's*, September 7, 1918.

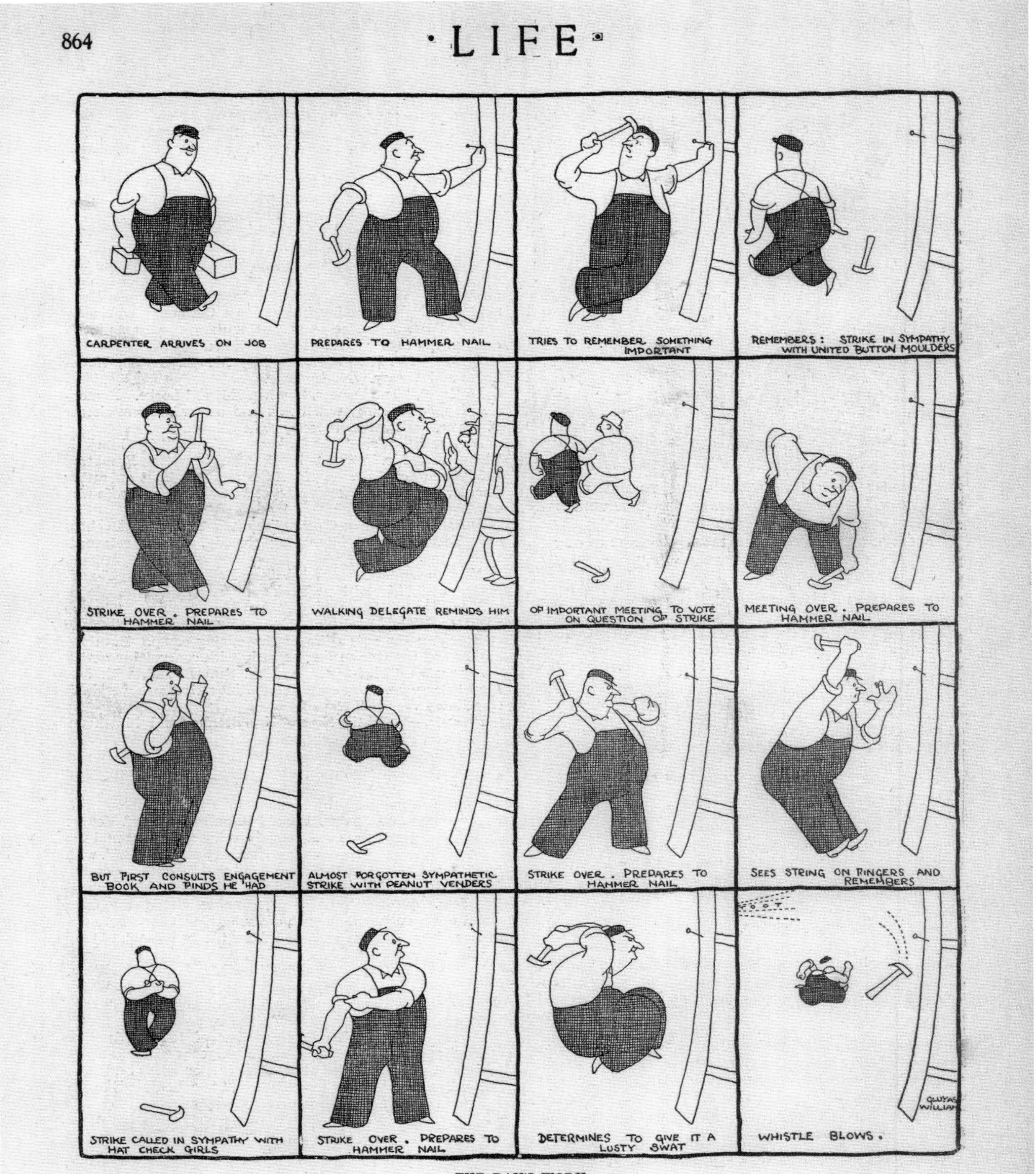
864
·LIFE·
CARPENTER ARRIVES ON JOB
PREPARES TO HAMMER NAIL
TRIES TO REMEMBER SOMETHING IMPORTANT
REMEMBERS: STRIKE IN SYMPATHY WITH UNITED BUTTON MOULDERS
STRIKE OVER. PREPARES TO HAMMER NAIL
WALKING DELEGATE REMINDS HIM
OF IMPORTANT MEETING TO VOTE ON QUESTION OF STRIKE
MEETING OVER. PREPARES TO HAMMER NAIL
BUT FIRST CONSULTS ENGAGEMENT BOOK AND FINDS HE HAD
ALMOST FORGOTTEN SYMPATHETIC STRIKE WITH PEANUT VENDERS
STRIKE OVER. PREPARES TO HAMMER NAIL
SEES STRING ON FINGERS AND REMEMBERS
STRIKE CALLED IN SYMPATHY WITH HAT CHECK GIRLS
STRIKE OVER. PREPARES TO HAMMER NAIL
DETERMINES TO GIVE IT A LUSTY SWAT
TOOT
WHISTLE BLOWS.
GLUYAS WILLIAMS
THE DAY'S WORK

"The Day's Work," *Life*, November 20, 1919.

SHORTLY AFTER the brouhaha over the *Fortune* article, Gluyas and Margaret Williams started becoming closer friends with Andy and Katharine White. Maine drew the two couples together. The Williamses bought a summer home in Deer Isle in 1929. In 1933, the Whites bought a house in nearby Brooklin. At first the Whites shuttled back and forth between Maine and New York but they made a more permanent move in 1938. The impetus for the move was Andy White's love of the countryside, and his desire to be a farmer-writer. In 1938, he started a monthly column in *Harper's* entitled "One Man's Meat," an impressionistic exploration of country life during a period of international crisis. These columns, collected in a book with the same title, established White as the 20th-century heir to Thoreau.

E.B. White's strong feeling for nature is palpable in the letters he wrote to Williams. "One thing I like about the country is the way everything moves indoors with you, come fall," White wrote in 1938. "Spiders, flies, hornets, dogs, crickets, bantams, lice, mice, everything. I don't see how we can be lonely with this company."

This letter provoked a strong response from Williams, who wrote, "I'd just as soon you didn't write such revoltingly cheerful letters about life in the country, because Boston is pretty hard to bear as it is. I feel about like my oculist who has just bought his cemetery lot and is planning to take a camp stool and a picnic lunch out to it, because it makes him happy to think how soon he will be resting peacefully and permanently in it."

The two families both loved the water. The Whites had a little cutter called *Astrid*, the Williamses a boat called *Tonga*. Roger Angell recalls that boating was a small-scale, family affair, far removed from the tony world of wealthy yachtsmen.

"Williams looked exactly like his drawings," Angell says. "He was very black and white, tall and clean-lined. He was nervous, always cautious rather than hopeful. His cartoons were taken almost exactly from life." When Angell looks at cartoons of the father reading in bed or a family vacationing in Maine, he can call up the original scenes that inspired them. "There was something vulnerable about Williams that made people want to protect him."

Another shared recreation was ping-pong. Williams would often play against Andy and Katharine's son, Joel. Williams would also bike through the Maine hills with his wife, although he was embarrassed by the fact that she could go uphill much more easily than he could.

The Williamses were also nature lovers. In the summer they could prowl though the woods of Deer Isle and pick berries. The pastoral life enjoyed by the Whites strongly tempted Williams: it is not too strong to say that the Whites were living the life the Williamses wanted. In several letters Williams mentions how much he envies the Whites.

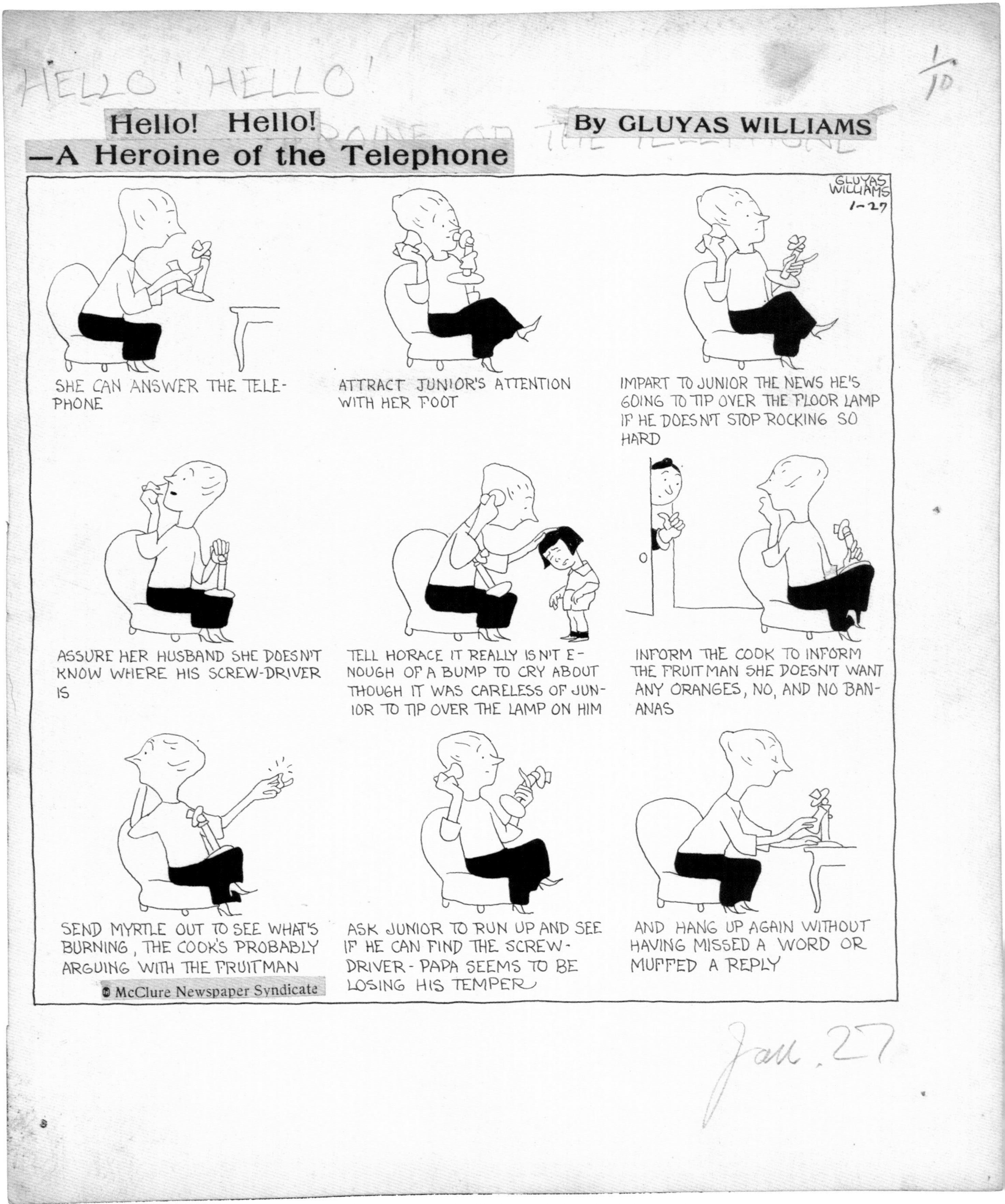
HELLO! HELLO!
1/10
Hello! Hello!
—A Heroine of the Telephone
By GLUYAS WILLIAMS
GLUYAS WILLIAMS 1-27
SHE CAN ANSWER THE TELEPHONE
ATTRACT JUNIOR'S ATTENTION WITH HER FOOT
IMPART TO JUNIOR THE NEWS HE'S GOING TO TIP OVER THE FLOOR LAMP IF HE DOESN'T STOP ROCKING SO HARD
ASSURE HER HUSBAND SHE DOESN'T KNOW WHERE HIS SCREW-DRIVER IS
TELL HORACE IT REALLY ISN'T ENOUGH OF A BUMP TO CRY ABOUT THOUGH IT WAS CARELESS OF JUNIOR TO TIP OVER THE LAMP ON HIM
INFORM THE COOK TO INFORM THE FRUITMAN SHE DOESN'T WANT ANY ORANGES, NO, AND NO BANANAS
SEND MYRTLE OUT TO SEE WHAT'S BURNING, THE COOK'S PROBABLY ARGUING WITH THE FRUITMAN
ASK JUNIOR TO RUN UP AND SEE IF HE CAN FIND THE SCREW-DRIVER - PAPA SEEMS TO BE LOSING HIS TEMPER
AND HANG UP AGAIN WITHOUT HAVING MISSED A WORD OR MUFFED A REPLY
McClure Newspaper Syndicate
Jan. 27

Original art for *Hello! Hello!—A Heroine of the Telephone*, daily panel, January 27, 1925. COURTESY OF CHRIS WARE.

Returning to Boston after a summer in Maine was always painful for Williams. "This is probably the lowest moment of my life to be writing to you two settling down for a winter in Maine while I'm getting ready for another 9 months in Boston," Williams wrote in 1938. "We came down yesterday and I'm ready to call the whole thing off right now. Everything I touch is grimy, everyone I speak to snaps at me, I have spent a full two hours at the telephone arranging dentists' & oculists' appointments for David & Peggy and calling back home to check and being called back because they can't go at that time and the streets are full of blowing newspaper and young men in knitted sport-shirts and suspenders and David on the eve of going to college feels that he'd rather study music and be a band leader. And I bet it's a golden day at Allen's Cove."

In 1939, the Williamses seriously considered buying a farm in Friendship, Maine. In a letter to Andy White, Williams referred to the farm they found as "the place of our dreams...12 acres on the harbor, good remodelled water house, tar road, swell pier, everything just as we had always wanted it. The only outs were the price which was stiff and the cellar which was bad and which would have entailed considerable remodelling of the house in order to get heat in."

After sleepless nights thinking about buying this farm, the Williamses decided not to do so. There were several factors at work. Williams had to think about his daily comic strip, his major source of income. In order to keep in touch with the suburban realities described in the strip, he felt he had to keep living in the suburbs. Williams was also worried about his sisters living in Sweden and Finland, dangerous places to be at the start of the Second World War. He wanted to have some financial reserves on hand in case his sisters and their families needed to come to the United States as refugees.

The decision not to buy the farm was one of the biggest heartbreaks of Williams's life. Perhaps fittingly, his son, who learned a love of nature from his summers in Deer Isle, fulfilled his father's unrealized dream by buying a farm after the Second World War.

Edward Streeter, who collaborated with Williams on two books, observed that the cartoonist wrote "fine, chatty, gloom-drenched epistles stuffed haphazardly with wit and wisdom." This is certainly true of the letters Williams wrote to Andy White—perhaps fittingly so. As the essayist Joseph Epstein once noted, "one has to search very sedulously indeed to find a gloomier writer than E.B. White." (The correspondence with Katharine is slightly more guarded.) The "gloom-drenched" quality that Streeter noticed is tempered by a sharp wit, which puts every dire situation into comic perspective.

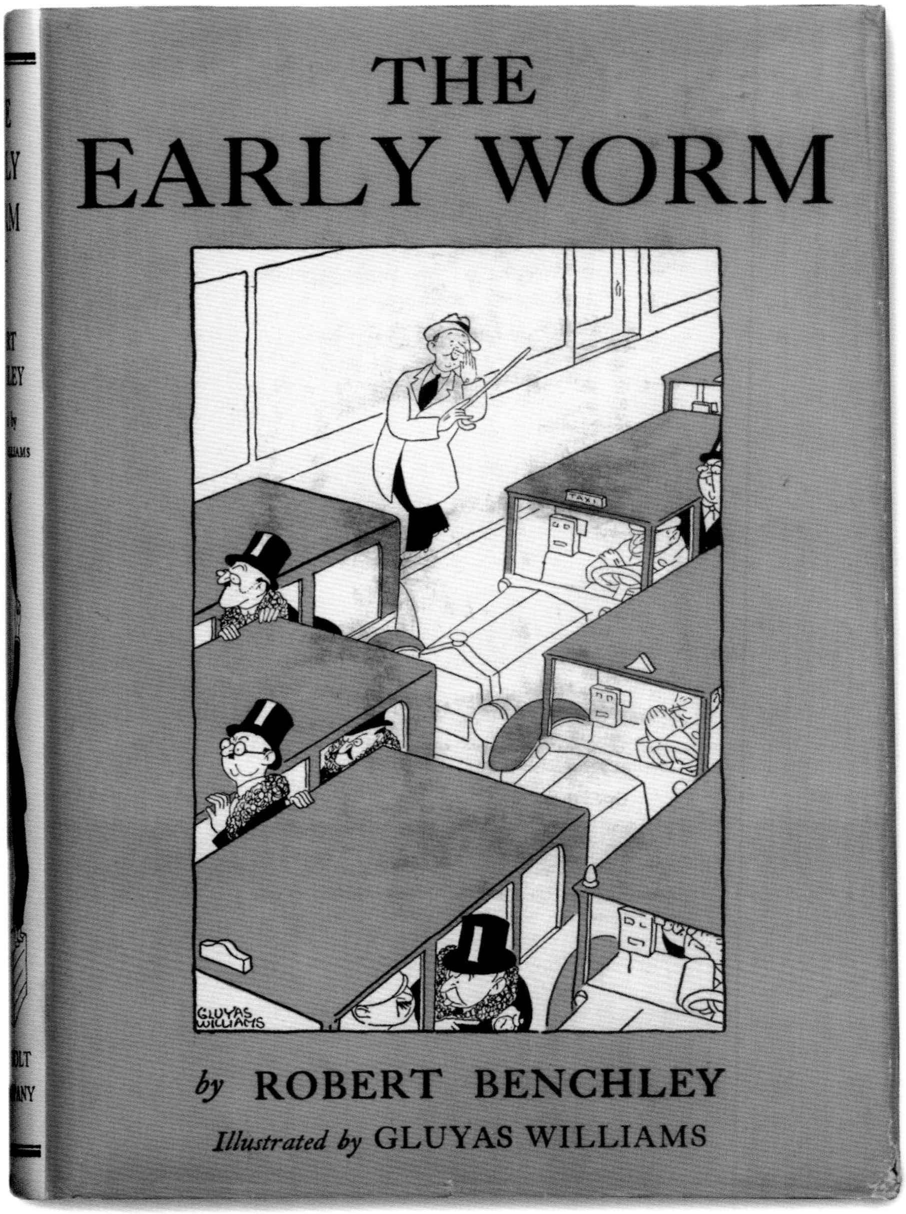
THE EARLY WORM
TAXI
GLUYAS WILLIAMS
by ROBERT BENCHLEY
Illustrated by GLUYAS WILLIAMS

RIGHT: Robert Benchley, *The Early Worm* (Henry Holt and Company, 1927). Illustrations by Williams.
COURTESY OF TODD HIGNITE.

OPPOSITE: "The Housewrecker Discovers He Has the Wrong Number," *The New Yorker*, June 19, 1926.

Williams's second cartoon for the publication. He had this to say on establishing his long relationship with *The New Yorker*: "[Editor] Harold Ross would write, but I'd say that I was based in Boston and I didn't know enough about New York to be of any use. And then finally he sent me a cartoon idea, about the house wrecker who has the wrong address. I did it, and sent it over, and Ross sent it back and said that it won't do; he said to get more fun into it—have a woman taking a bath while they're taking the bathtub out, and like that. He said to change it and put those things in it, and he'd buy it. I sent it back just as it was and said, No, I wouldn't touch it, because my idea of humor was understatement rather than slapstick, and Ross wrote—oh, how I wish I'd kept that letter!—it was a wonderful letter back saying, 'You're perfectly right, I'm going to change all my ideas on drawings. Of course that's much subtler your way and better.' And after that letter I thought to myself that this was an editor I'd like to work for."

—From a 1975 interview by Rick Marschall, *Nemo* #3 (Fantagraphics Books, 1983).

In a sense, Williams's letters are cartooning in prose. Here is a description of a family outing: "Our summer ended in a blaze of glory with a plugged radiator that boiled every few miles and that supplied work for the garages from Portsmouth to Topsfield. We finally got home about half past ten last night—nobody speaking to each other." It's easy to imagine this scene showing up in a daily strip or as a *New Yorker* panel.

During the War, Andy White asked Williams for advice on what school to send Joel to. In reply, he received a little lesson about home-schooling. "A man who spent some summers here disliked all schools to the extent that he wouldn't let any of his children go to them," Williams wrote. "He and his wife taught them at home; and at the ages that I knew the youngsters, thirteen to eighteen, they were without doubt the dumbest most insufferable pains in the neck I ever encountered."

Williams could be offhandedly dismissive of his own work. He referred to his strip as "my kind of daily claptrap." Yet his editors and collaborators remember him as being deeply committed to his art, holding himself to high standards. Certainly he had enough artistic pride to be hurt by criticism.

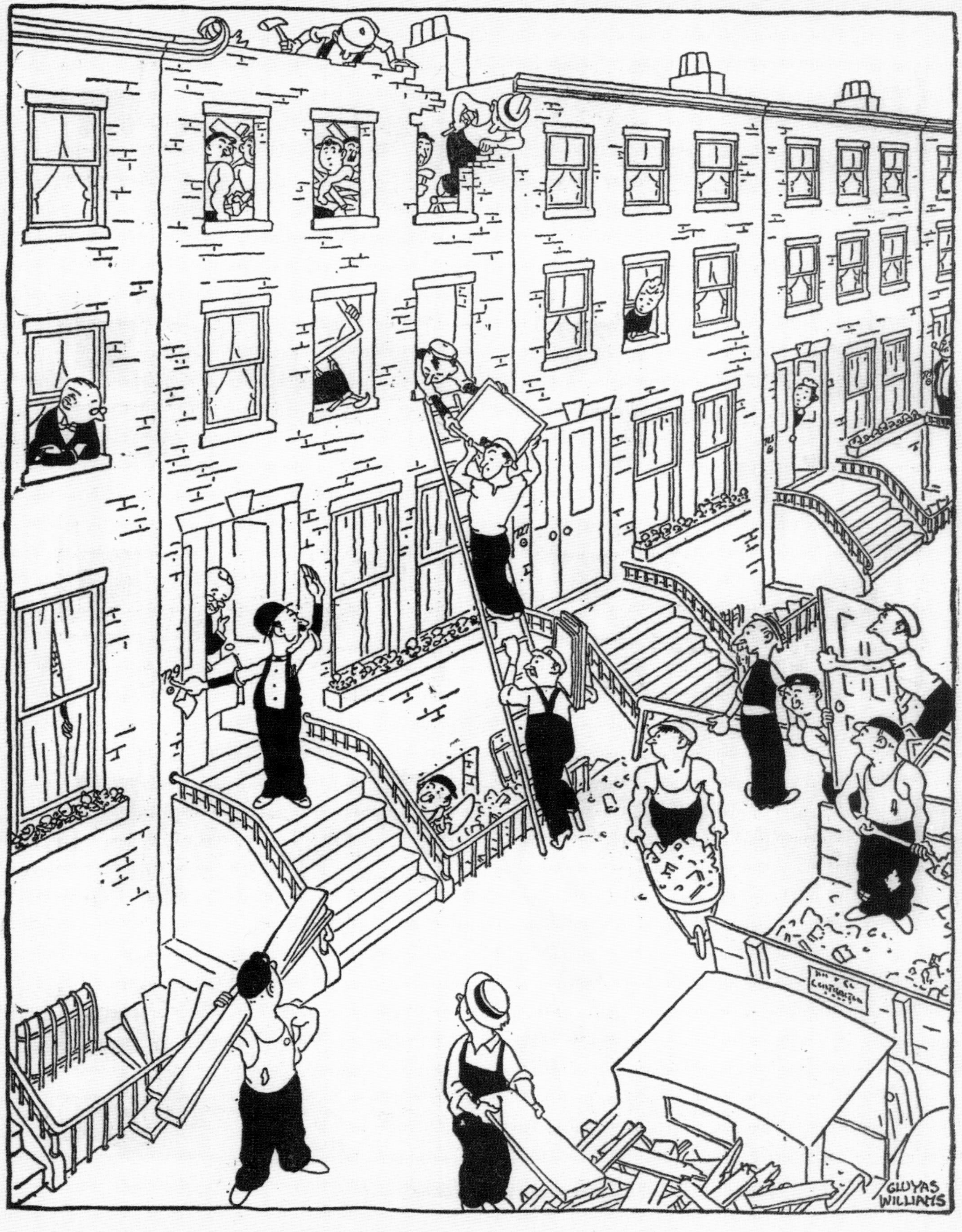
GLUYAS
WILLIAMS

The housewrecker discovers he has the wrong number

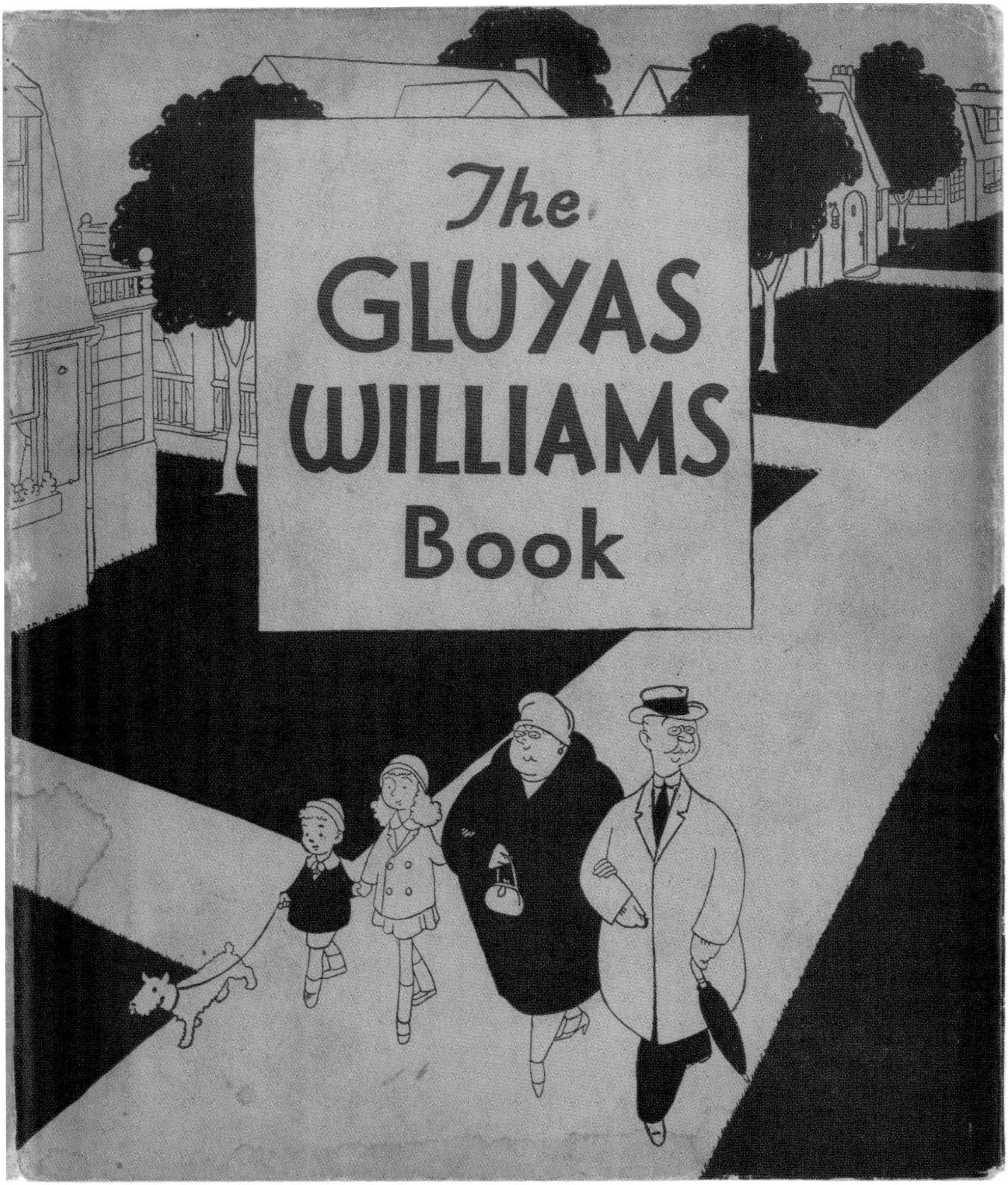
The
GLUYAS
WILLIAMS
Book

The Gluyas Williams Book (Doubleday, Doran & Company, 1929). Williams's first collection.
COURTESY OF WARREN BERNARD.

In 1943, Thomas Craven published *Cartoon Cavalcade*, a breezy, middle-brow guide to comics. In this book, he was dismissive of Williams. "Gluyas Williams, a veteran of *The New Yorker*, was influenced in technique in the wordless continuity by [H.M.] Bateman, of London," Craven wrote.

Williams is a droll fellow with a sturdy command of line, but I find his silent strips of a child getting ready for bed, or an old codger's pompous excursion to the vault of a bank only to find the safe-deposit box empty, long drawn out and monotonous. He is most amusing in the static humor of his Industrial Crises—the Day a Cake of Soap Sank at Procter & Gamble's, let us say—and in his pictures of Coolidge at the White House. With his dry, pawky style, Williams was perfectly equipped to work on Coolidge, and his drawing of the President's refusal to leave the Executive Mansion until his galoshes were mated will keep green the memory of a man who, otherwise, should be forgotten. I have only one serious grievance against Williams; the faces of his men tend to fall into one cast, and that cast reminds me of Calvin Coolidge—which is enough to take the joy out of life.

These observations, glib and superficial as they were, stung Williams. "I think my eyes are going bad which doesn't worry me much because I feel like an old has-been," Williams wrote to E.B. White in 1944. "After reading Thomas Craven's remarks in *Cartoon Cavalcade* I feel more like a never-was."

As a result of dimming eyesight, Gluyas Williams gave up cartooning in the early 1950s. There is no hint in his letters that he missed drawing. He and Margaret were ready to settle into a happy retirement. By this point, Dave and Peggy were both married and had kids of their own. Living in West Newton, the Williamses didn't own a TV set until very late in life. In Victorian fashion they would read books to each other, including the books of their friend E.B. White. Whenever a new White volume came out, Williams would quickly send off a congratulatory note.

By the late 1960s, the correspondence between Williams and the Whites took a darker turn. There were ailments all around: Andy's heart trouble and arthritis, Katharine's skin disease, a car accident that badly rattled Katharine, Gluyas's suffering from dimming eyesight as well as arthritis. In general, both the Williamses and the Whites bore their ailments with stoic fortitude. But the letters make clear that both couples felt life was hemming them in, foreclosing old freedoms and habits. The correspondence between the Williamses and the Whites became a round of mutual commiseration and medical news. After a car accident in the early 1970s, the Williamses gave up going to Deer Isle and eventually moved into a nursing home.

One by one their friends were dying off. Harold Ross, Carl Rose, Rea Irvin: each passing is marked with a note of condolence.

When Margaret died in 1976, Williams wrote a note to Katharine and Andy White that looked back to happier days. Tellingly, he focused on the years at Deer Isle.

You and Katharine have been wonderful in bringing so much comfort with your letter," Williams wrote. "You stressed Margaret's loving qualities. And so did the letters from the Islanders, for she did love every one of them. To read those letters was like living our 50 years on Deer Isle all over again for each one mentioned some little word or act by which Margaret had shown her love for them.

This essay draws on material found in the Gluyas Williams papers, Special Collections Research Center, Syracuse University Library; the E.B. White papers, The Division of Rare and Manuscript Collections, Cornell University; and the Katharine White papers at the Bryn Mawr College Library. Special thanks to the family of Gluyas Williams, to Christine Chambers, and to Roger Angell. ᏩᎾ

FOLLOWING TWO PAGES: Two-page letter from Harold Ross to Williams regarding the infamous *Fortune* magazine article. August 7, 1934.

THE
NEW YORKER
NO. 25 WEST 45TH STREET

EDITORIAL OFFICES
BRYANT 9-8200

August 7th, 1934

Dear Williams:

I have a note from Mrs. White today telling of your visiting her and expressing a determination not to accept ideas from others hereafter which distresses and alarms me. That damned, as I call it, Fortune piece has kicked up all sorts of unhappiness in subtle ways. It's got all the payroll figures wrong, or practically all, it says Steig's drawings are printed over Irvin's protest, that you don't have your own ideas, etc. I haven't read the thing, being afraid to, but I am hearing about it endlessly.

Now, to argue the ethics and advisability of an artist doing drawings which are not his idea I would cite the case of the Waring's Pennsylvanians idea. It was mine. I thought of it out of the clear air. I can't draw it. I'm employed by The New Yorker (although not at the $40,000 figure) largely as an idea man. That's what I regard myself as, at any rate and what I think my chief value to the magazine is. That's White's value partially, Mrs. White's and Thurber's. This magazine is run on ideas, God knows, and we naturally hire the people that have them and hire them for that purpose.

My God, a very large percentage of the contents of The New Yorker, drawings and text, are based on the ideas originating with the staff and suggested to writers. Now please reconsider your resolution. We don't ever try to cram an idea down an artist's throat. We always send it as a suggestion made on a take it or leave it basis. I'm flatly against our buying ideas as the old humorous magazines used to do and then sending them out to an artist to do at so much per picture. That is ruinous to humorous art, I think, or to anything creative. Our attitude, honestly observed, I think, in practice, is that we submit an idea to an artist and that if he sees fit to use it as a suggestion

for a picture into which he is going to put something of his
own he will proceed to draw it; otherwise not. It's the
same with our text pieces. We've suggested a lot in our time,
of course, and one significant thing is that I never remember
a writer announcing that he was through taking ideas from
someone else, although every artist seems to do it every once
in awhile. Or every really sensitive artist. All good artists,
either with pencil, pen or typewriter are hypersensitive,
thin-skinned, and apt to be influenced by crude observations.
I think Winchell's observations are all crude, I suppose most
of Fortune's were. I don't know whether Fortune said so or not,
but the one thing that has made The New Yorker successful is
that it is a collaborative effort, switching ideas back and
forth to find the man best adapted to doing them, and I hope
to high Heaven that you aren't going to be discouraged into
not being willing to work collaboratively. I'm a steadfast
believer in collaboration and The New Yorker is a monument,
or something to it. Please stick with us, and please remember
this: So help me, there's no sin, no harm, and nothing unethical
in drawing up an idea suggested by a man who can't possibly draw
it himself. You're just robbing the public of something enter-
taining. I hope you'll think it over and reconsider and do that
Pennsylvanians idea to begin with.

      We're desperately short of page drawings
and have been more or less depending on this and other things
from you. As a matter of fact this comes just after we had
resolved to put pressure on you somehow for more work.

      Don't bother to answer this. I'm going
out West at the end of the week to get away from it all and
wouldn't get it until I got back anyhow.

               Sincerely and hopefully,

               H. W. Ross

P.S.   I just happened to think. I was talking to E. V. Lucas
       of Punch a month or so ago and he told me that 90% of the
       Punch ideas are suggested to artists. (Our agerage is,
       of course, no where near so high) This proves that the
       honorable and ancient institution of Punch sees no sin
       in offering ideas to artists.

               H.W.R.

Gluyas Williams, Esq.,
Deer Isle, Maine

hwr/w

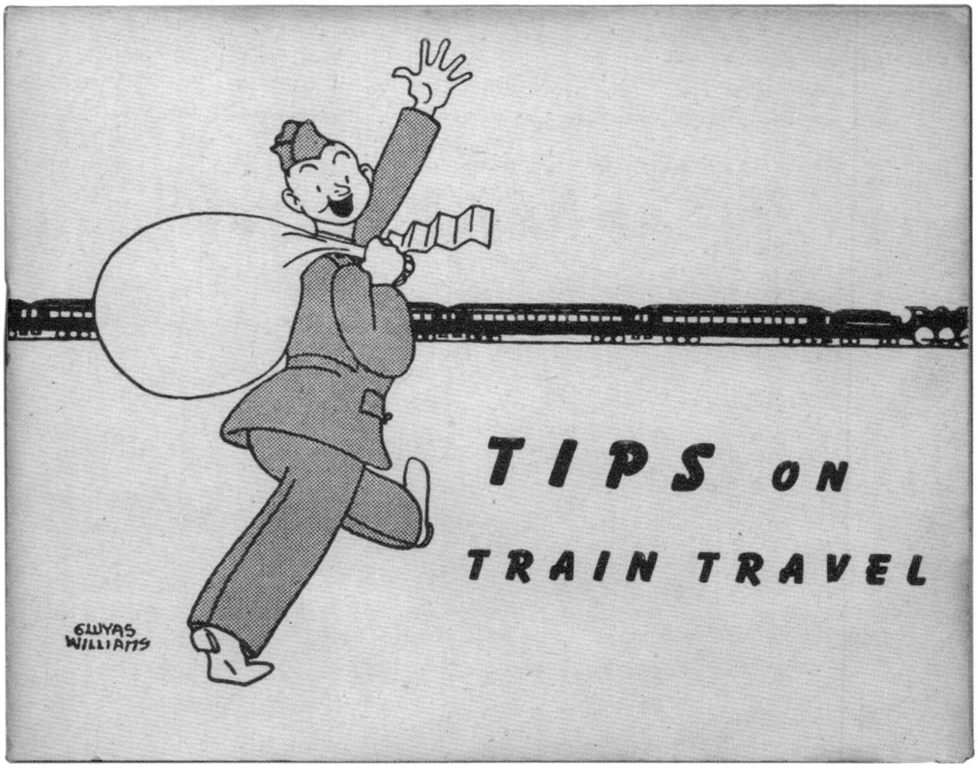
TIPS ON
TRAIN TRAVEL
GLUYAS WILLIAMS

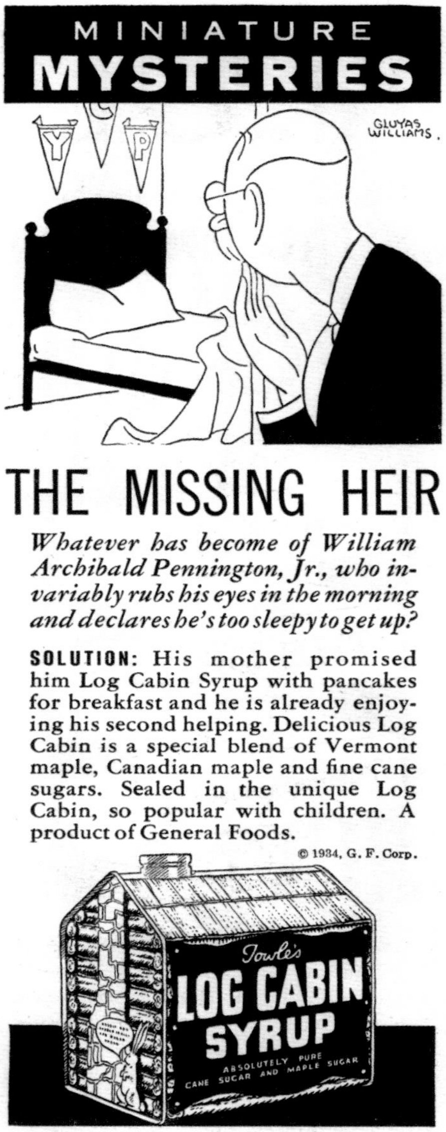
MINIATURE
MYSTERIES
GLUYAS WILLIAMS.
THE MISSING HEIR
Whatever has become of William Archibald Pennington, Jr., who invariably rubs his eyes in the morning and declares he's too sleepy to get up?
SOLUTION: His mother promised him Log Cabin Syrup with pancakes for breakfast and he is already enjoying his second helping. Delicious Log Cabin is a special blend of Vermont maple, Canadian maple and fine cane sugars. Sealed in the unique Log Cabin, so popular with children. A product of General Foods.
© 1934, G. F. Corp.
Towle's
LOG CABIN
SYRUP
ABSOLUTELY PURE
CANE SUGAR AND MAPLE SUGAR

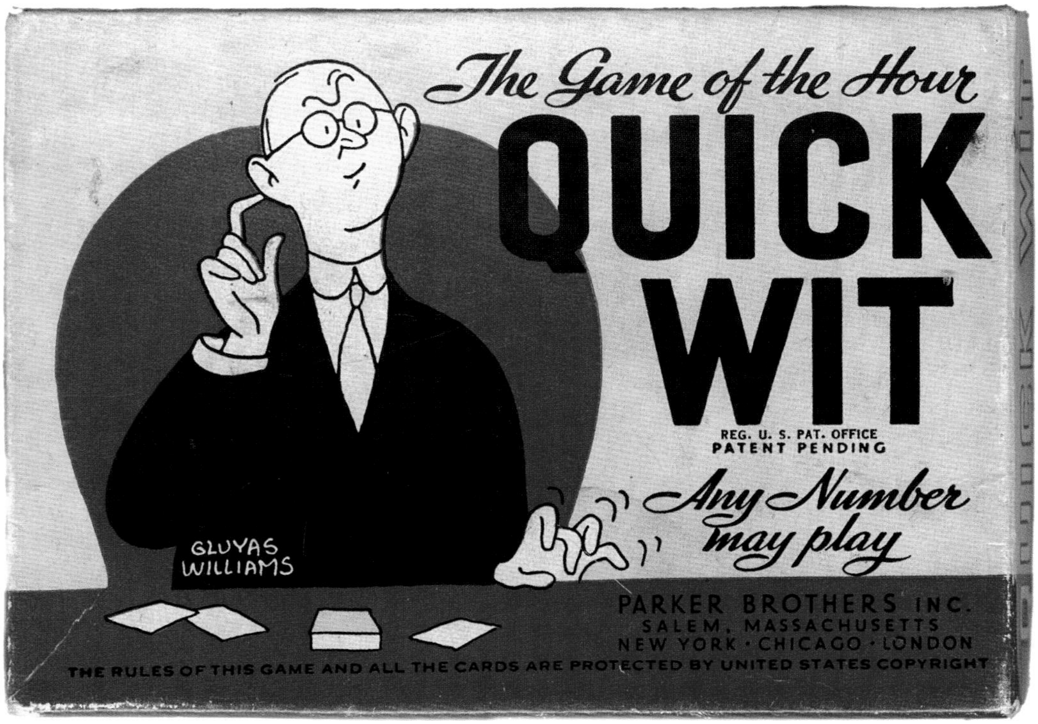
The Game of the Hour
QUICK
WIT
REG. U. S. PAT. OFFICE
PATENT PENDING
Any Number may play
GLUYAS WILLIAMS
PARKER BROTHERS INC.
SALEM, MASSACHUSETTS
NEW YORK · CHICAGO · LONDON
THE RULES OF THIS GAME AND ALL THE CARDS ARE PROTECTED BY UNITED STATES COPYRIGHT

Advertisement for Log Cabin Syrup, *The American Magazine*, February 1934.

TOP: *Tips on Train Travel*, c. late 1930s. Armed Forces Instructional Booklet. COURTESY OF CHRIS WARE.

BOTTOM: *Quick Wit*, card game (Parker Brothers, Inc., 1938). COURTESY OF CHRIS WARE.

OPPOSITE TOP: Original art for self-portrait sketch, undated. COURTESY OF ROB STOLZER.

OPPOSITE BOTTOM: Edward Streeter, *Daily—Except Sundays* (Simon & Schuster, 1938). Illustrations by Williams. COURTESY OF WARREN BERNARD.

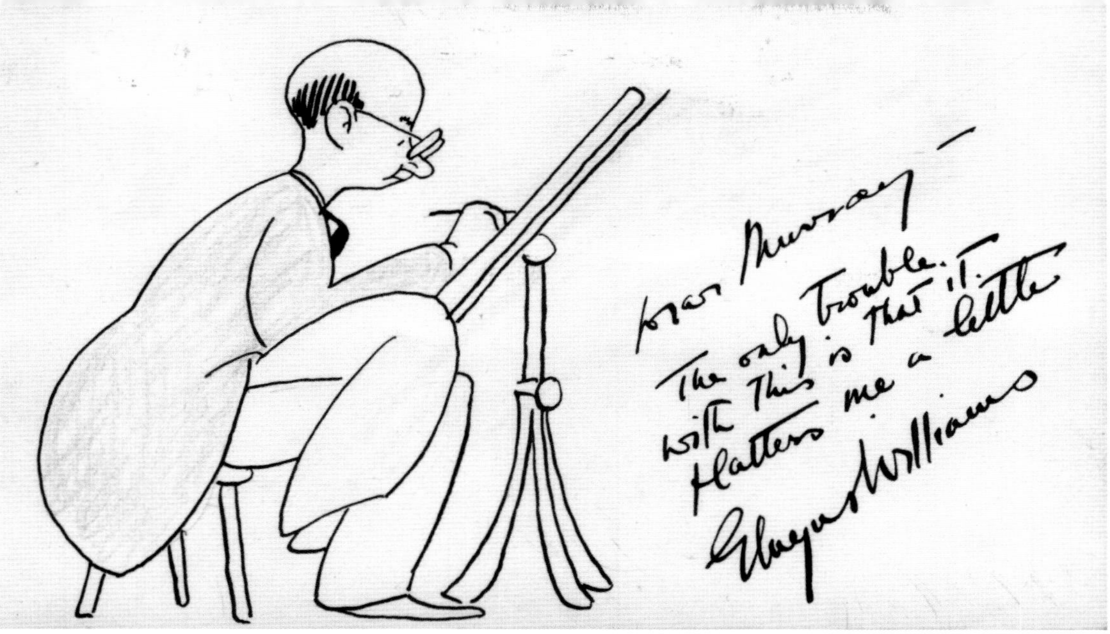
Dear Murray —
The only trouble with this is that it flatters me a little
Gluyas Williams

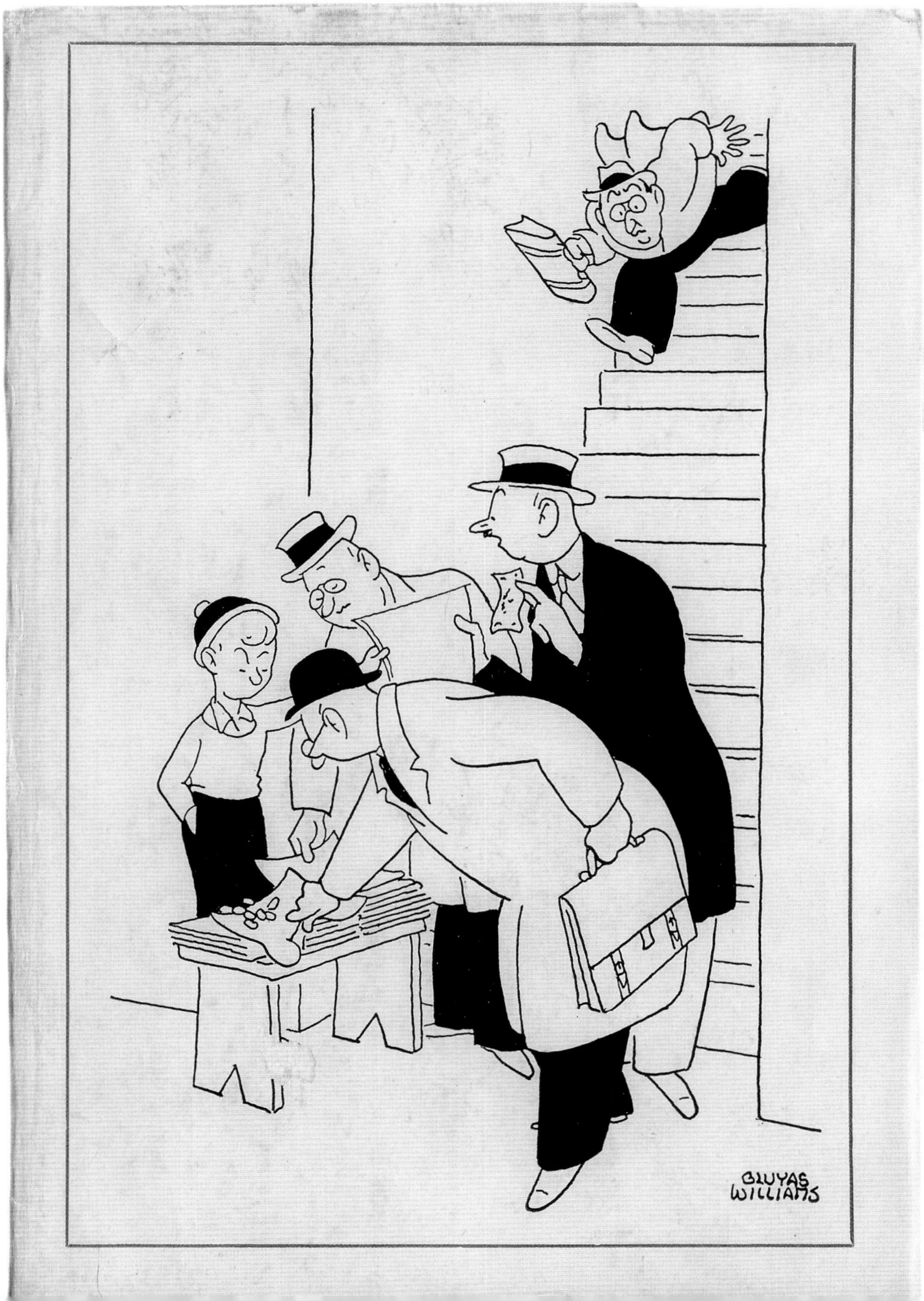
GLUYAS
WILLIAMS

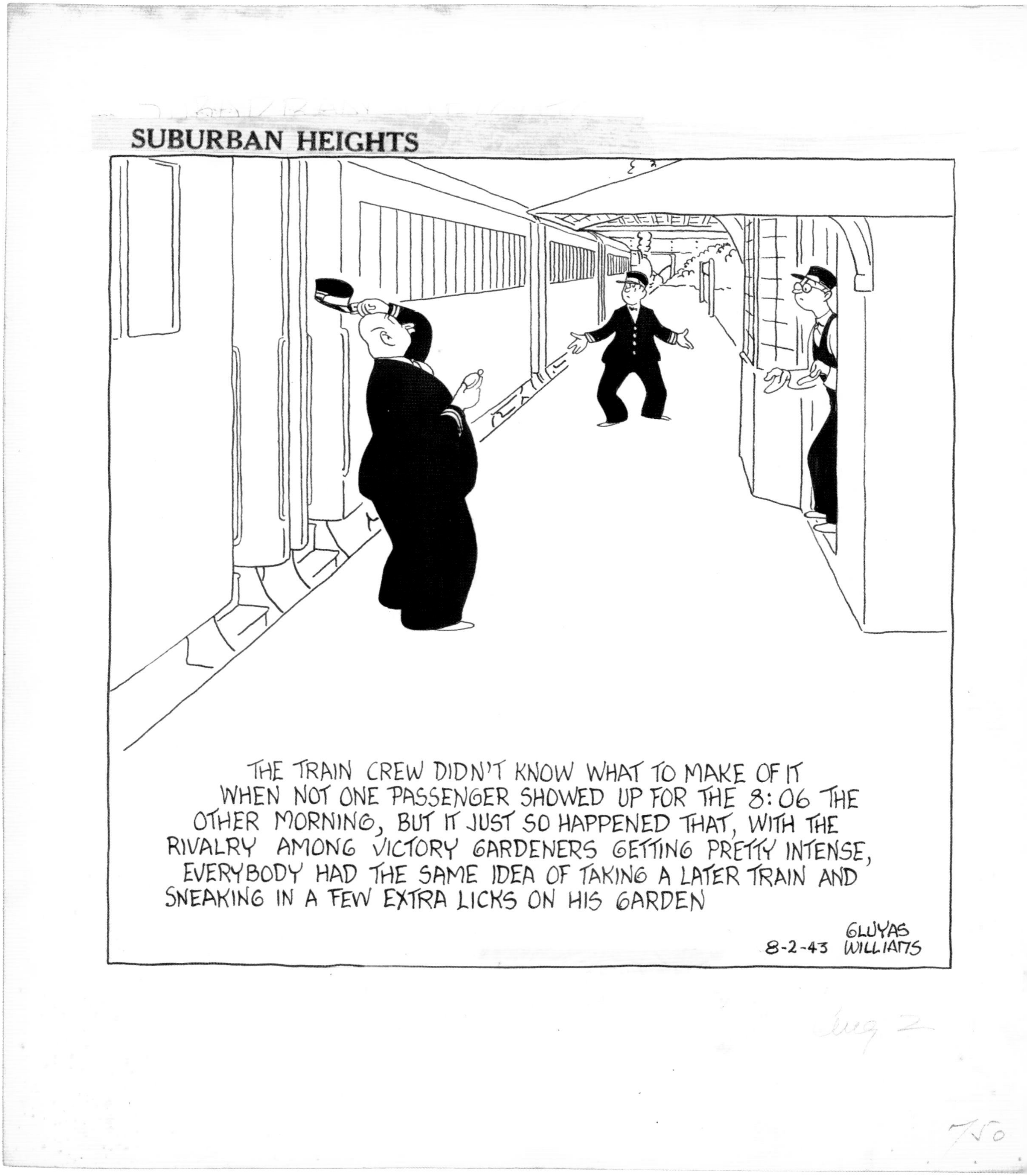
SUBURBAN HEIGHTS
THE TRAIN CREW DIDN'T KNOW WHAT TO MAKE OF IT WHEN NOT ONE PASSENGER SHOWED UP FOR THE 8:06 THE OTHER MORNING, BUT IT JUST SO HAPPENED THAT, WITH THE RIVALRY AMONG VICTORY GARDENERS GETTING PRETTY INTENSE, EVERYBODY HAD THE SAME IDEA OF TAKING A LATER TRAIN AND SNEAKING IN A FEW EXTRA LICKS ON HIS GARDEN
8-2-43
GLUYAS WILLIAMS
Aug 2
750

Original art for *Suburban Heights*, daily panel, August 2, 1943. COURTESY OF ROGER CLARK / WWW.ROGERCLARKART.COM.

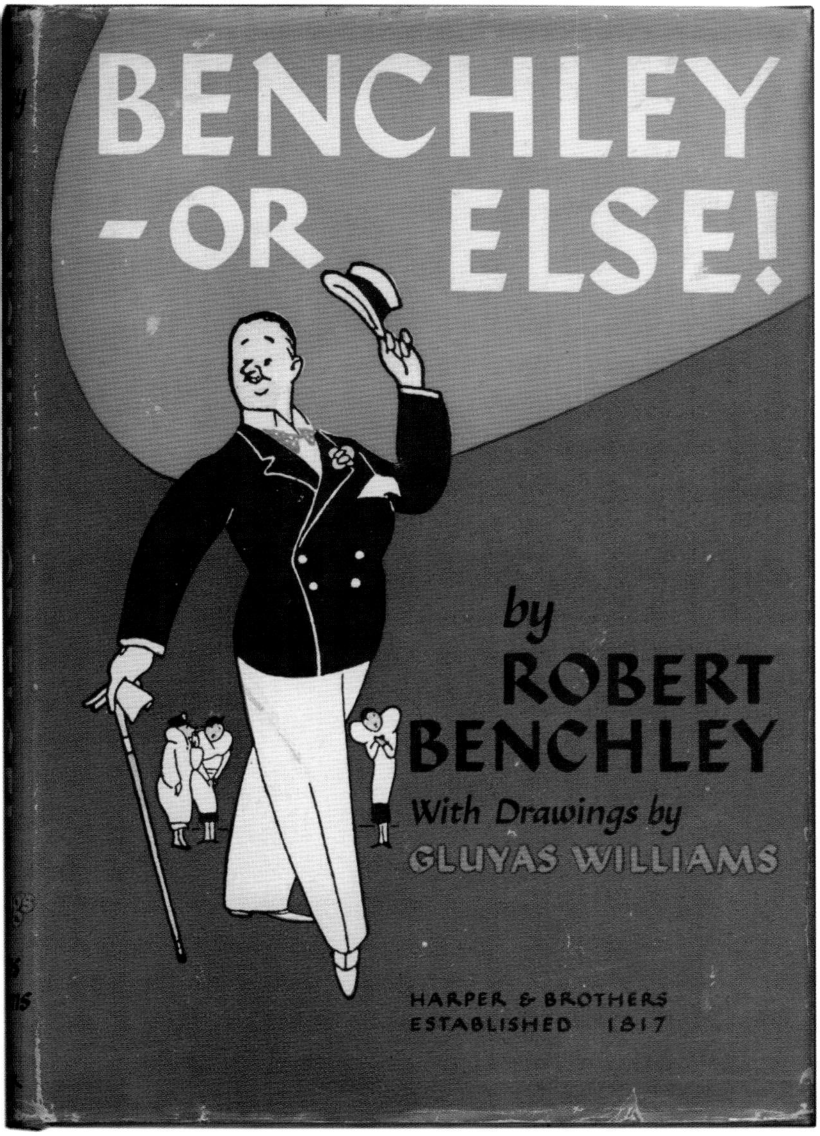
BENCHLEY
-OR ELSE!
by
ROBERT
BENCHLEY
With Drawings by
GLUYAS WILLIAMS
HARPER & BROTHERS
ESTABLISHED 1817

Robert Benchley, *Benchley—Or Else* (Harper & Brothers, 1947). Illustrations by Williams. COURTESY OF TODD HIGNITE.

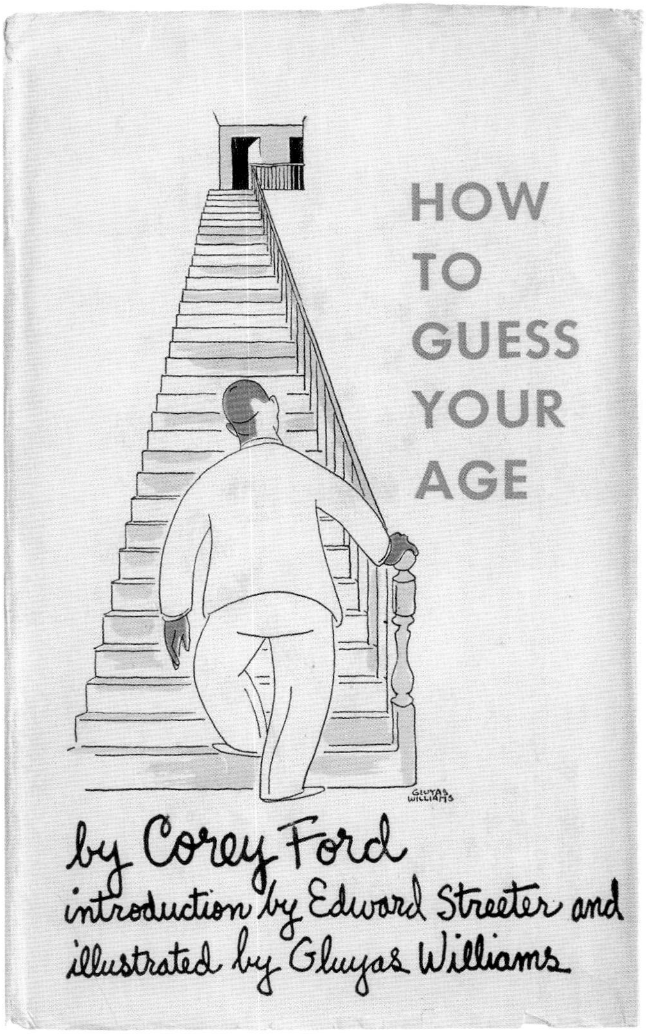
HOW
TO
GUESS
YOUR
AGE
GLUYAS WILLIAMS
by Corey Ford
introduction by Edward Streeter and
illustrated by Gluyas Williams

Corey Ford, *How to Guess Your Age* (Doubleday & Company, 1950). Illustrations by Williams. COURTESY OF WARREN BERNARD.

On the eleven pages following: a sampling of Williams's variously titled daily comic panel, which ran from 1922–1947. ALL COURTESY OF CHRIS WARE.

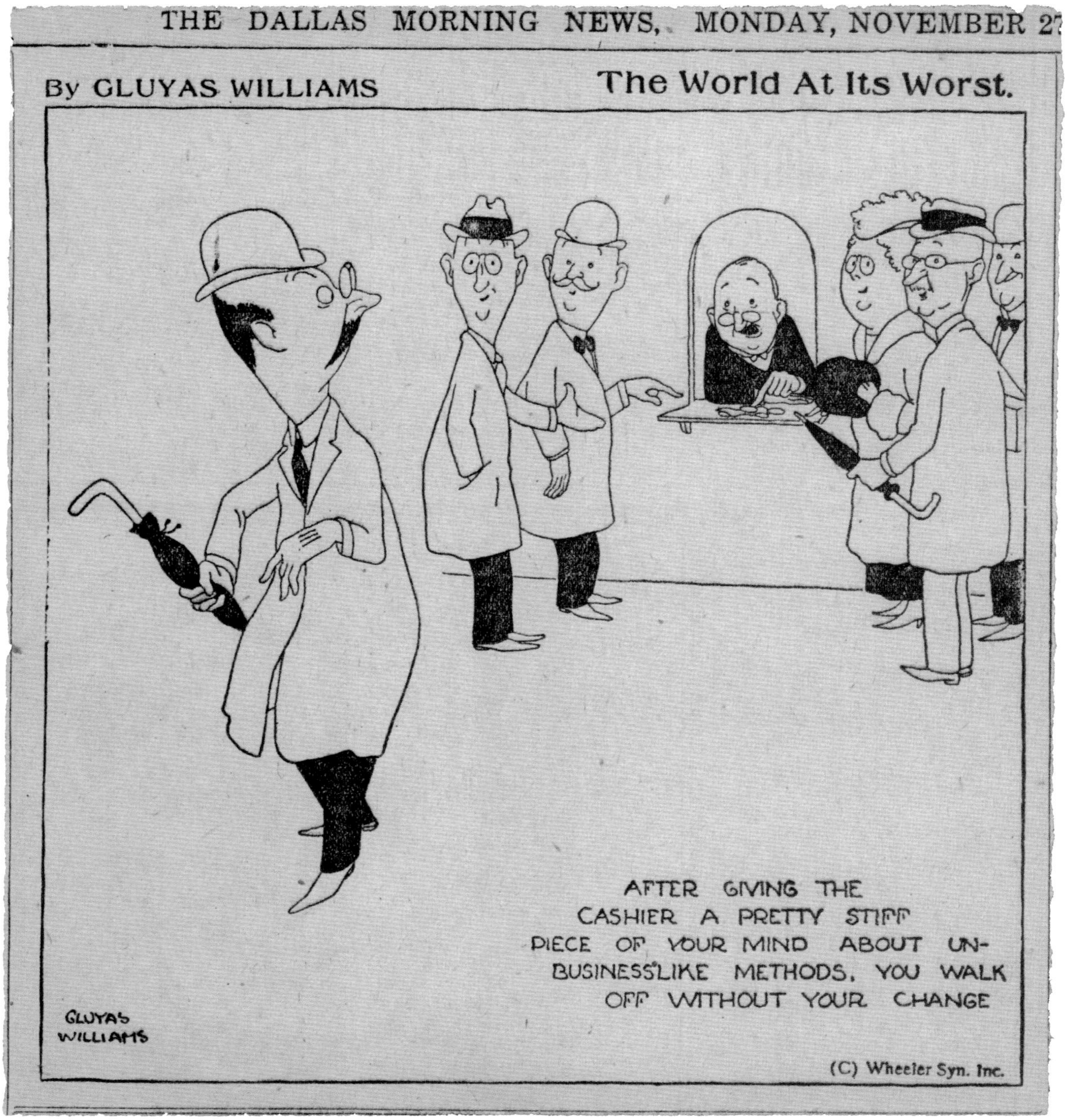
THE DALLAS MORNING NEWS, MONDAY, NOVEMBER 27
By GLUYAS WILLIAMS
The World At Its Worst.
AFTER GIVING THE CASHIER A PRETTY STIFF PIECE OF YOUR MIND ABOUT UN-BUSINESS-LIKE METHODS, YOU WALK OFF WITHOUT YOUR CHANGE
GLUYAS WILLIAMS
(C) Wheeler Syn. Inc.

The World At Its Worst, daily panel, November 27, 1922.

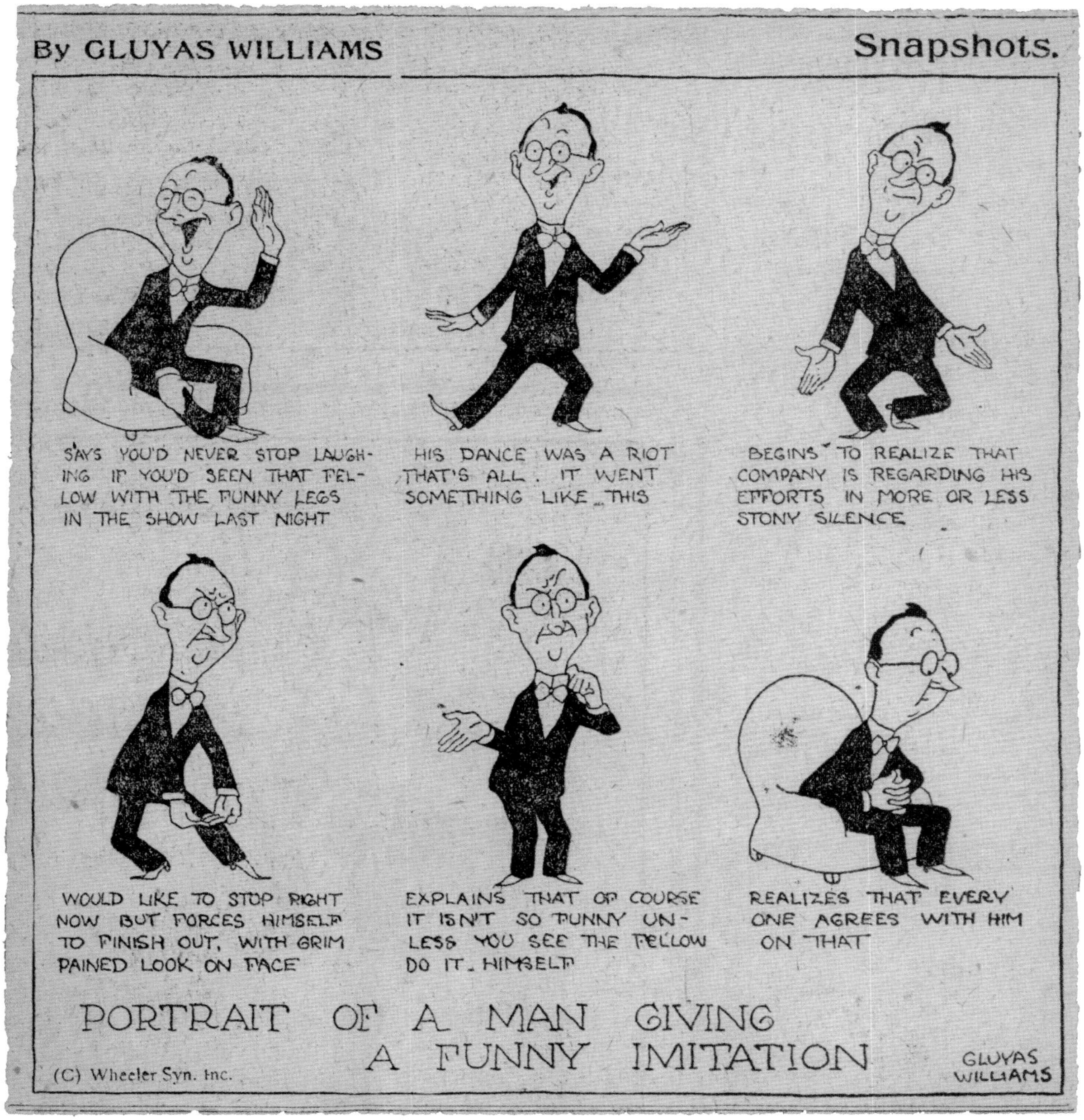

Snapshots, daily panel, 1923.

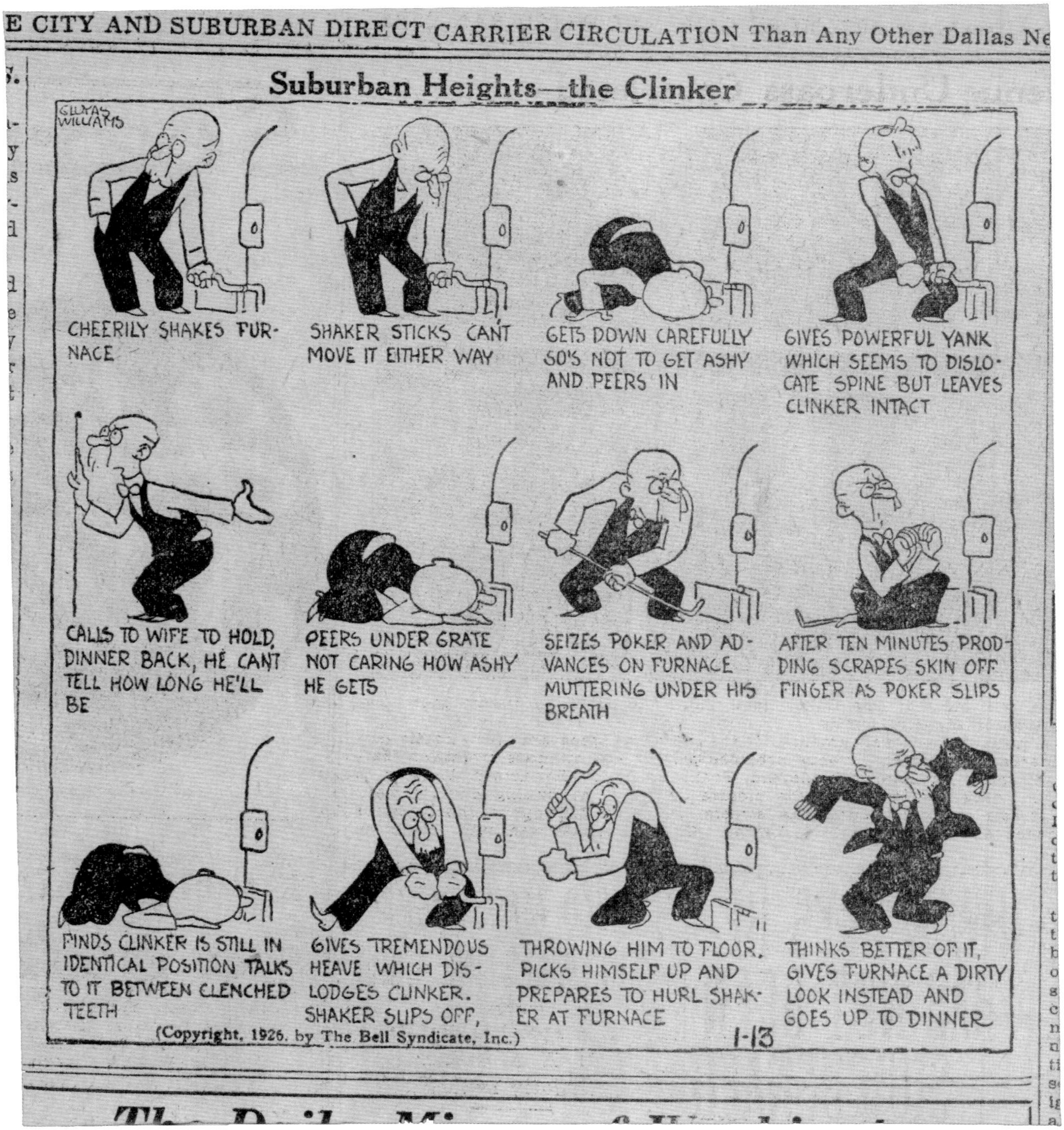
E CITY AND SUBURBAN DIRECT CARRIER CIRCULATION Than Any Other Dallas Ne
Suburban Heights—the Clinker
GLUYAS WILLIAMS
CHEERILY SHAKES FURNACE
SHAKER STICKS CAN'T MOVE IT EITHER WAY
GETS DOWN CAREFULLY SO'S NOT TO GET ASHY AND PEERS IN
GIVES POWERFUL YANK WHICH SEEMS TO DISLOCATE SPINE BUT LEAVES CLINKER INTACT
CALLS TO WIFE TO HOLD DINNER BACK, HE CAN'T TELL HOW LONG HE'LL BE
PEERS UNDER GRATE NOT CARING HOW ASHY HE GETS
SEIZES POKER AND ADVANCES ON FURNACE MUTTERING UNDER HIS BREATH
AFTER TEN MINUTES PRODDING SCRAPES SKIN OFF FINGER AS POKER SLIPS
FINDS CLINKER IS STILL IN IDENTICAL POSITION TALKS TO IT BETWEEN CLENCHED TEETH
GIVES TREMENDOUS HEAVE WHICH DISLODGES CLINKER. SHAKER SLIPS OFF,
THROWING HIM TO FLOOR. PICKS HIMSELF UP AND PREPARES TO HURL SHAKER AT FURNACE
THINKS BETTER OF IT, GIVES FURNACE A DIRTY LOOK INSTEAD AND GOES UP TO DINNER
(Copyright, 1926, by The Bell Syndicate, Inc.)
1-13

Suburban Heights—the Clinker, daily panel, January 13, 1926.

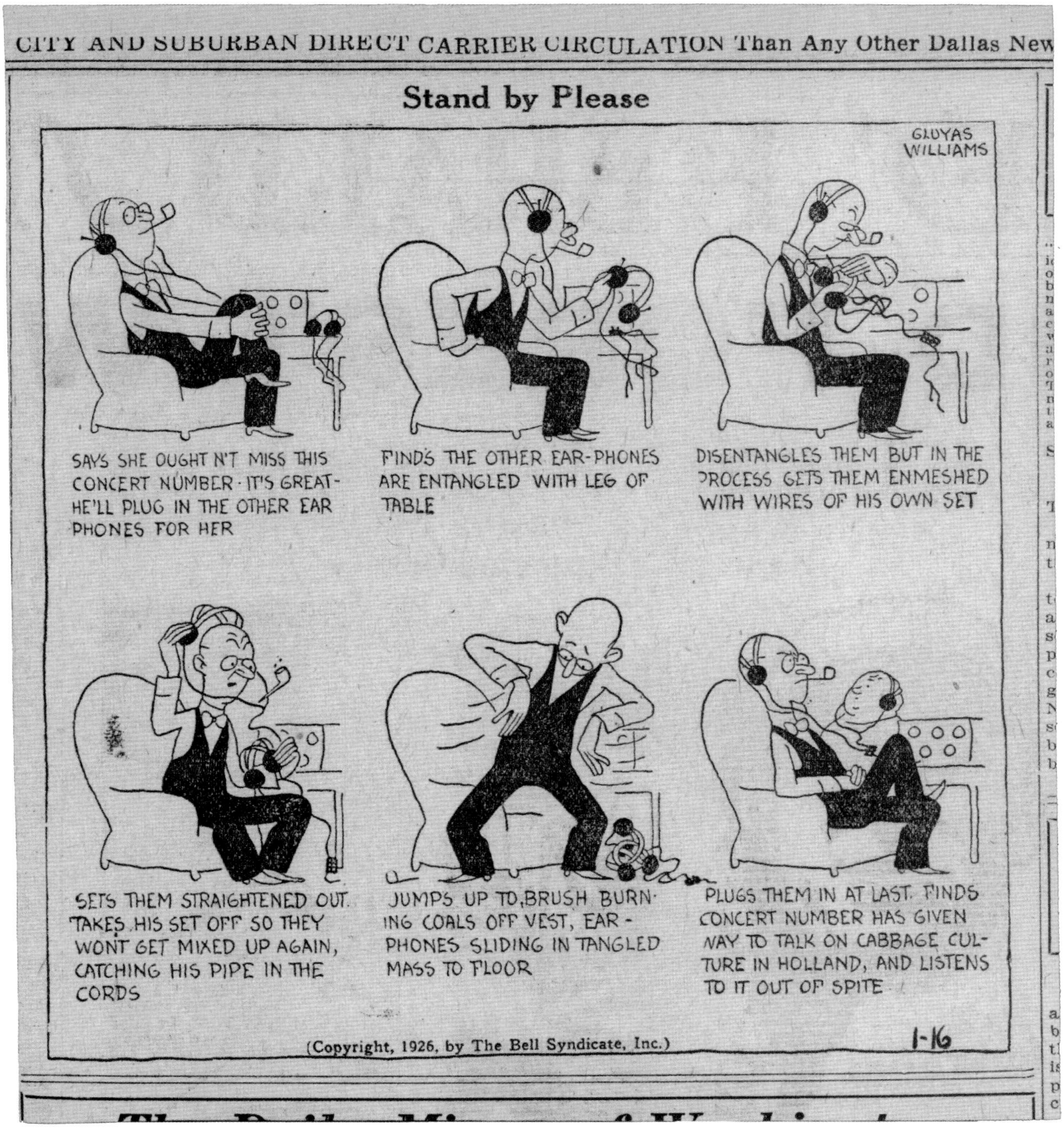
CITY AND SUBURBAN DIRECT CARRIER CIRCULATION Than Any Other Dallas New
Stand by Please
GLUYAS WILLIAMS
SAYS SHE OUGHT N'T MISS THIS CONCERT NUMBER - IT'S GREAT - HE'LL PLUG IN THE OTHER EAR PHONES FOR HER
FINDS THE OTHER EAR-PHONES ARE ENTANGLED WITH LEG OF TABLE
DISENTANGLES THEM BUT IN THE PROCESS GETS THEM ENMESHED WITH WIRES OF HIS OWN SET
GETS THEM STRAIGHTENED OUT. TAKES HIS SET OFF SO THEY WONT GET MIXED UP AGAIN, CATCHING HIS PIPE IN THE CORDS
JUMPS UP TO BRUSH BURNING COALS OFF VEST, EAR-PHONES SLIDING IN TANGLED MASS TO FLOOR
PLUGS THEM IN AT LAST. FINDS CONCERT NUMBER HAS GIVEN WAY TO TALK ON CABBAGE CULTURE IN HOLLAND, AND LISTENS TO IT OUT OF SPITE
(Copyright, 1926, by The Bell Syndicate, Inc.)
1-16

Stand by Please, daily panel, January 16, 1926.

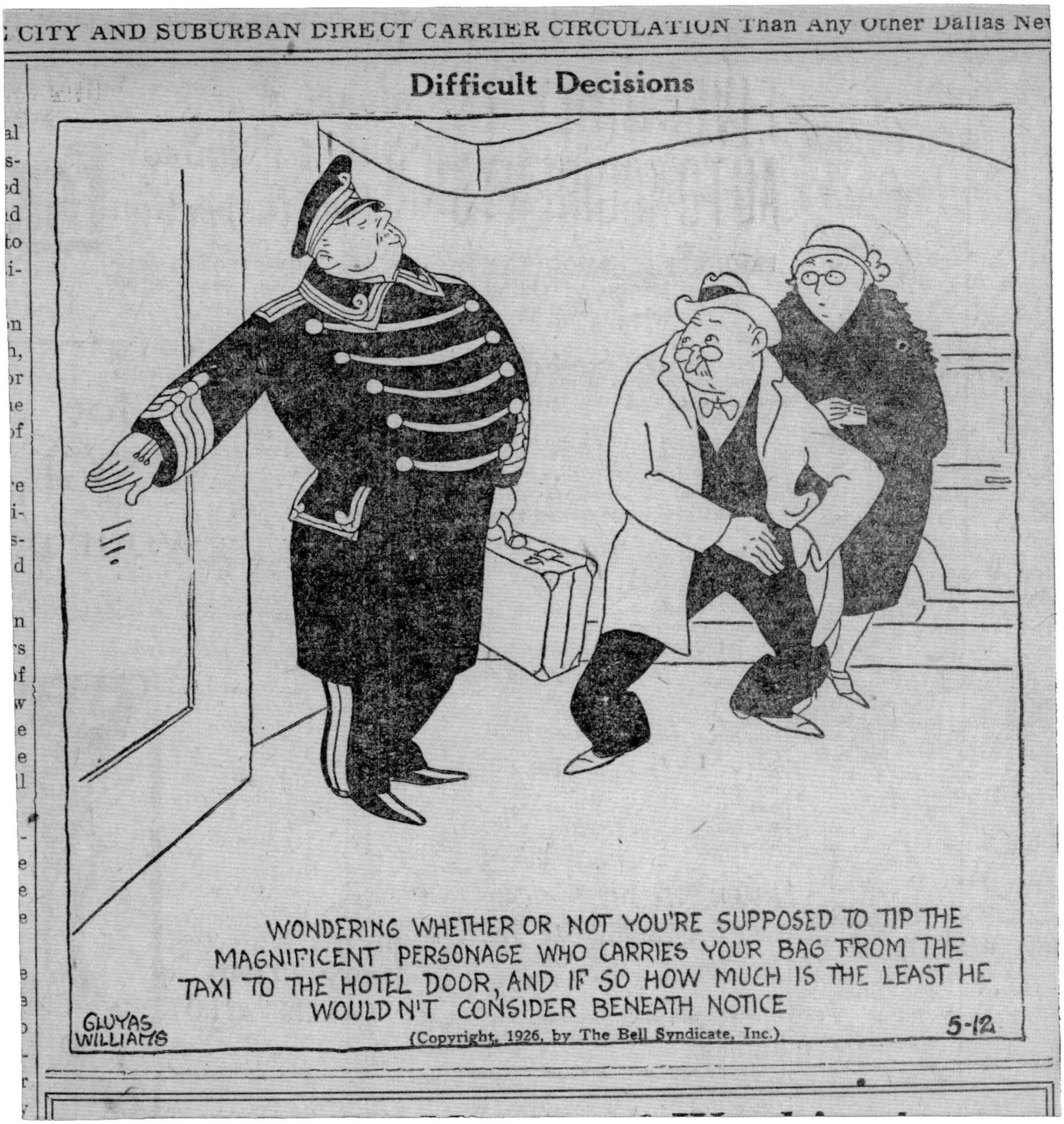
CITY AND SUBURBAN DIRECT CARRIER CIRCULATION Than Any Other Dallas Ne
Difficult Decisions
WONDERING WHETHER OR NOT YOU'RE SUPPOSED TO TIP THE MAGNIFICENT PERSONAGE WHO CARRIES YOUR BAG FROM THE TAXI TO THE HOTEL DOOR, AND IF SO HOW MUCH IS THE LEAST HE WOULD N'T CONSIDER BENEATH NOTICE
GLUYAS WILLIAMS
(Copyright, 1926, by The Bell Syndicate, Inc.)
5-12

Difficult Decisions, daily panel, May 12, 1926.

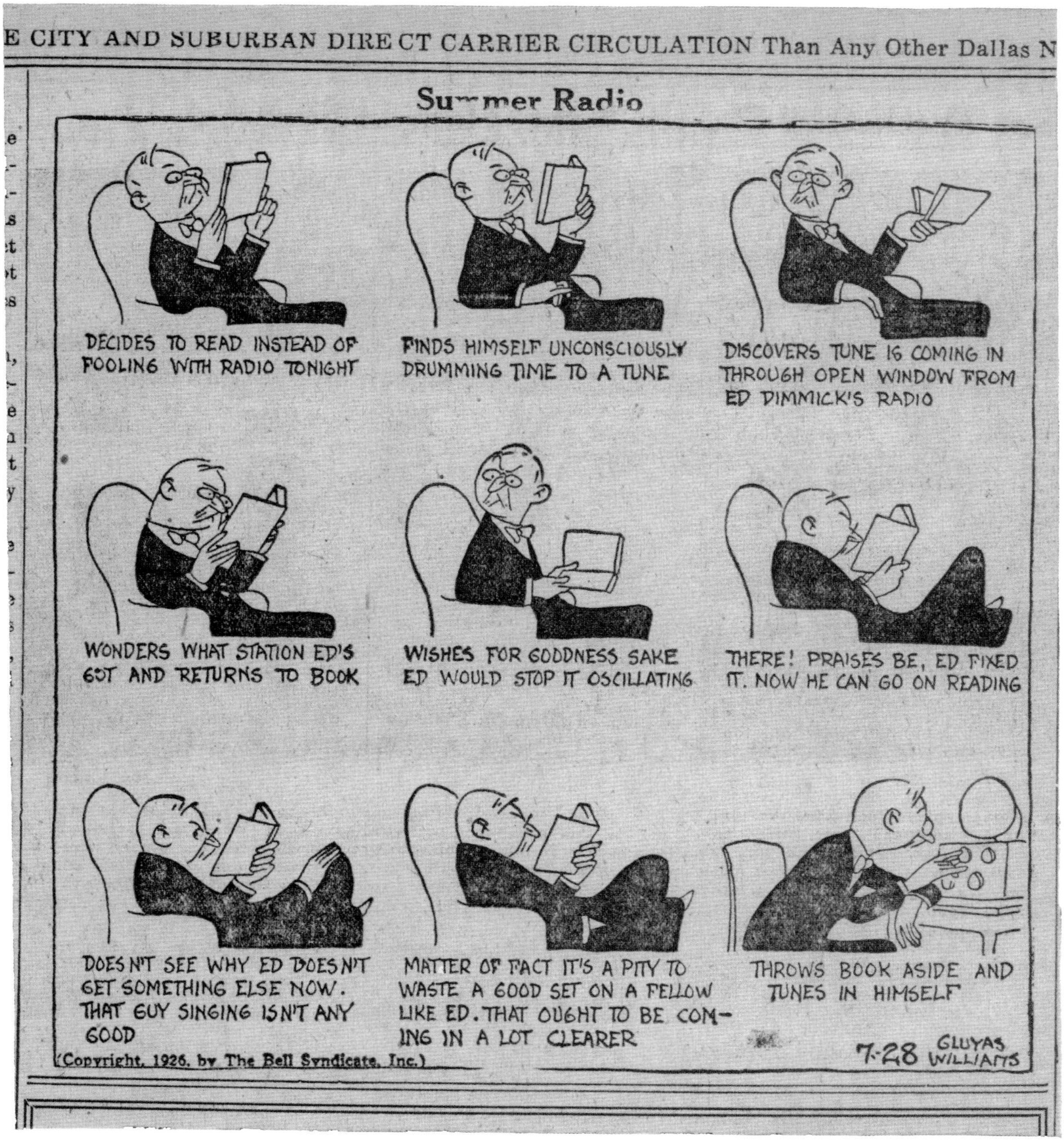
E CITY AND SUBURBAN DIRECT CARRIER CIRCULATION Than Any Other Dallas N
Summer Radio
DECIDES TO READ INSTEAD OF FOOLING WITH RADIO TONIGHT
FINDS HIMSELF UNCONSCIOUSLY DRUMMING TIME TO A TUNE
DISCOVERS TUNE IS COMING IN THROUGH OPEN WINDOW FROM ED DIMMICK'S RADIO
WONDERS WHAT STATION ED'S GOT AND RETURNS TO BOOK
WISHES FOR GODDNESS SAKE ED WOULD STOP IT OSCILLATING
THERE! PRAISES BE, ED FIXED IT. NOW HE CAN GO ON READING
DOES N'T SEE WHY ED DOES N'T GET SOMETHING ELSE NOW. THAT GUY SINGING ISN'T ANY GOOD
MATTER OF FACT IT'S A PITY TO WASTE A GOOD SET ON A FELLOW LIKE ED. THAT OUGHT TO BE COMING IN A LOT CLEARER
THROWS BOOK ASIDE AND TUNES IN HIMSELF
(Copyright, 1926, by The Bell Syndicate, Inc.)
7-28 GLUYAS WILLIAMS

Summer Radio, daily panel, July 28, 1926.

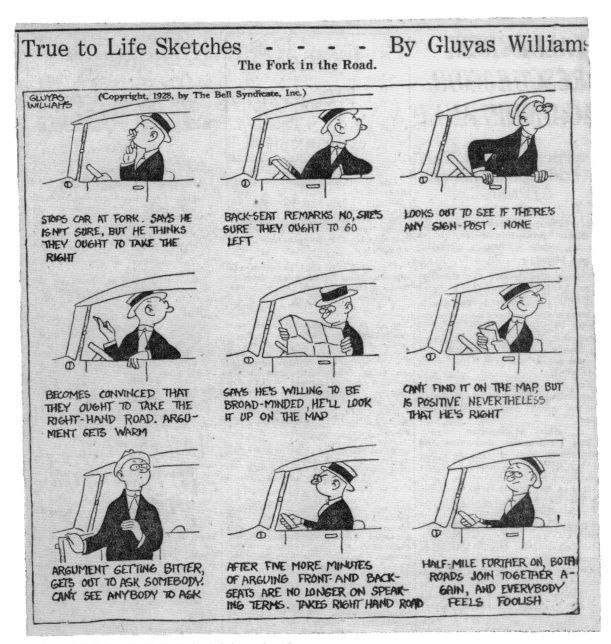

True to Life Sketches - - - - By Gluyas Williams
The Fork in the Road.
GLUYAS WILLIAMS
(Copyright, 1928, by The Bell Syndicate, Inc.)
STOPS CAR AT FORK. SAYS HE ISN'T SURE, BUT HE THINKS THEY OUGHT TO TAKE THE RIGHT
BACK-SEAT REMARKS NO, SHE'S SURE THEY OUGHT TO GO LEFT
LOOKS OUT TO SEE IF THERE'S ANY SIGN-POST. NONE
BECOMES CONVINCED THAT THEY OUGHT TO TAKE THE RIGHT-HAND ROAD. ARGUMENT GETS WARM
SAYS HE'S WILLING TO BE BROAD-MINDED, HE'LL LOOK IT UP ON THE MAP
CAN'T FIND IT ON THE MAP, BUT IS POSITIVE NEVERTHELESS THAT HE'S RIGHT
ARGUMENT GETTING BITTER, GETS OUT TO ASK SOMEBODY. CAN'T SEE ANYBODY TO ASK
AFTER FIVE MORE MINUTES OF ARGUING FRONT- AND BACK-SEATS ARE NO LONGER ON SPEAKING TERMS. TAKES RIGHT HAND ROAD
HALF-MILE FURTHER ON, BOTH ROADS JOIN TOGETHER AGAIN, AND EVERYBODY FEELS FOOLISH

True to Life Sketches. The Fork in the Road, daily panel, 1928.

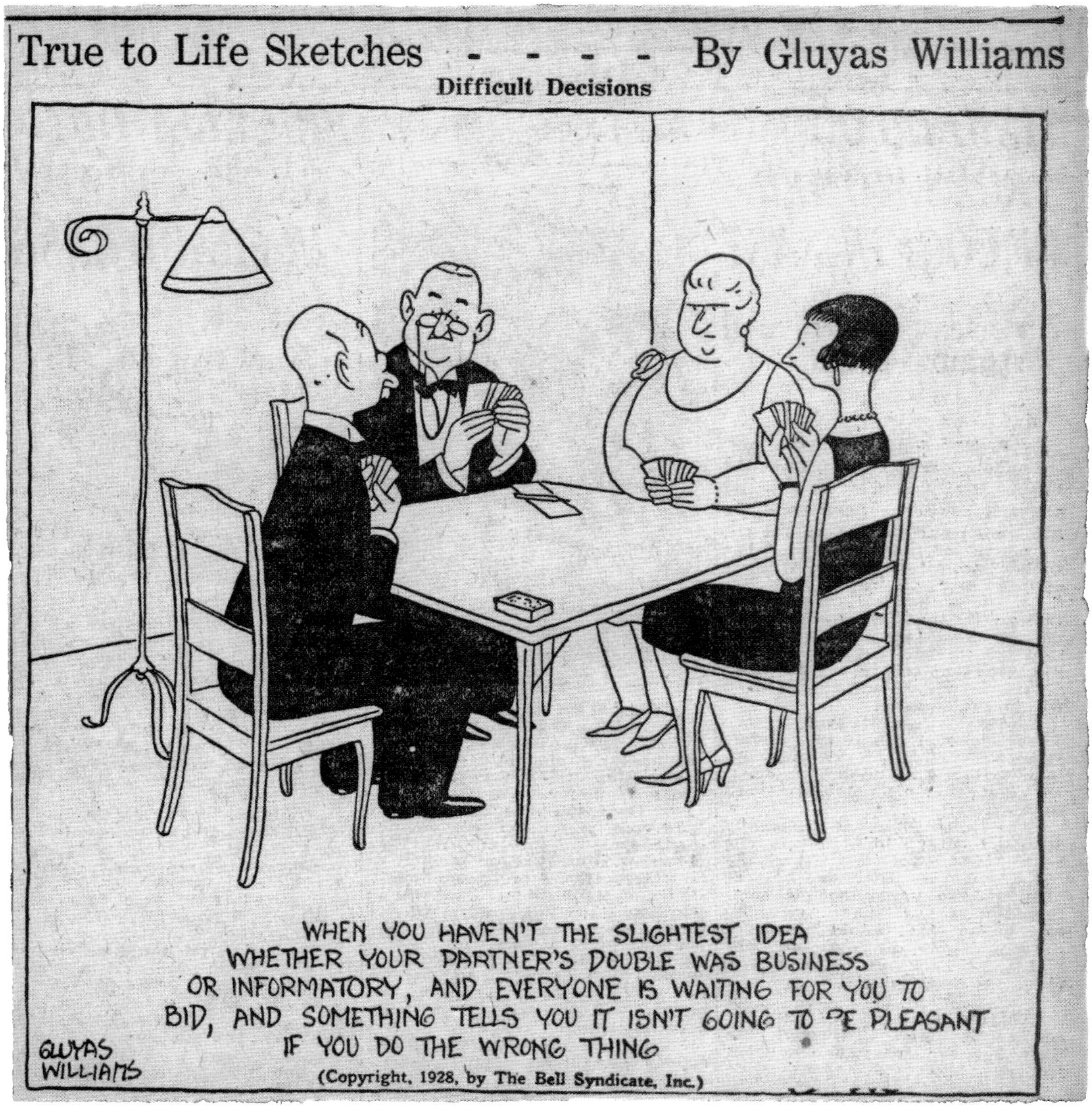
True to Life Sketches - - - - By Gluyas Williams
Difficult Decisions
WHEN YOU HAVEN'T THE SLIGHTEST IDEA WHETHER YOUR PARTNER'S DOUBLE WAS BUSINESS OR INFORMATORY, AND EVERYONE IS WAITING FOR YOU TO BID, AND SOMETHING TELLS YOU IT ISN'T GOING TO BE PLEASANT IF YOU DO THE WRONG THING
GLUYAS WILLIAMS
(Copyright, 1928, by The Bell Syndicate, Inc.)

True to Life Sketches. Difficult Decisions, daily panel, 1928.

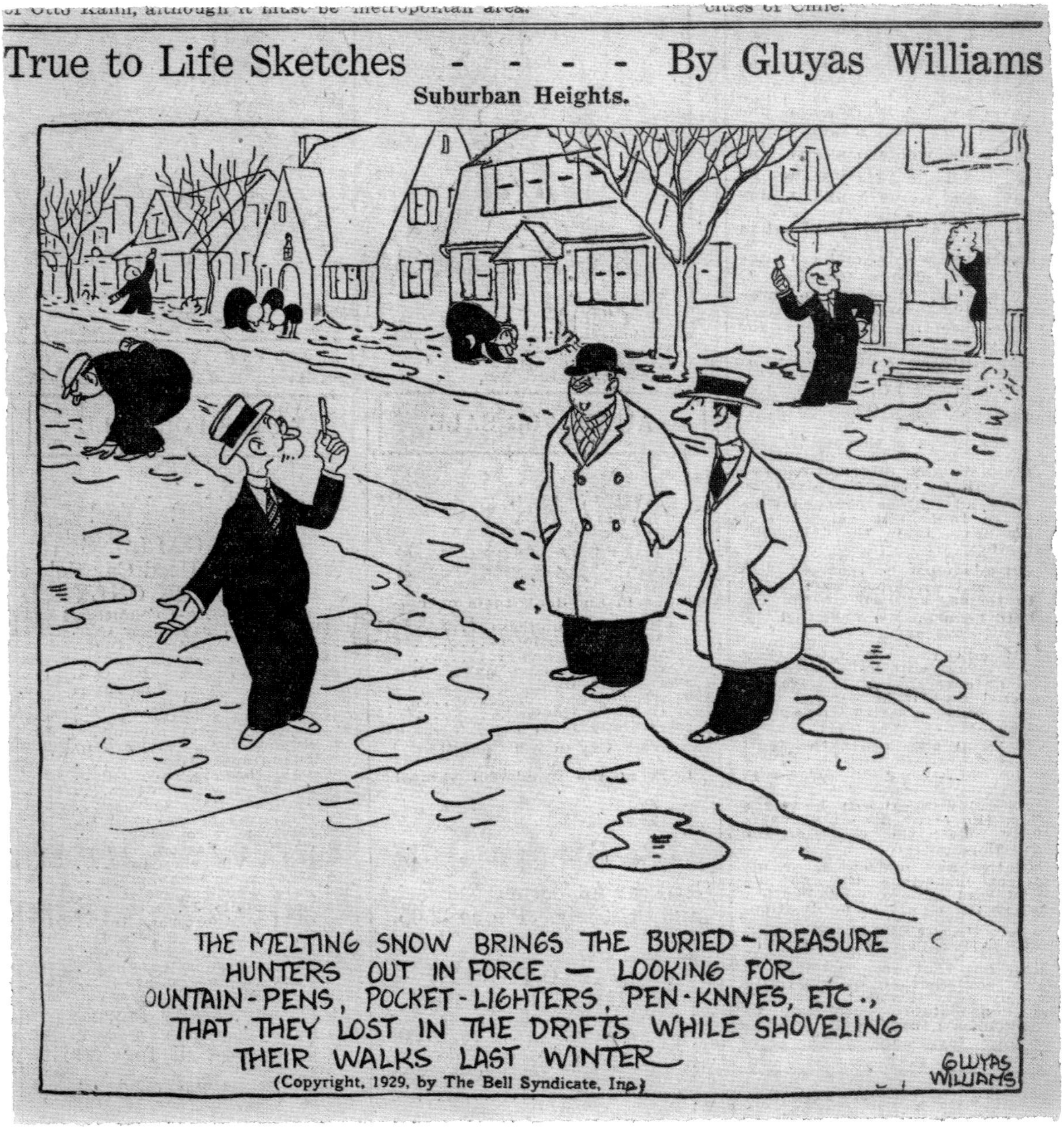
True to Life Sketches - - - - By Gluyas Williams
Suburban Heights.
THE MELTING SNOW BRINGS THE BURIED-TREASURE HUNTERS OUT IN FORCE — LOOKING FOR OUNTAIN-PENS, POCKET-LIGHTERS, PEN-KNIVES, ETC., THAT THEY LOST IN THE DRIFTS WHILE SHOVELING THEIR WALKS LAST WINTER
(Copyright, 1929, by The Bell Syndicate, Inc.)
GLUYAS WILLIAMS

True to Life Sketches, Suburban Heights, daily panel, March 1, 1929.

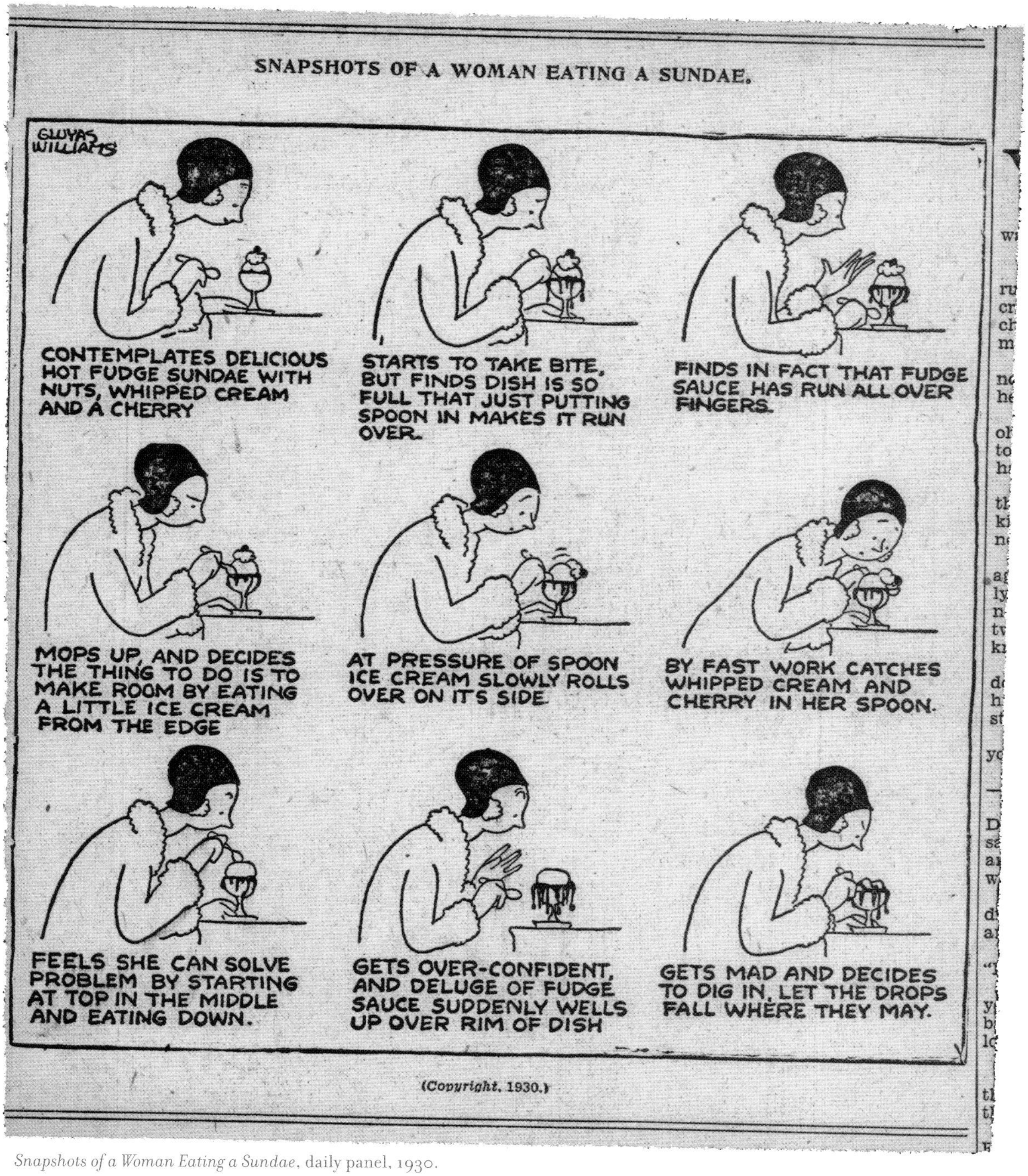
SNAPSHOTS OF A WOMAN EATING A SUNDAE.
GLUYAS WILLIAMS
CONTEMPLATES DELICIOUS HOT FUDGE SUNDAE WITH NUTS, WHIPPED CREAM AND A CHERRY
STARTS TO TAKE BITE, BUT FINDS DISH IS SO FULL THAT JUST PUTTING SPOON IN MAKES IT RUN OVER.
FINDS IN FACT THAT FUDGE SAUCE HAS RUN ALL OVER FINGERS.
MOPS UP, AND DECIDES THE THING TO DO IS TO MAKE ROOM BY EATING A LITTLE ICE CREAM FROM THE EDGE
AT PRESSURE OF SPOON ICE CREAM SLOWLY ROLLS OVER ON IT'S SIDE
BY FAST WORK CATCHES WHIPPED CREAM AND CHERRY IN HER SPOON.
FEELS SHE CAN SOLVE PROBLEM BY STARTING AT TOP IN THE MIDDLE AND EATING DOWN.
GETS OVER-CONFIDENT, AND DELUGE OF FUDGE SAUCE SUDDENLY WELLS UP OVER RIM OF DISH
GETS MAD AND DECIDES TO DIG IN, LET THE DROPS FALL WHERE THEY MAY.
(Copyright, 1930.)

Snapshots of a Woman Eating a Sundae, daily panel, 1930.

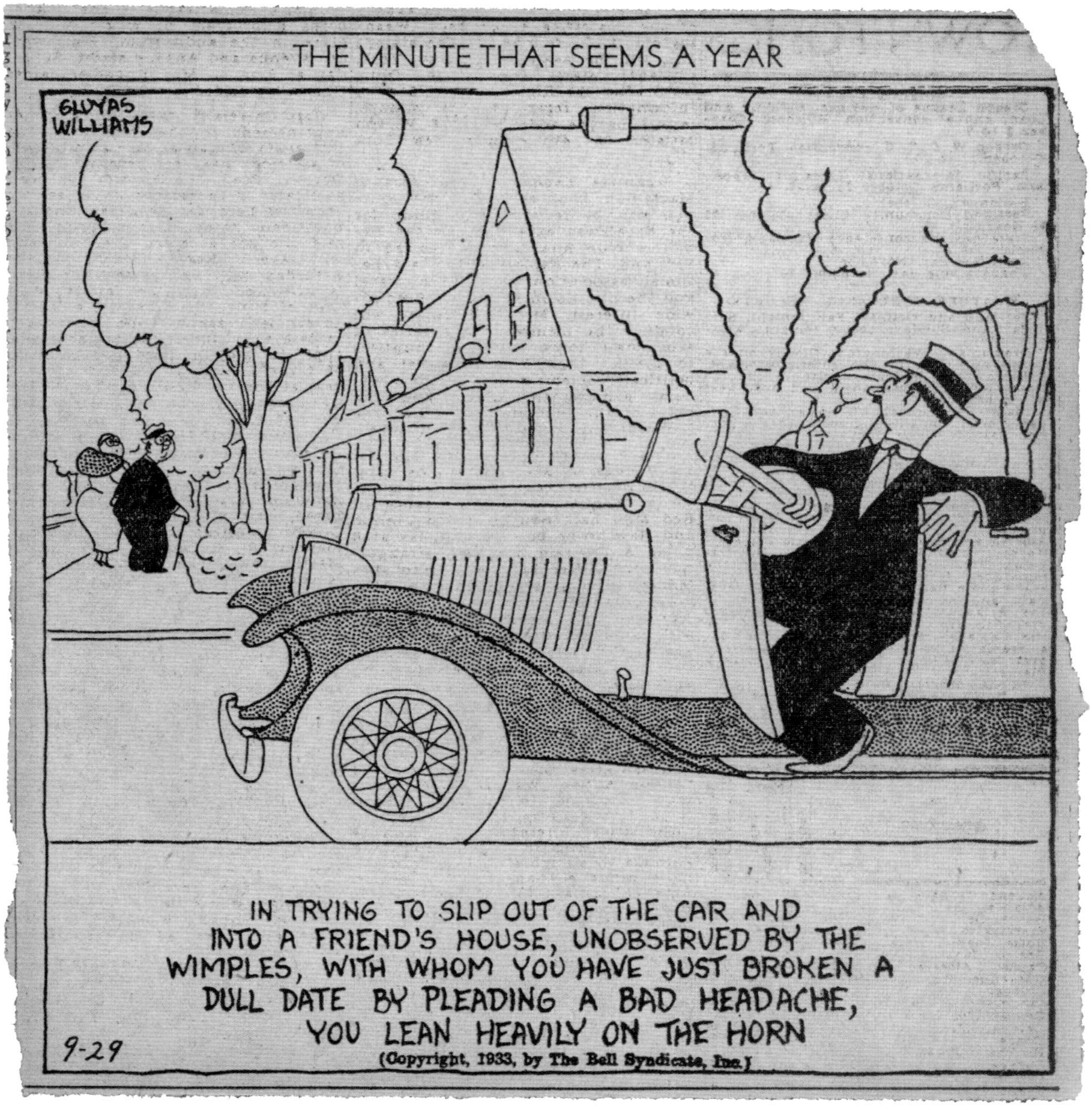
THE MINUTE THAT SEEMS A YEAR
GLUYAS WILLIAMS
IN TRYING TO SLIP OUT OF THE CAR AND INTO A FRIEND'S HOUSE, UNOBSERVED BY THE WIMPLES, WITH WHOM YOU HAVE JUST BROKEN A DULL DATE BY PLEADING A BAD HEADACHE, YOU LEAN HEAVILY ON THE HORN
9-29
(Copyright, 1933, by The Bell Syndicate, Inc.)

The Minute That Seems a Year, daily panel, September 29, 1933.

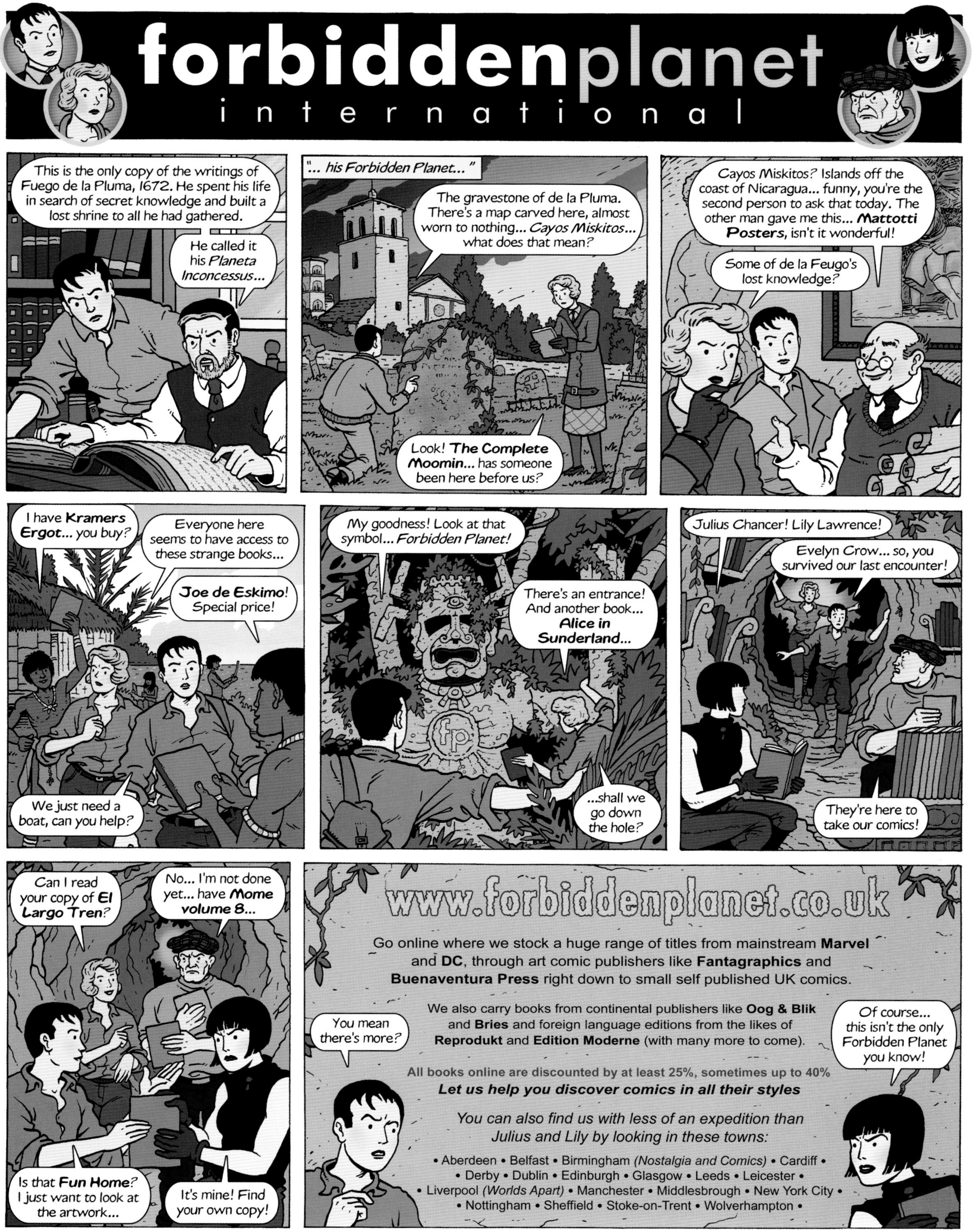
forbiddenplanet
international
This is the only copy of the writings of Fuego de la Pluma, 1672. He spent his life in search of secret knowledge and built a lost shrine to all he had gathered.
He called it his Planeta Inconcessus...
"... his Forbidden Planet..."
The gravestone of de la Pluma. There's a map carved here, almost worn to nothing... Cayos Miskitos... what does that mean?
Look! The Complete Moomin... has someone been here before us?
Cayos Miskitos? Islands off the coast of Nicaragua... funny, you're the second person to ask that today. The other man gave me this... Mattotti Posters, isn't it wonderful!
Some of de la Feugo's lost knowledge?
I have Kramers Ergot... you buy?
Everyone here seems to have access to these strange books...
Joe de Eskimo! Special price!
We just need a boat, can you help?
My goodness! Look at that symbol... Forbidden Planet!
There's an entrance! And another book... Alice in Sunderland...
...shall we go down the hole?
Julius Chancer! Lily Lawrence!
Evelyn Crow... so, you survived our last encounter!
They're here to take our comics!
Can I read your copy of El Largo Tren?
No... I'm not done yet... have Mome volume 8...
Is that Fun Home? I just want to look at the artwork...
It's mine! Find your own copy!
www.forbiddenplanet.co.uk
Go online where we stock a huge range of titles from mainstream Marvel and DC, through art comic publishers like Fantagraphics and Buenaventura Press right down to small self published UK comics.
We also carry books from continental publishers like Oog & Blik and Bries and foreign language editions from the likes of Reprodukt and Edition Moderne (with many more to come).
You mean there's more?
Of course... this isn't the only Forbidden Planet you know!
All books online are discounted by at least 25%, sometimes up to 40%
Let us help you discover comics in all their styles
You can also find us with less of an expedition than Julius and Lily by looking in these towns:
• Aberdeen • Belfast • Birmingham (Nostalgia and Comics) • Cardiff • • Derby • Dublin • Edinburgh • Glasgow • Leeds • Leicester • • Liverpool (Worlds Apart) • Manchester • Middlesbrough • New York City • • Nottingham • Sheffield • Stoke-on-Trent • Wolverhampton •

Garen Ewing www.rainboworchid.co.uk

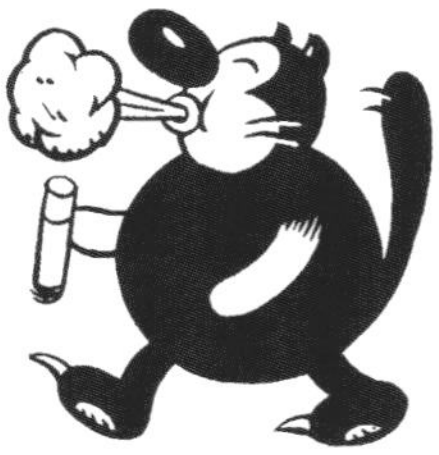

KING PUNKAROCKA

THE STORY OF

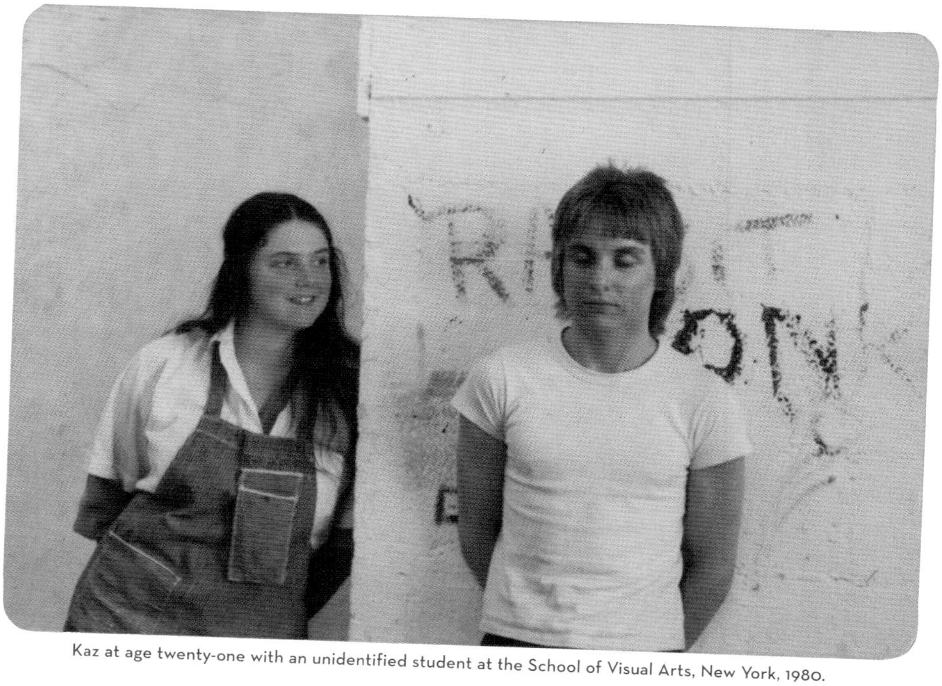

R
ON

Kaz at age twenty-one with an unidentified student at the School of Visual Arts, New York, 1980.

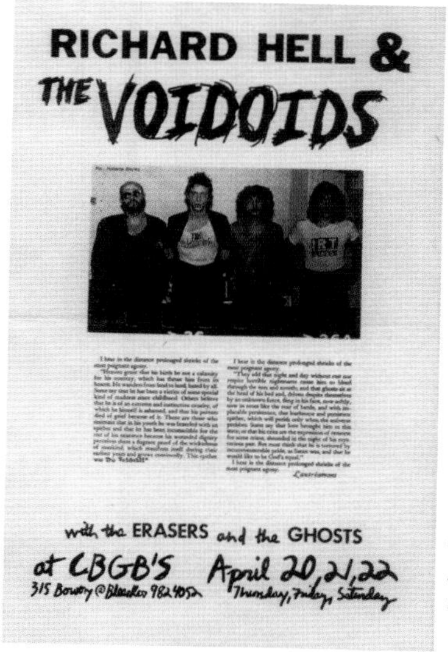
RICHARD HELL &
THE VOIDOIDS
with the ERASERS and the GHOSTS
at CBGB'S April 20,21,22
315 Bowery @ Bleecker 982-4052
Thursday, Friday, Saturday

Richard Hell and the Voidoids flyer, c. late 1970s.

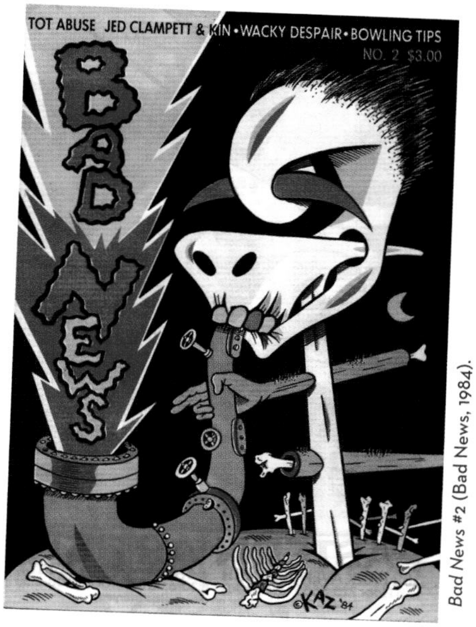
TOT ABUSE JED CLAMPETT & KIN • WACKY DESPAIR • BOWLING TIPS
NO. 2 $3.00
BAD NEWS
©KAZ '84

Bad News #2 (Bad News, 1984).

KAZ

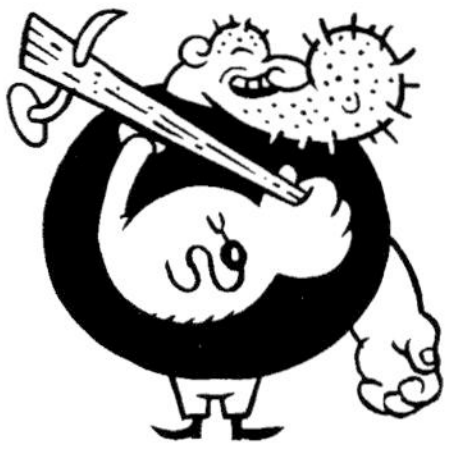

by BEN SCHWARTZ

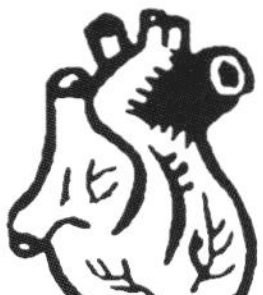

IN THE LATE, LATE HOURS of a winter night somewhere in 1977 or '78, the cartoonist known as Kaz, then eighteen, wandered into Penn Station at 8th Avenue and 31st Street, quite drunk, cold, and coming down from the adrenaline rush of a show at CBGB's. The club was at its peak, still a vibrant musical scene and home to the Ramones, Talking Heads, Blondie, Richard Hell and the Voidoids, the Dead Boys, and celebrity scenesters too big to play the tiny venue, such as Iggy Pop, Lou Reed, and Patti Smith. It hadn't been tagged "legendary" yet and still paid its rent as a club, not a T-shirt outlet. Kaz often found himself the only teenager in a room full of much older hipsters, just happy CB's served him beer.

Kaz had two ways of getting into Manhattan from his parents' house in Rahway, New Jersey. He either took the train or waited until his dad fell asleep and then snuck out in the family car. This night, Kaz had stayed late for a Dead Boys or Damned show (he can't remember exactly) and missed the last train home.

"It sucked to take the train," recalls Kaz. "The last one left at 1:40 A.M., and back then at CB's they did two shows. The wilder one was always the late show. You wanted to see that one with Richard Hell or the Ramones. I sometimes missed the train and had to spend the night with the homeless in the station. If you fell asleep, cops kicked your chair and woke you up."

Not that Kaz could ever fall asleep in such a creepy atmosphere. This night he sat for hours waiting for the first 7 A.M. train to New Jersey. Train or not, going home was always a letdown.

"I was pretty alienated back then. The temporary high I got from the punk rock energy of CBGB's dissipated as soon as I walked out onto the Bowery, ears ringing, and went back to New Jersey and my miserable factory job making air conditioners on an assembly line. The station looked like a halfway house for lost souls stuck forever in purgatory. I don't know, it reflected my feelings about life back then. I saw my own life as being hopeless. I wanted to be somehow part of the arts but didn't have a clue. I had no money. I was drifting."

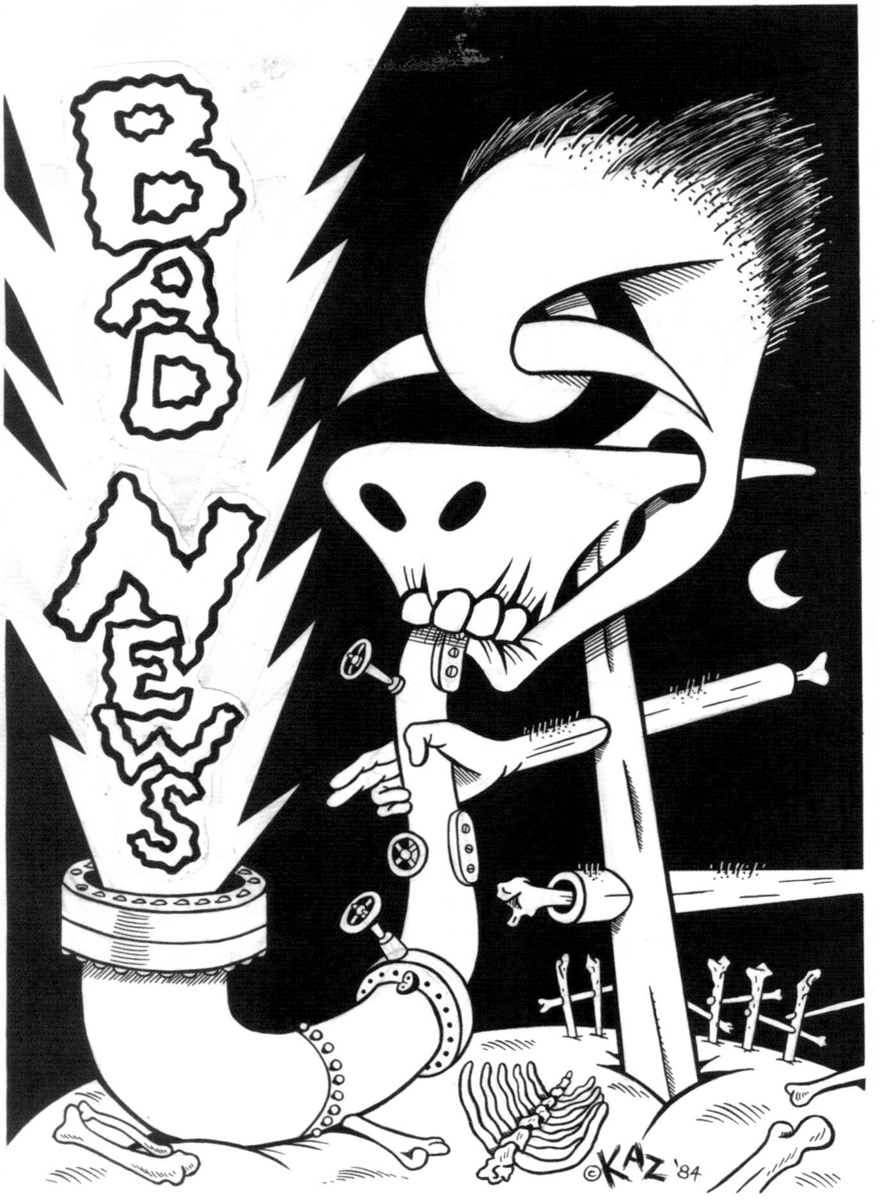
BAD NEWS
©KAZ '84

Original art for *Bad News* #2 cover (Bad News, 1984).

KAZIMIERAS GEDIMINUS Prapuolenis—Kaz—grew up in a family of immigrants as a first-generation American. "Gediminus, loosely translated, means 'goddamit!' in Lithuanian," says Kaz. His father, Joseph Prapuolenis, arrived first. "My dad came to America in the early '50s. He had been writing and printing a subversive anti-Communist underground newspaper in Lithuania when he was tapped by the CIA. He figured that if the CIA knew about him the KGB also knew, and so he, with the help of friends, escaped Lithuania and emigrated to America, settling in New Jersey."

Kaz's mother, Angelica Petkus, then eighteen, and her family lived in West Germany as Lithuanian refugees from the Second World War. The last place they wanted to live was Lithuania under Stalin. Kaz's father sponsored the Petkus family's immigration to America, and when they arrived, Joseph and Angelica soon got married and settled in Hoboken, where her relatives lived.

Kaz was born in St. Mary's Hospital, Hoboken, New Jersey, on July 31, 1959. "There were three babies in my mom's womb," says Kaz. "I was the first born, then my sister, Laima. Then the third came out dead. Stillborn. I like to think that my sister and I murdered him." If the idea of Kaz, underground cartoonist, son of the underground political rebel Joseph, sounds like the obvious inspiration for the underground artist as tot—well, life was less exciting than that. Joseph left his politics in Lithuania and took a job at a local factory. "He plated things," says Kaz. "They would get government contracts and plate everything from jeeps to warheads for all I know. Someone he worked with told me my dad almost fell into a giant plating vat. I had this image of him coming home like a giant pair of plated baby shoes."

The family lived in a boarding house. As Kaz recalls, it was "a roach-infested, cold-water flat. That apartment still makes me laugh. It looked like *The Honeymooners* apartment and even had the rolling-pin laundry machine in the kitchen. Sometimes when I had to pee in the middle of the night, I'd find homeless guys sleeping in our stairwell, and I'd have to get my dad to move them so I could go to the bathroom." By the time he was nine, the Prapuolenises settled in Rahway, where Kaz grew up. His parents never encouraged him in any creative direction whatsoever, but comics appealed to him from an early age. "There was a bookstore they used to have at Penn Station," he says, "and in the window they had that *Dick Tracy* book—the big blue one with his face on it, *The Celebrated Cases of Dick Tracy*—and I would stare at it. I never asked to have it; I already knew the answer to that, so I just stared and stared at that face, imagining what must be in it."

In the 1960s, Kaz read *MAD*, superhero comics, and newspaper strips. Most of the strips that one can find echoes of in *Underworld*, his current weekly strip, were Kaz's favorites by grade school: Gould's *Dick Tracy*, Lasswell's *Barney Google*, and *Krazy Kat*, via the anthology *George Herriman's Krazy Kat*, with an introduction by ee cummings. "I loved *Krazy Kat* because it was a mystery to me," says Kaz. "I never understood it. Was Krazy male or female? Why were the backgrounds changing? In the back of the book, or somewhere, I don't know where, I saw a picture of Herriman sitting at his drawing board in a suit and hat. I thought, 'Hey, if that guy can do it, I can.' I've always been like that—if he can do it, I can do it."

It was the kind of self-confidence needed if you're going to become an artist in the Prapuolenis household. Through a Bud Plant catalogue, Kaz ordered old comic strip reprints. Then, by the time he was in junior high school, he sent away for some underground comics and got copies of *Mr. Natural*, *Zap* #2, and *Big Ass Comics*. "They blew my mind. I couldn't believe it. I had to hide them. There was no way they'd allow me to read those. I collected all of Crumb's comics when I was a teenager. What I loved about Crumb was that he had a huge cast of characters and continued to create more new characters with each new comic book. He allowed his imagination to run wild and hit many different notes. Even when he was at his most mean, his work had a warm squishiness that I loved. *Fritz the Cat* was fantastic. *Mr. Natural* was the first Crumb comic I ever read. But I also loved the minor characters like Boingy Baxter and that fat kid with the fork. Mr. Snoid...Spider-Man went out the window at that point."

In high school, Kaz drew more and more. "I used to draw cartoons with a friend of mine. He was good at drawing cars. I could draw monsters. So, basically, we just drew lots of monsters driving cars. But that's what I liked about underground comics. They were funny and obviously only because the people making them thought so—not because anybody told them how to do it." At home, Kaz drew a copy of the cover of *Mr. Natural* #2 that his mother hung up in the living room. "She was just impressed that I could do anything halfway decent," says Kaz. At school one day, students were asked to write down the name of a person who did what they wanted to do for a living. Kaz put on a name tag that said, "Robert Crumb," and his junior high school English teacher said, approvingly, "Robert Crumb—he's some cartoonist, huh?"

That a teacher knew of Crumb actually made cartooning seem like a career choice. So far, that was all the encouragement Kaz had received as an artist. Except for his Mr. Natural sketch, his parents were clueless to his interests in pop culture. He still remembers vividly the time he got his father to take him to see *A Clockwork Orange*. "I could just feel him tense up during the movie. I was fourteen and I just said to him, 'We're not leaving.'" Still, Kaz sat down and thought up his first strip, *Mr. Roach*. "I thought I'd send it in and get it syndicated. I sent my strips off to all these cartoonists. The only one who wrote back was Russell Meyers, who did *Broom Hilda*. I was really excited because it came on stationery with all his characters on it. Basically, he said, 'Keep at it.'"

Besides comics, the other major discovery for the teenage Kaz was music. His uncle Alex had moved in with the family and played Kaz his copy of the New York Dolls album. "He was into the rock scene and somehow knew the Dolls. At first I was looking at that cover of them in makeup, and I was like, 'Whoa, I'm not ready for this.' But my uncle loved the whole idea of the Dolls making fun of what a rock band was supposed to look like. Then I got into it. He read the music magazines, like Lester Bangs's *Creem* from Detroit." The following excerpt from *Punk* magazine, read today, sounds like an *Underworld* gag between Creep Rat and Snuff.

RICHARD HELL: *Did you ever read Nietzsche?*

LEGS McNEIL: *Ha ha ha.*

RICHARD HELL: *Legs, listen to me, he said that anything that makes you laugh, anything, that's funny indicates an emotion that's died. Every time you laugh that's an emotion, a serious emotion that doesn't exist with you anymore...and that's why I think you and everything else is so funny.*

LEGS McNEIL: *Yeah, I do too, but that's not funny.*

RICHARD HELL: *That's cause you don't have any emotions [hysterical laughter].*

Unlike comics, which came from newspapers, catalogues, and San Francisco underground publishers, the New York music scene was a train ride away. Like so many people in the outlying New York area, Manhattan was the fantasy world you watched from across the river. From his bedroom window, Kaz saw the World Trade Center towers go up.

In 2007, punk music is a genre: it means spiky hair, three-minute power-pop songs, sneers from teenagers (or worse, paunchy forty-year-olds with spiky hair), strategically torn jeans, and hating record labels. In the winter of 1976, on Kaz's first trip to CBGB's, punk was an art-rock scene. Patti Smith, the Ramones, the pre-disco Blondie, Television, the Voidoids, Talking Heads, the Dead Boys, the Damned—only a few of them fit today's definition of punk.

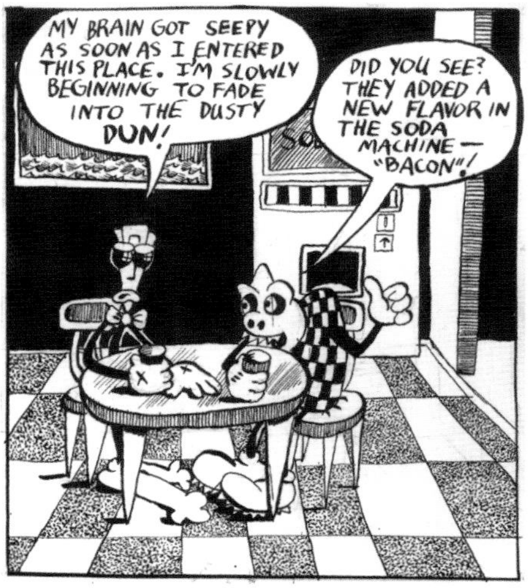
MY BRAIN GOT SEEPY AS SOON AS I ENTERED THIS PLACE. I'M SLOWLY BEGINNING TO FADE INTO THE DUSTY DUN!
DID YOU SEE? THEY ADDED A NEW FLAVOR IN THE SODA MACHINE — "BACON"!

Original art detail for "On the Avenue," unpublished, 1980. Kaz's first attempt at a weekly strip.

Kaz and his friends from Jersey saw shows like Queen, Aerosmith, and Emerson, Lake, & Palmer at Madison Square Garden. On his own, Kaz got high at home listening to Patti Smith's *Horses* again and again on his headphones. "I read in the *Village Voice* that she hung out at a dive bar called CBGB's," says Kaz. "I asked my friends to go into New York to see this 'punk music.' They told me 'punk is for fags.'" "So I went by myself," says Kaz, "took a train but forgot to bring my map of Manhattan. I got turned around exiting the F Train on 2nd Avenue and walked around in circles in the East Village for an hour, praying the winos wouldn't kill me. When I finally found CBGB's, it was like finding the lost tomb of King Punkarocka."

At his first show, Kaz saw the Ramones. He ended up seeing them maybe thirty times over the years. He tried Max's Kansas City, but they carded him and wouldn't sell him beer. At CB's he found himself one of the younger people in a punk scene then made up of older bohemians, intellectuals, and hipsters. "They wore shades inside," says Kaz. "There was no pogo or slam dancing back then. I remember sitting at the bar up by the stage, with everyone crowded together and I looked over and next to me was Patti Smith."

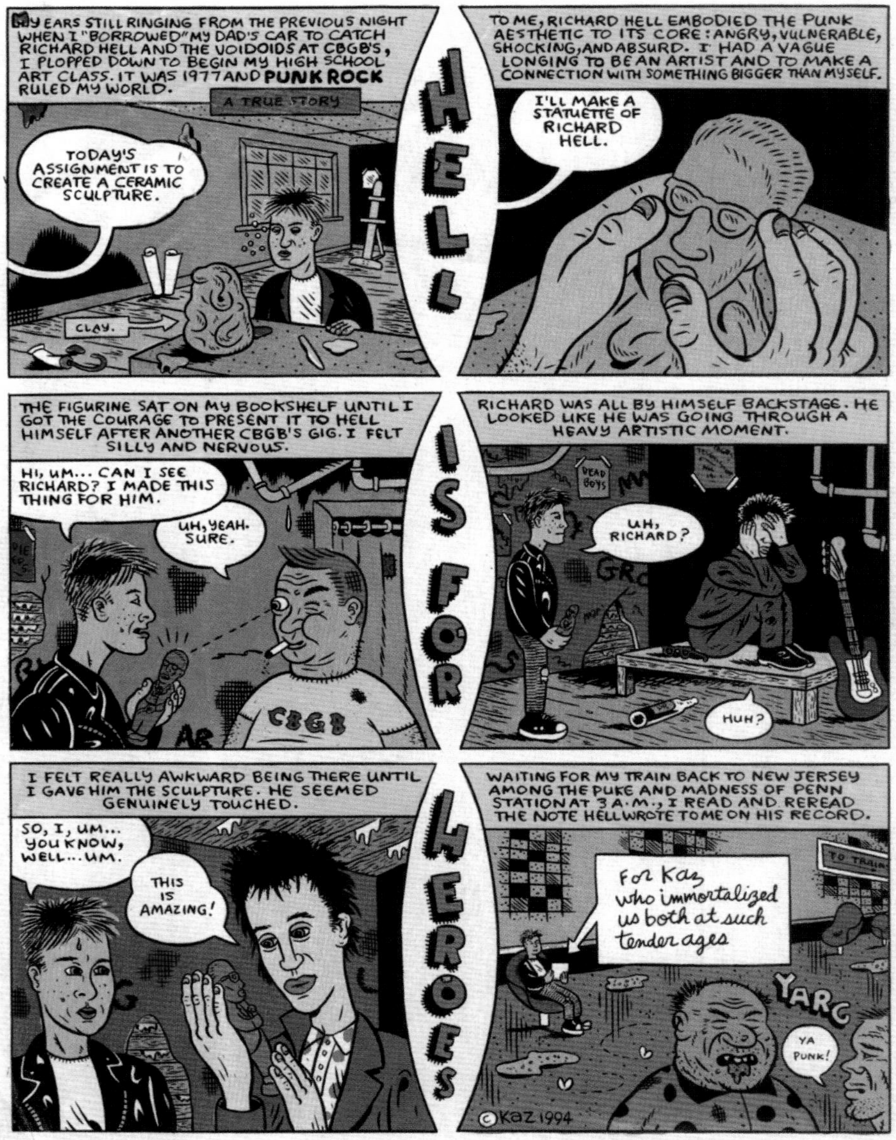

HELL IS FOR HEROES
MY EARS STILL RINGING FROM THE PREVIOUS NIGHT WHEN I "BORROWED" MY DAD'S CAR TO CATCH RICHARD HELL AND THE VOIDOIDS AT CBGB'S, I PLOPPED DOWN TO BEGIN MY HIGH SCHOOL ART CLASS. IT WAS 1977 AND PUNK ROCK RULED MY WORLD.
A TRUE STORY
TODAY'S ASSIGNMENT IS TO CREATE A CERAMIC SCULPTURE.
CLAY.
TO ME, RICHARD HELL EMBODIED THE PUNK AESTHETIC TO ITS CORE: ANGRY, VULNERABLE, SHOCKING, AND ABSURD. I HAD A VAGUE LONGING TO BE AN ARTIST AND TO MAKE A CONNECTION WITH SOMETHING BIGGER THAN MYSELF.
I'LL MAKE A STATUETTE OF RICHARD HELL.
THE FIGURINE SAT ON MY BOOKSHELF UNTIL I GOT THE COURAGE TO PRESENT IT TO HELL HIMSELF AFTER ANOTHER CBGB'S GIG. I FELT SILLY AND NERVOUS.
HI, UM... CAN I SEE RICHARD? I MADE THIS THING FOR HIM.
UH, YEAH. SURE.
CBGB
RICHARD WAS ALL BY HIMSELF BACKSTAGE. HE LOOKED LIKE HE WAS GOING THROUGH A HEAVY ARTISTIC MOMENT.
DEAD BOYS
UH, RICHARD?
HUH?
I FELT REALLY AWKWARD BEING THERE UNTIL I GAVE HIM THE SCULPTURE. HE SEEMED GENUINELY TOUCHED.
SO, I, UM... YOU KNOW, WELL... UM.
THIS IS AMAZING!
WAITING FOR MY TRAIN BACK TO NEW JERSEY AMONG THE PUKE AND MADNESS OF PENN STATION AT 3 A.M., I READ AND REREAD THE NOTE HELL WROTE TO ME ON HIS RECORD.
For Kaz who immortalized us both at such tender ages
YARG
YA PUNK!
©KAZ 1994

"Hell is for Heroes," *Details*, June 1994.

Punk was his social life and the focus of his creativity. "I did this drawing of the Ramones once. I saw Tommy Ramone standing at the bar one night, and I mumbled, 'Uh, I did this drawing of the Ramones.' And he said, 'That's really cool; we gotta show this to the guys.' He brought me to the dressing room, and there I am in this tiny room with the Ramones standing all around me looking at my drawing. And they're asking me all these questions, 'How come you gave us so much stubble? How come you drew it that way? Why am I so short?' They're *criticizing* my drawing. I just wanted to get out of there." The Ramones had just come back from England where they inspired the snarling genre version of punk popular now. Their album *Ramones* was out, and Kaz saw the arrival of the Dead Boys, an all-time favorite. They released *Young, Loud, and Snotty*, sporting such classics as "Caught With the Meat in Your Mouth" and "Sonic Reducer." Featuring clowns like Cheetah Chrome and Stiv Bators, Kaz loved that the Dead Boys parodied the whole idea of rock bands but could still really rock.

By 1977, Kaz was a high school graduate and had no idea about college, a future, or what to do with himself. He got factory jobs like his dad: in a bug spray plant (where, one guesses, dreams of *Mr. Roach* went to die), another building air conditioners, and another shipping boxes. He spent as much time as he could out drinking at clubs or getting high at work. It was the perfect frame of mind for a teen punk, and no doubt why Richard Hell was so important to Kaz's days haunting CBGB's. Critics like Lester Bangs, a holdover from the hippie days of believing rock could change the world, got more into the preachy morality "punk" of the Clash. The CB's scene Kaz loved saw it differently.

As filmmaker Mary Harron noted in the oral history *Please Kill Me*: "We didn't have anything to be idealistic about, and I was so sick of hippie culture...It was like you were forced to be optimistic and caring and good...I found it nauseating and prissy and sentimental, and smiley-faced. So Richard Hell just came over and said, 'This is what we are, we're the blank generation. It's over.'" Hell was an intimidating figure to many, but Kaz got the joke. "He was kinda funny looking. The music of the Voidoids was off-kilter in a churning, elastic way that I found really wacky and stimulating. Even the name Voidoids sounds silly. I loved Richard Hell's lyrics with their beatnik-by-way-of-dada cartoonist expressions. "Blank Generation" was the first song that expressed how I felt. It was pissed off, bemused, and misanthropic at the same time. On stage, Richard Hell and the Voidoids looked all wrong. The four members looked like they were from different bands. I liked the messiness of it. I was a mess."

At one point, Kaz literally idolized Hell by making a small statue of him, which he gave to Hell, depicted in Kaz's 1994 strip "Hell is for Heroes" in *Sidetrack City*. Years later, at a book signing, Kaz asked Hell if he remembered the statue. Hell had kept it, but had lost it when he moved. It was around this period, the blankest, when Kaz wandered drunk into the purgatory of Penn Station, the place where he discovered *Dick Tracy* as a kid and hated his new life as a freshly minted adult. The only thing he could think to do was express it creatively, but that wasn't working so well. That night, he let his imagination run wild during the hours-long wait for the train home.

"The game that I played with myself was that everything was art. I would memorize what I was looking at and take stock of my emotions. I would infuse my emotions into landscapes and architecture. The train ride back home at dawn would pass the industrial areas of the Northeast. The rusted, crumbling factories of Newark, New Jersey, became haunted houses where ghostly silent comedians played out their slapstick rituals inside. Some streets were angry while others stupid. I started drawing again. It was hard. I grew frustrated that my hand wasn't doing what my mind saw. I felt that I needed some guidance, some training. The idea of going to art school appealed to me. Thank God I hadn't dropped out of high school."

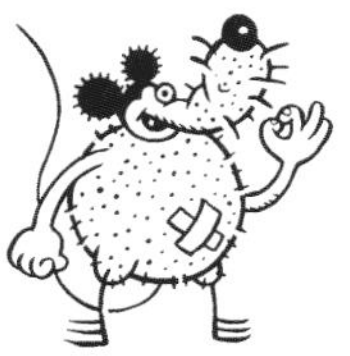

IN 1978, Kaz looked at Pratt in Brooklyn, but then saw the catalogue for the School of Visual Arts. He had soaked up enough comics history to see something important. "I saw Art Spiegelman's name, I saw Harvey Kurtzman's name, I saw Will Eisner's name. I knew I wanted to go there." Silas H. Rhodes and cartoonist Burne Hogarth founded the School of Visual Arts on 209 E. 23rd Street in 1947. It advertised itself as a trade school for cartoonists and illustrators and boasted a faculty who were all working professionals, meaning students learned from people who made a living at what they taught, not simply academics. Today SVA considers itself a fine-arts institution and names no cartoonists on its online alumni listings.

First-year cartooning students did not get to take any cartooning classes. They took everything but. "A little taste of everything," says Kaz. "Sculpting, painting, photography. Most cartoonists I knew hated it. But I gotta say, I *loved* it. I was like, 'You mean I get to take pictures and play around in this darkroom? You mean I get to mold this clay and stare at this naked model all day?' I never felt more like a cliché artist than when I was sculpting her butt with my hands." For a kid who had never been encouraged to do much creatively, SVA was a playground he had been waiting to get on all his life. Kaz met more punks like himself, including a girlfriend that he could share the scene with in Manhattan—which he had mainly done alone all through high school.

"It was a great place to go to college for people who didn't want to go to college," says Art Spiegelman today. "It was a very tiny cartooning department. Me, Eisner, and Kurtzman—and we never even met officially. I was kind of shocked that we didn't. We each had our own little school and did what we wanted." Spiegelman was surprised by more than that—he could barely communicate with most of his students. "I asked them to write a short essay on their favorite comic strip. Finding out they couldn't write was scary. Those that could had nothing to say—it was all on a level of Marvel Comics and *Garfield*."

Spiegelman made some decisions that had a profound effect on Kaz and the next generation of cartoonists. First, there were no required classes, meaning he didn't have to teach anyone who didn't want to be there. "I just didn't have anything to offer someone who wanted to draw Marvel Comics," he says. Second, Spiegelman thought out a new course, one intended to create a shared language of comics with his students. That is, create a frame of reference so that he could discuss comics with them at all. Comix 101, the lecture Spiegelman tours with today, is a microcosm of what his students got. "Where audiences today see a slide of McCay or Crumb," Spiegelman says, "at SVA I'd spend ninety minutes alone on McCay or Feininger." "I wanted to show how the boxes add up to a page as well as being individual boxes," says Spiegelman, and the form, history, and content of comics—with a canon heavy on newspaper strips and not superheroes—became that new frame of reference for his students.

Kaz also found himself with a group of students whose names are familiar to comics fans today, if not then: Drew Friedman, Mark Newgarden, Peter Bagge (in night classes), and later, Dan Clowes, taking the train over from Pratt to sit in on Spiegelman's lectures. Keith Haring was an art student at the time, as well as DC Comics editor Mike Carlin. *Punk* magazine founder John Holmstrom was in Kurtzman's class years before, and guest lecturers included Edward Sorel, Arnold Roth, Ralph Steadman, *New Yorker* artists, and visits from friends of the faculty like Crumb or Jay Lynch.

Kaz was exposed to a range of new ideas, from teacher Jerry Moriarty turning him on to the formal genius of Ernie Bushmiller's *Nancy* to Kaz walking in on a student video screening in which Keith Haring showed a video of himself having sex with a large black man. "Don't remind me," says Kaz. "Everyone in the room was *very* uncomfortable." He also met the Friedman-Newgarden clique of the cartooning department, who may have been the world's only art school bullies, or at least, class clowns with a mean bite.

"Kaz and I never officially 'met,'" says Friedman. "We just sort of encountered each other in Kurtzman's and Spiegelman's classes, fall 1980. I don't remember Kaz being funny in class. He was kind of quiet. We took an instant dislike to each other: he the sneering, Jersey City Punk in cutoff black T-shirts, and me, the smug Upper West Side privileged Jewboy. He had a couple of punky pals he'd hang with. I had my friends and he had his. I thought he was definitely talented, and he knew his comic history, too, from Segar to Kurtzman. But the punk style put me off." "Uh, that sounds about right," says Kaz. "Drew was a star right away; he had his style and never deviated from it. He had a lot of self-confidence that could come across as narcissism and ego, and it reflected in his friends, too, who weren't as talented. I kept my distance."

"Kaz looked like a punk," says Peter Bagge, who got to know Kaz around this time. "Though not of the retarded mohawk-and-safety-pins variety, he more or less had his own 'look,' in that from the waist down he was Joe Strummer, but from the belt up he was Wally Cox. And it worked! He was a sharp dresser, I thought."

Kaz sat through one Eisner lecture and never went back. The teacher Kaz connected with was Spiegelman. Kaz walked in knowing the classics Spiegelman taught as well as his teacher's underground work from *Arcade* and earlier, but it was all a jumble in Kaz's mind. "He gave me context for all that," says Kaz.

"Kaz was the best student I ever had at being a student. A great synthesizer," recalls Spiegelman. "But he didn't get stuck there, which is to say, show him Feininger and by god he's there—OK, he does little

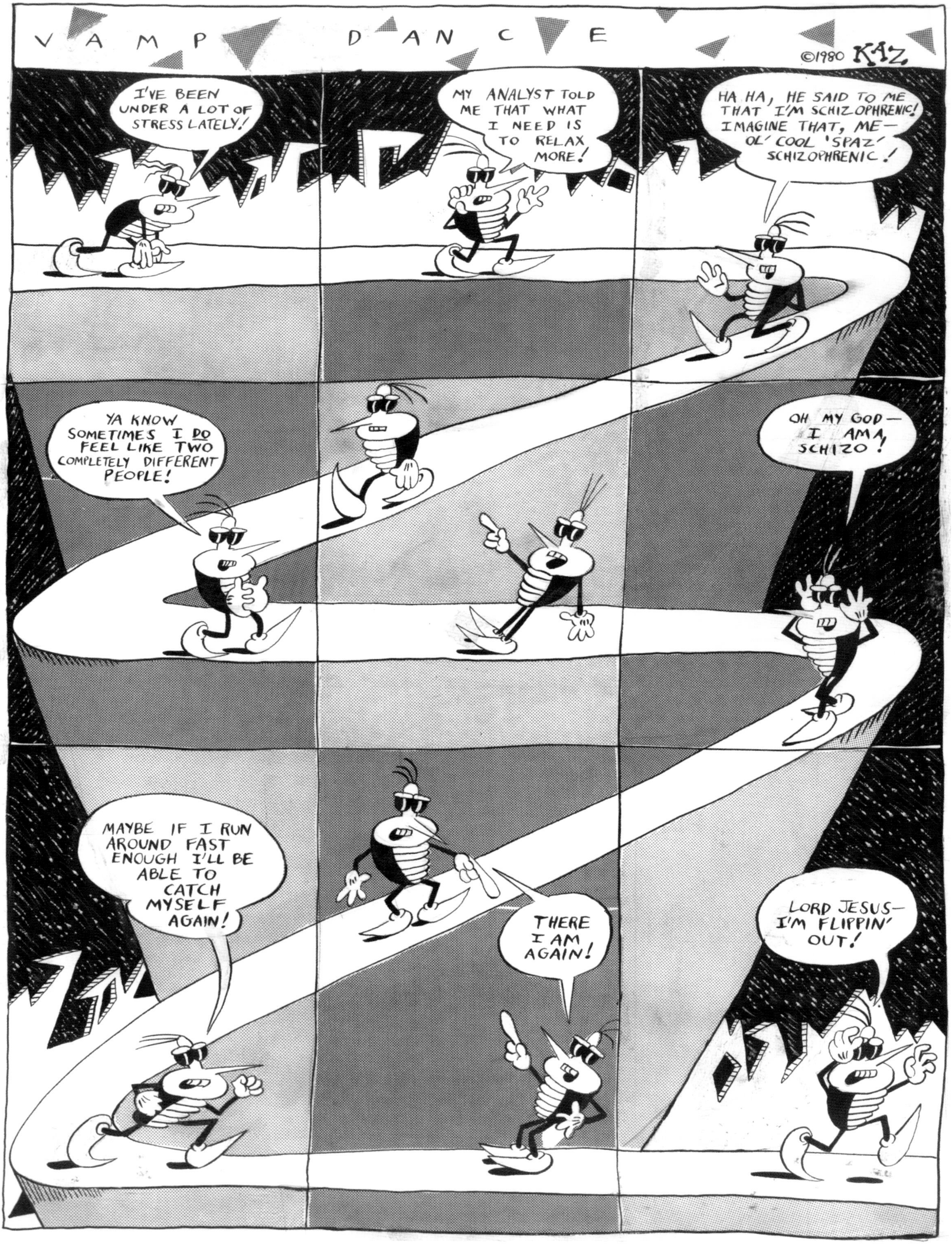
V A M P D A N C E
©1980 KAZ
I'VE BEEN UNDER A LOT OF STRESS LATELY!
MY ANALYST TOLD ME THAT WHAT I NEED IS TO RELAX MORE!
HA HA, HE SAID TO ME THAT I'M SCHIZOPHRENIC! IMAGINE THAT, ME— OL' COOL 'SPAZ' SCHIZOPHRENIC!
YA KNOW SOMETIMES I DO FEEL LIKE TWO COMPLETELY DIFFERENT PEOPLE!
OH MY GOD— I AM A SCHIZO!
MAYBE IF I RUN AROUND FAST ENOUGH I'LL BE ABLE TO CATCH MYSELF AGAIN!
THERE I AM AGAIN!
LORD JESUS— I'M FLIPPIN' OUT!

architectural drawings holding the page together, right. Backgrounds change in *Krazy Kat*, got it. Show a brush line from *Dick Tracy* and a diagrammatic approach to drawing, check! Kurtzman rhythmically builds up same-sized panels, got it! Segar, doodle drawing, got it. I can't remember anybody who was on the same frequency to pick up what I had to offer."

In Kurtzman's class, Kaz (like most who took it) was disappointed to find out the creator of *MAD* was not passing on what he knew best, sequential comics, nor was he passionate about teaching. He taught single-panel gag cartooning, and students stayed hoping to glean anything from him. Kaz did not have the rapport he did with Spiegelman. One story Kaz recalls sums it up: "Harvey was working on all these complex overlays, probably for a *Little Annie Fanny*, and I was looking over his shoulder as he worked on each one, page after page of them." Anyone who has seen the complexity of Kurtzman's *Annie* layouts for Will Elder knows what Kaz saw; many of them now sell as original art. They were done and redone and redone to help Kurtzman block out action and compose his dense panels, none of which made sense to his punky protégé. Looking over his shoulder, Kaz said, "If it was me, I'd just tear it up and start over."

Kurtzman stopped, sighed, and without looking up said in measured tone, "Yeah, I guess that's one way of doing it." Kaz took the hint and sat down. In his first collection, *Buzzbomb*, he quotes Kurtzman saying, "I never thought that guy would make it!" Says Spiegelman, "I remember a conversation one day where Harvey asked how Kaz was doing, and I said 'great.' 'Good,' Harvey said, 'I never knew what to do with him.' It wasn't that he thought Kaz lacked talent, he knew it was there, he just didn't know how to get to it."

One day Spiegelman asked Kaz if he would like to be part of a studio class where he would work with Spiegelman and a select group of other students like Friedman and Newgarden, and Kaz jumped at the chance. "It meant a lot to me that Art would ask me," says Kaz. "It was a real validation." Spiegelman's studio class involved comics history but also guest lecturers and assignments, like taking a page of Mark Twain and drawing it as a comic. He gave his students practical lessons in the profession, too, encouraging them to knock on doors and find magazines and newspapers and get in print. "He told us that seeing our work in print, published, was the best lesson we'd ever get. And he was right." Spiegelman says today, "As soon as you publish this thing, you get to find out what your black lines are looking like when they're reduced and whether your lettering is too small or your Zipatone has fingerprints on it, at least back in the day, when Zipatone still existed. It catapulted you ahead."

Unlike Kurtzman, whose class was like a party, Spiegelman's was a place to get serious or get out. "I remember Spiegelman's lectures and 'studio classes' being one in the same," says Friedman. "I was bored during the lectures. Art read the comics in a mind-numbing monotone." Spiegelman himself had little time for Friedman and Newgarden's heckling and sat them at opposite ends of the room like 4th graders. If Kurtzman ignored it, Spiegelman stopped the class cold and said, "I'm not here for the money, you know."

Guest lecturers like Mark Beyer visited the studio class. "I bought my first Mark Beyer comic off Mark Beyer, because he brought them," says Kaz. "I loved his stuff. To me it was punk rock, gothic, plus every kind of paranoia—in this one particular, fucked-up, flat, folk-art horror style—I don't even know how to talk about it properly. To me it was funny and scary at the same time. It influenced me. I saw that he was coming from places I was looking at, too." Spiegelman recalls, "Beyer didn't want to come because Beyer is painfully, painfully shy—I remember having to leave the class to have to coax him into the room. And he showed slides, mumbling, and at some point in the Q&A afterward, Kaz raised his hand and said, 'Do you draw that way because you want to or because you have to?' And then Beyer ends up clutching his beret and pulling it down almost over his eyes, as far down as it goes, and gets this agonized expression on his face and says, 'You're right, you're right, I don't know why I do it, I don't know!' And he just about scooted out of the classroom before I could get to him and almost had to run out to the street to bring him back. It just left him trembling. And poor Kaz was not at all being nasty. He loved the stuff and was just trying to understand it."

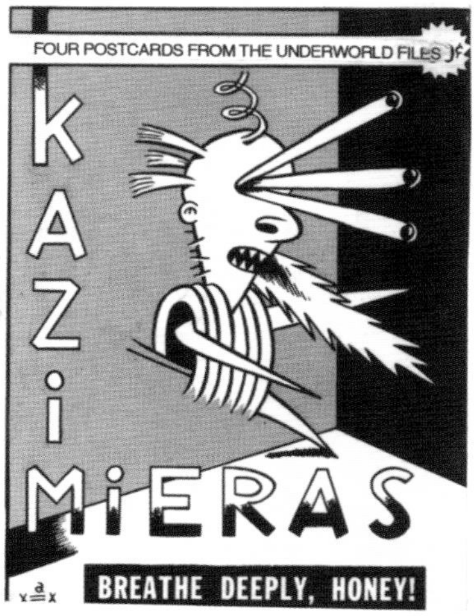
FOUR POSTCARDS FROM THE UNDERWORLD FILES
KAZi
MiERAS
BREATHE DEEPLY, HONEY!

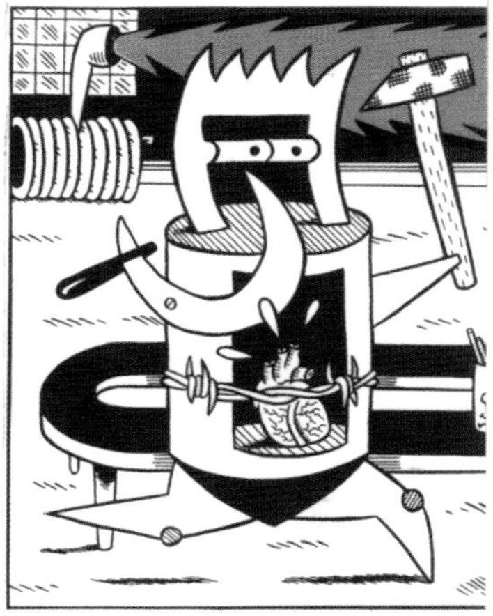

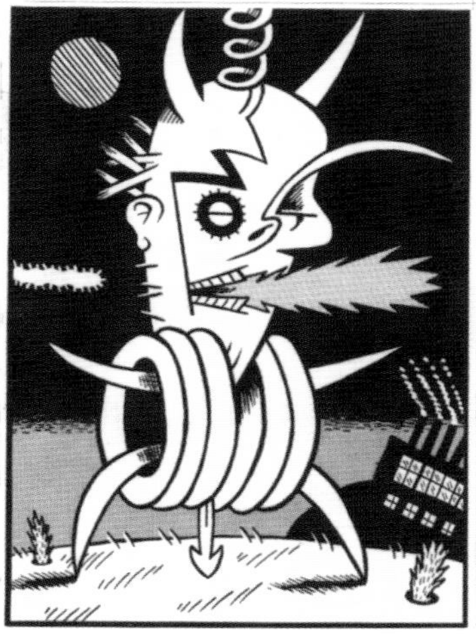

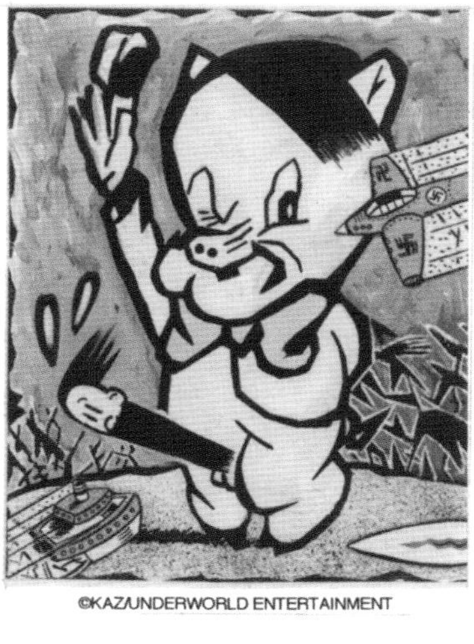

Opposite: Original art for "Vamp Dance," *RAW* #1 (RAW Books & Graphics, 1980).

Right: Postcard designs, 1980s.

Kaz began to actively incorporate the design elements and literal deconstructions that Spiegelman walked them through into his own work. That is, breaking the big box of a page into its little boxes and then rebuilding it. Beyer's style, for example, is incorporated in an early strip called "The Disappearance of Mr. Teeth." Kaz filled his work with goofy, punky characters—skeletons, bugs, ghouls. But he planted them in a classically rectangular full-page Sunday comics layout, as if his characters were squatters in once great buildings that had become slums when their original owners—Herriman, Sterret, Segar, and McCay—left the neighborhood years ago. The skeleton parade in "Vamp Dance," a riff on Buster Keaton's *Cops*, looks like a haunted Herriman house full of cartoon ghosts.

"Art was into deconstruction," says Kaz. "He liked taking the comics apart to teach you how it was done. What you see in those pages is me learning how to be a cartoonist, doing stuff you can look at for itself or commenting on itself." That kind of ironic deconstruction, which Kaz loved in the Dead Boys and the Ramones—bands making fun of rock but still delivering it—is a central theme and creative tool for Kaz that has lasted his whole career. He uses it to explore the medium as well as entertain readers who can follow him that way. Even if they can't, it's still just funny as a read.

"The nature of my lectures, which included very close readings of stories and pages of the cartoonists I introduced the students to, encouraged that kind of self-reflexiveness," says Spiegelman. "It's certainly been part of my own approach to comics for decades and, I guess, infected the classes." While at SVA, Kaz acted on Spiegelman's advice and came up with a strip he thought he could sell. Called *The Pests*, the strip depicted an insect rock band. He went down to the *East Village Eye*, which at one time published Crumb, Richard Hell, and other underground artists, and the *Eye* accepted them. A week went by, two, a month, and the strips never ran. Kaz, too shy to call, took it as a rejection. "So I went down to the *New York Rocker* and said, 'You gotta have cartoons in your paper.' They really liked them and accepted them. The next week, both the *New York Rocker* and the *East Village Eye* ran *The Pests*! The guys at the *Rocker* were really angry. They said they liked them but only wanted to run them if they could have it exclusively. So I said OK, but it has to run once a month, and they agreed."

The success continued. "I was still living at my parents' house in Rahway," recalls Kaz, "and the phone rang. I'll never forget, I was in my parents' kitchen and my dad came in and said, in that accent, 'Aht Shpee-gull-mun?' I was done with his studio class and never figured I'd see him again, but he said he was putting a new magazine together. I had been drawing strips and brought them in. He probably liked them because I was experimenting with ideas he taught us in class!" The new magazine Spiegelman and his wife, designer and publisher Françoise Mouly, were putting together was called *RAW*.

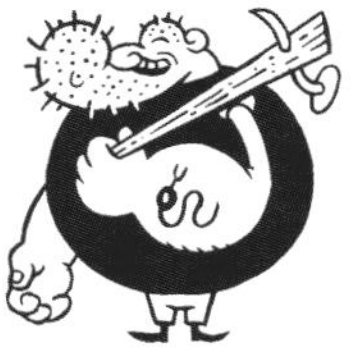

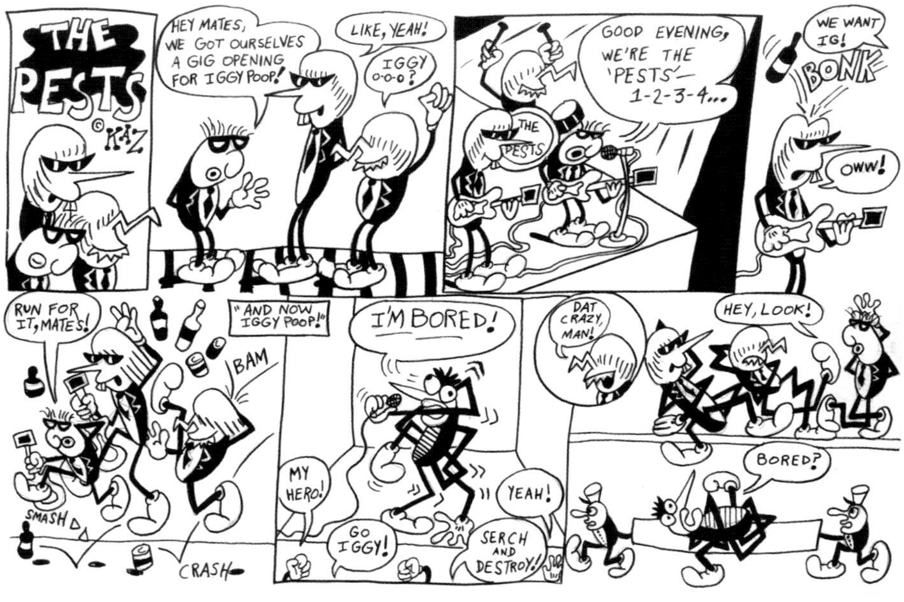
THE PESTS
©KAZ
HEY MATES, WE GOT OURSELVES A GIG OPENING FOR IGGY POOP!
LIKE, YEAH!
IGGY O-O-O?
GOOD EVENING, WE'RE THE 'PESTS'— 1-2-3-4...
THE PESTS
WE WANT IG!
BONK
OWW!
RUN FOR IT, MATES!
SMASH
BAM
CRASH
"AND NOW IGGY POOP!"
I'M BORED!
MY HERO!
GO IGGY!
YEAH!
SERCH AND DESTROY!
DAT CRAZY, MAN!
HEY, LOOK!
BORED?

Original art for "The Pests," *New York Press*, 1979

FOR DECADES, journalists have written variations of the lead "Bam! Biff! Ka-Pow! Comics Have Grown Up," when they discuss artists who don't draw capes. In 1980, *RAW* appeared. It knew this fact, assumed you did, and went from there. *RAW* #1 gives the impression that Spiegelman and Mouly saw so much untapped talent in 1980 that they just had to publish it all. "No," says Spiegelman definitively. "There was some, but in fact, we were kind of appalled, Françoise and I, when we started rooting around. There wasn't all that much, but if you put it all together, you could make this great Potemkin village and make it look like there was a world instead of a settlement. It wasn't like *Punk* magazine where there was this scene going on and they said, 'We should do a magazine.' With *RAW* the idea wasn't even to do an ongoing magazine, but just once and show people what could be done."

Spiegelman accepted Kaz's "Vamp Dance," a Sunday-sized strip, as well as work by Beyer, Joost Swarte, the Friedman brothers, Mark Newgarden, Jerry Moriarty, and Spiegelman's own insert, "Two-Fisted Painters." As Spiegelman and Mouly pulled the contents together, they called in Kaz, the other artists, and SVA students for "stapling parties." That is, the actual production of *RAW*. Kaz recalls, "They would have wine and cheese and we'd get together at their loft [for issue #1] and get to work."

"More or less," says Spiegelman, "we had chips and those horrible things that look like turds and make your hands orange. Cheese doodles. I think the first one might have been at our loft. At one point we used the Collective for Living Cinema's lobby during the day. For *RAW* #7 we used The Bindery, where they were especially appalled at what we did because we gave them such a hard time on the production, and paying throwaway flyer prices 'cause Françoise would negotiate to the point of them screaming, and then after all that fastidiousness, inviting people up to rip corners off the magazine (the 'torn again' issue)—they couldn't understand us."

At the parties, Kaz met other *RAW* contributors like Charles Burns, who lived in Philadelphia and stayed at Spiegelman's loft, or Sue Coe. "Some of the things she said just made me laugh," says Kaz, "like when she said she thought color was a capitalist tool." Kaz and Burns got to be friends and would go out for a beer when Burns was in town. Like so many of his artist friends, Kaz absorbed Burns into his own work, especially the inking. "Charles came to SVA," Kaz recalls, "and I remember seeing his stuff and thinking, 'Holy shit!' He wasn't even doing stories then. The first thing he ever did in *RAW* was more disassociated panels, like Lichtenstein, but the style was so amazing. Style was something that was extremely important to me. I would think about it all the time. I would think 'Who's style is it? What kind of style is it? How do I get more style? I need more style!' Clothing style, musical style, my hair style—everything was style."

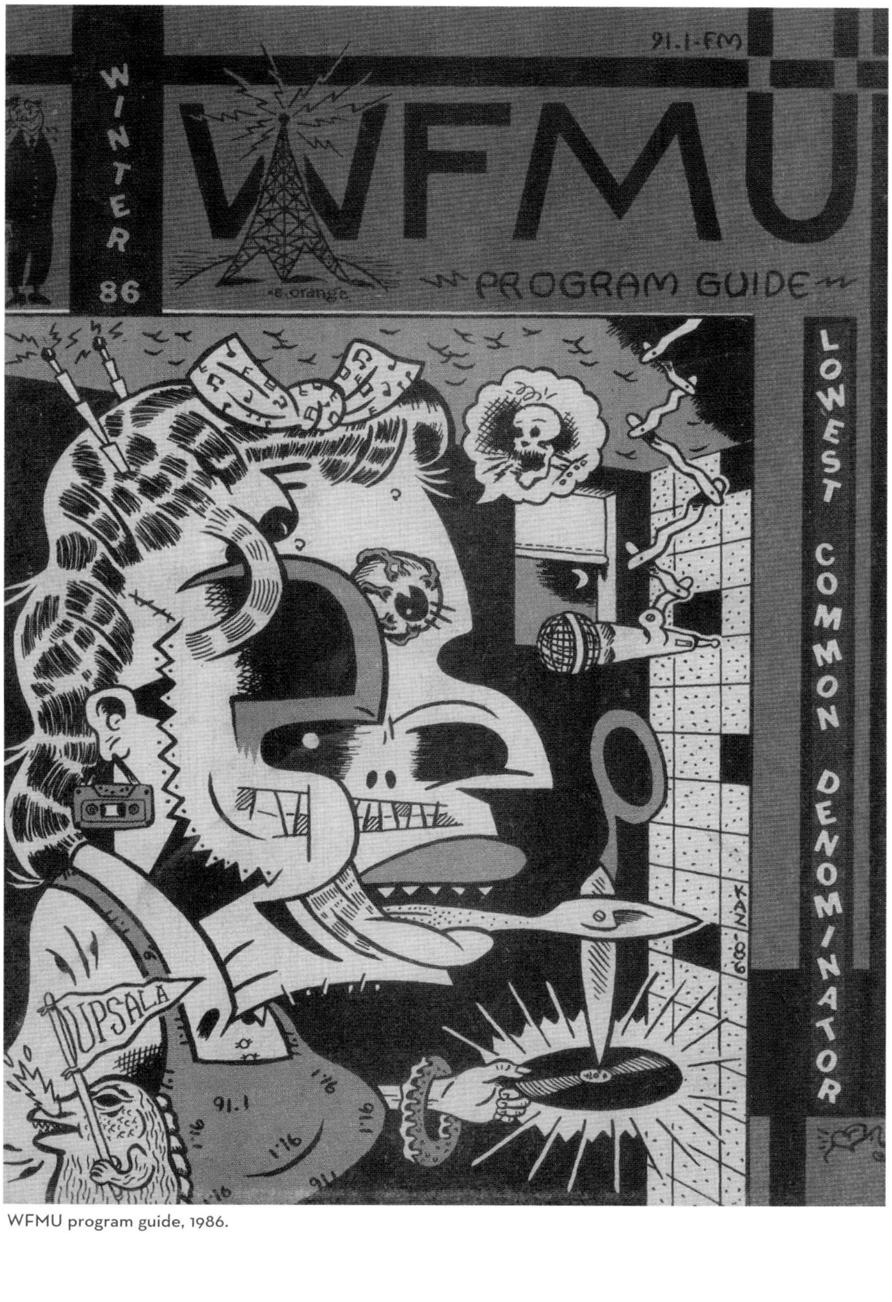
91.1-FM
WINTER 86
WFMU
PROGRAM GUIDE
LOWEST COMMON DENOMINATOR
UPSALA
KAZ '86
WFMU program guide, 1986.

As *RAW* #1 came together, Drew Friedman got to appreciate Kaz's sense of humor. "We saw each other at all the cartoonist parties in New York City throughout the '80s," says Friedman, "and he would also attend some of the VCR screenings I held at my apartment, not only *Plan 9*, but rare cartoons, old TV shows, Russ Meyer films...all that stuff was still incredibly rare at that time." If Kaz had first come to New York and hung out at the coolest scene in town as a fan, he was now part of one with *RAW*. Well, as far as comics were concerned. *RAW* sold out its 4,000-copy run quickly and a second issue was planned, as Spiegelman notes, "by popular demand of the artists."

As *RAW*'s cache grew, it made it easier to approach art directors for commercial work. "Oh, you're one of the *RAW* guys," Kaz recalls them saying while they looked over his portfolio. Appearing in *RAW* was a badge of honor in some circles, but an albatross around your neck in others. *RAW* made clear it saw comics as serious art and pop culture at the same time. It had humor in its ironic, Donald Barthelme self-awareness and its S.J. Perelman–level puns: "I Was a Saturday Evening Post-Modernist," "The Torn Again Graphix Magazine." But Spiegelman and Mouly aimed *RAW* at the intellectual reader, and the bias against fine arts was something Kaz had felt from his first days at SVA.

RAW opened up a critical debate still going on in comics, between the *RAW* ideal and those who think comics need to stick to their disposable, lowbrow roots. *RAW* was quickly answered by Holmstrom and Bagge's *Comical Funnies* and Crumb's *Weirdo*. "What was the difference between *RAW* and *Comical Funnies*?" says Bagge. "Everything! *CF* was extremely crude and ugly and dumb and amateurish compared to *RAW*. It was also better! I personally had mixed feelings about *RAW*, but I liked a lot of the artists in it, and Artie was pretty good to me for the most part, when he wasn't busy yelling at me for drawing willfully dumb comics, for hanging out with people like Holmstrom, and for always hitting him up for information."

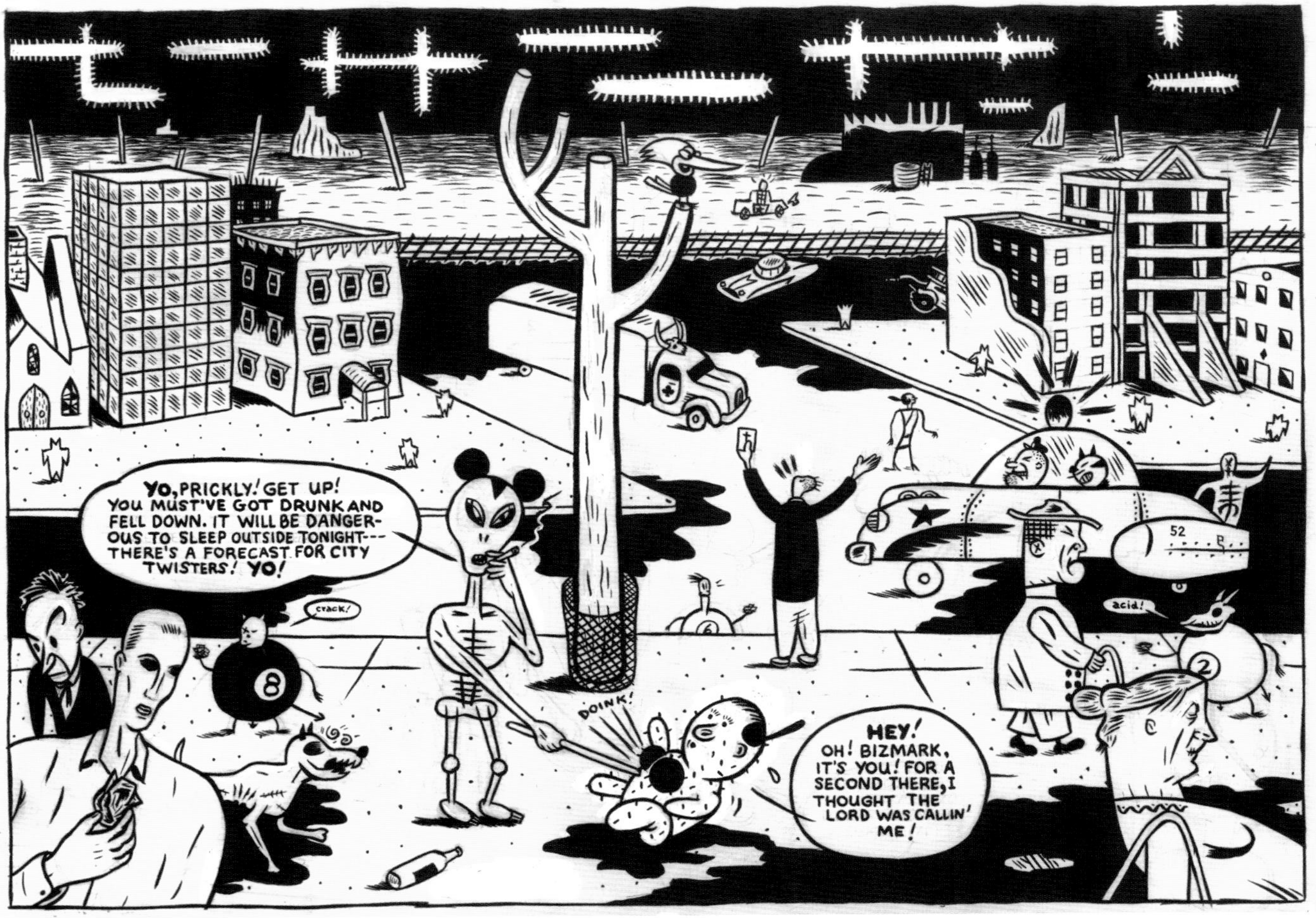
YO, PRICKLY! GET UP! YOU MUST'VE GOT DRUNK AND FELL DOWN. IT WILL BE DANGEROUS TO SLEEP OUTSIDE TONIGHT--- THERE'S A FORECAST FOR CITY TWISTERS! YO!
crack!
acid!
DOINK!
HEY! OH! BIZMARK, IT'S YOU! FOR A SECOND THERE, I THOUGHT THE LORD WAS CALLIN' ME!

Original art detail for *Sidetrack City and Other Tales* (Fantagraphics Books, 1997).

Bagge continues, "Kaz really looked up to Art, though. He really considered him a mentor. I might have given Kaz a hard time about that. I called him a 'spiegelboy,' a nickname for all the young cartoonists who worked closely with Art and were heavily influenced by him. But then he would give me an equally hard time about being willfully lowbrow. It really wasn't a big deal, though, as far as I was concerned. The other *CF* cartoonists might have been a bit more leery of Kaz because of his *RAW* association—mainly because they were more into defining separate 'camps' and indulging in 'us vs. them' talk than I was—but I never got the feeling that they disliked Kaz or his work. Quite the opposite, in fact. We were all just copping attitudes back then. It was stupid."

Few cartoonists fit both aesthetics, but Kaz is at the top of the list. "I picked up a copy of *Comical Funnies*. I thought it was funny," says Kaz, "and I was thinking about doing a humor strip along with the weirder, artier stuff I was doing. I called Peter Bagge up and said 'Hey, I'd like to do some comics for you.' At first I know he was a little tentative. He said, 'Well, this is humor,' and I said, 'Yeah, I know.' I remember going over to his apartment in Manhattan at the time, somewhere on the West Side. I brought over some comics I did that I thought were funny. And he read them. And I remember he said, 'Hey these are funny…' like you'd say, 'Hey, guess what?' Hey Mikey—they're funny. He didn't expect a *RAW* guy to be funny."

Bagge concurs. "I first met Kaz in person in late 1980 or early '81, when he stopped by my house and gave me some strips to use in *Comical Funnies*. He sorta had this surly 'punk' attitude, of the 'I'm-gonna-make-fun-of-you-first' variety, but he seemed like a nice guy in spite of it. A year later I moved to Hoboken, where Kaz was already living, and from that point on we hung out pretty regularly." "I was looking like a rough punk rocker," says Kaz, "And Pete always had a jaundiced eye for the rock scene in New York—for trendiness, artiness—set himself up as being against it. I got along with him, I thought he was funny. He was doing Junior, the Goon on the Moon, and later Martini Baton, and to me, I was like, this is funny. Through him I met J.D. King, John Holmstrom, Ken Weiner—who later on became an art director at *Screw*, where I did some covers."

Another plus to the *CF* crowd for Kaz was their parties. *RAW* parties meant wine and cheese (or cheese doodles), or long, fascinating, theory-filled conversations with Burns or Gary Panter, or hanging out at Friedman's apartment watching rare videos. It centered around being an artist, one way or the other. "The *Comical Funnies* guys were *fun* to hang around with," says Kaz. "They were very cutting. The art of the put-down was important to those guys. You couldn't turn your back without catching it. Completely different from the *RAW*/SVA crowd. Lots of beer. I loved that." "Yes, we *CF*-ers liked to throw parties," says Bagge today. "Our wives and girlfriends liked to cook and play hostess, while we guys would all eat and drink too much and insult each other and then fall down and break things. I don't know what *RAW* parties were like in

Opposite: Original art for *Sidetrack City and Other Tales* (Fantagraphics Books, 1997).

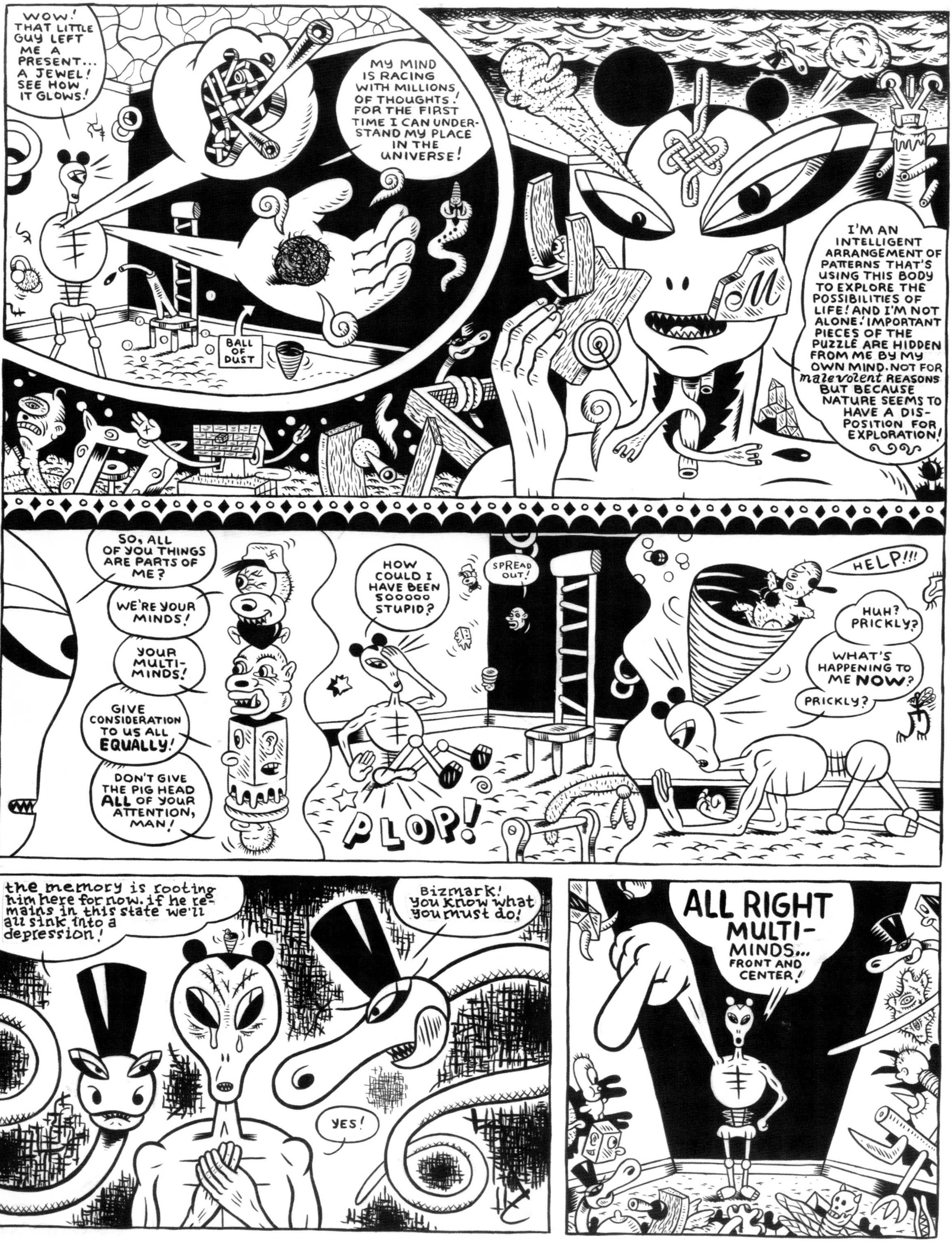
WOW! THAT LITTLE GUY LEFT ME A PRESENT... A JEWEL! SEE HOW IT GLOWS!
MY MIND IS RACING WITH MILLIONS OF THOUGHTS! FOR THE FIRST TIME I CAN UNDERSTAND MY PLACE IN THE UNIVERSE!
BALL OF DUST
I'M AN INTELLIGENT ARRANGEMENT OF PATTERNS THAT'S USING THIS BODY TO EXPLORE THE POSSIBILITIES OF LIFE! AND I'M NOT ALONE! IMPORTANT PIECES OF THE PUZZLE ARE HIDDEN FROM ME BY MY OWN MIND. NOT FOR malevolent REASONS BUT BECAUSE NATURE SEEMS TO HAVE A DISPOSITION FOR EXPLORATION!
SO, ALL OF YOU THINGS ARE PARTS OF ME?
WE'RE YOUR MINDS!
YOUR MULTI-MINDS!
GIVE CONSIDERATION TO US ALL EQUALLY!
DON'T GIVE THE PIG HEAD ALL OF YOUR ATTENTION, MAN!
HOW COULD I HAVE BEEN SOOOOO STUPID?
SPREAD OUT!
PLOP!
HELP!!!
HUH? PRICKLY?
WHAT'S HAPPENING TO ME NOW?
PRICKLY?
the memory is rooting him here for now. if he remains in this state we'll all sink into a depression!
Bizmark! you know what you must do!
YES!
ALL RIGHT MULTI-MINDS... FRONT AND CENTER!

KAZ
SIDETRACK CITY
and other tales

RAW
$7.95
NUMBER EIGHT
THE GRAPHIC ASPIRIN FOR WAR FEVER
Birth of the Bomb: THE BEGINNING OF THE END by Paul Boyer
JIMBO by Gary Panter
RAW GAGZ over 50 artists, over 99 laffs!
MAUS by art spiegelman
KAZ 1986

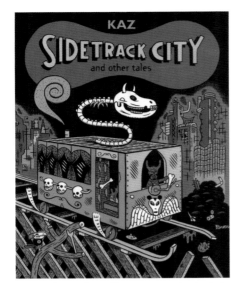

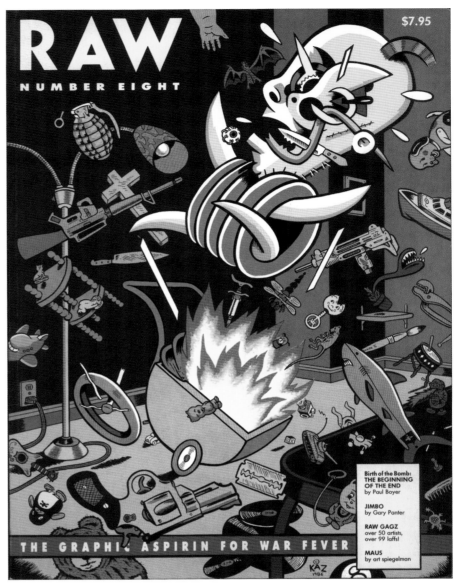

comparison since I never was invited to one. I wonder why?" "I found them frustrating at times, though," sighs Kaz. "This country loves to make fun of fine artists. They could be so close-minded about art and film and quick to dismiss. I've had that problem with people my whole life."

At a party in Edison, New Jersey, Kaz first encountered painter Joe Coleman and *Mutts* cartoonist Patrick McDonnell. "The Steel Tips were there for a Christmas party, and Patrick was the drummer for the Steel Tips. In the middle of the party Joe Coleman comes out and starts screaming all sorts of racist and sexist bullshit and how he wants to cut girls' tits off and everything and people at the party were like, 'What the fuck?' And then he opened up his jacket and lit some fireworks and it just—boom-boom-boom—blew up right there, and he just disappeared in a cloud of smoke. And everyone was running out the front door thinking they would get blown up—and that's where I first met Patrick McDonnell. And he was laughing his head off."

"I think that was a New Year's Eve party at Tom O'Leary's (lead singer of Steel Tips) apartment," says McDonnell today, who was at the time illustrating Russell Baker's column for the *New York Times*. "A very small apartment—around 1979. It was very crowded, very loud, and very out of control. If I remember correctly, my drum set was set up in the kitchen. On occasion Kaz would come to see Steel Tips at CBGB's. We all went to see Pee-wee Herman (before *Pee-wee's Playhouse*) at a comedy club in the city. Kaz and I got to know each other when we both lived in Hoboken. Peter Bagge and his wife, Joanne—a great chef—threw some wild parties for all the cartoonists that lived there."

ENTERING THE '80s, Kaz found himself less and less a fan of the fading scene at CBGB's and more into post-punk, the East Village fine art scene, and living in New Jersey with a girlfriend. Kaz contributed to *RAW*, *Comical Funnies*, new anthologies like *Bad News*, the *New York Rocker*, and *Weirdo*, as well as making a living as a commercial illustrator. Kaz's clients included *Entertainment Weekly* and *Modern Bride*. The cover of 1984's *Bad News* #2 is a breakthrough for Kaz. It features a strange, abstractly conceived creature, made up of bones, sticks, and a hand, and yet it still has hair. It's blowing a giant steam pipe *shofar* that blares out the magazine's title, "Bad News," in giant, vibrant lettering. The orange desert graveyard set against a black sky makes it look the kind of zombie Herriman might have drawn to devour his own cast...who knows, maybe the bones at its feet are what's left of Offisa Pup.

It's weird and hilarious. Kaz had seen a number of cartoon-style paintings by artists like Kenny Scharf and Keith Haring that he felt "weren't strong enough. I wanted that cover to be something I wanted to look at, like a painting, where you follow the contours of it. I wanted it to be funny, goofy,

Left: *Sidetrack City and Other Tales* (Fantagraphics Books, 1997).

Right: *RAW* #8 (RAW Books & Graphics, 1986).

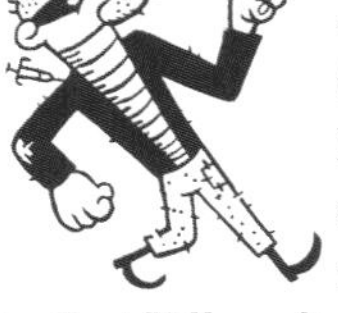

Snake Eyes
Post-Popeye Picto-Fiction

Snake Eyes
Post-Popeye Picto-Fiction
SANDLIN
KAZ
HEAD
TOMPKINS
BUKOWSKI
PIXIE MEAT
& More
Spicy Delights
No. 1

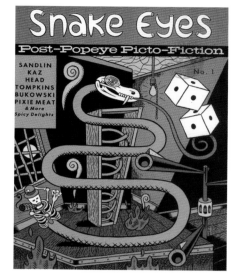

and scary." The cover of *Bad News* #2 is his answer to them. The creature's parts make no sense but, added up, they form what Kaz wanted. It looks like the Picasso sculptures in which the artist made a baboon out of a toy car (*Baboon and Young*, 1951). Kaz is not the first artist to introduce a talking object as a comics character, but those were much more literal. Kaz's are piles of unrelated junk—a lead pipe attached to a skull attached to flower pot—imbued with recycled personalities.

"I'd been doing abstract characters since my first year at SVA," says Kaz. "I had seen drawings by Max Ernst and Dalí with these constructs walking around, then Joan Miró, Picasso. I thought they could be done as cartoon characters. It's pure creativity, creating something from something else. Like when you're a kid and you're using your imagination and saying, 'Ok, this garbage can is a space ship and that bush is a monster.'" It was the *Bad News* cover that set Kurtzman back on his heels to exclaim, "Wow, I never thought that guy would make it." If Kaz ever needed an SVA diploma, that was it.

That period of cartooning for Kaz comes together in *Buzzbomb* (1987), published by Fantagraphics (still his publisher today). Looking back, Kaz says, "It's me learning how to be a cartoonist." The progression is impressive, from his 1980 *New York Rocker* "Vamp Dance" strips to the explosive 1987 abstract character cover. It starts with his SVA design experiments from Spiegelman's class, where they questioned the nature of the boxes adding up to the big box—the questions Herriman and King and Sterret once asked. And it closes on Kaz's own questions about the abstract nature of the cartoon character itself. In "Two Nuts in Search of a Bolt," Kaz drew his first abstract character, Crank Case, who appears on the cover of *Buzzbomb* in an even wilder rendering, now made of flesh, blood, metal, and shapes made of—what?

"His early comics had a very distinct arty edge," says Bagge, "which was also very 'punk,' when you think about where the whole punk scene's roots *really* came from." Gary Panter says of the early Kaz: "I was knocked out. He seemed self-spawned and played with the page composition, conventions, and devices of cartooning in a smart way like Herriman or Bobby London could." *Buzzbomb* includes his riffs on Herriman; "The Dreams of the Pork Rind Fiend" and "The Bath Between"; his Beyer strip "The Disappearance of Mr. Teeth"; and his character Norman Endless, a rare human character, in "Way Out West." Set in a cemetery full of cartoonists' graves (Herriman, Opper, DeBeck, Feininger, McCay), Norman is a mama's boy whose mama has died. The panels are done as bones set against a black infinite space. Herriman crawls from his grave to shout "Be hushed!" at Norman for his whining, and even his own mother comes back from the dead to tell him to grow up.

Buzzbomb's cover, however, shows where Kaz's imagination went. It features Crank Case, introduced as a minor character

Left: Original art for *Snake Eyes* #1 cover (Fantagraphics Books, 1991).

Right: *Snake Eyes* #1 (Fantagraphics Books, 1991).

Sketches of the character Bill Beak, 1991.

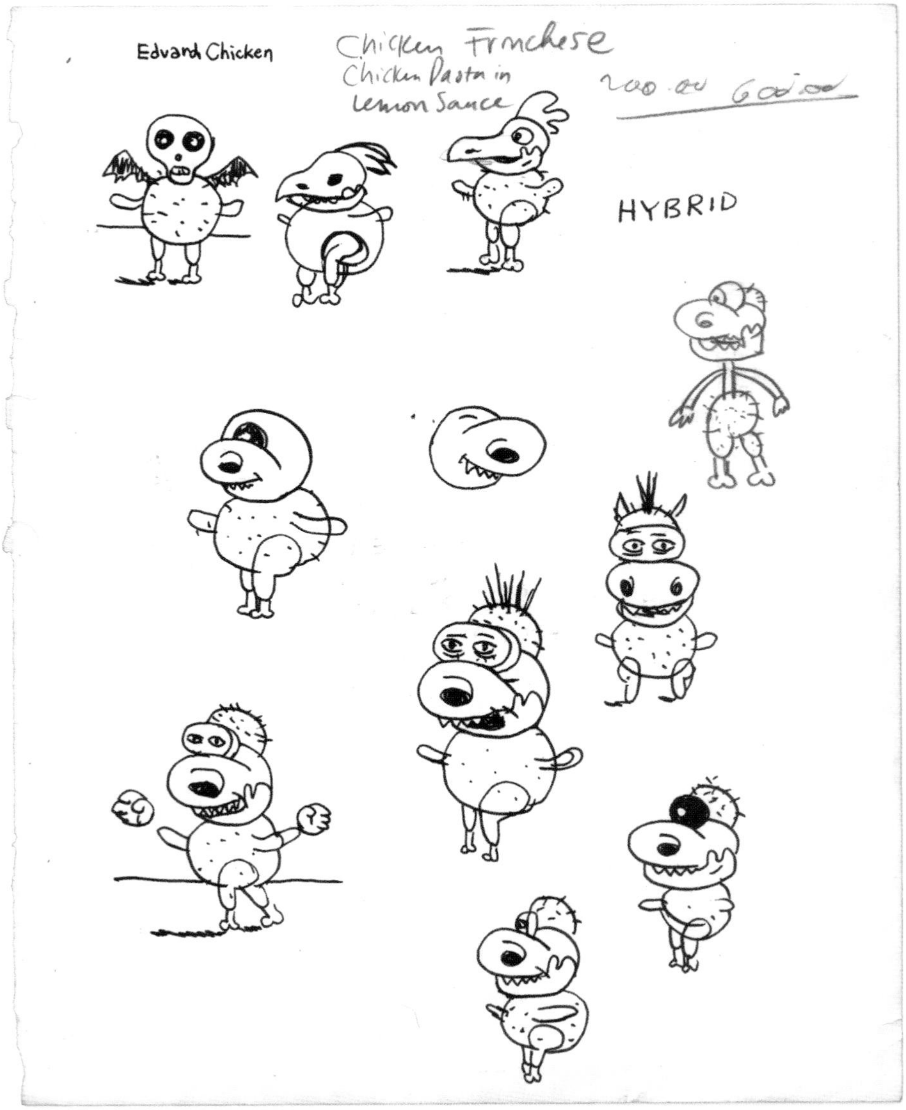
Edvard Chicken
Chicken Pasta in
Lemon Sauce
HYBRID

in one strip, and now the dynamic center of Kaz's cover. It states his post-SVA ideas clearly. Finally, Kaz published it in a large format size, 15 1/4 x 10 1/2", for one specific reason: so he could always say, "Bigger than *RAW*!" Meek mama's boy Norman Endless falling into the old cartoonists' graveyard is a fitting SVA graduation speech, done Kaz-style. In *Buzzbomb* he's moving on, finally at home in the medium. "I used all of that to find my own voice," says Kaz. "I experimented to see what I could do with it."

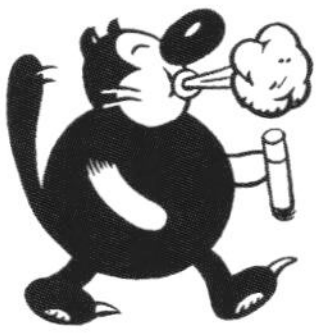

AS *Buzzbomb* ARRIVED from Fantagraphics, Kaz was hosting his own radio show on college station WFMU with Chris T., of the Nihilistics. The two met in Bagge's old apartment, where Kaz was goofing around with some other WFMU people, taping station promos. Chris T., now on Sirius satellite radio, says "Kaz and I hit it off right away. Our show was a combination of music, pranks, interviews, talk—we played whatever we liked. He brought in lots of left-field gems I had never heard. He had a healthy love of the absurd and was willing to try anything. Pretty fearless."

Guests included Joe Coleman, bands Missing Foundation and Woodpecker, and any number of Kaz's friends like Gary Panter, Peter Bagge, and Mark Newgarden, all invited in to play the music they liked. The Friedman brothers took listener calls and brought in their Jim Nabors collection. "He was always very hip to all the latest underground-y bands," says Bagge, "like he'd be the first person to tell me about Flipper and the Butthole Surfers and all those other post-punk '80s bands that I totally hated and still do. But he was hip to 'em first!"

Kaz hosted for two years, until he felt that the station was eating up time where he was presenting other people's art instead of creating his own. At the same time, he had moved to Jersey City after a break-up with a girlfriend. Mutual friends introduced him to a new roommate, fine arts painter Alexander Ross (not the glossy superhero illustrator). They lived in a tough, African-American neighborhood where the two skinny, young white artists were confronted more than once by local thugs. Both remember the Public Enemy CD *Yo! Bum Rush the Show* playing constantly, and just as often from their own apartment. "I'll never forget the park across the street at night," says Kaz. "It was beautiful. When there was a full moon, the sidewalk would sparkle and shine. That was because of all the broken beer bottles the winos smashed there."

"I was a fine artist who was interested in comics," says Ross. "I had a fine arts background, the books…I knew where the shows were and showed him a fine art appreciation." All of which Kaz wanted to study. For two years the two exchange endless amounts of graphics theory, music, and opinion. "Before your coffee some mornings, you got theory thrown at you," says Kaz. And they dropped lots of acid. Kaz's love of self-medication has been well documented elsewhere, but he was coming to some conclusions as to the age-old question of how drugs aided creativity. "Well," he says, "life becomes an instant layered art cake. Later, in *Sidetrack City*, you can see that psychedelic mindset, of a reality beyond reality that we see, played out as that story evolves."

And then, acid was just fun to do. If anything, the drug world itself gave him more ideas than actual drug use. Kaz sums up his views on the subject in one of his more popular *Underworld* characters: Nuzzle, the junkie with the permanent syringe in his shoulder. An addled buffoon who knows he's wasting his life, Nuzzle's zero willpower means he has about as much chance of kicking heroin as Charlie Brown does kicking that football. Toward the end of his years with Ross, the two remember there was a bad acid trip that perhaps was a sign

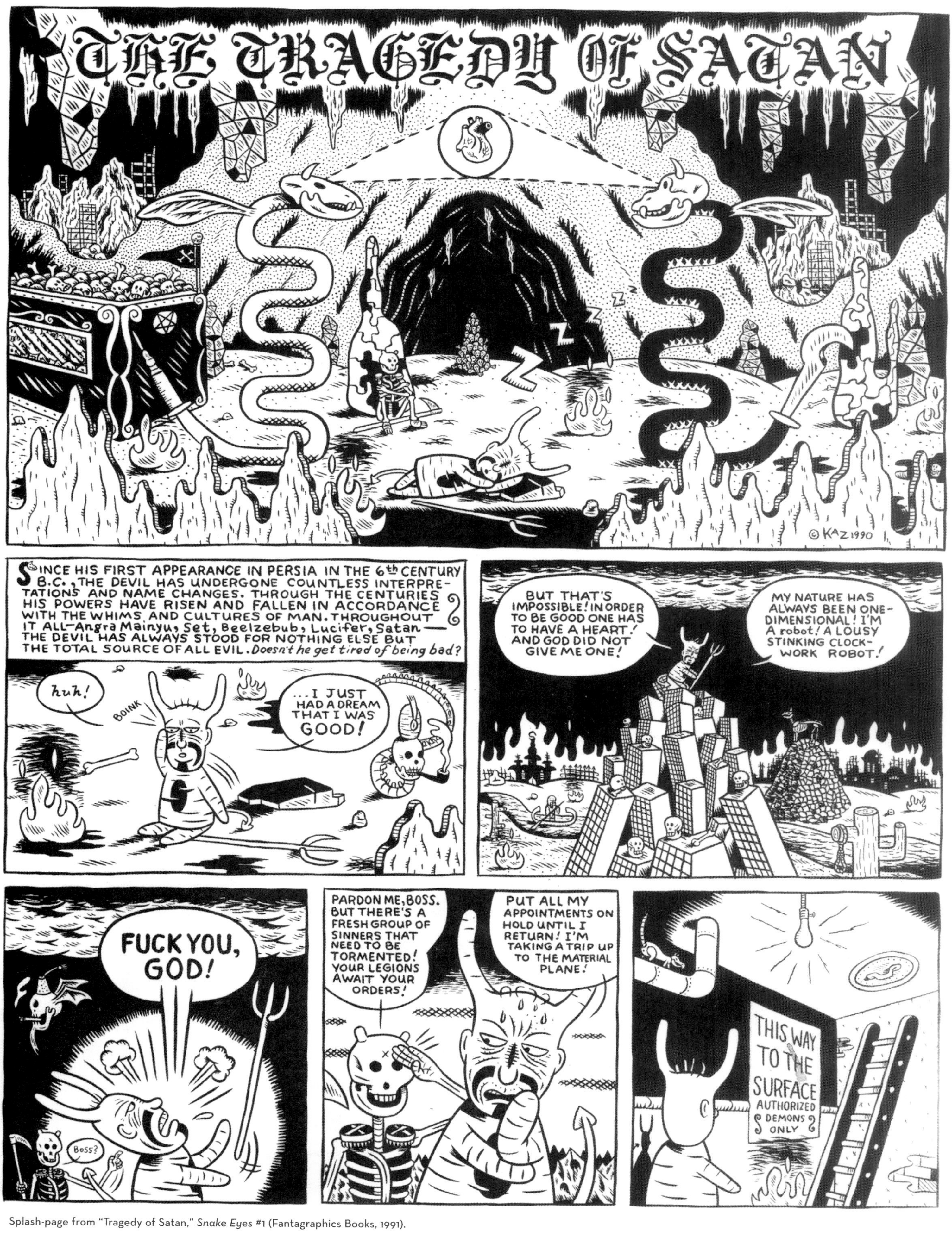
THE TRAGEDY OF SATAN
Z Z Z
© KAZ 1990
SINCE HIS FIRST APPEARANCE IN PERSIA IN THE 6th CENTURY B.C., THE DEVIL HAS UNDERGONE COUNTLESS INTERPRETATIONS AND NAME CHANGES. THROUGH THE CENTURIES HIS POWERS HAVE RISEN AND FALLEN IN ACCORDANCE WITH THE WHIMS AND CULTURES OF MAN. THROUGHOUT IT ALL—Angra Mainyu, Set, Beelzebub, Lucifer, Satan— THE DEVIL HAS ALWAYS STOOD FOR NOTHING ELSE BUT THE TOTAL SOURCE OF ALL EVIL. Doesn't he get tired of being bad?
huh!
BOINK
...I JUST HAD A DREAM THAT I WAS GOOD!
BUT THAT'S IMPOSSIBLE! IN ORDER TO BE GOOD ONE HAS TO HAVE A HEART! AND GOD DID NOT GIVE ME ONE!
MY NATURE HAS ALWAYS BEEN ONE-DIMENSIONAL! I'M A robot! A LOUSY STINKING CLOCKWORK ROBOT!
FUCK YOU, GOD!
BOSS?
PARDON ME, BOSS. BUT THERE'S A FRESH GROUP OF SINNERS THAT NEED TO BE TORMENTED! YOUR LEGIONS AWAIT YOUR ORDERS!
PUT ALL MY APPOINTMENTS ON HOLD UNTIL I RETURN! I'M TAKING A TRIP UP TO THE MATERIAL PLANE!
THIS WAY TO THE SURFACE
AUTHORIZED DEMONS ONLY

Splash-page from "Tragedy of Satan," *Snake Eyes* #1 (Fantagraphics Books, 1991).

DEAD ED
RIP ED
POP
©Kaz'93

NEWTON
UM, PETER, I'D LOVE TO HAVE SEX WITH MY NEW GIRL-FRIEND. BUT... I'M AFRAID MY you-know-what IS TOO SMALL!
WELL, HOW SMALL IS IT?
pissst, pissst
OOOH. TOO BAD.
BUT, WHAT DO YOU WANT ME TO DO?
Pissst Pissst
NO.
NO.
NO.
ALL RIGHT. I'LL DO IT.
LATER...
HONEY, YOUR 'BACK DOOR MAN' IS HERE!
I'M READY, BABY!
NEWTON! NO WAY!
© KAZ '94

to move on. Ross's interests were shifting, and he got more into other art scenes and put away all his cartoon-inspired work. "Maybe there was a sense of Kaz feeling left behind, a sense of betrayal," says Ross. Sort of. "I thought he was trying to kill me," says Kaz. "I had broken up with my girlfriend and was paranoid. I thought the whole world was trying to kill me for about a month. It was one of the worst periods of my life."

By 1989, Kaz left his radio show and he and Ross decided to move to Manhattan and separate apartments, although they remain good friends. The last time Kaz saw their Jersey City apartment was in an episode of *The Sopranos*. Tony Soprano returns to his old neighborhood with his son to visit a beautiful church in the Season 4 episode "Watching Too Much Television." "This neighborhood used to be 100 percent Italian," says a disgusted Tony. "Look at these buildings around here, most of them falling down to the ground." "That's when Tony looks at the building across the street," says Kaz, "windows boarded up, crates and a mattress in the front yard, shit everywhere—it was our house!"

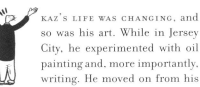

KAZ'S LIFE WAS CHANGING, and so was his art. While in Jersey City, he experimented with oil painting and, more importantly, writing. He moved on from his one-shot Sunday pages to the comic book proper. One of the best is his contribution to *Snake Eyes* #1, 1990's "The Tragedy of Satan." Reading biography into art is, to say the least, an inexact science. But Kaz was living in a violent, ugly neighborhood and had just gone through a wrenching break-up worsened by negative acid trips—much of which comes into play in "The Tragedy of Satan," perhaps the most poignant example of Kaz's nihilism to date.

In his youth, Kaz's nihilism meant getting drunk and going to CBGB's. "Yeah, we're fucked up and fuck you. That was perfect for my seventeen-year-old teenage ego," he says now. By 1990, Kaz gained more perspective on it. He found the world to be an amoral place, not purely evil, nor purely good, but always comical. And so, Kaz's Satan is not the omnipresent evil of *The Exorcist* or *The Omen*. He's a *schlemiel*, a *nudnik*, a *schmuck*, not so much Jack Chick as Garfield. "That's because no one believes in him anymore," says Kaz. "He's lost his power, so he isn't scary. He isn't big. He isn't a threat." Visually, Kaz is somewhere between his *Buzzbomb* period and where he is today in *Underworld*, with a mix of characters, creepy humans and monsters along with his first truly "cute" character, appropriately for Kaz, Satan. "The Tragedy of Satan" basically asks: in an amoral world, what place is there for the devil? And Satan is as bored with the good-evil issue as Kaz, exclaiming, "My nature has always been one-dimensional. I'm a robot. A lousy stinking clockwork robot! FUCK YOU, GOD!"

Rather than spend another meaningless day in hell, Satan climbs to Earth through the "poop hatch," which a caption tells us is Lithuanian folklore. "Actually, I made that up," Kaz admits today. "Nobody knows anything about Lithuania, so I thought, what the hell?" On Earth, Satan falls for his evil ideal—a whore. "A perfect choice for the old snake," says the caption. "Meet Virus Slunk, the worst woman in the world." "Fifty dollars for a half hour," Virus tells Satan, "Then get lost." Desperate to win her, Satan creates a ten-foot-tall diamond, but she gives him the finger. "You can't refuse me! I'm Satan! The devil himself! You must love me!" "Don't tell me what I must do! I'll never love anything!" says Slunk. "Both you and God can go fuck yourselves!" Enraged and heartbroken, Satan leaves, and Virus's pimp can't wait to sell the diamond and retire. When it disappears in a puff of smoke, the pimp kills Virus. At first Satan can't wait to have her in hell, which is now cooling down because Satan has lost interest in his work. Then, a cow-skulled demon, chilly in a royal, fur-lined bathrobe and ear muffs, explains, "She's in purgatory. As bad as she was, she never fully accepted you."

Purgatory, Penn Station, now Jersey City: Like the teenage Kaz sitting hours on end with the lost souls of Midtown Manhattan, the true nihilists have no place in either world. Upon learning Virus Slunk's fate, and worse, his own lonely one, Satan breaks down crying. In one of the greatest panels Kaz has ever drawn, Satan stands alone sobbing, in hell—a hell that Popeye or Sluggo might end up in, but a hell nonetheless. His downfall is that he really

Original art for "Dead Ed," 1993, *Underworld vol. 1: Cruel and Unusual Comics* (Fantagraphics Books, 1995).

Original art for "Newton," 1994, *Underworld vol. 2: Bare Bulbs* (Fantagraphics Books, 1997).

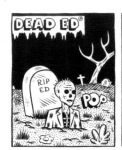

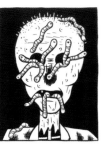

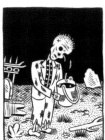

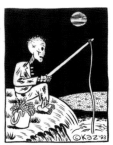

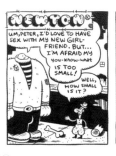

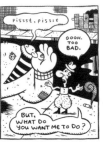

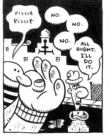

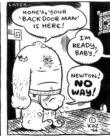

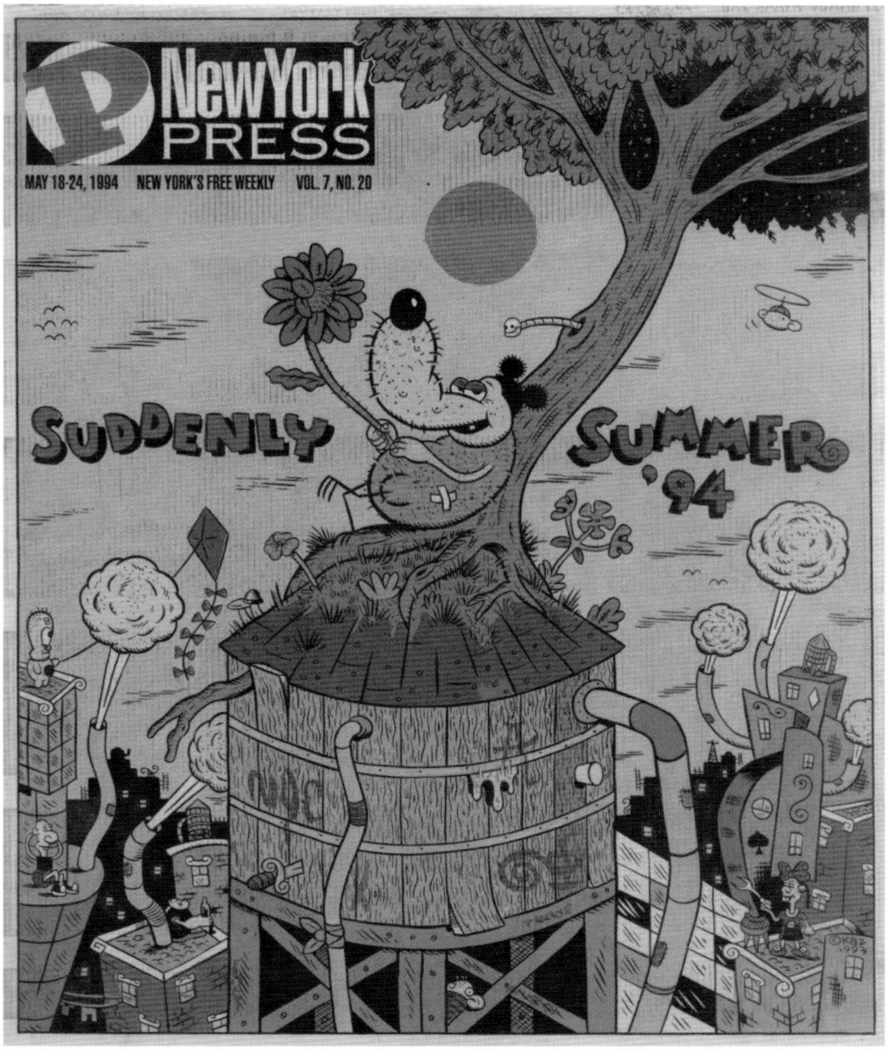
New York PRESS
MAY 18-24, 1994 NEW YORK'S FREE WEEKLY VOL. 7, NO. 20
SUDDENLY SUMMER '94

does believe in a simplistic black-and-white world, a purely good and evil existence—one Kaz never believed. Kaz leaves us with the line, "Hell falls apart when the devil gets a heart."

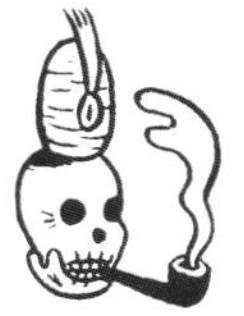

IN THE EARLY 1990S, Kaz got a call from Drew Friedman, now the comics editor for the *National Lampoon*. "All the editors at the *Lampoon* were confused by everyone I brought in, including Dan Clowes and Chris Ware," says Friedman. "But the first piece Kaz did, 'Kiss of Shame,' about a tough seaport town where all the 'mean and dirty' men had tits, was a big hit. I remember when I invited Kaz to be a regular contributor. He told me I was the first person to hire him to be *funny*, which surprised me. I had thought his work was funny for quite a few years."

Both *Lampoon* and *Heavy Metal* were owned by the same publisher, and Kaz did a strip for *Heavy Metal* called "Skully and Mandabelle," made up of his unique abstract characters. The strips are about Skully and Mandabelle's hijinks. Like Friedman, Kaz got in on the loophole of *HM* allowing funny strips as long as they were science-fiction themed. Kaz offered them a post-apocalyptic *Katzenjammer Kids*. The sun flickers on them like a loose light bulb, they get scolded for playing in the malignant zone, their house breaks up into an army of decaying goblins, and they find that if you throw pieces of junk together—a coffee cup, a pencil, and some bones—they come to life and run away. The family itself is made of skull heads, various objects for torsos, and cactus legs. These, and a short story featuring Little Bastard, a piece of cable from a factory "in the juicy junkyard of disjointed dreams," are the last abstract characters Kaz would create. "I stopped using those characters at some point," he says, "because people found it harder to identify with something that abstract, something not human at all."

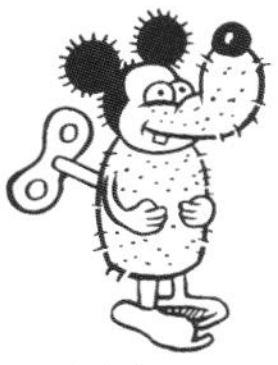

"KAZ ONCE PROPOSED to me collaborating on a regular gag strip," says Bagge, "with me being mainly the writer and him doing most of the art, which were our presumed 'strengths' at the time. But as it turned out, his own gags wound up being so much better than mine that I didn't see what point there was in our collaborating. In fact, for all of his cutting-edge, artsy-fartsy pretensions, he went on to become one of the best joke-telling machines in the history of comics, a regular punk rock Joey Adams. Who knew? It was a gift that even he wasn't fully aware he had at the time, I don't think."

In 1992, Kaz created the weekly strip he has worked on for the last fifteen years, *Underworld*. He moved to New York City, near Columbia University. Two life-changing events took place for him that year. He met Linda Marotta and, soon after, created *Underworld*. Marotta, the chief book buyer for Shakespeare and Co. and a horror critic for *Fangoria*, has been with Kaz ever since. They were married in 2001, on Halloween.

Creating *Underworld* was a major decision, since in 1992 Kaz had no idea if he ever wanted to draw a comic again. He certainly wasn't making any money on *RAW*, *Comical Funnies*, *Sidetrack City*, or much else that he loved to do. Paying jobs came from commercial illustration or design work on merchandising for *Pee-wee's Playhouse* through Gary Panter. "Kaz and Mark Newgarden and J.D. King, Wayne White, Ric Heitzman and a whole lot of people did art for Pee-wee products," says Panter, "and when they did, it was great. I wish that the talking toothbrush, plastic tea set, and play phone that Kaz and Mark designed had made it to the stores and into the hands of the children of the world. Luckily, the sheets and the bubble-gum cards and the Colorforms and the Matchbox Playhouse did."

Underworld also emerged in a pop culture in which Kaz could finally see a place for himself. In the '70s, much of what he liked was underground. In 1992, Kaz says, "Matt Groening and Tim Burton were doing really cool stuff through TV networks and movie studios. I thought, hey, if they can do it..." As Kaz got ambitious, an editor

Cover for *New York Press*, May 18–24, 1994.

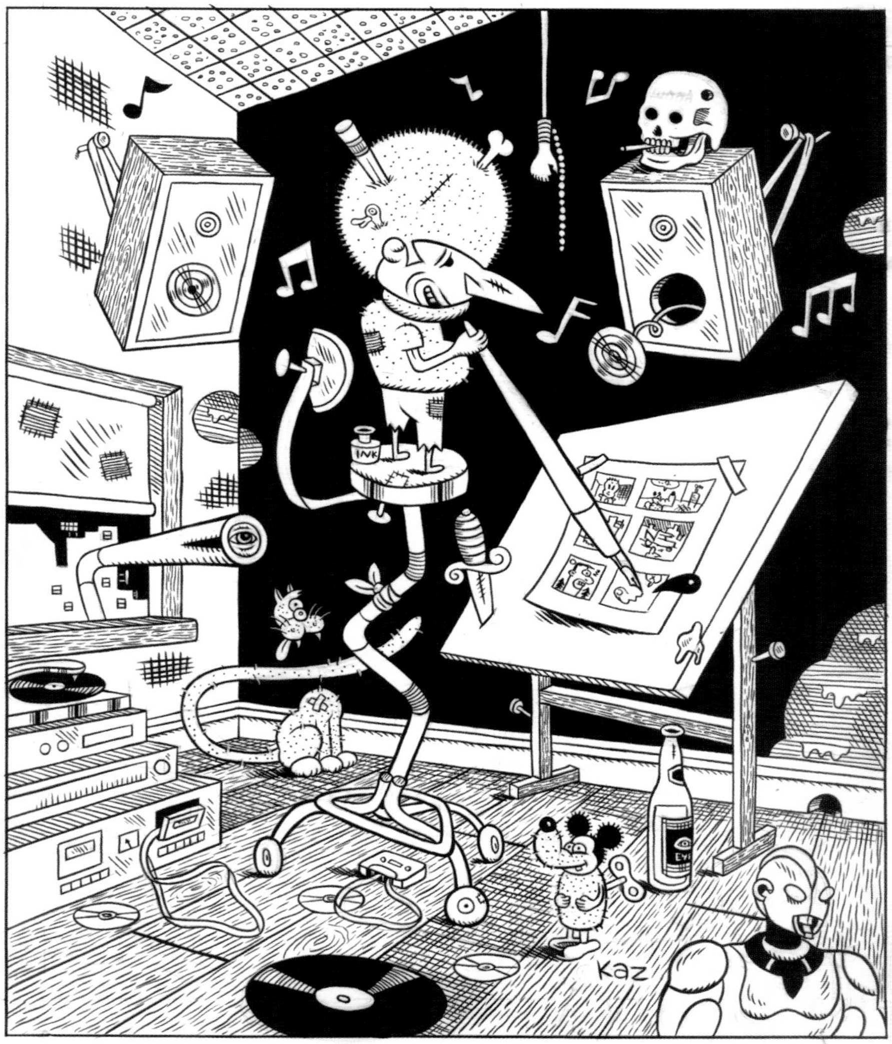
INK
KAZ

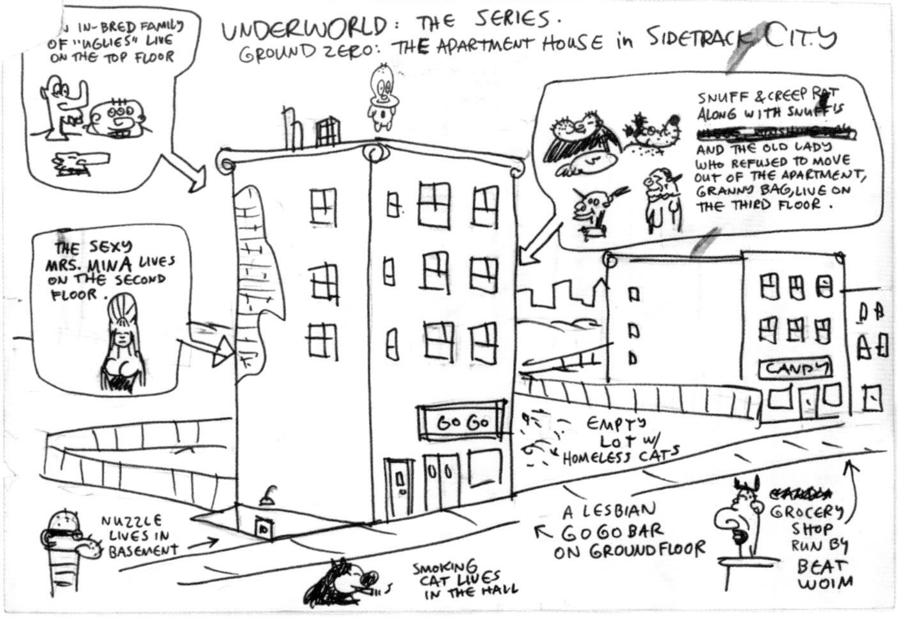
UNDERWORLD: THE SERIES.
GROUND ZERO: THE APARTMENT HOUSE in SIDETRACK CITY
IN-BRED FAMILY OF "UGLIES" LIVE ON THE TOP FLOOR
SNUFF & CREEP RAT ALONG WITH SNUFF'S AND THE OLD LADY WHO REFUSED TO MOVE OUT OF THE APARTMENT, GRANNY BAG, LIVE ON THE THIRD FLOOR.
THE SEXY MRS. MINA LIVES ON THE SECOND FLOOR.
GO GO
EMPTY LOT W/ HOMELESS CATS
CANDY
NUZZLE LIVES IN BASEMENT
A LESBIAN GO GO BAR ON GROUND FLOOR
SMOKING CAT LIVES IN THE HALL
GROCERY SHOP RUN BY BEAT WOIM

Original art for "Cartoonist at Work" illustration, *Pulse* (Tower Records, 1996).

Original sketch for a dreamt-of *Underworld* animated series, 1998.

at the *New York Press* asked him if he would do a weekly strip for the Press. Kaz said yes. "*Underworld* became a lifeline to me for comics," says Kaz. "I knew I couldn't do the pages I had done before in the *Rocker* because weeklies don't want full-page comics anymore. They want to sell ad space. It was also good to have a weekly because you had a flag out there. You always had something new to talk about when you met art directors or whoever."

Underworld was a highly calculated project. Having given up his Sunday page vistas, Kaz minimized in the extreme and created a four-panel strip. Lynda Barry and Matt Groening got more space each week, but Kaz chose to make his strip as easy as possible for editors to run. "When I created *Underworld* I decided to have a comedy team, Creep Rat and Snuff, that were the stars of the strip," says Kaz. "Then, whenever I felt like it, I would create new characters and even name the strip after them from time to time. All in the spirit of R. Crumb's comic books. I wasn't nailed down to drawing and writing the same three or four characters over and over again."

The major creative concession for Kaz, besides a looming weekly deadline, was the loss of cartoon real estate compared to the *Buzzbomb* era. If the widescreen look was gone, Kaz made up for it in the space he had in composition and layout. Says Spiegelman, "I think those four-panels are very well designed. It has that *Nancy* quality of 'Oh, I'll read this before I know it.' That is, in a line I've stolen from Wally Wood, '*Nancy* was the most read comic in the world, not the most popular—because it took more work to not read it than to read it.' He does the work for you instead of you having to do the work of what symbol means what and where is it. All the signs are in place so that as you go through it you get it and it delivers. That makes it very unusual in the alt-comics newspaper wing." Says Panter, "I think that if you can do a masterpiece a week for years in four panels, nothing is lost at all. Kaz has fine compositional skills, hitherto only observed in *Nancy*. He has an early period, to me; and a changing, dark, experimental period when he was studying with Spiegelman and for a while there after; then, the ambitious newly extra-clear composed comics; and then the tight four-panel era; and his Hollywood era when he is working so much that he decides to loosen up and let the energy vary."

To be sure, *Underworld* is all Kaz, but it exists in a world synthesized from his favorite cartoonists. "Kaz's early *RAW* magazine work was quite surreal, and there is a touch of *Krazy Kat*," says Patrick McDonnell. "But it pales in comparison to what he would do later in *Underworld*. Kaz is a modern traditionalist in that he knows how to tell a great gag. Punch lines with punch. The toughest thing to do is to be consistently funny, and Kaz nails it. In his own weird way, Kaz carries on the grand tradition of Elzie Segar, Milt Gross, and Bill Holman." One could also add touches of Gould, Bushmiller, Lasswell, Sterrett, Charles Burns, and whomever Kaz happens to absorb that week. But Kaz is no imitator. He invites them all into *Underworld*—Dick Tracy beats up a kid until he confesses that comics made him commit crimes; Nuzzle's oracle is a little black-girl version of Nancy; a nude Snuffy Smith and Maw are shown in bed; Tweety Birds battle in the wimp army; Hanna-Barbera's Baba Looey appears; and finally, there are Snuff and Creep Rat themselves. "For the record," says Kaz, "Creep Rat's look is a combination of Mickey Rat, Rat Fink, and Ignatz Mouse. Snuff is a combo of Popeye and Brutus."

Underworld is reflective, not derivative. In *Bare Bulbs*, the second *Underworld* collection, there are at least twenty strips that directly reference comedy types (hillbillies, funny animals), jokes about jokes themselves, or actual cartoon characters. The *RAW* deconstructionist Kaz now took apart the daily four-panel strip and held each component to the light. As he forced a killer gag out of himself each week, he adapted the daily strip's comic clichés as his own. "In *Underworld* it was an arty way of approaching comedy," says Kaz, "because unlike the strips in *Buzzbomb*, I was getting into narrative and comedy 'types.' I was very self-conscious. It was like I had to get through two or three layers of history to make myself laugh. And I had to do it really fast because I only had four panels to make you laugh. It was a stepping back and saying, 'Isn't it weird that these comedy types

Original art for *Underworld vol. 4: Duh* (Fantagraphics Books, 2001).

exist?' It was a way of making fun of the art I had chosen as my mode of expression. It was a shorthand to humor. Then I would imagine what these 'types' would have thought about their predicament. How would I feel? Like in that strip where the characters become aware that they can't die. What would they do? Take drugs and have fun."

Underworld feels like it occupies a bad neighborhood of your daily comics page, like you got off on the wrong subway stop. Drugs, sex, violence, murders, perversion, and quite often just excrement are the subject matter of many of the jokes, and yet the strip never feels mean-spirited. "He deals with all of that and yet it never feels scatological," says Charles Burns. "His point is not to shock."

Not that Kaz hasn't offended readers; his website currently runs a long list of mail

from Arizonans so appalled by *Underworld* that they had it pulled from their local alternative paper. But Kaz's use of those subjects for jokes is the beginning of the conversation, not the end of it. That is, to him it's a given that his characters live in such a seedy place. It's the point of view of the kid finding a homeless man in his bathroom or Keith Haring sex videos in class or thinking his roommate is going to kill him. Kaz starts in such places and then finds the punch line—he finds a way to laugh at all that. "He's not stopping there; he's going toward something else," says Spiegelman. "In a world in which it's a given that everyone absorbs this stuff by the time we're twelve, what you do with it in a comic strip is fine. And they're real characters as opposed to just a tool to shove something in your face that smells bad. The word that

"The Terrorists Upstairs," c. 2002.

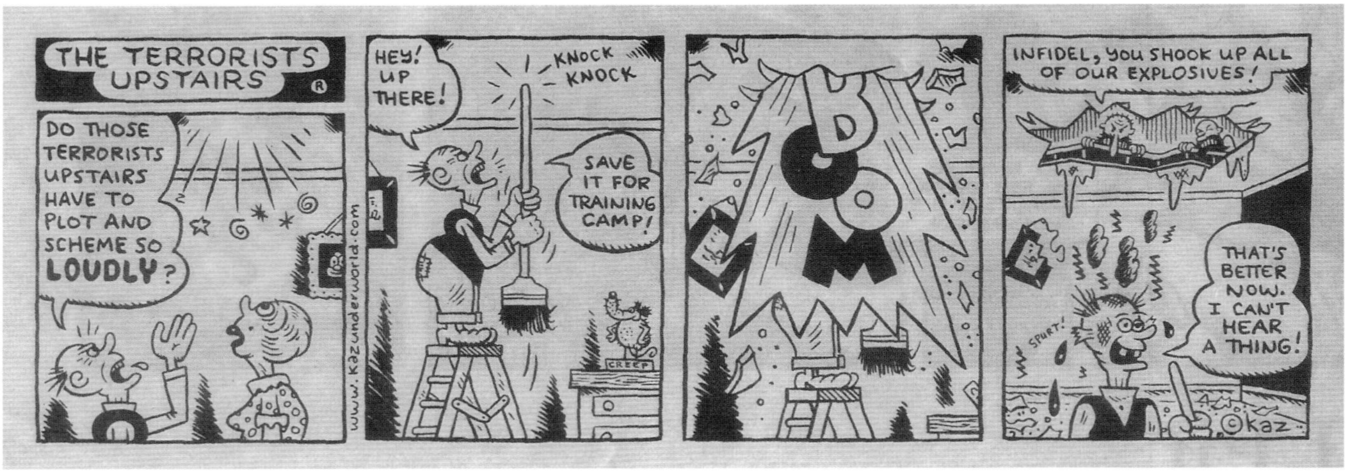
THE TERRORISTS UPSTAIRS ®
DO THOSE TERRORISTS UPSTAIRS HAVE TO PLOT AND SCHEME SO LOUDLY?
www.kazunderworld.com
HEY! UP THERE!
KNOCK KNOCK
SAVE IT FOR TRAINING CAMP!
CREEP
BOOM
INFIDEL, YOU SHOOK UP ALL OF OUR EXPLOSIVES!
THAT'S BETTER NOW. I CAN'T HEAR A THING!
SPURT!
©KAZ

comes up for me, and I don't mean this in any emo-boy put down, but Kaz is genuinely sensitive. While the strips tend to be about junkies and caca, they don't feel like they're there to maim and hurt someone. It seems no different to him than jokes about alcohol were to '20s and '30s cartoonists. But that puts him in a very different place than some of the more mean-spirited stuff that keeps surfacing from the underground these days."

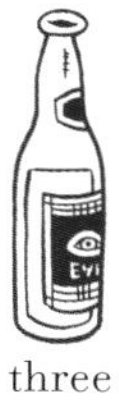

TWENTY YEARS AFTER RAW, Kaz found himself working with Spiegelman and Mouly again, this time on the *Little Lit* series. Between 2000 and 2003, Kaz created short stories for all three volumes of Spiegelman and Mouly's *Little Lit*. He is the only cartoonist whose work from all three volumes was collected in the 2006 "Best of" collection. During that time he also began focusing on his writing. Kaz went back to school and took two screenwriting classes at NYU. But it was an *Underworld* strip, "Lumberger," that got him the attention of Steve Hillenburg, creator of *Spongebob Squarepants*, in Los Angeles. "My band had a rehearsal space and 'Lumberger' was stuck up on the wall," says Hillenburg. "We all loved it, and then I started buying his *Underworld* collections when they came out. And *RAW* before that. At some point I was talking to Derek Drymon about it and wondering if we could get Kaz to write for our show. I said, 'Do you think we could get him? He lives in New York.' And Derek said, 'He's an underground cartoonist. He probably needs the money.'"

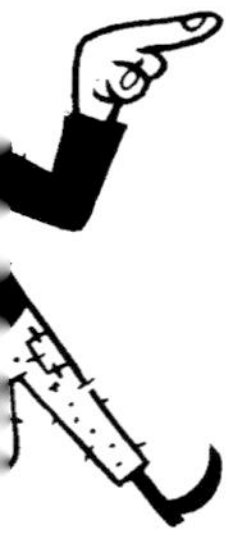

Kaz could indeed use the money, but he was excited to go. He had wanted to work in animation since he became a cartoonist. Pages like *RAW*'s "Voo Doo" are designed as a comics animation layout. Kaz was hired for Season 3 as a *Spongebob* writer to work out gags, and he came out to Los Angeles. For his first show, he couldn't have found a crew with sensibilities closer to his own. They wanted the pace and level of funny found in Warner Bros. cartoons and with the same silly, subversive world of Pee-wee Herman.

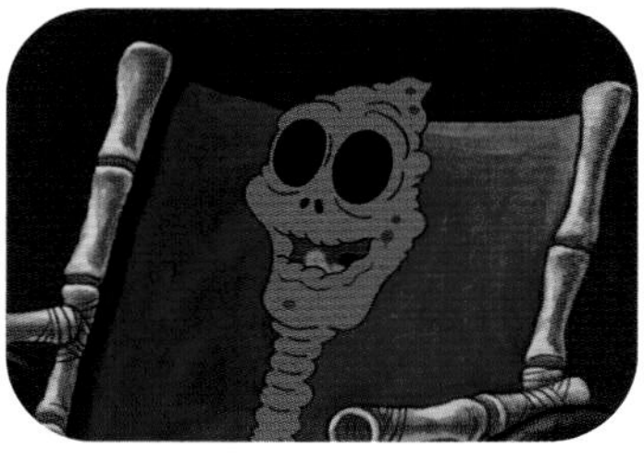

An example of Kaz's work for *Spongebob Squarepants*: the character "Ma," c. 2002.

In the downtime between episodes, Kaz sat in with the show's creators to add gags to animatics. He co-wrote outlines and co-directed storyboards. "The storyboard director is the one closest to the script," says Hillenburg. "The actual animation director is the one trying to get what's on those boards animated."

What's notable about Kaz's work on *Spongebob* is that on his cartoons, he's both a writer and director, something not unheard of, but less common in *Spongebob* episodes since outlines are created by the staff and then given to the storyboard directors best suited for their tone. To be sure, Kaz did not create the *Spongebob* characters. But actor Tom Kenny—the voice of Spongebob and many other characters—compares Kaz to the old Warner Bros. cartoon directors. "Friz Freleng, Chuck Jones, and Bob Clampett, they didn't always create Bugs, Daffy, and Porky, but they each had their own style. Kaz did on *Spongebob*. As someone who has played that part many times, I can tell a Kaz storyboard without ever seeing his name on it."

Episodes that stand out as particularly Kaz include "Chocolate with Nuts" and "The Nasty Patty." If Hillenburg hoped to get the flavor of *Underworld*, he got it. In "Chocolate with Nuts" (co-written with Paul Tibbitt), Spongebob and Patrick the Starfish sell chocolate bars door-to-door, meeting one disturbing liar, lunatic, or pathetic resident of their neighborhood after the next. The crazy neighbor screaming "chocolate" is a running gag in the cartoon, where you think he's going to kill Spongebob and Patrick, until he reveals himself as an addict and takes everything they have. "Kind of twisted in all those people they meet," is how Hillenburg recalls it, "twisted, especially the one screaming 'Chocolate!' at them." "The borders between *Underworld* and Spongebob's Bikini Bottom definitely blurred in that one," says Kenny. "Particularly his character, Ma."

Indeed, the creepiest characters are the elderly, limbless, wheelchair-bound Ma (played by Kenny) and Lazy Mary, Ma's adult daughter who takes care of her invalid mother. The crew assumed Ma was an eel or a fish—she seems to be decomposing already, and Kaz only describes her as "a shrunken head on an esophagus." When Mary refuses to buy Ma chocolate, Ma screams back, in a line one imagines rarely heard on Nickelodeon, "Ah, you're just waiting for me to die!" "That image is strongly Kaz," says Hillenburg. "Easily one of those disturbing, *Wizard of Oz*–flying-monkey-type moments that a kid is going to take with them well into adulthood," says Kenny, "and I'm not saying that's a bad thing. But that clearly came out of Kaz's underground background."

It's when Spongebob and Patrick realize that successful salesmen lie in order to make sales that the money comes pouring in. They return to everyone promising that their chocolate will make you—among other things—rich, smarter, prettier, and, in the case of their return to Ma's house, help you live forever if you rub it all over yourself. Lazy Mary cringes upon hearing that, and Kaz spares us the disgusting image, in what Tom Kenny calls "a David Lynchian moment where it happens behind a door and you hear Ma saying, 'Start rubbing me with that chocolate!'" In the end, Spongebob and Patrick make lots of money and take their dates—Lazy Mary and Ma, naturally—out to a fancy dinner. Says Kenny, "Yeah, Kaz turned them into grifters. You never know what will be cut by the censors and what won't. In different episodes, Kaz has managed to get through Ma, flesh-eating zombies, and Mr. Krabs—one of the major characters in the franchise—defiling a grave to rob it. You're not going to see that on *Clifford the Big Red Dog*. But Steven Hillenburg's creation allows you to find those corners and, so far, only Kaz seems to want to go there."

"The Nasty Patty" (also written with Tibbett) is another Kaz classic, in which a health inspector drops in at the restaurant where Spongebob works. When he and Mr. Krabs, the owner, think the inspector is a fraud trying to con them, they concoct a disgusting hamburger full of grime, muck, and human waste. When the inspector chokes on a fly and passes out, Spongebob and Mr. Krabs don't call for help—they

think they've murdered him, so they spend the episode trying to find a place to bury the body and not get caught. In the end he wakes up (several times, but is hit in the head with a shovel) and everything eventually works out. For children's entertainment, Kaz cartoons don't offer much of a moral lesson, except that lying, violence, mortality, and elder abuse are all ahead of you. The fun Kaz had with the Dead Boys, the Ramones, Crank Case, "The Tragedy of Satan," and *Underworld* is what makes his voice so obvious in his *Spongebob* work.

 IN 2006, Kaz was nominated for an Emmy for his work on *Camp Lazlo*, a cartoon about a summer camp attended by a group of animal characters. "Some '90s show called *The Simpsons* won," says Kaz, who is currently at work on his own pilot, *Zoot Rumpus*. Since moving to LA, he has also worked with Gary Panter on their own animation project, with *Corpse Bride* co-director Mike Johnson on a film project, and with Derek Drymon on an animation pilot.

This is the teen nihilist come full circle, the one who accepts amorality as a given and what you do with it afterward as the punch line. If Kaz remains one of the few active voices from punk's early days—and not just comics, but really all of American pop culture—he couldn't care less. He was there, but he's never wanted to spend his life in any one place. "The New York punk thing was a desperate cry from the next generation overshadowed by their older brothers—'kill the hippies!'" says Kaz today. "If the generation after punk said 'Kill the punks!' I'd be totally with them too. But they didn't. The grunge generation held up punk as a standard of authenticity. Now, *that's* funny." ᴳᴬ

Thanks to the following for all their time and help in putting this story together: Peter Bagge, Glenn Bray, Charles Burns, Brian Doherty, Robin Edgerton, Fantagraphics, Drew Friedman, Richard Gehr, Steve Hillenburg, Kaz, Tom Kenny, Linda Marotta, Michelle McCarthy, Patrick McDonnell, Mark Newgarden, Karen O'Connell, Gary Panter, Eric Reynolds, Alex Ross, Art Spiegelman, Chris T., and always, Bridie and Archer.

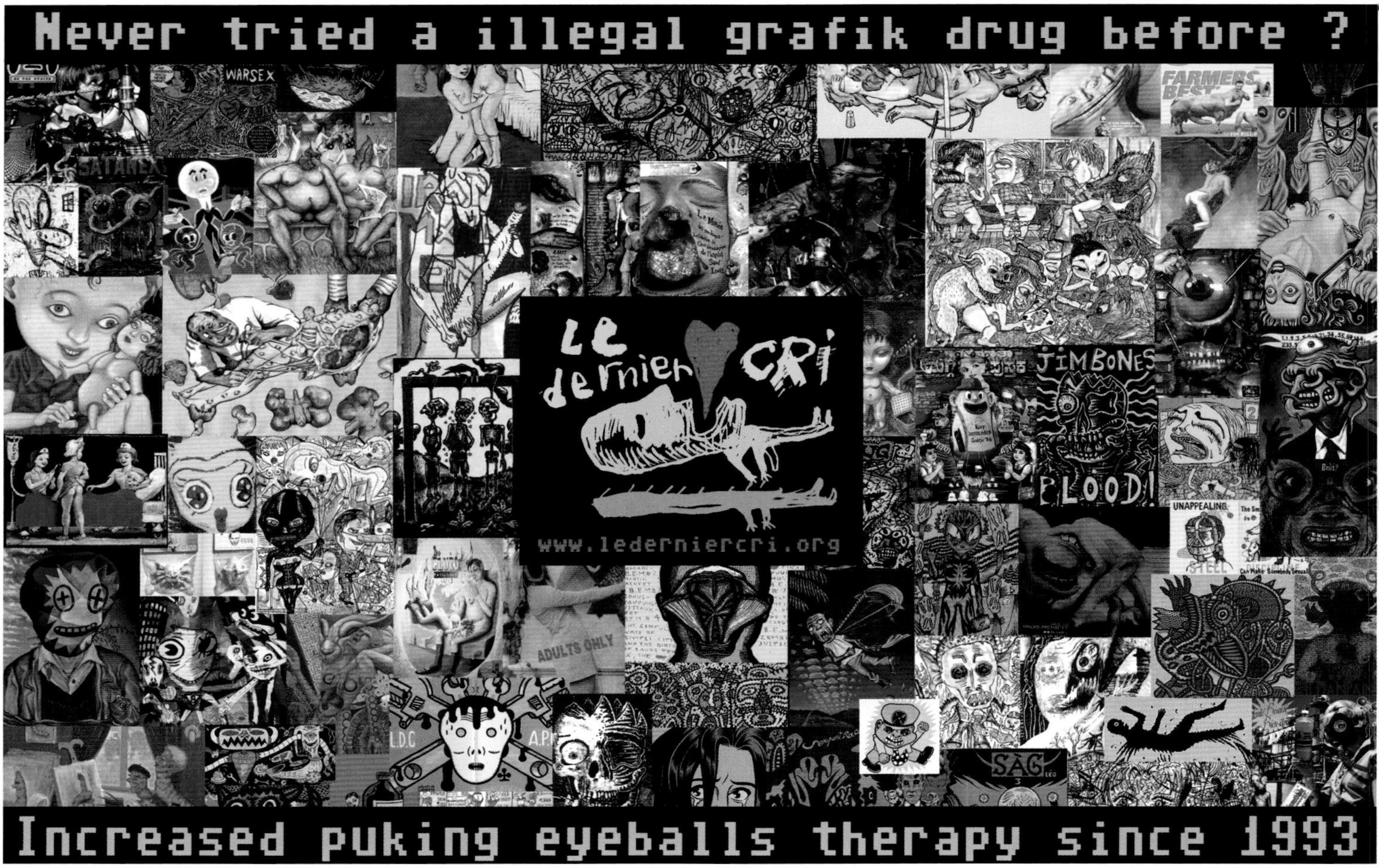

Never tried a illegal grafik drug before ?
le dernier cri
www.ledernier cri.org
Increased puking eyeballs therapy since 1993

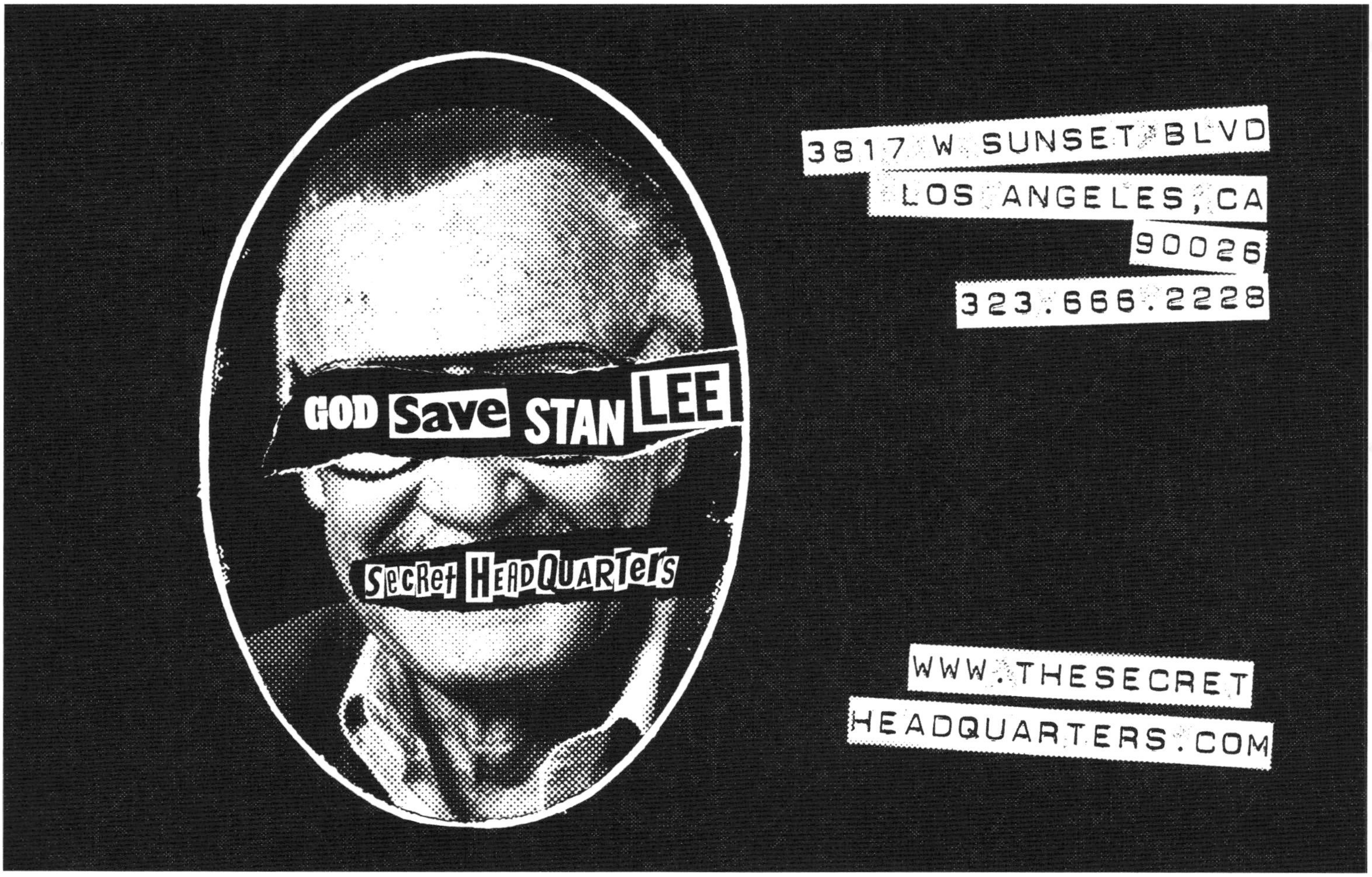

GOD Save STAN LEE
Secret HEADQUARTERS
3817 W SUNSET BLVD
LOS ANGELES, CA
90026
323.666.2228
WWW.THESECRET
HEADQUARTERS.COM

SPIRIT DUPLICATOR

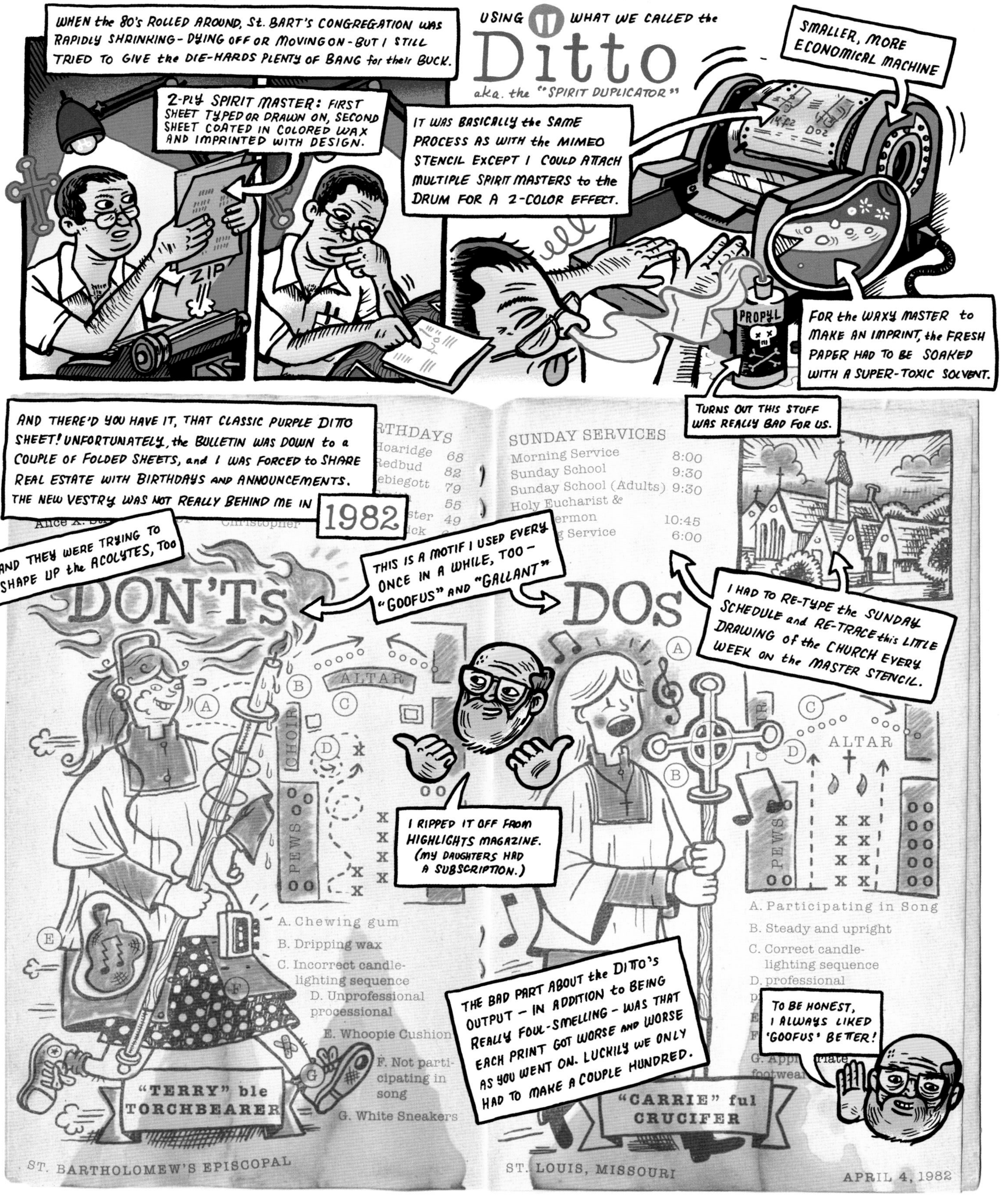

WHEN the 80's ROLLED AROUND, St. BART'S CONGREGATION WAS RAPIDLY SHRINKING - DYING OFF OR MOVING ON - BUT I STILL TRIED TO GIVE the DIE-HARDS PLENTY OF BANG for their BUCK.
USING WHAT WE CALLED the
Ditto
aka. the "SPIRIT DUPLICATOR"
SMALLER, MORE ECONOMICAL MACHINE
2-PLY SPIRIT MASTER: FIRST SHEET TYPED OR DRAWN ON, SECOND SHEET COATED IN COLORED WAX AND IMPRINTED WITH DESIGN.
ZIP
IT WAS BASICALLY the SAME PROCESS AS WITH the MIMEO STENCIL EXCEPT I COULD ATTACH MULTIPLE SPIRIT MASTERS to the DRUM FOR A 2-COLOR EFFECT.
PROPYL
FOR the WAXY MASTER to MAKE AN IMPRINT, the FRESH PAPER HAD TO BE SOAKED WITH A SUPER-TOXIC SOLVENT.
TURNS OUT THIS STUFF WAS REALLY BAD FOR US.
AND THERE'D YOU HAVE IT, THAT CLASSIC PURPLE DITTO SHEET! UNFORTUNATELY, the BULLETIN WAS DOWN to a COUPLE OF FOLDED SHEETS, and I WAS FORCED to SHARE REAL ESTATE WITH BIRTHDAYS AND ANNOUNCEMENTS. THE NEW VESTRY WAS NOT REALLY BEHIND ME IN
1982
BIRTHDAYS
Hoaridge 68
Redbud 82
ebiegott 79
55
ster 49
SUNDAY SERVICES
Morning Service 8:00
Sunday School 9:30
Sunday School (Adults) 9:30
Holy Eucharist &
Sermon 10:45
g Service 6:00
AND THEY WERE TRYING TO SHAPE UP the ACOLYTES, TOO
THIS IS A MOTIF I USED EVERY ONCE IN A WHILE, TOO - "GOOFUS" AND "GALLANT"
I HAD TO RE-TYPE the SUNDAY SCHEDULE and RE-TRACE this LITTLE DRAWING of the CHURCH EVERY WEEK ON the MASTER STENCIL.
DON'Ts
DOs
ALTAR
CHOIR
PEWS
I RIPPED IT OFF FROM HIGHLIGHTS MAGAZINE. (MY DAUGHTERS HAD A SUBSCRIPTION.)
A. Chewing gum
B. Dripping wax
C. Incorrect candle-lighting sequence
D. Unprofessional processional
E. Whoopie Cushion
F. Not participating in song
G. White Sneakers
A. Participating in Song
B. Steady and upright
C. Correct candle-lighting sequence
D. professional
THE BAD PART ABOUT the DITTO'S OUTPUT - IN ADDITION to BEING REALLY FOUL-SMELLING - WAS THAT EACH PRINT GOT WORSE AND WORSE AS YOU WENT ON. LUCKILY WE ONLY HAD TO MAKE A COUPLE HUNDRED.
TO BE HONEST, I ALWAYS LIKED 'GOOFUS' BETTER!
"TERRY" ble TORCHBEARER
"CARRIE" ful CRUCIFER
ST. BARTHOLOMEW'S EPISCOPAL
ST. LOUIS, MISSOURI
APRIL 4, 1982

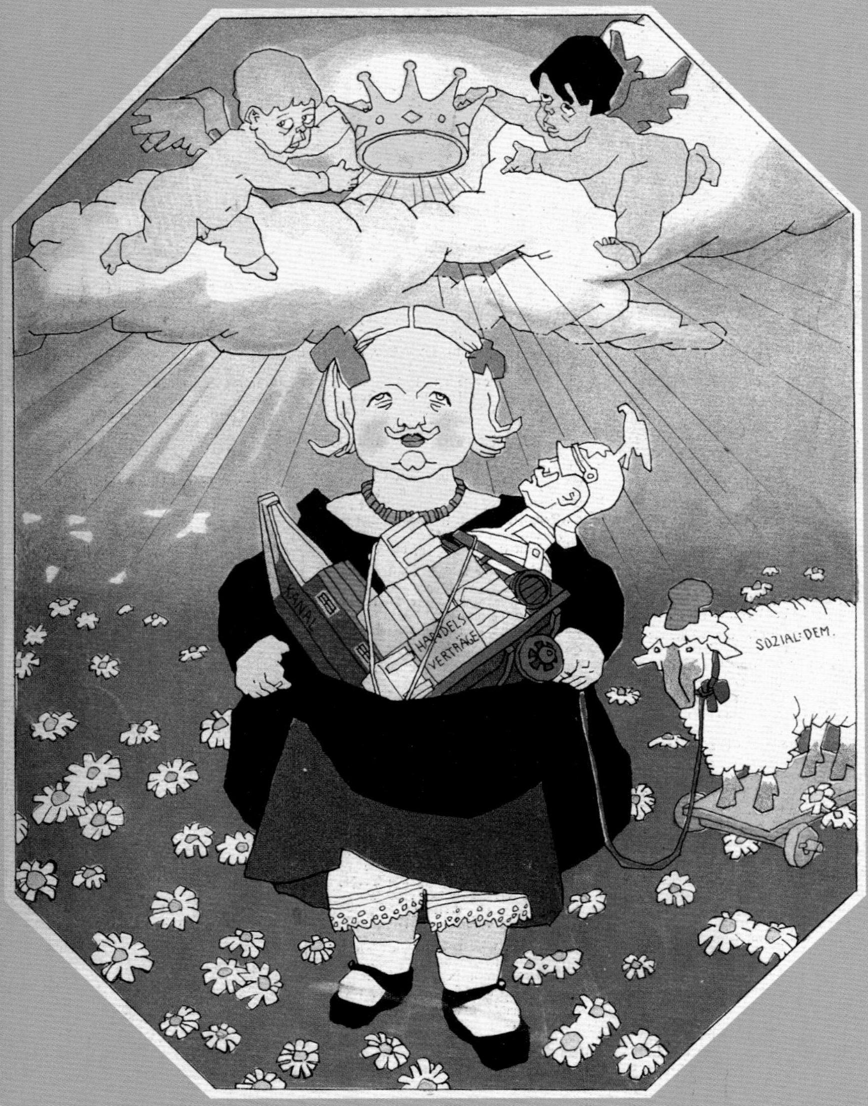
KANAL
HANDELS VERTRÄGE
SOZIAL-DEM.

Lustige Blätter, April 5, 1905.

LYONEL FEININGER'S LOST CONTINENT

1871–1956

by

THIERRY SMOLDEREN

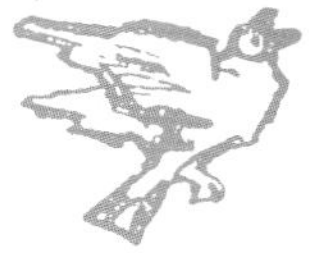

IN THE 1910s, Lyonel Feininger invented his own version of cubism, rubbed shoulders with Matisse, Pascin, Kubin, Gropius, and Kandinsky, and was a Bauhaus stalwart who was to become one of the major painters of the first half of the twentieth century. However, from 1890 to 1910 he devoted the early years of his career to illustration and caricature, and even went on a memorable excursion into the field of American comic strips.

This is the tale of an unusual exile set in the golden age of international caricature, which would lead the young American to publish his drawings at the highest levels in Paris, Berlin, New York, and Chicago...[1]

From *City at the Edge of the World* (1965), by T. Lux Feininger, photographs by Andreas Feininger. "All the long evenings I have been creating demons, pixies, 'Mysterious Petes,' and lantern-jowled professors, to pass the hours..." Letter from October 12, 1953. Some of the carved and drawn apparitions made by Feininger up to the end of his life harkened back half a century to the cast of his *Kin-der-Kids* pages.

1887—1890: New York - Hamburg - Berlin
Family Bathtub Sets Sail—Kids Aboard

IN OCTOBER 1887, Lyonel Feininger left America for the first time. He was sixteen, fond of bicycles, boats, and trains, and had just spent a good part of his New York childhood watching the city undergo radical changes at lightning speed. During those years Manhattan and Brooklyn engineers had constructed towering metal bridges spanning the water, started sending out elevated trains over the horizon, and prided themselves on erecting a fifty-meter-tall statue from Paris, inaugurated on Bedloe Island the previous October.

The immense human throng, the sirens' cacophony, and the exploding fireworks accompanying the inauguration ceremony still rung in the young boy's ears while the ocean steamer that was taking him onwards to Europe chugged past the Statue of Liberty. The first image in the *Kin-der-Kids*, drawn twenty years later in Germany, evokes this departure, albeit in a fantastical re-working. In the image, Lady Liberty frenetically waves a giant handkerchief to mark the leave-taking of the Kids in their floating bathtub.

At first glance, however, there was not much to justify such a noisy farewell—Lyonel's mother and sisters were in Germany and he was joining them, a somewhat mundane exercise in the life of a family of internationally renowned musicians perpetually on tour. In the streets of lower Manhattan, familiar ground to the young lad and his much-used bicycle, there were as yet no skyscrapers. As he watched his city's skyline disappear he could not have suspected the degree of change that would greet him on his return to New York. Nor could he have anticipated the length of time he would have to wait for this homecoming.

Lyonel's father, who had studied music in Leipzig, had foisted a violin onto the lad from his earliest age and still hoped to see him start out on serious musical study in the same town. He was perturbed to note his son's passion lay elsewhere, in observing the axles turn on a 4-4-0 American locomotive, watching an aboveground train on Second Avenue, or admiring the clean lines of the miniature yachts Lyonel and childhood friend Francis Kortheuer would test out on the pond in Central Park under the watchful and critical eyes of three old retired captains, likewise smitten with model boats.

If his virtuoso violinist father had not so violently despised everything that smacked of technology and science, Lyonel would surely have imitated his friend Francis who enrolled to study engineering, and the problem would have been solved. But the Feiningers' family life had been interrupted over the last few years as a result of his parents' never-ending travel: he often found himself alone without any real professional or scholarly direction, his father seeking to ensure his training as a violinist between tours. The year before his departure for Germany saw the young man working as an office hand for a firm in Brooklyn; his life seemed to be made of waiting and stop-gap solutions.

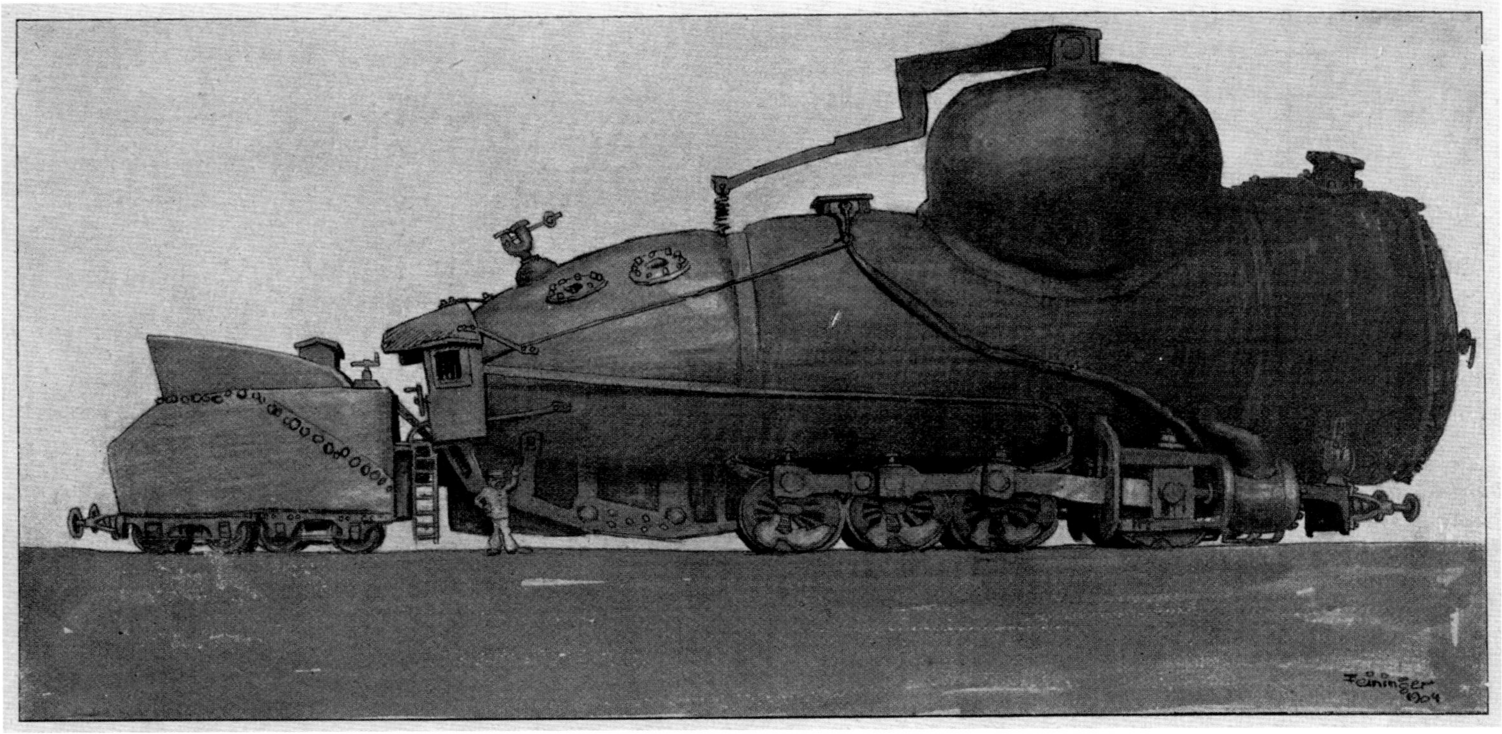
Feininger 1904

The Aunt, Hamburg School of Arts and Professions—The First Ghosts

ARRIVING IN HAMBURG at the end of October 1887, Lyonel immediately found himself pushed into another ill-defined, typically Feininger family situation: he stayed with an aunt while his parents continued to tour until Christmas. Obliged to find an occupation for his first winter in Hamburg, he enrolled in the town's art school.

Feininger had drawn a considerable amount in New York—numerous Atlantic locomotives sketched on the platforms of Grand Central Station, careful diagrams of schooners detailed to the last rivet, and an abundance of cartoons. He suddenly found himself caught up in a typical European art program: eight hours of drawing (charcoal, life-study, plaster, and watercolors) per day, taught, of course, as an exact science following the academic rules of art—and in German. At a very early stage in those months, Feininger wrote to Francis Kortheuer that he had realized he would be "a watercolor landscape artist or nothing at all," taking the opportunity to boast of the praise he was receiving from his teachers; his progress in drawing was swift.

Despite the homesickness that started to seriously gnaw at him, the young man was sketching out an artistic career for himself, quite unlike the one his musical parents hoped for. However, his vocation was as yet hesitant: although he was blossoming academically and dreamt of becoming a watercolorist, he spent most of his free time drawing caricatures. In letters sent to Francis, a great number of cartoons in the style of Wilhelm Busch were mixed in with his more usual sketches of nautical and railroad machinery. He had just discovered Busch, author of *Max and Moritz*, and bought himself several albums for his birthday. He did not find them particularly well drawn but he was won over by their vitality and exuberant humor. Enthused, he invented a prank for the two mischievous rascals, and slipped it into one of his letters. All this did not prevent him from declaring his preference for American caricature, in particular for the work of Zim [Eugene Zimmerman] in *Judge* magazine.

Feininger was starting to see the benefits of his European exile. Francis Kortheuer, who well knew his preferences in caricature and had a keen eye himself, could help him keep up-to-date with all the recent interesting American developments and sent him books, articles, newspaper cuttings, and, importantly, illustrated periodicals such as *Puck*, *Harper's New Monthly*, *Scribner's*, and *Judge*. For his part, Lyonel found in the art schools he attended (first at Hamburg, then subsequently, in 1888, Berlin) excellent information on what was happening graphically in Europe. In fact, Germany was at that time considered to be a center of excellence for caricature. Wilhelm Busch's picture stories had made famous *Fliegende Blätter*, a Munich humor weekly launched in 1848. Busch managed to invent a new humorous voice that was the admiration of caricaturists on both sides of the Atlantic; his impertinent and childlike tone was mixed with cruelty and grotesqueness, in contrast with the satire focused on social and political matters that had dominated cartooning for several decades, confining the genre to the national sphere. In France, the *Chat Noir* artists were affected by this evolution and specialists such as Arsène Alexandre openly admitted the debt French illustrators owed to Wilhelm Busch and Adolf Oberländer (Busch's successor at *Fliegende Blätter*); in America the great A.B. Frost was inspired by Busch's pantomimes in

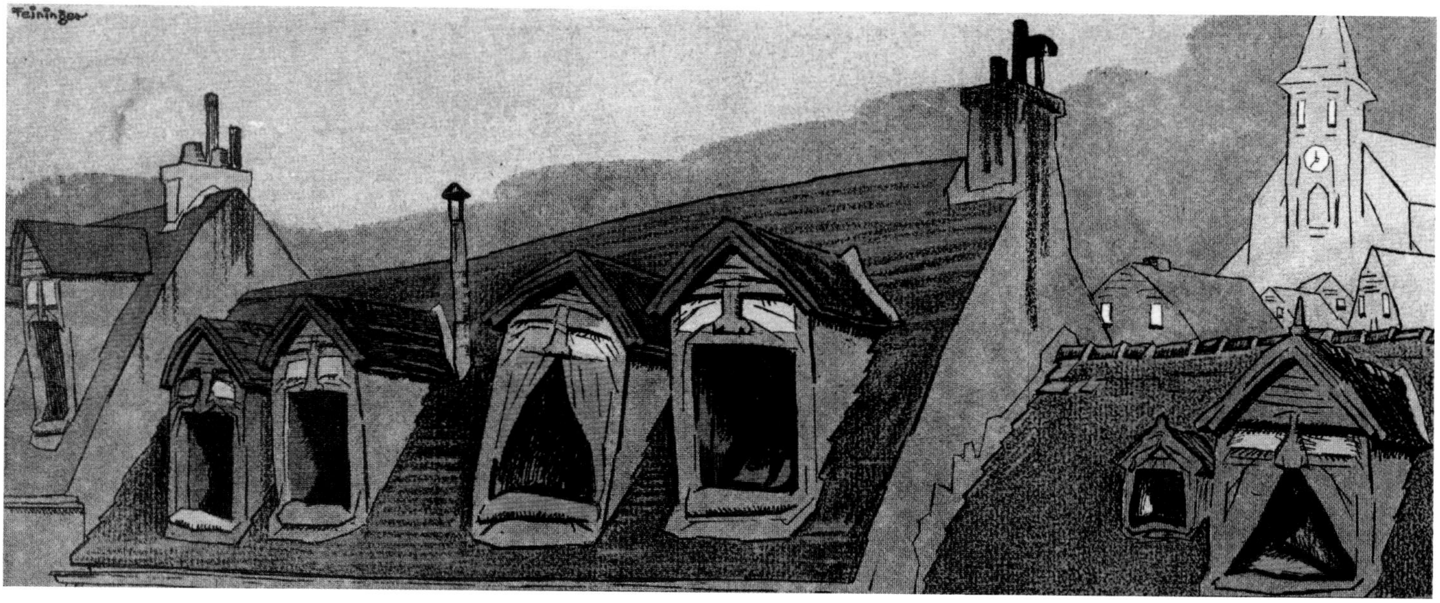
Feininger

Above: Detail from *Wee Willie Winkie's World*, Sunday strip, September 16, 1906. ***Wee Willie Winkie's World*** **is one of the most fascinating strips ever published. Probably inspired by Feininger's fascination for Old World architecture and countryside, it follows Wee Willie, a small boy who has the uncanny ability of transforming objects—trees, clouds, houses, rocks, etc.—into anthropomorphic, resonating shapes. The series offers precious glimpses into the inner-workings of Feininger's artistic mind, and possibly offers one of the most revealing discourses ever attempted on the analytic and figural processes at the core of the modernist revolution.**

Opposite: If some of Feininger's drawings, like this one, were directly influenced by his scale-modeling hobby, his love of carved lines and sculpted volumes can be felt everywhere in his graphic work.

his comics of the early 1880s. During the following decade, Feininger would have the unique advantage of experiencing the German tradition at the highest professional level while cultivating his natural affinity with the American school.

After a number of months in Hamburg, Lyonel spent his first German summer in Berlin, still left to his own devices as his parents were in Brazil. In October 1888, he enrolled in Berlin's Prussian Royal Academy of Art. The following year he passed his exams with flying colors, well ahead of his fellow pupils. That year he published some drawings, again very influenced by Busch, in the Berlin publication *Humoristische Blätter*.

His initial academic and professional successes, of which he was proud, were encouraging, but this did not stop him from experiencing darker thoughts calling him to return to New York. The young artist was nostalgic by nature and memories of his American childhood came back to haunt him incessantly in the form of spectral visions, ghostly moments charged with emotion. These included an image, remembered from a trip to South Carolina, of mysterious silhouettes standing out against the shining water of a canal at sunset and, more troublingly, the ethereal pale faces of the passengers riding on an elevated Third Avenue train, which he saw slip by one day, like an apparition.

These iconic phantoms and many others were by Feininger's own admission (his sons T. Lux and Andréas have devoted a very beautiful book to the subject) central to his pictorial work. One of the paradoxes of Feininger's work as an artist enthralled by trains, bikes, and the period's flourishing high-speed technology was the static nature of his art, which sought to capture, to "photograph," purely contemplative non-narrative moments as true emotional and artistic fetishes. This figural tension was exactly what was to make his graphic work so grippingly modern.

But, in 1890, homesickness still rankled and caused real physical suffering. Germany was a prison; America a beckoning utopia. In June, buoyed up by his first professional and academic achievements, Lyonel explained his plan to his parents who were back from Brazil: if he could manage to get published in *Judge* or *Life*, or in the worst case scenario, work to pay the monthly bills in a Wall Street office, he thought he could earn a living in New York.

Lyonel's father gave his consent. Lyonel was nineteen and his German exile had only lasted two years. His return was set for September.

1890–1894: Liège - Berlin
Belgian Gothic

THAT SUMMER DID NOT pan out as expected, however. By a cruel turn of fate, the young man who had so often been left to his own devices was to be sanctioned almost immediately after returning to his family's sphere of influence. In order to help out a friend he had pawned his watch, and suddenly parental wrath came down upon him. Treated as the black sheep and accused of cultivating a bohemian lifestyle, he wasn't allowed to return happily to America; instead, his father condemned him to finishing his studies in a Catholic college in Liège, Belgium. Though Feininger was blissfully unaware of it at the time, the incident meant his exile in Europe had just been prolonged for forty-seven years.

With a reaction that was as much a result of survival instinct as the discovery of his own very real spirituality, the young

Caran d'Ache (illustrations), A. Millaud (text), *La Comédie du Jour* (Plon, 1886). **After a trip to Paris in 1892, Feininger praised French pen work as "superb." The artist he had most prominently in mind, at the time, must have been Caran d'Ache, whose wacky illustrations for *La Comédie du Jour* clearly made a lasting impression on him: note the melodramatic conspiratorial character—an early prototype for Mysterious Pete and, more importantly, the angular, unsentimental pen work with its ironic slant towards children's drawing and carved toys. Even Caran d'Ache's typical lettering seems to have influenced Feininger's.**

man was to surmount this enormous disappointment. He would even end up thanking his father for having entrusted him to the priests of Collège St. Servais in Liège.

Perhaps he was tired of continually dealing with his American ghosts; in any case, the few months he spent in Belgium from the fall of 1890 to the spring of '91 were to leave other images, typically European this time, engraved on his memory. At one point he hid away for an unforgettable week in the streets of Gothic Brussels, which were all lit up like the rooms of a gigantic castle: scowling cathedrals and medieval houses half-drenched in shadow concealed strange curved deformities, crooked chimneys whispered secrets to each other, and gutters frowned like eyebrows above the wide-open eyes of rectangular windows. And then there was the local countryside with its anachronistic thatched roofs, rekindling his flame for the magical Europe of his childhood, the Europe of the Brothers Grimm and Peter Schlemiel, the man who sold his own shadow. It was a chance to dive into another time and another world, deeper still than his personal memories, paving the way for the anthropomorphic world of *Wee Willie Winkie*, one of the two great comic strips he was to publish in America in the following decade.

Belgium filled a void: it was an image world worthy of replacing the neurosis of exile. The homesickness lessened in the tranquility and reflection of the Liège school. When Feininger returned to Berlin at the beginning of summer 1891, he was still every bit the yankee and would remain so during the many decades to come, but he was no longer quite as American as before. Images of old world Europe and its fairy tales were to remain implanted.

The Berlin Academy— Praise of American Illustration

FROM THEN ON, Feininger lived with his mother and sisters in a comfortable Berlin apartment. After years of tension his parents had separated and the young man experienced for the first time a degree of family stability. In the winter of 1891, he studied under Adolf Schlabitz, a teacher who particularly favored watercolor and decorative design. In 1892, he managed to get into the most advanced class in the Berlin Academy and quickly became an outstanding pupil placed under the tutelage of the town's best art teacher, Woldemar Friedrich, who introduced him to the great German tradition. As the star pupil he easily obtained a number of commissions and started earning his living illustrating six-penny novels and publishing caricatures in various illustrated periodicals.

In November 1892 he disappeared for six or eight months to Paris where he immersed himself in his drawing. His budget did not always allow him to enjoy all the capital's cultural riches, but he could do studies of the moving folds of elegant ladies' dresses, which had a marvelous feel of liberty and ease. This trip must have been the occasion for a hitherto undisclosed artistic influence that was to have lasting effects on Feininger's comic strips. In a letter to a friend, he praised French pen work as *superb*. There's no doubt that the artist he had most prominently in mind at the time was Caran d'Ache, whose early illustrative work contained uncanny prototypes of Feininger's future cast of *Kin-der-Kids* characters, and seems to have inspired even his highly recognizable lettering.

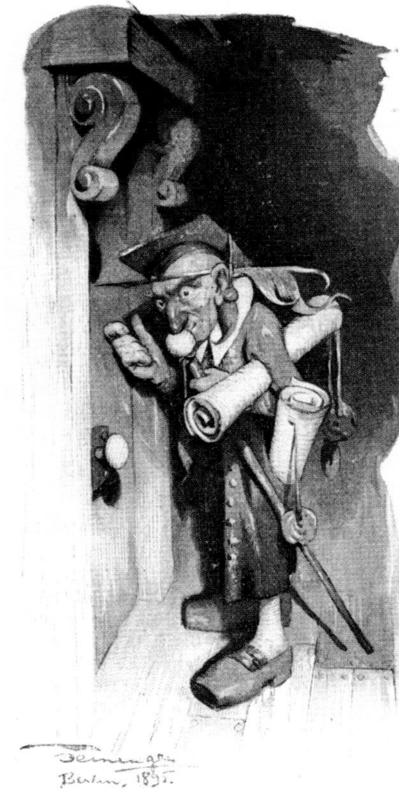
Feininger
Berlin, 1895.

Illustration for *Gorgonzola, The Author*, by John Kendrick Bangs, *Harper's Round Table*, February 9, 1897.

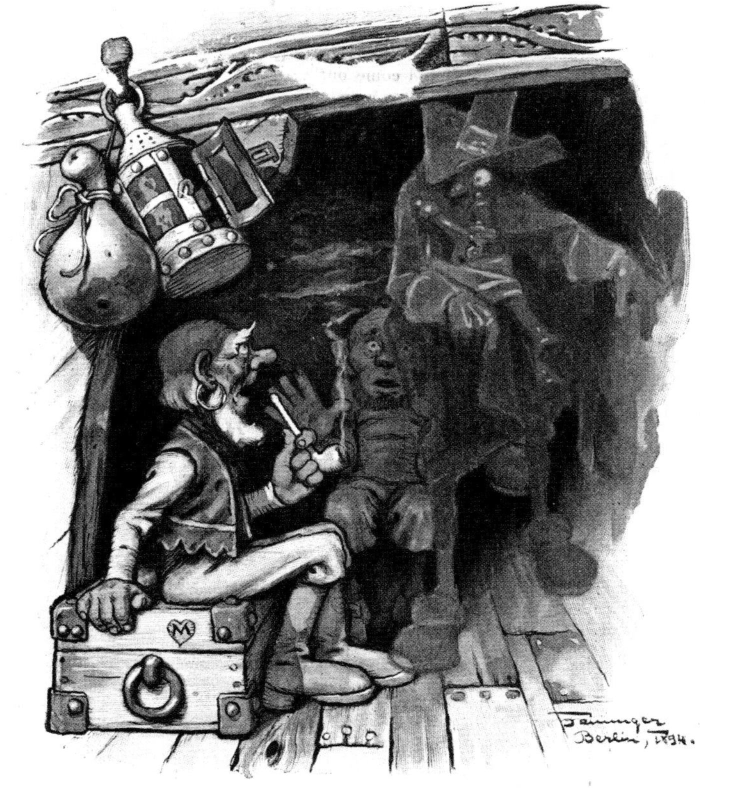
Feininger
Berlin, 1894.

Illustration for *The Loss of the "Gretchen B,"* by John Kendrick Bangs, *Harper's Round Table*, July 27, 1897. **The ghost is a clear link between the conspiratorial silhouette in Caran d'Ache's *La Comédie du Jour* and the Mysterious Pete character in *The Kin-der-Kids*.**

On returning to Berlin, Feininger started again selling illustrations and caricatures to various local publications. His study and free research sought to consolidate his professional know-how. He was quite clear from now on which direction he wanted to take:

> *Of course book-illustration is my aim and zwar [what is more] for the present, at least, illustrations of fantastic subjects as: Fairy Stories, Nonsense stories...and Children's Books; I find in this field everything to call out my powers and feel happy in my work; which is the Hauptsache [main thing] ...I think without pride of vanity that I may claim to be alone in my line of work in America.*
>
> APRIL 6, 1894, SCHEYER

In another letter sent at the same time to Francis Kortheuer, Feininger was even more precise:

> *You know that although there are in Germany some splendid fairy-tale illustrators: Hermann Vogel, Richter, etc., yet none of them have paid much [attention] to anything more than the decorative and glamorous part of fairy- or wonder Tale depiction...I get on a distinctly different, very individual, un-traditional mission, such as is after all, the only thing to do where the country for which I work and always mean to work (America) is itself in these matters so little traditional...*
> *I mean to assure the position of the Nonsense-Story, which title does not preclude the possibility of its containing pure humor, feeling, etc., by any means!...*
> *I have an idea for an entire book, a series of quaint chronicles, to be written and illustrated by myself.*
>
> JUNE 22, 1894, SCHEYER

At the beginning of 1894, Feininger was still fixated with his initial goal of returning to America to work there as an illustrator or even author of stories in images. After a long interruption, his correspondence with Francis Kortheuer was to start up again more intensely. As before, the two friends exchanged periodicals and books. Sending copies of *Fliegende Blätter* to his friend, Lyonel wrote:

> *We have nothing like them in America (I mean in their style or as good), although Frost and Opper are just as fine in a different branch of humor. Frost is the king of American illustrators of humorous subjects. Howard Pyle, E.A. Abbey, W.T. Smedley, C.S. Reinhardt are the "big ones."*
>
> MARCH 10, 1894, SCHEYER

The very high opinion that he held of the humorist A.B. Frost is particularly interesting, given his project for an "entire book" in the nonsense vein. A.B. Frost was in fact the author of an album entitled *Stuff and Nonsense* (1884), which combined stories in images and illustrated limericks.[2] The book Feininger dreamt of was possibly a similar compilation, composed of comics and limericks. It would display the international medley of influences the young man had been exposed to, among which Caran d'Ache's graphic style had probably weighed more than any other.

Of course, all the clues also point to the fact that this original pet project ultimately became the source for the American comic strip he would draw a dozen years later for the *Chicago Tribune*.

Lustige Blätter, November 15, 1905.
One of Feininger's self-portraits.

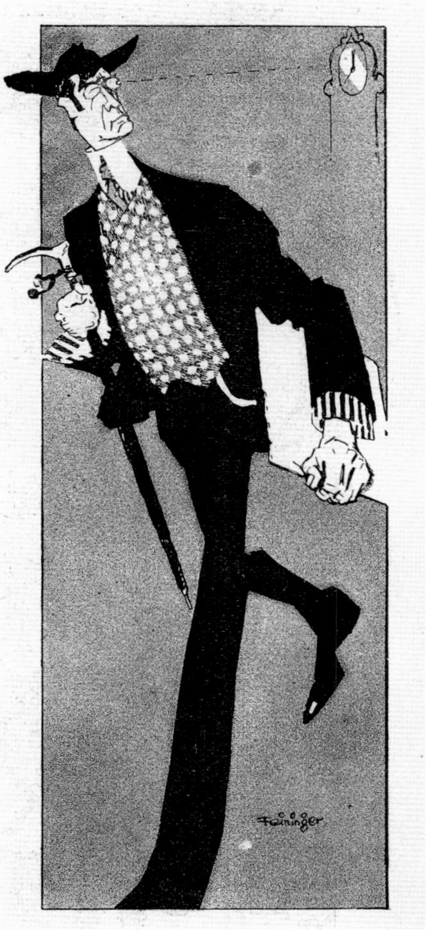

Harper's Young People

ALL THE ILLUSTRATORS named in the quote above worked for the biggest American publisher of the day, Harper & Brothers. It is clear that Feininger hoped to become one of the fold as soon as he could return to the country. At the beginning of 1894, a decisive step was made in this direction: in January, he sent a series of drawings to *Harper's*; in April, he received a letter full of praise commissioning other drawings on the theme of fairies, gnomes, goblins, etc. The editor asked him to illustrate John Kendrick Bangs's short stories meant for *Harper's Young People*, the house's periodical for children. Bangs was a prolific and popular author specialized in ghost tales. This theme had been a subject of predilection for Lyonel ever since he had seen the anonymous and ghostly faces of the passengers of the aboveground train on Third Avenue passing by.

Moreover, John K. Bangs worked with the two American illustrators Feininger admired the most, A.B. Frost and Peter Newell, a newcomer whose style was round and rich and whose ink washes were illuminated with a very particular light. *Harper's Young People* had been publishing Peter Newell's work for some time and his influence is noticeable in one of the earliest Feininger pieces published in the same magazine in 1895. It is also detectable in certain illustrations dating from the early 1900s published in German newspapers.

In addition to this drawing, we have located some John K. Bangs stories illustrated by Feininger and we are delighted to be able to reproduce these images, which have not been published since their original appearance in *Harper's Young People/Harper's Round Table* from 1894 to 1897 (the magazine changed its title in November 1894).

IN A LETTER to Kortheuer, dated April 1894, Feininger announces this American commission:

> *My drawings for Harper's are "slightly" caricatured, but in a way which, I flatter myself, does not cause repulsion but only adds to vividness of the characterization. And the secret of their not impressing one as being deformed, is because they are obviously represented as being "pygmies" or a little race of (principally) dutch and "olde Englishe."*
>
> APRIL 2, 1894, SCHEYER

The secret to which Feininger alludes is particularly interesting: it is one of the major keys of a trend noticeable in American humor illustration over the preceding fifteen years and which directly participated in the stylistic revolution of the American comic strip at the end of the 1890s.

FIGURES SHARING certain physical characteristics—small stature, giant hands and feet, and big heads—as if belonging to a sort of dwarf race, had been current in humorous drawings for children in Germany and England since the middle of the century. In the U.S. during the 1880s, the best-selling children's series was Palmer Cox's *The Brownies*, published in the *St. Nicholas* periodical—a direct competitor of *Harper's Round Table*. *The Brownies* were a group of diminutive dwarf people with round heads. Their oversized saucer eyes are direct descendants of Frost's and Cruikshank's ghosts.

The Brownies played an important role in the establishment of a typology that would become specific to comic strip characters in the age of the *Funnies*,[3] and it is quite significant that Feininger's description of an imaginary pygmy race perfectly encapsulates a stylistic shift the main consequence of which was to replace the repulsive effect of traditional caricature with a different kind of deformation that conveyed attractive cuteness. Cuteness is not a subjective quality. In a famous article, Konrad Lorenz defines it as the set of physical characteristics typical of human babies that triggers a positive feeling of protection and sympathy in us.[4] This innate mechanism evolved for understandable reasons and is quite uncontrollable, which explains why it may be triggered by decoys of all sorts (including animals, inanimate objects, or graphic creatures). This happens when the decoys possess some of the following attributes, listed by Lorenz—a relatively disproportionate cranium with huge eyes that are situated low in the face, and well-rounded cheeks (with marked corners at the mouth). The arms and legs should be short and thick, the consistency firm and elastic. All these characteristics were present in Feininger's pygmies.

1894–1906: Berlin
Ulk, Lustige Blätter, Narrenschiff...

WHEN FEININGER'S German career finally got off the ground, after eight years on the Old Continent, it was to a flying start. At the beginning of 1895, the liberal Berlin daily, the highly regarded *Berliner Taggeblatte*, opened its doors to him. The daily was accompanied once a week by a color comic supplement named *Ulk*. Feininger could now congratulate himself on being published on either side of the Atlantic in two periodicals with a very high circulation. The recognition of his talent was undeniable; however he was still not truly famous. The American editor published his drawings in dribs and drabs; 1895 went by and *Harper's Round Table* used but one of his illustrations in a tiny

Opposite: *Lustige Blätter*, October 18, 1905.
Vision of a green future? In the 1890s, Feininger often played with futuristic landscapes full of flying machines, but some of his drawings, like this view of *Leipzigerstrasse 1995*, played on intriguingly prescient themes.

Leipzigerstrasse 1995. (Zum Projekt der „Großen Berliner“.)

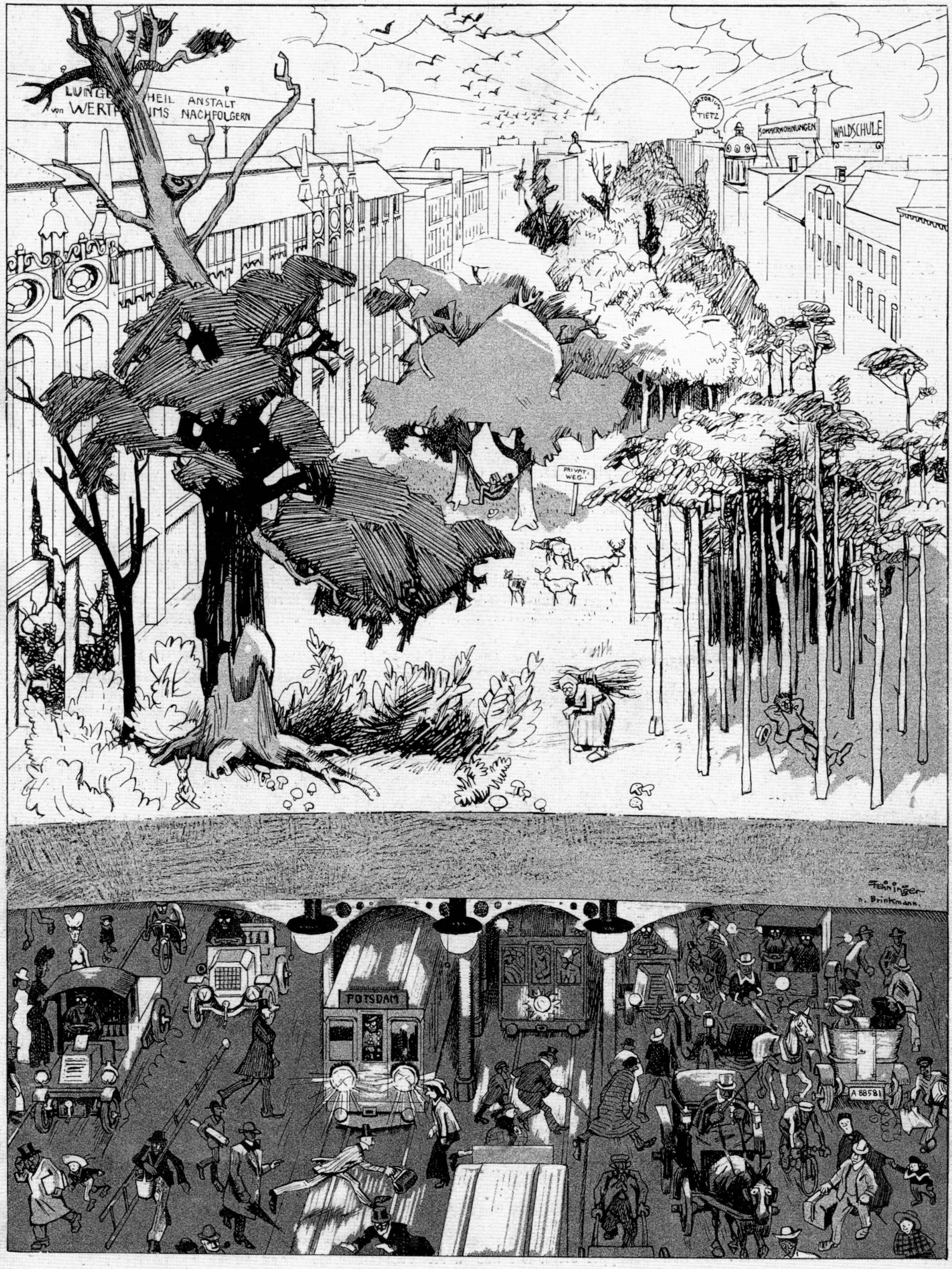
LUNGE HEIL ANSTALT
von WERT IMS NACHFOLGERN
SANATORIUM TIETZ
SOMMERWOHNUNGEN
WALDSCHULE
PRIVAT-WEG!
Feininger
v. Brinkmann
POTSDAM
A 88581

Tief die Welt verworren schallt,
Oben einsam Rehe grasen — —

Eichendorff.

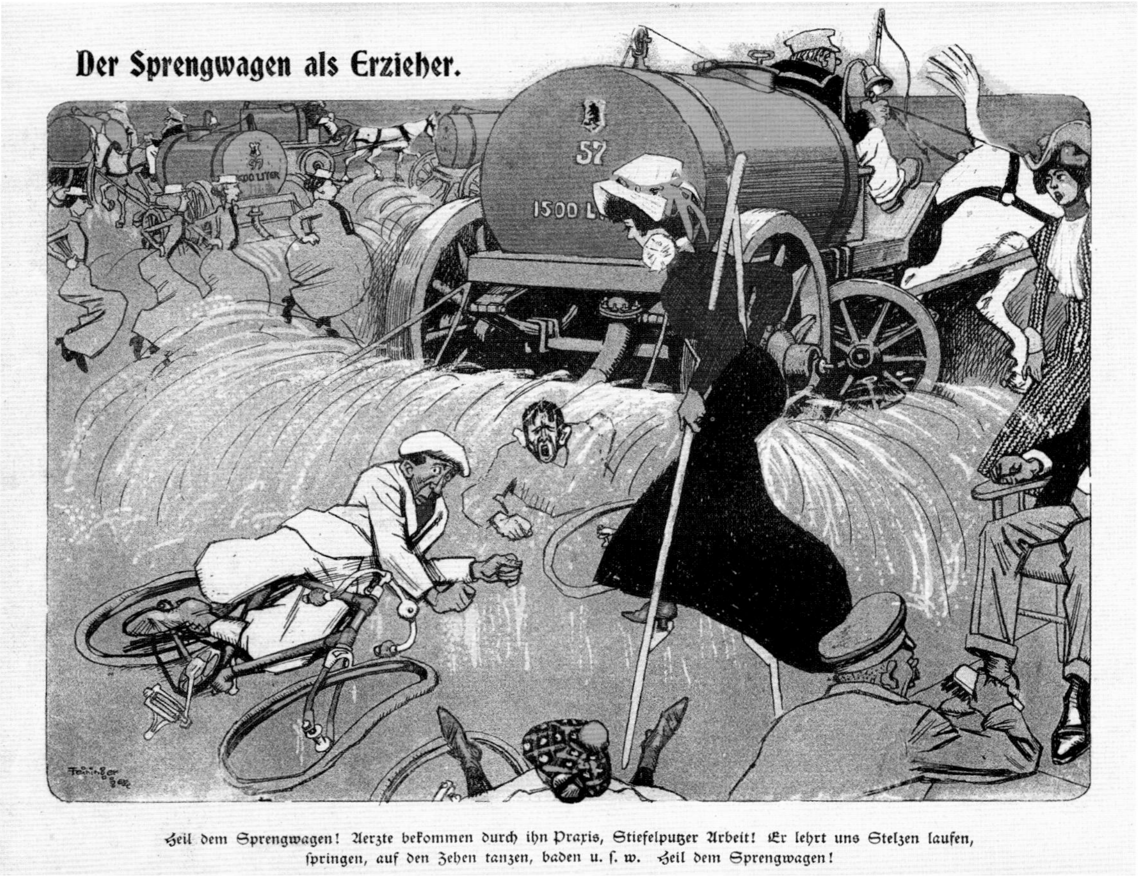
Der Sprengwagen als Erzieher.
57
1500 L
Heil dem Sprengwagen! Aerzte bekommen durch ihn Praxis, Stiefelputzer Arbeit! Er lehrt uns Stelzen laufen, springen, auf den Zehen tanzen, baden u. s. w. Heil dem Sprengwagen!

Ulk, color supplement to the *Berliner Taggenblatte*, August 1, 1902. Feininger's childhood fascination with boats, trains, bicycles, and automobiles was always central to his interest in drawing. His cartoons often displayed the diagrammatic precision of the engineer.

pantomime in the humorous assortment of the magazine's final pages. A great number of his John K. Bangs illustrations, drawn in 1894 and '95, would not appear for another two years. Undoubtedly frustrated by this disappointing and erratic treatment, the artist was forced once again to shelve his plan to return to the U.S. It was now the satirical Berlin newspapers that provided the most significant and regular part of his income. In 1896 he was earning 200 Marks a month in comparison to 50 Marks fourteen months prior. Over the following twelve years, he lived in Berlin on the money he earned for the drawings he regularly published in *Ulk*, *Lustige Blätter*, *Narrenschiff*, and a few other humorous publications.

At first he was mainly admired for his futuristic fantasies (a particularly popular theme at the end of the century). During his stay in Liège he had admired the splendid illustrations of Riou in Jules Verne's novels; he was well aware of European tradition. But his own personal tastes led him rather to the likes of F.B. Opper, whose cartoon work in the 1890s often included weirdly comic inventions, absurd gadgets, and other highly fantastical flight machinery. Again, this kind of imagery probably sprang from the work of the great illustrator George Cruikshank, whose humorous prints, toward 1850, depicted detailed (albeit absurd) flying machines in a sort of semi-diagrammatic representation that could be animated in the reader's mind's eye, despite their actual impossibility of working; similar contraptions can be found in numerous comic strips of the 1900s, like Feininger's own *Kin-der-Kids*, McCay's *Little Nemo*, Herriman's *Major Ozone*, and Harry Grant Dart's *Explorigator*.

Another Feininger idiosyncrasy, at the end of the 1890s, was a turn towards a child-like drawing style, an effect Adolf Oberländer was fond of using in *Fliegende Blätter*, but which was to take on a very different plastic meaning for the American artist. In fact, all of Feininger's style tends towards a simplification of form, a process of which children's art and naive graffiti seem to hold the original secret. All through his long life he would often come back to this concept. The young man's caricatures quietly raised important pictorial issues.

Despite the continued rankling homesickness, his early days as a caricaturist of some caliber were probably thrilling. Feininger often depicted himself and his colleagues in *Ulk* or *Lustige Blätter*'s offices, positive proof of his enjoyment in being involved in the publishing world. He was very much sought after and his work was no longer rejected. There were, however, certain limiting factors: editors asked him to illustrate rather coarse jokes or expected him to illustrate one topical theme or another. This did not prevent him from

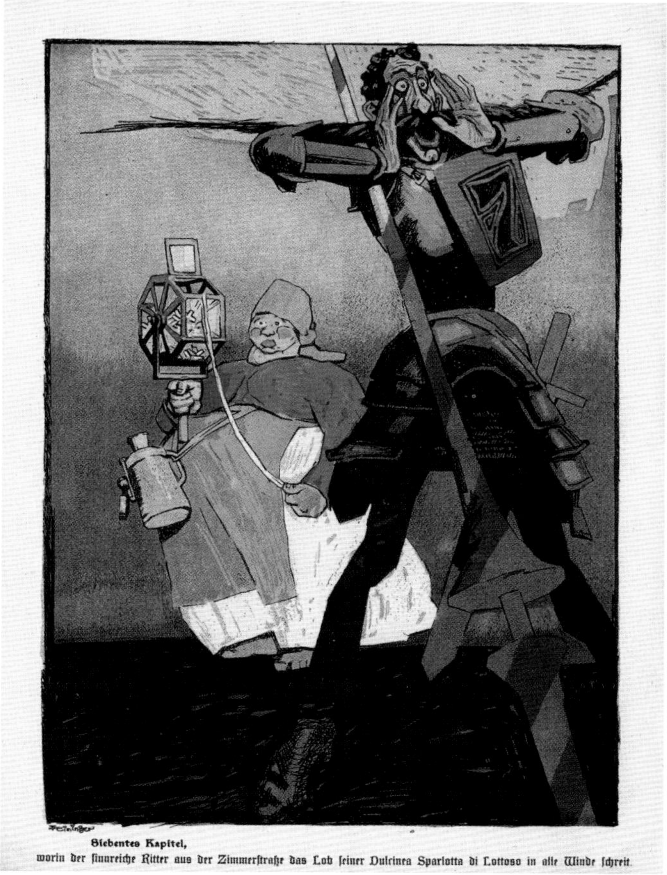
Siebentes Kapitel,
worin der sinnreiche Ritter aus der Zimmerstraße das Lob seiner Dulcinea Sparlotta di Lottoso in alle Winde schreit.

Lustige Blätter, January 11, 1905.

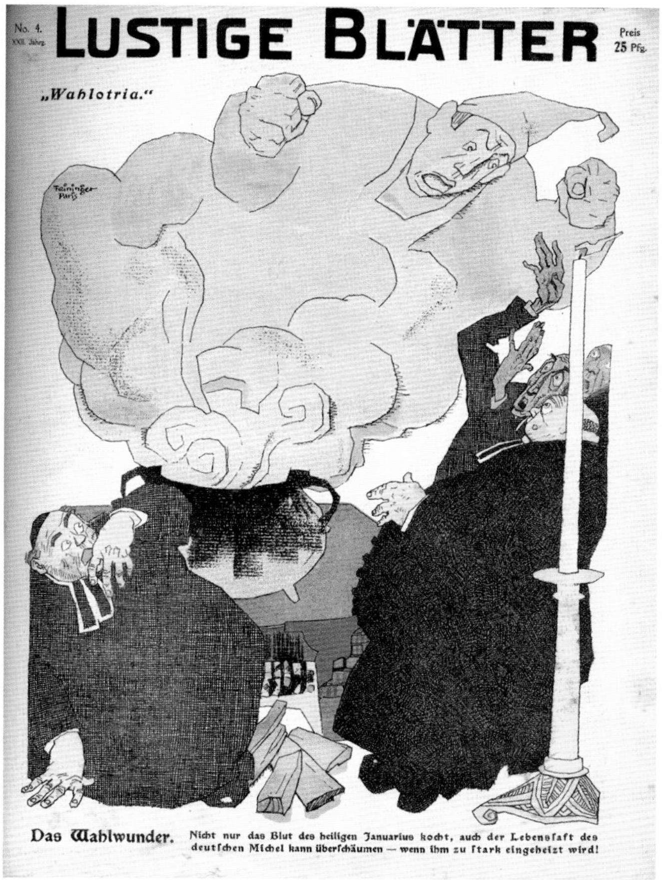
No. 4.
LUSTIGE BLÄTTER
Preis 25 Pfg.
„Wahlotria."
Das Wahlwunder.
Nicht nur das Blut des heiligen Januarius kocht, auch der Lebenssaft des deutschen Michel kann überschäumen — wenn ihm zu stark eingeheizt wird!

Lustige Blätter, January 23, 1907.

producing images whose line work continually sought to invent and sculpt forms faithful to his own aesthetic ideal. The essence of Feininger's line work has much to do with a universe of angles, broken lines, and flattened curves, which was probably a throwback to the innocent art of his New York golden days, when he gauged and carved the lines of his boats and tried them out on Central Park's pond.

Jugendstil

IN 1896, two important Munich periodicals, *Die Jugend* and *Simplicissimus*, published their first issues. *Simplicissimus*, especially, became the launching pad for a particularly flourishing school of young German artists doubling as political cartoonists or illustrators, such as Olaf Gulbransson, Rudolf Wilke, Bruno Paul, and Pascin. Feininger's strong, modernist sense of composition and line matched theirs (he was to meet Pascin in the circle of German artist expatriates who attended the Café du Dôme in Paris in the second half of the 1900s).

But, even compared to their powerful work, his own displayed an extraordinary variety of style and techniques. As if in reaction to the increasingly uncomfortable burden of imposed subjects, he continually invented new challenges more worthy of his artistic ethics. He was gradually working his way towards what he called "free painting," even when defining the lithographic process used by the magazines, at the time, for printing colors:

> *Do not think exclusively of the key-stone [which gives the design its contourlines]. The whole [printing process] must be conducted like an orchestra. Only this way can you achieve the magic integration of the hues and their values with the rich complementing function of shades, textures and blots. Without this integration, your work will always remain just a contour-drawing to which color has been added. To utilize to the fullest the potentialities of the technical process of printing is a necessary prerequisite of success in this art.*
>
> UNDATED, SCHEYER

Toward 1906, Feininger felt more and more distanced from the editorial direction of the publications he had been working with for over ten years. Although he had as yet not tried it out, the challenge of serious painting became an irresistible temptation. He well knew that it would take several years to achieve anything suitable for showing. He also knew there was only one city where he could flourish as an artist. But at the very moment when he had decided to take the risk of going to live in Paris an unexpected visitor offered him the chance to pack his bags and return to the U.S., all expenses paid. *continues on page 142*

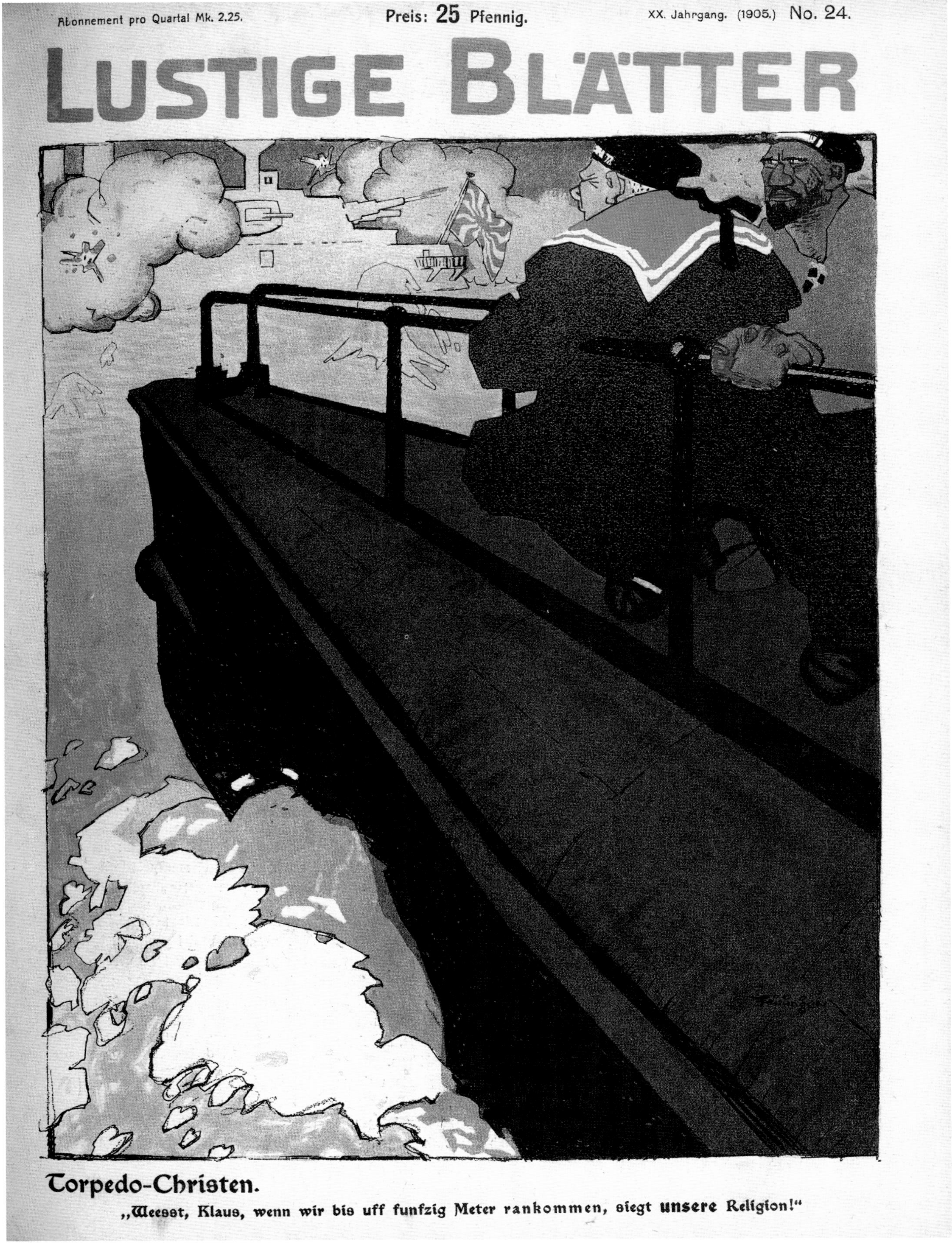
Abonnement pro Quartal Mk. 2.25. Preis: 25 Pfennig. XX. Jahrgang. (1905.) No. 24.

LUSTIGE BLÄTTER

Torpedo-Christen.

„Weesst, Klaus, wenn wir bis uff funfzig Meter rankommen, siegt **unsere** Religion!“

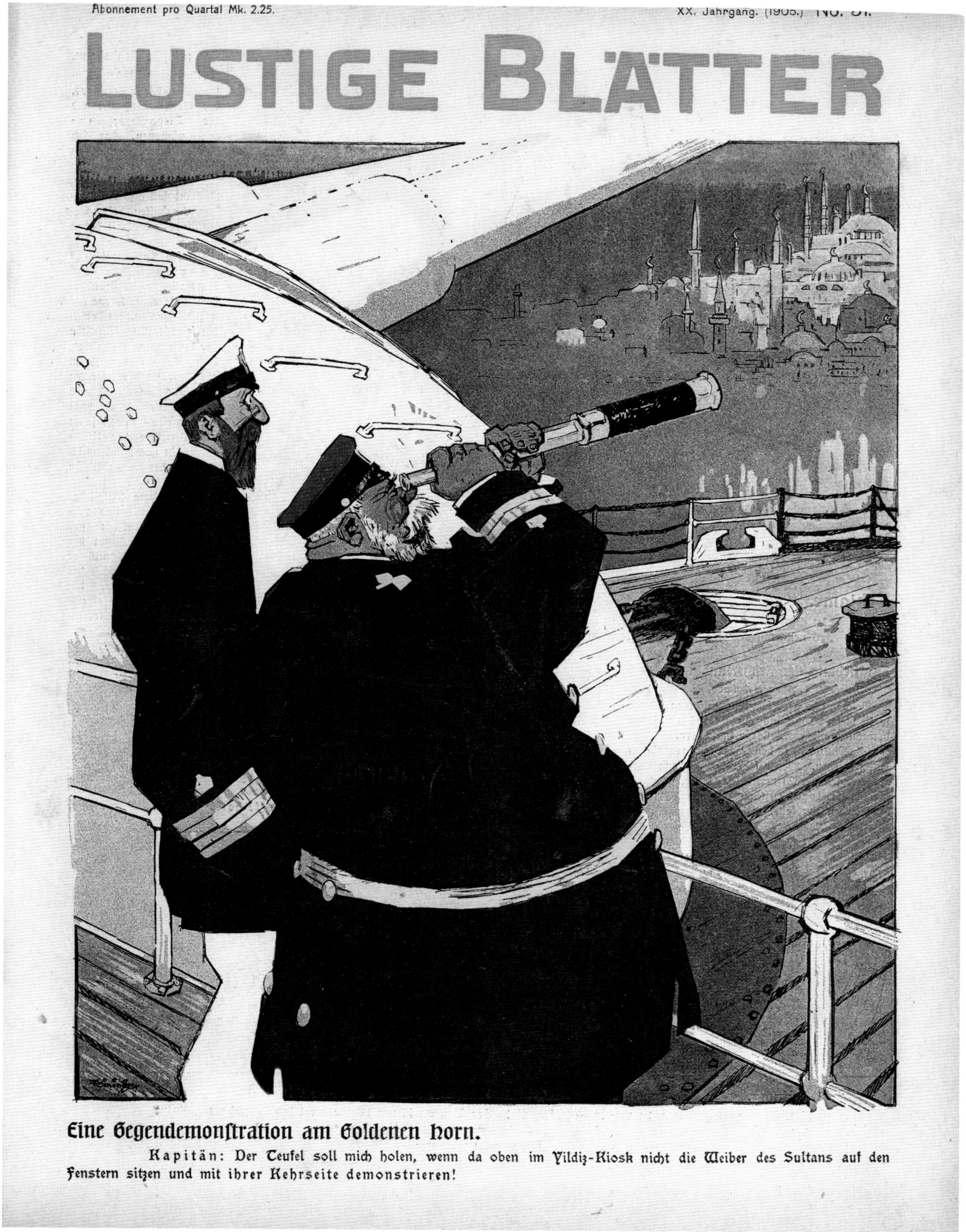

Abonnement pro Quartal Mk. 2.25. XX. Jahrgang. (1905.) No. 51.

LUSTIGE BLÄTTER

Eine Gegendemonstration am Goldenen Horn.

Kapitän: Der Teufel soll mich holen, wenn da oben im Yildiz-Kiosk nicht die Weiber des Sultans auf den Fenstern sitzen und mit ihrer Kehrseite demonstrieren!

Opposite: *Lustige Blätter*, June 14, 1905. Above: *Lustige Blätter*, December 20, 1905. Always the modernist, Feininger loved to fiddle with the conventional rules of composition, cramming a lot of visual information into an upper corner, and leaving the rest of the picture to the formal interplay of shapes and empty space.

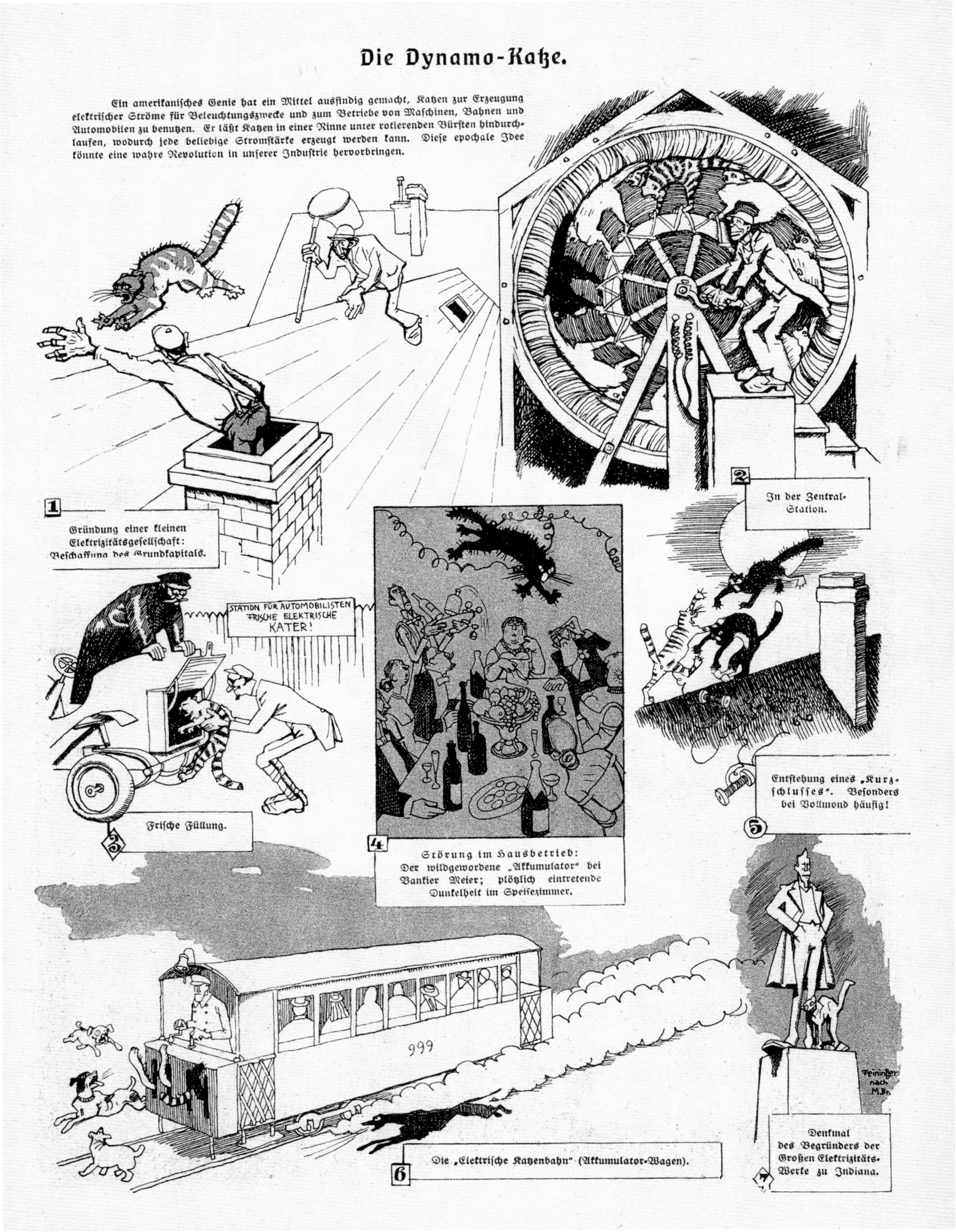
Die Dynamo-Katze.
Ein amerikanisches Genie hat ein Mittel ausfindig gemacht, Katzen zur Erzeugung elektrischer Ströme für Beleuchtungszwecke und zum Betriebe von Maschinen, Bahnen und Automobilen zu benutzen. Er läßt Katzen in einer Rinne unter rotierenden Bürsten hindurchlaufen, wodurch jede beliebige Stromstärke erzeugt werden kann. Diese epochale Idee könnte eine wahre Revolution in unserer Industrie hervorbringen.
1
Gründung einer kleinen Elektrizitätsgesellschaft: Beschaffung des Grundkapitals.
2
In der Zentral-Station.
STATION FÜR AUTOMOBILISTEN FRISCHE ELEKTRISCHE KATER!
3
Frische Füllung.
4
Störung im Hausbetrieb: Der wildgewordene „Akkumulator“ bei Bankier Meier; plötzlich eintretende Dunkelheit im Speisezimmer.
5
Entstehung eines „Kurzschlusses“. Besonders bei Vollmond häufig!
999
6
Die „Elektrische Katzenbahn“ (Akkumulator-Wagen).
Feininger nach M. Br.
7
Denkmal des Begründers der Großen Elektrizitäts-Werke zu Indiana.

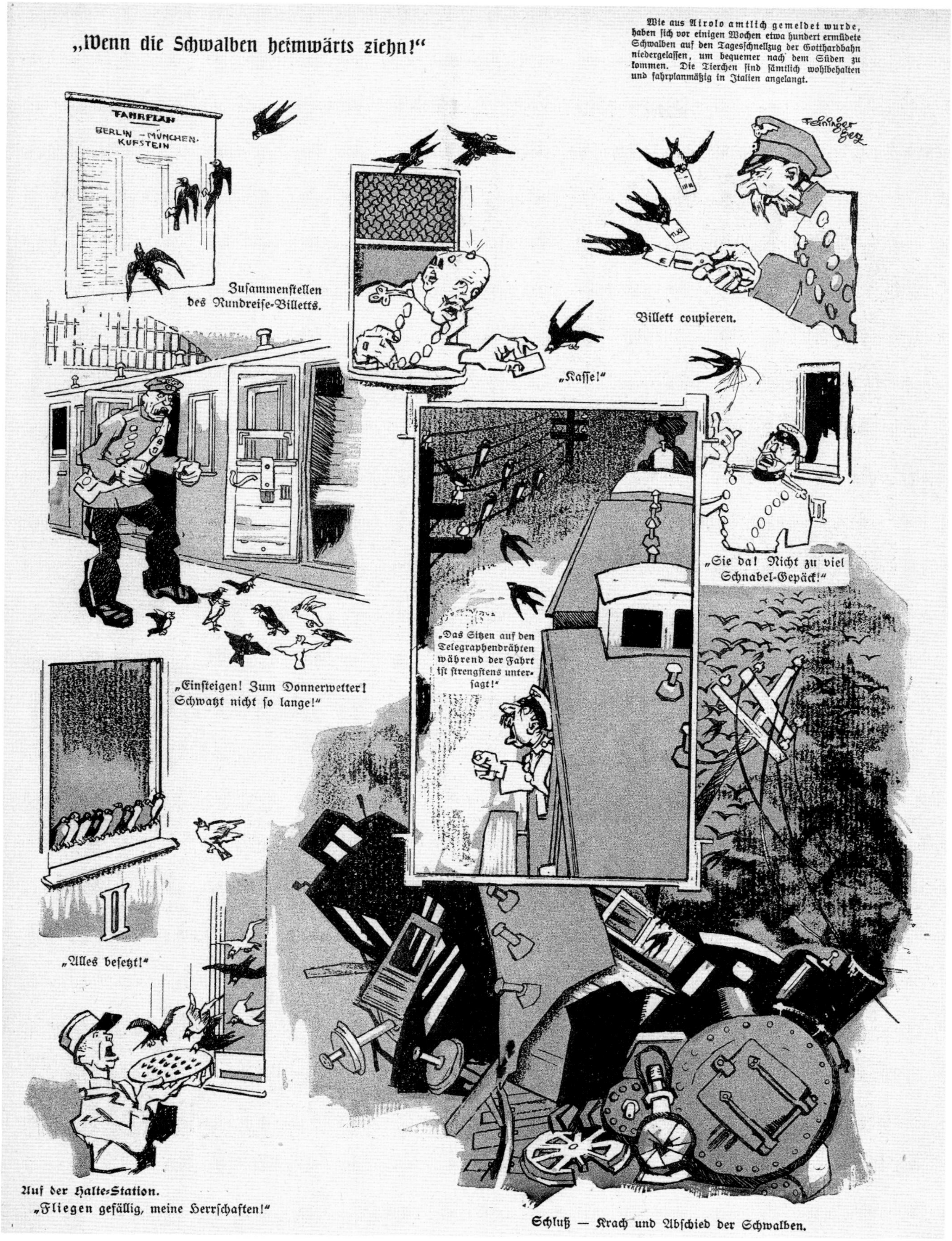
„Wenn die Schwalben heimwärts ziehn!"
Wie aus Airolo amtlich gemeldet wurde, haben sich vor einigen Wochen etwa hundert ermüdete Schwalben auf den Tagesschnellzug der Gotthardbahn niedergelassen, um bequemer nach dem Süden zu kommen. Die Tierchen sind sämtlich wohlbehalten und fahrplanmäßig in Italien angelangt.
FAHRPLAN
BERLIN – MÜNCHEN. KUFSTEIN
Zusammenstellen des Rundreise-Billetts.
„Kasse!"
Billett coupieren.
„Einsteigen! Zum Donnerwetter! Schwatzt nicht so lange!"
„Sie da! Nicht zu viel Schnabel-Gepäck!"
„Das Sitzen auf den Telegraphendrähten während der Fahrt ist strengstens untersagt!"
„Alles besetzt!"
Auf der Halte-Station. „Fliegen gefällig, meine Herrschaften!"
Schluß — Krach und Abschied der Schwalben.

Opposite: *Lustige Blätter*, August 23, 1905. Above: *Lustige Blätter*, December 13, 1905. Sequential pages drawn in *Lustige Blätter* in 1905, a year before Feininger was contacted by the *Chicago Tribune*. A page with multiple panels was often approached as an exercise in composition by European artists. The post-Muybridgeian "kinetoscopic" matrix that dominated the American comic strips at the time—with their "mechanically" repetitive framings, equal-sized panels, and pleasant wallpaper gestalt—clearly played no part in Feininger's aesthetics.

1906–1907: Berlin - Paris - Chicago
The Kin-der-Kids and Wee Willie Winkie's World

THE MAN, sent by the *Chicago Tribune*, was named James Keeley. In February 1906, he had been sent on a mission by his newspaper, with a proposition that seemed like Feininger's twenty-year-old fantasy come true. The famous midwestern daily was losing ground to its competitors, whose color Sunday supplements were drawing readers (many of which were German immigrants) away in droves. The newspaper's bold plan was to hire some of the best German illustrators in an attempt to beat competitors at their own game. Having worked for an important Berlin daily for twelve years, Feininger was one of the first artists to be approached. Feininger's surprise must have been matched by that of his visitor when the *Chicago Tribune* agent first met this American sportsman, who had learned the art of cartooning by studying the work of Busch, Opper, and Frost, and had been dreaming for ten years of producing a book of typically American nonsense.

EXACTLY HOW AWARE Feininger was of the rapid changes occurring in American comic strips at that time is difficult to know with any degree of certainty, but when you consider the artists—of the highest international caliber—who were making comics at the time, it would be a safe bet to guess that his knowledge of the fast-evolving medium must have been quite good. He probably had access to pages or indeed albums of F.B. Opper (*Happy Hooligan*), Rudolph Dirks (*Katzenjammer Kids*), Winsor McCay (the *International Herald Tribune* published *Little Nemo* in Europe), and R.F. Outcault (*Buster Brown*). And by retracing, as we have, the major steps in his life, one also realizes that he had been awaiting this kind of chance for a long time. No wonder he enthusiastically agreed to draw a series for the *Chicago Tribune*.

However, despite Keeley's insistence, he refused point blank to return home to America. There were probably very personal reasons for this, as Feininger was in the midst of a painful separation at the time (a situation he depicted in a curious allegorical picture story, in *Lustige Blätter*). He had just met a married woman, Julia Berg,

also a painter, who, according to Ulrich Luckhardt, was ready "to support his search for his own path in art, and cope with the artist's doubt about what he had achieved so far." He said that he would work on the strip in Paris or not at all. Keeley agreed and the contract was signed. For a few days, late in 1905, both men worked on the storyline for the strip. Probably looking for familiar ground, Feininger fell back on a little tribe of "specters," some of which had been old friends for years, like *Strenuous Teddy*, a reference to Teddy Roosevelt, whom he had already caricatured dozens of times in the German periodicals, or *Mysterious Pete*, who rode his flying cloud like a *deus ex machina* from some baroque pantomime. *Mysterious Pete* had already shown his shadowy silhouette in one of the John K. Bangs stories Feininger had illustrated ten years before. A quite similar figure also appeared in the seminal Caran d'Ache album Feininger had bought in Paris in the early 1890s, so he was, quite literally, a ghost from the past. The other characters in the gang probably sprang from the same personal mythology, although the formulaic idea of putting together a team of well-differentiated kids (the Fat guy, the Strong one, the Brainy one, etc.) possibly came from Keeley. The strip would be a rhapsodic, open-ended adventure, whose episodes would be connected by the slightest hint of a storyline: a bunch of kids embarking on a grandiose ocean trip in the family bathtub.

IN TERMS OF pictorial invention, *The Kin-der-Kids* has few rivals. A beautiful blend of American pop culture and European avant-gardism, the short, unfinished run of twenty-nine pages is now, for good reason, iconic. Some intriguing similarities between the *Kin-der-Kids* and George Herriman cartoons published during the same period are worth noting, however. The image in which Feininger caricatures himself introducing the *Kin-der-Kids* is eerily reminiscent of some of Herriman's sketches published in the Hearst sports section. In 1906, Feininger was producing work for a magazine by the name of *Sportshumor* on a regular basis and it would not be that surprising if he was familiar

with the work of his New York counterpart. If anyone could suggest to Feininger what was possible in America in terms of unbridled graphic invention, Herriman would have been the man to watch. Conversely, one might also wonder whether this influence was a two-way process. Some early *Kin-der-Kids* pages that feature primitive and geometric design prefigure *Krazy Kat* layouts of later years.

Similarities in their work possibly sprang from the fact that neither Feininger nor Herriman was particularly inspired by the era's dominant model of the comic strip layout based on a repetitive grid also typical of Muybridge's chronophotographic plates. In color American strips, the graphic impact of repetitive patterns produced by this kind of composition gave a sort of joyfully colored "wallpaper" effect, but Herriman and Feininger tended to favor another solution, derived from romantic illustration, where a decorative theme unifies the page. This type of layout was often favored in Europe by the German illustrators of Feininger's generation (when they drew sequential pages for *Simplicissimus* or *Lustige Blätter*, in particular), or in the French publications of *Le Chat Noir* and the Imprimeries Quantin at the turn of the century. All of this goes back to book illuminators' vine leaves, whose twists and turns linked one image to the next, making a graphic, decorative whole out of the different elements of the page. Some of Feininger's spreads for *Ulk* plainly illustrate this romantic heritage, which became even more obvious in *Wee Willie Winkie's World*, the second series Feininger drew for the *Chicago Tribune*. *continues on page 147*

(Opposite and following spread)

Lustige Blätter, May 4, 1904.

Ulk, color supplement to the *Berliner Taggenblatte*, July 11, 1902.

Ulk, color supplement to the *Berliner Taggenblatte*, July 18, 1902.

Feininger, like many European turn-of-the-century artists in France and Germany, often referred to Baroque decorative compositions in their multi-paneled pages. Similar solutions were also found in playful newspaper layouts on both sides of the Atlantic. Winsor McCay's *Tale of the Jungle Imps* is a good example of this trend—an Art Nouveau extension of the romantic and ubiquitous Gothic Revival approach that had permeated popular illustration since the middle of the 19th century.

Stilllegung der Zechen im Ruhrgebiet.

„Alle Räder stehen still,
Wenn's der Kapitalismus will!"

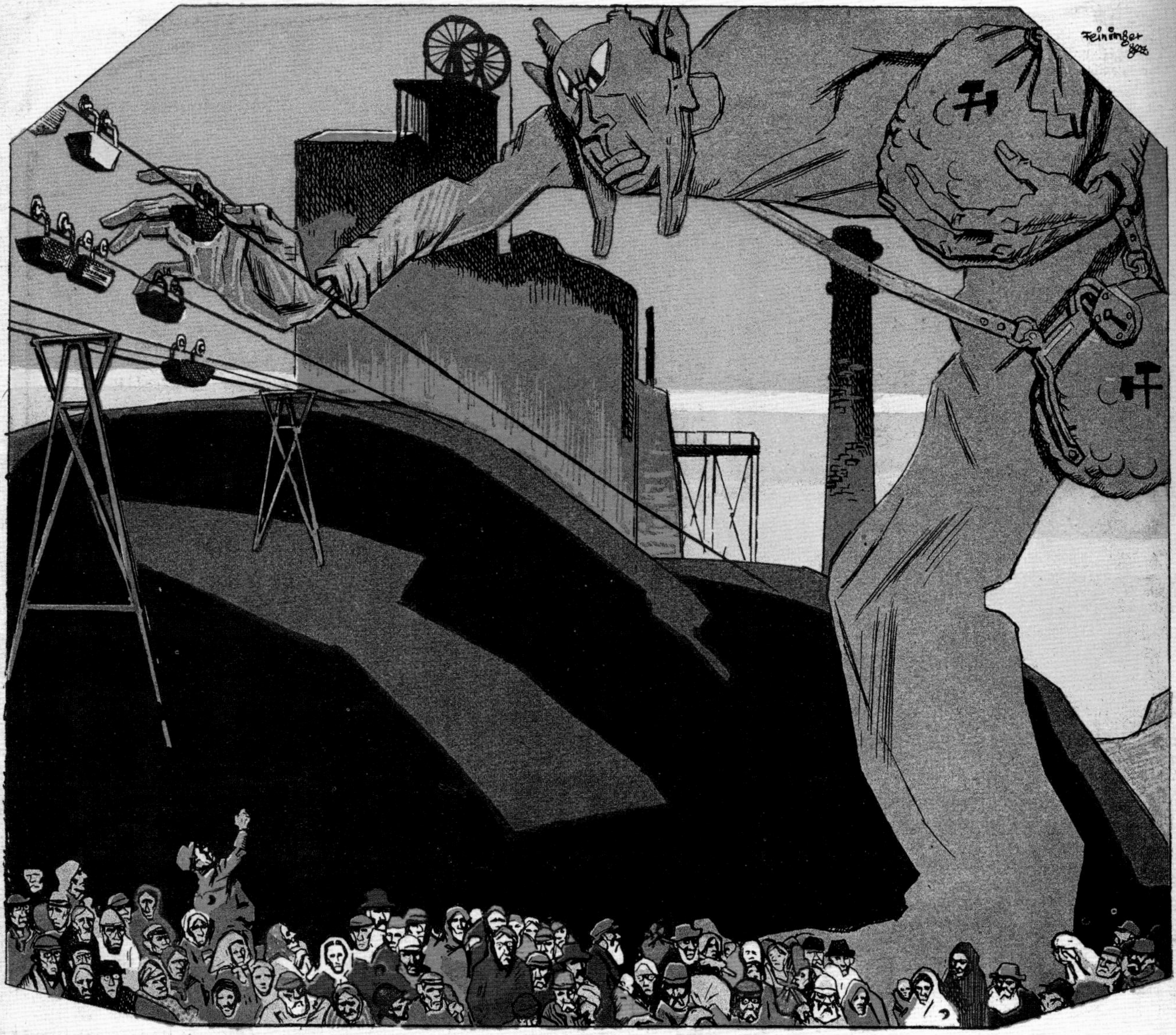
Feininger

Das Syndikat kauft — aber der Arbeiter bezahlt die Zeche!

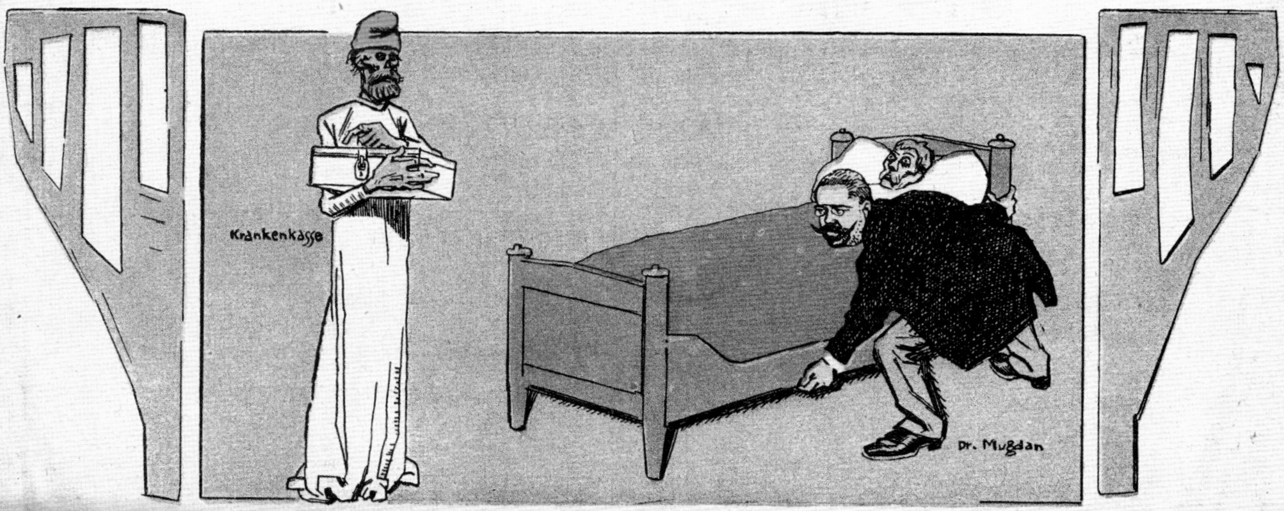
Krankenkasse
Dr. Mugdan

Gevatter Tod.

(Ein Märchen vom Grimm der Aerzte gegen die Krankenkassen.)

„. . . . Als der Arzt aber an das Bett trat, so stand der Tod zu den Füssen des Kranken. Ei, sagte der Arzt, da drehe ich das Bett herum und verändere die Lage des Kranken; denn solange der immer nur auf den — Kassenvorstand sieht, kann ihm nicht geholfen werden!"

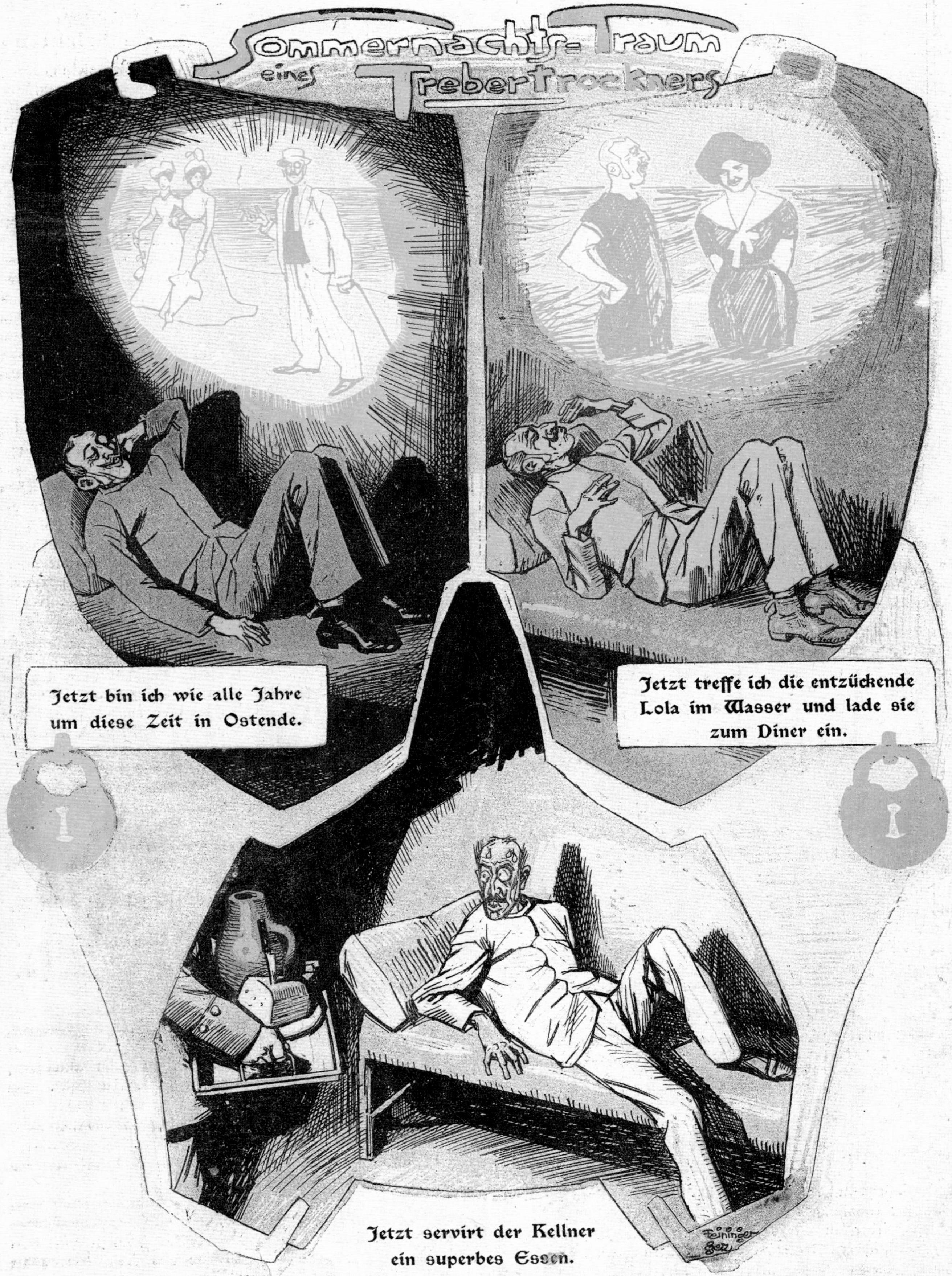
Sommernachts-Traum
eines
Trebertrockners
Jetzt bin ich wie alle Jahre um diese Zeit in Ostende.
Jetzt treffe ich die entzückende Lola im Wasser und lade sie zum Diner ein.
Jetzt servirt der Kellner ein superbes Essen.

"Der Roland von Berlin"

Der Steinerne Gast

Leoncavallo

Leoncavallo

Er denkt an ihn zu jeder Frist.
Selbst wenn er speist — —

— — selbst wenn er küsst.

Auch Nachts schreckt ihn
der Mann von Stein,

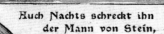

Nur wenn er bei der Arbeit ist,
Da lässt der Roland ihn allein.

Fertig ist die Laube!

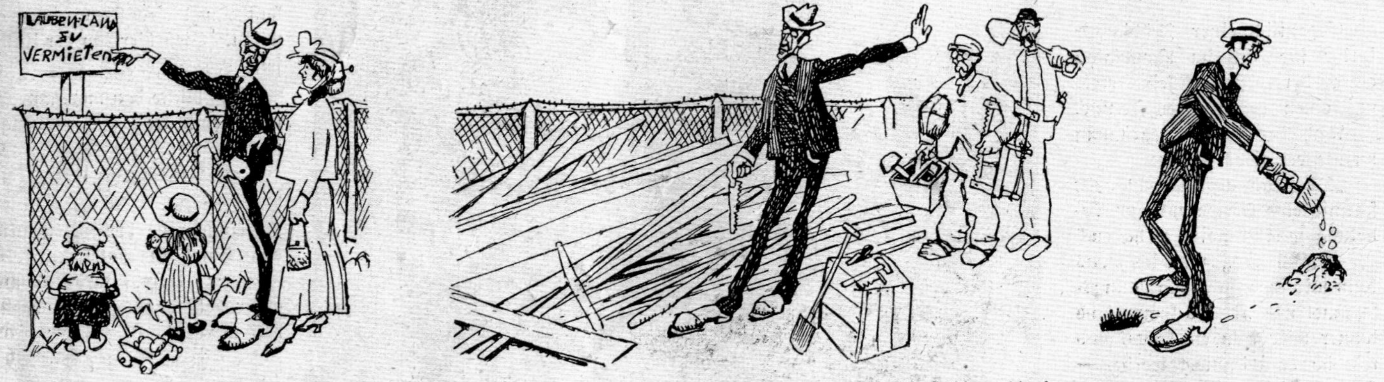

LAUBEN-LAND ZU VERMIETEN

Hier dieses Plätzchen mieten wir, Die Laube mach' ich selber hier!

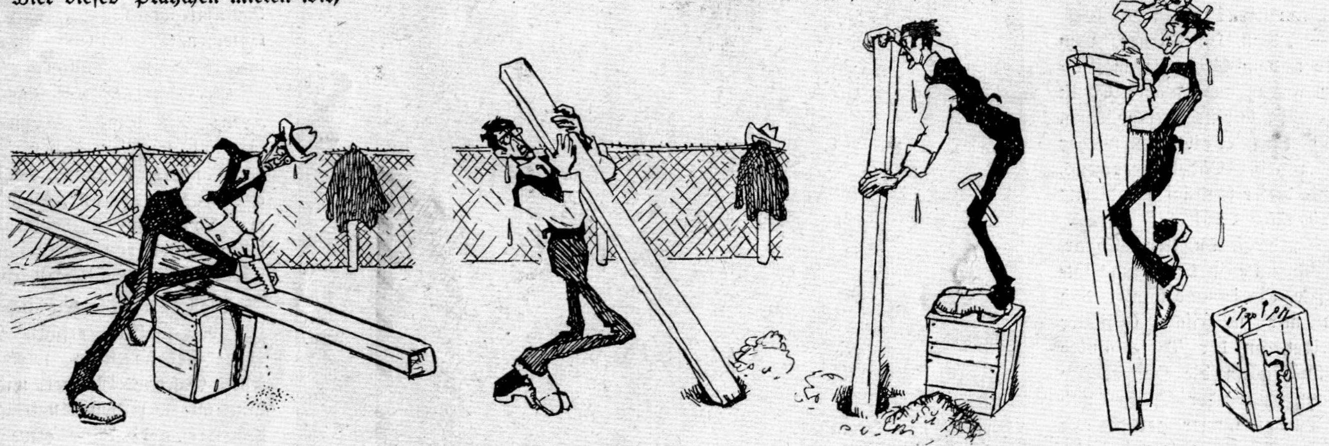

Die Latten her — zur Laubenstütze! Ich bin der reine Lattenfritze!

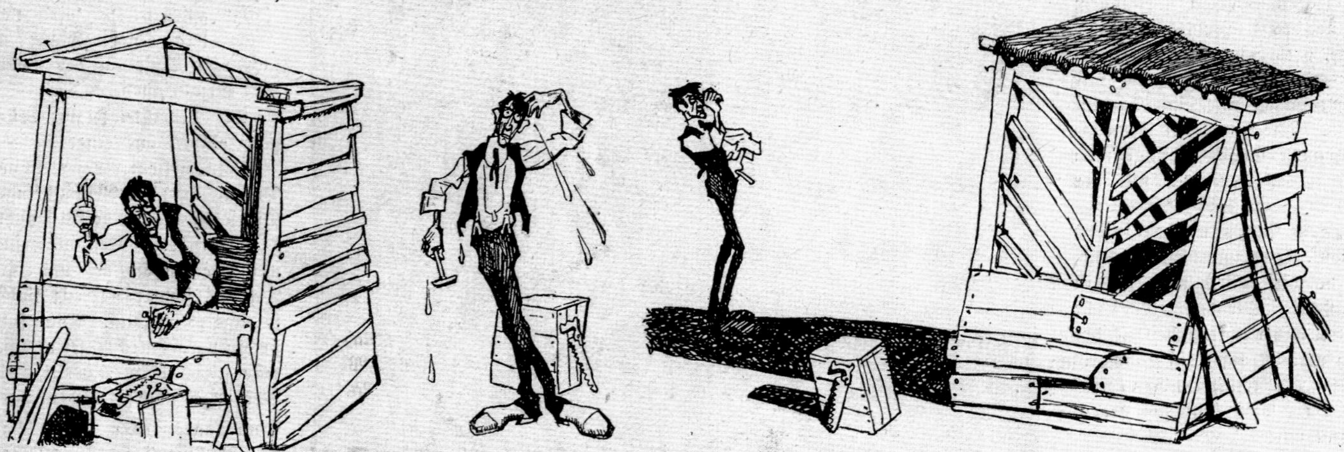

Das Werk, es muß den Meister loben Herrje, wie steht das da, verschroben!

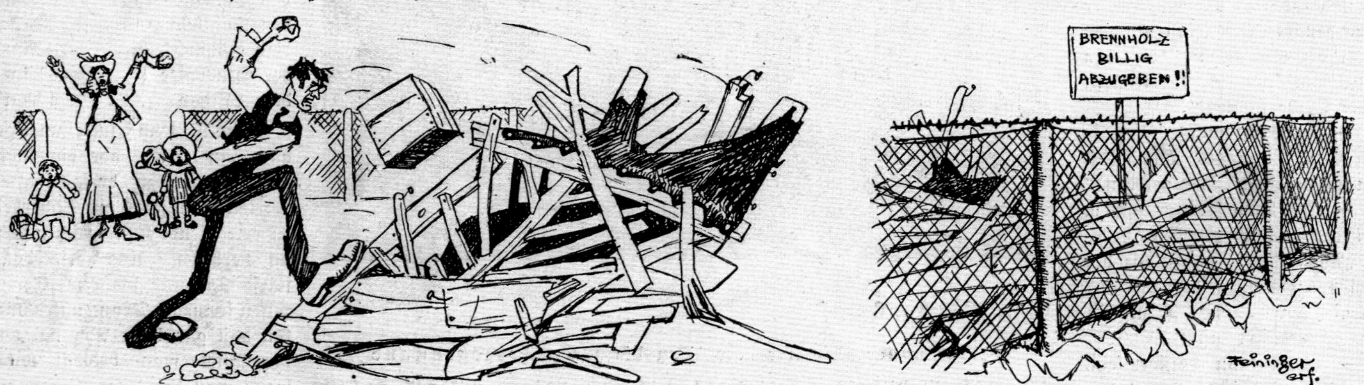

BRENNHOLZ BILLIG ABZUGEBEN!!
Feininger gez.

Das Zeugs in Klumpen werfe ich, Ex est die Laube! — Na denn nich!

Wee Willie Winkie's World is probably one of the most fascinating strips ever published in the so-called "Platinum" period. There's barely anything narrative about it, and it should be read, I believe, as a bona fide tutorial in the art of seeing, given by one of the master painters of the 20th century. In it, we're invited to follow the exchange between the narrator, Uncle Feininger, and Wee Willie, a small boy who has the uncanny ability of transforming objects—trees, clouds, houses, rocks, etc.—into anthropomorphic, resonating shapes. It offers precious glimpses into the inner-workings of Feininger's artistic mind, and possibly offers one of the most revealing discourses ever attempted on the analytical and figural processes at the core of the modernist revolution.

The hesitant and improvised nature of the narration in the *Kin-der-Kids* series, however, was also quite striking. It probably reflects both the haste with which the project took flight and the unfamiliarity of the medium in which Feininger had to express his old ideas. The use of speech balloons must have been particularly perplexing to him. It was a subtle art—and quite a new one at the time—to make the dialogue blend seamlessly with the action, sometimes becoming the action itself, as in F.B. Opper's *Alphonse and Gaston* and *Happy Hooligan* series, which first demonstrated to the world how to work with speech balloons in a sequential strip, and transform it into a virtual *audiovisual* experience. Separated from the teeming American brew of technological ideas and innovations, Feininger was probably not in sync with that revolution, and his dialogues reflect it. The balloons never really drive or *become* the action: what they do, mostly, is to comment on, paraphrase, or explain, passively, what's happening in the picture. They read more or less like the labels in George Cruikshank's etchings, or in Outcault's early *Yellow Kid* Sunday pages.[5]

The series may also have been hindered by the lack of immediate feedback from the readers. All great authors have said that such response is essential for the success of this kind of serial. Feininger, unfortunately, being abroad, could not rub shoulders with his readers on a daily basis. How could he have known that in choosing Paris rather than Chicago he would lose out on any chance of building up a fantasy world in interaction with his audience?

In any case, the "German" experiment at the *Tribune* was stopped after a year as the readership continued to decline. It is difficult to know how Feininger felt when his last American dream crumbled—the contract ended in the later part of 1906. It would be wrong to say, as certain critics have, that he wearied of comic strips, abandoning them in favor of "free painting," as from 1907. His involvement in the comic strip world shows us an intensely personal imagination that is quite inseparable from the bigger picture of his life story, just like the model wooden figurines he continued to carve all through his life, particularly during the seemingly never-ending First World War, which he spent under house arrest in a Berlin suburb. Model figures of the *Kin-der-Kids* and *Wee Willie Winkie's World* were among the family of toys he never tired of producing. The figurines accompanied him like old friends, ever ready to distract or inspire him in his austere and often tortuous artistic quest: his houses, bell towers, windmills, bridges, his much cherished trains, yachts, and flying machines—each time, the magic mixture of art and technology met with his desire to re-conjure the beautiful, fleeting images of the phantom continent he had lost when he was sixteen.

Opposite: *Lustige Blätter*, June 28, 1905. According to Ulrich Luckhardt, this allegorical page expressed Feininger's recognition of the failure of his first marriage. At the time, he was in the midst of a painful separation.

Below: *Lustige Blätter*, October 18, 1905. Another self-portrait, and, possibly, another indirect allusion to Feininger's extra-marital affair...

Das schlaue Professorentöchterlein.

„Papa, wie machten es denn nur gleich die alten Römer, wenn sie ihr Ende herannahen fühlten?"

„„Sie hüllten sich in ihre Toga, mein Kind!""

The Kin-Der-Kids The Relief-Expedition Meets With Base Ingratitude

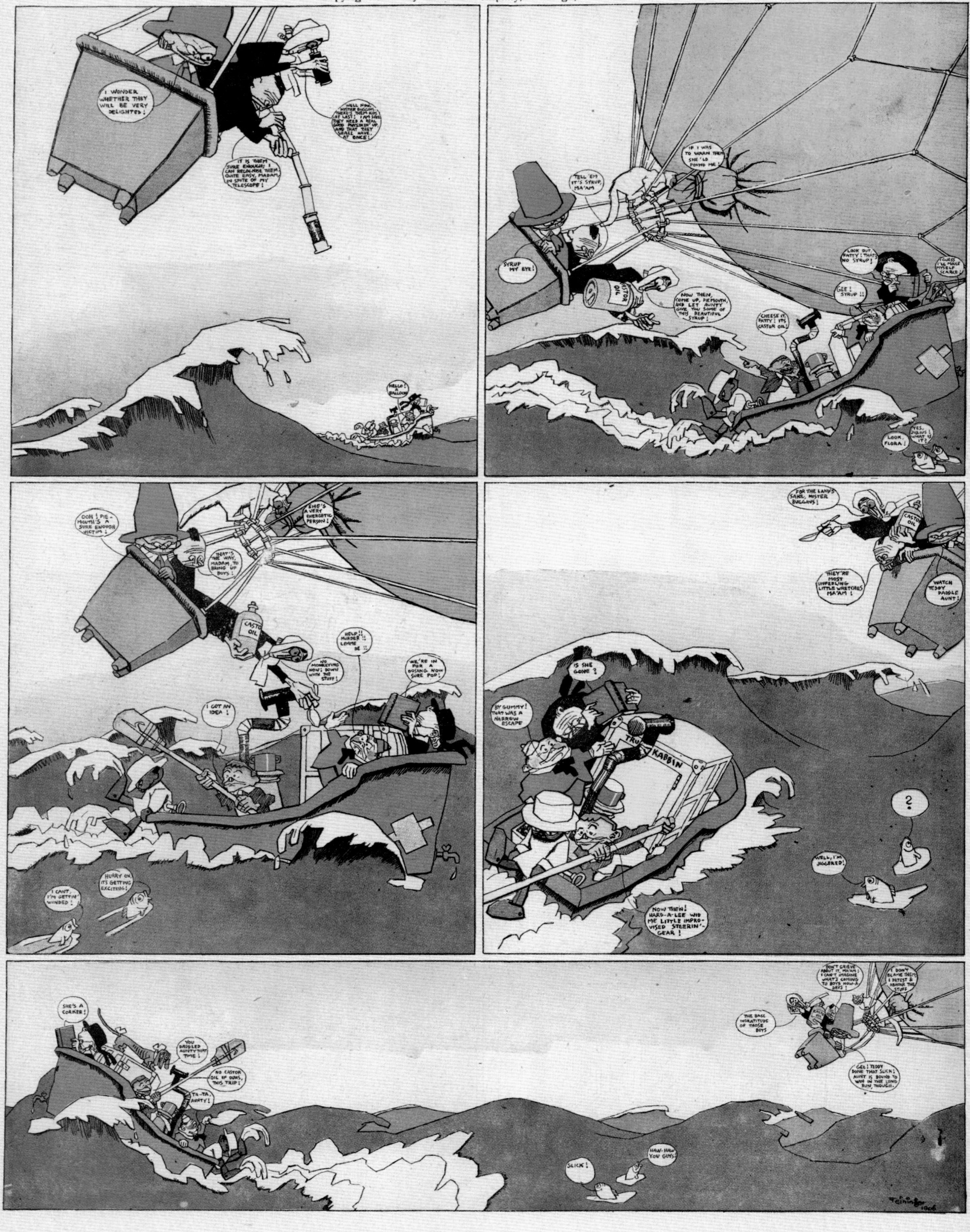
I WONDER WHETHER THEY WILL BE VERY DELIGHTED!
WELL NOW, MISTER BUGGINS, THERE'S THEM KIDS AT LAST! I AM SURE THEY NEED A REAL GOOD PHYSIKIN' UP, AND THAT THEY SHALL HAVE, AT ONCE!
IT IS THEM SURE ENOUGH; I CAN RECOGNISE THEM QUITE EASY, MADAM, IN SPITE OF MY TELESCOPE!
HELLO! A BALLOON
IF I WAS TO WARN THEM SHE'LD POUND ME!
TELL 'EM IT'S SYRUP, MA'AM
SYRUP MY EYE!
CASTOR OIL
NOW THEN, COME UP, PIEMOUTH, AND LET AUNTY GIVE YOU SOME OF THIS BEAUTIFUL SYRUP!
LOOK OUT, FATTY! THAT'S NO SYRUP!
I GUESS I'LL MAKE MYSELF SCARCE!
GEE! SYRUP!!
CHEESE IT, FATTY! ITS CASTOR OIL!
LOOK, FLORA!
YES, JULIUS! WHAT IS IT?
OOH! PIE-MOUTH'S A SURE ENOUGH VICTIM!
SHE'S A VERY ENERGETIC PERSON!
THAT'S THE WAY, MADAM, TO BRING UP BOYS!
CASTOR OIL
HELP!! MURDER!! LEMME BE!!
NO MONKEYING NOW! DOWN WITH THE STUFF!
WE'RE IN FOR A DOSING NOW SURE POP!
I GOT AN IDEA!
HURRY ON, IT'S GETTING EXCITING!
I CANT, I'M GETTIN' WINDED!
FOR THE LAND'S SAKE, MISTER BUGGINS!
CASTOR OIL
THEY'RE MOST UNFEELING LITTLE WRETCHES MA'AM!
WATCH TEDDY PADDLE AUNT!
IS SHE GONE?
BY GUMMY! THAT WAS A NARROW ESCAPE
KABBIN
?
WELL, I'M JIGGERED!
NOW THEN! HARD-A-LEE WID ME LITTLE IMPROVISED STEERIN'-GEAR!
SHE'S A CORKER!
YOU DADDLED AUNTY THAT TIME!
NO CASTOR OIL IF OURS, THIS TRIP!
TA-TA, AUNTY!
DON'T GRIEVE ABOUT IT, MA'AM! I CAN'T IMAGINE WHAT'S COMING TO BOYS NOW-A-DAYS!
I DON'T BLAME THEM; I DETEST & ABHOR THE STUFF
THE BASE INGRATITUDE OF THOSE BOYS
GEE! TEDDY DONE THAT SLICK! AUNT IS BOUND TO WIN IN THE LONG RUN, THOUGH.
SLICK!
HAW-HAW YOU GUYS!
Feininger 1906

1937–1956: New York
Master of Forms

LYONEL FEININGER finally arrived with his entire family in New York on June 17, 1937, half a century after having left as a child. At sixty-six years old, the painter was practically penniless. The Nazis had declared him decadent and he found himself obliged to start his life over once again—exactly as he had had to start afresh in the summer of 1907, thirty years previously, when he had arrived in Paris for the love of painting, to study with Matisse, make friends with Jules Pascin, and talk art into the small hours in the murky light of the Café du Dôme with other equally passionate German artists. Memorable years indeed, his last years as a professional illustrator and the first of his life as an artist. In 1907, his caricatures were still being published in Berlin's *Lustige Blätter* and Paul Iribe's *Le Témoin* in Paris; and of course, each Sunday in Chicago newsstands you could buy his brightly colored comics. That would be enough for most lifetimes, but not for Lyonel Feininger, who still had many

mountains to climb—needless to say, his American nationality became problematic because of the conflict with Germany—before he truly made an impression on the young up-starts of the avant-garde art scene. He was yet to accept Walter Gropius's invitation, at the beginning of the 1920s, to become involved, as Master of Forms, with the magnificent experiment that was the first Bauhaus art school at Weimar.

And in that fine summer of 1937, he still had twenty years of drawing, painting, ghosts, and mini-regattas around the pond of Central Park to come. All to be enjoyed on his lost continent, now finally regained. ⚙

Translated from the French by Libbie McQuillan, Glasgow, 2005.
(First published in 9e Art 10, April 2004.)

Many thanks to Shirley Smolderen for additional help with the translation.

Thanks to Yves Cotinat for his friendly help.

Notes

[1] Most of the biographical facts compiled in the present essay come from the following secondary sources. Extracts from Feininger's correspondence are from Scheyer's excellent book about Feininger's early career, which was particularly useful in the writing of this essay:

E. Scheyer, *Lyonel Feininger, Caricature and Fantasy* (Detroit: Wayne State University Press, 1964).

T.L. and A. Feininger, *Lyonel Feininger: City at the Edge of the World* (New York: Frederick A. Praeger, 1965).

U. Luckhardt, *Lyonel Feininger* (Munich: Prestel-Verlag, 1989).

B. Blackbeard, ed., *The Comic Strip Art of Lyonel Feininger* (Amherst, Massachusetts: Kitchen Sink Press, 1994).

[2] A.B. Frost, *Stuff and Nonsense* (Seattle: Fantagraphics Books, 2003).

[3] T. Smolderen, "Why the Brownies Are Important," www.coconino-classics.com, 1999. http://www.coconino.fr/s_classics/pop_classic/brownies/brow_eng.htm

[4] K. Lorenz, *Evolution and Modification of Behavior* (Chicago: University of Chicago Press, 1965).

[5] T. Smolderen, "Of Labels, Loops, and Bubbles: Solving the Historical Puzzle of the Speech Balloon," *Comic Art* #8 (Buenaventura Press, 2006).

Opposite: The Kin-der-Kids, Sunday strip, July 15, 1906.
Courtesy of Peter Maresca.

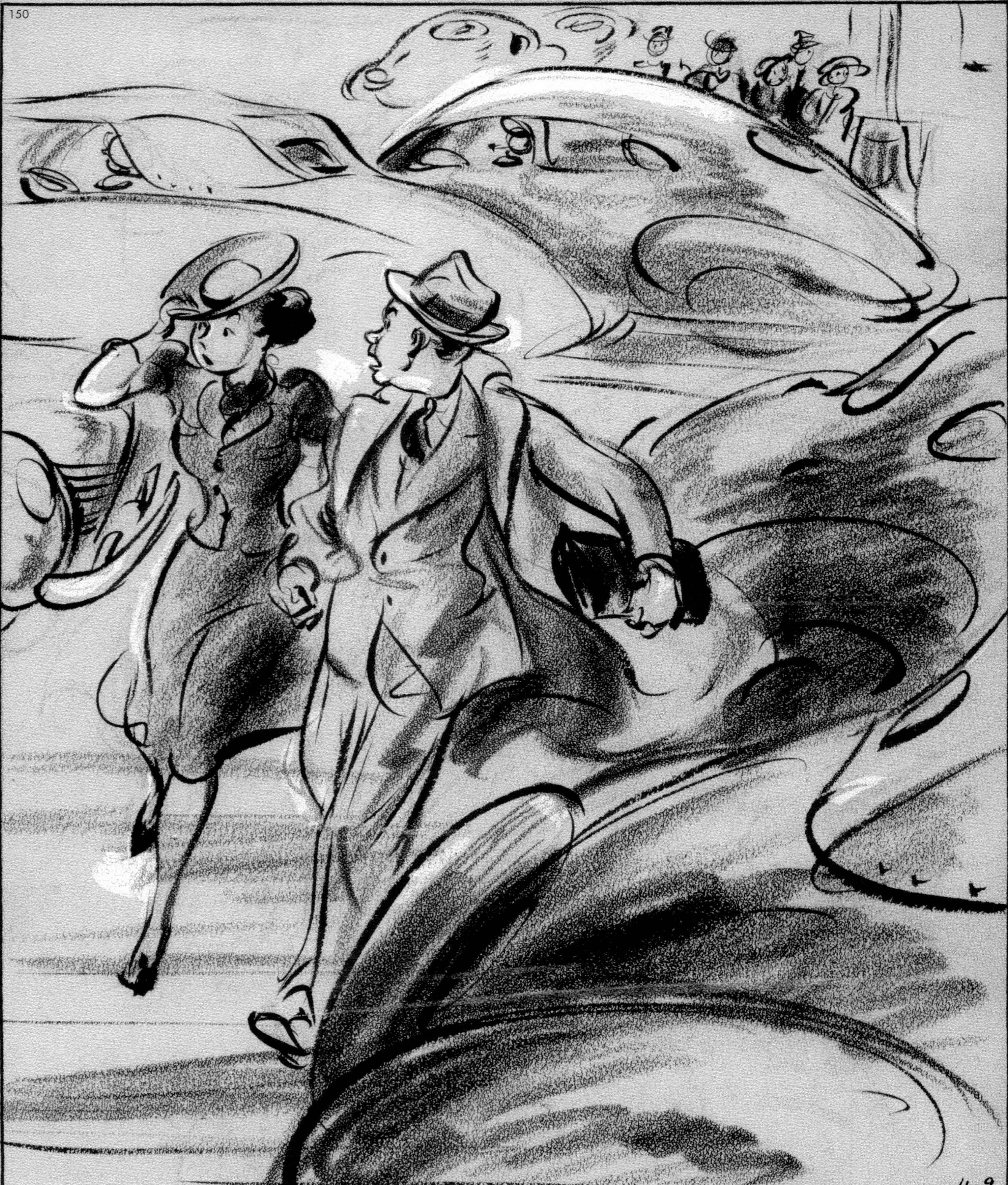
4-9
Reg. U. S. Pat. Off.:
Copyright, 1941, by News Syndicate Co. Inc.

"We'd better get our bank's advice on these bonds. Never pays to take chances when we're ~~......~~ planning for our future."

PICTURE WINDOWS:
The Discreet Smile of George Clark's Americana

by Donald Phelps

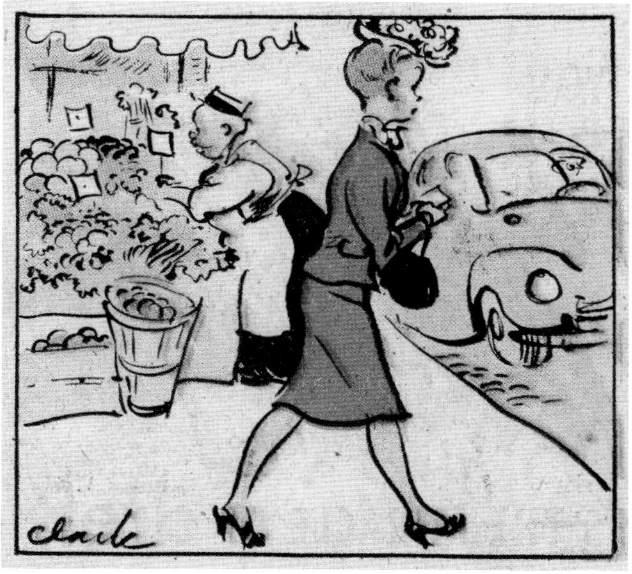
clark

Above: *The Ripples*, Sunday strip detail, June 16, 1946.

Opposite: Original art for *The Neighbors*, daily panel, April 9, 1941. Courtesy of Rob Stolzer.

On page four of the *New York Daily News*, April 17, 1939, a youngish father, seated at what appears to be a recently cleared dinner table, raises one arm in either a yawn, a gesture of exasperated authority, or something of both. His attractive blond wife is chiding several cavorting youngsters: "Come, children. It must be past your bed-time. Daddy is getting tired and fussy." One's vision is nudged, as by one of those terse, pungent headlines so familiar then on the *News*'s front pages, along with—should one so choose to perceive it—a faint but definite erotic twinkle. Readers at the time might have recalled, associatively, such radio song hits as "Let's Put Out the Lights and Go to Bed," later bowdlerized, at the insistence of then radio critic Ring Lardner and other press-side Puritans, replacing "bed" with "sleep." Dead on the heels of such observations, one might be struck by the casual intimacy of the image's tone: the unstudied aspect of the scene, defined as it is in brisk, emphatic, yet discreetly mobile black strokes; the fresh vitality of the children's faces, as against the hieroglyphic knot (suppressed yawn? repressed shout?) of the father's countenance.

Successive appearances of George Clark's daily single-panel contribution, *The Neighbors*, marked the first entrance into the *News* comics supplement of (for all I know, a now archaic term) genre art. The phrase carries with it a supposition of a placid terrain, a serene suspension of humanity's more negative energies, whereas the realism originally proposed for his comic supplement by Captain Joseph Patterson was lean, rugged, largely blue collar; decidedly not (primarily) for the kids. George Clark's contribution was the only single panel featuring human action (excepting the satiric olios of W.E. Hill) to appear; The Captain, obviously, being hooked on the possibilities of sequential movement. In contrast with the dramas—romantic, farcical, explosive—surrounding it, *The Neighbors* offered—what?

A prospect like that of picture windows—as contrasted with the tenement: narrow panes decorated with soot, food smears, flyspecks, bird shit—of the surrounding terrain. There cohabits in Clark's series a seeming placidity of surveillance, and a prickling, nervous animation, that recalls the work of such a film director as, say, Hollywood's George Cukor. An abiding sense of composition hovers, like a gentle governess; yet, the attention is always being refocused on some fleeting glint of not-quite-caustic observation. "They'd have us down more often," lectures a wife to her husband, "If you'd just agree with them when they discuss politics." Side by side, in

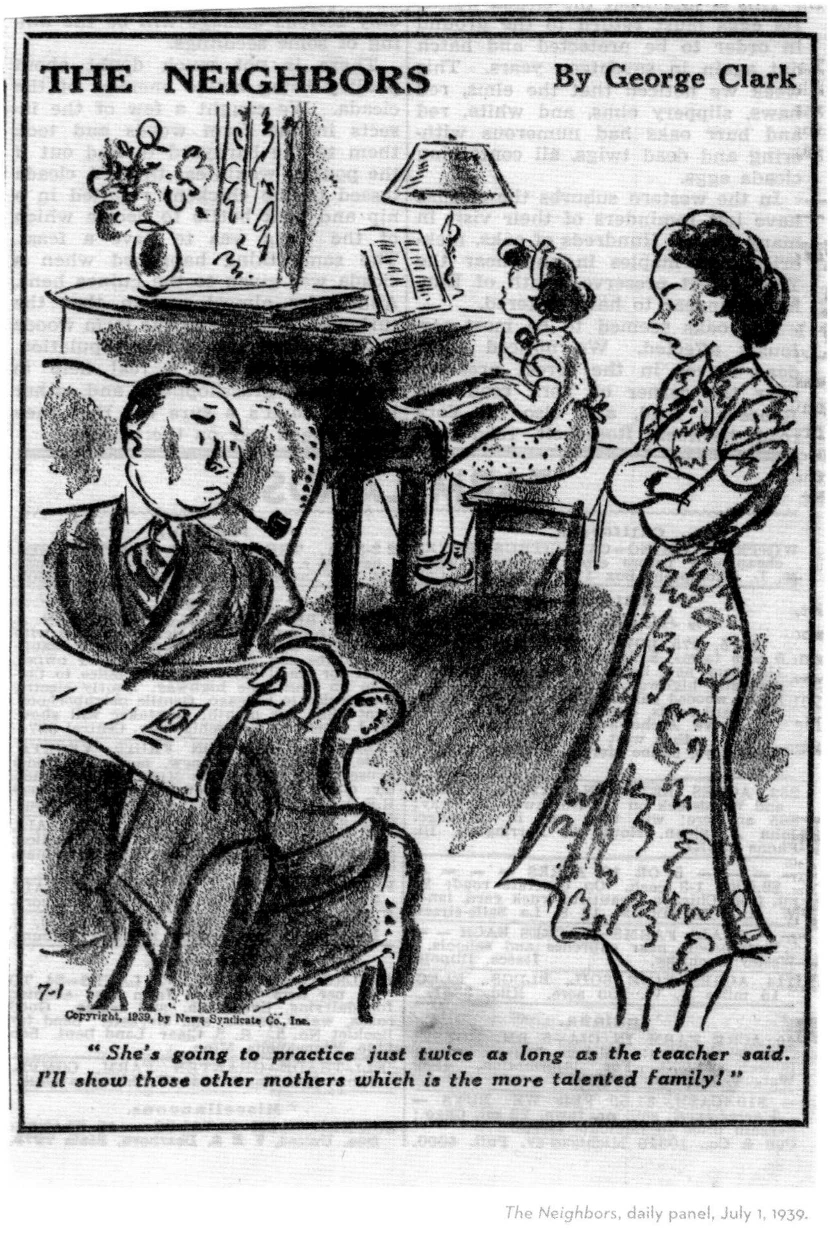
THE NEIGHBORS
By George Clark
7-1
Copyright, 1939, by News Syndicate Co., Inc.
" She's going to practice just twice as long as the teacher said. I'll show those other mothers which is the more talented family! "

The Neighbors, daily panel, July 1, 1939.

Our Neighbors the Ripples, Sunday strip detail, August 20, 1939.

the family car: one discerns, in the background, the handsome country house that they are just now departing. "If I give you your week's allowance now," a mother proposes to her young son, "Will you promise not to do the first thing you think of?" The seeming non sequitur pulses with the inanity of desperation.

Such appeals and proposals abound in the ever slightly strained gentility of Clarksville. The prevalent tone evokes two designations from eras prior to George Clark's 1940s. "Genre art": depictions and commemorations of "typical" quotidian life; and "comedy of manners": a theatrical genre, usually featuring the aristocracy or upper middle classes in crises of "good form" or "delicacy." The designations shiver like disturbed cobwebs in George Clark's mini-dramas, at once sustained and menaced by the shuddering pulsations of radically changing times: on the eve, by

autumn of 1940, of devastating emphases. The recurrent notes of minor but genuine desperation, of wistfulness, shading sometimes into forlornness; such moods lend Clark's work its curious tang, its delicate darkness. On July 9 of 1939, a bearded husband stands, irresolute and forlorn, in his workshop. His wife, with a female visitor, beholds him through the open door. Says she: "Bill's kinda lonesome here, now. The children have outgrown the things he likes to do." The featured couple lag behind, by some years, the elders in, say, Paul Osborn's *Morning's at Seven*; but the faint leitmotif is familiar. Fractional awareness and gnat-like, darting insights, are common in George Clark territory. In a subsequent panel, a young mother, diapering her infant son amid an entourage of females (club members?) remarks: "They say he's sick and tired of being around women all the time."

As in this latter example, one might repeatedly feel of Clark's drawings: "This is the working material of a gag by, say, Syd Hoff, or by Gluyas Williams." Such is the essence of Clark's glowing miniaturism—of definitive genre art. The bathroom-tile pristineness of Williams's *New Yorker* vignettes sometimes, in fact, approaches Clark; much more so, the genius of William Steig's tenement scenes (Steig repeatedly displays an access to fantasy, as Clark, to my knowledge, does not).

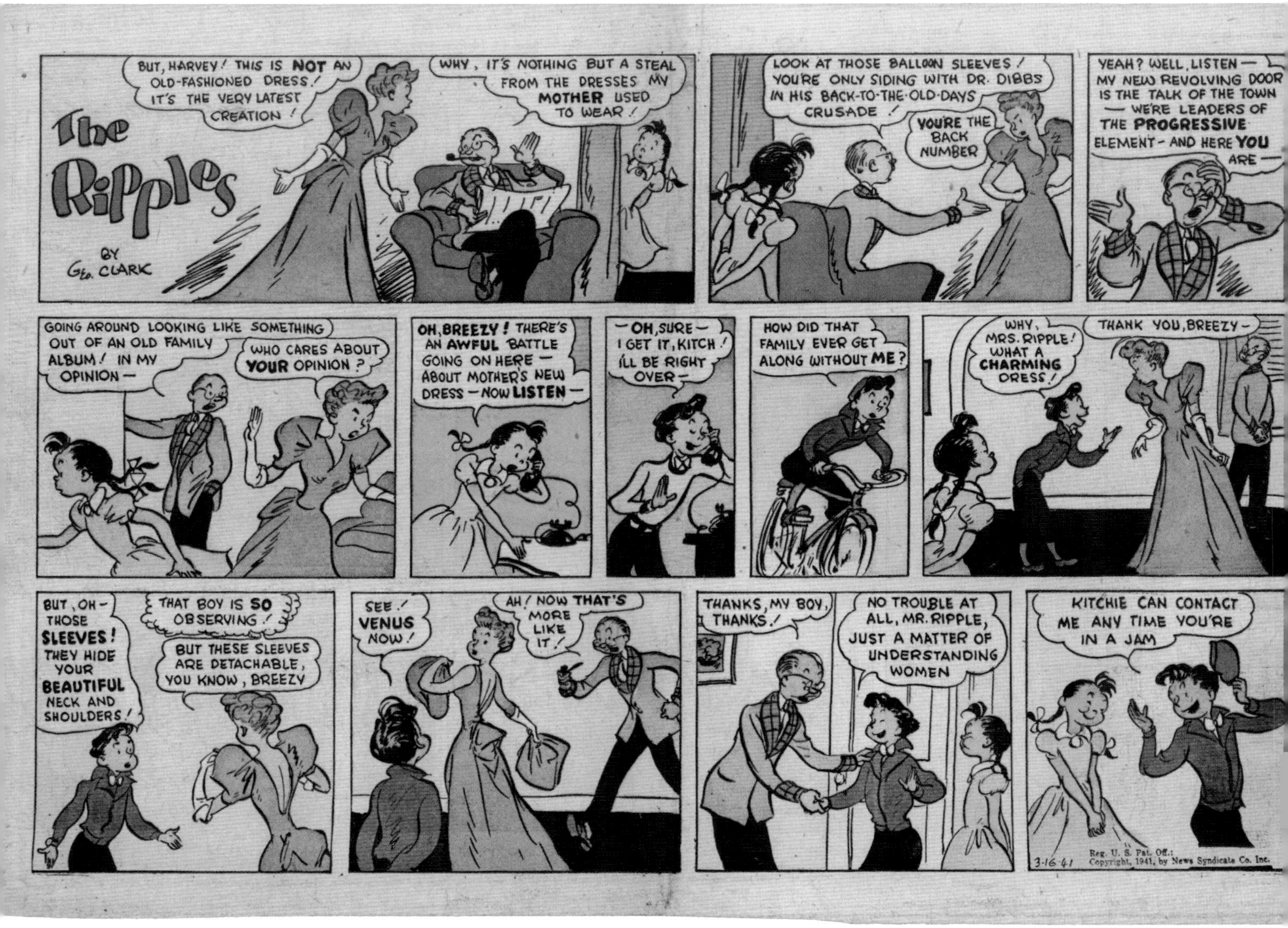
The Ripples
BY Geo. CLARK
BUT, HARVEY! THIS IS NOT AN OLD-FASHIONED DRESS! IT'S THE VERY LATEST CREATION!
WHY, IT'S NOTHING BUT A STEAL FROM THE DRESSES MY MOTHER USED TO WEAR!
LOOK AT THOSE BALLOON SLEEVES! YOU'RE ONLY SIDING WITH DR. DIBBS IN HIS BACK-TO-THE-OLD-DAYS CRUSADE!
YOU'RE THE BACK NUMBER
YEAH? WELL, LISTEN — MY NEW REVOLVING DOOR IS THE TALK OF THE TOWN — WE'RE LEADERS OF THE PROGRESSIVE ELEMENT - AND HERE YOU ARE —
GOING AROUND LOOKING LIKE SOMETHING OUT OF AN OLD FAMILY ALBUM! IN MY OPINION —
WHO CARES ABOUT YOUR OPINION?
OH, BREEZY! THERE'S AN AWFUL BATTLE GOING ON HERE — ABOUT MOTHER'S NEW DRESS — NOW LISTEN —
— OH, SURE — I GET IT, KITCH! I'LL BE RIGHT OVER —
HOW DID THAT FAMILY EVER GET ALONG WITHOUT ME?
WHY, MRS. RIPPLE! WHAT A CHARMING DRESS!
THANK YOU, BREEZY —
BUT, OH — THOSE SLEEVES! THEY HIDE YOUR BEAUTIFUL NECK AND SHOULDERS!
THAT BOY IS SO OBSERVING!
BUT THESE SLEEVES ARE DETACHABLE, YOU KNOW, BREEZY
SEE! VENUS NOW!
AH! NOW THAT'S MORE LIKE IT!
THANKS, MY BOY, THANKS!
NO TROUBLE AT ALL, MR. RIPPLE, JUST A MATTER OF UNDERSTANDING WOMEN
KITCHIE CAN CONTACT ME ANY TIME YOU'RE IN A JAM
3-16-41
Reg. U. S. Pat. Off.: Copyright, 1941, by News Syndicate Co. Inc.

The Ripples, Sunday strip, March 16, 1941.

Clark's studies fairly rustle with the tatters of mistimed or otherwise fumbled occasions, and attempts to restore or compensate for them. Some of his best glow with a nostalgia for *shapeliness*, in some occasion or other, in the style of their lives. A minor example: a wife asks her husband, in full huntsman's gear, whether he will prefer sardines or baked beans for the evening meal. On the farcical level: a handsome Miss in tailored attire explains to the butcher that "they pulled me in here." "They," i.e., two strapping dogs panting for the butcher's wares, have bound her smartly in their leashes. We stand to be threatened, our dignity upended, at the simplest levels of decorum. Or, occasions of a venerable sort may seem to exist solely in order to be exploited. Against a wintry landscape, on a tree-lined lane leading to the university, a collegiate youth, in the fedora hat and sweater of the late '30s student body, entreats his elderly, van Dyke-bearded professor for a passing grade, on a plea of an impending family reunion, "with lots of songs and stories" and, of course, Mother: "How d'you think she'll feel when she finds out I'm flunking?"

On the reverse side is a cultural nostalgia, nodding to the still lively ghost of Sinclair Lewis. In a panel of July 1, 1939, a mother, fiercely obdurate, commands her young daughter, seated at a piano: "She's going to practice just twice as long as the teacher said. I'll show those other mothers which is the more talented family!" Or, a matron circulates a sheath of verses to her cultural circle,

with a paean to "Gloria"—Daughter? Niece? Neighbor? The slender, fair-haired Gloria sits a little apart from the ladies and a single academic-looking gentleman, head bowed, hands clasped, like an object of outraged denigration in a Quaker meeting hall of days past.

It's the nostalgia for art in life, for eternally fugitive Form, that gives so much of George Clark's work its distinctive cachet of humor—particularly in the seemingly unlikely environs of the *Daily News*. Yet, were they—need one perceive them now—so very unlikely? The headlines of 1939, closely adjoining *The Neighbors*, announce the arming of England and France to confront the Germans; Hitler commanding his army. The familiar past workaday realism of Winnie Winkle and Skeezix and Moonshine and Dick Tracy: had it not acquired something of a glaze, over those years (or, as with *The Gumps*, decades) past? The comic strip entourage of the terminal '30s and burgeoning '40s sounds varying themes of mistrust, challenged and/or altered relationships, domesticity reconsidered and re-evaluated. The teenage Skeezix of *Gasoline Alley* finds his new car enviously courted by two doubtful cronies: Gootch and Tops. Meanwhile, Moon Mullins, as hospital patient, discovers a new woman-chasing replacement—Sir Stymie—for the absent Plushbottom. George Bailey, chief executive, notifies his erstwhile office boy and confidant, Smitty, that he is going undercover—disguised, that is, with a hairpiece on his bald pate—to investigate

mysterious shenanigans in the supply room. Meanwhile, among the harder breathing adventure strips, Smilin' Jack, attempting to flee a tropical penal colony, re-encounters a nefarious duo: The Head, a Peter Lorre look-alike, and his creature, The Claw: bald of head and waist, with a right-handed iron hook that recalls *Captain Easy*'s Bull Dawson. Chester, precocious scion of *The Gumps*, is found fleeing Bedouin kidnappers in a Sahara-like desert. And Dick Tracy, fatigued by recent exploits, seeks R and R at Pop's Health Farm—a haven threatened by the criminal subterfuges of the owner's son, whose face bears a black birthmark: Cain, updated?

The earliest unmistakable allusion to contemporary realities was probably Harold Gray's Little Orphan Annie, pursued cross-country by a Mephistophelian villain named Axel (Axis?). Yet, the reverberations of world events might be observed in certain notable changes among Annie's comic strip contemporaries. In any case, from the present distance, the breadth and diversity of actuality seem to have been demanding their due. One might also note that the beginning of the '40s saw the death (all but unprecedented in American comics) of a popular featured character: Raven Sherman, the Norma Shearer—like beauty of Milton Caniff's *Terry and the Pirates*. Presently, Smilin' Jack would lose his bride (resurrected, unconvincingly, later) in a plane crash. The *News* artists found themselves increasingly in strained competition with the march of world events.

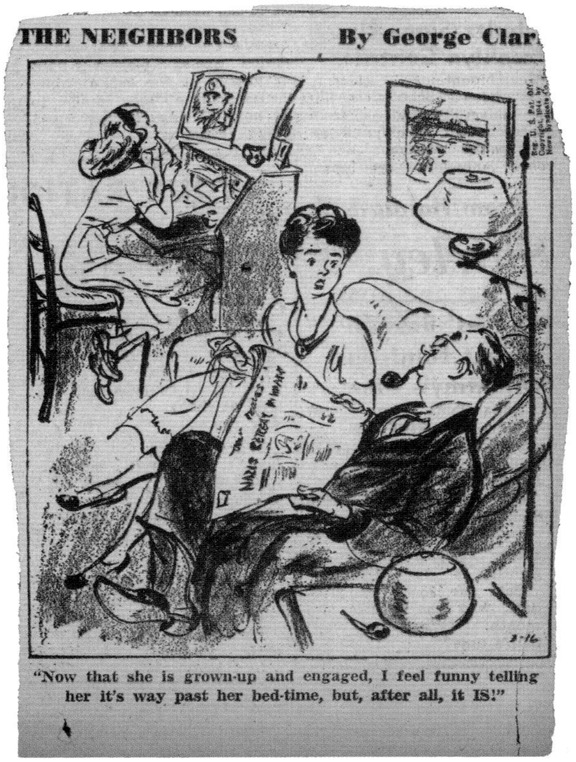
THE NEIGHBORS
By George Clar
3-16
"Now that she is grown-up and engaged, I feel funny telling her it's way past her bed-time, but, after all, it IS!"

The Neighbors, daily panel, March 16, 1944.

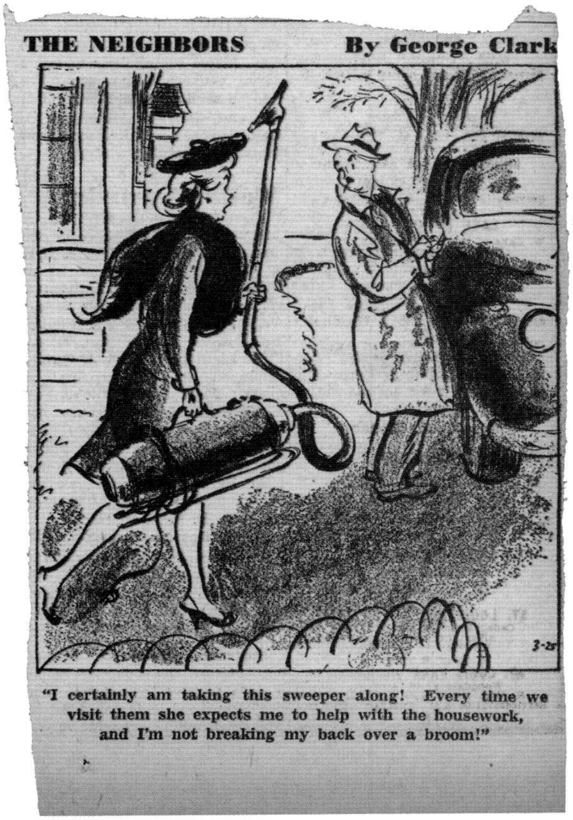
THE NEIGHBORS
By George Clark
3-25
"I certainly am taking this sweeper along! Every time we visit them she expects me to help with the housework, and I'm not breaking my back over a broom!"

The Neighbors, daily panel, March 25, 1944.

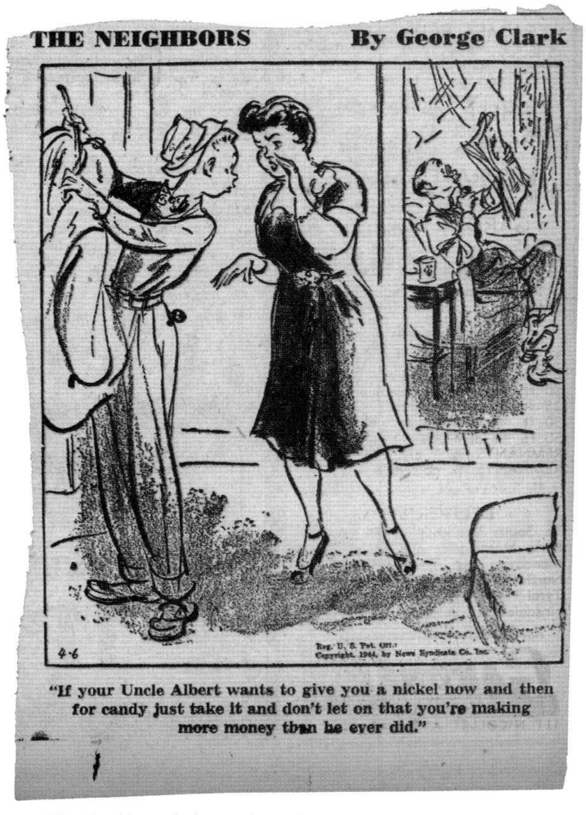
THE NEIGHBORS
By George Clark
4-6
"If your Uncle Albert wants to give you a nickel now and then for candy just take it and don't let on that you're making more money than he ever did."

The Neighbors, daily panel, April 1, 1944.

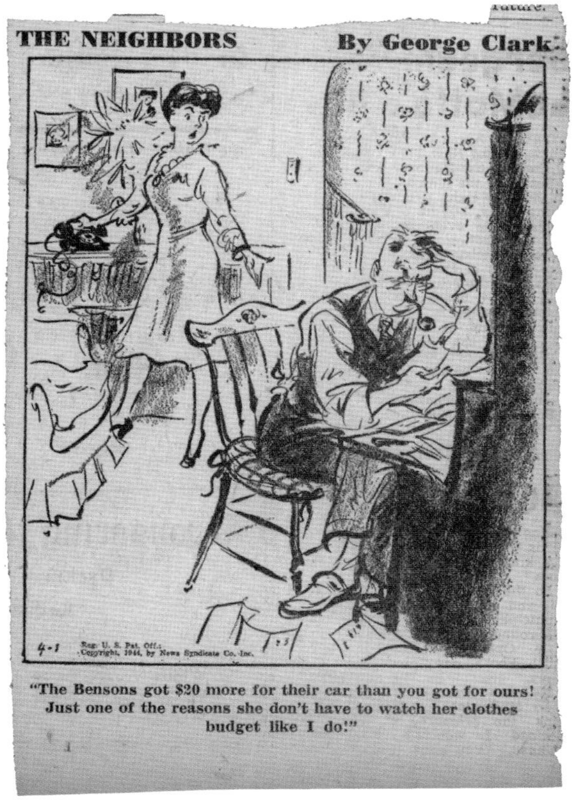
THE NEIGHBORS
By George Clark
"The Bensons got $20 more for their car than you got for ours! Just one of the reasons she don't have to watch her clothes budget like I do!"

The Neighbors, daily panel, April 6, 1944.

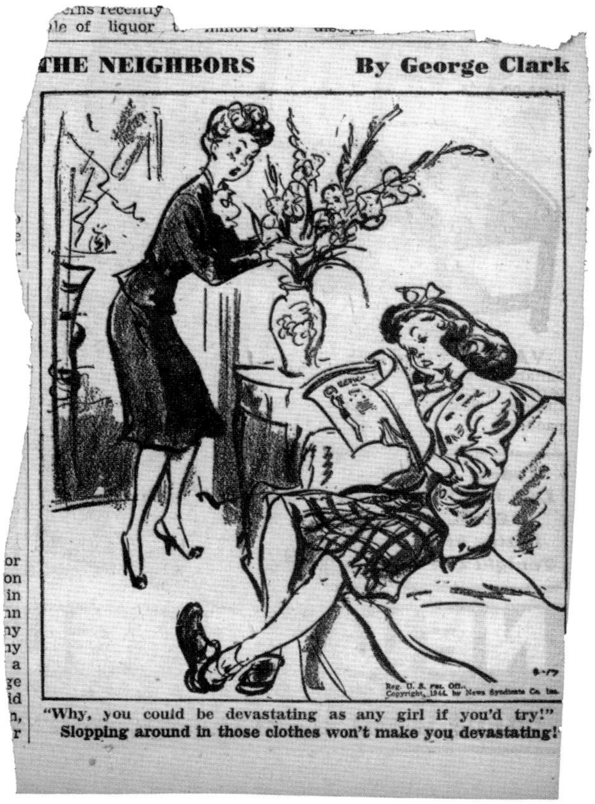
THE NEIGHBORS
By George Clark
"Why, you could be devastating as any girl if you'd try!" Slopping around in those clothes won't make you devastating!

The Neighbors, daily panel, April 14, 1944.

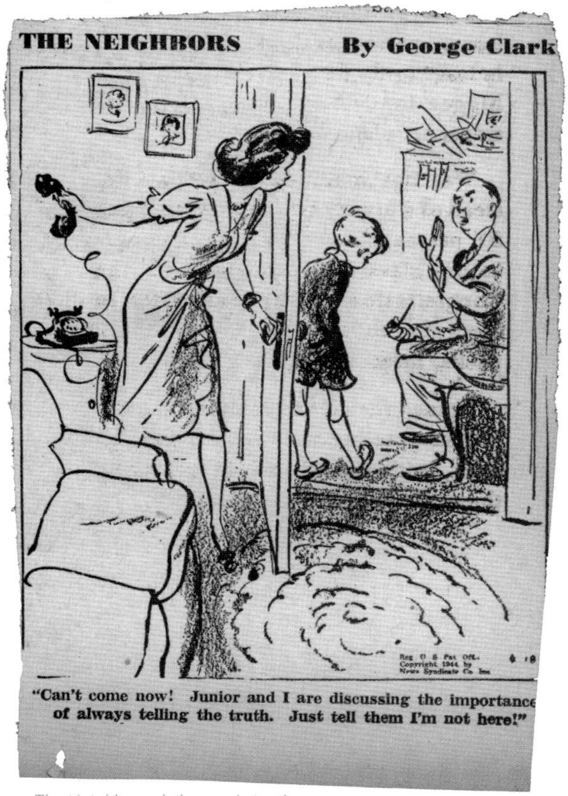
THE NEIGHBORS
By George Clark
"Can't come now! Junior and I are discussing the importance of always telling the truth. Just tell them I'm not here!"

The Neighbors, daily panel, April 17, 1944.

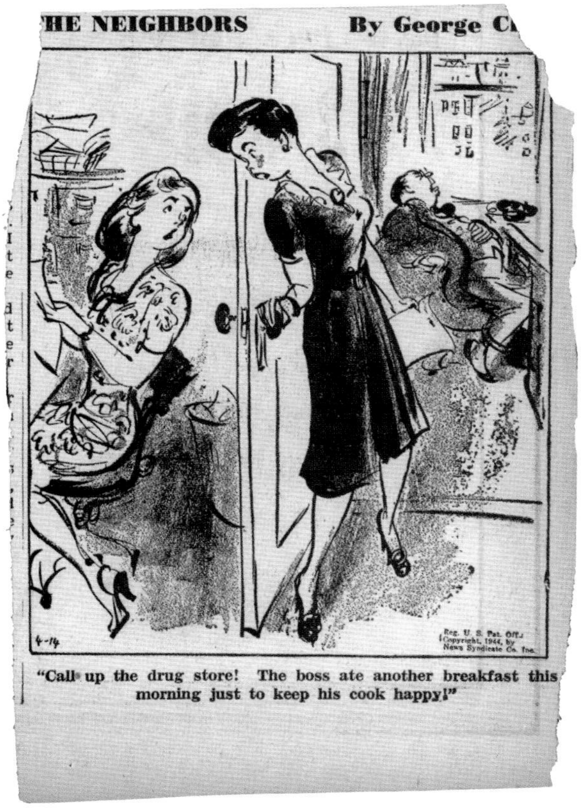
THE NEIGHBORS
By George C
"Call up the drug store! The boss ate another breakfast this morning just to keep his cook happy!"

The Neighbors, daily panel, April 18, 1944.

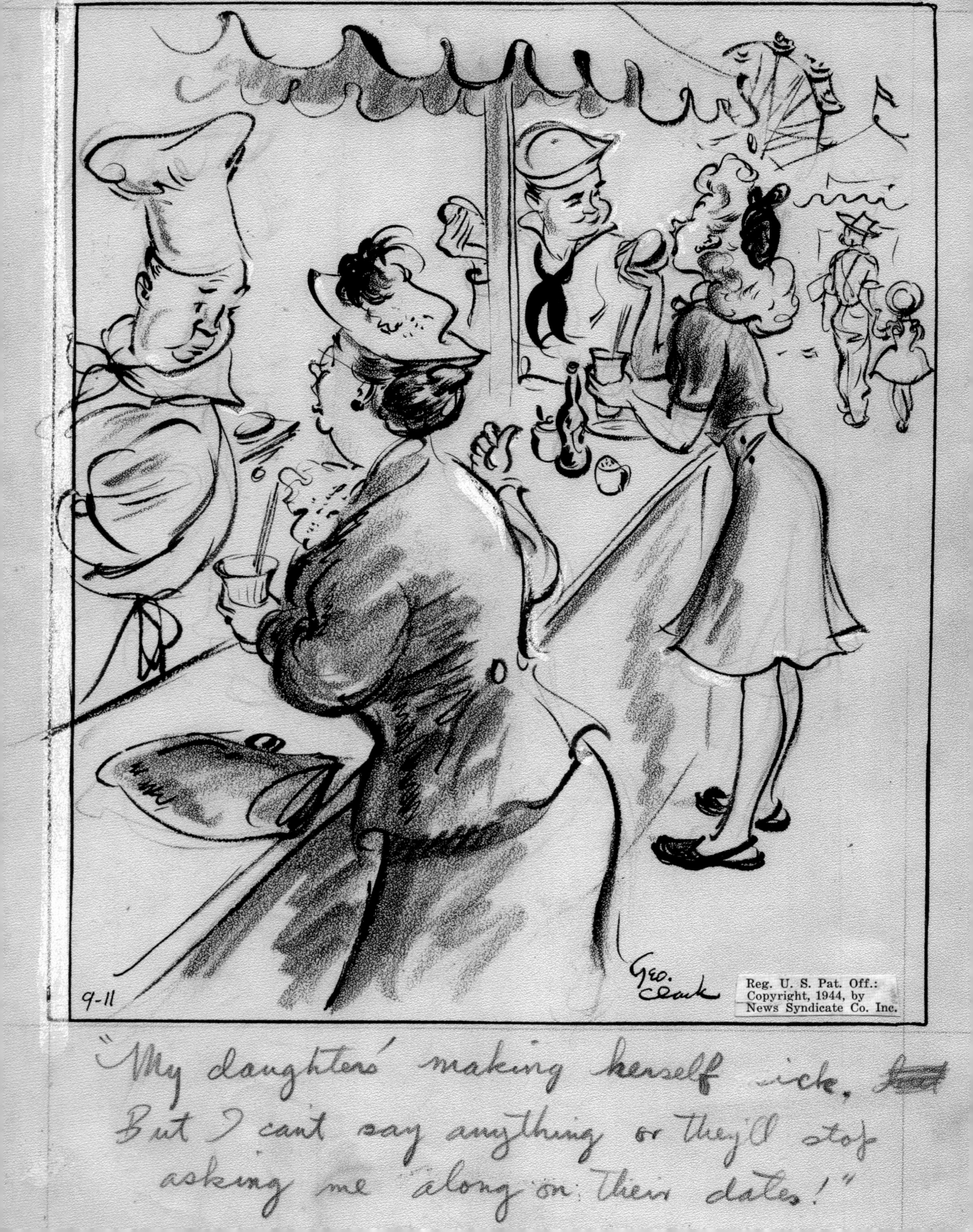
9-11
Geo. Clark
Reg. U. S. Pat. Off.: Copyright, 1944, by News Syndicate Co. Inc.

"My daughter's making herself sick. But I can't say anything or they'll stop asking me "along on their dates!"

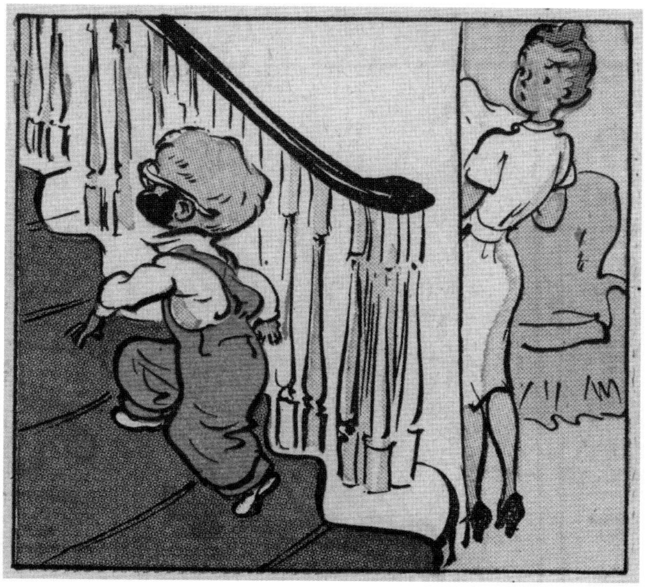

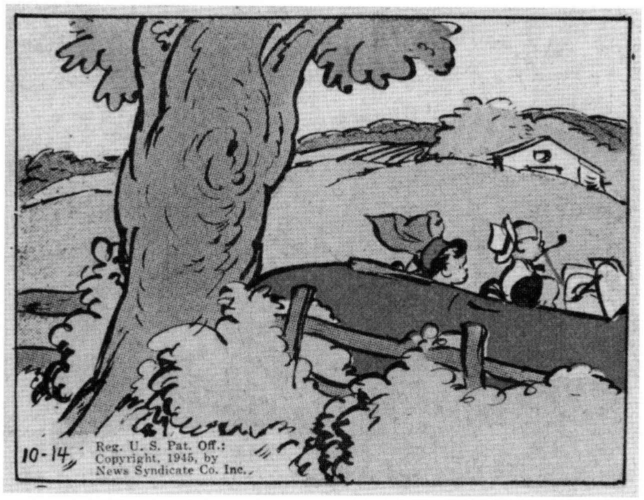
10-14
Reg. U. S. Pat. Off.:
Copyright, 1945, by
News Syndicate Co. Inc.

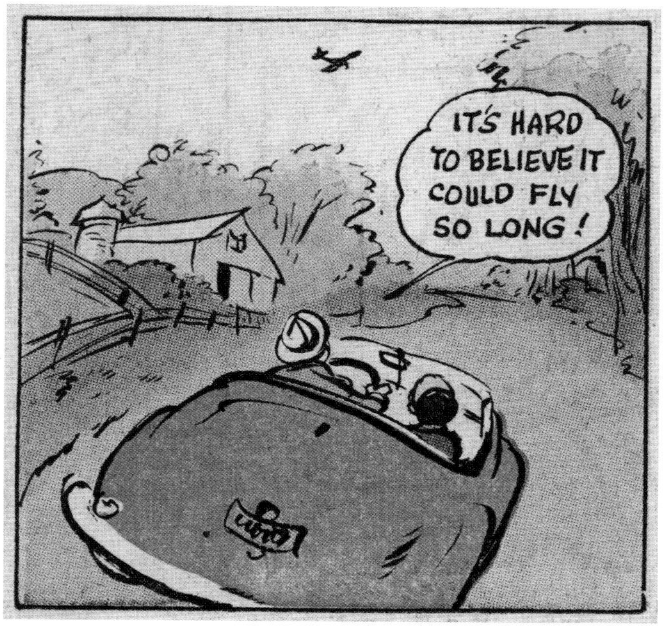
IT'S HARD TO BELIEVE IT COULD FLY SO LONG!

Top: *The Ripples*, Sunday strip detail, August 18, 1946.

Above: *The Ripples*, Sunday strip detail, October 14, 1945.

Right: *The Ripples*, Sunday strip detail, October 21, 1945.

Opposite: Original art for *The Neighbors*, daily panel, September 11, 1944. Courtesy of Rob Stolzer.

Even when males are featured, women may preempt the conversation. "Now listen, Emery," one of two males corners a third, in the host's kitchen: "Are you going out again this Xmas, and buy your wife something none of us can afford?" While a poker player turns from his game to reassure his spouse: "No, dear, they won't try and call me. They know I wouldn't bluff with you standing there!"

Women occasionally spark the sauntering serenity of Clark's graphic meditations with glintings of acerbity, although the diffuseness of his focus prevents their assuming the status of permanent debunkers. The pores of civility are always open, in the body of Clark's comedy—too much so for the cozy stereotyping of standard domestic humorists. Yet, Clark's boundlessly roving eye will not blink the inevitable possibilities of bitchery.

"He has no enemies, but he's the type whose best friends cordially detest him." This, from one of several gracious ladies surrounding a tea table. During the latter '40s (his work for the *News* halted in 1948), a certain glaze surfaces on occasion: the recurrent strain of erotica—usually an unobtrusive vein, in early

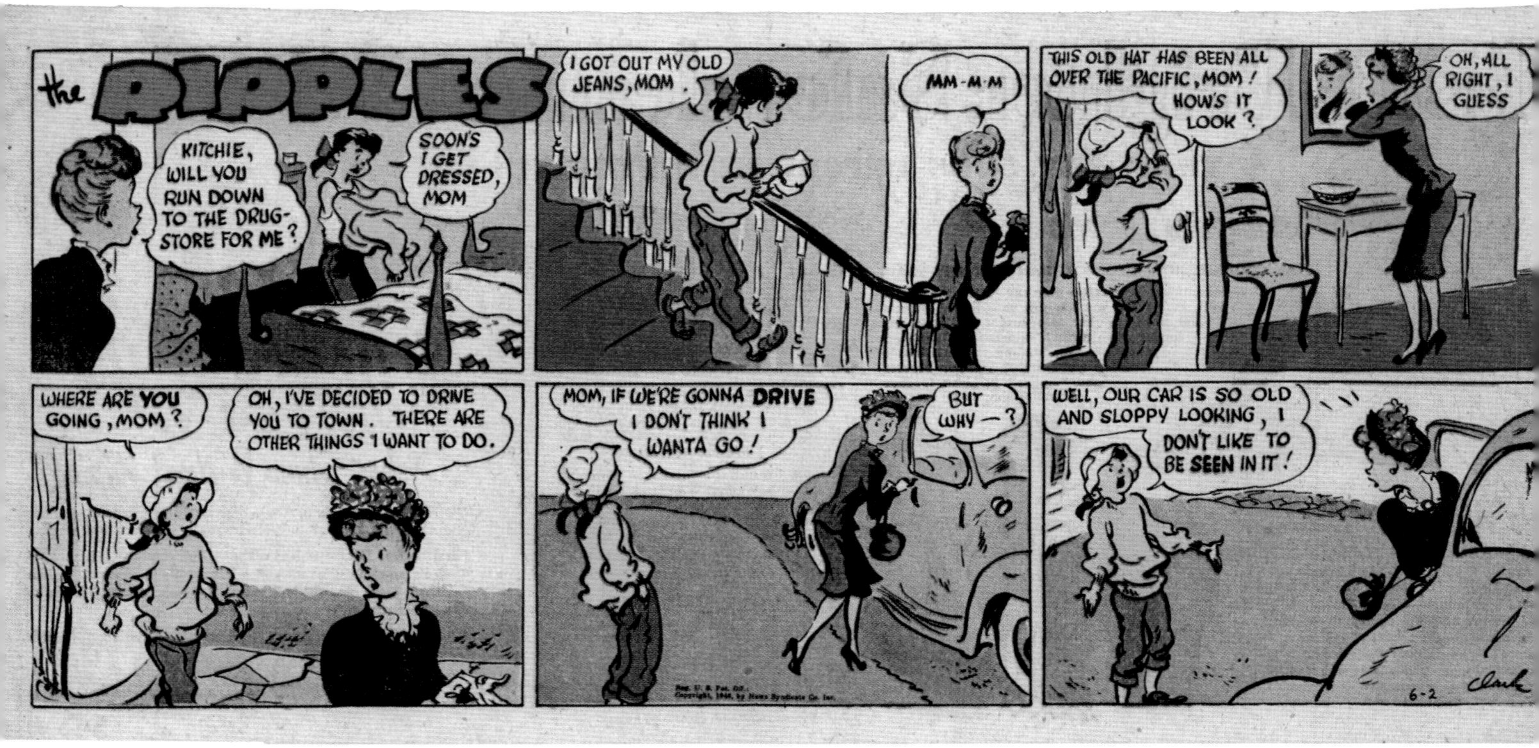
the RIPPLES
KITCHIE, WILL YOU RUN DOWN TO THE DRUG-STORE FOR ME?
SOON'S I GET DRESSED, MOM
I GOT OUT MY OLD JEANS, MOM.
MM-M-M
THIS OLD HAT HAS BEEN ALL OVER THE PACIFIC, MOM! HOW'S IT LOOK?
OH, ALL RIGHT, I GUESS
WHERE ARE YOU GOING, MOM?
OH, I'VE DECIDED TO DRIVE YOU TO TOWN. THERE ARE OTHER THINGS I WANT TO DO.
MOM, IF WE'RE GONNA DRIVE I DON'T THINK I WANTA GO!
BUT WHY—?
WELL, OUR CAR IS SO OLD AND SLOPPY LOOKING, I DON'T LIKE TO BE SEEN IN IT!
6-2
Clark

Above: *The Ripples*, Sunday strip, June 2, 1946.

Opposite: *The Ripples*, Sunday strip, July 14, 1946.

years, it materializes later, here and there, as near crudity. A youngster of, say, seven, warns his teacher he does not wish to alarm her, but: "My daddy says that if I don't get a passing grade, somebody's gonna get spanked." Teacher, let it be noted, is a nubile blonde, clad in an angora sweater: she could pass for nineteen. In another instance of Clark spark, a blonde of riper years is roped securely, with what appears to be professional expertise, to a chair; wearing a look of extreme perturbation, as her little son—a possible six—informs a caller on the telephone that Mama cannot come because she is in jail.

Such misdemeanors—possible side products of Clark's advance, with America, into the '40s (he was born in 1902)—may also be seen to highlight his lack, or perhaps, denial, of that urbanity, typical of Noel Coward, say, that subsumes and manipulates vulgarity. Clark, as noted, rejects such urbanity, as he does other manifestations of showbiz sophistication: he embraces a casualness that is largely venom-free, and in like degree, raunch-free.

It seems something of an anticlimax—the kind frequently wrought by publishers and kindred opportunists—that Clark, in the ninth month of his eye-opening and -expanding illustrative career, should have (so one assumes) been prevailed upon to introduce a half-page Sunday strip into the *News* comics supplement: engaging in a form that typically embodied antic consequence and studied attention to characters. *Our Neighbors the Ripples*, as the strip was initially titled, was indeed, even at outset, more zap-free and amiably diffuse and low-key than its immediate neighbors.

It proved a rather opportune showcase, however, for a manifest stylistic interest, i.e., Clark's concern with telltale postures and positioning: expressive waves of hands, cockings of heads—homegrown histrionics. In the very first episode, December 1, 1939, lanky, bespectacled Harvey, husband and father, is displayed in several looming

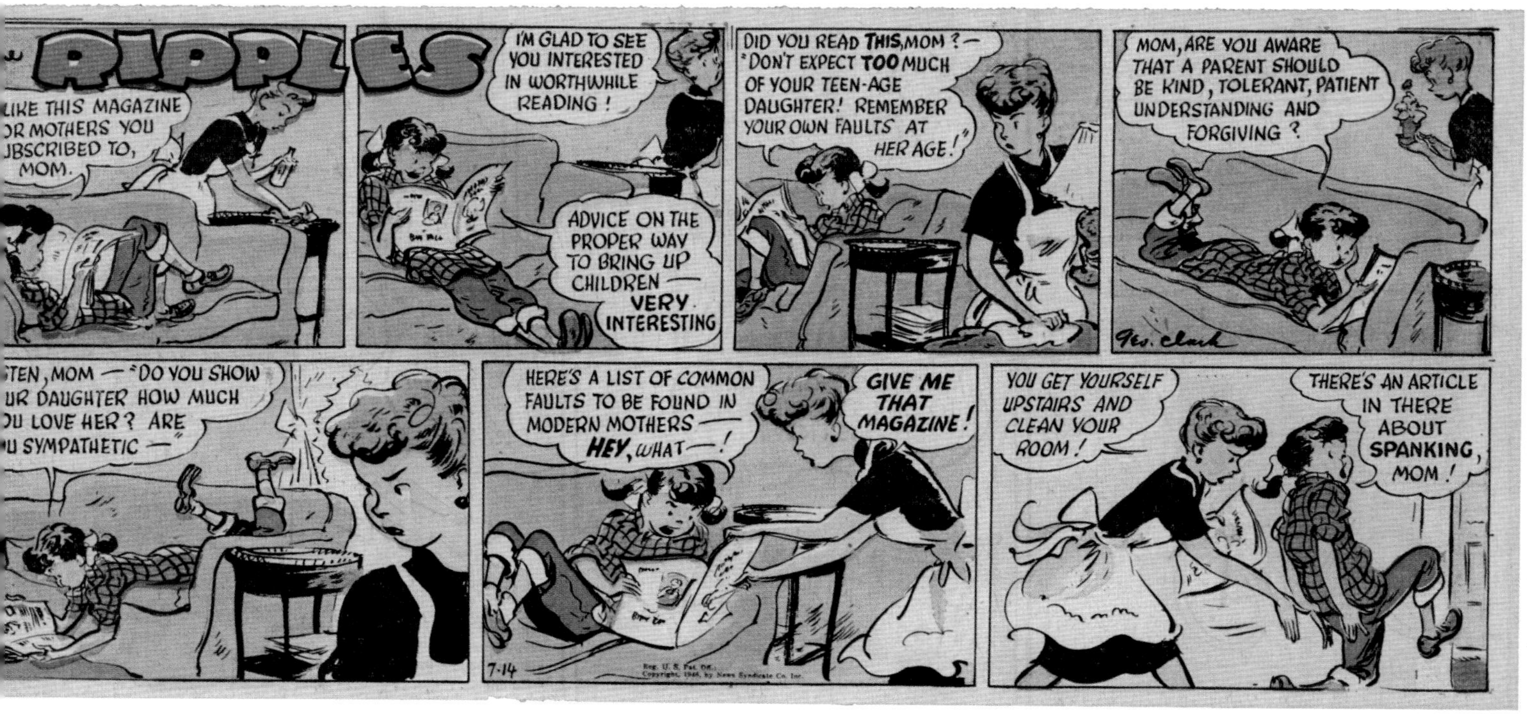
RIPPLES
IKE THIS MAGAZINE
OR MOTHERS YOU
JBSCRIBED TO,
MOM.
I'M GLAD TO SEE YOU INTERESTED IN WORTHWHILE READING !
ADVICE ON THE PROPER WAY TO BRING UP CHILDREN — VERY. INTERESTING
DID YOU READ THIS, MOM ? — "DON'T EXPECT TOO MUCH OF YOUR TEEN-AGE DAUGHTER! REMEMBER YOUR OWN FAULTS AT HER AGE !"
MOM, ARE YOU AWARE THAT A PARENT SHOULD BE KIND, TOLERANT, PATIENT UNDERSTANDING AND FORGIVING ?
Geo. Clark
TEN, MOM — "DO YOU SHOW
UR DAUGHTER HOW MUCH
OU LOVE HER ? ARE
U SYMPATHETIC —"
HERE'S A LIST OF COMMON FAULTS TO BE FOUND IN MODERN MOTHERS — HEY, WHAT — !
GIVE ME THAT MAGAZINE !
7-14
YOU GET YOURSELF UPSTAIRS AND CLEAN YOUR ROOM !
THERE'S AN ARTICLE IN THERE ABOUT SPANKING, MOM !

close-ups—quite rare in any Captain Patterson comic strip at that time—as, following his wife Clara's behest, he telephones an elaborate alibi (a mysterious fainting spell) to prospective visitors. A little smile of self-felicitation tilts Harvey's modest mouth. Later in the strip's course, a dinner table scene will feature cross-talk—trading in personal critiques—between the dark-haired, thirteen- year-old (?) daughter, and her younger (ten?) brother. Harvey's gamboling stride is a character emblem, as is Clara's ever-purposeful march step. And Clark's unfailing deadpan tone exacts hilarity from a wintry chestnut: Harvey somersaulting on a snowy slope, down which the kids are confidently tobogganing.

A signal triumph of Clark's comic grace is the delectable mobility of that daughter—a visual exemplar of the lovely old word "coltish." Her prancing trot commended her to the strip's foreground and, in one segment, presented with a (holiday? birthday?) gift of a movie camera, she proceeds to act out her cherished dreams of directing her own film. This she does by enlisting her gangling father and the dumpy, bearded little family M.D., to play bank robbers in a pseudo documentary staged in the neighborhood bank. In they stride, brandishing toy pistols at the clerk, who—tipped off in advance, of course—obediently raises hands in air, grinning from ear to ear. In the next panel, as the bogus bandits depart, the clerk is viewed, behind the desk, silently guffawing his head off. The entire sequence presented, at once, a definitive glimpse of prophetic perception: George Clark forecasting the New Woman (as the Victorian-era phrase was newly perceived and affirmed in the feminism of the 1960s)—and a lovely recollection of the not-quite-yet expiring style of humane film comedy once summoned by the names of Leo McCarey and George Stevens. As well, one might hope, the non-cinematic minor genius of George Clark.

Thanks abiding to Dale Thomajan, for guidance through the New York Public Library's microfilm division, and to the Library staff.

NBM 30 Years of Pretty Good GNs...

FOREVER NUTS
CLASSIC SCREWBALL STRIPS
The Early Years of Mutt&Jeff
By Bud Fisher
Edited by Jeffrey Lindenblatt
NBM

INTRODUCING

FOREVER NUTS
CLASSIC SCREWBALL STRIPS

Classic off-the-wall early strips

I'LL HAVE SOME, FILET MIGNON—
SOME WHAT?
SOME FILET MIGNON
SOME WHO?
FILET MIGNON! F-I-L-E-T M-I-G-N-O-N!
OH, YES! F-I-L-E-T- M-I-G-N-O-N, SURE!
AND SOME CHOUX EN CREME
COME AGAIN ON THAT LAST ONE

A different one in each volume.
Just as goofy fun as ever!

CHOUX EN CREME!
WHO IS?
CHOUX EN CREME! C-H-O-U-X E-N- C-R-E-ME
OH, SURE! CHOKES IN CREAM-CERTAINLY!
AND SOME CAPON AUX CHAMPIGNON
GOOD NIGHT!
CAFE
AW, WHAT'S THE USE?

NBM returns to classic comic strip reprints which it pioneered with Terry & the Pirates in 1983. Inaugurating a new series of handsomely designed classic strip reprints showcasing early daily comics so ingeniously nutty they're forever fresh and off the wall.

FOREVER NUTS:
Classic Screwball Strips
The Early Years of MUTT & JEFF
Bud Fisher

One of the most long lasting and popular humor strips in history, Mutt and Jeff had many memorable moments of serious goofiness and irreverence. Here's a rediscovery of a true oddball classic maybe only outdone by the antic high living of its own creator.
2007 marks the 100th anniversary of this strip.

11x6 1/2, 192pp., B&W, jacketed hardcover, $24.95
ISBN 978-1-56163-502-3

NBM, 40 Exchange Place, Ste. 1308, New York, NY 10005, 1-800-886-1223
MC, VISA, Amex accepted, add $3 P&H for 1st item, $1 each additional.

See previews and more at
www.nbmpublishing.com

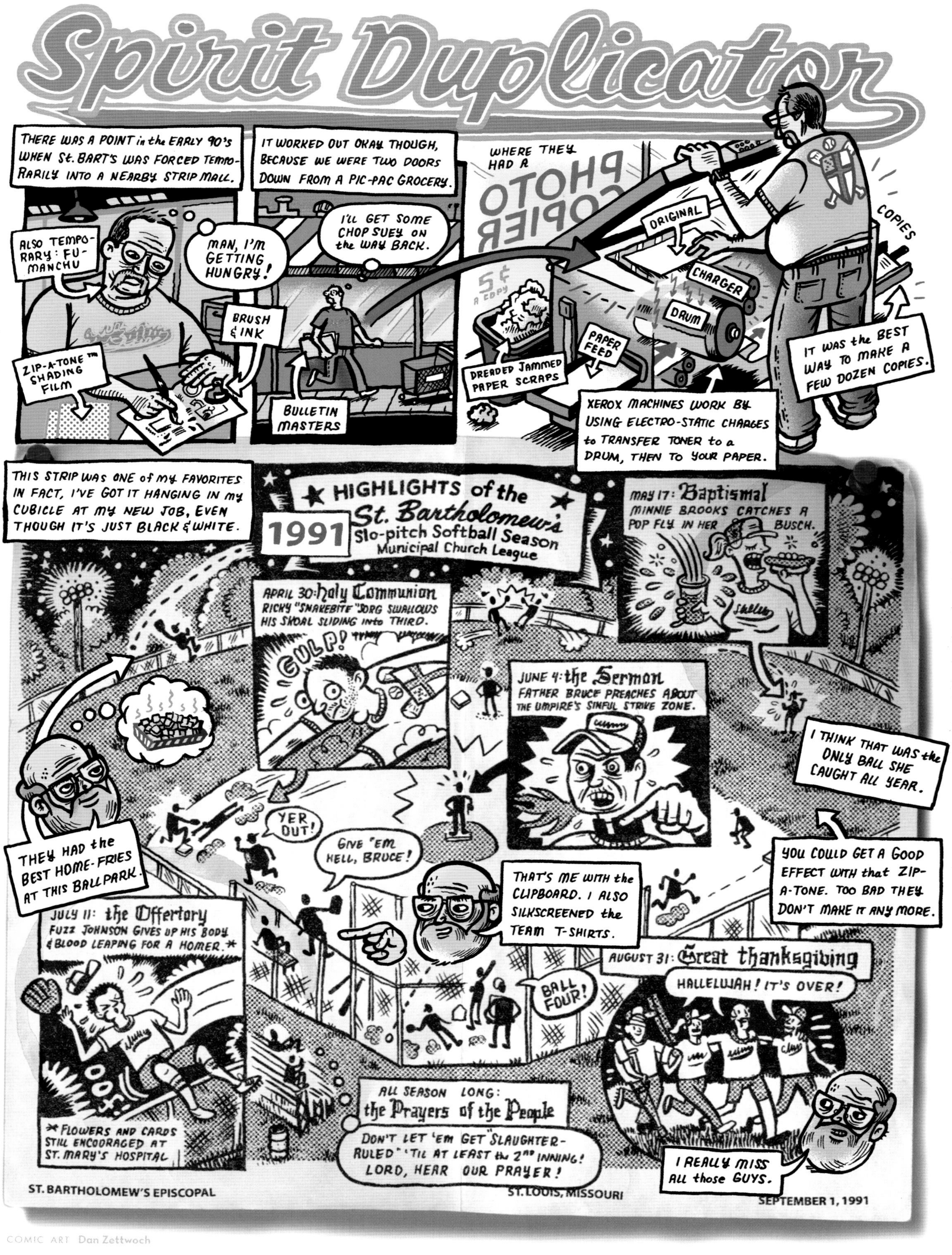
Spirit Duplicator
THERE WAS A POINT in the EARLY 90's WHEN St. BART'S WAS FORCED TEMPORARILY INTO A NEARBY STRIP MALL.
ALSO TEMPORARY: FU-MANCHU
MAN, I'M GETTING HUNGRY!
BRUSH & INK
ZIP-A-TONE™ SHADING FILM
IT WORKED OUT OKAY THOUGH, BECAUSE WE WERE TWO DOORS DOWN FROM A PIC-PAC GROCERY.
I'LL GET SOME CHOP SUEY ON the WAY BACK.
BULLETIN MASTERS
WHERE THEY HAD A
PHOTO COPIER
5¢ A COPY
ORIGINAL
CHARGER
DRUM
COPIES
PAPER FEED
DREADED JAMMED PAPER SCRAPS
IT WAS the BEST WAY TO MAKE A FEW DOZEN COPIES.
XEROX MACHINES WORK BY USING ELECTRO-STATIC CHARGES to TRANSFER TONER to a DRUM, THEN TO YOUR PAPER.
THIS STRIP WAS ONE of MY FAVORITES IN FACT, I'VE GOT IT HANGING IN MY CUBICLE AT MY NEW JOB, EVEN THOUGH IT'S JUST BLACK & WHITE.
HIGHLIGHTS of the St. Bartholomew's 1991 Slo-pitch Softball Season Municipal Church League
APRIL 30: Holy Communion RICKY "SNAKEBITE" JORG SWALLOWS HIS SKOAL SLIDING into THIRD.
GULP!
MAY 17: Baptismal MINNIE BROOKS CATCHES A POP FLY IN HER BUSCH.
JUNE 4: the Sermon FATHER BRUCE PREACHES ABOUT THE UMPIRE'S SINFUL STRIKE ZONE.
I THINK THAT WAS the ONLY BALL SHE CAUGHT ALL YEAR.
THEY HAD the BEST HOME-FRIES AT THIS BALLPARK.
YER OUT!
GIVE 'EM HELL, BRUCE!
THAT'S ME WITH the CLIPBOARD. I ALSO SILKSCREENED the TEAM T-SHIRTS.
YOU COULD GET A GOOD EFFECT WITH that ZIP-A-TONE. TOO BAD THEY DON'T MAKE IT ANY MORE.
JULY 11: the Offertory FUZZ JOHNSON GIVES UP HIS BODY & BLOOD LEAPING FOR A HOMER.*
*FLOWERS AND CARDS STILL ENCOURAGED AT ST. MARY'S HOSPITAL
BALL FOUR!
AUGUST 31: Great thanksgiving
HALLELUJAH! IT'S OVER!
ALL SEASON LONG: the Prayers of the People
DON'T LET 'EM GET "SLAUGHTER-RULED" 'TIL AT LEAST the 2nd INNING! LORD, HEAR OUR PRAYER!
I REALLY MISS ALL those GUYS.
ST. BARTHOLOMEW'S EPISCOPAL
ST. LOUIS, MISSOURI
SEPTEMBER 1, 1991

COMIC ART Dan Zettwoch

Jesse

A HISTORY *of* HIS WORK IN COMICS

by Ron Goulart

VIRTUALLY UNKNOWN and unsung during his relatively short lifetime, Jesse Marsh remains today, forty years after his death, one of the least recognized of the major 20th-century comic book artists. A giftedly inventive cartoonist, he turned out over a hundred and fifty issues of the *Tarzan* comic book from the late 1940s until the middle 1960s. In addition, he produced a great many western titles, notably those dealing with singing cowboy Gene Autry, and found time, throughout the 1950s and early 1960s, to draw the *Walt Disney's Treasury of Classic Tales* Sunday page. Marsh managed, for most of his career, to be both prolific and good. When Alex Toth died recently, several obituary accounts referred to him as "an artist's artist," a term that implies quality but not necessarily vast popularity. Since Marsh was one of Toth's lifelong favorites, that would make him "an artist's artist's artist."

Marsh drew all his comic books for the Southern California office of Western Printing, the outfit that produced the Dell comic books. Because of the clean cut material they published, including the Disney and Looney Tunes titles, Western is usually considered a sedate and conservative organization, a comic book company that had no need to subscribe to the Comics Code in the 1950s. However, they also employed several of the most innovative artists ever to work in the field. The top three, in my view, were Carl Barks, Alex Toth, and Jesse Marsh. Unlike Barks and Toth, Marsh inspired no immediate disciples or imitators, and his unique style remained unique and died with him.

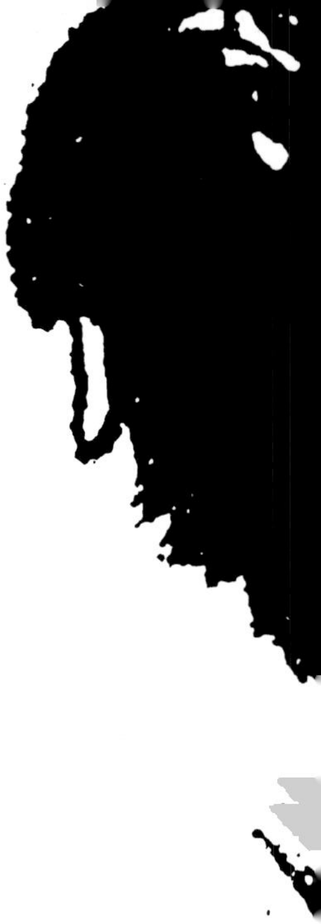

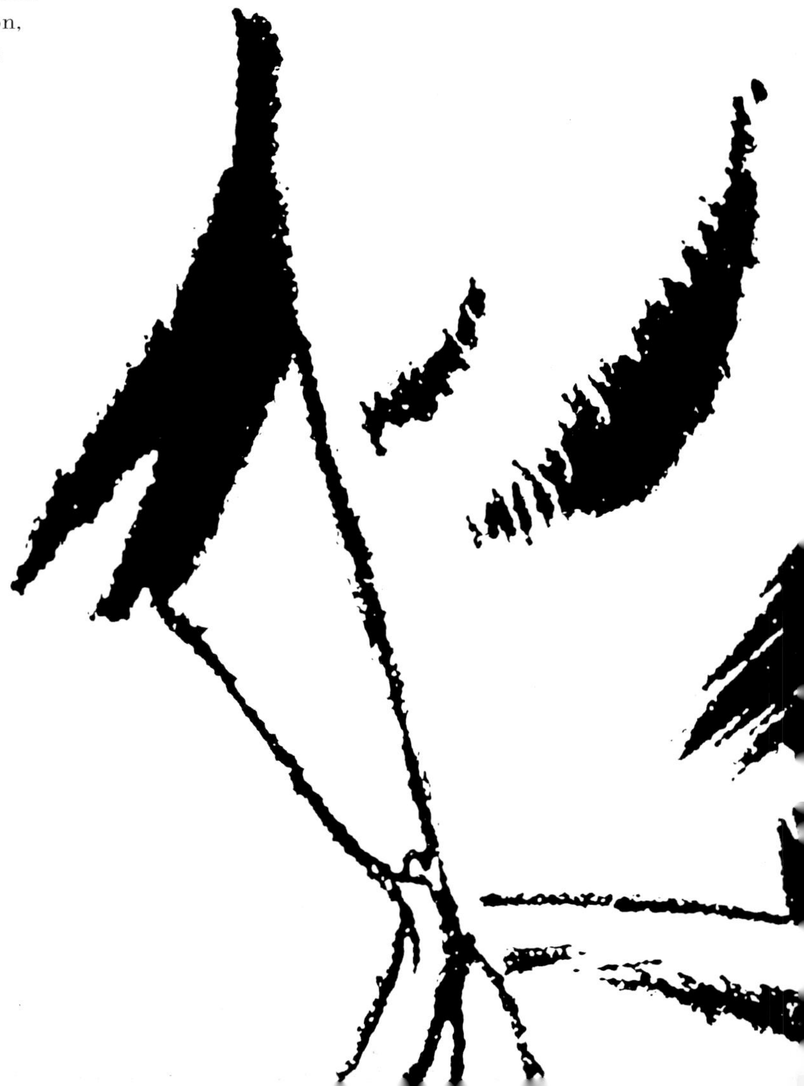

Marsh

A Q&A WITH GILBERT HERNANDEZ

by Adrian Tomine

ADRIAN TOMINE: How did you first come into contact with Jesse Marsh's work? If I'm doing my math correctly, his career was well under way before you were even born.

GILBERT HERNANDEZ: All I remember is that those late '50s/early '60s Dell, then Gold Key, comics were around the house, *Tarzan* being the favorite "superhero" of Latinos at the time. Up until high school, the few "superhero" comics the Latino kids at school looked at were jungle adventure comics. I noticed if a Latino was reading a comic book on the bus, it was almost always a *Tarzan* comic book. I don't know if that's at all significant, or because my world was pretty small at the time, but there it is. It's possible I identified with those Jesse Marsh *Tarzan* comics because characters looked Latino to me.

AT: How important do you think it is for a reader to see something of himself in the characters he's reading about?

GH: It was a big deal to me and other Latinos, I'm sure. Kids in the 'hood would watch a movie or TV show with a dark-haired, swarthy guy, like Tyrone Power in *The Mark of Zorro* (did you know Zorro stories take place in LA?!?) or Victor Mature in anything, and the kids were convinced those guys were Mexican. It was all projecting, of course. Role models were always looked for, and I took that very seriously.

AT: Do you think about this at all when you're creating the characters in your own comics?

GH: That's why I chose to use Latinos for my comics: not only because it pleases me, but I happen to agree with the notion that the more ethnic a work of art is, the more universal. The more Swedish Ingmar Bergman was, or [the more] Japanese Kurosawa and Ozu were, the more their work had resonance for everybody who can absorb it.

Life drawing from Marsh's days at Disney. Courtesy of Dylan Williams.

HOW TO WEAR CLOTHES BY MARSH

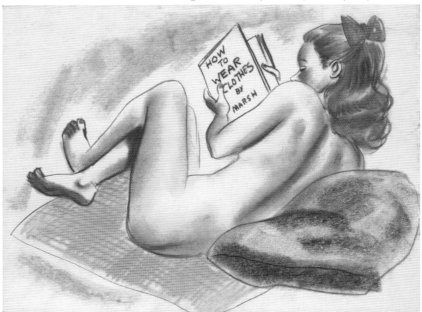

Born in Alabama in 1907, Jesse Mace Marsh moved to Southern California with his family (including a twin sister) when he was sixteen. Fascinated with drawing from his earliest years, his ambition was to become a painter and he devoted quite a lot of time in local libraries to poring over art books. In 1939, Marsh got a job with the Walt Disney studio. He worked in animation and later as a story man. He was one of the many Disney employees who worked on *Pinocchio* and *Fantasia*, and was also involved with projects that never made it to the screen, including an animated version of *Don Quixote*.

After serving in the Air Force during World War II, Marsh, who'd been seriously wounded while overseas, returned to Disney. This time he worked on ideas and storyboards for both cartoon shorts and feature-length animated films, including *Make Mine Music*. Marc Davis, a vet-eran Disney artist, said of him, "He was a very talented draftsman and he used to decorate the doors of our studios with huge color nudes drawn on wrapping paper. He was very good." It's likely that Marsh, who enjoyed drawing slim, pretty women, was an admirer of the work of Fred Moore, who designed the slim, pretty lady-centaurs in *Fantasia* and helped create the basic 1940s Disney cute girl.

Marsh began his association with Western Printing late in 1944, while still employed by Disney. By this time Western had already established a business relationship with the Walt Disney organization. They began publishing Mickey Mouse Big Little Books under their Whitman colophon in 1933, adding a Donald Duck series in 1937. In the comic book field, they started *Mickey Mouse Magazine* in 1935, which turned into *Walt Disney's Comics and Stories* in 1940. Carl Barks, a Disney studio employee since the middle 1930s, drew the first original-material Disney comic book, *Donald Duck Finds Pirate Gold*, in 1942 and began drawing ten-page Donald Duck adventures in *WDC&S* early in 1943. Marsh was recruited to handle somewhat more serious fare for Western toward the end of the following year.

Initially he was put to work on Wild West yarns, namely the ongoing *Gene Autry* title. The first truly successful singing cowboy of the movies, Autry had commenced his career in 1935 and had been appearing in Big Little Books since 1938. He moved into a comic book of his own late in 1941. Fawcett Publications, who'd launched such heroes as Captain Marvel, Spy Smasher, and Bulletman, published the first ten issues of *Gene Autry Comics* and then, possibly

A DELL COMIC
DELL
JAN.-FEB.
EDGAR RICE BURROUGHS'S
10¢
TARZAN
in The Valley of the Monsters

Tarzan #7 (Dell Publishing Co., 1949).

AT: Did Marsh's style appeal to you right away? I always wondered if there were some comics fans in the '50s who would be attracted to those painted covers on *Tarzan* and then open it up and be kind of flabbergasted.

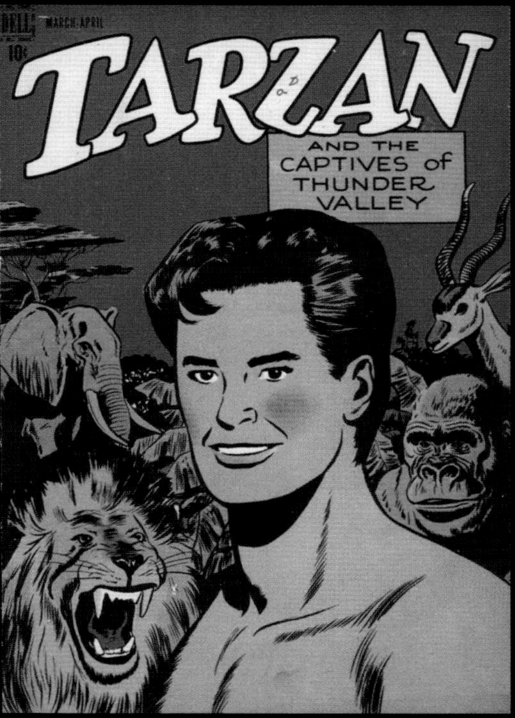
DELL
MARCH-APRIL
10¢
TARZAN
AND THE CAPTIVES of THUNDER VALLEY
Tarzan #2 (Dell Publishing Co., 1948).

GH: Again, the way Marsh drew Tarzan, Jane, and Boy looked like my relatives. I know not a lot of comics fans "get" Marsh's art, but I liked his thick line and direct approach to his storytelling, even when I was a tyke. I loved DC and Marvel comics, but when I compared them to *Tarzan*, they seemed unrealistic and ignorant. *Tarzan* simply seemed more like "home."

AT: What was it about Marsh's style that grabbed you? Is there any difference in the way you appreciate his artwork now, as opposed to when you were first discovering it?

GH: The thick, thick ink line and basic layouts and pacing of the stories. I understand he would finish an entire issue over a weekend, but for me, that gave the art its urgency.

AT: Has this influenced your methods at all? Your amazing level of productivity makes me think you might've been able to keep pace with Marsh in his heyday.

GH: Marsh had a background in art training, which I believe gave him a bit of confidence in himself to blast the stuff out. He had a great library of research materials and loved to use them when necessary. I have neither of those things to speak of. I'm more into using my imagination, and rarely get to use it as much as I'd like to. So, no, I would be up against too much to produce what I was "supposed" to do.

AT: Like so many of those comic book artists from his era, Marsh seems to have worked almost entirely uncredited. I'm curious about when you started recognizing his style, and how you were able to eventually put an artist's name to that style.

GH: My brother Mario probably came across his name in a fanzine somewhere. One of the biggest compliments I've ever gotten for my art was from the late comics fan/critic Don Thompson. He didn't like my work very much at all, but he did compliment my art by saying it looked like Jesse Marsh's a little.

AT: Marsh seems to be often grouped in with artists like Toth, Caniff, Sickles, etc. Where do you think he ranks in that pantheon?

GH: I think Marsh is a giant among the best comic book artists ever. I like that school of art very much (let's not forget Lee Elias's *Black Cat* comics for Harvey). I've talked to a few "hot," pencil-neck, neurotic cartoonists who are repulsed by Caniff's work, et al. It's not like I don't respect their opinions, it's just that they seem to be the spokespeople for comics these days, and—I take it back. I don't respect their opinions.

AT: Do you think someone could not share your influences and still produce work you enjoy? Or are the two inextricable?

GH: Yes, actually I do enjoy artists that do work I would never do. Or could do. Frank Cho, Chaykin, Romita, John Buscema, Neal Adams, Corben; these are artists I've enjoyed from time to time who are on a different plane than I'm on. They're also my superiors in basic draftsmanship, that's for damn sure. I, uh, think that answers your question.

AT: Are you a fan of the actual stories that Marsh was illustrating, or is it mostly a visual/cartooning appeal?

GH: I do enjoy the stories for their simplicity and directness, and sheer charm. They were written by a gentleman named Gaylord Dubois, I believe. It is the art I'm more attracted to, but I do like the stories.

feeling uncomfortable with a hero who couldn't fly, relinquished the title to Dell/Western in 1943. Till Goodan, the authentic cowboy artist who'd drawn the Fawcett issues, moved with the title; in fact, he drew the cover of Marsh's debut issue. This first comic book work by Marsh appeared early in 1945, titled *Gene Autry and the Trail of Terror*. The twenty-six-page adventure involved Gene and his horse Champion in the hunt for a notorious bank robber, a man who "left a trail of terror through three states." Although Autry's Republic films usually took place in the contemporary climate, the comic book had him functioning in a post–Civil War Old West.

In addition to their regular monthly titles, Dell/Western maintained a showcase series, *Four Color* comics, comprised of one-shots and tryouts. There were over 1,300 issues published from 1942 to 1962, and Jesse Marsh's first five Autry books were a part of this series, with two more appearing in 1945 and another two early in 1946. (A regular Gene Autry title, which soon became a monthly, was introduced in the spring of '46; Marsh continued to illustrate the imaginary Old West exploits of the millionaire cowboy until the early 1950s.) The second of the *Four Color* batch, #75, *Gene Autry and the Wildcat*, had a June 1945 publication date and sported Marsh's very first cover.

At the risk of jumping to obvious conclusions based on his earlier film work, Marsh's maiden effort, that twenty-six-page yarn from *Four Color* #66 about a bank robber known as the Black Hawk, has considerable affinities to a storyboard. The story demonstrates a simpler style than Marsh later developed and the action in this tale of twin bank robbers, murder, and kidnapping is broken down cinematically: for the most part, medium, long, and extreme long shots are favored. In addition to demonstrating a strong sense of what later came to be called sequential storytelling, logically guiding the reader from panel to panel, Marsh already displayed obvious skill at pacing and setting up scenes. The Disney animators and technicians had already developed the multi-plane camera, which allowed the character animation to unfold a couple of layers in front of the background, and Marsh uses a similar approach in his comic landscapes, paying considerable attention to the dry, bleak Western countryside—its yellow sands, rocky trails, stunted trees, and distant mountains and mesas. The action always unfolds in front of well-rendered backgrounds, and in the extreme long shots, while his figures are sometimes only a fraction of an inch high, their poses always manage to convey attitude and feeling.

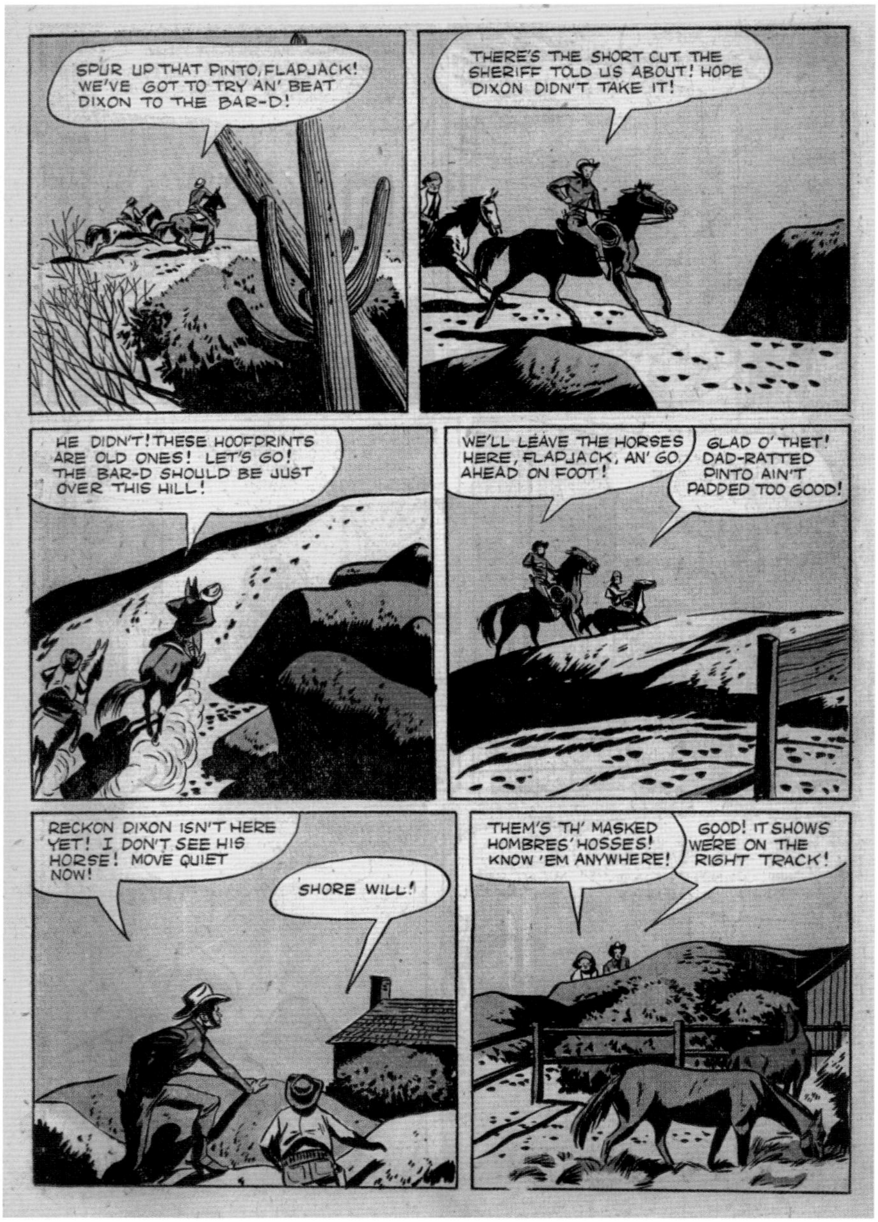
SPUR UP THAT PINTO, FLAPJACK! WE'VE GOT TO TRY AN' BEAT DIXON TO THE BAR-D!
THERE'S THE SHORT CUT THE SHERIFF TOLD US ABOUT! HOPE DIXON DIDN'T TAKE IT!
HE DIDN'T! THESE HOOFPRINTS ARE OLD ONES! LET'S GO! THE BAR-D SHOULD BE JUST OVER THIS HILL!
WE'LL LEAVE THE HORSES HERE, FLAPJACK, AN' GO AHEAD ON FOOT!
GLAD O' THET! DAD-RATTED PINTO AIN'T PADDED TOO GOOD!
RECKON DIXON ISN'T HERE YET! I DON'T SEE HIS HORSE! MOVE QUIET NOW!
SHORE WILL!
THEM'S TH' MASKED HOMBRES' HOSSES! KNOW 'EM ANYWHERE!
GOOD! IT SHOWS WE'RE ON THE RIGHT TRACK!
Page from Gene *Autry Comics* #16 (Dell Publishing Co., 1948). Courtesy of Dylan Williams.

Although Marsh's earliest drawing has been described as "primitive" and little concerned with accurate anatomy, this is not at all the case. From the beginning, he displayed considerable sophistication and he was quite adept at rendering a figure accurately and with a minimum of lines. *Trail of Terror* contains a sequence in which the Black Hawk, disguised as a passenger, holds up the stage coach that Autry is riding on. He grabs a young woman passenger—Marsh's first slim, dark-haired girl—drags her out of the coach as a hostage and then abandons her. After the bank robber escapes, Autry picks up the unconscious young woman and carries her back inside the coach. Marsh handles this all simply, but accurately and effectively. While a great many of his contemporaries were capable of drawing a superhero leaping off a tall building, not all of them could create a sequence like this with the naturalness that Marsh brings to it.

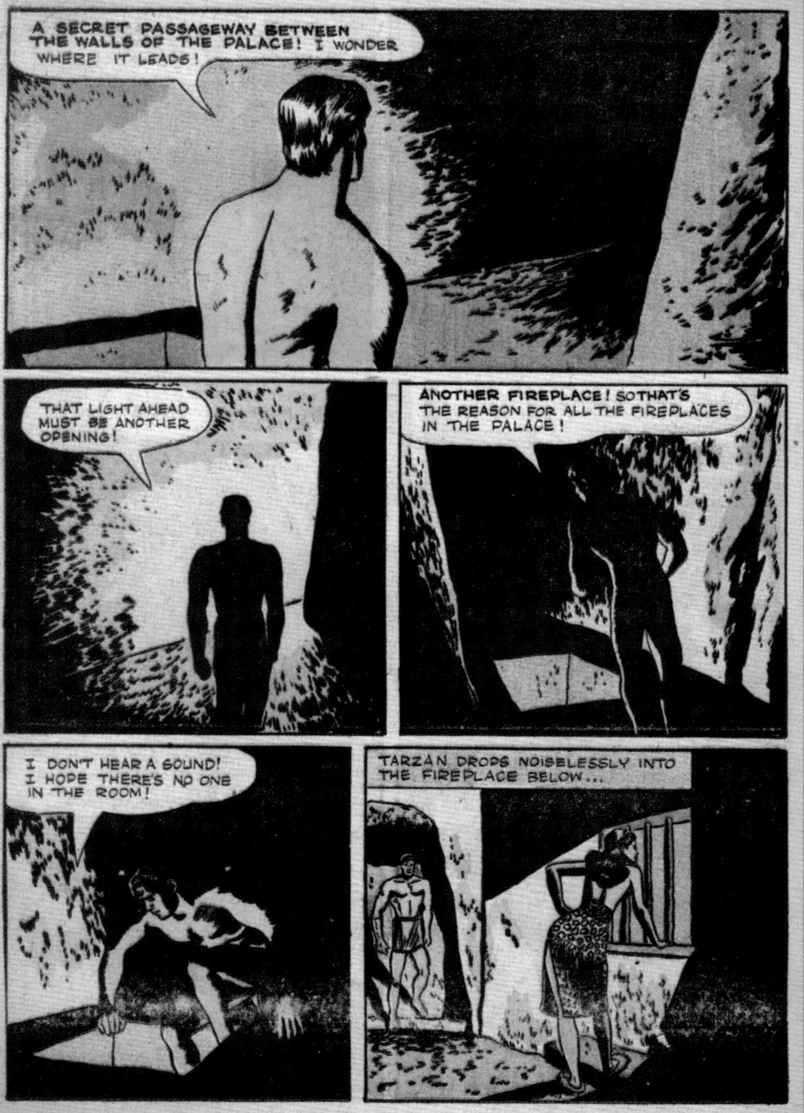
A SECRET PASSAGEWAY BETWEEN THE WALLS OF THE PALACE! I WONDER WHERE IT LEADS!
THAT LIGHT AHEAD MUST BE ANOTHER OPENING!
ANOTHER FIREPLACE! SO THAT'S THE REASON FOR ALL THE FIREPLACES IN THE PALACE!
I DON'T HEAR A SOUND! I HOPE THERE'S NO ONE IN THE ROOM!
TARZAN DROPS NOISELESSLY INTO THE FIREPLACE BELOW...

Page from *Tarzan* #1 (Dell Publishing Co., 1948).

AT: Can you think of (and describe) any specific ways that Marsh has influenced your own work?

GH: All of the above.

AT: I think Marsh's influence might be more immediately apparent in your work, but can you see it at all in Jaime's work? I ask because I think he was the one who brought up Marsh in your first *Comics Journal* interview.

GH: Jaime's ink line hides the Marsh influence, but if you look at Jaime's early "jungle" stories (*Love & Rockets* vol. 1, #2 and 3), it's clearly there.

AT: Do you think the influence of people like Toth and Marsh can be applied effectively to more personal, naturalistic comics? Or is that style just inherently more suited to action/adventure stories?

GH: Marsh's style is absolutely suited for everyday living–type stories: look at me, or James Sturm, Jessica Abel, Caniff, '50s/early '60s Kirby, Elias, in our "quiet" scenes.

AT: The two modern cartoonists you mentioned are James Sturm and Jessica Abel. Do you see them as kind of torchbearers for the Marsh/Caniff/Toth style of cartooning?

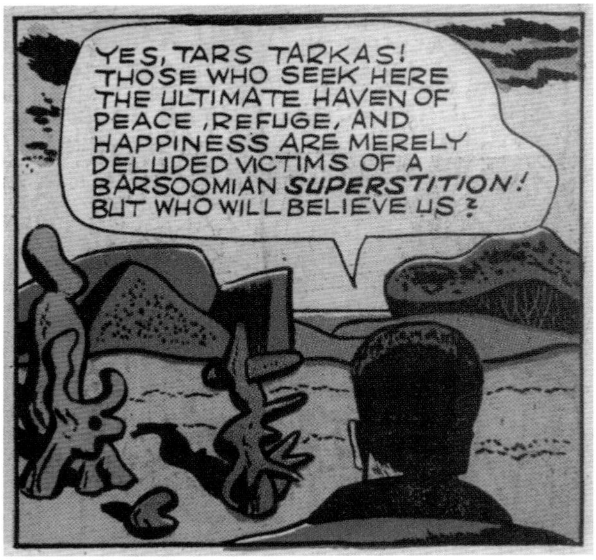
YES, TARS TARKAS! THOSE WHO SEEK HERE THE ULTIMATE HAVEN OF PEACE, REFUGE, AND HAPPINESS ARE MERELY DELUDED VICTIMS OF A BARSOOMIAN *SUPERSTITION!* BUT WHO WILL BELIEVE US?

Panel from "John Carter of Mars in The Black Pirates of Omean," *Four Color* #437 (Dell Publishing Co., 1952).

Already Marsh, who was just starting to learn the comic book trade, was establishing an undeniably individual style that owed little to what was going on in the industry of the time, and despite the breakneck speed at which he was working, his storytelling was always perceptively thoughtful. Russ Manning, a talented but much more conventional Dell/Western cartoonist, was a friend and admirer, and years after Marsh's death, he singled out *Gene Autry* #16 from 1948 as being an especially impressive effort: "Clear-cut, finely designed shapes fit within and against each other in a quite unique illusion of reality, and the overall impression is very pleasing...the artist has done the original. I don't remember anything like this style in any comic book or strip. It may come partially from a study of the 19th-century French painter-draftsman Ingres, whom our artist had long admired, but it most likely reflects his own particular beliefs and way of seeing." Marsh continued to do impressive work on the Autry book from the late 1940s to the early 1950s, but possibly the great leap forward on his horse operas was caused by adding Dell/Western's new *Tarzan* comic book to his work load in 1947. He would thrive in this jungle venue.

By the time Western Publishing introduced their *Tarzan* comic book, the first to use original material, they had been doing business with Edgar Rice Burroughs, Inc., for well over a decade. Their original Big Little Book about the Lord of the Jungle was entitled *Tarzan of the Apes* and appeared in 1933. Nearly twenty more Tarzan titles followed in the '30s and '40s, as well one devoted to John Carter of Mars in 1940. Up until Marsh's rendering, Tarzan had been depicted in the movies, on book jackets, and in newspaper funnies as a muscular chap, rendered in an illustration style that grew out of the work of such giants as Howard Pyle, N.C. Wyeth, and J. Allen St. John. Burne Hogarth, who took over the Sunday page from Hal Foster in 1937, was a great devotee of musculature, and his Tarzan, once he gave up trying to follow in Foster's footsteps, looked like he'd stepped out of a

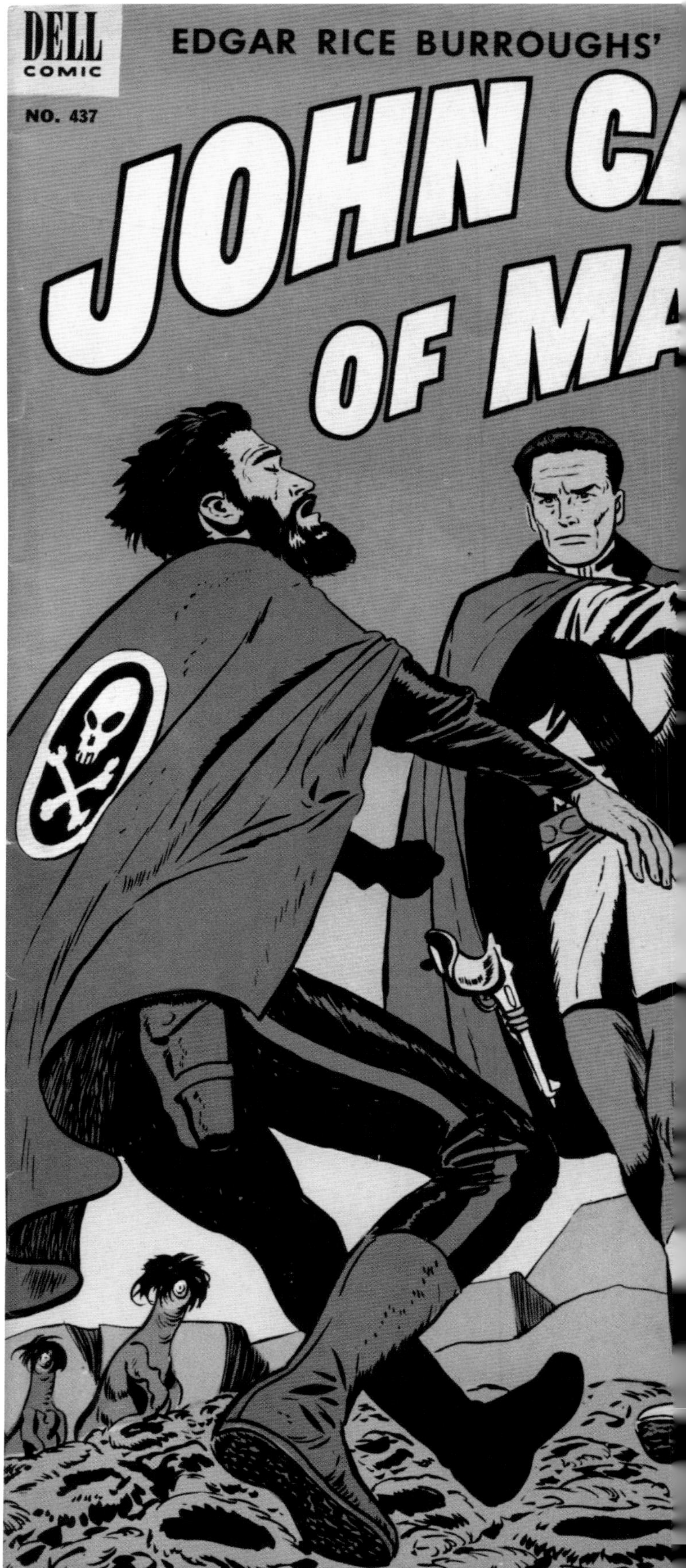
DELL COMIC
EDGAR RICE BURROUGHS'
NO. 437
JOHN CA
OF MA

"John Carter of Mars in The Black Pirates of Omean," *Four Color* #437 (Dell Publishing Co., 1952).

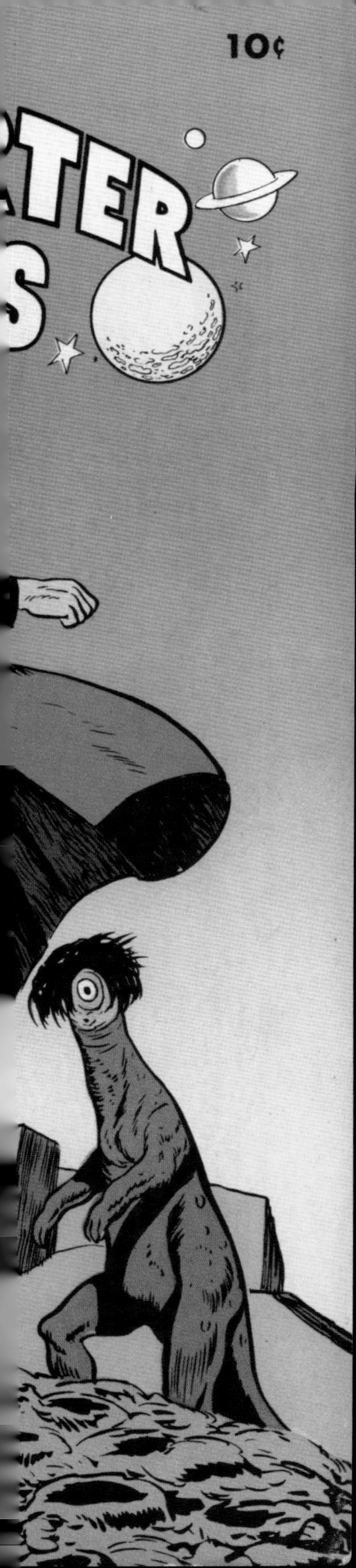
10¢

GH: Actually, they're the only two I could think of off the top of my head; there are people in mainstream comics that use a heavy brushline, like Paul Pope and Cliff Chiang, for example. So is that the criteria? Heavy brushlines? Fuck, I'm shallow.

AT: I imagine the first thing someone would notice about Marsh's work is his bold and eccentric inking style, but I understand that he was also his own penciler and letterer. How important are those steps in his process to the overall result?

GH: It's all him on the page and that's what I'm looking for.

AT: I remember reading an essay by Toth in which he criticized Marsh's drawing ability with regards to human anatomy. Do you think this is an accurate (or relevant) criticism?

GH: No, Toth must have been thinking of Burne Hogarth. Seriously, I find Marsh's rushed "stylizing" more "realistic" than Toth's precise approach.

AT: Do you know anything about Jesse Marsh beyond his work? Did he ever enjoy any kind of recognition in his lifetime?

GH: His name is on the story credits of the Disney cartoon film *Melodytime*, but I don't know about recognition.

AT: What do you think the young cartoonists of today could learn from Jesse Marsh?

GH: Pacing, tone, mood, direct storytelling.

AT: If someone wanted to seek out some of Marsh's work, what would you recommend as a starting point, and why?

GH: *Tarzan* comics of the '50s, and maybe the couple of issues he did of *John Carter of Mars* [reprinted] in the '60s, just because they're almost like David Lynch versions of those stories. Thing is, if the interested parties are looking for some kind of epiphany or payoff with his work, forget it. Real art doesn't work that way. CA

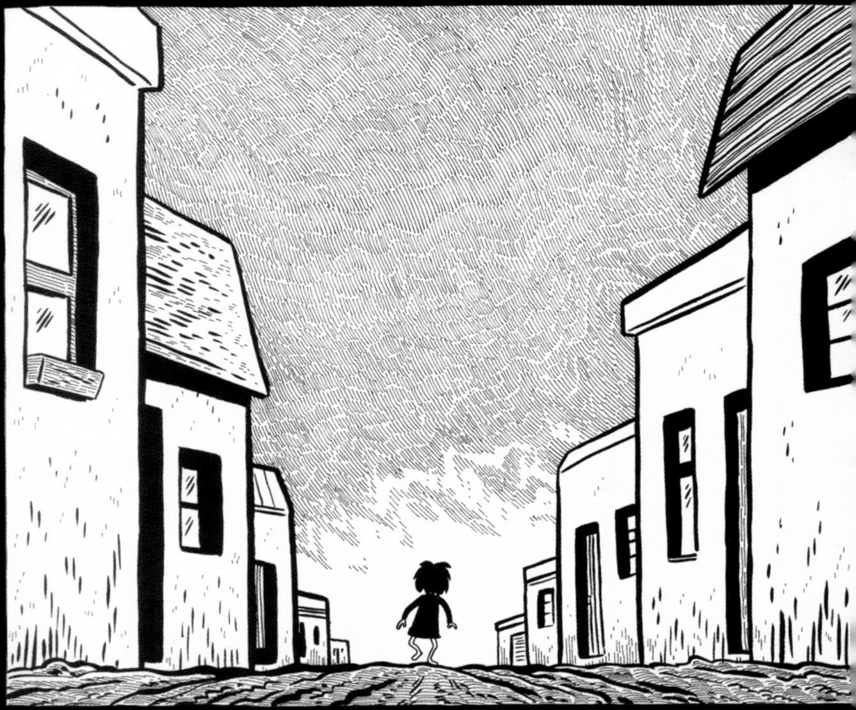

Gilbert Hernandez, panel from *New Tales of Old Palomar* #1 (Fantagraphics Books and Coconino Press, 2006

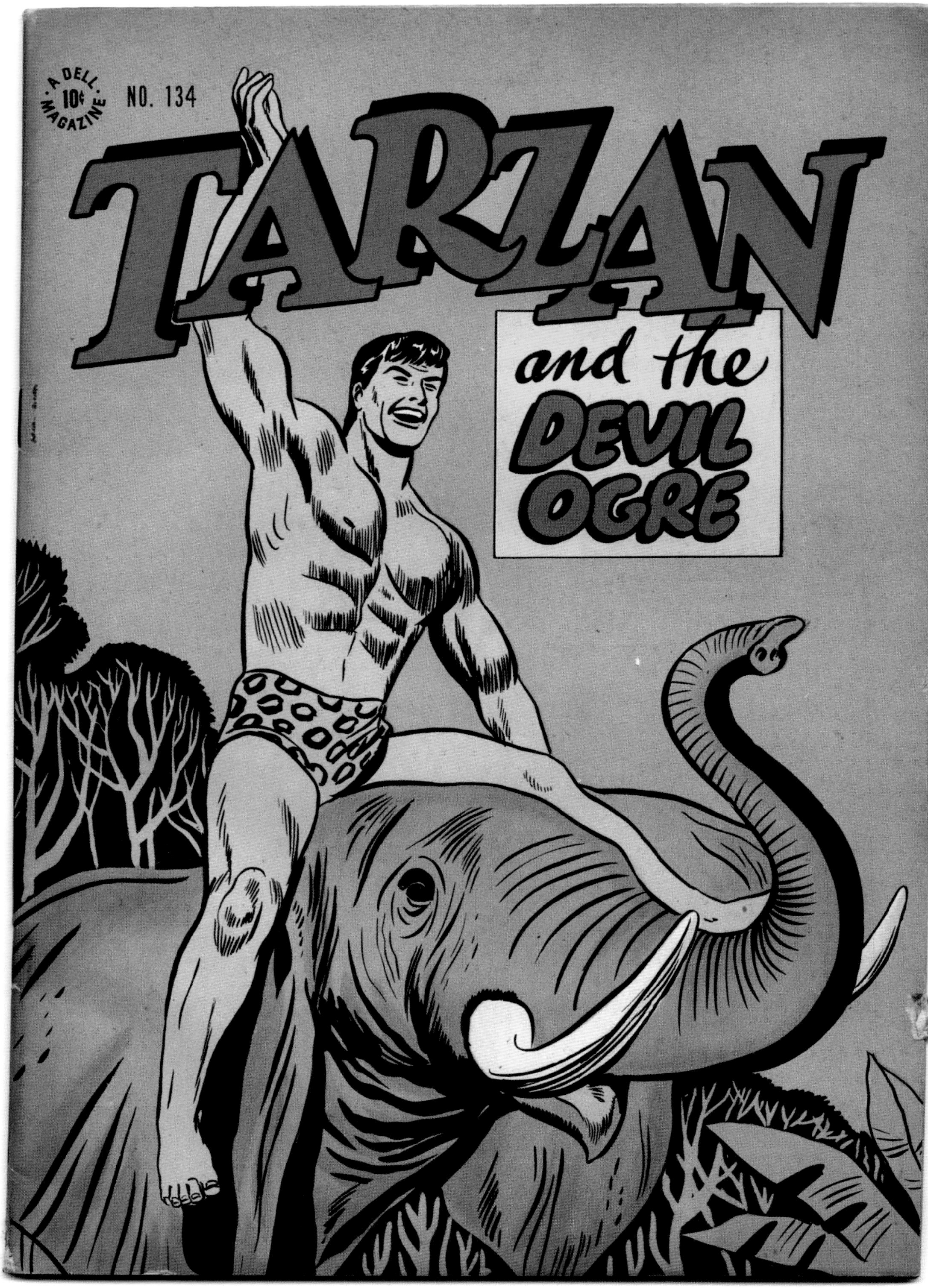
A DELL 10¢ MAGAZINE
NO. 134
TARZAN
and the
DEVIL OGRE

"Tarzan and the Devil Ogre," *Four Color* #134 (Dell Publishing Co., 1947).

bodybuilding magazine (in fact, most of Hogarth's women were also highly toned and even his trees had muscles). Only Rex Maxon, the artist on the daily strip from the early 1930s to the mid-'40s, drew in a looser, less formal style (Edgar Rice Burroughs himself loathed Maxon's work and made several attempts to get the United Feature Syndicate to dump him). The daily strip, which began in 1929, didn't use word balloons, rather chunks of copy adapted from Burroughs's novels were set in type (later hand-lettered) and ran beneath the panel illustrations. This practice was considered a more dignified way to present literature and when the Sunday page began in 1931 balloons were also avoided. Until the Dell *Tarzan* came along, nary a word balloon had ever appeared in a graphic ape man narrative, so the Jesse Marsh version was quite probably a shock to longtime Tarzan buffs. Marsh also broke with other traditions, as his jungle lord was muscular, but not in the pumped up manner Hogarth was promoting on Sundays and nowhere near as grim, even smiling now and then.

Whereas the newspaper Sunday pages often resembled a collection of book illustrations or the plans for a series of tableaux, Marsh's comic book pages were laid out flowingly, incorporating multiple points of view. Turning his back on the Foster and Hogarth traditional illustrative approach, Marsh adapted the impressionistic style introduced by Noel Sickles and Milton Caniff in newspaper adventure strips of the mid-1930s: his inking on *Tarzan* was more lush than it had been on his cowboy stuff and while the jungle often threatened to close in on his characters, he also demonstrated a fondness for wide open spaces, veldts, dangerous rapids, stormy skies, and—these being Burroughs-inspired tales—convincingly designed lost cities and civilizations. Marsh taught himself to be an expert on the flora and fauna of Africa, and unlike the workers in the Jerry Iger shop who were turning out jungle girl epics for such Fiction House titles as *Jumbo Comics*, he drew believable Africans and made few mistakes as to their manner of dress or their manner of living.

The Dell *Tarzan* began with two *Four Color* tryout issues. *Tarzan and the Devil Ogre* (#134) reached newsstands early in 1947 and *Tarzan and the Fires of Tohr* (#161) followed six months later. Sales of both were good and the first issue of a regular series, with a January-February 1948 cover date, arrived at the tail end of 1947. Marsh developed an even bolder style as the book began its regular schedule. He even managed, in a few early issues, to sign his name to his work (the West Coast Dells didn't allow artist or writer credits, and Barks, Toth, Manning, and all the others worked anonymously). Toth, who went to work for Western a few years after Marsh, was a dedicated admirer and champion of Marsh's *Tarzan* run. In a 1981 appreciation he wrote for John Benson's *Panels*, he praised the "broad picture-making vistas encompassing the whole of Africa and its peoples, tribes, costumes, customs, terrain and wildlife," further observing that "it was a delight to see [Marsh] grow with the series established as a hit—each issue a surprise—for he became enmeshed in his subject and, with an ever growing personal library on Africa (rumored to have topped 2,000 volumes), Jesse documented his people and places to a faretheewell, more than any other *Tarzan* strip artist had (before, during, or after his tenure)!"

A DELL 10¢ MAGAZINE
NO. 161
TARZAN
and the FIRES of TOHR

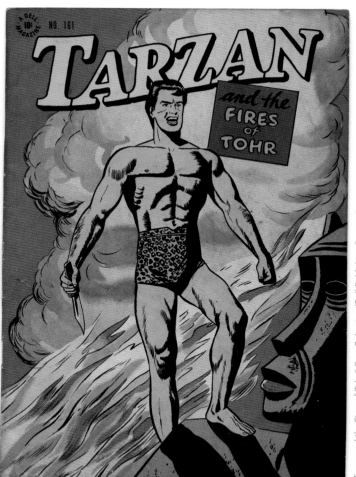

"Tarzan and the Fires of Tohr," *Four Color* #161 (Dell Publishing Co., 1947).

DELL COMIC
JULY-AUG.
EDGAR RICE BURROUGHS'S
10¢
TARZAN
K-6-16
and The Lone Hunter

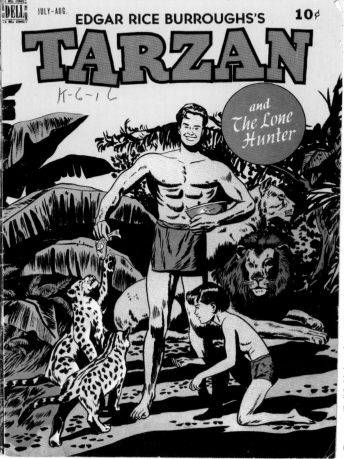

Tarzan #4 (Dell Publishing Co., 1948).

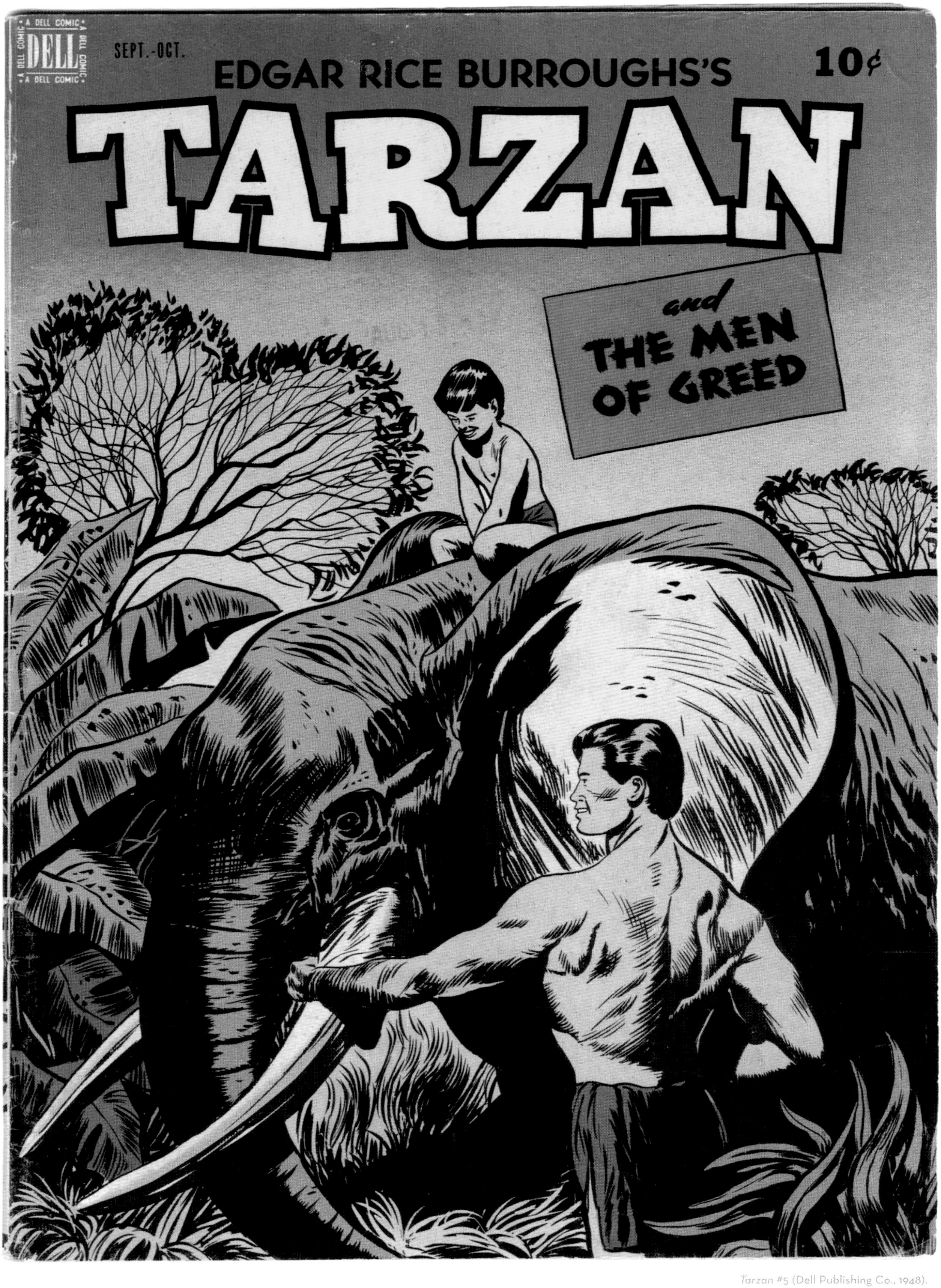
A DELL COMIC
DELL
SEPT.-OCT.
EDGAR RICE BURROUGHS'S
10¢
TARZAN
and
THE MEN
OF GREED

Tarzan #5 (Dell Publishing Co., 1948).

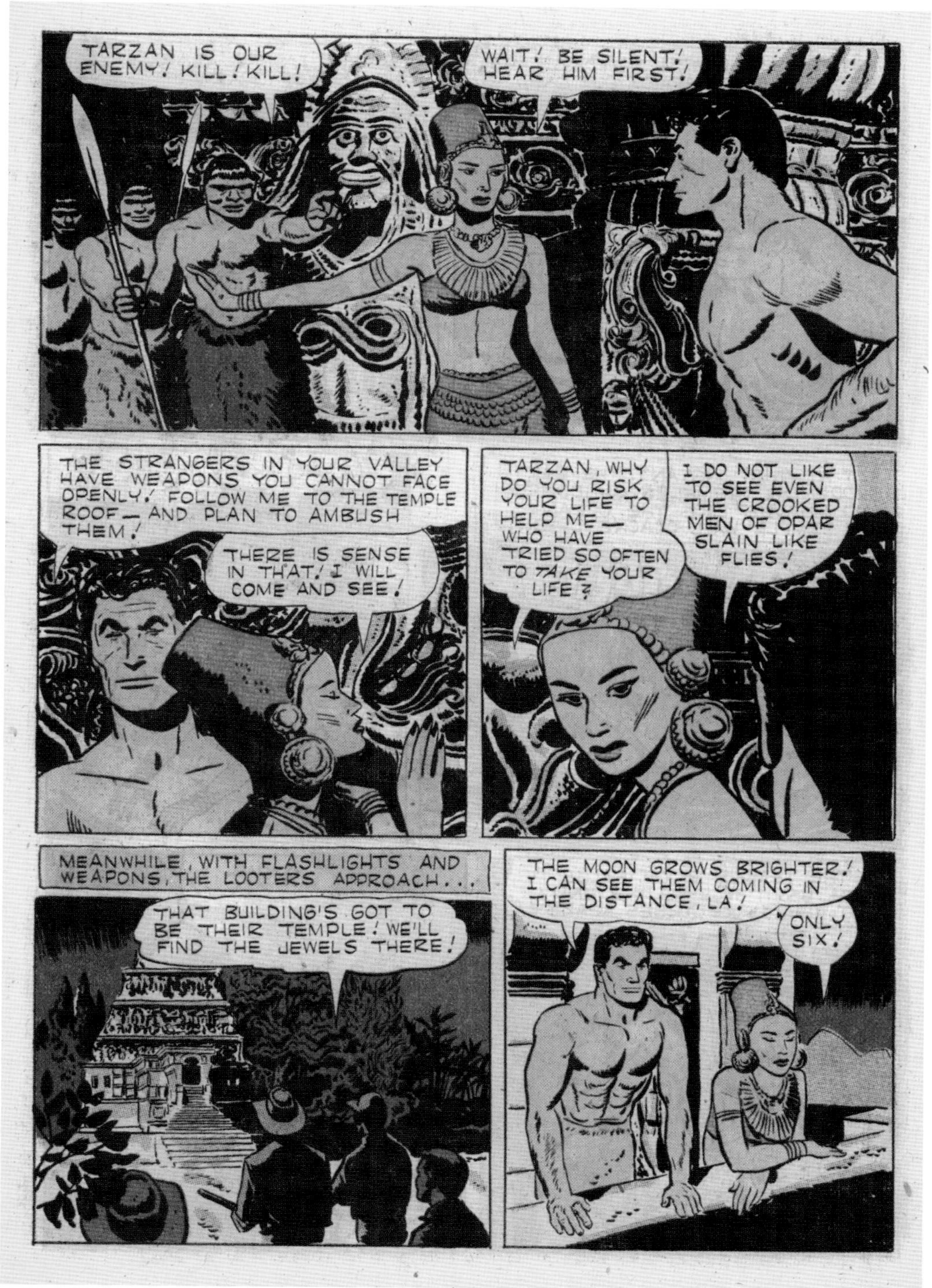

TARZAN IS OUR ENEMY! KILL! KILL!
WAIT! BE SILENT! HEAR HIM FIRST!
THE STRANGERS IN YOUR VALLEY HAVE WEAPONS YOU CANNOT FACE OPENLY! FOLLOW ME TO THE TEMPLE ROOF— AND PLAN TO AMBUSH THEM!
THERE IS SENSE IN THAT! I WILL COME AND SEE!
TARZAN, WHY DO YOU RISK YOUR LIFE TO HELP ME— WHO HAVE TRIED SO OFTEN TO TAKE YOUR LIFE?
I DO NOT LIKE TO SEE EVEN THE CROOKED MEN OF OPAR SLAIN LIKE FLIES!
MEANWHILE, WITH FLASHLIGHTS AND WEAPONS, THE LOOTERS APPROACH...
THAT BUILDING'S GOT TO BE THEIR TEMPLE! WE'LL FIND THE JEWELS THERE!
THE MOON GROWS BRIGHTER! I CAN SEE THEM COMING IN THE DISTANCE, LA!
ONLY SIX!

Page from *Tarzan* #82 (Dell Publishing Co., 1956). Courtesy of Dylan Williams.

During his tenure with the ape man, Marsh was able to include numerous attractive young women in his pages. The dark-haired ones were most often queens of lost cities and the blondes usually the daughters or nieces of explorers, zoologists, botanists, archaeologists, and assorted treasure seekers. While not an exponent of what's come to be called Good Girl Art, Marsh was quite good at depicting women in a relatively natural, believable manner. Toth once told me that Marsh had a habit of asking some of the female employees of the Western Publishing offices if he might sketch them; those who agreed probably served as models for some of those lost city queens and explorer relatives. When Jane began appearing in the jungle tales, it was evident that Marsh had given considerable thought to how to depict her. She comes across not as an actress pretending to do her housekeeping in a tree house, but as a capable woman who could actually function in the complex, sometimes fantasy-tinged, milieu in which Tarzan existed.

While the first Tarzan scripts were written by a fellow named Rob Thompson who'd been involved with the *Tarzan* radio show a decade earlier, from the second regular issue onward, the majority of the stories were written by Gaylord Dubois. Since the comic was edited out of Western's Southern California office, it's unlikely that he had much one-on-one contact with his editors or Marsh, and in an autobiographical piece written late in his career, Dubois makes no mention of Marsh. His method of scripting *Tarzan* he explained thusly: "First I describe the picture the artist is to draw, in detail, which includes color, action, expression, background, angle of view, etc. Then I write out the dialogue balloons, and finally I write the caption or narrative line." Admitting that "the artist is free to use or not use my instructions for each panel," and that "half the story's popularity" is due to the artist, he adds that "usually, though, the art department follows my script fairly close." Dubois apparently had no appreciation of how Marsh continually enhanced his scripts through myriad approaches and techniques.

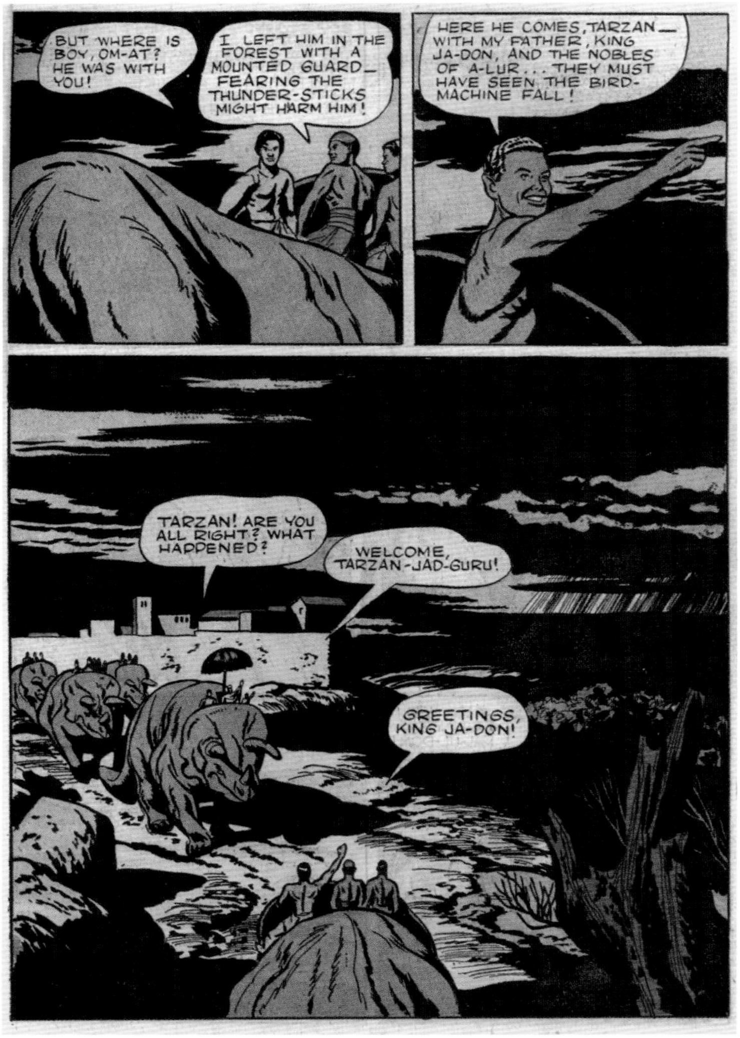
BUT WHERE IS BOY, OM-AT? HE WAS WITH YOU!
I LEFT HIM IN THE FOREST WITH A MOUNTED GUARD— FEARING THE THUNDER-STICKS MIGHT HARM HIM!
HERE HE COMES, TARZAN— WITH MY FATHER, KING JA-DON, AND THE NOBLES OF A-LUR... THEY MUST HAVE SEEN THE BIRD-MACHINE FALL!
TARZAN! ARE YOU ALL RIGHT? WHAT HAPPENED?
WELCOME, TARZAN-JAD-GURU!
GREETINGS, KING JA-DON!

Above: Page from *Tarzan* #16 (Dell Publishing Co., 1950). Courtesy of Dylan Williams.

Right: Page from *Tarzan, Lord of the Jungle* #1 (reprinted from *Tarzan* #13, 1950; Gold Key, 1965). Courtesy of Dylan Williams.

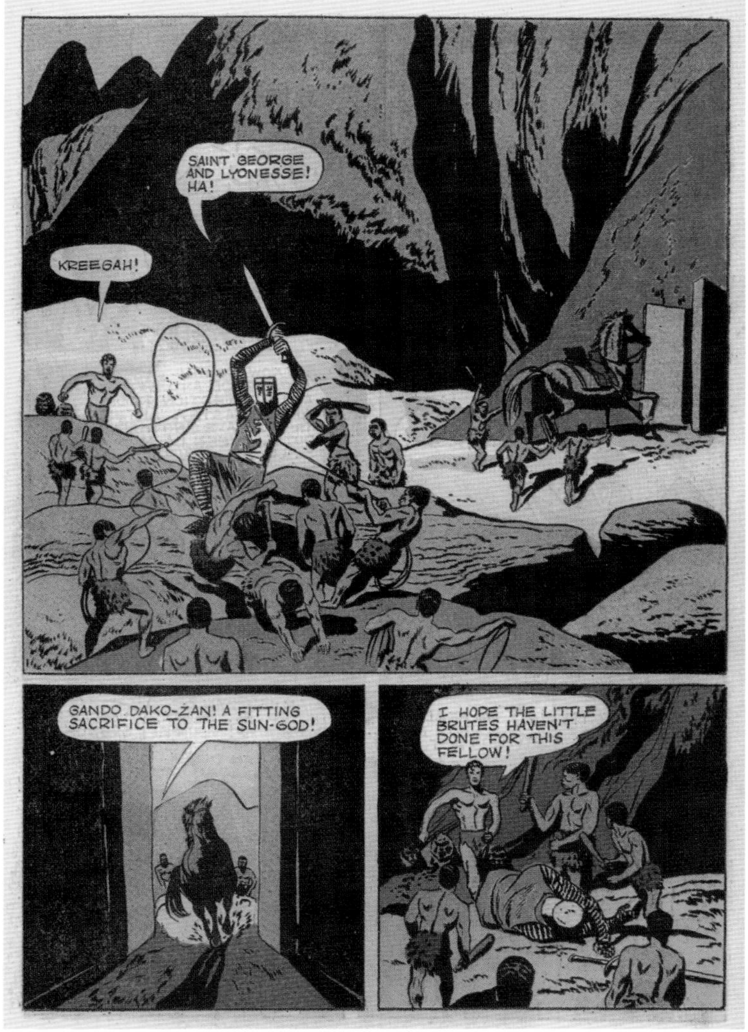
SAINT GEORGE AND LYONESSE! HA!
KREEGAH!
GANDO DAKO-ZAN! A FITTING SACRIFICE TO THE SUN-GOD!
I HOPE THE LITTLE BRUTES HAVEN'T DONE FOR THIS FELLOW!

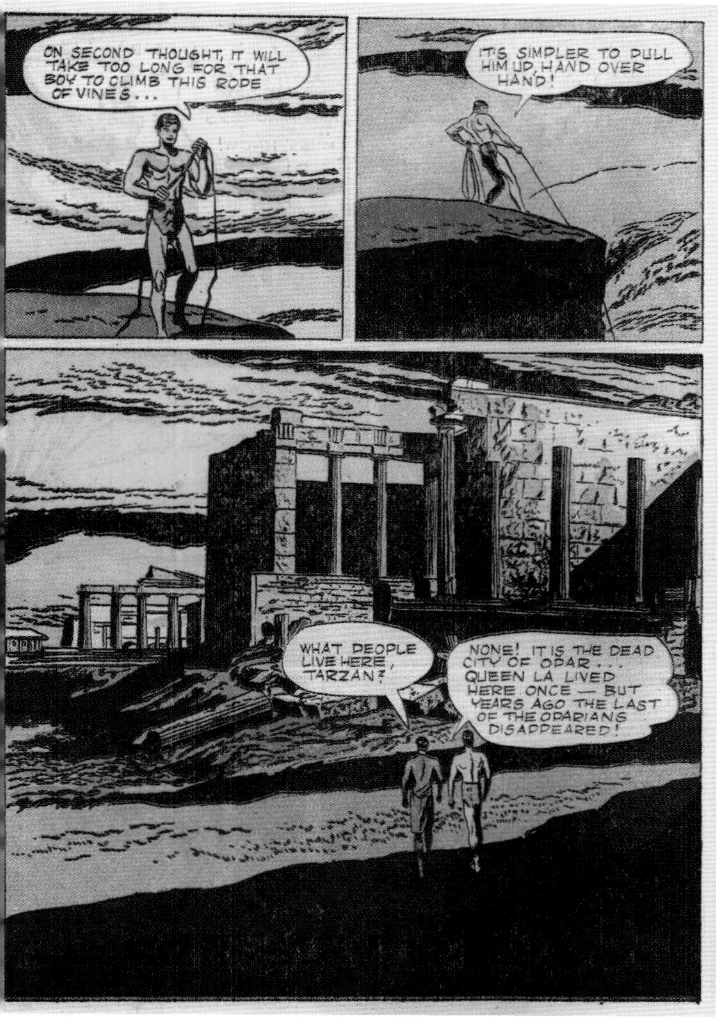
ON SECOND THOUGHT, IT WILL TAKE TOO LONG FOR THAT BOY TO CLIMB THIS ROPE OF VINES...
IT'S SIMPLER TO PULL HIM UP, HAND OVER HAND!
WHAT PEOPLE LIVE HERE, TARZAN?
NONE! IT IS THE DEAD CITY OF OPAR... QUEEN LA LIVED HERE ONCE — BUT YEARS AGO THE LAST OF THE OPARIANS DISAPPEARED!

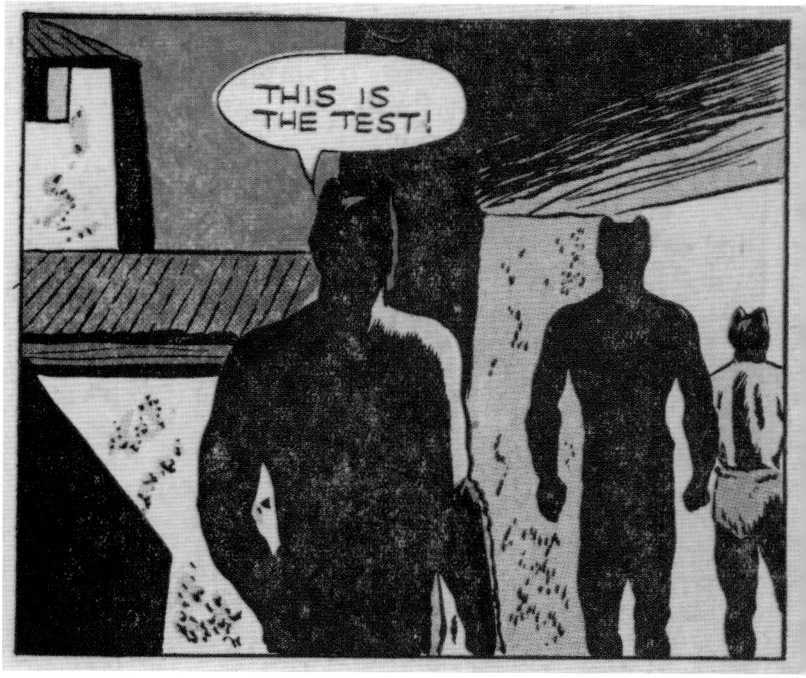
THIS IS THE TEST!

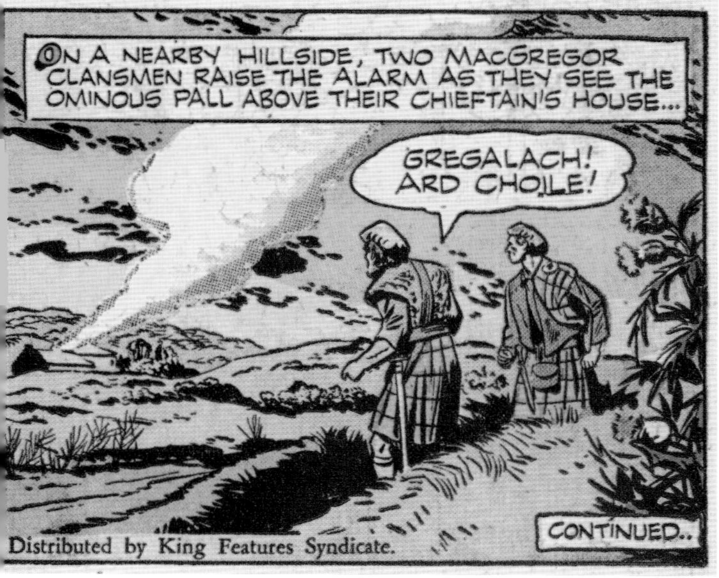
ON A NEARBY HILLSIDE, TWO MACGREGOR CLANSMEN RAISE THE ALARM AS THEY SEE THE OMINOUS PALL ABOVE THEIR CHIEFTAIN'S HOUSE...
GREGALACH! ARD CHOILLE!
Distributed by King Features Syndicate.
CONTINUED..

Above: Panel from *Tarzan* #53 (Dell Publishing Co., 1954).

Top left: Page from *Tarzan, Lord of the Jungle* #1 (reprinted from *Tarzan* #13, 1950; Gold Key, 1965). Courtesy of Dylan Williams.

Bottom left: Panel from "John Carter of Mars in The Black Pirates of Omean," *Four Color* #437 (Dell Publishing Co., 1952).

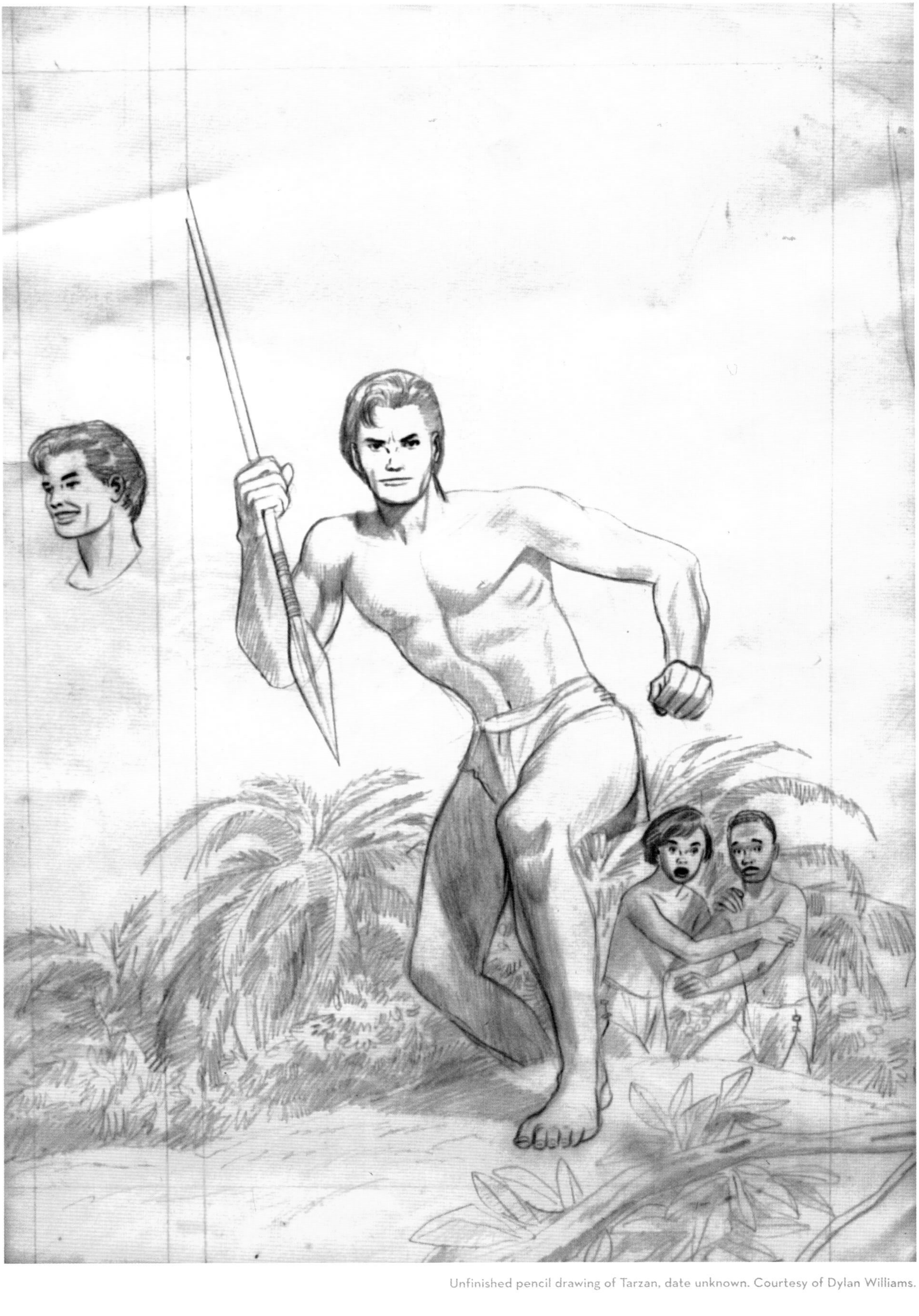

Unfinished pencil drawing of Tarzan, date unknown. Courtesy of Dylan Williams.

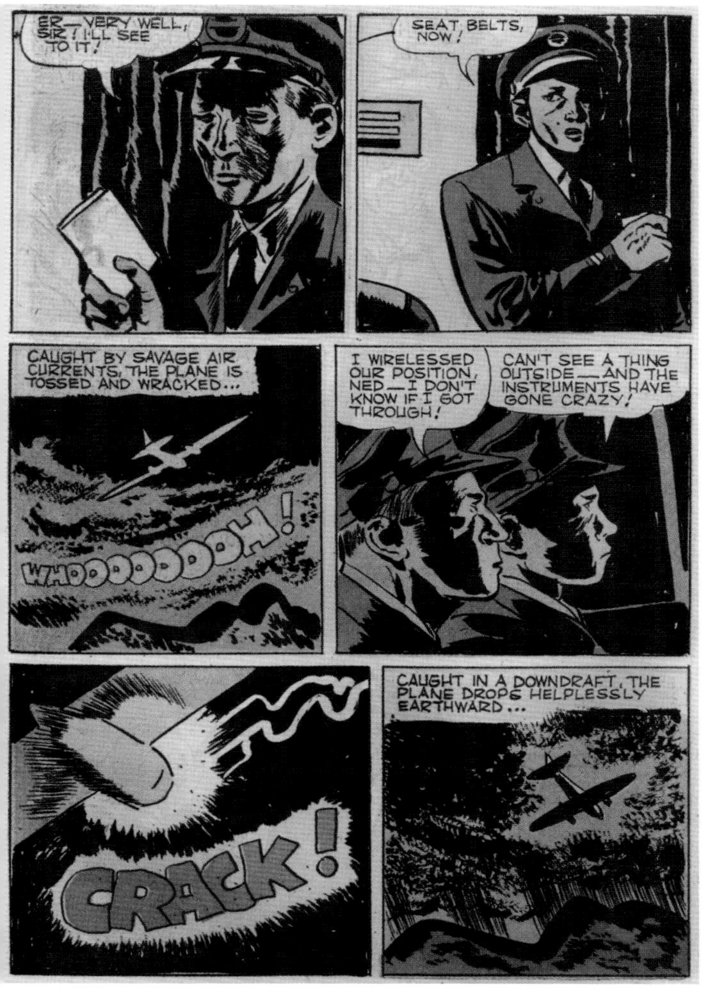
ER—VERY WELL, SIR! I'LL SEE TO IT!
SEAT BELTS, NOW!
CAUGHT BY SAVAGE AIR CURRENTS, THE PLANE IS TOSSED AND WRACKED...
WHOOOOOOOOOH!
I WIRELESSED OUR POSITION, NED—I DON'T KNOW IF I GOT THROUGH!
CAN'T SEE A THING OUTSIDE—AND THE INSTRUMENTS HAVE GONE CRAZY!
CRACK!
CAUGHT IN A DOWNDRAFT, THE PLANE DROPS HELPLESSLY EARTHWARD...

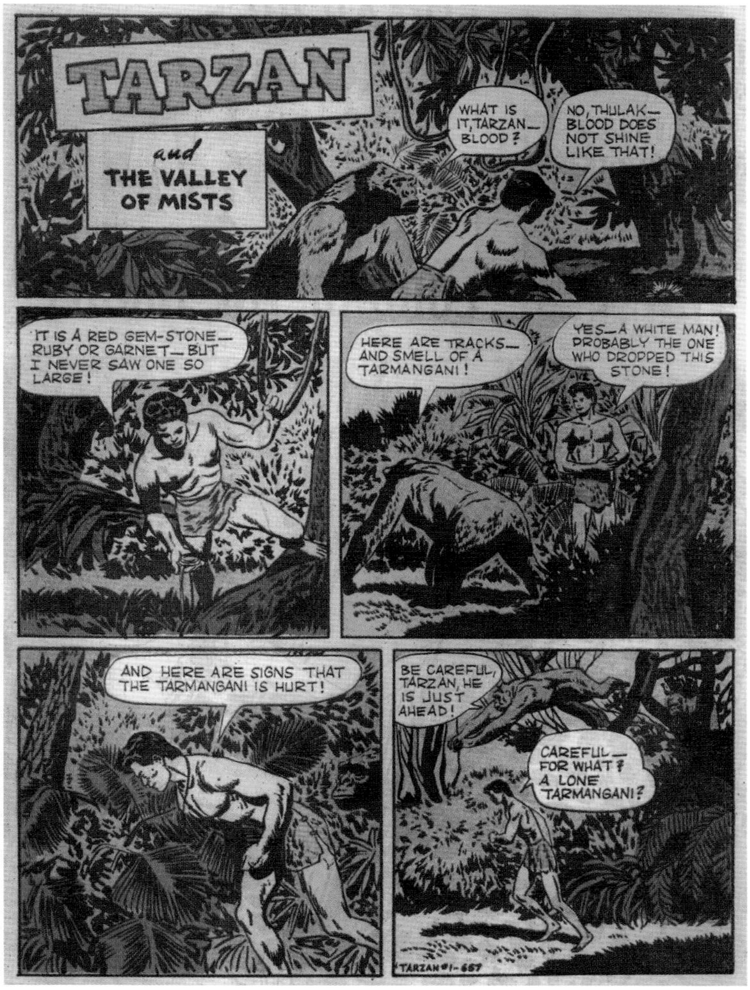
TARZAN
and
THE VALLEY OF MISTS
WHAT IS IT, TARZAN—BLOOD?
NO, THULAK—BLOOD DOES NOT SHINE LIKE THAT!
IT IS A RED GEM-STONE—RUBY OR GARNET—BUT I NEVER SAW ONE SO LARGE!
HERE ARE TRACKS—AND SMELL OF A TARMANGANI!
YES—A WHITE MAN! PROBABLY THE ONE WHO DROPPED THIS STONE!
AND HERE ARE SIGNS THAT THE TARMANGANI IS HURT!
BE CAREFUL, TARZAN, HE IS JUST AHEAD!
CAREFUL—FOR WHAT? A LONE TARMANGANI?

Left: Page from "Tarzan's Jungle World," *Dell Giant* #25 (Dell Publishing Co., 1959). Courtesy of Dylan Williams.

Right: Page from *Tarzan, Lord of the Jungle* #1 (reprinted from *Tarzan* #18, 1950; Gold Key, 1965). Courtesy of Dylan Williams.

The early and mid-1950s were busy years for Marsh. He continued to provide at least two dozen *Tarzan* pages every month, never ceasing to experiment. As Toth pointed out, "the primitive beauty of African design/art affected him deeply, for he focused on them and adapted stylistic line treatments and patterns and textures into his panels, lending great pictorial variety to them." Late in 1951, Marsh also began drawing a new invention of Dubois, a six-page backup story titled *Brothers of the Spear*. The feature dealt with one black and one white protagonist, each a deposed king from a mythical jungle kingdom, and Marsh relinquished it to Russ Manning after fourteen issues. Marsh also added the drawing of two new cowboy titles to his chores in the early part of the decade. He did his usual thoughtful job on the handful of issues devoted to Johnny Mack Brown, and he worked equally well on a few stories for the Buck Jones comic book that began at about the same time. The power of licensing was such that it could raise the dead: a popular movie cowboy in the 1930s, Jones, who rode a horse named Silver before the Lone Ranger ever took to the airwaves, had died in a nightclub fire in Boston in 1942. Western Publishing issued several Buck Jones Big Little Books while Jones was still above the ground and they brought him back to life to take advantage of the current enthusiasm for cowboy comic books.

In 1952 Marsh took on Edgar Rice Burroughs's other long-lived hero, John Carter of Mars, and drew three issues of a *John Carter* title. The Martian swordsman had appeared briefly in comic books and in an unsuccessful Sunday page a decade earlier. Marsh ignored the approach used by Burroughs's artist son, John Coleman Burroughs, on both those earlier versions, and his Mars was a well-designed place that had a distinctly alien look: Marsh obviously had fun working out the idiosyncratic buildings, costumes, and fantastic creatures Burroughs had invented decades before.

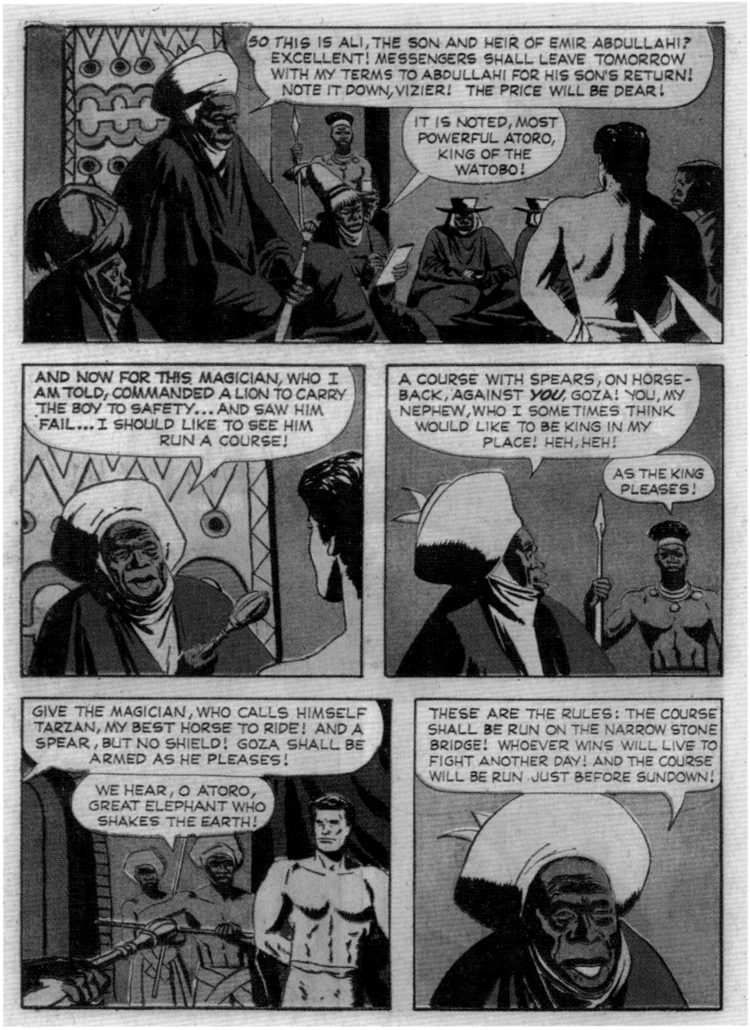
SO THIS IS ALI, THE SON AND HEIR OF EMIR ABDULLAHI? EXCELLENT! MESSENGERS SHALL LEAVE TOMORROW WITH MY TERMS TO ABDULLAHI FOR HIS SON'S RETURN! NOTE IT DOWN, VIZIER! THE PRICE WILL BE DEAR!
IT IS NOTED, MOST POWERFUL ATORO, KING OF THE WATOBO!
AND NOW FOR THIS MAGICIAN, WHO I AM TOLD, COMMANDED A LION TO CARRY THE BOY TO SAFETY... AND SAW HIM FAIL... I SHOULD LIKE TO SEE HIM RUN A COURSE!
A COURSE WITH SPEARS, ON HORSEBACK, AGAINST YOU, GOZA! YOU, MY NEPHEW, WHO I SOMETIMES THINK WOULD LIKE TO BE KING IN MY PLACE! HEH, HEH!
AS THE KING PLEASES!
GIVE THE MAGICIAN, WHO CALLS HIMSELF TARZAN, MY BEST HORSE TO RIDE! AND A SPEAR, BUT NO SHIELD! GOZA SHALL BE ARMED AS HE PLEASES!
WE HEAR, O ATORO, GREAT ELEPHANT WHO SHAKES THE EARTH!
THESE ARE THE RULES: THE COURSE SHALL BE RUN ON THE NARROW STONE BRIDGE! WHOEVER WINS WILL LIVE TO FIGHT ANOTHER DAY! AND THE COURSE WILL BE RUN JUST BEFORE SUNDOWN!

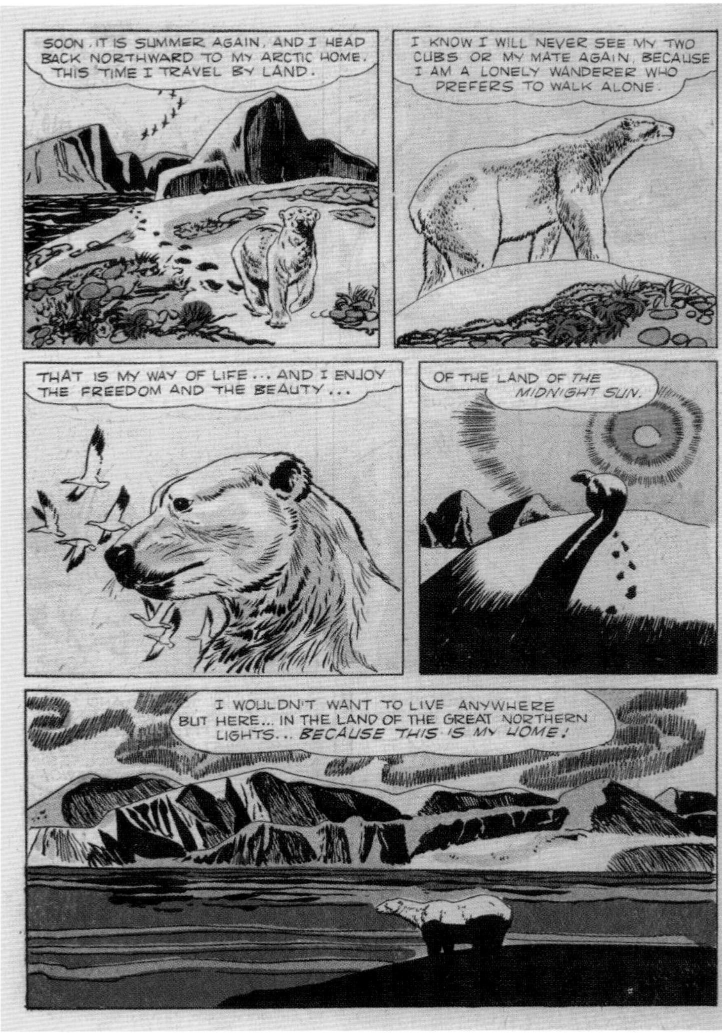
SOON, IT IS SUMMER AGAIN, AND I HEAD BACK NORTHWARD TO MY ARCTIC HOME. THIS TIME I TRAVEL BY LAND.
I KNOW I WILL NEVER SEE MY TWO CUBS OR MY MATE AGAIN, BECAUSE I AM A LONELY WANDERER WHO PREFERS TO WALK ALONE.
THAT IS MY WAY OF LIFE... AND I ENJOY THE FREEDOM AND THE BEAUTY...
OF THE LAND OF THE MIDNIGHT SUN.
I WOULDN'T WANT TO LIVE ANYWHERE BUT HERE... IN THE LAND OF THE GREAT NORTHERN LIGHTS... BECAUSE THIS IS MY HOME!

THE SUMMER of 1954 found the artist adding what for some cartoonists would've been a full-time assignment in itself. The Disney studio had expanded into producing live action movies, and a newspaper Sunday page, syndicated by King Features, was created to promote and publicize them. Titled *Walt Disney's Treasury of Classic Tales*, it was edited and written by Frank Reilly, a former feature editor with the Associated Press, who headed up the Disney newspaper comics department. The first tale was *20,000 Leagues Under The Sea*, which ran for four months (the main characters had virtually no resemblance to the movie's stars, Kirk Douglas and James Mason, who portrayed Captain Nemo). Marsh remained the artist until 1962, illustrating Sunday pages of such Disney novel adaptations as *Rob Roy*, *Robin Hood*, *Pollyanna*, *Swiss Family Robinson*, *Johnny Tremain*, and *Darby O'Gill and the Little People*. Since the Disney policy about credits was the same as Western's, Marsh's name never appeared on the feature. He did a serviceable job, but his Sunday pages were never as inventive or varied as his comic book art.

By the late 1950s Marsh, a diabetic, was having trouble with his eyesight. His work on *Tarzan* in the early 1960s still exhibits a typically strong design sense, but the drawing is not as assured and is marked by a lack of experimentation. Tarzan became a chunkier, unsmiling fellow. The book had always sold well, and in 1965, Marsh's final year with it, each bimonthly issue was selling an average of 350,000 copies. Mark Evanier has reported that in the early '60s, Edgar Rice Burroughs, Inc., "began demanding an artist with a more sophisticated style...someone who could draw a slicker, more muscular Tarzan like the one seen in the newspaper strips." Western stuck by Marsh, however. "Knowing that Marsh was in poor health," continued Evanier, "the Burroughs folks elected to wait him out on the condition that [Russ] Manning would succeed him."

The ailing Jesse Marsh retired in the autumn of '65 and his final issue of *Tarzan* was #153, cover-dated October. Russ Manning did indeed replace him. Marsh had announced that he intended to devote himself to painting once he was through with comics and had sufficient time, but he died in spring of '66, some months short of his fifty-ninth birthday.

Opposite left: Page from *Tarzan* #144 (Gold Key, 1964). Courtesy of Dylan Williams.

Opposite right: Page from "Walt Disney's The Nature of Things," *Four Color* #842 (Dell Publishing Co., 1957). Courtesy of Dylan Williams.

Below: Panel from *Korak, Son of Tarzan* #11 (Dell Publishing Co., 1965). Courtesy of Dylan Williams.

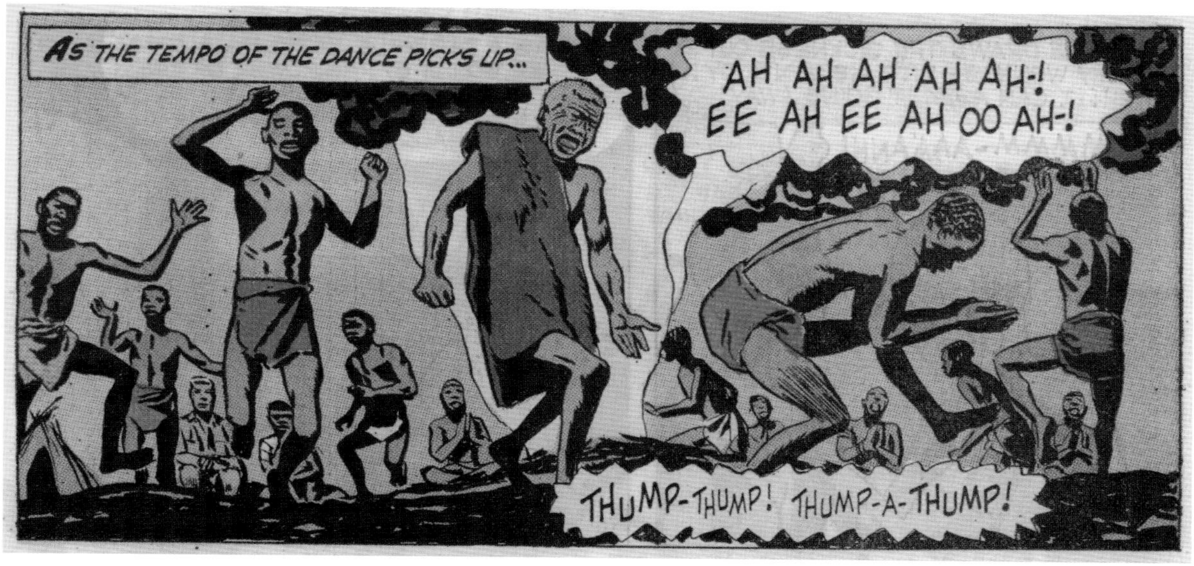
AS THE TEMPO OF THE DANCE PICKS UP...
AH AH AH AH AH-! EE AH EE AH OO AH-!
THUMP-THUMP! THUMP-A-THUMP!

It is known that Marsh lived at 652 West King Street in the Southern California town of Monrovia during his peak years working for Dell, but there are few personal accounts of him during the period. According to Toth, Marsh was rather elusive when it came to social encounters. He was only able to talk to Marsh at the Western offices on a dozen or so occasions. "Jesse had a wall up and few of us could penetrate it, but I kept at it. At the time, I lived in Pasadena, just minutes from his digs in Monrovia. So, I phoned him to invite him to my place, or to meet at his. He'd met and knew my wife long ago for she was a receptionist at Whitman/Western (where, of course, I met her), so it'd be a kick for us to have him over for dinner or lunch or coffee and kick the gong around—and, at last he agreed, then cancelled, then postponed, cancelled again, until it was clear that he just wasn't about to be colleague/neighbor... so I let go."

Since Marsh labored anonymously for most of his years, he received little attention during his lifetime. He died while the Silver Age of comic books was in full flower and a hyperactive, flamboyant approach to storytelling—as epitomized by Jack Kirby, Carmine Infantino, Gil Kane, etc.—was what got the attention of fans. Friends of his, notably Manning and Toth, wrote in praise of him in specialized publications aimed at comic book fans and/or Burroughs admirers, and I appraised his career in my 1986 entry on him in *The Great Comic Book Artists*, but he remained an outsider to mainstream histories of the medium's great innovators. Recently, the internet has helped Marsh's cause somewhat: blogs and assorted fan websites have been taking note of him, and contemporary cartoonists have expressed praise for his work. In his piece on Marsh back in the early 1980s, Toth told how Marsh, living alone since his parents' deaths, had "died unattended in that family home—where he was found days later." He then complained that Marsh was "unheralded by then-emerging fandom which hardly knew of the man or his work, or worse, dismissed both." Perhaps, over a half century later, the situation is changing.

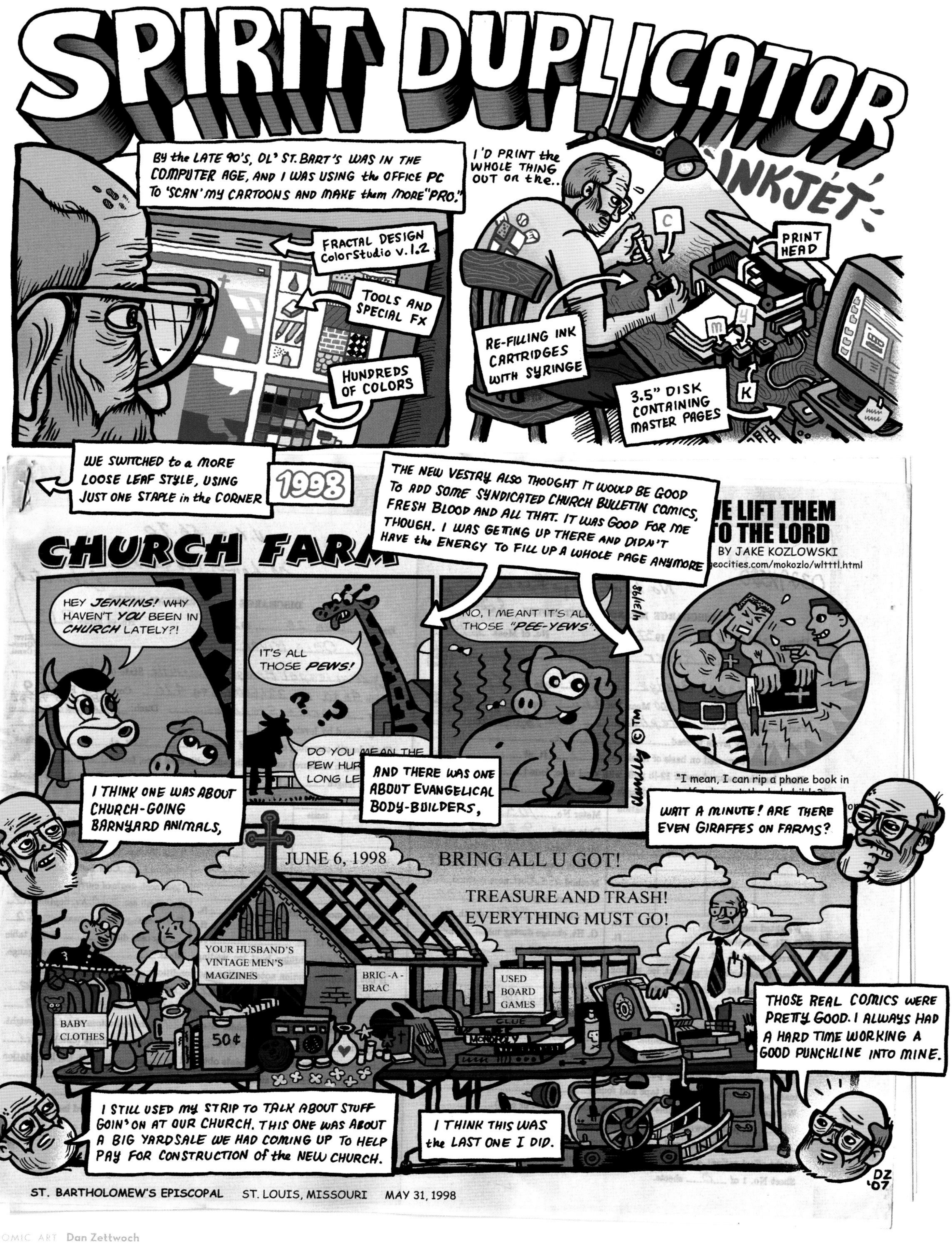
SPIRIT DUPLICATOR
By the LATE 90'S, OL' ST. BART'S WAS IN THE COMPUTER AGE, AND I WAS USING the OFFICE PC TO 'SCAN' MY CARTOONS AND MAKE them MORE "PRO."
FRACTAL DESIGN ColorStudio v.1.2
TOOLS AND SPECIAL FX
HUNDREDS OF COLORS
I'D PRINT the WHOLE THING OUT on the..
INKJET
C
PRINT HEAD
RE-FILLING INK CARTRIDGES WITH SYRINGE
M
Y
K
3.5" DISK CONTAINING MASTER PAGES
WE SWITCHED to a MORE LOOSE LEAF STYLE, USING JUST ONE STAPLE in the CORNER
1998
THE NEW VESTRY ALSO THOUGHT IT WOULD BE GOOD TO ADD SOME SYNDICATED CHURCH BULLETIN COMICS, FRESH BLOOD AND ALL THAT. IT WAS GOOD FOR ME THOUGH. I WAS GETTING UP THERE AND DIDN'T HAVE the ENERGY TO FILL UP A WHOLE PAGE ANYMORE
CHURCH FARM
HEY JENKINS! WHY HAVEN'T YOU BEEN IN CHURCH LATELY?!
IT'S ALL THOSE PEWS!
DO YOU MEAN THE PEW HUR LONG LE
NO, I MEANT IT'S ALL THOSE "PEE-YEWS".
4/12/1998
©TM
WE LIFT THEM TO THE LORD
BY JAKE KOZLOWSKI
geocities.com/mokozlo/wltttl.html
"I mean, I can rip a phone book in
I THINK ONE WAS ABOUT CHURCH-GOING BARNYARD ANIMALS,
AND THERE WAS ONE ABOUT EVANGELICAL BODY-BUILDERS,
WAIT A MINUTE! ARE THERE EVEN GIRAFFES ON FARMS?
JUNE 6, 1998
BRING ALL U GOT!
TREASURE AND TRASH! EVERYTHING MUST GO!
YOUR HUSBAND'S VINTAGE MEN'S MAGZINES
BRIC-A-BRAC
USED BOARD GAMES
BABY CLOTHES
50¢
CLUE
MEMORY
THOSE REAL COMICS WERE PRETTY GOOD. I ALWAYS HAD A HARD TIME WORKING A GOOD PUNCHLINE INTO MINE.
I STILL USED MY STRIP TO TALK ABOUT STUFF GOIN' ON AT OUR CHURCH. THIS ONE WAS ABOUT A BIG YARDSALE WE HAD COMING UP TO HELP PAY FOR CONSTRUCTION OF the NEW CHURCH.
I THINK THIS WAS the LAST ONE I DID.
DZ '07
ST. BARTHOLOMEW'S EPISCOPAL ST. LOUIS, MISSOURI MAY 31, 1998

Preis 30 Pfg.   Wilhelm Busch-Nummer

München, 15. April 1907   12. Jahrgang   No. 3

SIMPLICISSIMUS

Abonnement vierteljährlich 3 Mt. 60 Pfg.   Herausgeber: Albert Langen   In Oesterreich-Ungarn vierteljährl. K 4.40

(Alle Rechte vorbehalten)

Der Fall Max und Moritz

(Zeichnungen von Th. Th. Heine)

Das Urteil: Fall Bolte, Sachbeschädigung und Bandendiebstahl, §§ 303, 243 des R.St.G.B., Gefängnisstrafe von 2 Jahren und Zuchthausstrafe von 8 Jahren, zusammengezogen in 9 Jahre Zuchthaus. — Fall Böck, Körperverletzung, § 223 des R.St.G.B., 3 Jahre Gefängnis. — Fall Zuckerbäcker, Einbruchsdiebstahl, § 243 des R.St.G.B., 10 Jahre Zuchthaus. — Fall Lämpel, Verbrechen gegen § 6 des Sprengstoffgesetzes, 9 Jahre Zuchthaus. Schwere Körperverletzung, §§ 225, 229 des R.St.G.B., 10 Jahre Zuchthaus. — Insgesamt 38 Jahre Zuchthaus und 3 Jahre Gefängnis, zusammengezogen in 40 Jahre Zuchthaus.
Trotz der glänzenden Verteidigungsrede Wilhelm Buschs mußten leider mildernde Umstände versagt und fast durchgängig auf die Maximalstrafe erkannt werden, da die Angeklagten ihre moralische Verkommenheit dem hohen Gerichtshof aufs neue vor Augen führten, indem sie wilde Maikäfer, welche sie sich auf unbegreifliche Weise zu verschaffen gewußt hatten, auf die Richter hetzten.

Zur Feier des fünfundsiebzigsten Geburtstages Wilhelm Buschs ist durch einen Gnadenakt des Landesfürsten den Büßern Max und Moritz gestattet worden, dem Jubilar persönlich ihre Glückwünsche darzubringen. Unter sicherer Begleitung erscheinen sie dort in ihrer schmucken Zuchthauskleidung. Fast ist zu befürchten, daß Meister Busch sich im Laufe der Jahre selbst von der Schuld der Verbrecher überzeugt hat und über das Wiedersehen nicht recht erfreut sein mag.

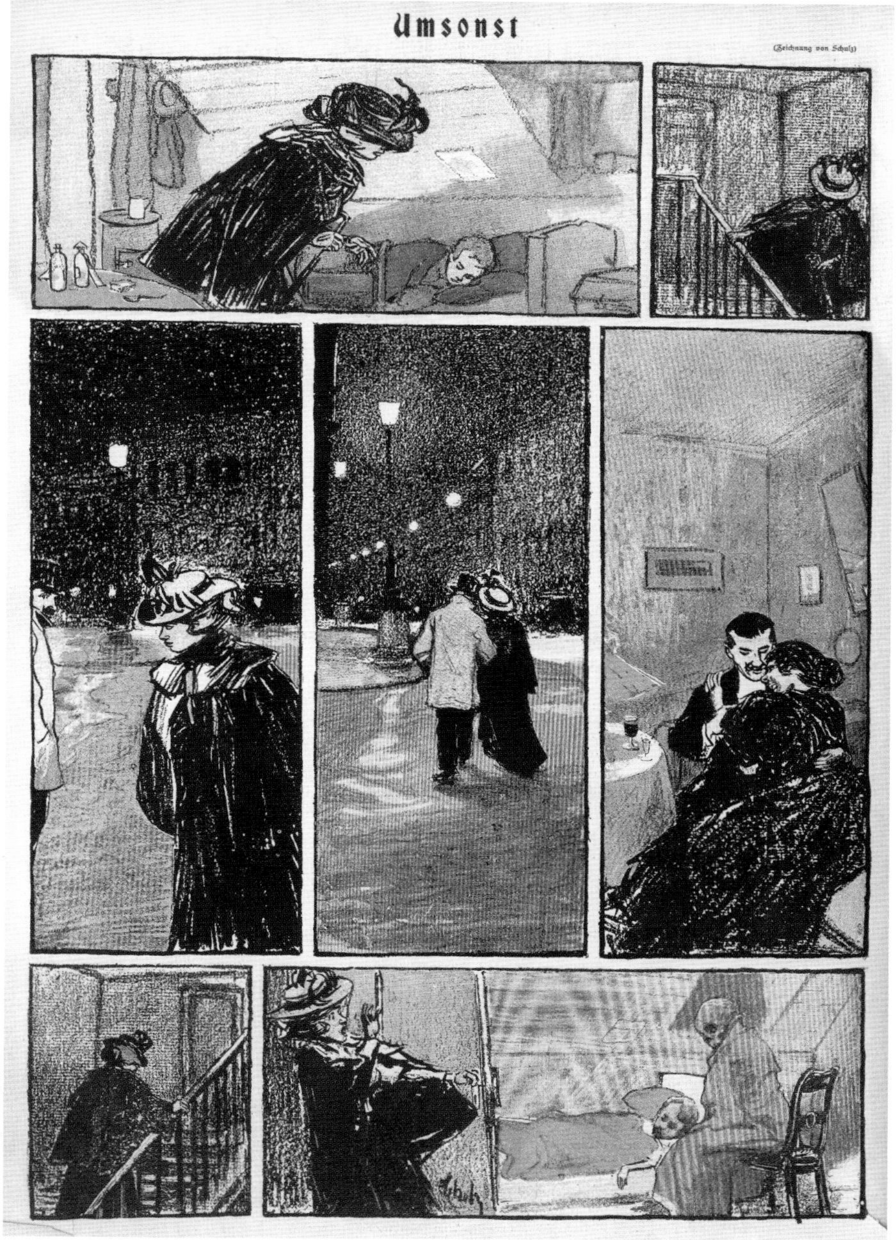
Umsonst
(Zeichnung von Schulz)

Wilhelm Schulz, October 31, 1897.

SIMPLICISSIMUS

By Thierry Smolderen and Josepe,
for the Coconino World website
www.coconino-world.com
& www.coconino-classics.com

In partnership with *Comic Art*, the Coconino Classics website is proud to present this portfolio of comic strip pages and cartoons by the great German graphic artists of the turn-of-the-century publication *Simplicissimus*—surely one of the best satirical magazines ever.

Looking at the comic strip pages in this *Simplicissimus* portfolio (most of them designed by the great Olaf Gulbransson), it is worth noting that these German artists were perfectly conscious of the long tradition of the comic strip in Germany, and, in particular, of the farcical *Fliegende Blätter* stories that were so popular in the last decades of the 19th century. Thomas Heine's cover for the April 15, 1907, issue of *Simplicissimus* was dedicated to Wilhelm Busch, as was the whole commemorative issue, full of stories drawn by Wilhelm Schulz, Gulbransson, and Heine, in the manner of the father of German comic strips. Despite this tip of the hat, it is clear that the *Simplicissimus* gang wasn't competing on the same field as their *Fliegende Blätter* colleagues. Having no interest in slapstick and farcical comedy, they only used the comic strip form when it suited their satirical agenda.

To these sequential pages (relatively rare in the magazine), we've added a sample of the much more common single cartoon works by the greatest names of the magazine—Rudolf Wilke, Ragnvald Blix, Bruno Paul, Eduard Thony, and Karl Arnold. One of the main goals of the Coconino World Website—and, I'm sure, one of the main goals of *Comic Art* magazine—is to add DNA to the global graphic gene pool, hoping for richer stylistic combinations and experiments. We know that this peek into the largely forgotten Munich school of modernist rebels will not leave any true lover of comic art indifferent.

Bonner Nachtleben

(Zeichnungen von Bruno Paul)

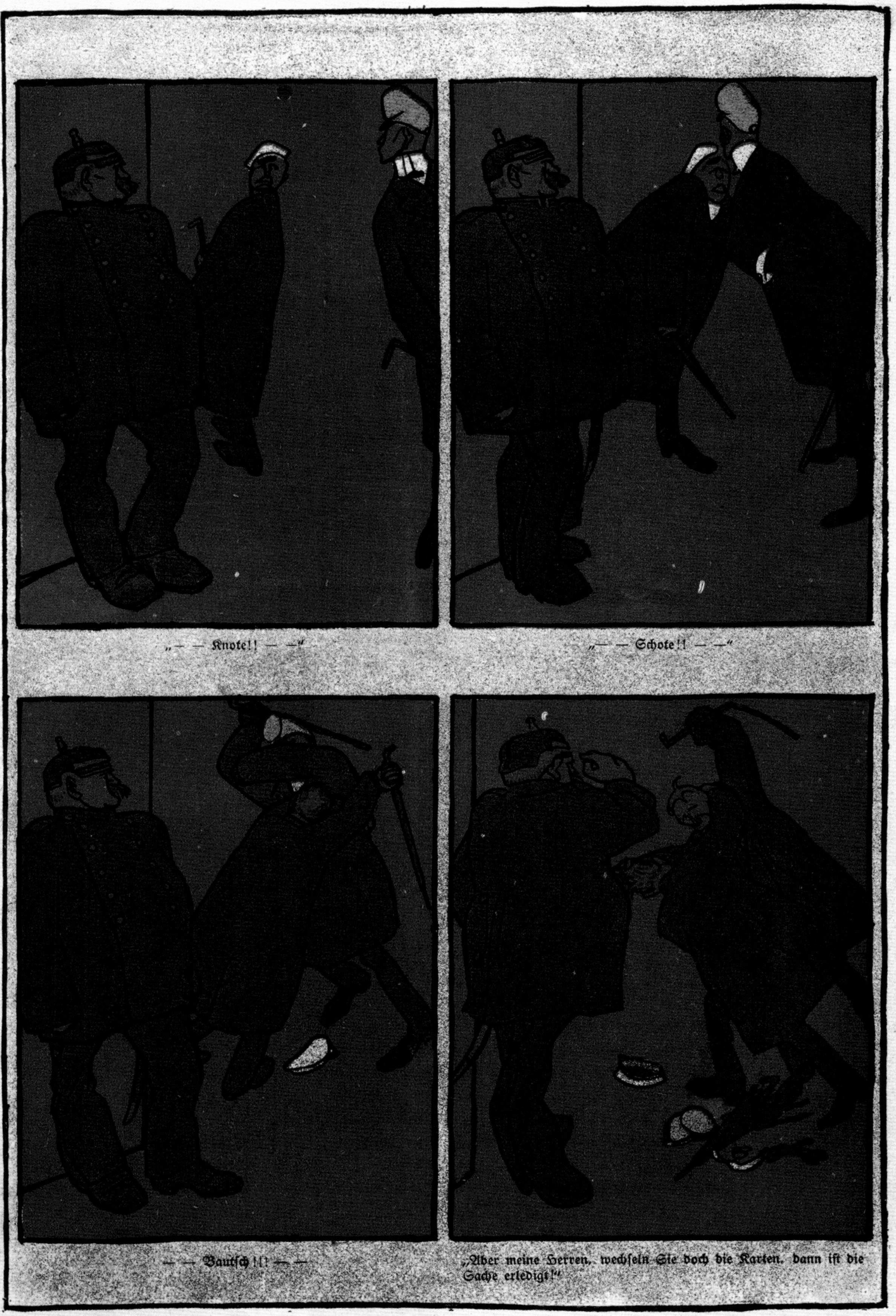
„— — Knote!! — —"
„— — Schote!! — —"
— — Bautsch!!! — —
„Aber meine Herren, wechseln Sie doch die Karten, dann ist die Sache erledigt!"

Bruno Paul, April 2, 1906.

Sein Glück

(Zeichnung von E. Thöny)

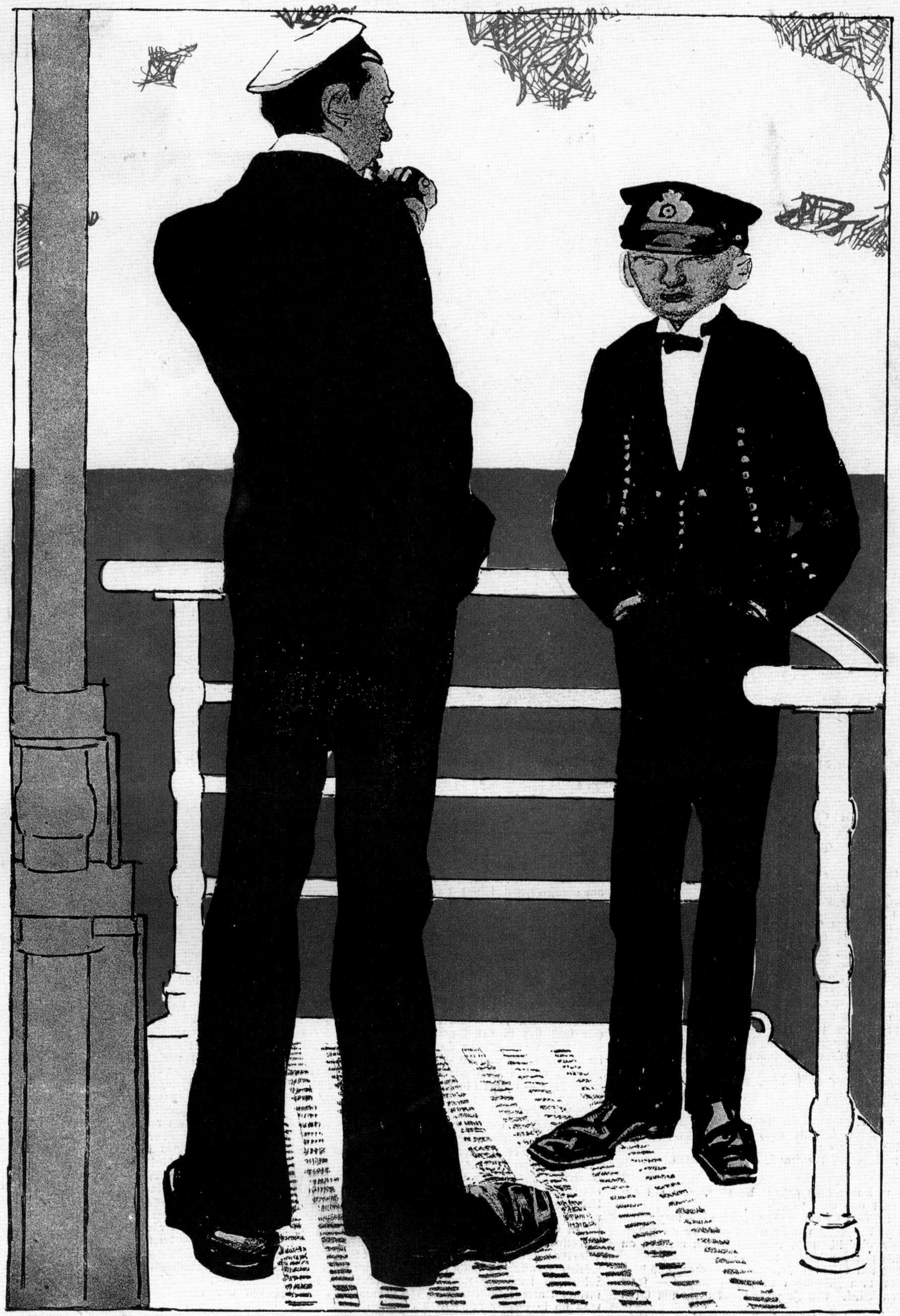

„Mein Vetter Hans wollte auch mal Wechsel ausstellen. Aber er war schon zehn Jahre bei den Deutzer Kürassieren, und da konnte er natürlich seinen Namen nicht mehr schreiben.“

Eduard Thony, August 12, 1907.

Der griechische Delegierte im Haag

(Zeichnung von E. Thöny)

„Wenn die Konferenz noch länger dauert, würde ich mir doch ein zweites Paar Strümpfe schicken lassen, Herr Karamopulos."

Eduard Thony, August 12, 1907.

Karl Arnold, March 14, 1910.

Entgegenkommen

(Zeichnung von Karl Arnold)

„Ich gebe Ihnen meine älteste Tochter, Herr Sekretär, weil sie ein kleines Magenleiden und also sehr wenig Appetit hat — denn für meine Paula würden Ihre zweihundertfünfzig Mark monatlich wohl kaum ausreichen."

Liebeswerben

(Zeichnung von Rudolf Wilke)

„Bal' ich dir aba drei Maß zahl', Kaspar?!" — „Fünf Ziehgar'n, wenn'st zuawi tuast, nacha mag' i, weil i a starker Raucher bin."

Zwangslage

(Zeichnung von Rudolf Wilke)

„Na, Korl, nu segg man bloß mal, worum hest denn du di verfriet?" — „Ja, wie dat nu woll so kömmt. Erst heff ick mi von ehr en Dahler leiht, un denn heff ick ehr ja woll heiraten möten."

Rudolf Wilke, August 26, 1907.

Rudolf Wilke, August 12, 1907.

Das süße Geheimnis

(Zeichnung von Blix)

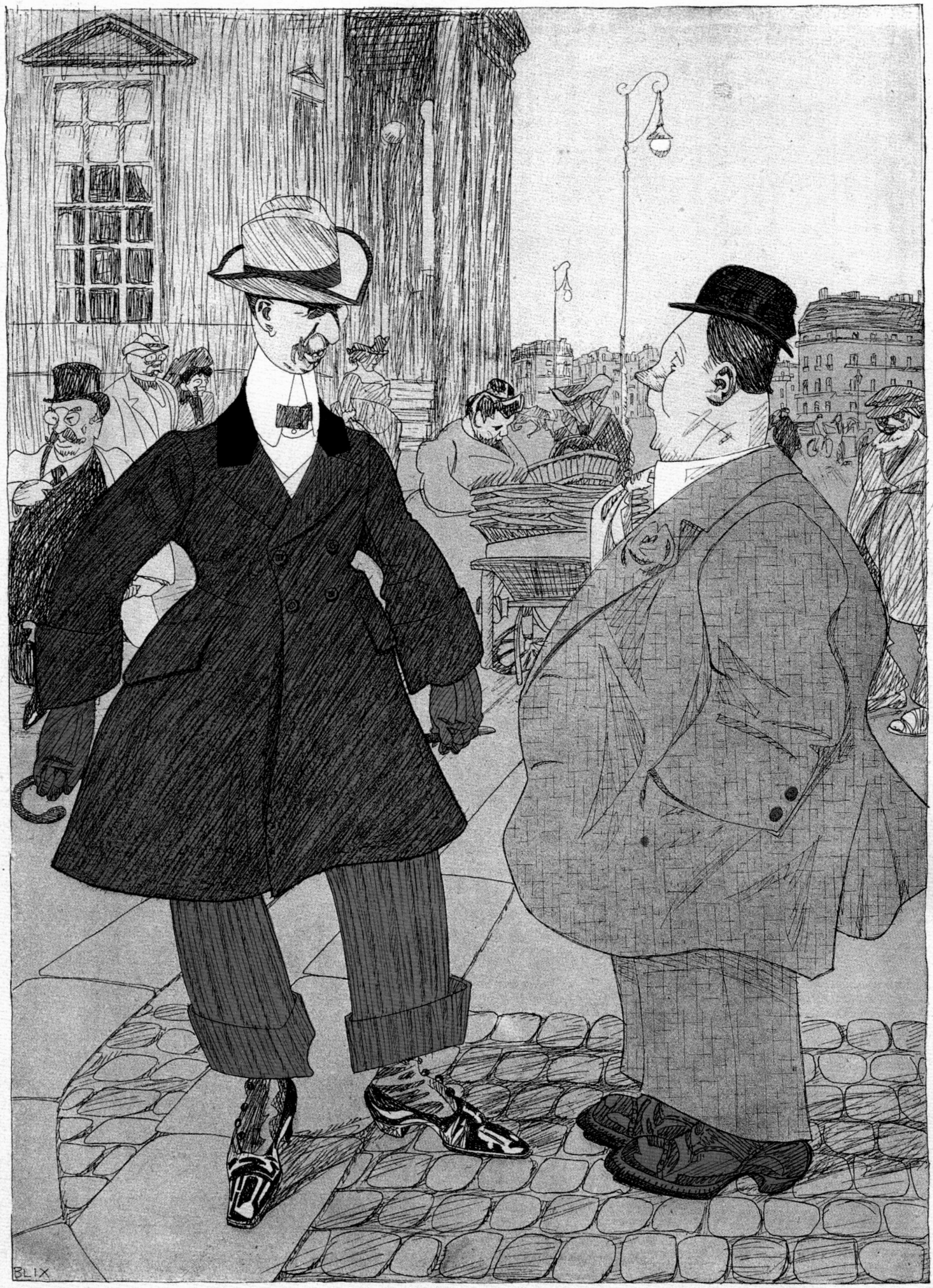
BLIX

„Denken Sie sich — erhalte eben Depesche — bin Vater jeworden." — „Na — und Jnädigste wohlauf?" — „Wenn die bloß nischt von erfährt."

Ragnvald Blix, February 14, 1910.

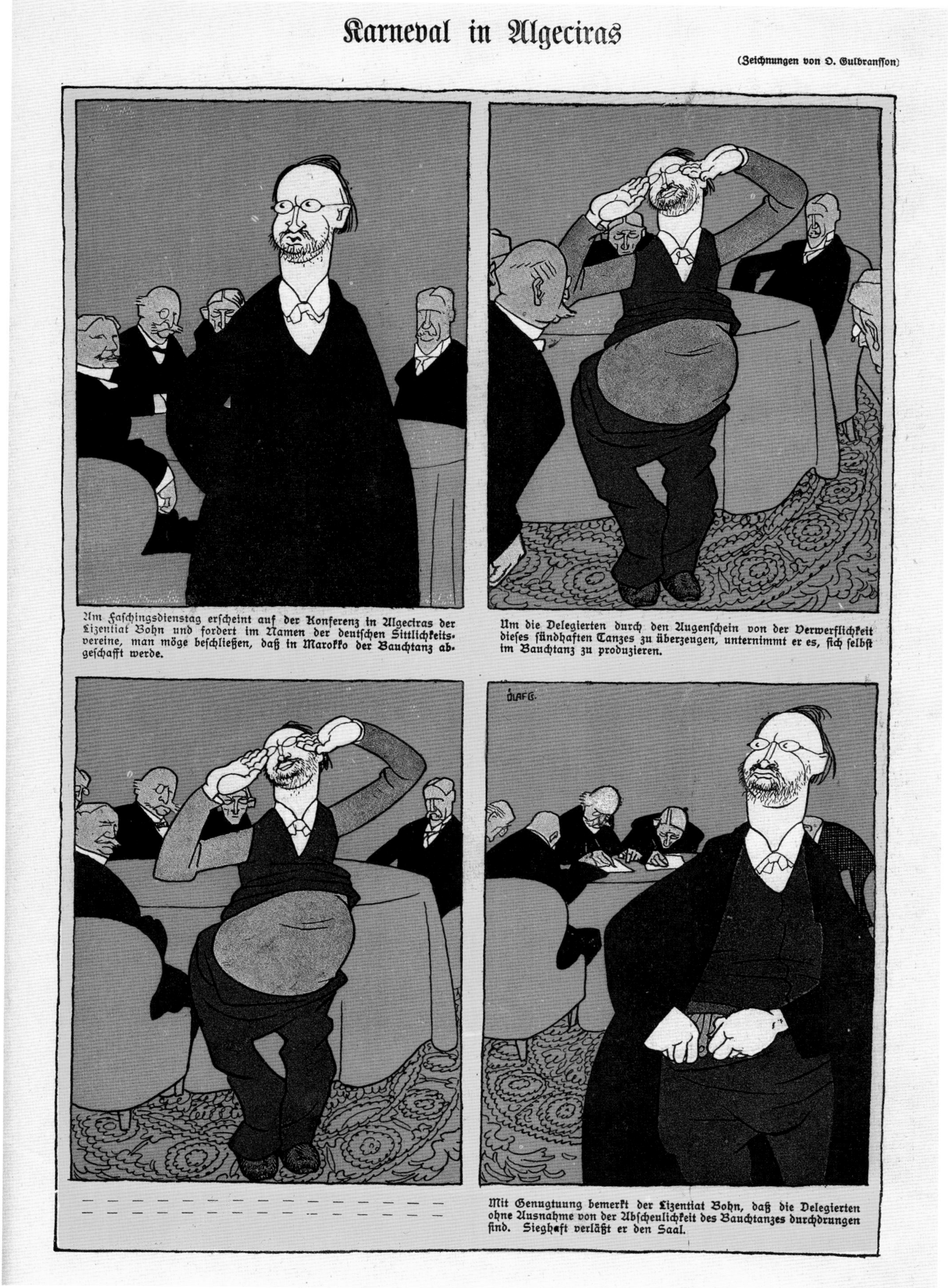
Karneval in Algeciras
(Zeichnungen von O. Gulbransson)
Am Faschingsdienstag erscheint auf der Konferenz in Algeciras der Lizentiat Bohn und fordert im Namen der deutschen Sittlichkeitsvereine, man möge beschließen, daß in Marokko der Bauchtanz abgeschafft werde.
Um die Delegierten durch den Augenschein von der Verwerflichkeit dieses sündhaften Tanzes zu überzeugen, unternimmt er es, sich selbst im Bauchtanz zu produzieren.
OLAF G.
Mit Genugtuung bemerkt der Lizentiat Bohn, daß die Delegierten ohne Ausnahme von der Abscheulichkeit des Bauchtanzes durchdrungen sind. Sieghaft verläßt er den Saal.

Olaf Gulbransson, February 19, 1906.

Die Geschichte der Familie Huber

III.

Die Kreuzzüge

(Zeichnungen von O. Gulbransson)

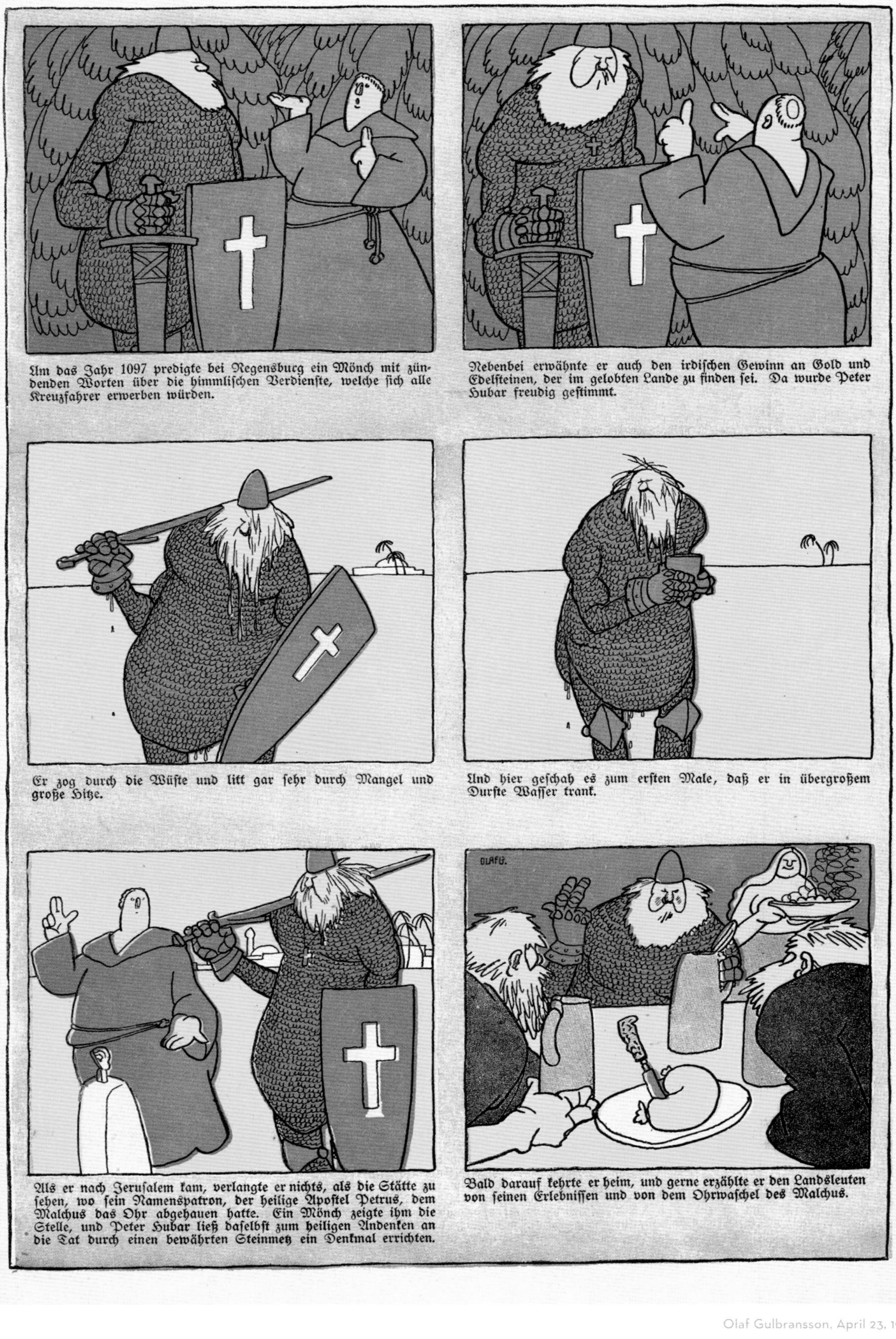
OLAF G.

Um das Jahr 1097 predigte bei Regensburg ein Mönch mit zündenden Worten über die himmlischen Verdienste, welche sich alle Kreuzfahrer erwerben würden.

Nebenbei erwähnte er auch den irdischen Gewinn an Gold und Edelsteinen, der im gelobten Lande zu finden sei. Da wurde Peter Hubar freudig gestimmt.

Er zog durch die Wüste und litt gar sehr durch Mangel und große Hitze.

Und hier geschah es zum ersten Male, daß er in übergroßem Durste Wasser trank.

Als er nach Jerusalem kam, verlangte er nichts, als die Stätte zu sehen, wo sein Namenspatron, der heilige Apostel Petrus, dem Malchus das Ohr abgehauen hatte. Ein Mönch zeigte ihm die Stelle, und Peter Hubar ließ daselbst zum heiligen Andenken an die Tat durch einen bewährten Steinmetz ein Denkmal errichten.

Bald darauf kehrte er heim, und gerne erzählte er den Landsleuten von seinen Erlebnissen und von dem Ohrwaschel des Malchus.

Olaf Gulbransson, April 23, 1906.

Wo ist noch Sicherheit?

(Zeichnungen von O. Gulbransson)

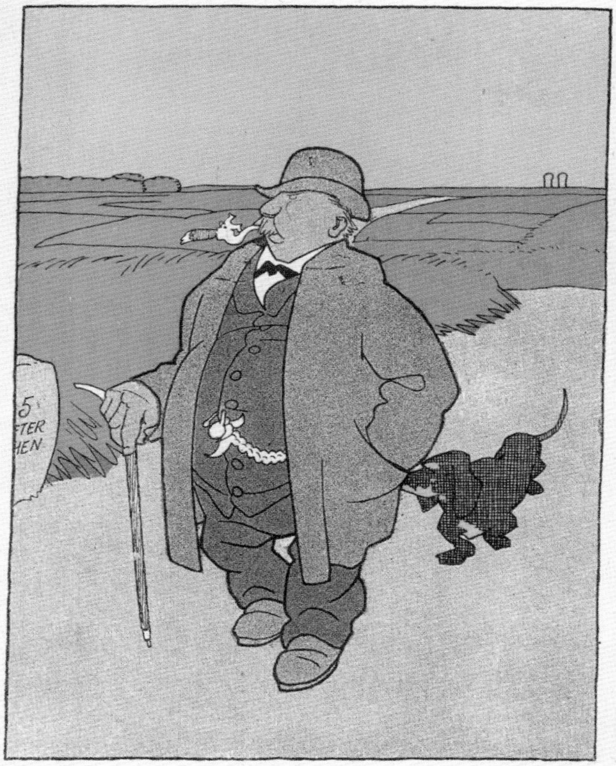

Der Privatier Xaver Schlederer aus München begab sich am 27. Oktober, nachmittags 2 Uhr nach Harlaching.

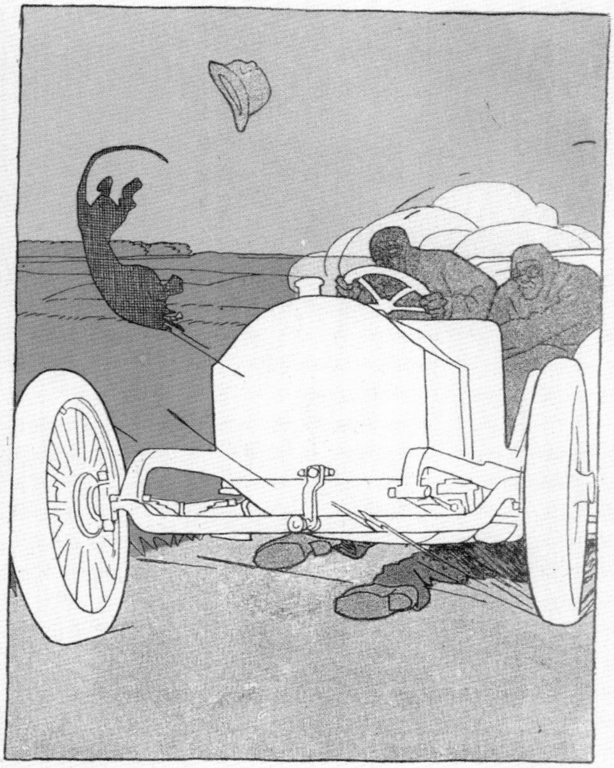

Der nichts Ahnende wurde von einem dahinrasenden Automobil erfaßt und auf der Stelle getötet.

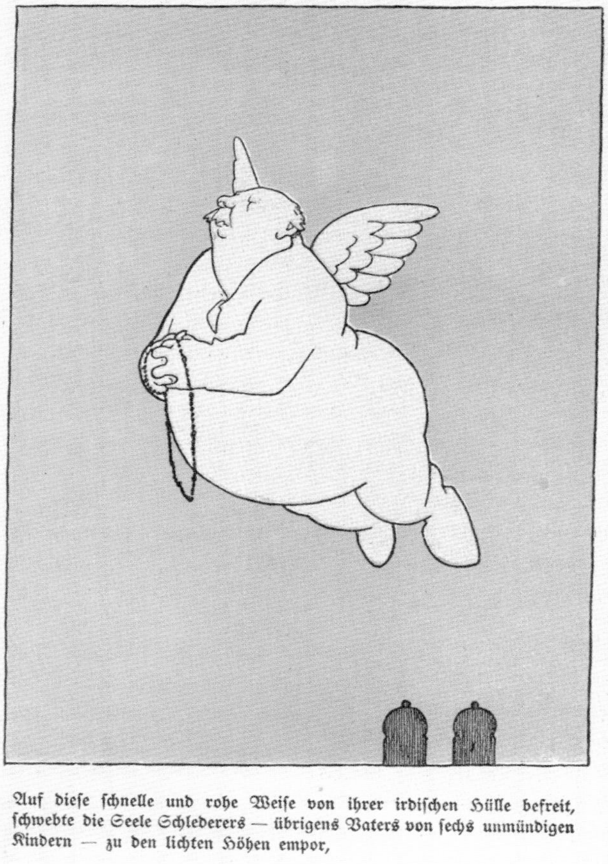

Auf diese schnelle und rohe Weise von ihrer irdischen Hülle befreit, schwebte die Seele Schlederers — übrigens Vaters von sechs unmündigen Kindern — zu den lichten Höhen empor,

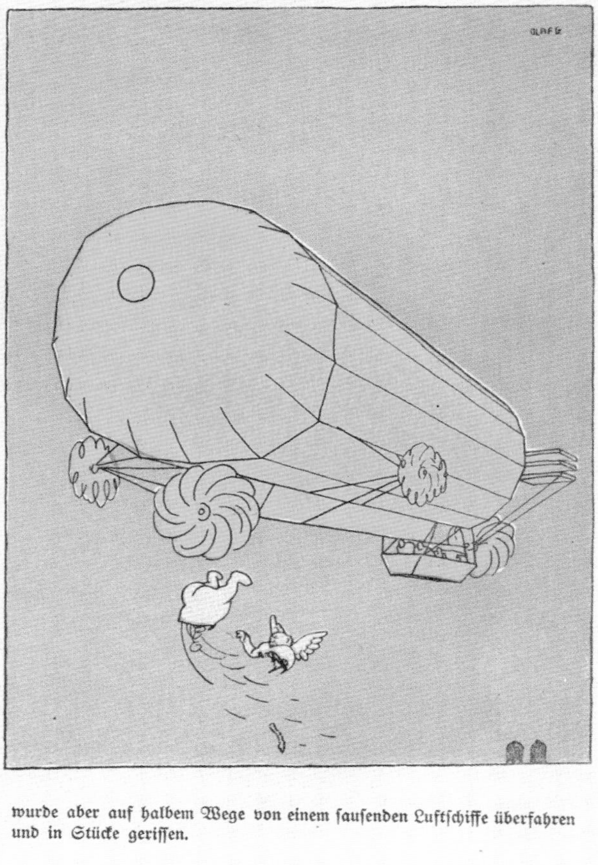

wurde aber auf halbem Wege von einem sausenden Luftschiffe überfahren und in Stücke gerissen.

Olaf Gulbransson, November 4, 1906.

Ein Schwächeanfall

(Zeichnungen von O. Gulbransson)

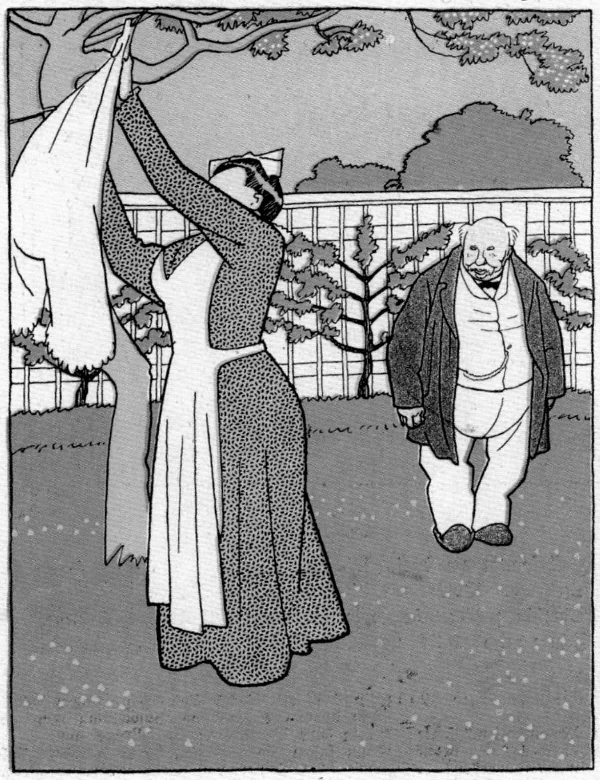

„Schau, schau!“

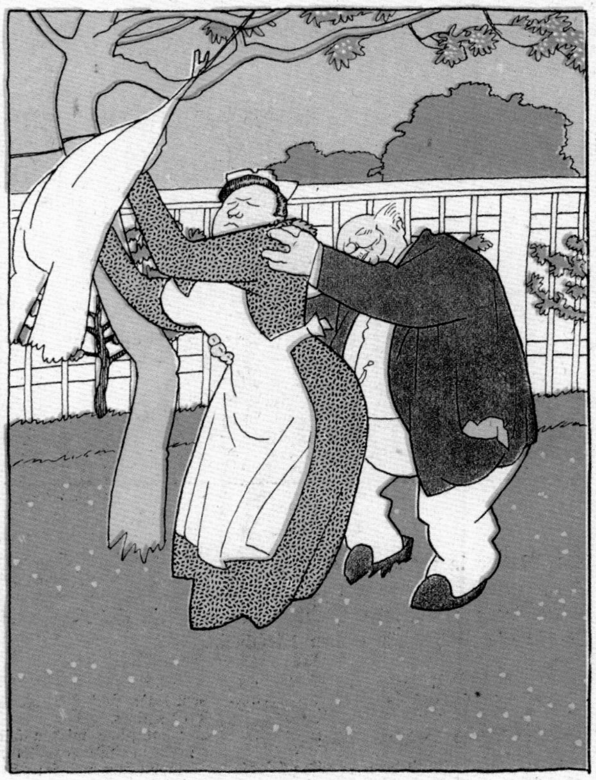

– – – –

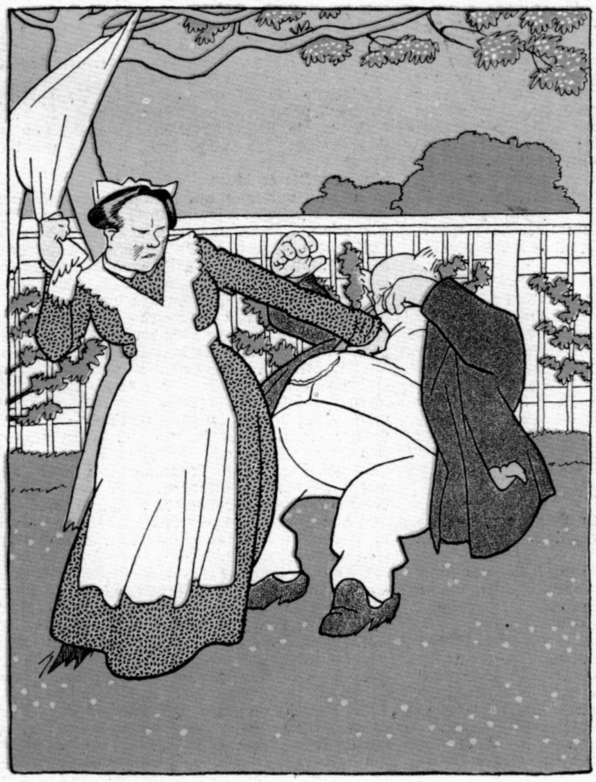

– – – –

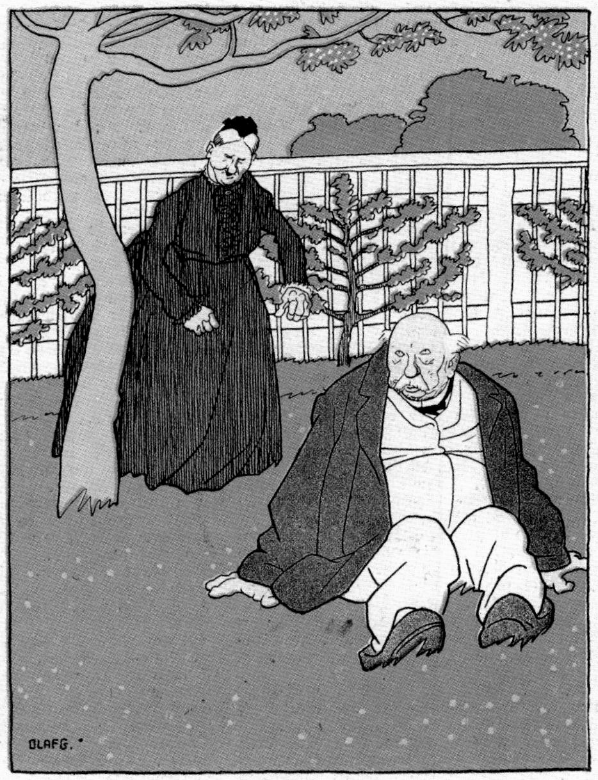
OLAFG.

„Gelt, Alterchen, jetzt muß ich dir wieder auf die Beine helfen?“

Olaf Gulbransson, May 17, 1909.

Der Sieger von Treptow

Ein Ruhmesblatt

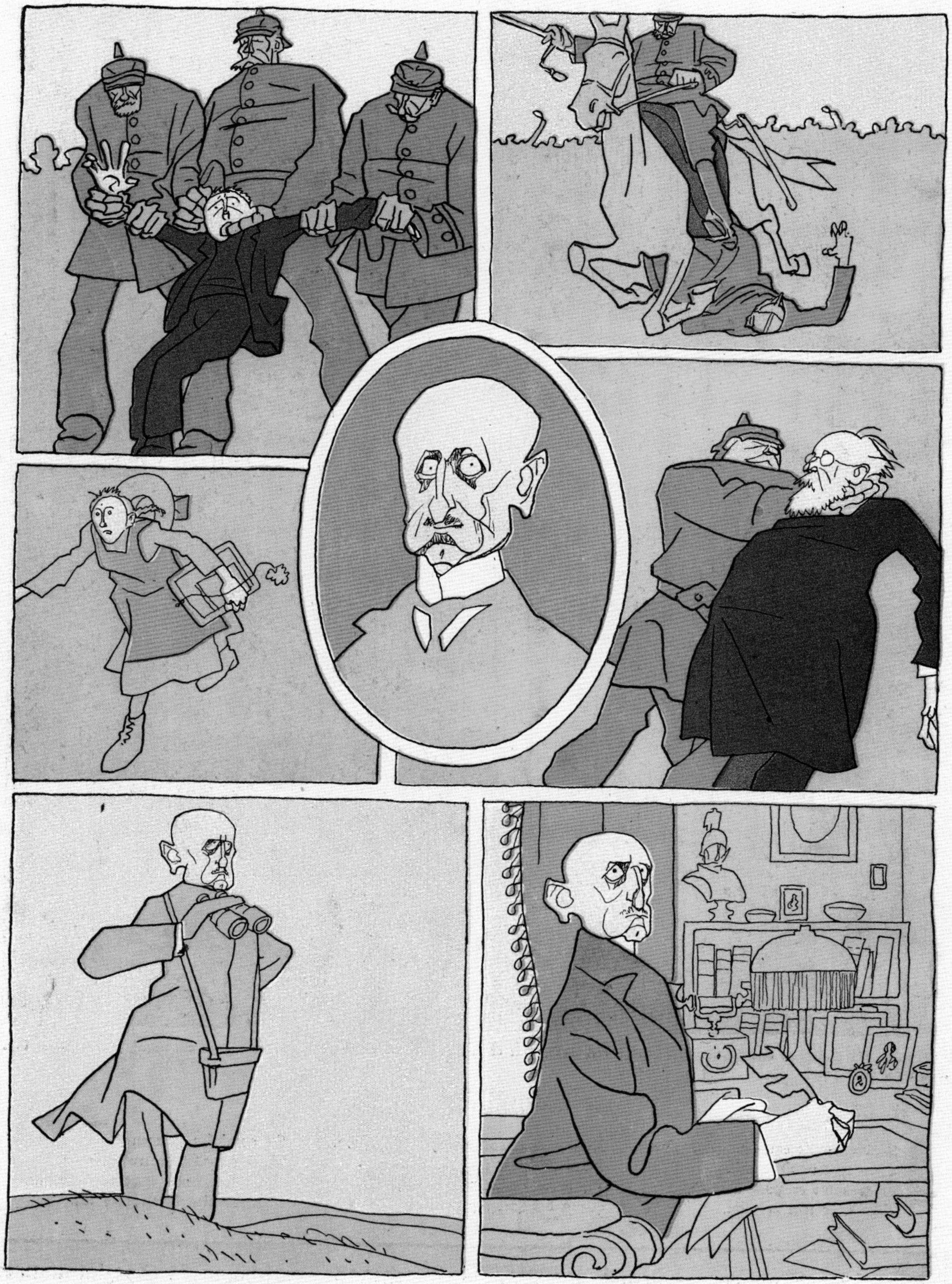

1. Gelungener Ueberfall
2. Der Feind gibt Treptow preis
3. Jagow sucht Sozi

Er

4. Der Todesritt von Treptow
5. Vae victis!
6. Jagow schreibt das 29. Siegesbulletin

Olaf Gulbransson, March 28, 1910.

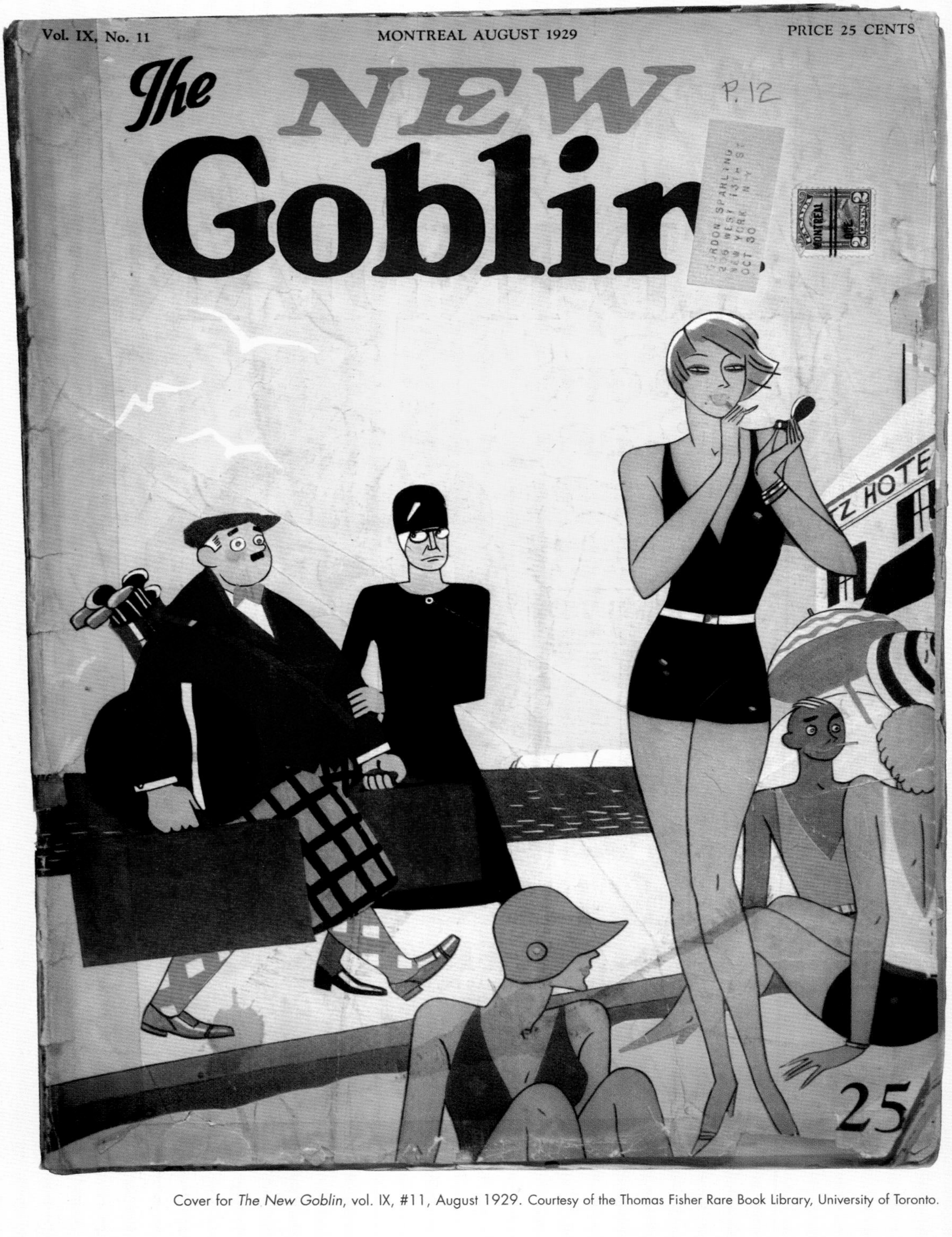
Vol. IX, No. 11
MONTREAL AUGUST 1929
PRICE 25 CENTS
The NEW
Goblin
P. 12
25

Cover for *The New Goblin*, vol. IX, #11, August 1929. Courtesy of the Thomas Fisher Rare Book Library, University of Toronto.

MYSTERY MAN —

The Early Comic Art of Richard Taylor

Mystery is the wisdom of blockheads
—HORACE WALPOLE

by **Bryan Munn**

IT IS SURPRISING how often the lives of even the most familiar cartoonists remain hazy and mysterious. Richard Taylor is a well-known figure to those acquainted with 20th-century magazine illustration and especially the cartoons of *The New Yorker*. Beginning in the 1930s, Taylor's distinctive cartoon figures, recognizable by their heavily lidded eyes and droll attitude, were mainstays of *The New Yorker*, *Collier's*, and *The Saturday Evening Post* for decades. In fact, Taylor's trademark style has been so closely linked with *The New Yorker* and its pantheon of iconic artists that his origins and early career have generally been mired in obscurity, overshadowed by the relative success of his mature work. Yet it is Taylor's early career, as a young cartoonist trying to make his mark on the burgeoning publishing world of 1920s Toronto, that hides one of the most fascinating episodes in the history of comic strips in North America.

The Mystery Men, daily strip, May 16, 1924.

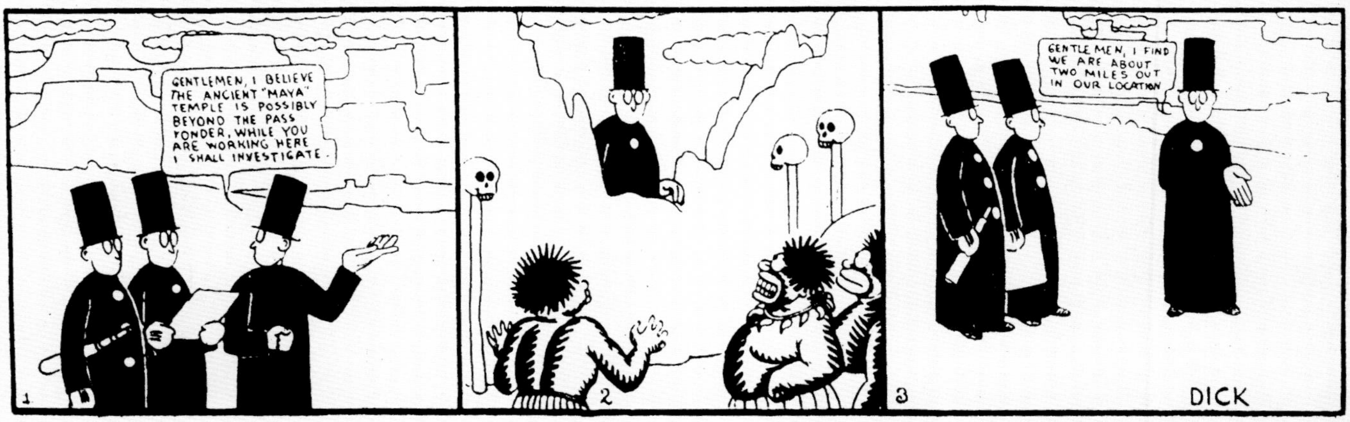
GENTLEMEN, I BELIEVE THE ANCIENT "MAYA" TEMPLE IS POSSIBLY BEYOND THE PASS YONDER, WHILE YOU ARE WORKING HERE I SHALL INVESTIGATE.
GENTLEMEN, I FIND WE ARE ABOUT TWO MILES OUT IN OUR LOCATION
DICK

In 1924, Toronto was home to six daily newspapers, each competing for a larger share of a paying audience made up of a potential half-million readers. The two leading combatants in this circulation war were the *Daily Star* and the *Evening Telegram*, each selling for two cents a copy. Bitter enemies, the two papers vied for readers using a stable of Hearst-like stunts, contests, crusades, and muckraking, coupled with genuine innovative and informative reporting. Founded in 1876 by John Ross Robertson, the *Evening Telegram* was one of the first modern papers in Canada and Robertson was one of the first Canadian press barons. Where previous publishers had relied on political patronage, graft, and a pious tone, Robertson established a publishing empire built on cheap classified advertising and colorful local reporting geared towards a working-class readership. The upstart *Star* and its publisher, "Holy Joe" Atkinson, on the other hand, had clambered to the top of the circulation heap through a combination of crime reporting, sensationalism, and a mild social justice policy that championed government reforms like pension plans and the abolition of capital punishment. Where the *Telegram* usually supported Conservative Party candidates and flew the Union Jack on its masthead, the *Star* had close ties to the Liberal government. One of the chief innovations of the *Star* was the creation in 1910 of a national magazine, the *Star Weekly*, which included general articles, humor pieces, serialized fiction, and, beginning in the 1920s, a large color comics insert.

It is hard to ignore the prominence given to comic strips by the *Star*. In addition to a full page of syndicated U.S. strips in the daily edition, the paper had hired folksy cartoonist Jimmy Frise in 1911, and by 1921 he was working exclusively for the *Star Weekly*. When the *Star* stopped buying the U.S. strip *Among us Mortals* by W.E. Hill, Frise created a replacement, a half-page cartoon panel called *Life's Little Comedies*. The strip was initially modeled on its predecessor but soon evolved into a gently humorous and nostalgic paean to rural life, along the lines of J.R. Williams's *Out Our Way*, but with a more regular cast of characters. Retitled *Birdseye Center*, the strip became a huge hit, driving the sales of the paper and making Frise a minor celebrity.

The *Telegram*'s cartoon content, by contrast, was spotty and ill-considered. It had no major cartooning stars and instead made due with a hodgepodge of syndicated material from the U.S.—two or three odd strips scattered throughout the paper that luckily included Rube Goldberg's daily panel. Determined to change this situation, the *Telegram*'s editors initiated a series of cartoon contests to cultivate some homegrown talent of their own. Beginning early in 1924, the paper began soliciting humorous drawings and gag cartoons from its readers with the promise of small cash prizes for published entries.

When this initial effort received enthusiastic response, the *Telegram* contest became a regular event, an early form of

THE MYSTERY MEN —

Fifty Dollars to Find Names for the Three Funny Fellows in The "Tely's" Prize Strip

First Prize $25.00   Second Prize $10.00
Third Prize $5.00
And Ten Additional Prizes of One Dollar Each

IN THIS ISSUE

"Goodbye," said the dog, "but I'm warning you—"

"The story so far"

reader participation that had the added benefit of bringing promising artistic talent to light and adding a much-needed graphic punch to its pages. For a few dollars every week, the paper generated enormous reader reaction and a page full of drawings. Eventually, the *Telegram* ran a contest for comic strips, with a cash prize of $25 promised to the best contribution. The contest closed on March 31 and the paper began running some of the more successful entries on April 5 under the headline, "Out of Queen City Ink Bottles New Funny Folk Are Created."

The resulting strips vary in quality but can be quite charming—to the modern eye the published submissions reveal a refreshing love of simple cartooning and an untutored humor almost entirely lacking in cynicism. Rendered in variations of the style of the day, the dozen or so strips featured during the following weeks usually aped the clichés and genres of American cartooning, combining mostly amateurish drawing styles with strict adherence to

the gag-a-day (or gag-a-week) formula. However clumsily rendered, these earnest strips nevertheless parrot the pacing and urbanity of their more adult role models, illustrating the degree to which the tropes of American strip cartooning had begun to be codified and ritualized for an entire generation.

Enter the Mystery Men

IF THE RUNNER-UP strips were a trifle unoriginal, the actual winner of the *Telegram* contest was anything but; indeed, it was the most deserving of the editor's attention. The contest winner began appearing as a daily strip on May 3, 1924. With great fanfare and bold headlines, the young man responsible for all this excitement was also featured prominently on the same page. In a short article printed below the strip, it was revealed that the cartoonist who signed his work "DICK" was really Richard Taylor, a Toronto illustrator. Born in Fort William (now Thunder Bay), Ontario, in 1902, Taylor's family moved to

Left: Advertisement for *The Mystery Men* naming contest, May 3, 1924.

Middle: Contents page illustration from *The New Goblin*, vol. IX, #11, August 1929. Courtesy of the Thomas Fisher Rare Book Library, University of Toronto.

Right: Interior gags from *The New Goblin*, vol. IX, #11, August 1929. Courtesy of the Thomas Fisher Rare Book Library, University of Toronto.

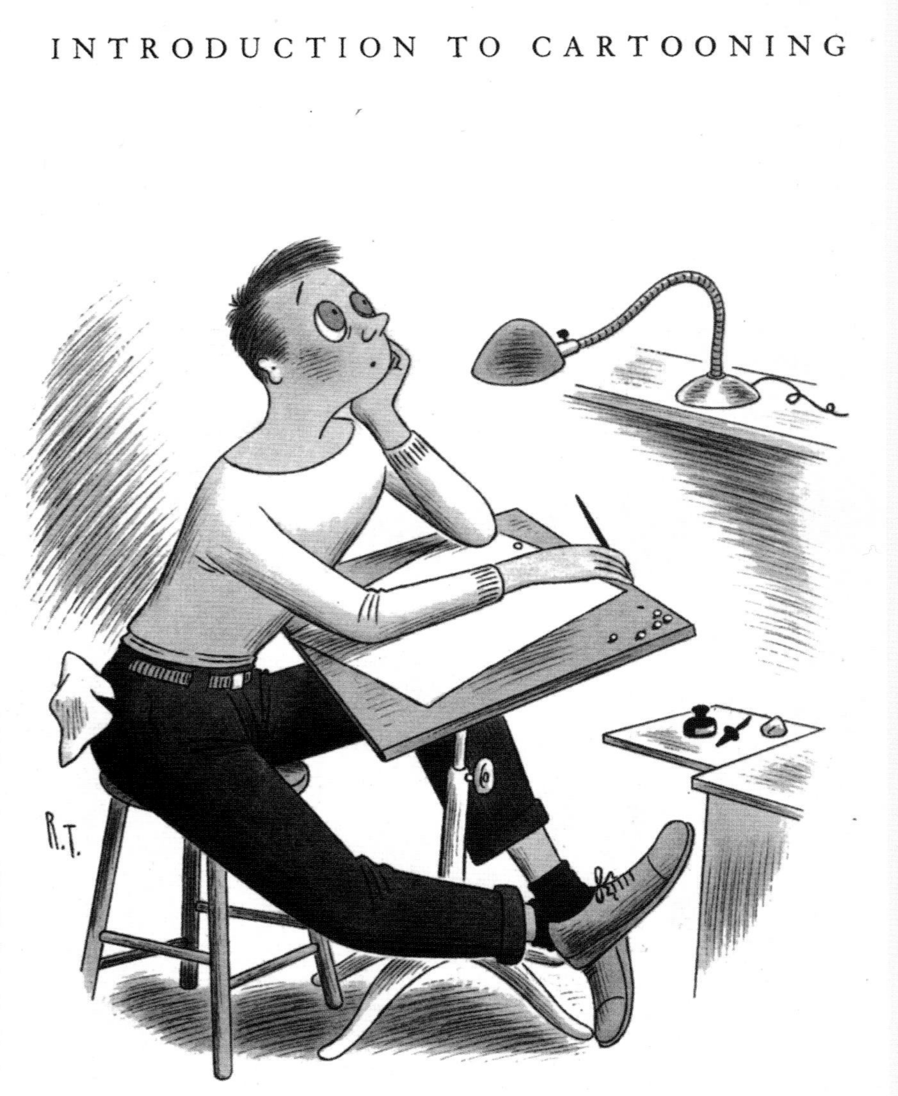
INTRODUCTION TO CARTOONING
R.T.

Cartoon self-portrait from Taylor's *Introduction to Cartooning* (Watson-Guptill, 1947).

Toronto in 1904. He received early tutoring in art from local painters, members of the Royal Canadian Academy, and took classes at Central Tech and the Ontario College of Art. His family occasionally wintered in California and Taylor also studied briefly at the Los Angeles School of Art and Design (his first job was as a sign painter in the Mexican quarter of Los Angeles). The twenty-one-year-old Taylor was exactly the sort of raw talent the *Telegram* was looking for, and the accompanying photo of the artist shows a sly, expectant glimmer around the eyes of the clean-cut youth. The *Telegram*'s profile also includes a note about his style and use of word balloons that says a little bit more about the editors' taste in comic strips: "In making their award the judges were impressed by the bold originality of idea and vigorous technique shown. Ability to get the idea over with little or no letterpress counted high with the judges. The first and second prize winning cartoons and those in the third place show this quality well. Many otherwise excellent efforts were overburdened with lettering."

Taylor's boldly original idea, to use the *Telegram*'s phrasing, was a bizarre strip entitled simply "? ?? ???" and introducing an odd trio of nearly identical, expressionless cartoon ciphers—The Mystery Men. Clad in long black coats and tall stovepipe hats, the three nameless characters were nearly indistinguishable except by the number of buttons (ranging from one to three) on their coats. This strange group moved in lock-step and spoke with an antiquated vocabulary reminiscent of Frederick Opper's *Alphonse and Gaston*. Their alien appearance lent even their most pedestrian adventure a patina of charming weirdness unlike anything on display in other newspapers. And they lived up to their name: every aspect of the strip was a mystery. Who are they? Where did they come from? What is their relationship to each other? Why don't they have any hair (or pupils, for that matter)? How did they arrive at their singular form of dress? These questions were never really answered.

The Mystery Men (henceforth billed as *The "Tely" Mystery Men*) ran as a daily strip for several months in the *Telegram* and created something of a sensation. At the same time as the strip premiered the editors launched another contest to name the "Three Funny Fellows." Prizes totaling $50 were offered to the lucky readers who could give names to the trio, and banner ads ran alongside the strip for weeks. By way of promotion, the *Telegram* published lyrics singing the praises of the strip and also inserted spot illustrations of the different Mystery Men reminding readers of the contest. According to the *Telegram*, "the judges had three or four thousand entries to consider" and received entries for days after the contest closed "from all over and around Toronto, and even from Winnipeg, Saskatchewan and New York." By May 31, the *Telegram* was announcing a winner—a Mr. W. Hargreaves took the top prize of $25 for suggesting "The Pickwick Hicks: Pick, Hick and Wick. Being so much alike, so are their names. Their humor is somewhat akin to the innocent homeroom adventures of Dickens' Pickwick Club. One of them generally leads and picks the action, another is quick (Wick) to execute the action. The other is generally the 'Hick' of the joke or humor." It is likely the judges (including Taylor) recognized the ultimate clunkiness of this name, for they introduce the winning entries with this caveat: "Quite possibly they will remain 'The Mystery Men,' although plenty of clever suggestions for their names appear in the prize list."

Eventually the daily *Mystery Men* would fall into an alternating pattern, used as stand-alone filler or incorporated into a fuller page of imported strips, sandwiched between Chic Young's *Dumb Dora* and British import *Pop* by J. Millar Watts. Taylor created two continuities for the strip, a Middle-East adventure and a serial devoted to the antics of the Mystery Men's visiting country cousins—a blank-eyed clan of moochers. In general, the Oriental adventure is the more successful, although both display the artist's love of puns and a growing propensity for drawing cute flapper girls. The strip ran for several months and was used in many of the the *Telegram*'s promotions (notably, a live appearance at the Canadian National Exhibition). The final strip appeared October 27, 1924, after which the Mystery Men, and Richard Taylor, vanished from the pages of the *Evening Telegram*, replaced by the *"Tely" Snuggle Pups*, created by the American cartoonist Frank Hopkins and syndicated by the John F. Dille Co.

Taylor continued to work as an illustrator in Toronto, producing advertisements and drawings for a number of different clients. In 1927 he joined the staff of the humor magazine *The Goblin* as art director. Founded in 1921 by students at the University of Toronto, *The Goblin* quickly grew into a national success in the mold of *Life* or *The New Yorker*. Taylor contributed a batch of cartoons for each issue in a variety of styles. After the magazine folded with the onset of the Depression, Taylor became a self-described "bohemian" and political radical, producing cartoons and woodcuts for various left-wing publications, including the weekly *Masses* magazine. Under the name "Ric," Taylor began producing a weekly strip called *Dad Plugg* for *The Worker*, the organ of the Communist Party of Canada.

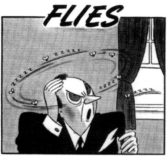

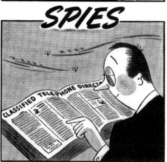

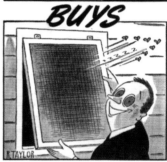

FLIES
SPIES
BUYS
R.TAYLOR
MORAL: When you want a screen for a window, fire-place, or movie projector, look in the Classified.
You save a lot of time and energy when you look in the Classified section of your Telephone Directory before you buy things or have them repaired.
You get useful shopping information about local tradespeople through the Classified. Many of them tell whether they deliver, whether their service men are factory-trained, what hours their stores are open.
Look in the Classified now. See for yourself.
Make the Classified your buying guide

Classified Telephone Directory advertisement, *Collier's*, June 20, 1942.

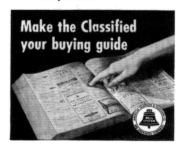

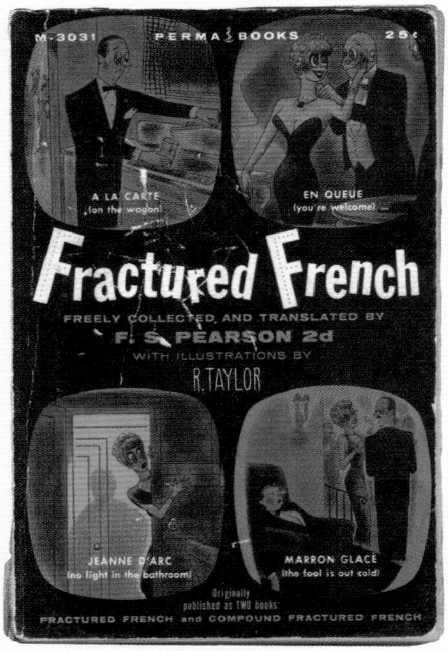
M-3031
PERMA BOOKS
25¢
A LA CARTE
(on the wagon)
EN QUEUE
(you're welcome)
Fractured French
FREELY COLLECTED, AND TRANSLATED BY
F. S. PEARSON 2d
WITH ILLUSTRATIONS BY
R. TAYLOR
JEANNE D'ARC
(no light in the bathroom)
MARRON GLACE
(the fool is out cold)
Originally published as TWO books:
FRACTURED FRENCH and COMPOUND FRACTURED FRENCH

By the mid-'30s, Taylor came into contact with Clifton Fadiman, an editor at Simon and Schuster in New York, who urged him to submit work to *The New Yorker*. Beginning in 1935, Taylor worked for months trying to crack the *New Yorker* market, finally being rewarded with a $15 check for a small spot illustration. More and more checks followed and Taylor moved to the U.S. in 1936 to be closer to the action. He married fellow Canadian Maxine MacTavish, the daughter of a prominent art critic and editor, and the couple eventually settled in Bethel, Connecticut. From there his cartooning career essentially took off. He expanded his market to include other magazines, book illustration, and advertising.

In 1947, Taylor, now very successful and considerably less mysterious, wrote and illustrated a "how-to" book entitled *Introduction to Cartooning*, published by Watson-Guptill. His final words to his students, while illustrating a degree of self-deprecating humor and sophistication typical of his later work, serve also as something of a coda to his early years in Canada: "To those who really try hard to develop, and who possess all the requirements, I wish success, and say that when next you look upon the drawings by a famous cartoonist in the pages of the press, just remember that there is the work of someone like yourself who experienced the same discouragements, went through exactly the same growing-pains and, many times perhaps, wished he'd taken up plumbing instead." CA

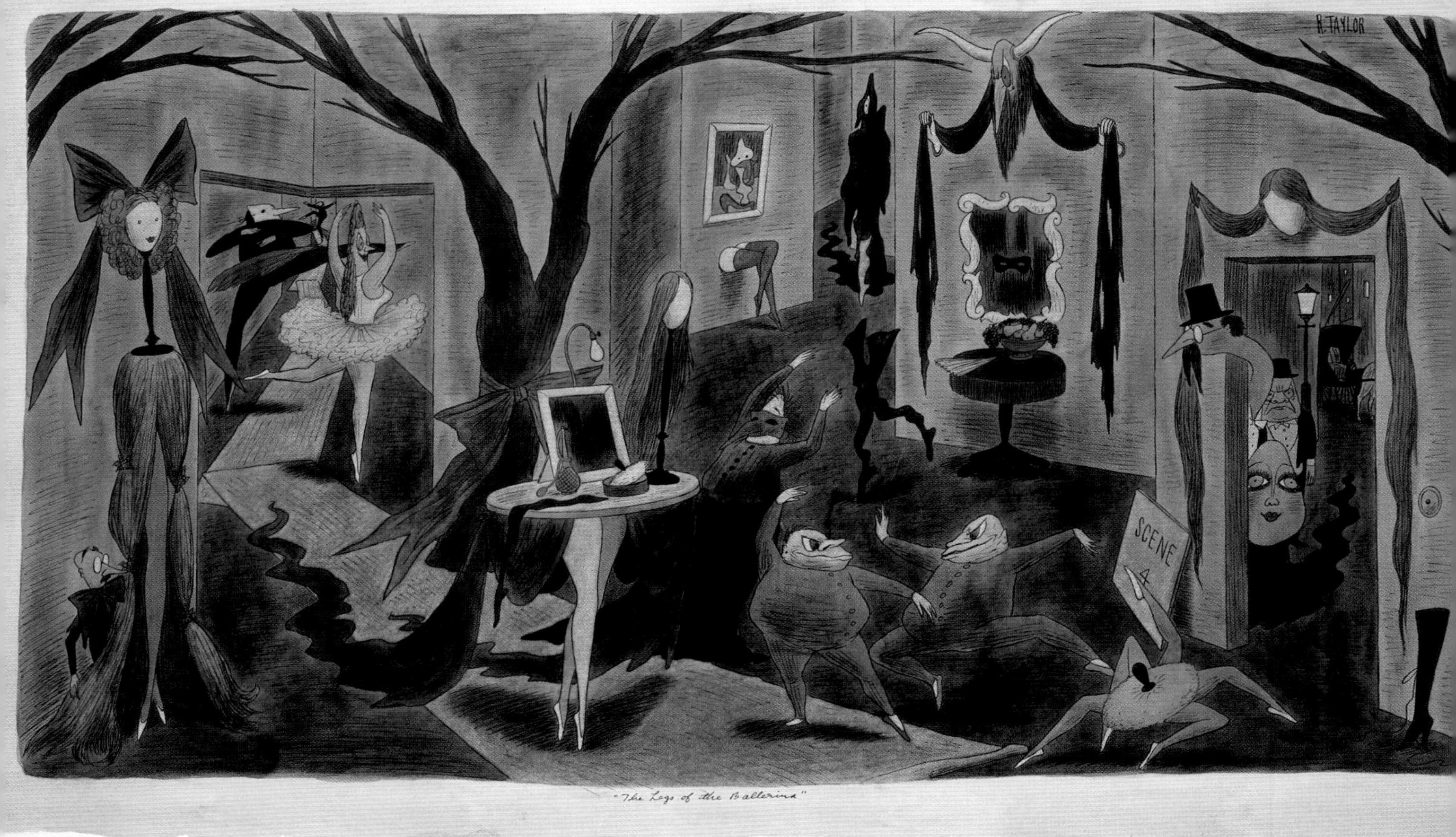
R. TAYLOR
SCENE 4
"The Legs of the Ballerina"

Top: *Fractured French* by F.S. Pearson 2nd, with illustrations by Taylor (Perma Books, 1956).

Above: *The Legs of the Ballerina*, ink and watercolor painting, 1960. Courtesy of Glenn Bray.

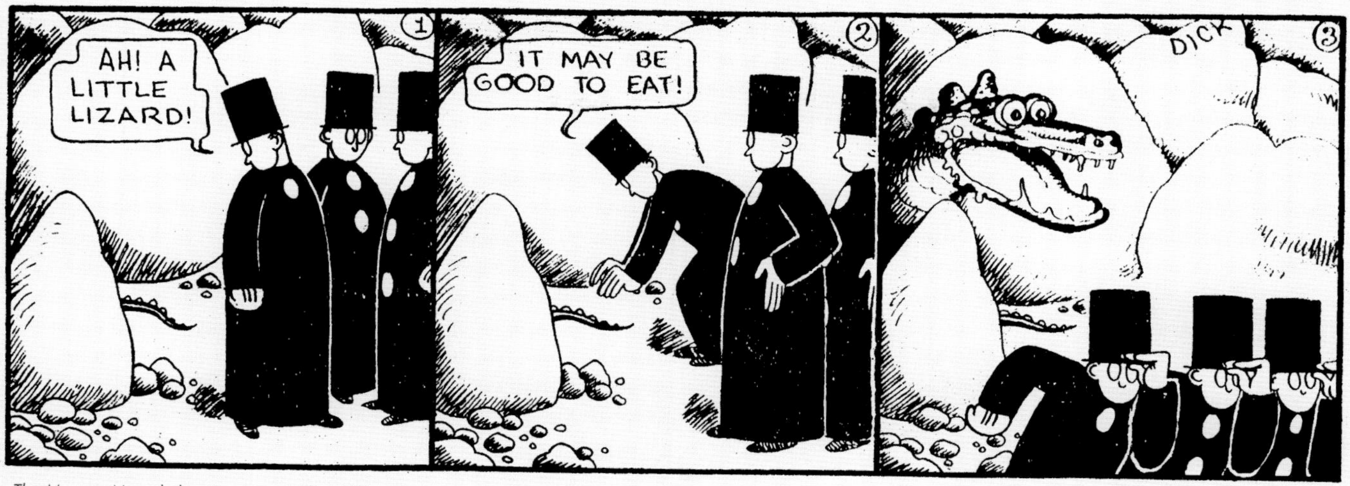
AH! A LITTLE LIZARD!
IT MAY BE GOOD TO EAT!
DICK

The Mystery Men, daily strip, August 19, 1924.

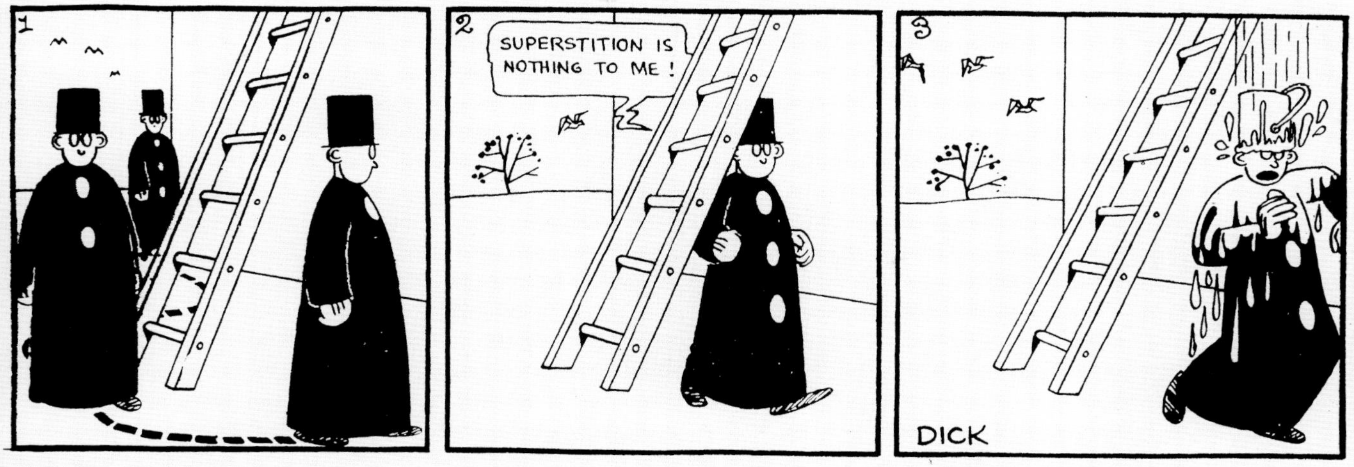
SUPERSTITION IS NOTHING TO ME!
DICK

The Mystery Men, daily strip, August 26, 1924.

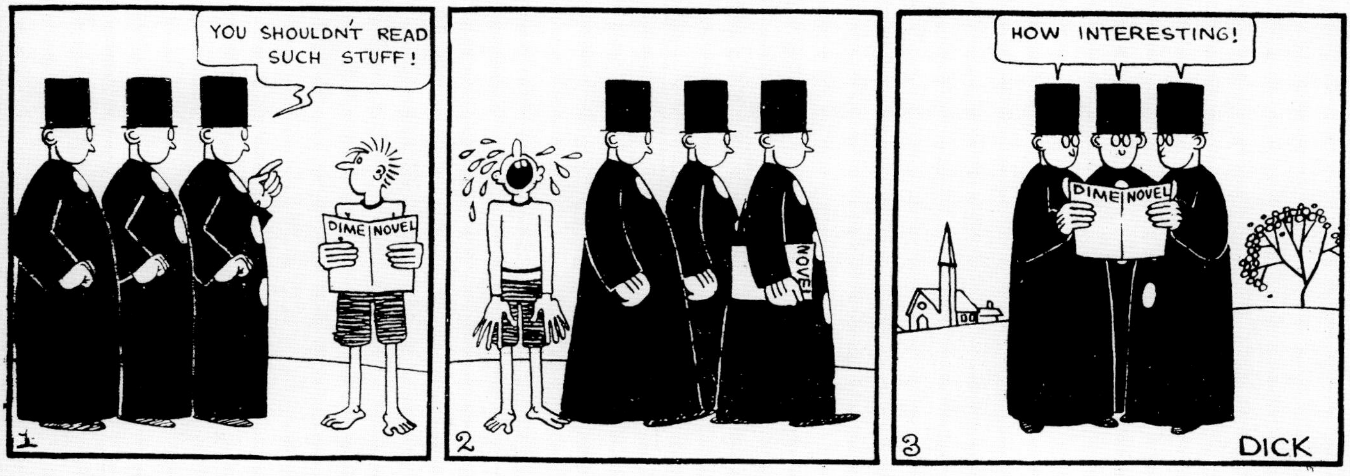
YOU SHOULDN'T READ SUCH STUFF!
DIME NOVEL
NOVEL
HOW INTERESTING!
DIME NOVEL
DICK

The Mystery Men, daily strip, August 27, 1924.

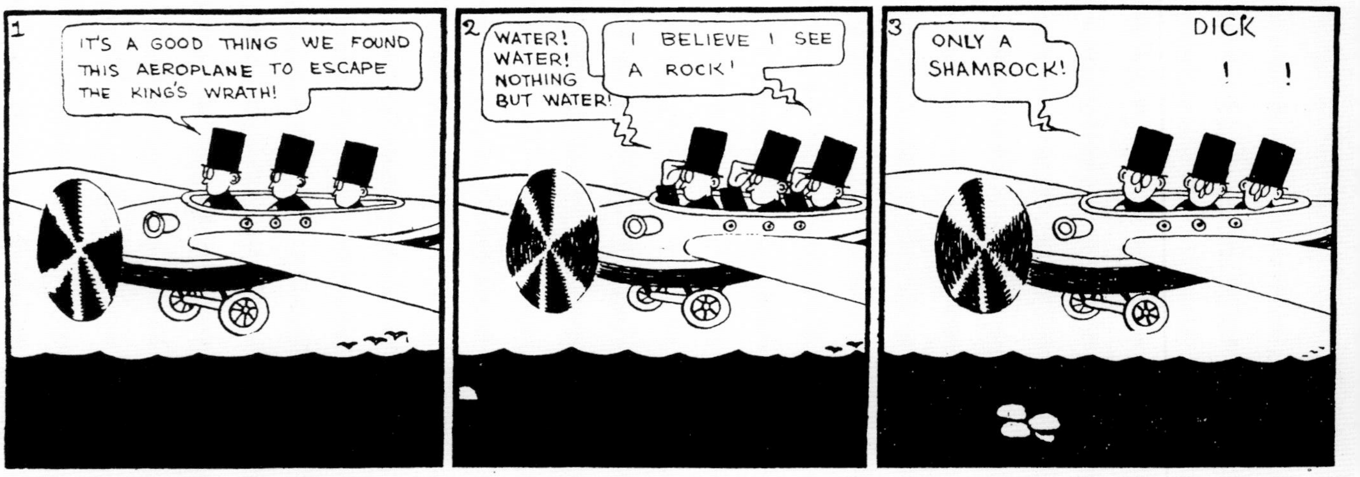
1
IT'S A GOOD THING WE FOUND THIS AEROPLANE TO ESCAPE THE KING'S WRATH!
2
WATER! WATER! NOTHING BUT WATER!
I BELIEVE I SEE A ROCK!
3
ONLY A SHAMROCK!
DICK
! !

The Mystery Men, daily strip, August 28, 1924.

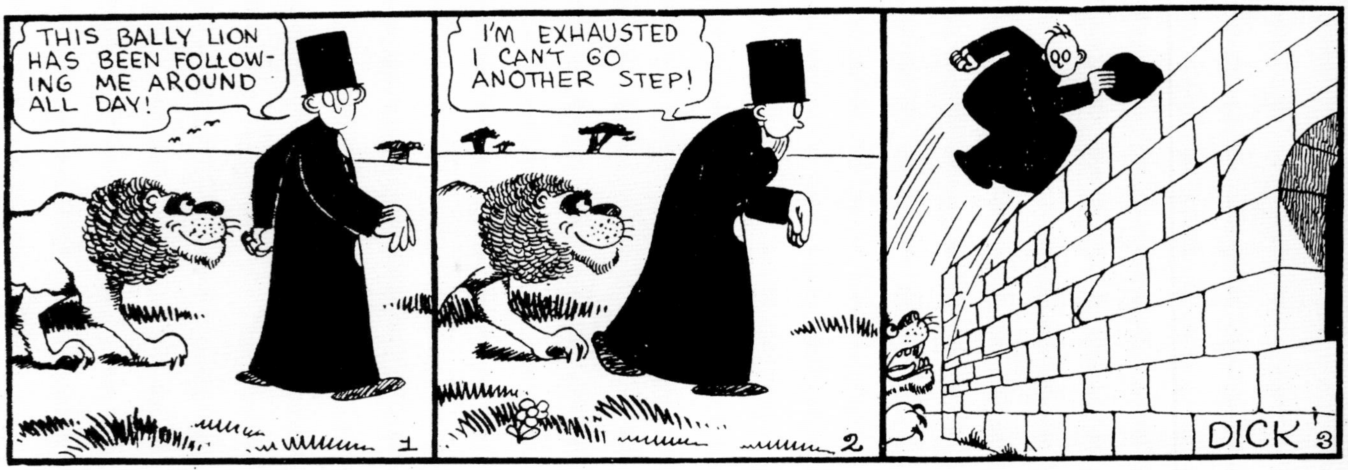
THIS BALLY LION HAS BEEN FOLLOWING ME AROUND ALL DAY!
1
I'M EXHAUSTED I CAN'T GO ANOTHER STEP!
2
DICK
3

The Mystery Men, daily strip, August 29, 1924.

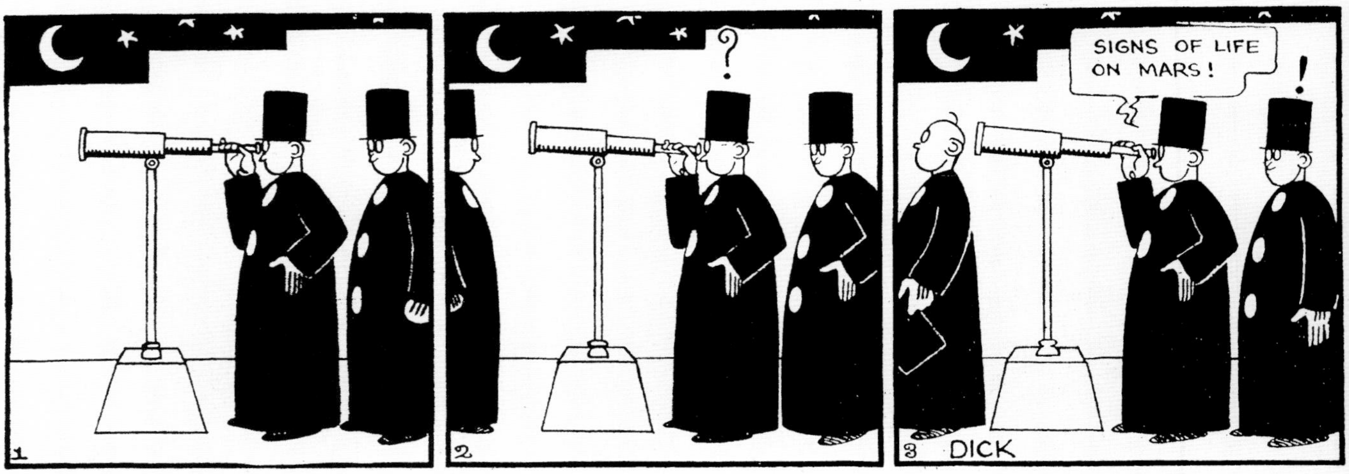
1
?
2
SIGNS OF LIFE ON MARS!
!
3
DICK

The Mystery Men, daily strip, August 30, 1924.

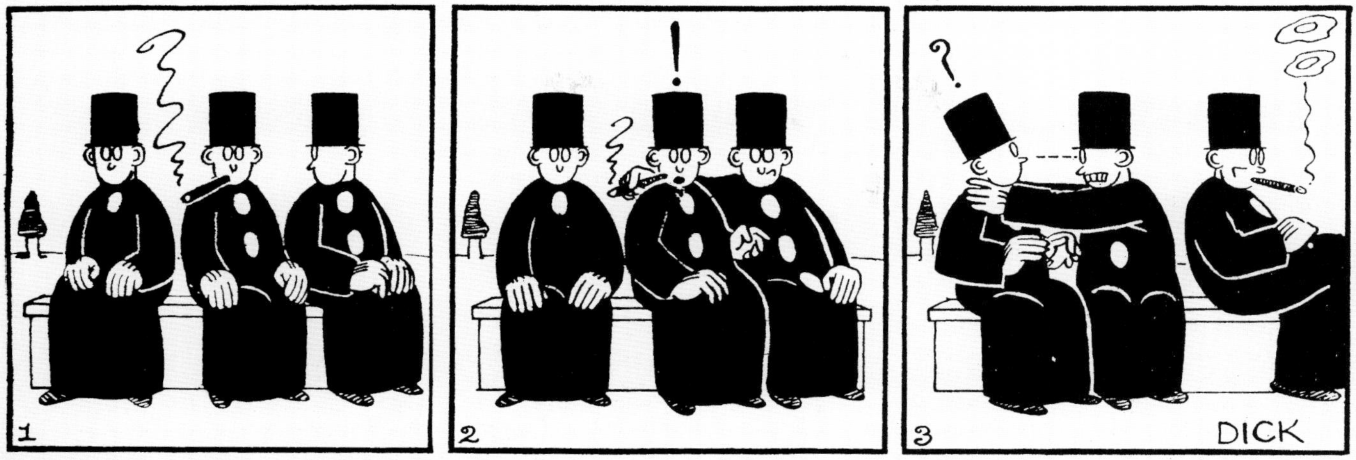
DICK

The Mystery Men, daily strip, September 3, 1924.

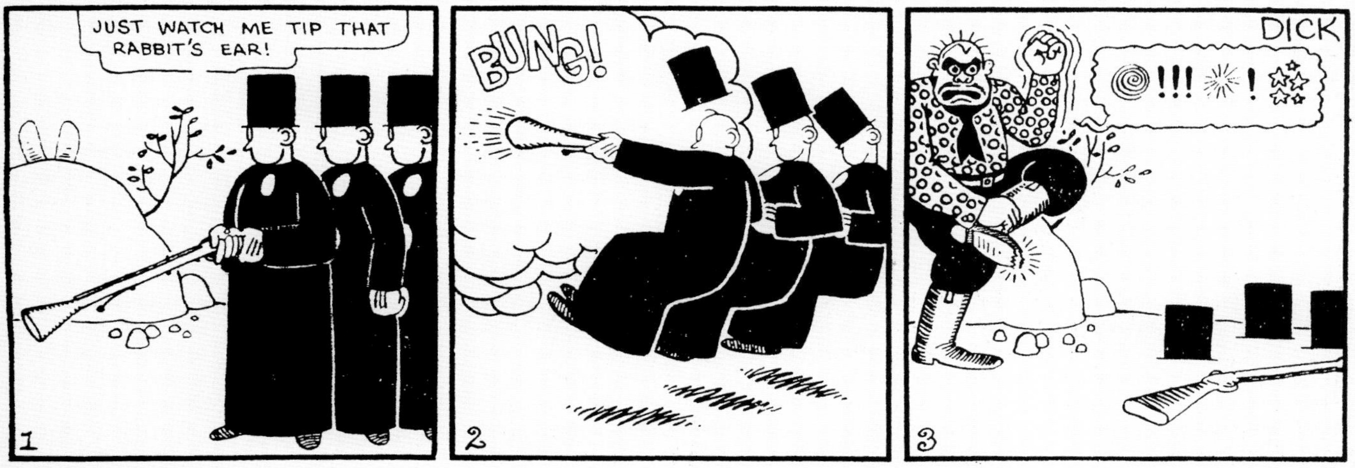
JUST WATCH ME TIP THAT RABBIT'S EAR!
BUNG!
DICK
!!! !

The Mystery Men, daily strip, September 5, 1924.

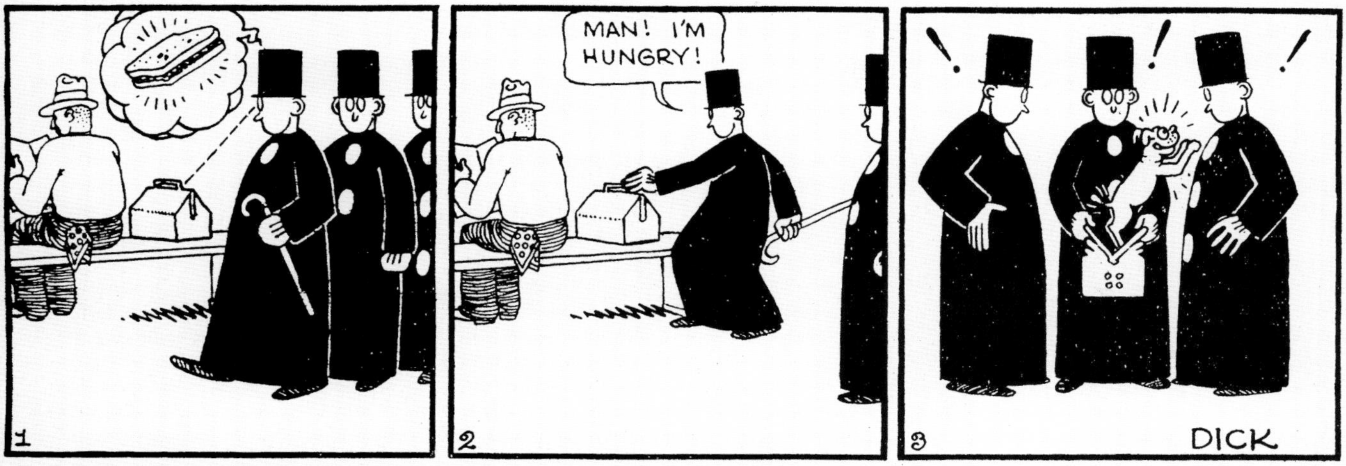
MAN! I'M HUNGRY!
DICK

The Mystery Men, daily strip, September 6, 1924.

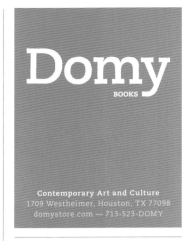

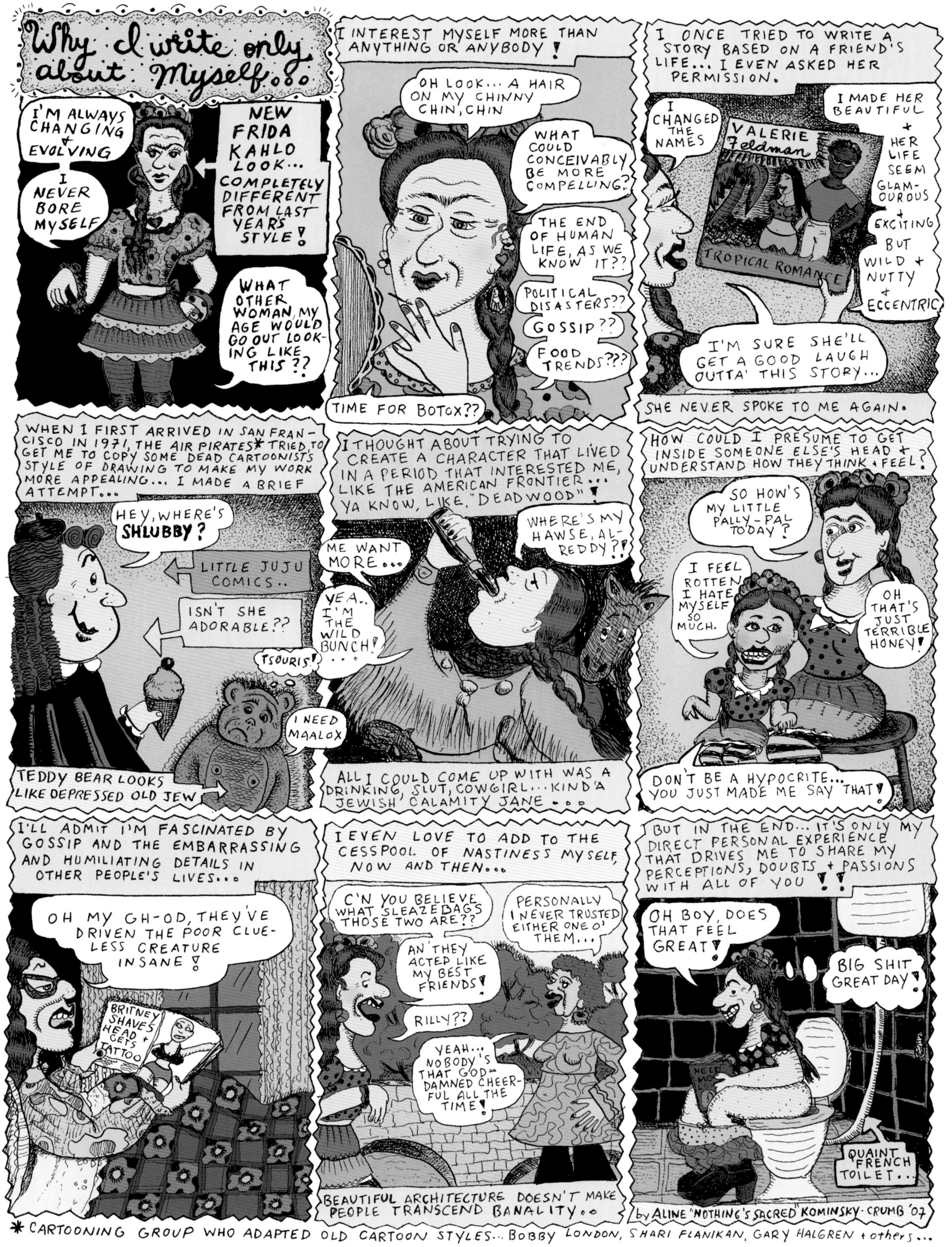

Why I write only about Myself...
I'M ALWAYS CHANGING + EVOLVING
I NEVER BORE MYSELF
NEW FRIDA KAHLO LOOK... COMPLETELY DIFFERENT FROM LAST YEAR'S STYLE!
WHAT OTHER WOMAN MY AGE WOULD GO OUT LOOKING LIKE THIS??
I INTEREST MYSELF MORE THAN ANYTHING OR ANYBODY!
OH LOOK... A HAIR ON MY CHINNY CHIN, CHIN
WHAT COULD CONCEIVABLY BE MORE COMPELLING?
THE END OF HUMAN LIFE, AS WE KNOW IT??
POLITICAL DISASTERS??
GOSSIP??
FOOD TRENDS???
TIME FOR BOTOX??
I ONCE TRIED TO WRITE A STORY BASED ON A FRIEND'S LIFE... I EVEN ASKED HER PERMISSION.
I CHANGED THE NAMES
VALERIE Feldman
TROPICAL ROMANCE
I MADE HER BEAUTIFUL + HER LIFE SEEM GLAMOUROUS + EXCITING BUT WILD + NUTTY + ECCENTRIC
I'M SURE SHE'LL GET A GOOD LAUGH OUTTA' THIS STORY...
SHE NEVER SPOKE TO ME AGAIN.
WHEN I FIRST ARRIVED IN SAN FRANCISCO IN 1971, THE AIR PIRATES* TRIED TO GET ME TO COPY SOME DEAD CARTOONIST'S STYLE OF DRAWING TO MAKE MY WORK MORE APPEALING... I MADE A BRIEF ATTEMPT...
HEY, WHERE'S SHLUBBY?
LITTLE JUJU COMICS..
ISN'T SHE ADORABLE??
TSOURIS!
I NEED MAALOX
TEDDY BEAR LOOKS LIKE DEPRESSED OLD JEW
I THOUGHT ABOUT TRYING TO CREATE A CHARACTER THAT LIVED IN A PERIOD THAT INTERESTED ME, LIKE THE AMERICAN FRONTIER... YA KNOW, LIKE, "DEADWOOD"!
ME WANT MORE...
WHERE'S MY HAWSE, ALREDDY?!
YEA.. I'M THE WILD BUNCH!...
ALL I COULD COME UP WITH WAS A DRINKING, SLUT, COWGIRL... KIND'A JEWISH CALAMITY JANE...
HOW COULD I PRESUME TO GET INSIDE SOMEONE ELSE'S HEAD + UNDERSTAND HOW THEY THINK + FEEL?
SO HOW'S MY LITTLE PALLY-PAL TODAY?
I FEEL ROTTEN I HATE MYSELF SO MUCH.
OH THAT'S JUST TERRIBLE HONEY!
DON'T BE A HYPOCRITE... YOU JUST MADE ME SAY THAT!
I'LL ADMIT I'M FASCINATED BY GOSSIP AND THE EMBARRASSING AND HUMILIATING DETAILS IN OTHER PEOPLE'S LIVES...
OH MY GH-OD, THEY'VE DRIVEN THE POOR CLUELESS CREATURE INSANE!
BRITNEY SHAVES HEAD + GETS TATTOO
I EVEN LOVE TO ADD TO THE CESSPOOL OF NASTINESS MYSELF, NOW AND THEN...
C'N YOU BELIEVE WHAT SLEAZEBAGS THOSE TWO ARE??
PERSONALLY I NEVER TRUSTED EITHER ONE O' THEM...
AN' THEY ACTED LIKE MY BEST FRIENDS!
RILLY??
YEAH... NOBODY'S THAT GOD-DAMNED CHEERFUL ALL THE TIME!
BEAUTIFUL ARCHITECTURE DOESN'T MAKE PEOPLE TRANSCEND BANALITY..
BUT IN THE END... IT'S ONLY MY DIRECT PERSONAL EXPERIENCE THAT DRIVES ME TO SHARE MY PERCEPTIONS, DOUBTS + PASSIONS WITH ALL OF YOU!!
OH BOY, DOES THAT FEEL GREAT!
BIG SHIT GREAT DAY!
QUAINT FRENCH TOILET...
by ALINE "NOTHING'S SACRED" KOMINSKY-CRUMB '07

* CARTOONING GROUP WHO ADAPTED OLD CARTOON STYLES... BOBBY LONDON, SHARI FLANIKAN, GARY HALGREN + others...

CONTRIBUTORS

TOM DE HAVEN is the author of sixteen books, including *Freaks' Amour*, *It's Superman!*, and the Derby Dugan Trilogy: *Funny Papers*, *Derby Dugan's Depression Funnies*, and *Dugan Under Ground*. He teaches in the graduate creative writing program at Virginia Commonwealth University in Richmond.

RON GOULART has been a professional writer for over a half century. Since he escaped from the ad game in 1968, he has been a full-time freelancer. Thus far Goulart has written over two hundred books, including novels in the science fiction, mystery, horror, Western, and historical genres, and nonfiction books that deal with popular culture—comic books, comic strips, and pulp fiction. He's also turned out something like seven hundred short stories and articles. Goulart has been nominated twice for an MWA Edgar award, once for an SFWA Nebula, and once for an Eisner Award. His latest mystery novel is *Groucho Marx, King of the Jungle*. This year has seen a handsome and profusely illustrated reissue of his pioneering pulp history, *Cheap Thrills*, and the appearance of his new tome about comic books, *Good Girl Art*, both published by Hermes Press.

JEET HEER is writing a doctoral thesis on the cultural politics of Harold Gray's *Little Orphan Annie*. With Kent Worcester, he has co-edited *Arguing Comics*, an anthology that charts how 20th-century intellectuals have regarded comics. With Chris Ware and Chris Oliveros, Heer is the co-editor of the multi-volume *Walt and Skeezix* series published by Drawn & Quarterly. He's also written the afterwords to the recent reprinting of Clare Briggs's *Oh Skin-nay: The Days of Real Sport*, and the introduction to several volumes of the *Krazy and Ignatz* reprint series. His last feature for *Comic Art* was "Cartoonists in Navajo Country."

TIM HENSLEY is a cartoonist and musician living in Los Angeles, California. His work has appeared in numerous anthologies and mini-comics, and he currently contributes regular installments of his "Wally Gropius" stories to *Mome*, published by Fantagraphics Books. He also has a new strip in the forthcoming issue of *Kramers Ergot* from Buenaventura Press.

ALINE KOMINSKY-CRUMB began making comics in the early 1970s after moving to San Francisco. She is an autobiographical and feminist comix pioneer and her idiosyncratic voice has proven widely influential. Collections of her work include *Love That Bunch* and, with her husband Robert Crumb and daughter Sophie Crumb, *The Complete Dirty Laundry Comics*. She, Robert, and Sophie also collaborate regularly on strips for *The New Yorker*. Her latest book is *Need More Love: A Graphic Memoir*. She lives in the lovely south of France.

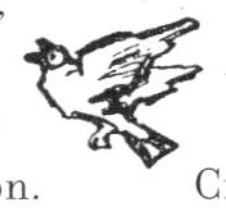

BRYAN MUNN lives in Canada. He is one of the organizers of the Doug Wright Awards and writes about comics for the Sequential news blog, sequential.spiltink.org.

KEN PARILLE is Assistant Professor of English at East Carolina University. He has published essays on the rivalry between William Wordsworth and Lord Byron, Louisa May Alcott's *Little Women*, and boyhood in antebellum America. His writing has appeared in *Tulsa Studies in Women's Literature*, *New Literary History*, *Children's Literature*, *The Journal of Popular Culture*, *Children's Literature Association Quarterly*, *Papers on Language and Literature*, *GuitarOne*, and *The Boston Review*. His last feature for *Comic Art* was on Daniel Clowes's *David Boring*.

DONALD PHELPS has been writing about the arts for forty years. He published his own guerilla cultural magazine in the 1960s, and his writings have appeared in *Pulpsmith*, *The Nation*, *The Comics Journal*, and *Film Comment*. His collected essays on comics, *Reading the Funnies*, published by Fantagraphics Books, received an American Book Award. An essay by him, "The Runners," was included in the 2006 anthology *American Movie Critics: From the Silents Until Now*, edited by Phillip Lopate and published by Library of America.

BEN SCHWARTZ lives in Los Angeles, California, and has written for movies and television as well as the *New York Times*, the *Los Angeles Times*, the *Washington Post*, *Salon*, and the *Huffington Post*, and he is currently on assignment for *Vanity Fair*. His past features for *Comic Art* focused on Charles M. Schulz and Drew Friedman.

THIERRY SMOLDEREN teaches the history of the comic strip and gives workshops on image-oriented writing at the École Supérieure de l'Image in Angoulême, France. He has written texts for dozens of *bandes dessinées* albums (including a bio-fiction of Winsor McCay with J-P. Bramanti entitled *McCay*, published by Editions Delcourt). He is also the co-founder of www.coconino-world.com, a website dedicated to the history of the comic strip (in the largest sense of the term) and contemporary graphic art.

ADRIAN TOMINE writes and draws the comic book series *Optic Nerve*, and his illustrations appear with some regularity in *The New Yorker*. His book *Shortcomings* will be published by Drawn & Quarterly in the fall of 2007.

DAN ZETTWOCH lives in St. Louis, Missouri, and earns a living making illustrations, diagrams, and maps. In addition to several handmade booklets, his comics have appeared in *Kramers Ergot*, *Drawn & Quarterly Showcase*, *Bogus Dead*, and the *Riverfront Times*. He is hard at work on his forthcoming comic book series *Redbird*, to be published by Buenaventura Press.